T0367233

DUMBARTON OAKS
MEDIEVAL LIBRARY

Daniel Donoghue, General Editor

THE OLD ENGLISH
PASTORAL CARE

DOML 72

The Old English
Pastoral Care

Edited and Translated by

R. D. FULK

Dumbarton Oaks
Medieval Library

HARVARD UNIVERSITY PRESS
CAMBRIDGE, MASSACHUSETTS
LONDON, ENGLAND
2021

First Printing

Library of Congress Cataloging-in-Publication Data
Names: Gregory I, Pope, approximately 540–604. | Gregory I, Pope,
    approximately 540–604. Regula pastoralis. English (Old English) |
    Gregory I, Pope, approximately 540–604. Regula pastoralis. English. |
    Fulk, R. D. (Robert Dennis), editor, translator.
Title: The Old English Pastoral care / edited and translated by R. D. Fulk.
Other titles: Dumbarton Oaks medieval library ; 72.
Description: Cambridge, Massachusetts : Harvard University Press, 2021. |
    Series: Dumbarton Oaks medieval library; DOML 72 | Includes
    bibliographical references and index. | Texts in Old English with
    English translation following.
Identifiers: LCCN 2021010893 | ISBN 9780674261150 (cloth)
Subjects: LCSH: Pastoral theology—Early works to 1800.
Classification: LCC BR65.G53 R4413 2021 | DDC 253—dc23
LC record available at https://lccn.loc.gov/2021010893

Contents

CONTENTS

Introduction

Pope Gregory I, also known as Saint Gregory the Great, born in approximately 540, was pontiff from 590 to 604, during a crucial period in which the papacy provided civil government (attending especially to the needs of the poor who thronged Rome), religious authority, and military force in central and southern Italy, and during which Rome faced daunting obstacles to its authority, pressed on opposing sides by the Lombard invaders of Italy and the Byzantine emperor. Among his accomplishments, Gregory effected a degree of monastic discipline in the Lateran Palace, instituted liturgical reforms, brought the Visigoths of Spain and the Lombards into the ambit of Roman Christianity, cultivated ties with the north of Europe, and produced a number of religious works, both practical and exegetical.

The title *Liber regulae pastoralis* assigned to the Latin text from which the Old English *Pastoral Care* is translated, is apparently the one intended by its author, Gregory. It may be rendered *Book of Pastoral Rule,* in reference to the duties of a "shepherd," or bishop. The book is also sometimes called *Liber pastoralis curae (Book of Pastoral Care),* or some variant thereof, apparently on the basis of its opening words. The work was completed at the start of Gregory's pontificate, in 590 or 591, and it fulfilled an intention that Gregory had earlier expressed of composing for speakers of Latin a resource already available in Greek: an account of the qualities required of a bishop and of the best methods to be employed in dealing with the diverse sorts of people under a bishop's care.[1] There is abundant evidence of the esteem in which Gregory's book was held throughout the Christian world. It is highly praised in a letter to Gregory from Licinianus, the learned bishop of Carthagena in Spain. The Byzantine emperor Maurice had it translated into Greek by Anastasius, the patriarch of Antioch, an admirer of the work. It came to play a prominent role in the Frankish Church, where a series of Church councils required bishops to study it, and where in the ninth century a copy apparently was placed in the hands of bishops before the altar at their consecration.

It may be deduced from the verse prologue to the Old English translation that Augustine of Canterbury took a copy of the work with him to England when Gregory sent him to begin the work of converting the English in 597. Gregory's responsibility for the conversion no doubt made the choice of this work for translation natural when King Alfred (r. 871–899), known as Alfred the Great since the sixteenth century, initiated his program of translating important works from Latin into English. Yet it is also an especially apt choice because of its potential utility in respect to the larger aim of Alfred's reform, which, it may be inferred from what he says in his prefatory letter to his bishops (addressed, in the present text, to Bishop Wærferth), was to rebuild the English Church, ravaged by years of neglect and by invasions from Scandinavia.

The letter to Wærferth, composed sometime between 890 and 896, has attracted more scholarly comment than any other portion of the work, in part because of its strikingly dire depiction of the state of England's preeminent public institution, the Church, during Alfred's reign. It is equally enlightening in its straightforward explanation that the translation is one of a projected series intended to be the cornerstone of an effort instigated by Alfred and his ecclesiastical advisers to restore to vitality the learning in which England had once flourished and which was now hampered by general illiteracy in Latin among the clergy, and even among bishops. The prefatory letter, however, is also much admired for its prose style, which evinces a marked suppleness and an evident aptness for the expression of complex ideas that is superior to that of the translation itself, though the latter, to a remarkable degree, manages to render the complexity and length of many of Gregory's periods without undue simplification. Relatively little of the surviving corpus of Old English is not translated from Latin, and so this prefatory letter is one of a small number of sources by which to gauge the language's capability for refined scholarly expression, unfettered by the requirements of translation. The translation of Gregory's work itself is more faithful than the Old English renderings of Boethius's *De consolatione philosophiae* and Augustine of Hippo's *Soliloquia*, two other works often accredited to Alfred, though a fourth work commonly ascribed to him, the prose translation of the first fifty Psalms, is also by necessity fairly literal. The fidelity of the *Pastoral Care* to its source may be a result of its being, in the opinion of most scholars, the earliest of the Alfredian translations. Yet it is by no means slavish, and although some of the discrepancies must be due to misconstrual of the Latin, at many places it is evident that conveying the spirit of Gregory's text weighed more heavily than adhering to the letter.

On the basis of what is said in the prefaces and epilogues to this and other Alfredian works, and in Asser's Latin life of the king, it is to be concluded that Alfred in the last six years of his life learned Latin and translated these works, even though for half of that time he was engaged in conducting a defensive war against Scandinavian invaders.[2] This is so remarkable an accomplishment that it has inevitably raised doubts among scholars. M. R. Godden has been the most outspoken critic of trust in Alfred's authorship of any of the translations ascribed to him, pointing out how commonplace a practice it was in the early Middle Ages to claim the authorship of a monarch for a text that is patently of another's devising.[3] Janet Bately has responded effectively to claims that linguistic differences among the Alfredian texts point to differences in authorship, but even if common authorship is credited, it cannot be denied, as she concludes, that Alfred was probably never working alone.[4] Certainly, the claim of Alfred's authorship asserted in the epistolary preface to the *Pastoral Care* is exceptionally difficult to dismiss, especially as the king credits the assistance of four of his advisers, an admission without parallel among the cases of pseudepigraphy cited by Godden, and one hard to explain very convincingly if the king's authorship, or significant involvement, were purely a fiction.

The only prior complete edition and translation of the Old English *Pastoral Care* was prepared by Henry Sweet, the great philologist and phonetician (and the inspiration for the character Henry Higgins in Shaw's *Pygmalion*), who prepared the work while an undergraduate at Oxford. It was published in 1871 for the Early English Text Society. Sweet's important introduction to the book laid the groundwork for the study of Old English dialectology. The present edition owes much to Sweet's, though it also not infrequently furnishes corrections to his text and his interpretation of it.

A word may be said about some of the principles that inform the present translation. The *Pastoral Care* is a work of moral instruction. To convey the gravity of its ethical dictates, the translation aims for a somewhat elevated register, though not one that is oppressively archaic. Additionally, although the Old English translator tended to render words in the Latin text by the same Old English word in each instance, it was one of the aims of the present translation to offer a more varied diction. It is a well-known linguistic principle that there is no one-to-one semantic correspondence between lexemes in different languages, and proceeding as if there were such a correspondence may result in conveying an inaccurate impression of the style of the text to be translated. This is particularly true when a text is to be put into English. Because of its history, English is a language especially rich in synonyms and near synonyms, and as a result, speakers of the language tend to regard repetitive diction as a mark of inferior writing, even when no such stigma is to be attached to such redundancy in the source language.

In not a few instances, varied diction serves to convey the polysemy of words in languages less rich in synonyms than English is. An example of the problem is the Old English expression *to manianne,* used in this text frequently in the general sense "to be warned," referring to what is to be done for members of a bishop's flock in need of spiritual guidance. Like the Latin word *ammonendi* that it renders, it has a range of meanings, and the action referred to may amount to instructing, warning, reminding, exhorting, advising, admonishing, guiding, suggesting, or counseling, among other possibilities. Certainly, neither Gregory nor his Old English translator intended just one of these meanings in every instance, and even if the precise shade of meaning cannot be determined in a given context, variation in the way the expression is rendered serves the purpose of conveying the range of attitudes toward their charges that Gregory expected bishops to assume. Similarly, translating one word in various ways may serve the purpose of rendering more comprehensible conceptions and attitudes that time and cultural difference have tended to obscure. An example is the use of the Old English word *reccend* to refer to a bishop, a word which in other texts is most usually and conveniently to be translated "ruler." To be sure, variation in the rendering of individual words may seem a drawback to those who, not knowing Old English, are particularly concerned to tease out the precise meaning of the Old English text by comparison to the translation. It may then be regarded as a compensating factor that although the translation inevitably must depart from the word order of the Old English text, an effort has been made to align the syntax of the two texts to the extent that it is feasible.

It is sometimes advised that certain words of Old English be rendered as literally as possible. Yet to identify the literal meaning of Old English words is not so straightforward a matter as such advice presupposes. For example, where Old English *ondrædan* is here sometimes translated "worry," other translators might prefer "fear" or "dread," presumably because the word is reflected as "dread" in Modern English. But etymologically the meaning of the word is "advise against" *(and-rædan),* and surely the word's semantic range must have encompassed some less impassioned feeling like this. Because of the smaller vocabulary of Old English, a single word in that language must have had a wider range of meaning than most words in Modern English, and the present translation accordingly strives to suggest nuance when that seems appropriate. Certainly, a bishop may be expected to feel terror when contemplating the eternal consequences of sin in this world, but terror is probably not what he should be expected to have felt about the possibility of censuring his charges' misbehavior too harshly (see 21.5).

It is a pleasure to acknowledge the debt owed to those patient souls who read this book carefully in typescript and offered much helpful advice. They include Daniel Donoghue, Christopher A. Jones, Peter S. Baker, Nicole Eddy, Hannelore Segers, and John Kee. The author himself, of course, bears responsibility for any remaining errors and infelicities.

Notes

1 The evidence for the date of composition is summarized in Bruno Judic, Floribert Rommel, and Charles Morel, eds. and trans., *Grégoire le grand: Règle pastorale,* 2 vols., Sources Chrétiennes 381, 382 (Paris, 1992), vol. 1, pp. 21–22. On the Greek work, see the note to the translation of 23.1.

2 For the other prefaces and epilogues, see Susan Irvine and Malcolm R. Godden, eds. and trans., *The Old English Boethius, with Verse Prologues and*

Epilogues Associated with King Alfred, Dumbarton Oaks Medieval Library 19 (Cambridge, MA, 2012). For the Latin life of Alfred, see William Henry Stevenson, ed., *Asser's Life of King Alfred: Together with the Annals of Saint Neots Erroneously Ascribed to Asser* (Oxford, 1904; repr., 1959), and for a translation of Asser's work, see Simon Keynes and Michael Lapidge, *Alfred the Great: Asser's "Life of King Alfred" and Other Contemporary Sources* (Bungay, Suffolk, 1983).

3 Malcolm Godden, "Did King Alfred Write Anything?," *Medium Ævum* 76 (2007): 1–23.

4 Janet Bately, "Did King Alfred Actually Translate Anything? The Integrity of the Alfredian Canon Revisited," *Medium Ævum* 78 (2009): 189–215.

VERSE PROLOGUE

Augustine brought this message north to islanders over the salt sea, in such form as that champion of the Lord had composed it beforehand, the pope in Rome. Sharp-sighted Gregory was versed in many an upright lesson by his perceptive nature, his fund of subtle thinking. For that reason he won over the greatest mass of humankind for the guardian of the heavens, foremost among Romans, best endowed of humans in character, most celebrated for his praiseworthy achievements. Subsequently King Alfred turned every word of me into English and sent me south and north to his scribes, asked them to bring him more of such after the exemplar, so that he could send it to his bishops, since certain of them had need of it, those who least comprehended the Latin tongue.

EPISTOLARY PREFACE

Ðeos boc sceal to Wiogora ceastre.

Ælfred kyning hateð gretan Wærferð biscep his wordum luflice ond freondlice, ond ðe cyðan hate ðæt me com swiðe oft on gemynd hwelce wiotan iu wæron giond Angelcynn, ægðer ge godcundra hada ge woruldcundra; ond hu gesæliglica tida ða wæron giond Angelcynn; ond hu ða kyningas ðe ðone onwald hæfdon ðæs folces Gode ond his ærendwrecum hiersumedon; ond hie ægðer ge hiora sibbe ge hiora siodo ge hiora onweald innanbordes gehioldon, ond eac ut hiora eðel rymdon; ond hu him ða speow ægðer ge mid wige ge mid wisdome; ond eac ða godcundan hadas, hu giorne hie wæron ægðer ge ymb lare ge ymb liornunga, ge ymb ealle ða ðiowotdomas ðe hie Gode scoldon; ond hu man utanbordes wisdom ond lare hieder on lond sohte, ond hu we hie nu sceoldon ute begietan gif we hie habban sceoldon. Swæ clæne hio wæs oðfeallenu on Angelcynne ðæt swiðe feawa wæron behionan Humbre ðe hiora ðeninga cuðen understondan on Englisc, oððe furðum an ærendgewrit of Lædene on Englisc areccean; ond ic wene ðætte noht monige begiondan Humbre næren. Swæ feawa hiora wæron ðæt ic furðum anne anlepne ne mæg geðencean be suðan Temese ða ða ic to rice feng. Gode ælmihtegum sie ðonc ðætte we nu ænigne onstal habbað lareowa.

2   Ond forðon ic ðe bebiode ðæt ðu do swæ ic geliefe ðæt ðu wille, ðæt ðu ðe ðissa worulððinga to ðæm geæmetige swæ

EPISTOLARY PREFACE

This book is to go to Worcester.

King Alfred, with expressions of cordiality and amiability, directs that greetings be extended to Bishop Wærferth, and instructs that you be informed how very often it has come to mind what sages there once were among the English, both religious and lay; and how blessed the times were then among the English; and how the kings who had the governance of the people heeded God and his ministers; and they maintained order and morals and governance domestically, and also enlarged their domain; and how they excelled both in warfare and in erudition; and also the religious orders, how scrupulous they were as to teaching and learning, and as to all the services that they owed God; and how sagacity and education were sought out here in this country from abroad, and how we should now have to obtain them abroad if we were to have them. So entirely were they decayed among the English that there were very few on this side of the Humber who could make sense in English of their services, or translate even one missive from Latin into English; and I expect that there were by no means many beyond the Humber. There were so few of them that I cannot think of even a single one south of the Thames when I came to the throne. Thanks be to almighty God that we now have any fund of teachers.

And therefore I direct you to do as I believe you would like, to disengage yourself from these worldly concerns as 2

5

ðu oftost mæge, ðæt ðu ðone wisdom ðe ðe God sealde ðær ðær ðu hiene befæstan mæge, befæste. Geðenc hwelc witu us ða becomon for ðisse worulde, ða ða we hit nohwæðer ne selfe ne lufodon ne eac oðrum monnum ne lefdon: ðone naman ænne we lufodon ðætte we Cristne wæren, ond swiðe feawe ða ðeawas.

3   Ða ic ða ðis eall gemunde, ða gemunde ic eac hu ic geseah, ær ðæm ðe hit eall forhergod wære ond forbærned, hu ða ciricean giond eall Angelcynn stodon maðma ond boca gefylda ond eac micel mengeo Godes ðiowa, ond ða swiðe lytle fiorme ðara boca wiston, forðæm ðe hie hiora nan wuht ongiotan ne meahton, forðæm ðe hie næron on hiora agen geðiode awritene, swelce hie cwæden, "Ure ieldran, ða ðe ðas stowa ær hioldon, hie lufodon wisdom, ond ðurh ðone hie begeaton welan ond us læfdon. Her mon mæg giet gesion hiora swæð, ac we him ne cunnon æfter spyrigean. Ond forðæm we habbað nu ægðer forlæten ge ðone welan ge ðone wisdom, forðæm ðe we noldon to ðæm spore mid ure mode onlutan."

4   Ða ic ða ðis eall gemunde, ða wundrade ic swiðe swiðe ðara godena wiotona ðe giu wæron giond Angelcynn, ond ða bec ealla be fullan geliornod hæfdon, ðæt hie hiora ða nænne dæl noldon on hiora agen geðiode wendan. Ac ic ða sona eft me selfum andwyrde ond cwæð: "Hie ne wendon ðætte æfre menn sceolden swæ reccelease weorðan ond sio lar swæ oðfeallan. For ðære wilnunga hie hit forleton, ond woldon ðæt her ðy mara wisdom on londe wære ðy we ma geðeoda cuðon." Ða gemunde ic hu sio æ wæs ærest on Ebrisc geðiode funden, ond eft, ða hie Creacas geliornodon, ða wendon hie hie on hiora agen geðiode ealle, ond eac ealle

often as you can, with the aim of applying the understanding which God bestowed on you wherever you can apply it. Think what punishments plagued us before all the world when we neither loved it ourselves nor passed it down to other people: we loved the name alone of being Christians, and very few loved the practices.

When I remembered all this, I recalled also how I had 3 seen, before it was all plundered and reduced to ashes, how the churches throughout the English realm stood filled with riches and books, and likewise a great throng of God's servants, and they derived very little profit from those books, because they could comprehend nothing of them, since they were not written in their own tongue, as if they were to say, "Our elders, who once inhabited these parts, loved learning, and through it they amassed wealth and left it to us. Here their track can still be seen, yet we cannot follow it. And we have now forfeited both the riches and the learning, because we would not incline our understanding to the track."

When I remembered all this, I was wholly astonished 4 that the good scholars who once walked among the English, and who had studied all those books in full, did not care to turn any share of them into their own tongue. But then I answered myself promptly, saying, "They did not suppose that people would ever grow so negligent and learning so decayed. On purpose they left it undone, since they expected that there would be the greater erudition in the country the more languages we knew." Then I remembered how the law was first disclosed in the Hebrew tongue, and, in turn, when the Greeks studied it, they translated all of it into their own tongue, and all other books, as well. And in

7

oðre bec. Ond eft Lædenware swæ same, siððan hie hie geliornodon, hie hie wendon ealla ðurh wise wealhstodas on hiora agen geðiode. Ond eac ealla oðra Cristna ðioda sumne dæl hiora on hiora agen geðiode wendon.

5   Forðy me ðyncð betre, gif iow swæ ðyncð, ðæt we eac suma bec—ða ðe niedbeðearfosta sien eallum monnum to wiotonne—ðæt we ða on ðæt geðiode wenden ðe we ealle gecnawan mægen, ond gedon swæ we swiðe eaðe magon mid Godes fultume, gif we ða stilnesse habbað, ðætte eall sio gioguð ðe nu is on Angelcynne friora monna, ðara ðe ða speda hæbben ðæt hie ðæm befeolan mægen, sien to liornunga oðfæste, ða hwile ðe hie to nanre oðerre note ne mægen, oð ðone first ðe hie wel cunnen Englisc gewrit arædan; lære mon siððan furður on Lædengeðiode ða ðe mon furðor læran wille ond to hieran hade don wille.

6   Ða ic ða gemunde hu sio lar Lædengeðiodes ær ðissum afeallen wæs giond Angelcynn, ond ðeah monige cuðon Englisc gewrit arædan, ða ongan ic ongemang oðrum mislicum ond manigfealdum bisgum ðisses kynerices ða boc wendan on Englisc ðe is genemned on Læden *Pastoralis,* ond on Englisc *Hierdeboc,* hwilum word be worde, hwilum andgit of andgiete, swæ swæ ic hie geliornode æt Plegmunde minum ærcebiscepe ond æt Assere minum biscepe ond æt Grimbolde minum mæsseprioste ond æt Iohanne minum mæssepreoste. Siððan ic hie ða geliornod hæfde, swæ swæ ic hie forstod, ond swæ ic hie andgitfullicost areccean meahte, ic hie on Englisc awende, ond to ælcum biscepstole on minum rice wille ane onsendan; ond on ælcre bið an æstel, se bið on fiftegum mancessa. Ond ic bebiode on Godes naman ðæt nan mon ðone æstel from ðære bec ne do, ne ða boc from

turn those of the Latin nations likewise, after they studied it, through discerning translators turned it all into their own language. And also all other Christian nations turned a certain portion of it into their own tongue.

Therefore it seems to me better, if it seems so to you, that 5 we turn certain books—those most essential for all people to know—into that tongue that we can all comprehend, and arrange, as we very readily can with God's aid, if we have cessation of hostilities, that the present English youth of the class of freemen who have the wherewithal to commit to it, be applied to learning for as long as they cannot be put to any other employment, until such time as they can well read English writing; let those be instructed further in the Latin tongue whom it is desirable to instruct further and to appoint to a higher office.

When I remembered how decayed the teaching of Latin 6 had grown among the English, and yet many could read English writing, I began, amid other various and manifold affairs of this state, to render into English the book that is called in Latin *Pastoralis,* and in English *Shepherd's Book,* at times word for word, at times sense for sense, just as I had studied it with Plegmund my archbishop and with Asser my bishop and with Grimbold my chaplain and with John my chaplain. After I had studied it, in accordance with my understanding of it, and as sensibly as I could render it, I translated it into English, and to each episcopal seat in my kingdom I intend to send one copy; and in each there will be a certain pointer which will be valued at fifty crowns. And I direct in God's name that no one remove the pointer from the book, nor the book from the minster: there is no knowing

ðæm mynstre: uncuð hu longe ðær swæ gelærede biscepas sien, swæ swæ nu, Gode ðonc, welhwær siendon. Forðy ic wolde ðætte hie ealneg æt ðære stowe wæren, buton se biscep hie mid him habban wille, oððe hio hwær to læne sie, oððe hwa oðre bi write.

how long there will be such learned bishops there as, God be thanked, are now everywhere. Accordingly, I desire that they always remain in that location, unless the bishop wishes to have it with him, or it is somewhere on loan, or someone is making a copy of it.

TABLE OF CONTENTS

TABLE OF CONTENTS

x. Huelc se beon sceal ðe to reccenddome cuman sceal.

xi. Huelc se beon sceal se ðærto cuman ne sceal.

xii. Hu se se ðe gedafenlice ond endebyrdlice to cymð, hu he ðæron drohtian scyle.

xiii. Hu se lareow sceal beon clæne on his mode.

xiiii. Hu se lariow sceal beon on his weorcum fyrmesð.

xv. Hu se lariow sceal beon gesceadwis on his suigean ond nyttwyrðe on his wordum.

xvi. Hu se lariow sceal bion eallum monnum efnðrowiende ond foreðencende on hira earfeðum.

xvii. Hu se reccere sceal bion ðæm weldoendum monnum fore eaðmodnesse gefera, ond wið ðara yfelena unðeawas stræc for ryhtwislecum andan.

xviii. Hu se lariow ne sceal ða inneran gimenne gewanian for ðære uterran abisgunge, ne eft ða uterran ne forlæte he for ðære innerran.

xviiii. Ðætte se reccere his godan weorc fore gielpe anum ne do, ac ma for Godes lufan.

xx. Ðætte se reccere sceal geornlice witan ðætte oft ða unðeawas leogað ond licettað ðætte hi sien gode ðeawas.

xxi. Hu gesceadwis se reccere sceal bion on his ðreaunga ond on his oleccunga, ond eac on his hatheortnesse ond on his manðwærnesse.

xxii. Hu suiðe se reccere sceal bion on his smeaunga abisgod on þære halgan æ.

xxiii. Hu micel scyle bion ðæt toscead, ond hu mislice mon scyle men læran, mid ðæm cræfte ðæs lareowdomes.

xxiiii. Ðætte on oðre wisan sint to manianne weras, on oðre wiif.

xxv. Ðætte on oðre wisan sint to manianne ða iungan, on oðre ða ealdan.

xxvi. Ðætte on oðre wisan sint to manianne ða welegan, on oðre ða wædlan.

xxvii. Ðætte on oðre wisan sint to manianne ða gladan, on oðre ða unrotan.

xxviii. Ðætte on oðre wisan sint to monianne ða aldor-men, on oðre wisan ða hiremen.

xxviiii. Ðætte on oðre wisan sint to monianne ða hlafordas, on oðre wisan ða ðegnas ond eac ða ðeowas.

xxx. Ðætte on oðre wisan sint to monianne ða dolan, on oðre ða wisan.

xxxi. Ðætte on oðre wisan sint to monianne ða scam-fæstan, on oðre ða scamleasan.

xxxii. Ðætte on oðre wisan sint to monianne ða ofermo-dan ond ða upahafenan on hira mode, on oðre wisan ða earmheortan ond ða wacmodan.

xxxiii. Ðætte on oðre wisan sint to monianne ða un-geðylðegan, ond on oðre ða geðyldegan.

xxxiiii. Ðætte on oðre wisan sint to moniane ða welwil-lendan, ond on oðre ða æfstegan.

xxxv. Ðætte on oðre wisan sint to monianne ða bilwitan, on oðre ða ðweoran ond ða lytegan.

xxxvi. Ðætte on oðre wisan sint to monianne ða halan, on oðre ða unhalan.

xxxvii. Ðætte on oðre wisan sint to monianne ða ðe him ondrædað Godes suingellan oððe monna, ond forðy for-lætað ðæt hi yfel ne doð; on oðre wisan ða ðe bioð sua ahear-dode on unryhtwisnesse ðæt hi mon ne mæg mid nanre ðreaunge geðreatian.

XXXVIII. Ðætte on oðre wisan sint to monianne ða ðe to suiðe suige beoð, on oðre wisan ða ðe willað to fela idles ond unnyttes gesprecan.

XXXVIIII. Ðætte on oðre wisan sint to monianne ða ðe bioð to late, on oðre ða ðe bioð to hrade.

XL. Ðætte on oðre wisan sint to monianne ða monðwæran, on oðre ða grambæran.

XLI. Ðætte on oðre wisan sint to monianne ða eaðmodan, on oðre wisan ða uppahæfenan on hira mode.

XLII. Ðætte on oðre wisan sint to monianne ða anwillan, on oðre ða ungestæððegan ond unfæsðrædan.

XLIII. Ðætte on oðre wisan sint to monianne ða ðe hi selfe forgiefað gifernesse, on oðre wisan ða ðe doð forhæfdnesse.

XLIIII. Ðætte on oðre wisan sint to monianne ða ðe hira agenu ðing mildheortlice sellað, ond on oðre wisan ða ðe ðanne git willniað oðerra monna gereafian.

XLV. Ðætte on oðre wisan sint to monianne ða ðe nohuæðer ne oðra monna ne wilniað, ne hira agen nyllað sellan; on oðre wisan ða ðe willað sellan ðæt hi gestrinað ond ðeah nyllað geswican ðæt hi oðre men ne reafien.

XLVI. Ðætte on oðre wisan sint to monianne ða geðwæran, on oðre ða ungeðwæran.

XLVII. Ðætte on oðre wisan sint to moniane ða wrohtgeornan, on oðre ða gesibsuman.

XLVIII. Ðætte on oðre wisan sint to moniane ða ðe ða halgan æ ryhtlice ongitan ne cunnan, on oðre wisan ða ðe hi ryhtlice angietað ond ðeah for eaðmodnesse swigiað ðæt hi hie ne bodiat.

XLVIIII. Ðætte on oðre wisan sint to monianne ða ðe medomlice cunnon læran, ond ðeah for miclum ege ond for micelre eaðmodnesse forwandiað, ond on oðre wisan ða ðe ðanne giet to ðæm gewintrede ne beoð ne geðigene, ond ðeah for hrædhydignesse beoð to gegripene.

L. Ðætte on oðre wisan sint to monianne ða ðe worold-are wilniað, ond hi ðonne orsorglice habbað, ond on oðre wisan ða ðe woroldare wilniað, ond ðonne hi gewilnode hab-bað, hi ðonne mid micelre earfoðnesse ond mid micle broce onwuniað.

LI. Ðætte on oðre wisan sint to monianne ða ðe beoð ge-bundene mid sinrædenne, on oðre wisan ða ðe freo beoð ðara benda.

LII. Ðætte on oðre wisan sint to monianne ða ðe gefan-dod habbað ðara flæsclicra synna, on oðre wisan ða ðe ðæs nowiht ne cunnan.

LIII. Ðætte on oðre wisan sint to monianne ða ðe ða ge-worhtan synna wepað, on oðre ða ðe ða geðohtan wepað.

LIIII. Ðætte on oðre wisan sint to moniane ða ðe ðurh-togena scylda wepað, ond hi suaðeah ne forlætað, on oðre wisan ða ðe hi no ne hreowsiað, ond ðeah forlætað.

LV. Ðætte on oðre wisan sint to monianne ða ðe ða un-aliefedan ðing ða ðe hi doð herigeað, on oðre ða ðe hi tælað ond suaðeah doð.

LVI. Ðætte on oðre wisan sint to monianne ða ðe suiðe hrædlice beoð ofersuiðde mid sumere unryhtre gewilnunge, on oðre wisan ða ðe longe ær ymbðeahtiað, ond hit ðonne on lasð ðurhteoð.

LVII. Ðætte on oðre wisan sint to monianne ða ðe ofthrædlice lytla scylda wyrceað, on oðre wisan ða ðe hi

gehealdað wið þa lytlan scylda, ond ðeah hwiltidum afealleð on hefegum scyldum.

LVIII. Ðætte on oðre wisan sint to monianne ða ðe nan wuht godes ne onginnað, on oðre wisan ða ðe hit onginnað ond wel ne geendiað.

LVIIII. Ðætte on oðre wisan sint to monianne ða ðe deogollice yfel doð, ond god openlice, on oðre wisan ða ðe willað helan ðæt hi to gode doð, ond of sumum ðingum openlice kyðað ðæt hi willað ðæt men wenen ðæt hi yfele bion.

LX. Ymbe ðæt, hu man monige scyndan scyle to ðæm ðætte his godan dæda ne weorðen to yfelum dædum.

LXI. Ymbe ðæt, hu mon ænne mon scyndan scile ðonne he yfle costunga monige ðrowað.

LXII. Ðætte hwilum ða leohtan scylda beoð beteran to forlætan, ðy læs ða hefegran weorðen ðurhtogen.

LXIII. Ðætte ða untruman mod mon ne scyle eallinga to helice læran.

LXIIII. Be ðæm weorcum ðæs lareowes ond be his wordum.

LXV. Ðonne hwa ðis eall gefylled hæbbe, hu he ðonne sceal hine selfne geðencean ond ongietan, ðy læs hine auðer oððe his lif oððe his lar to up ahebbe.

DEDICATORY LETTER
OF GREGORY

Þu leofusta broður, suiðe freondlice ond suiðe fremsum-
lice ðu me tældesð, ond mid eaðmode ingeðonce ðu me cid-
desð, forðon ic min mað, ond wolde fleon ða byrðenne ðære
hirdelecan giemenne. Ðara byrðenna hefignesse, eall ðæt ic
his geman, ic awrite on ðisse andweardan bec, ðy læs hi
hwæm leohte ðyncen to underfonne; ond ic eac lære ðæt
hira nan ðara ne wilnie ðe hine unwærlice bega; ond se ðe hi
unwærlice ond unryhtlice gewilnige, ondræde he ðæt he hi
æfre underfenge.

2   Nu ic wilnige ðætte ðeos spræc stigge on ðæt ingeðonc
ðæs leorneres, suæ suæ on sume hlædre, stæpmælum near
ond near, oð ðæt hio fæstlice gestonde on ðæm solore ðæs
modes ðe hi leornige. Ond forðy ic hi todæle on feower: an is
ðara dæla hu he on ðone folgoð becume; oðer hu he ðæron
libbe; ðridda is hu he ðæron lære; feorðe is hu he his agene
unðeawas ongietan wille ond hira geðæf bion, þy læs he for
ðy underfenge his eaðmodnesse forlæte, oððe eft his lif sie
ungelic his ðenunga, oððe he to ðriste ond to stið sie for ðy
underfenge his lareowdomes. Ac gemetgige hit se ege his
agenra unðeawa, ond befæste he mid his lifes bisenum ða
lare ðæm ðe his wordum ne geliefen. Ond ðonne he god
weorc wyrce, gemyne he ðæs yfeles ðe he worhte, ðette sio
unrotnes, ðe he for ðæm yflan weorcum hæbbe, gemetgige

DEDICATORY LETTER
OF GREGORY

Dearest brother, in friendly and kindly fashion you reproved me, and with humble intent you chided me for having hidden myself and for having wished to escape the burden of pastoral care. The oppressiveness of those burdens,
all that I remember of it, I will write of in this present book,
to prevent their seeming to anyone light to assume; and I
likewise advise that no one covet them who will take them
up without caution; and let whoever desires them rashly and
improperly tremble at ever having assumed them.

Now I intend for this discourse to ascend in the mind of 2
the learner as if on a certain ladder, step by step, nearer and
nearer, until it stands firmly on the sunny uppermost floor
of the mind that studies it. And therefore I divide it into
four parts: one of the parts is how he shall attain the office;
the second how he should conduct his life in it; third is how
he should teach in it; fourth is how he should wish to recognize his own vices and contend with them, so that he not
lose his humility on account of taking office, or his life in
turn be incommensurate with his duties, or he be too inflexible and too stern for the assumption of his teaching duties.
But let the fear of his own vices temper it, and by the example of his life let him affirm his teaching to those who may
not believe his words. And when he does a good deed, let
him remember the bad that he has done, so that the discom-
fort he feels for those evil acts may temper the satisfaction

ðone gefean ðe he for ðæm godan weorcum hæfde, ðy læs he beforan ðæs dieglan deman eagum sie ahafen on his mode ond on his ofermettum aðunden, ond ðonne ðurh ðæt selflice his godan weorc forleose.

3   Ac monige sindon me suiðe onlice on ungelærednesse: ðeah ðe hi næfre leorningcnihtas næren, wilniað ðeah lareowas to beonne, ond ðyncet him suiðe leoht sio byrðen ðæs lareowdomes, forðon ðe hi ne cunnon ðæt mægen his micelnesse. From ðære dura selfre ðisse bec—ðæt is from onginne ðisse spræce—sint adrifene ond getælde ða unwaran ðe him agniat ðone cræft ðæs lareowdomes ðe hi na ne geleornodon.

which he might have had in the good deeds, to prevent his being high-flown in his mind and conceited in his pride before the eyes of the unseen judge, and through that self-regard vitiate his good works.

But many are quite like me with respect to want of learn- 3 ing: though they were never disciples, they wish nonetheless to be teachers, and the burden of teaching seems to them very light, because they cannot recognize its immensity. From the very door of this book—that is, from the beginning of this treatise—the unwary who appropriate the craft of teaching without having learned it are expelled and reproved.

BOOK ONE

Chapter 1

1. Ðætte unlærde ne dyrren underfon lareowdom.

Forðon ðe nan cræft nis to læranne ðæm ðe hine ær geornlice ne leornode, for hwon beoð æfre suæ ðriste ða ungelære-
dan ðæt hi underfon ða heorde ðæs lariowdomes, ðonne se
cræft ðæs lareowdomes bið cræft ealra cræfta? Hua nat ðæt
ða wunda ðæs modes bioð digelran ðonne ða wunda ðæs lic-
haman? Ond ðeah ða woroldlecan læcas scomaþ ðæt hi
onginnen ða wunda lacnian ðe hi gesion ne magon, ond huru
gif hi nouðer gecnawan ne cunnan ne ða medtrymnesse ne
eac ða wyrta ðe ðærwið sculon. Ond hwilon ne scomað ða ðe
ðæs modes læceas beon scoldon, ðeah ðe hi nane wuht ongitan ne cunnon ðara gæstlecena beboda, ðæt hie him onteoð
ðæt hie sien heortan læcas. Ac forðon ðe nu eall se weorðscipe ðisse worolde is gecierred, Gode ðonc, to weorðscipe
ðæm æwfæstum, ðæt ða sindon nu weorðoste ðe æwfæst-
oste sindon, forðon licet suiðe monig ðæt he æwfæsð lareow
sie, ðe he wilniað micle woroldare habban. Be ðam Crisð
selfa cleopode, ond ðus cwæð: "Hi secað ðæt hi mon ærest
grete ond weorðige on ceapstowum ond on gebeorscipum,
ond ðæt hie fyrmest hlynigen æt æfengieflum, ond ðæt
ieldesðe setl on gemetengum hi secað." Forðon hie sua on

BOOK ONE

Chapter 1

1. That the untutored not presume to undertake teaching.

Because no craft is to be taught by someone who has not already learned it, why are the uneducated so presumptuous as to undertake the responsibility of teaching, when the craft of teaching is the craft of all crafts? Who does not know that the wounds of the spirit are more perplexing than the wounds of the body? And yet mundane physicians are ashamed at setting out to heal wounds they cannot see, and especially if they neither recognize nor know how to deal with either the complaint or the herbal remedies to be applied. And sometimes, though those who would be physicians of the soul are at a loss how to interpret spiritual precepts at all, they feel no compunction at taking it on themselves to be healers of the heart. But because all the esteem of this world is now converted, thanks be to God, to esteem of the pious, so that now those are most revered who are the most devout, many pretend to be pious teachers because they wish to have grand worldly honors. Christ himself cried out against such and spoke thus: "They aim to be approached first and paid homage in marketplaces and at banquets, and to be the first to recline at suppers, and they claim the foremost seat at assemblies." Because they thus

ofermettum ond mid upahafenesse becumað to ðære are
ðære hirdelecan giemenne, hi ne magon medomlice ðenian
ða ðenunga, ond ðære eaðmodnesse lareowas bion; ac sio
tunge bið gescinded on ðam lariowdome ðonne hio oðer
lærð, oðer hio liornode. Suelcum monnum Dryhten cidde
ðurh ðone witgan, ond him suelc oðwat, ða he cuæð, "Hie
ricsedon—næs ðeah mines ðonces. Ealdormen hi wæron,
ond ic hie ne cuðe." Ða ðe sua ricsieað, hi ricsiað of hira
agnum dome, næs of ðæs hiehstan deman, ðonne hi ne beoð
mid nanre sylle underscotene ðæs godcundlican mægenes,
ne for nanum cræfte gecorene, ac mid hira agenre gewilnunge hie bioð onbærnede, ðæt hie gereafiað sua heane la-
riowdom suiðor ðonne hi hine geearnien. Hie ðonne se eca
ond se diegla dema up ahefeð suelce he hi nyte, ond
geðafiende he hit forbireð for ðam dome his geðylde. Ac
ðeah hi on ðam hade fela wundra wyrcen, eft ðonne hi to
him cumað, he cuið, "Gewitað from me ge unryhtwyrhtan;
nat ic hwæt ge sint." Eft he hie ðreade ðurh ðone witgan for
hira ungelærednesse, ða he cuæð, "Ða hierdas næfdon ondgit: hie æfdon mine æ, ond hi me ne gecniowon." Se ðe
Godes bebodu ne gecnæð, ne bið he oncnawen from Gode.
Ðæt ilce cuæð *sanctus* Paulus: "Se ðe God ne ongit, ne ongit
God hine."

2   Unwise lareowas cumað for ðæs folces synnum. Forðon
oft for ðæs lareowes unwisdome misfarað ða hieremenn,
ond oft for ðæs lareowes wisdome unwisum hieremonnum
bið geborgen. Gif ðonne ægðer bið unwis, ðonne is to geðencanne hwæt Crisð self cuæð on his godspelle; he cwæð, "Gif
se blinda ðone blindan læt, hi feallað begen on ænne pytt."
Be ðæm ilcan se sealmscop cuæð, "Sien hira eagan aðistrode

attain to the dignity of pastoral care in pride and with self-aggrandizement, they cannot adequately perform the duties and be teachers of humility; but in instructing, the tongue is abused teaching one thing when it has learned another. The Lord reprimanded such people through the prophet and charged them with such when he said, "They ruled—not, however, by my consent. They were princes, and I did not know them." Those who so rule govern by their own authority, not that of the highest judge, when they are not sustained by any foundation of divine strength, nor chosen for any achievement, but they are inflamed with their own desire, so that they thus usurp the high office of teacher more than they earn it. The eternal and unseen judge then makes them eminent as if he did not know them, and patiently he allows it for the dignity of his forbearance. And though they may work many wonders in that office, when at length they come to him, he will say, "Depart from me, you malefactors. I do not know who you are." Again he censured them through the prophet for their want of learning when he said, "These shepherds have no understanding: they had my law, and they did not know me." Whoever does not know God's commandments is unknown to God. Saint Paul said just the same: "Whoever does not recognize God, God does not recognize him."

Ignorant teachers arise on account of the people's sins. 2
For that reason followers often are led astray on account of the teacher's fatuity, and often foolish followers are spared because of the teacher's wisdom. If both are foolish, then what Christ himself said in his gospel is to be kept in mind: he said, "If the blind lead the blind, the two will fall into one and the same pit." About the same the psalmist said, "May

ðæt hi ne geseon, ond hiora hrygc simle gebieged." Ne cuæð
he ðæt forðy ðe he ænegum men ðæs wyscte oððe wilnode,
ac he witgode sua sua hit geweorðan sceolde. Soðlice ða eagan, ðæt beoð ða lareowas, ond se hrygc, ðæt sint ða hieremenn, forðan ða eagan bioð on ðam lichoman foreweardum
ond ufeweardum, ond se hrycg færð æfter ælcre wuhte; sua
gað ða lareowas beforan ðæm folce, ond ðæt folc æfter.
Ðonne ðam lareowum aðistriað ðæs modes eagan, ðe beforan gan scoldon mid godum bisenum, ðonne gebigð ðæt
folc hira hrycg to hefegum byrðenum manegum.

Chapter 2

11. Ne eft ða gelæredan, ðe swa nyllað libban swa hie
on bocum leornedon, ðæt hi scoldon ne underfon ða
are ðæs lareowdomes.

Monige eac wise lareowas winnað mid hira ðeawum wið
ða gæsðlecan bebodu ðe hi mid wordum lærað, ðonne hie on
oðre wisan libbað on oðre hi lærað. Oft ðonne se hirde gæð
on frecne wegas, sio hiord, ðe unwærre bið, gehrist. Be suelcum hirdum cwæð se witga, "Ge fortrædon Godes sceapa
gærs ond ge gedrefdon hiora wæter mid iowrum fotum,
ðeah ge hit ær undrefed druncen." Sua ða lareowas: hi drin-
cað suiðe hluter wæter, ðonne hi ðone godcundan wisdom
leorniað, ond eac ðonne hie hiene lærað; ac hie hit gedrefað

their eyes be dimmed so that they cannot see, and their back always bent." He did not say that because he wished or intended it of any person, but he prophesied as to how it should chance to be. In truth, the eyes are the teachers and the back is the followers, for the eyes are in front and upward in the body, and the back comes behind each creature; thus, the teachers go before the people, and the people behind. When the mind's eyes, which should lead with good examples, grow dim in teachers, the people bend their back to many heavy burdens.

Chapter 2

2. And, in turn, that the educated who will not live as they have learned in books should not assume the dignity of teaching.

Many learned teachers likewise by their actions wage a struggle against the spiritual precepts that they teach with their words when they live in one fashion and teach in another. Often, when the shepherd walks in perilous ways, the herd, which is less wary, topples over. About such shepherds the prophet said, "You trampled the grass of God's sheep, and you sullied their water with your feet, though you had already drunk it unsullied." Thus the teachers: they drink very pure water when they learn divine wisdom, and also when they teach it; but they foul it with their own vices

mid hira agnum unðeawum, ðonne ðæt folc bisenað on hira
unðeawum, nals on hira lare. Ðeah ðæt folc ðyrste ðære lare,
hie hie ne magon drincan, ac hio bið gedrefed mid ðam ðe ða
lareowas oðer doð oðer hie lærað. Be ðæm Dryhten cwæð
eft ðurh ðone witgan, "Yfle preostas bioþ folces hryre."

2   Ne dereð nan mon suiðor ðære halgan Gesomnunge
ðonne ða ðe ðone noman underfoð ond ða endebyrdnesse
ðæs halgan hades ond ðonne on woh doð, forðon hie nan
monn ne dearr ðreagean ðeah hie agylten, ac mid ðam beoð
synna suiðe gebrædda ðe hie beoð sua geweorðade. Ac hie
woldon selfe fleon ða byrðenne sua micelre scylde, ða ðe his
unwierðe wæron, gif hie mid hiora heortan earum woldon
gehieran ond geornlice geðencan ðone Cristes cuide, ða he
cuæð, "Se ðe ænigne ðissa ierminga besuicð, him wære
betere ðæt him wære sumu esulcweorn to ðæm suiran ge-
tiged, ond sua aworpen to sæs grunde." Ðurh ða cweorne is
getacnod se ymbhwyrft ðisse worolde ond eac monna lifes
ond hira gesuinces, ond ðurh ðone sægrund hira ende ond se
siðemesða demm. Ðonne bið sio cweorn becierred ðonne se
monn bið geendod; ðonne bið sio micle cweorn becierred
ðonne ðeos weorld bið geendod. Se ðonne ðe to halgum
hade becymð, ond ðonne mid yflum bisnum oððe worda
oððe weorca oðre on won gebringð, betre him wære ðæt he
on læssan hade ond on eorðlicum weorcum his lif geendode;
forðæm gif he on ðæm wel deð, he hæfð ðæs god lean; gif he
yfle deð, læsse wite he ðrowað on helle, gif he ana ðider
cymð, ðonne he do, gif he oðerne mid him ðider bringð.

when they give example to the people by their own bad ways, not at all by their instruction. Though the people thirst for that instruction, they cannot drink from it, but they are defiled by teachers' conducting themselves in one fashion and teaching another. About this the Lord said again through the prophet, "Bad priests are the people's ruin."

No one does more harm to holy Church than those who assume the name and the grade of holy orders and then conduct themselves disgracefully, since no one will dare upbraid them when they are guilty, but sins are promoted in proportion as these people are so revered. But those who were unworthy of it would themselves want to break free of the onus of such a grave offense if with their heart's ears they would listen and contemplate earnestly Christ's verdict when he said, "Whoever beguiles any of these innocents, it would be better for him if a certain millstone were tied to his neck and tossed thus to the bottom of the sea." By the millstone is expressed the course of this world and of the life of humans and their labors, and by the bottom of the sea their conclusion and the final damnation. When the mill is turned, the man has reached his end; when the great mill is turned, this world will have reached its end. Whoever attains to holy orders and then by bad example of either words or deeds brings others to woe, it would be better for him if he ended his life in a position of lower status and in mundane work, because if he does well at that, he will have good reward for it; if he does ill, he will suffer less misery in hell if he goes there alone than he will do if he takes another there with him.

Chapter 3

111. Be ðære byrðenne ðæs reccenddomes, ond hu he
scyle eall earfoðu forsion, ond
hu forht he sceal beon for ælcre
orsorgnesse.

Forðon we ðiss feawum wordum sædon, ðy we woldon ge-cyðan hu micel sio byrðen bið ðæs lareowdomes, ðy læs ænig hine underfon durre ðara ðe his unwierðe sie, ðy læs hie ðurh ða wilnunga ðære woroldare underfo ðone latteowdom ðæs forlores. Suiðe medomlice Iacobus se apostol his stirde, ða he cuæð, "Broðor, ne beo eower to fela lareowa." Forðæm se wealhstod self Godes ond monna—ðæt is Crist—fleah eorðrice to underfonne. Se se ðe ealne ðone wisdom ðara uferrenna gæsta oferstigð ond ær worolde ricsode on hefe-num, hit is awriten on ðæm godspelle, Iudeas comon ond woldon hine don niedenga to cyninge. Ða se hælend ðæt ongeat, ða becierde he hie ond gehydde hiene. Hwa meahte ieð monnum rædan butan scylde, ðonne se ðe hi gescop? Ne fleah he ðy rice ðy his ænig monn bet wyrðe wære, ac he wolde us ða bisene astellan, ðæt we his to suiðe ne gitseden; ond eac wolde for us ðrowian. He nolde beon cyning, ond his agnum willan he com to rode gealgan. Ða weorðmynde cynehades he fleah, ond ðæt wite ðæs fraceðlecestan deaðes he geceas, forðam ðætte we, ðe his liomu sindon, leornedon æt him ðæt we flugen ða oliccunga ðisses middangeardes,

Chapter 3

3. Of the burden of governance, and how the teacher shall hold all vicissitudes as nothing, and what dread he ought to feel of all easy circumstances.

We have said this in brief words, for the reason that we wished to make plain how great the burden of the office of a teacher is, so that anyone who is unworthy of it should not presume to accede to it, lest through desire for worldly honor he should undertake to lead the way to perdition. Quite aptly the apostle James discouraged it when he said, "Brother, do not let too many of you be teachers." For that reason, the mediator himself between God and humans— that is, Christ—refused to accept earthly rule. It is written in the gospel about the one who transcends all the wisdom of the higher spirits and ruled in heaven before the world was, that the Jews came and would make him king by compulsion. When the savior perceived that, he avoided them and hid himself. Who could rule humans more easily without fault than the one who created them? He did not refuse governance because any person would be worthier of it, but he wished to set us the example that we not hunger for it too much, and also because he intended to suffer for us. He declined to be king, and of his own will he came to the gallows of the cross. He shunned the dignity of kingship, and he embraced the torment of the vilest death so that we, who are his limbs, should learn from him to shun the allurements of

ond eac ðæt ðæt we his ege ond his brogan us ne ondreden, ond for soðfæsðnesse ðæt we lufigen gesuinc, ond orsorgnesse we us ondræden, ond hi forðy forbugen, forðam for ðære orsorgnesse monn oft aðint on ofermettum, ond ða earfeðu ðurh sar ond ðurh sorge hiene geclænsiað ond geeaðmedað. On ðæm gesundfulnessum ðæt mod wierð up ahafen; ond on ðæm earfeðum, ðeah hit ær up ahafen wære, hit bið geeaðmedd. On ðære gesundfulnesse mon forgiett his selfes; on ðæm gesuincum he sceal hine selfne geðencean, ðeah he nylle. On ðære orsorgnesse oft ðæt he to gode gedyde he forliesð; on ðæm earfoðum oft ðæt he longe ær to yfle gedyde, he gebett.

2   Suiðe oft monn bið ðære earfoðnesse lareowdome underðieded, ðeah he ær nolde his lareowes ðeawum ond larum bion. Ac ðeah hine ðonne ða brocu getyn ond gelæren, sona, gif he on rice becymð, for ðære weorðunge ðæs folces, he bið on ofermettu awended, ond gewunað to ðæm gielpe. Sua sua Saul se cyning, æresð he fleah ðæt rice, ond tealde hine selfne his suiðe unwierðne. Ac sona sua he ðone anwald onfeng ðæs rices, he astag on ofermetto, ond hine bealg wið ðone ilcan Samuel ðe hine ær on ðæm rice gebrohte, ond hine to gehalgode, forðam ðe he him sæde beforan ðam folce his unðeawas, ða he him ær hiera ðonces gestieran ne meahte; ond ða he him from wolde, ða gefeng he hine, ond toslat his hrægl, ond hine geunarode. Sua eac Dauit, ðe folneah on eallum ðingum Gode licode, sona sua he ða byrðenne næfde sua monegra earfeða, he wæs mid ofermettum gewundad, ond ðæt suiðe wælhreowlice gecyðde on Urias slæge his agenes holdes ðegnes, for ðære scamleaslecan gewilnunge his wifes. Se ilca se monegum yfelum wið

this world, and, too, that we not shrink from its intimidation and its terrors, and that for piety we love labor, and that we detest prosperity, and therefore avoid it, because through prosperity one is often elated with pride, and through pain and sorrow his trials purify and humble him. In well-being the spirit is raised, and in vicissitudes, even if it were earlier exalted, it is humbled. In easy circumstances one forgets oneself; in labor he shall engage in introspection, even if he wishes otherwise. In insouciance he will often spoil what he has done to the good; faced with reverses, he will often amend what of ill he has long done before.

Quite often one is made subject to the instruction of adversity, even if before that he was unwilling to be subject to the morals and instruction of his teacher. But though these tribulations may instruct and educate him, all at once, if he comes to a position of authority, by the reverence of the people he is diverted to pride and habituates himself to ostentation. Just so King Saul at first refused governance and counted himself fully unworthy of it. But as soon as he assumed the rule of the realm, he rose in pride and grew incensed with the same Samuel who had brought him to power and consecrated him, because he told him his vices before the people, seeing as before that he was not able to control him with their consent; and when he wanted to depart from him, he seized him and ripped his clothing and dishonored him. So, too, as soon as David, who pleased God in nearly all respects, was rid of the burden of so many difficulties, he was wounded by pride, and he showed it in extremely cruel fashion by the killing of Uriah, his own loyal officer, out of shameless lust for his wife. This same one who had forgiven many ills committed against him

39

hine selfne forworhtum ær gearode, he wearð eft sua ungemetlice grædig ðæs godan deaþes, butan ælcre scylde ond
ælcre wiðerweardnesse wið hine. Se ilcan Dauid ðe forbær
ðæt he ðone kyning ne yfelode, ðe hine on sua heardum
wræce gebrohte, ond of his earde adræfde, ða he his wel geweald ahte on ðæm scræfe, he genom his loðan ænne læppan
to tacne ðæt he his geweald ahte, ond hine ðeah for ðam
ealdan treowum forlet. Se ilca Dauid miclum his agenes
herges pleah, ond monigne forsende, ðær he ymb his getreowne ðegn unsynnigne sierede. Sio scyld hine suiðe feorr
of ealra haligra rime atuge, ðær him eft ða gesuinc ond ða
earfeðu ne gehulpen.

Chapter 4

IIII. Ond hu oft sio bisgung ðæs rices ond ðæs
recedomes toslit ðæt mod ðæs recceres.

Suiðe oft gedrefeð ða heortan sio manigfealde giemen ðæs
underfangenan lareowdomes, ond ðonne ðæt mod bið on
monig todæled, hit bið on anes hwæm ðe unfæstre, ond eac
ðe unnyttre. Bi ðam cuæð Salomonn se snottra, "Sunu min,
ne todæl ðu on to fela ðin mod, ond ðin weorc endemes."
Forðan oft ðonne mon forlæt ðone ege ond ða fæsðrædnesse
ðe he mid ryhte on him innan habban scolde, hine spænð his
mod to suiðe manegum unnyttum weorce. He sorgað ymb

grew so unreservedly desirous of the good man's death without a single offense or a single act of defiance against him. This same David, who refrained from harming the king who had sent him into such hard exile and driven him from his homeland, when he had him completely in his power in the cave, took one corner of his mantle as a sign that he had had control of him and yet had released him for their alliance of old. This same David exposed his own army to great danger and betrayed many in plotting against his true, guiltless officer. The crime would have distanced him quite far from the communion of all saints if his labors and struggles had not helped him back.

Chapter 4

4. And how the affairs of state and of governance often divide the attention of one who governs.

Quite frequently the multiple cares of the position of teacher, once assumed, disturb the heart, and when the mind is drawn in many directions it is less intent on each thing, and also less effective. About this the wise Solomon said, "My son, do not disperse your attention too widely, and likewise your efforts." For often when a person casts aside the reverence and the resolve that he ought rightly to have within him, his way of thinking commits him to excessively numerous pointless undertakings. He frets about them and

ða, ond bið ðara suiðe gemyndig, ond forgiett his selfes, ðonne he suiðor his mod gebint to ðam unnyttran weorcum ðonne he ðyrfe. Him bið sua sua ðam menn ðe bið abisgod on færelde mid oðrum cierrum, oð ðæt he nat hwider he ær wolde, ne geðencan ne con hwæt him losað on ðære gælinge ðe he ða hwile amierreð, ond hu suiðe he on ðam gesyngað. Ne wende na Ezechias Israhela kyning ðæt he gesyngade, ða he lædde ða ællðeodgan ærenddracan on his maðmhus, ond him geiewde his goldhord. Ac he onfunde ðeah Godes ierre on ðam hearme ðe his bearne æfter his dagum becom. Ond ðeah he wende ðæt hit nan syn nære.

2   Oft ðonne hwæm gebyreð ðæt he hwæt mærlices ond wundorlices gedeð, ond his ðonne wundriað ða ðe him un-derðiedde bioð, ond hine heriegeað, ðonne ahefð he hine on his mode, ond his deman ierre fullice to him gecigð, ðeah ðe he hit on yfelum weorcum ne geopenige. Suaðeah mid ðy selflice se dema bið genieded to ðæm ierre, ond se dema se ðe ðæt inngeðonc eall wat, he eac ðæm inngeðonce demð. We magon monnum bemiðan urne geðonc ond urne willan, ac we ne magon Gode. Hwæt, se Babylonia cyning wæs suiðe up ahafen on his mode for his anwalde ond for his ge-limpe, ða he fægnode ðæs miclan weorces ond fægernesse ðærre ceastre, ond hine oðhof innan his geðohte eallum oðrum monnum, ond suigende he cwæð on his mode, "Hu ne is ðis sio micle Babilon ðe ic self atimbrede to kynestole ond to ðrymme, me selfum to wlite ond wuldre, mid mine agne mægene ond strengo?" Ða suigendan stefne suiðe hraðe se diegla dema gehirde, ond him suiðe undeogollice geondwyrde mid ðam witum ðe he hit suiðe hrædlice wræc. Ða upahafenesse he arasode ond hie getælde, ða he hine

is overly concerned with them, and he forgets himself when he devotes his attention more to those inconsequential pursuits than he need do. He is like someone on a journey who is occupied by other matters, until he forgets where he had intended to go, and he cannot imagine what he is losing by the time he squanders in that delay, and how badly he thus goes astray. Hezekiah, king of Israel, never supposed that he sinned when he admitted the foreign emissaries to his treasury and showed them his hoard of gold. Nonetheless, he experienced God's wrath in the harm that fell to his child's lot after his days. And yet he did not believe that it was any sin.

Often when a person succeeds in doing something nota- 2 ble and wonderful, and those subject to him are amazed at him and sing his praises, he exalts himself in his mind, and he utterly calls down his judge's anger on him, though he does not reveal it by ill deeds. Nonetheless, by that self-regard the judge is compelled to anger, and the judge who knows all one's thoughts judges those thoughts, as well. We can conceal our thoughts and our desires from humans, but we cannot from God. Now, the Babylonian king was quite conceited at heart over his power and his good fortune when he exulted in the tremendous accomplishment and the splendor of his city, and he exalted himself in his mind before all other people, and without speaking aloud he said in his heart, "Is this not the great Babylon which I myself constructed as a royal seat and as a mark of majesty, to my own brilliance and glory, with my own power and strength?" The unseen judge at once heard the private voice and answered him very publicly with the torments with which he quite soon avenged it. This hubris God corrected and reproved

ascead of ðam woroldrice, ond hine gehwyrfde to un-
gesceadwisum neatum, ond sua awende mode he hine
geðiedde to feldgongendum deorum; ond sua ðy ðearlan
dome he forleas his mennisce. Se ilca se ðe wende ðæt he
wære ofer ealle oðere menn, him gebyrede ðæt he nyste self
hwæðer he monn wæs. Suaðeah, ðeah ic nu ðis recce, næ
tæle ic na micel weorc ne ryhtne anwald, ac ic tæle ðæt hine
mon forðy up ahebbe on his mode; ond ða untrymnesse
hiera heortan ic wolde getrymman, ond gestiran ðære wilnunge ðæm unmedemum, ðæt hiera nan ne durre gripan sua
orsorglice on ðæt rice ond on ðone lareowdom, ðy læs ða
gongen on sua frecne stige, ða ðe ne magon uncwaciende
gestondan on emnum felda.

Chapter 5

v. Bi ðæm ðe magon on ealdordome nytte beon
on bisnum ond on cræftum,
ond ðonne for hira agenre
ieðnesse ðæt fleoð.

Ac monige siendun mid miclum giefum monegra cræfta
ond mægene geweorðode, forðon ðe hie hie scoldon monegum tæcan, ond for oðerra monna ðearfe onfoð ðyllica giefa:
ðæt is ðæt hie gehealdað hira lichoman firenlusta clænne;

when he sundered him from earthly rule and turned him to an irrational beast of burden, and, his mind so altered, he consigned him to the field animals; and so by that severe judgment he lost his humanity. To the very one who had supposed that he was above all other people it happened that he did not himself know whether he was human. Nonetheless, though I recount this now, I deplore neither great works nor legitimate authority, but I deplore that a person should on that account exalt himself in his mind, and I would fortify the weakness of the heart, and curb the desire in the unfit, so that none of them presume to grasp at authority and the position of teacher so confidently, lest those walk so perilous a path who cannot stand on level ground without staggering.

Chapter 5

5. Of those who in governance can be productive in the way of setting an example and in the way of virtues, and yet who for their own convenience shun it.

But there are many endowed with great gifts of numerous virtues and with ability, for the purpose that they should teach them to many, and it is for the need of other people that they receive such gifts: that is that they keep their

oðer is ðæt hi beoð on færhæfdnesse strenge strange; ðridde
is ðæt hi beoð mid lara suetmettum gefylde; feorðe is ðæt
hi beoð on ælengum ðingum ond ælcre longunge geðyldige,
ond on forebyrde eaðmode; fifte is ðæt hie habbað ða arod-
nesse ond ða bieldo ðæt hie magon anweald habban; siexte
is ðæt hi beoð fremsume; siofoðe is ðæt hi beoð reðe ond
stræce for ryhtwisnesse. Ða ðe ðonne ðyllice beoð, ond him
mon suelcne folgað beodeð, ond hie him wiðsacað, oft him
gebyreð ðæt hie weorðað bereafod ðara giefa ðe him God for
monigra monna ðingum geaf, næs for hiera anra. Ðonne hie
synderlice ðenceað hu hie selfe scylen fullfremodeste weorðan, ond ne giemað to hwon oðerra monna wise weorðe,
mid ðy hi bereafiað hie selfe ðara goda ðe hie wilniað synderlice habban. Be suelcum monnum Crist on his godspelle
cuæð, "Ne scyle nan mon blæcern ælan under mittan." Ond
eft he cuæð to Petre ðæm apostole, "Petrus, lufastu me?" He
cuæð: "Ðu wast ðæt ic ðe lufige." Ond ða cuæð Dryhten:
"Fed ðonne min sceap, gif ðu me lufige." Gif ðonne seo fed-
ing ðara sceapa bið ðære lufan tacen, hwi forcwið ðonne se
ðe him God suelce cræftas giefð ðæt he ne fede his heorde,
buton he cueðan wielle ðæt he ne lufige ðone Hlaford ond
ðone hean hierde eallra gesceafta? Be ðam Paulus se apostol
cuæð, "Gif Crist for us eallum dead wæs, ðonne weorðað
ealle menn deade. Hwæt is ðonne betere ða hwile ðe we libben, ðonne we ures flæsces lustum ne libben, ac ðæs bebodum ðe for us dead wæs ond eft aras?"

2   Be ðam cuæð Moyses, "Gif hwa gefare ond nan bearn ne
gestriene, gif he broðor læfe, fo se to his wife. Gif he ðonne
bearn ðærbig gestriene, ðonne cenne he ðæt ðam gefarenan

bodies undefiled by lust; a second is that they are self-disciplined in the rigor of abstinence; a third is that they are filled with the sweet delicacies of learning; a fourth is that they are patient about tedious matters and every delay, and humble in authority; a fifth is that they have the spirit and the self-confidence to hold onto power; a sixth is that they are benign; a seventh is that they are severe and inflexible in the cause of righteousness. When those, then, who are of that sort are offered authority and they refuse it, often it happens to them that they are deprived of the gifts that God gave them for many people's sake, not for their own. When they consider only how they themselves can become most perfect, and they pay no heed to what other people's condition may amount to, they thereby deprive themselves of the benefits which they wish to have to themselves. About such people Christ said in his gospel, "No one ought to light a lamp under a bushel." And further he said to Peter the apostle, "Do you love me, Peter?" He said, "You know that I love you." And then the Lord said, "Then feed my sheep if you love me." If the feeding of the sheep is a token of love, why then does he whom God gives such talents refuse to feed his flock unless he wishes to say that he does not love the Lord and the high shepherd of all creation? About this Saint Paul said, "If Christ died for the sake of us all, then all people shall die. What is better, then, during the time we are alive, than to live not for the pleasures of our flesh, but after the commandments of the one who died for us and rose again?"

About this Moses said, "Should someone die and produce 2 no offspring, if he leaves a brother, let him take his wife. If he then conceives a child with her, let him beget it for the

breðer ðe hie ær ahte. Gif he ðonne ðæt wif wille forsacan, ðonne hræce hio him on ðæt nebb foran, ond his mægas hine anscogen oðre fet, ðæt mon mæge siððan hatan his tun ðæs anscodan tun." Ðis wæs ryht dom on ðære ealdan æ, ond is nu us to bispelle. Se ær gefarena broðor getacnað Crist. He hine ætiede æfter ðære æriste, ond cuæð, "Farað ond cyðað minum broðrum ðæt hie cumen to Galileum, ðær hie me geseoð." He gefor suelce he butan bearnum gefore, forðon he næfde gefylled ða giet ðone rim his gecorenra. Sua sua ðæs gefarenan broðor wif on ðære ealdan æ wæs geboden ðæm lifiendan breðer to onfonne, sua is cynn ðæt sio giemen ðære halgan ciricean—ðæt is Cristes folces gesomnung—sie ðam beboden ðe hie wel ofer mæge, ond hiere wel rædan cunne. Gif hire ðonne se wiðsace, ðonne is cynn ðæt him spiwe ðæt wif on ðæt nebb—ðæt is ðæt hine tæle ðæs folces gesomnung, emne suelce hie him on ðæt nebb spæten, forðon ðe he nyle giefan ðæt him God geaf, ond helpan ðæs folces mid ðam ðe he his healp. Sua is cynn ðæt sio halige gesomnung tæle ælces ðara god ðe hit him anum wile to gode habban, ond nyle oðera mid helpan. Se við eac mid ryhte oðre fet anscod, ond hine mon scyle on bismer hatan se anscoda. Be ðæm cuæð Crist on his gospelle, "Sceawiað iowre fet, ðæt ge sien gearwe to ganganne on sibbe weg æfter minra boca bebodum." Gief we ðonne habbað sua micle sorge ond sua micle gieman urra niehstena sua sua ure selfra, ðonne hæbbe we begen fet gescode suiðe untællice; gif we ðonne agiemeleasiað urra niehstena ðearfa, ond ðenceað ymbe ure synderlice, ðonne bið us suiðe fracoðlice oðer fot unscod.

departed brother who had had her. If, then, he chooses to refuse the woman, let her spit in his face, and let his kinsmen remove one of his shoes, so that his house can afterward be called the house of the unshod." This was lawful judgment under the old law, and now it is a prefiguration to us. The first-departed brother stands for Christ. He revealed himself after the resurrection and said, "Go and announce to my brothers that they should come to Galilee, where they will see me." He passed away as if he did so without children, because he had not yet filled the ranks of his elect. Just as the wife of the deceased brother under the old law was offered for the surviving brother to take, so it is natural that the care of holy Church—that is, the congregation of Christ's own people—be offered to one who can well preside over it and knows how to guide it well. If, then, he refuses her, it is natural that the woman should spit in his face—that is, that the congregation of the people berate him, just as if they were to spit in his face, because he will not render up what God gave him, and help the people with that with which God gave help to him. Just so, it is natural that holy Church censure the gift of each who wishes to have it as a gift for himself alone and is unwilling to help others with it. He is likewise rightly unshod on one foot, and he ought to be called "the unshod" in disgrace. About such a one Christ said in his gospel, "See to your feet, that you be prepared to go on the way of peace after the precepts of my books." If, then, we have as much conscientiousness and as much care of our neighbors as of ourselves, we will have both feet shod quite irreproachably; if, then, we neglect our neighbors in need and think about ourselves exclusively, one of our feet is very disgracefully unshod.

3   Monige menn siendon, sua sua we ær cuædon, ðe beoð geweorðode mid miclum ond mid monegum Godes giefum, ond ðonne beoð onælede mid ðære gierninge ðara smeaunga Godes wisdomes anes, ond fleoð ðonne ða nyttwyrðan hiersumnesse ðære lare, ond nyllað ðæs ðencean hu hie mægen nyttweorðuste bion hiera niehstum, ac lufiað diegla stowa, ond fleoð monna onsiena. Gif him ðonne God ryhtlice ond stræclice deman wile, ond he him for his mildheortnesse ne arað, ðonne beoð hie sua monegum scyldum scyldige sua hie manegra unðeawa gestiran meahton mid hiora larum ond bisenum, gif hi ongemong monnum beon wolden. Hwæt ðenceað ða ðe on suelcum weorcum scinað, ond magon hiera niehstum sua nytte beon, hwy hie ðara geearnunga hiora diegelnesse ond anette bet truwigen ðonne ðære hu hie oðerra monna mæst gehelpen? Hwæt se ancenneda Godes sunu of his Fæder bosme wæs ferende to urre andweardnesse ðæt he ure gehulpe?

Chapter 6

VI. Bi ðæm ðe for eaðmodnesse fleoð ða byrðenne ðæs lareowdomes; ðonne hie beoð ryhtlice eaðmode ðonne hie ne winnað wið ðone godcundan dom.

Ðonne siendon monige ðe fleoð for eaðmodnesse anre, forðon hie noldon ðæt hie mon ahofe ofer ða ðe him beteran ðynceað ðonne hie selfe. Nis ðæs ðonne nan tweo, gif suelc

There are many people, as we said earlier, who are distin- 3 guished by great and numerous gifts from God, and then they are inflamed with longing for the study of God's wisdom alone, and consequently resist beneficial submission to instruction, and they refuse to consider how they could be most serviceable to their neighbors, but they love secluded places, and they avoid being seen. If God will justly and strictly judge them, and will not out of his benignity excuse them, they will be guilty of as many trespasses as the vices they could have corrected by their teaching and example if they had been willing to be in society. What do they think, those who are brilliant at such accomplishments, and can be so useful to their neighbors: for what reason should they trust better in the rewards of their seclusion and solitude than of how they can best assist other people? Did not the only begotten son of God proceed from his Father's embrace into our midst in order to help us?

Chapter 6

6. Of those who for humility evade the burden of teaching; they will be properly humble when they do not contend with divine will.

Then there are many who shirk solely out of humility, because they do not wish to be raised above those who seem to them better than themselves. There is in that case no doubt

eaðmodnes bið mid oðrum godum ðeawum begyrded, ðæt
ðæt bið beforan Godes eagum soð eaðmodness, ðonne he
for nanre anwielnesse ne wiðcuið ðam nyttan weorcum ðe
him mon beodeð to underfonne. Ne bið ðæt na soð eaðmodnes, gif mon ongiett ðæt ðæt Godes willa sie ðæt he
ofer oðre beon scyle, ðæt he ðonne wiðsace, ac beo underðieded Godes willan ond his dome, ond forlæte ða uncyste
ðære anwielnesse. Ðonne he oferstæled bið, ond him gereaht bið ðæt he oðrum mæg nytt bion on ðam ðe him mon
ðonne bebeodeð, mid his mode he hit sceal fleon, ond ðeah
for hiersumnesse he hit sceal underfon.

Chapter 7

VII. Ðætte oft ðæs lareowdomes ðenung bið swiðe
untælwyrðlice gewilnad, ond eac swiðe
untælwierðlice monige beoð to geniedde.

Þeahhwæðre monige wilniað folgoðes ond ealdordomes
suiðe untælwierðlice, ond monige beoð to geniedde eac
suiðe untælwierðlice. Ðæt we magon sueotole ongietan, gif
we geðenceað ða twegen witgan ðe God wolde sendan to
læranne. Oðer hiene his selfes willum gebead to ðære lare
ond to ðæm færelte. Oðer for ðæm ege, ðe he ondred ðæt he
hit sua medomlice don ne meahte, him wiðsoc. Ðæt wæs
Heremias. Ða he hine sendan wolde, ða bæd he eaðmodlice
ðæt he hiene ne sende ond cuæð, "Eala, eala, eala, Dryhten,

about it, if such humility is reinforced by other good practices, it will be in God's eyes true humility when it is for no self-will that one refuses to undertake the useful work which he is asked to accept. In the event it is perceived that it is God's will that he should be above others, it is not true humility for him then to refuse, but let him be subservient to God's will and his judgment, and put aside the fault of obstinacy. When he is persuaded, and it is demonstrated to him that he can be of use to others concerning what is asked of him, in his heart he ought to shun it, and yet for obedience' sake he ought to accept it.

Chapter 7

7. That the vocation of teaching is often quite blamelessly desired, and also many very blamelessly are compelled to it.

Nonetheless, many desire authority and governance quite blamelessly, and many are likewise compelled to it blamelessly. This we can perceive plainly if we consider the two prophets whom God wished to send to preach. One of them offered himself of his own accord for teaching and traveling. The other refused it out of dread, inasmuch as he feared that he could not do it so adequately. That was Jeremiah. When he intended to send him, he prayed humbly that he would not send him and said, "Oh, oh, oh, Lord, I

ic eom cnioht. Hwæt conn ic sprecan?" Ac Essaias, ða
Dryhten acsode hwone he sendan meahte, ða cuæð Essaias,
"Ic eom gearo. Send me." Loca nu hu ungelic spræc eode
of ðissa tuega monna muðe. Ac hio wæs of suiðe gelicum
willan, forðon hio aweoll of anum wille; ðeah heo an tu te-
fleowe, ðeah wæs sio æspryng sio soðe lufu. Ymb ða we habbað tua bebodu: an is ðæt we lufigen God, oðer ðæt we lufien
ure niehstan. For ðære lufan Essaias wilnode hu he nyttosð
meahte beon his nihstum on ðys earfeðlican life, ond forðon
he wilnode ðære ðegnunga ðæs lariowdomes. Hieremias
ðonne wilnode singallice hine geðiedan to ðære lufan his
scippendes, ond forðam he forcwæð, ond nolde ðæt hine
mon sende to læranne. Ðæt ilce ðæt he untælwyrðlice ondred to underfonne, ðæt ilce se oðer swiðe hergeondlice
gewilnode. Oðer ondred ðæt he forlure sprecende ða ge-
strion ðe he on ðære swigean geðencan meahte; oðer ondred
ðæt he ongeate on his swygean ðæt he sumne hearm geswi-
gode ðær ðær he freme gecleopian meahte, gif he ymb ðæt
geornlice swunce.

2   Ac we sculon swiðe smealice ðissa ægðer underðencean,
forðon ðe se ðe ðær wiðcwæð, na fullice ne wiðcwæð, ond se
se ðe wolde ðæt hine mon sende, he geseah ær hine clænsian
ðurh ða colu ðæs alteres, ðy læs ænig unclænsod dorste on
swa micelne haligdom fon ðære clænan ðegnenga ðæs sa-
cerdhades, oððe eft ænig durre on eaðmodnesse hiwe hit
ofermodlice forcweðan, swelce he licette eaðmetto, ond doo
ðeah for gilpe, gif hine gecist sio uplice gifu. Ac forðæm ðe
hit swa earfoðe is ænegum menn to witanne hwonne he geclænsod sie, he mæg ðy orsorglicor forbugan ða ðegnunga;
ond næs swaðeah to anwillice ne forbuge he, swa we ær

am a lad. What do I know about speaking?" But Isaiah, when the Lord asked whom he could send, said, "I am ready. Send me." Observe, now, what different speech came out of the mouths of these two people. But it was out of a very similar intent, because it welled up from a single spring: though it flowed out in two streams, the source was genuine love. About that we have two commandments: one is that we love God, the other that we love our neighbor. Out of love, Isaiah desired to be as useful as he could be to his neighbors in this life of difficulties, and therefore he desired the service of being a teacher. Jeremiah, then, wished to apply himself constantly to the love of his creator, and therefore he refused and wished not to be sent to teach. The very thing that he blamelessly feared to undertake, the other very commendably desired. One feared that in speaking he would profane those precious things that he had been able to meditate upon in silence; the other feared that he would feel that by not speaking he would be passing over in silence some ill about which he could cry out to advantage if he took up the task in earnest.

Yet we ought to examine these two quite closely, because 2 the one who refused did not refuse entirely, and the one who wished to be sent saw that he was first purified with the coals of the altar, so that no one unpurified should dare assume such great sanctity of the pure service of the priesthood, or else someone should dare under pretense of humility refuse it out of pride, such that he should feign humility and yet do it for vainglory, if heavenly grace should select him. But since it is so difficult for anyone to know when he is pure, he can the more confidently decline service; and yet let him not at all decline too decidedly, as we said before,

cwædon, ðonne he ongiete ðone ufancundan willan ðæt he hit don scyle. Ægðer ðissa gefylde Moyses ða he wiðsoc swa miclum ealdordome. Ægðer ge he wolde ge he nolde, ond ðeah for eaðmodnesse geðafode. We witon ðæt he nære eaðmod, gif he underfenge ðone ealdordom swelces unrim-folces buton ege; ond eft he wære ofermod, gif he wiðcwæde ðæt he nære underðidd his scippende. Ac ægðer ðissa he dyde for eaðmodnesse ond for underðidednesse. He scea-wode hine selfne, ond pinsode, ða ða him ðuhte ðæt he hit doon ne meahte, ond swaðeah geðafode, forðam ðe he ge-truwode ðæs mægene ðe hit him bebead.

3   Hwæt, se haliga wer ongeat þæt he hæfde Godes fultom, ond swaðeah ondred ðæt he underfenge ðone lattiowdom ðæs folces; ond nu him ne ondrædað ða dolan for hiera agnum scyldum ðæt hie sien ofer oðre, ond ne magon him gegaderian on ðyllicum bisene hu micel synn ond hu micel frecennes hit bið. God selfa tyhte Moyses on ðone folgoð, swaðeah he him ondred; ond nu fundiað swelce wræccan ond teoð to, woldon underfon ðone weorðscipe ond eac ða byrðenne; ond ða ðe beoð mid hira agnum byrðennum ofðrycte ðæt hie ne magon gestondan, hie willað lustlice un-derfon oðerra monna, ond unniedige hie underlutað mid hira sculdrum oðerra byrðenna toeacan hiera agnum. He ne mæg his agne aberan, ond wolde ðeah maran habban.

when he perceives the divine will to be that he should do it. Moses fulfilled both of these conditions when he refused such great dominion. He both was and was not willing, and yet out of humility he consented. We know that he would not have been humble if he had accepted sovereignty over such a vast nation without trepidation, and, conversely, he would have been arrogant had he refused to be subject to his creator. But he did both of these things for humility and for subservience. He examined himself and reflected when it seemed to him that he could not do it, and yet consented because he trusted in the might of the one who asked it of him.

Now, the holy man perceived that he had God's assistance, and yet he was afraid to take up the instruction of the people; and now the foolish are not afraid on account of their own faults to have charge of others, and cannot gather from such an example how great a sin and what an enormous peril it is. God himself urged leadership upon Moses, yet he was afraid; and now such wretches try for it and approach it intending to assume the honor and also the burden; and as for those who are so weighed down by their own burdens that they cannot stand, they are all too willing to assume other people's, and without any coercion they shoulder others' loads in addition to their own. They cannot sustain their own and yet would have a greater. 3

Chapter 8

VIII. Be ðæm ðe wilniað biscephad to underfonne,
hu hie gegripað ðone cwide ðæs apostoles Paules
hiora gitsunge to fultome.

Ac ða ðe willað gripan on swelcne folgað for hiera gitsunge, hie doð him to leafe ðone cwide ðe *sanctus* Paulus
cwæð: "Se ðe biscephad gewilnað, god weorc he gewilnað."
Gif he hit ða herede ond ontyhte, eft he stierde ðære gewilnunge ða he cwæð, "Biscepe gedafnað ðæt he sie tælleas."
Ðærbufan is geteald hwelc he beon sceal, gif he untælwierðe
bið. Mid oðrum worde he hierte, mid oðrum he bregde,
swelce he openlice cwæde, "Ic herige ðæt ge secað, ac leorniað ðæt ge witen hwæt hit sie. Ac gif ge agiemeleasiað ðæt
ge ameten eow selfe hwelce ge sien, sua eow on hierran
folgoðe ahebbað, swa ge sweotolran ond widmærran gedoð
eowre tælweorðlicnesse." Sua se micla cræftiga hiertende
toscyfð, ond egesiende stierð ofermetta mid ðære tælinge
his hieremonnum, ðæt he hie gebringe on life.

2   Eac is to geðencanne ðæt on ða tiid ðe se biscephad swa
gehered wæs, sua hwelc swa hine underfeng, he underfeng
martyrdom. On ða tiid wæs to herigeanne ðæt mon wilnode
biscephades, ða ðe nan twio næs ðæt he ðurh ðone sceolde
cuman to hefegum martyrdome. Ðæt is to tacne ðæt mon
endebyrðlice ðone biscepdom healde, ðæt he hine on godum weorcum geendige. Forðon hit is gecweden, "Se ðe

Chapter 8

8. How those who desire to undertake pastoral authority seize upon the words of the apostle Paul to justify their cupidity.

But those who for their acquisitiveness wish to arrogate to themselves such a dignity take as their justification what Saint Paul said: "Whoever desires the episcopacy desires noble work." If he at that point extolled it and recommended it, in turn he constrained the desire when he said, "It is incumbent upon a bishop to be above reproach." It is besides told of what sort he ought to be if he will be above reproach. With one remark he encouraged, with the other he discouraged, as if he plainly said, "I commend you for seeking it, but be certain that you know what it is. But if you neglect to take measure yourself of what sort you are, in proportion as you elevate yourself to higher office you will make your blameworthiness plainer and more notorious." Thus, the great craftsman spurs on with encouragement and curbs with warnings the presumption of his disciples by rebuking it, that he may bring them to life.

There is also this to consider, that at the time when the episcopate was so highly regarded, whoever accepted it accepted martyrdom. At that time it was praiseworthy that someone would desire to be bishop, when there was no doubt that in doing so he should achieve crushing martyrdom. It is a sign that one has held the episcopacy in the appropriate manner if he finishes it in good works. Therefore

biscephad gewilnað, god weorc he gewilnað." Se ðonne for
ðære gewilnunge swelcra weorca biscopdom ne secð, he bið
ðonne him self gewita ðæt he wilnað him selfum gielpes;
ne deð he ðonne ðæt an yfel ðæt he ne lufað ða halgan
ðegnunga, ac eallinga he hie forsiehð. Ond ðonne he fundað
to ðæm weorðscipe ðæs folgoðes, his mod bið afedd mid
ðære smeaunga ðære wilnunga oðerra monna hiernesse ond
his selfes upahæfenesse, ond fægenað ðæs hu hiene mon
scyle herigean. Ahefð ðonne his heortan forðy, ond for ðære
genyhte ðæs flowendan welan he blissað. He licet eaðmodnesse, ond secð mid ðam ðisses middangeardes gestreon. On
ðæm hiewe ðe he sceolde his gielpes stieran on ðæm he his
strienð. Mid ðy ðe he sceolde his gestreon toweorpan, mid
ðy he hie gadrað. Ðonne ðæt mod ðenceð gegripan him to
upahefenesse ða eaðmodnesse, ðæt ðæt he utan eowað innan he hit anwent.

Chapter 9

VIIII. Hu ðæt mod ðætte wilnað for oðre beon, lihð
him selfum ðonne hit ðencð fela godra weorca to
wyrcanne, ond ðæt licett oðrum monnum,
gif he worldare hæbbe, ond wile hit ðonne
oferhebban siððan he hie hæfð.

Ac ðonne he wilnað to underfonne ða are ond ðone ealdordom, he ðencð on ðam oferbrædelse his modes ðæt he

it is said, "Whoever desires the episcopacy desires noble work." Then whoever does not seek the office of bishop out of desire for such works is himself witness that he desires vainglory for himself; then he does not merely commit the offense of not loving holy ministry, but he despises it entirely. And when he aspires to the honor of leadership, his mind is glutted with contemplation of the desire for other people's obedience and his own exaltation, and he exults in how he will be lionized. For that he lifts up his heart, and for the abundance of flowing wealth he is elated. He feigns humility and under cover of that runs after the riches of this world. In the pretense of curbing his vanity he intensifies it. While he ought to distribute his wealth, he amasses it. When an individual thinks to seize upon humility for the sake of his self-regard, what he shows outwardly he perverts inwardly.

Chapter 9

9. How the individual who desires authority over others deceives himself when he plans to perform many good works, and makes a pretense of it in the sight of others in pursuit of worldly preeminence, and prefers to neglect them once he has it.

But when they desire to assume the honor and the authority, they think on the surface of their consciousness that

sciele monig god weorc ðæron wyrcan, ond he ðencð mid
innewearde mode ðæt he gierneð for gilpe ond for upahafenesse ðæs folgoðes; smeageað ðeah ond ðeahtigað on hiera
modes rinde monig god weorc to wyrcanne, ac on ðam piðan
bið oðer gehyded. Ac on uteweardum his mode he liehð him
selfum ymbe hine selfne bie ðæm godum weorcum; licet ðæt
he lufige ðæt he ne lufað: ðisses middangeardes gilp he lufað,
ond he licett swelce he ðone onscunige, ond hine him ondræde. Ðonne he wilnað on his mode ðæt he sciele ricsian,
he bið swiðe forht ond swiðe behealden; ðonne he hæfð ðæt
he habban wolde, he bið swiðe ðriste. Ðonne he to fundað,
he ondræt ðæt he ne mote to cuman, ond sona swa he to
ðære are cymð, swa ðyncð him ðæt se hie him niedscylde
sceolde se se hie him sealde, ond brycð ðære godcundan are
woruldcundlice, ond forgitt swiðe hræðe ðæt he ær æfæst-
lices geðohte. Hu mæg hit butan ðam beon ðætte ðæt mod
ðe ær wæs aled of his gewunan for ðære wilnunge ðære
worldare, ðæt hit ne sie eft to gecirred ðonne hit hæfð ðætte
hit ær wilnode? Ac sona beoð ðæs modes eagan eft gewende
to ðæm weorcum ðe hit ær worhte.

2   Ac ðence ælc mon ær hu nytwyrðe he sie ond hu gehier-
sum ðæm ðe he ðonne mid ryhte hieran scyle on ðam ðe he
ðonne deð. Ðonne mæg he witan be ðy, gif he hierran folgað
habban sceal, hwæðer he ðonne don mæg ðæt ðæt he ær
ðencð ðæt he don wolde, forðon seldun mon geleornað on
miclum rice eaðmodnesse, gif he ær on læssan folgoðe ofermod wæs ond recceleas. Hu mæg he ðonne ðæt lof ond ðone
gilp fleon ðonne he onahæfen bið, se his ær wilnode ða he
butan wæs? Hu mæg he ðonne beon butan gitsunge, ðonne

in office they shall perform many a good work, and they think in the depths of their being that they yearn for the glory and the exaltation of office; yet in the bark of their mind they deliberate and ponder performing many a good work, but inside the bole something else is concealed. But in the outward portion of his mind he is deceived about himself regarding those good works; he pretends to love what he does not love: he loves the glory of this world, and he lets on as if he were avoiding it and were in dread of it. When he desires in his mind that he should rule, he is very timid and very cautious; when he has what he wanted to have, he will be supremely audacious. While he aspires to it, he fears that he will not be allowed to attain it, and as soon as he secures the honor, it seems to him that whoever gave it to him did so out of necessity, and he enjoys the sacred privilege in profane fashion and forgets very soon whatever of a pious nature he had had in mind. How can it be otherwise than that the mind that has been diverted from its usual habits by the desire for worldly privilege should not revert when it has what it desired? But the mind's eyes will all at once be turned back to former occupations.

But let everyone consider beforehand how serviceable he   2 is and how compliant to those he ought rightly to obey in what he does. For if he is to have higher authority, he can ascertain by that whether he can do what he had thought he wanted to do, since a person seldom learns humility in a position of great power if, in a position of lesser authority, he had already been proud and headstrong. How can he then resist adulation and self-aggrandizement when he gains a higher station if he desired them when he was without it? How can he then be free of cupidity when he has to think of

he sceal ymb monigra monna are ðencan, gif he nolde ða ða he moste ymb his anes? Healde hine ðæt hine his agen geðanc ne biswice, ðæt he ne truwige ðæt he on ðæm folgoðe wille wel don, gif he nolde on ðæm læssan; forðæm ðe oftor on ðæm hieran folgoðe mon forlæt goodne gewunan, ðonne he hine ðæron geleornige, gif he hine ær næfde on læssan folgoðe ond on maran æmettan. Swiðe eaðe mæg on smyltre sæ ungelæred scipstiera genoh ryhte stieran, ac se gelæreda him ne getruwað on ðære hreon sæ ond on ðæm miclan stormum. Hwæt is ðonne ðæt rice ond se ealdordoom butan ðæs modes storm, se simle bið cnyssende ðæt scip ðære heortan mid ðara geðohta ystum, ond bið drifen hider ond ðider on swiðe nearwe bygeas worda ond weorca, swelce hit sie ongemong miclum ond monigum stancludum tobrocen?

3   Hwæt is nu ma ymbe ðis to sprecenne, buton se se ðe swelc ongieten sie ðæt he ða cræftas hæbbe ðe we ær bufan cwædon, ðæt he ðonne to foo, gif he niede sciele, ond se se ðe swelc ne sie, ðær no æt ne cume, ðeah hiene mon niede? Se ðonne, se ðe ðeonde bið on swelcum cræftum ond geearnungum, swelce we ær spræcon, ond ðonne to swiðe wiðsceorað ðæm ealdordome, healde hine ðæt he ne cnytte ðæt underfongne feoh on ðæm swatline ðe Xrist ymbe spræc on his godspelle—ðæt is ðæt he ða Godes gifa ðe he onfeng ge on cræftum ge on æhtum ðæt he ða ne becnytte on ðæm sceate his slæwðe, ond he for his swongornesse hie ne gehyde, ðy læs hit him sie eft witnod. Ða ðonne ðe idle beoð swelcra giefa, ond ðeah wilniað ðæs ealdordomes, healden hie ðæt hie mid hiera unryhtum bisenum ða ne screncen ða ðe gað on ryhtne weg toweard ðæs hefonrices, swa dydon Fariseos: naðer ne hie selfe on ryhtne weg gan

the welfare of many people if he did not care to be so when he was entitled to think only of his own? Let him take care not to let his own thoughts deceive him into believing that he will do well in office if he did not care to in a lower station, since more frequently a good practice is abandoned in higher office than learned there, supposing it has not been acquired in lower office and at greater leisure. An inexperienced helmsman can quite easily steer a ship true enough on a calm sea, but an experienced one does not have confidence in himself on a rough sea and in a great tempest. What, then, are power and overlordship but a tempest of the mind, which perpetually tosses the ship of the heart with waves of thoughts, and it is driven this way and that on singularly narrow straits of words and works, as if it were broken up on shoals of rocks both huge and countless?

What more is there to say about this but that one who is 3 perceived to have the skills that we described above is then to come to office, if he is so obliged, and that one who is not of that sort is not to approach it, even if compelled? Whoever excels in such virtues and merits as we mentioned earlier, and then refuses leadership too decidedly, let him take care that he not knot up the money he received in the napkin that Christ spoke of in his gospel—that is, that he not bind up the gifts of God that he received in the form of virtues and valuables in the kerchief of his sloth, and not conceal them for his indolence, or he will be punished for it. Then as for those devoid of such gifts who nonetheless hunger after authority, let them take care not to lead astray by their devious example those who are on the true way to the heavenly kingdom, as did the Pharisees: they would neither themselves travel the true way nor consent that others

noldon, ne oðrum geðafigean. Ymb ðyllic is to geðencenne ond to smeaganne, forðam se ðe biscephad underfehð, he underfehð ðæs folces mettrymnesse, ond he sceal faran gind lond swa swa læce æfter untrumra monna husum. Gif he ðonne giet geswicen næfð his agenra unðeawa, hu mæg he ðonne oðerra monna mod lacnian, ðonne he bireð on his agnum moniga opena wunda? Se læce bið micles to beald ond to scomleas ðe gæð æfter oðra monna husum læcnigende, ond hæfð on his agnum nebbe opene wunde unlacnode.

Chapter 10

x. Hwelc se bion sceal ðe to reccenddome cuman sceal.

Ac ðone monn scyle ealle mægene to bisscephade teon, ðe on monigum ðrowungum his lichoman cwilmð, ond gæstlice liofað, ond ðisses middangeardes orsorgnesse ne gimð, ne him nane wiðerweardnesse ne andræt ðisse worolde, ac Godes anne willan lufað. Suelcum ingeðonce gerist ðæt he for licuman tiedernesse ne for woroldbismere anum wið ða scire ne winne, ne he ne sie gietsiende oðerra monna æhta, ac sie his agenra rummod, ond his breosð sien simle onhielde for arfæstnesse to forgiefnesse, næfre ðeah suiðor ðonne hit gedafenlic sie for ryhtwisnesse. Ne sceal he naht unaliefedes don, ac ðæt ðætte oðre menn unaliefedes dot he sceal wepan sua sua his agne scylde, ond hira untrymnesse

should. Such things demand contemplation and deliberation, because whoever assumes pastoral authority assumes care of the people's maladies, and he is obliged to go about the countryside like a physician among the houses of the indisposed. If, then, he still has not routed his own vices, how can he tend to other people's consciences when he harbors in his own many open wounds? The physician is all too brazen and shameless who goes among other people's houses healing, and has on his own face an untreated open sore.

Chapter 10

10. What sort he shall be who ought to come to a position of authority.

But by every effort is to be enticed to the episcopate one who mortifies his body with numerous punishments and lives spiritually, and holds as nothing the prosperity of this earth, nor is daunted by any adversity of this world, but loves God's will only. It befits such a nature neither for weakness of the body nor for mere shame before the world to resist the appointment, and not to be desirous of other people's possessions, but to be generous of his own, and for his breast to be always inclined to the virtue of clemency, though never more than is proper to righteousness. He shall do nothing forbidden, but the forbidden things that other people do he shall grieve over as if for his own transgressions, and for

he sceal ðrowian on his heortan, ond ðæs godes his nihstena he sceal fægnian sua sua his agnes. His weorc sceolon beon ðæs weorðe ðæt him oðre menn onhyrien. He sceal tilian sua to libbanne sua he mæge ða adrugodan heortan ge-ðwænan mid ðæm flowendan yðon his lare. He sceal geleornian ðæt he gewunige to singallecum gebedum, oð he ongite ðæt he mæge abiddan æt Gode ðæt he ongienne, suelce him mon to cueðe, "Nu ðu me cleopodesð: nu ic eom her."

2   Hwæt wenstu nu, gif hwelc forworht monn cymð, ond bitt urne hwelcne ðæt we hine læden to sumum ricum menn, ond him geðingien ðonne he wið hine iersað? Gif he me ðonne cuð ne bið, ne nan monn his hiredes, ic wille him suiðe ræðe andwyrdan ond cueðan, "Ne mæg ic ðæt ærendigean; ic ne eom him sua hiwcuð." Gif we ðonne scomiað ðæt we to uncuðum monnum suelc sprecen, hu durre we ðonne to Gode suelc sprecan? Oððe hu dear se gripan on ða scire ðæt he ærendige oðrum monnum to Gode se se ðe hine selfne hiwcuðne ne ongiet Gode ðurh his lifes geearnunga? Oððe hu dearr he ðingian oðrum monnum, ond nat hwæðer him selfum geðingod bið? He mæg ondrædan ðæt he for his ægnum scyldum mare ierre gewyrce. Ealle we witon bi monnum, se se ðe bitt ðone monn ðæt him ðingie wið oðerne ðe he bið eac ierre, ðæt irsigende mod he gegremeð, ond wierse ierre he astyreð. Geðencen ðæt, ða ðe ðonne giet ðisse worolde wilniað, ond healden hie ðæt hie mid hira ðingengum hefigre ierre ne astyrien ðæs ðearlwisan deman. Healden hie hie ðonne hie gitsiað sua micles ealdordomes ðæt hie ne weorðen ealdormenn to forlore hira hieramonnum. Ac pinsige ælc mon hiene selfne georne, ðy læs he

their frailty he shall suffer in his heart, and his neighbors' good fortune he shall celebrate as if his own. His works shall be worthy of other people's emulation. He shall endeavor to live in such a way that he can moisten the arid heart with the flowing waves of his teaching. He shall accustom himself to remaining in unceasing prayer until he perceives that he can obtain from God what he proposes, as if it were said to him, "You summoned me just now; now I am here."

What do you suppose, if some criminal comes and asks 2 one of us to lead him to a certain powerful individual and intercede for him because he is angry with him? If, then, he is not an acquaintance of mine, nor anyone of his household, I will very promptly answer him and say, "I cannot undertake that responsibility; I am not on such intimate terms with him." Then if it shames us to speak thus to people we do not know, how dare we speak thus to God? Or how dare he arrogate to himself the office of intercessor with God for other people who does not know himself to be God's intimate by virtue of a life of merit? Or how dare he curry favor for other people not knowing whether he is favored? He can expect that on account of his own offenses he will provoke greater anger. We all know it about people that when someone asks to be interceded for with another by a person with whom the other is likewise angry, he embitters the irritable mind and occasions worse anger. Let those who still have their heart set on this world consider that, and take care not to elicit by their intercession weightier ire from the stern judge. Let them see to it, then, that they not long for such great authority that they become overlords to the ruin of their dependents. But let everyone examine himself meticulously, so that he will not dare assume the office of

durre underfon ðone lareowdom ðæs folces ða hwile ðe him ænig unðeaw on ricsige. Ne wilnige se na beon ðingere for oðerra scylde se ðe bið mid his agenum gescinded.

Chapter 11

XI. Hwelc se beon sceal se ðe ðærto cuman ne sceal.

Bi ðon cuæð sio uplice stemn to Moyse ðæt he sceolde beodan Arone ðæt nan monn hiera cynnes ne hiera hieredes ne offrode his Gode nanne hlaf, ne to his ðegnunga ne come, gif he ænig wom hæfde: gif he blind wære oððe healt, oððe to micle nosu hæfde, oððe to lytle, oððe eft wo nosu oððe tobrocene honda oððe fet, oððe hoferede wære, oððe torenige, oððe fleah hæfde on eagan oððe singale sceabbas oððe teter oððe healan.

2   Se bið eallenga blind, se ðe noht ne ongiet be ðam leohte ðære uplecan sceawunge, ond se se ðe bið ofseten mid ðæm ðistrum ðisses anweardan lifes, ðonne he næfre ne gesiehð mid his modes eagum ðæt to

 towearde leoht, ðy ðe he hit lufige, ond he nat hwider he recð mid ðæm stæpum his weorca. Be ðæm witgode Anna, ða hio cuæð, "Dryhten gehilt his haligra fet, ond ða unryhtwisan sicettað on ðam ðiestrum." Se bið eallenga healt se ðe wat hwider he gaan sceal, ond ne mæg for his modes untrymnesse; ðeah he geseo lifes weg, he ne mæg medomlice ongan, ðonne he hæfð to godum weorce

teacher of the people as long as any vice has power over him. Let him not desire to be intercessor for the sins of others who is tainted with his own.

Chapter 11

11. What sort he shall be who ought not to come thereto.

The supernal voice told Moses to caution Aaron that none of their kin or of their household should offer his God any bread, or come to his rites, if he had any blemish: if he were blind, or lame, or had too big a nose, or too small, or similarly a crooked nose, or broken hands or feet, or if he were hunchbacked, or purblind, or with a white spot in the eye, or chronic scabs or impetigo or hydrocele

He is entirely blind who perceives nothing by the light of sublime revelation, and who is suffocated in the gloom of this present life, when he never observes with his mind's eyes the light ahead so that he might love it, and he does not know what direction he takes with the steps of his conduct. Hannah prophesied about him when she said, "The Lord will direct the feet of his saints, and the unrighteous will groan in the darkness." He is entirely lame who knows where he ought to go and cannot for frailty of will; though he may see the path of life, he cannot adequately follow it

gewunad, ond læt ðonne ðæt aslacian, ond hit nyle up aræran to ðam staðole fulfremedes weorces; ðonne ne magon ðider fullice becuman ða stæpas ðæs weorces ðieder ðe he wilnað. Be ðæm cuæð Paulus, "Astreccað eowre agalodan honda ond eowru cneowu, ond stæppað ryhte, ne healtigeað leng, ac beoð hale."

3   Ðonne is sio lytle nosu ðæt mon ne sie gescadwis; forðæm mid ðære nose we tosceadað ða stencas, forðam is sio nosu gereaht to gesceadwisnesse. Ðurh ða gesceadwisnesse we tocnawað good ond yfel, ond geceosað ðæt god ond aweorpað ðæt yfel. Be ðæm is gecueden on ðære bryde lofe, "Ðin nosu is suelc suelce se torr on Liuano ðæm munte." Forðæm sio halige gesomnung ðurh gesceadwisnesse gesiehð ond ongietað of huan ælc costung cymeð, ond ðæt towearde gefeoht ðara uncysta, hwonon hie ðæs wenan sculon. Ac monige menn beoð ðe noldon ðone hlisan habban ðæt hie unwiese sien; angiennað ðonne oftrædlice mare secgean ond smeagean suiðor ðonne him ðearf sie to begonganne, ond rædað sume leasunge on ðære smeaunge. Ðæt is sio micle nosu ond sio woo, se ðe wile ungemetlice gesceadwis beon, ond secð ðæt smealicor ðonne he ðyrfe; se æfð to micle nosu ond to woo, forðon sio gesceadwisnes hie selfe gescind mid ðære ungemetgodan smeaunge.

4   Ðæt is ðonne se foreda foot ond sio forude hond ðæt mon wite Godes biboda weg, ond ðær nylle on gan, ac sie bedæled ond aidlad ælces godes weorces, nals na sua sua healt monn oððe untrum—hwilum hie gað, hwilum hie restað—ac se foreda fot a bið ælces feðes bedæled. Se ðonne bið hoferede se ðe sio byrðen ofðrycð ðisse eorðlican gewilnunge, ond næfre ne besyhð to ðære uplican are; ac ealne weg fundað to ðeosum eorðlecum, ond ðonne hie gehierað

when he has accustomed himself to a good work and then lets it decay, and does not care to raise it to the level of a perfect work; then the steps of that work cannot arrive finally where he desires. About this Paul said, "Reach forth your disused hands and your knees and step properly and be lame no longer, but be sound."

Then to have a small nose is to lack discernment; given 3 that with the nose we distinguish odors, the nose signifies discrimination. Through discrimination we recognize good and bad and choose the good and refuse the bad. About that it is said in praise of the bride, "Your nose is as the tower on Mount Lebanon." Therefore, holy Church through discernment perceives and understands the source of each temptation, and from what direction the impending attack of vices ought to be expected. Yet there are many people who wish not to have the reputation of being foolish, and therefore they frequently take up explaining and contemplating more than there is need for them to do, and they reach false conclusions in their contemplation. That is the big nose and the crooked, which chooses to be immoderately discriminating and scrutinizes more subtly than one need do; he has too large and too crooked a nose because discernment is marred by intemperate study.

The broken foot and the broken hand signify that one 4 knows the way of God's precepts and will not walk in it but is deprived and devoid of every good work, not at all like the lame person or the frail—at times they walk, at times they rest—but the broken foot is always deprived of the ability to walk. The one who is hunchbacked is someone whom the burden of this earthly desire oppresses, and who never looks up to heavenly favor but is always intent on earthly, and

awuht be ðæm gode ðæs hefonlican rices, ðonne ahefegiað hira heortan ða byrðenna ðæs forhwirfdan gewunan ðætte hie ne magon hiera geðohtes staðol up aræran. Be ðæm se salmsceop cwæð, "Ic eom gebiged, ond æghwonon ic eom gehiened." Ond eft be ðæm ilcan scyldum sio Soðfæstnes ðurh hie selfe cwæð: "Hiera sæd gefeollon on ða ðornas— ðæt sindon ða ðe gehierað Godes word, ond mid ðære geornfulnesse ond mid ðære wilnunge ðisse worlde ond hiere welena bið asmorod—ðæt sæd Godes worda, ðeah hie up apryttæn, ðæt hie ne moten fulgrowan ne wæstmbære weorðan."

5   Se ðonne bið siwenige se ðe his ondgit bið to ðon beorhte scinende ðæt he mæge ongietan soðfæstnesse, gif hit ðonne aðistriað ða flæsclican weorc. Hwæt, on ðæs siwenigean eagum beoð ða æpplas hale, ac ða bræwas greatigað, forðam hie beoð oft drygde for ðæm tearum ðe ðær gelome of flowað, oð ðæt sio scearpnes bið gewird ðæs æpples. Swa sindon wel monege ðara ðe gewundiað hiera mod mid ðæm weorcum ðisses flæsclican lifes, ða ðe meahton smealice ond scearplice mid hiera ondgite ryht geseon, ac mid ðæm gewunan ðara wona weorca ðæt mod bið adimmod. Se bið eallinga siwenige ðonne his mod ond his ondgit ðæt gecynd ascirpð, ond he hit ðonne self gescient mid his ungewunan ond wom wilnungum. Be ðæm wæs wel gecweden ðurh ðone ængel, "Smiriað eowre eagan mid sealfe ðæt ge mægen geseon." Ðonne we smierewað ure heortan eage mid sealfe ðæt we mægen ðy bet geseon, ðonne we mid ðæm læcedome godra weorca gefultumað urum ondgite ðæt hit bið ascirped to ongietenne ða bierhtu ðæs soðan leohtes. Se ðonne hæfð eallinga fleah on his modes eagum, ðe on nane wisan ne mæg ryhtwisnesse geseon, ac bið ablend mid unwisdome ðæt he

when such hear anything about the good of the heavenly kingdom, the burdens of perverted habits weigh down their heart, so that they cannot elevate the condition of their mind. About such the psalmist said, "I am bowed, and on all sides I am abased." And again about that same trespass, Truth in person spoke: "Their seed fell among the thorns — that is, those who hear God's word and are smothered with devotion to and desire for this world and its riches — so that the seeds of God's word, though they sprout, are not permitted to flourish or bear fruit."

One whose understanding is so brightly radiant that he 5 can perceive truth is purblind if bodily works then dim it. Now, in the eyes of the partly blind the pupils are healthy, but the eyelids swell because they are often desiccated on account of the tears that frequently flow from them, until the sharpness of the pupil is impaired. Like this are quite many of those who impair their judgment with the works of this fleshly life, those who, with their intellect, can see in detail and sharply what is right, but with the habit of deficient works, the judgment is clouded. He is altogether purblind when nature sharpens his judgment and his understanding, and he himself impairs it with his bad habits and twisted desires. About this it was well said through the angel, "Anoint your eyes with salve, so that you can see." We anoint our heart's eye with salve so that we can see better when we lend aid to our understanding with the medicine of good works, so that it is made sharp enough to perceive the radiance of the true light. Then he altogether has a white spot in his mind's eyes who cannot in any degree see righteousness but is blinded with ignorance, so that he does not

ne ongit ða uplican ryhtwisnesse. Ðurh ðone æpl ðæs eagan mon mæg geseon, gif him ðæt fleah on ne gæð; gif hine ðonne ðæt fleah mid ealle ofergæð, ðonne ne mæg he noht geseon. Sua eac bi ðæs modes eagum is gecueden, gif ðæt ondgit ðæs menniscan geðohtes ongiett ðæt hit self dysig sie ond synfull, ðonne gegripð hit ðurh ðone wenan ðæt andgit ðære incundan byrhto; gif he ðonne self wenð ðæt he sie wis ond gescadwislice ryhtwis, mid ðy he hiene bedælð ðære oncnawnesse ðæs uplecan leohtes, ond micle ðy læs he ongiet ða bierhto ðæs soðan leohtes ðonne he hiene up ahefeð on his mode on suelc gielp ond on suelc selflice. Sua sua be sumum monnum cueden is, "Hie sædon ðæt hie wæren wiese, ond ða wurdon hie dysige forðam."

6   Soðlice se hæfð singalne sceabb se ðe næbre ne ablinð ungestæððignesse. Ðonne bi ðam sceabbe suiðe ryhte sio hreofl getacnað ðæt wohhæmed. Ðonne bið se lichoma hreof, ðonne se bryne ðe on ðæm innoðe bið ut aflihð to ðære hyde. Sua bið sio costung æresð on ðæm mode, ond ðonne fereð utweardes to ðære hyde, oð ðæt hio ut asciet on weorc. Butan tweon gif ðæt mod ær ðæm willan ne wiðbritt, se wielm ðæs innoðes ut abiersð ond wierð to sceabbe, ond moniga wunda utane wyrcð mid ðæm won weorcum. Forðon wilnode *sanctus* Paulus ðæt he ðære hyde giocðan of adrygde mid ðæm worde, ða he cuæð, "Ne gegripe eow næfre nan costung buton menniscu"; suelce he openlice cuæde: mennisclic is ðæt mon on his mode costunga ðrowige on ðæm luste yfles weorces, ac ðæt is deofullic ðæt he ðone willan ðurhteo. Se ðonne hæfð teter on his lichoman se hæfð on his mode gitsunga; gif hiere ne bið sona gestiered, hio wile weahsan mid ungemete. Butan tueon se teter, butan sare he ofergæð ðone lichoman, ond suaðeah ðæt lim geunwlitegað;

recognize sublime justice. Through the pupil of the eye one can see, if albugo does not permeate it; if, then, albugo spreads entirely over his eye, he can see nothing. So, likewise, it is said of the mind's eyes, if the understanding of human intellect perceives that it is itself filled with folly and sin, it will grasp through that perception the idea of the light within; if, on the other hand, one supposes himself wise and discriminatingly just, with that he distances himself from recognition of the supernal light, and he much less perceives the radiance of the true light when he exalts himself in his mind with such self-aggrandizement and such self-love. Just so is it said of certain people, "They said that they were wise, and thereby they were rendered foolish."

In truth, he has a chronic scab who never leaves off frivolity. For by the scab, skin disease quite properly signifies fornication. When the body is scabrous, the inflammation on the inside emerges on the skin. Likewise, temptation is first in the mind and then is transmitted outward to the surface, until it bursts out as action. Without a doubt, if the mind does not curb the will beforehand, the turbulence in the interior will burst out and emerge as a scab, and will produce many eruptions on the surface in the form of miserable doings. For that reason Saint Paul desired to stanch the flux of the skin's running sores with this dictum, when he said, "Never let any temptation seize you unless human"; as if his meaning plainly put were: it is human to suffer temptation in the mind from the pleasure of wrong behavior, but it is satanic to fulfill the desire. Then he who has impetigo on his person has cupidity in his mind; if it is not tamed at once, it will grow without measure. To be sure, impetigo will spread over the body without pain, and yet the limb is disfigured;

6

se giecða bið suiðe unsar, ond se cleweða bið suiðe row, ond ðeahhwæðere gif him mon to longe fylgð, he wundað ond sio wund sarað. Sua eac sio gitsung ðæt mod ðæt hio gebindeð mid ðære lustfulnesse hio hit gewundað, ðonne hio wyrpð on ðæt geðoht hwæthugu to bigietene. Hio gehæt him æghwæs genog; ðeah ðæt ðonne ðæm mode licige ond lust-fullige, ðeah hit gewundað mid ðæm ðe hit wyrcð feond-scipe. Ðurh ða wunde he forliest ðone wlite his lioma, ðonne he ðurh ðæt woo weorc forliest ðone wlite oðerra godra weorca, gelicost ðæm ðe he gewemme ealne ðone lichoman, ðonne he ðurh ealle uncysta ðæt mod gescrencð. Ðæt try-mede *sanctus* Paulus ða he cuæð ðæt ælces yfeles wyrttruma wære ðæt mon wilnode hwelcre gitsunge.

7   Se ðonne ðe bið healede ne mæg mid weorce began ða scondlicnesse, ond suaðeah bið ahefegod mid ðæm singalum geðohte butan ælcum gemete; ond suaðeah næfre ne mæg ðurhteon ðæt unryhtlice weorc, ond hwæðere ðæt mod hæfð fulfremedne willan to ðære wrænnesse butan ælcre steore ond wearne, gif he hit ðurhteon meahte. Ðonan cymeð sio mettrymnes ðæm healedum, ðe se wæta ðara in-noða astigð to ðæm lime; ðonne asuilð hit ond ahefegað ond unwlitegað. Se bið eac eallenga healede se se ðe eall his mod bið aflogen to gæglbærnesse ond to dole, ðonne he bierð on his heortan ða byrðenne ðæs bismeres, ond suaðeah mid won weorcum hit to ðweorlice ne fremeð, ðeah he hit on his mode forlætan ne mæge, ne fullice gewunian to godum weorcum, forðon sio byrðen ðære sconde hine diogollice hefegað.

8   Sua hwelc ðonne sua ðissa uncysta hwelcre underðieded bið, him bið forboden ðæt he offrige Gode hlaf, forðæm hit

the incrustation is quite painless, and the itching is quite mild, and yet if it is left untreated for too long, lesions will appear, and the lesions will cause pain. So, also, cupidity wounds the mind that it enthralls with desirousness when it presents to the imagination something to be obtained. It promises it plenty of everything, and although it pleases the mind and fills it with desire, it wounds inasmuch as it causes enmity. Through that wound one spoils the fineness of his limbs when by that crooked deed he vitiates the fineness of other good deeds, quite like his corrupting the entire body when he ruins the mind through all his bad practices. Saint Paul confirmed that when he said that the root of every evil was giving way to any avarice.

Then one who is afflicted with hydrocele cannot accom- 7 plish his vileness in deed, and still he is burdened beyond all bounds with the incessant thought of it; and yet he can never compass the wrongful act, and still the mind retains unalloyed desire for lasciviousness without any restraint or hesitation, if only the man could carry it through. The condition of hydrocele results when fluid from the interior rises to the member; then it bloats and grows heavy and becomes deformed. Likewise, he is altogether bloated with hydrocele whose entire mind is addicted to lechery and folly, when he bears in his heart the burden of shame, and yet he does not carry it through too perversely with vile acts, though he cannot rid his mind of it, nor wholly accustom himself to good works, because the burden of shame privately weighs on him.

Whoever, then, is subject to any of these vices is forbid- 8 den to offer bread to God, because it is to be expected that

79

is wen ðæt se ne mæge oðerra monna scylda of aðuean, se se ðe hine ðonne giet his agena onherigeað.

9 Ær ðioson we sægdon feam wordum hwelc se bion scolde ðe medome hierde ond lareow bion sceolde, ond eac hwelc se bið ðe him ondrædan sceal ðæt he unmedome sie. Ær ðiosum we rehton hwelc se beon sceolde ðe to ðæm biscepdome cuman sceolde; nu we willað reccan, gif he ðær suelc to cyme, hu he ðæron libban scyle.

he will not have the capacity to wash away other people's sins who is continually plagued by his own.

Up to now we have said a few words about what sort he ought to be who should be a competent pastor and teacher, and also about what sort he is who ought to beware turning out to be incompetent. Up to now we have been discussing what sort he ought to be who should attain to the episcopate; now we intend to discuss, once he who is of that sort has secured it, how he should conduct his life in office. 9

BOOK TWO

Chapter 12

XII. Hu se se ðe gedafenlice ond endebyrdlice to cymð, hu he ðæron drohtian scyle.

Þæs biscepes weorc sceolon bion ofer oðra monna weorc sua micle beteran sua hit micel bið betwux ðæs hirdes life ond ðære heorde. Him gedafenað ðæt he geðence ond geornlice smeage hu micel niedðearf him is ðæt he sie gebunden to ðære ryhtwiesnesse mid ðy rape ðæt he ongite for hwæs geðyncðum ðæt folc sie genemned heord. Hwæt, ðæm hierde ðonne wel gerisð ðæt he sie healic on his weorcum, ond his word sien nyttwyrðu, ond on his suigean he sie gescadwis; him sculan eglan oðerra monna brocu suelce he efnsuiðe him ðrowige; he sceal sorgian ymbe ealle ond fore ðencean; he sceal bion for eaðmodnesse hira gefera ælces ðara ðe wel doo; he sceal bion stræc wið ða ðe ðær agyltað, ond for ryhtwisnesse he sceal habban andan to hira yfele; ond ðeah for ðara bisgunge ne sie his giemen na ðy læsse ymb ða gehirsuman; ne eac for hira lufan geornfulnesse ne forlæte he ða ungehirsuman. Ac ðis ðæt we nu feam wordum arimdon we willað hwene rumedlicor heræfter areccean.

BOOK TWO

Chapter 12

12. How he who comes to it fittingly and by due process ought to conduct himself therein.

The bishop's conduct should be superior to other people's conduct as much as the shepherd's life to the flock's. It is incumbent on him to contemplate and consider to the full how great the need is for him to be bound to righteousness with such a cord that he may recognize for whose dignity the people are called a flock. Now, it is proper for the shepherd to be towering in his conduct, and that his words be efficacious, and that he be discreet in his silences. Other people's trials should grieve him as if he suffered them just as much; he ought to have a care for and devote attention to all; for their humility he should be an associate of everyone who conducts himself well; he ought to be severe with those who transgress in that respect, and out of justice he ought to be indignant over their wrongdoing; and yet in ministering to them, not to let his care for the obedient be any the less; nor likewise in the diligence of his care for those should he neglect the disobedient. But these things that we have enumerated in a few words we intend to explain at somewhat greater length in what follows.

Chapter 13

XIII. Hu se lareow sceal bion clæne on his mode.

Se reccere sceal bion simle clæne on his geðohte, ðætte nan unclænnes hine ne besmite ðonne he ða ðegnunga underfehð, forðæm ðæt he mæge adrygean of oðra monna heortan ðæt ðæron fules sie. Hit is ðearf ðæt sio hond sie ær geclænsad ðe wille ðæt fenn of oðerre aðierran; gif sio ðonne bið eac fennegu, ðonne is wen ðæt hio ða oðre wiers besmite gif hio hire anhrinð. Forðæm wæs ðurh ðone witgan gecueden, "Dooð eow clæne, ge ðe berað Godes fatu." Ða ðonne berað Godes fatu, ða ðe oðerra monna saula underfooð to lædanne on ða treowa hira agenra gearnunga to ðæm innemestan halignessum. Geðencen hie ðonne betwuh him selfum hu suiðe hie sculon beon geclænsode, ða ðe berað on hira greadum ða a libbendan fatu to ðæm ecean temple on hira agenne borg.

2   Forðy wæs ðurh ða halgan stemne beboden ðætte on Arones breostum sceolde beon awriten sio racu ðæs domes on ðæm hrægle ðe mon hæt *rationale,* ond mid noslum gebunden, forðæm ðætte sio oferflownes ðara geðohta ne meahte ofsittan ðæs sacerdes heortan, ac hio sciolde beon gebunden mid ðære ilcan race, ðætte he ne ðohte nawuht ungesceadwislices ne unnetlices. Forðæm he bið gesett to bisene oðrum monnum, simle he sceal ætiewan on his lifes gestæððignesse hu micle gesceadwisnesse he bere on his breostum. On ðæm selfan hrægle, ðe he on his breostum wæg, wæs eac awriten ða naman ðara twelf heahfædera.

Chapter 13

13. How the teacher ought to be pure of mind.

The leader ought always to be pure in his thoughts, so that no corruption defile him when he undertakes his ministry, to the end that he have the ability to wipe away what is foul in other people's hearts. The one hand needs to be cleansed first that is going to clear mud from the other; if it, too, is spattered with mud, then it is to be expected that it will soil the other worse if it touches it. For that reason, it was said through the prophet, "Make yourselves clean, you who bear God's vessels." Those bear God's vessels who undertake to lead other people's souls to the inmost sanctum in the faith of their own merits. Let them consider among themselves, then, how thoroughly those ought to be purified who carry in their embrace the ever-living vessels under their own care to the eternal temple.

For that reason it was commanded by the sacred voice 2 that there should be inscribed on Aaron's chest the elucidation of judgment, on the garment that is called a *rationale,* and tied with bands, so that a deluge of thoughts could not assail the priest's heart, but it should be bound with that same rationale so that he should entertain no indiscreet or inapposite thoughts. Because he is set as an example to other people, he ought always to show in the constancy of his life what great discernment he bears in his breast. On that same garment that he wore on his chest were also inscribed the names of the twelve patriarchs. The priest quite

Ðonne birð se sacerd suiðe untællice awriten ðara fædra naman on his breostum, ðonne he singallice geðencð hiera lifes
bisene. Ðonne stæpð se sacerd suiðe tælleaslice on ðone
weg, ðonne he ða bisene ðara forðgefarenra federa geornlice
ond unablinnendlice sceawað, ond on ðæt suæð ðara haligra
singallice winnað to spyriganne, ond unaliefde geðohtas
ofðrycð, ðy læs he ofer ðone ðerscold his endebyrdnesse
stæppe. Suiðe ryhte ðæt hrægl is gehaten, ðæt se sacerd beran sceolde ðæs domes racu, forðam se sacerd scolde ond git
sceal simle smealice geðencean ðæt he cunne god ond yfel
tosceadan, ond siððan geornlice geðence hu he gehwelcne
læran scyle, ond hwonne, ond hwæt him gecopust sie, ond
nowuht him selfum synderlice wilnige, ac his niehstena god
he sceal tellan him selfum. Be ðam is awriten ðæt mon
sceolde writan on ðæm hrægle ðe Aron bær on his breostum,
ðonne he inn eode beforan Gode, ða lare ond ða domas ond
ða soðfæsðnesse. Ða domas he bær on his breostum beforan
Gode Israhela bearna simle. Sua sceal se sacerd giet simle
beran ða domas awritene on his breostum Israhela bearna—
ðæt is ðæt he ðara ðing ðe him underðiodde bioð for ðæm
ege anum ðæs innecundan deman inweardlice undersece,
ðætte sio mennisce oliccung for nanum freondscipe ðærto
ne gemencge, forðon he bið to Cristes bisene ond to his anlicnesse ðær aset.

3   Ond ðeah for ðære geornfulnesse ðære ryhtinge ne sie he
to hræd ne to stið to ðære wrace, ac ðonne he bið ongieten
æfstig wið oðra monna yfelu, anscunige he eac his agenu, ðy
læs ða smyltnesse ðæs domes gewemme oððe se dierna æfst
oððe to hræd ierre. Ac gif he geðencð ðone ege ðæs deman

blamelessly bears the fathers' names written on his chest when he incessantly considers the example of their life. The priest will tread the path entirely free of blame when he scrupulously and without cease observes the example of the departed fathers and continually strives to follow the track of the saints and suppresses illicit thoughts, to avoid stepping beyond the threshold of his rank. Very proper is the name of that garment, that the priest should bear the rationale of judgment, because the priest was obliged, and still is ever, to study assiduously to know how to distinguish good and evil, and subsequently to consider attentively how he should instruct each, and when, and what would be most fitting for them, and desire nothing solely for himself, but the well-being of his neighbors he must account his own. About that it is written that there should be inscribed on the garment that Aaron bore on his chest, when he went in before God, doctrine and judgments and truth. Before God he bore always on his chest the judgments of the children of Israel. So ought the priest still always to bear the judgments of the children of Israel inscribed on his chest—that is, that he inwardly attend to the interests of those entrusted to his care out of reverence for the indwelling judge, so that no human desire to please be intermixed with it on account of any friendship, since he is placed there as the example and likeness of Christ.

And yet out of scrupulousness about correction let him 3 not be too hasty or too harsh in regard to the penalty, but at the same time that he is perceived to be severe about other people's wrongs, let him detest his own, so that neither concealed vehemence nor overhasty anger will mar the composure of judgment. But if he keeps in mind fear of the judge

ðe ofer eall sitt, ðonne ne stierð he no his hieremonnum butan miclum ege. Ac se ege ðonne he geeaðmed ðæt mod he
hit geclænsað, ðy læs sio gedyrstignes his modes hine to upp
ahebbe, oððe ðæs flæsces lusðfulnes hiene besmite, oððe
ðurh ða wilnunga ðissa eorðcundlicra ðinga ðæt mod aðis-
trige se forhwierfeda gewuna gemalicnesse, sio oft ðæt mod
ðæs recceres astyreð. Ac hit is micel ðearf ðæt mon hire
suiðe hrædlice wiðbregde, ðy læs sio scyld ðe hiene ðurh
scienesse costað for his luste ond for his wacmodnesse hine
ofersuiðe; forðon gif hio ne bið hrædlice aweg adrifen, he
bið ofslægen mid ðæm sueorde ðære geðafunge.

Chapter 14

XIIII. Hu se lareow sceal beon
on his weorcum fyrmest.

Se lareow sceal bion on his weorcum healic, ðæt he on his
life gecyðe lifes weg his hieremonnum, ðætte sio hiord se ðe
folgað ðæm wordum ond ðæm ðeawum ðæs hierdes, ðætte
sio heord mæge bet gan æfter his ðeawum ðonne æfter his
wordum. He bið genied mid ðæm folgoðe ðæt he sceal
healice sprecan; geðence he ðonne ðæt him is efnmicel nied,
siððan he hit gesprecen hæfð, ðæt he eac sua doo sua sua he
lærð, forðon sio stefn ðæs lariowes micle ðe ieðelicor ðurhfærð ða heortan ðæs gehirendes, gif he mid his ðeawum hi

who sits over all, he will never shepherd those entrusted to him without considerable fear. But when fear humbles the mind, it cleanses it, to prevent the boldness of one's mind from making him too conceited, or the cravings of the flesh from corrupting him, or the perverse habit of unrestraint, which often troubles the mind of the leader, from clouding the mind through desire for worldly things. But it is a firm requirement that it be deterred with all haste, so that the sin that for his desirousness and his pliancy tempts him through its suggestiveness should not get the upper hand of him, because if it is not driven off at once, he will be struck by the sword of consent.

Chapter 14

14. How the teacher ought to be preeminent in his demeanor.

The teacher ought to be a towering example in his conduct, so that by his manner of living he shows the way of life to his charges, to the end that the flock that attends to the words and the practices of the shepherd be better able to follow his practices than his words. He is required to speak high-mindedly with the flock; let him imagine, then, that he is equally required, after he has spoken, to practice as he preaches, because the voice of the teacher much more easily penetrates the heart of one who attends to him if he secures

ðæron gefæsðnað; ðæt is ðæt he sprecende bebiet ðæt he
ðæt wyrcende oðiewe, ðæt hit ðurh ðone fultum sie forð-
genge. Bi ðæm wæs gecueden ðurh ðone witgan, "Ðu ðe wilt
godspellian Sion, astig ofer heane munt." Ðæt is ðætte
se sceal, se ðe wile brucan ðara godcundra ðinga ond ðara
hefonlicra lara, forlætan ðas niðerlican ond ðas eorðlecan
weorc, forðam he bið gesewen standende on ðam hrofe godcundra ðinga. Sua micle he mæg ieð his hieremenn geteon to
beteran, ond he bið sua micle sel gehiered sua he ufor
gestent on his lifes geearnungum.

2   Forðam bebiet sio halige æ ðæt se sacerd scyle onfon
ðone suiðran bogh æt ðære offrunge, ond se sceolde bion
asyndred from ðæm oðrum flæsce. Ðæt ðonne tacnað ðæt
ðæs sacerdes weorc sculon beon asyndred from oðerra
monna weorcum—nalles na ðæt an ðæt he god doo gemang
oðrum monnum, ac eac synderlice sua suæ he on ðyncðum
bið furður ðonne oðre, ðæt he eac sie on his weorcum ond
ðeawum sua micle furður. Eac him mon scolde sellan ða
breosð ðæs neates toeacan ðæm boge—ðæt is ðæt he geleornige ðæt he selle Gode his agne breosð, ðæt is his inngeðonc—nalles na ðæt an ðæt he on his breostum ðence
ðætte ryht sie, ac eac ða spone ðe his ðeawa giemað to
ðæm illcan mid his godum biesenum. Ne wilnige he nanes
eorðlices ofer ðæt, ne he him ne ondræde nanne eorðlicne
ege ðyses andweardan lifes, ac geðence he ðone inncundan
ege Godes, ond forsio ælce olicunge ðisses middangeardes,
ond eac his ege, for ðære wynsuman suetnesse Godes.

3   Forðon ðurh ða uplecan stefne wæs beboden on ðære æ
ðæt se sacerd scolde beon fæste bewæfed on bæm sculdrum
mid ðæm mæssehrægle—ðæt is ðæt he bio simle getrymed

it there with his conduct—that is, that he prescribe in speaking what he demonstrates in doing, so that with that support it may be effective. About this it was said through the prophet, "You who intend to preach to Zion, ascend a lofty mountain." That is, whoever intends to deal with religious matters and heavenly instruction ought to renounce these low and earthbound doings, so that he will be seen to stand on the summit of things divine. He can lead his charges the more easily to a better condition, and will be the better obeyed, the higher he stands on the merits of his life.

For that reason holy scripture dictates that the priest shall receive the right shoulder from the sacrifice, and it shall be kept separate from the remaining flesh. This, then, indicates that the priest's works ought to be distinguished from other people's works—not only that he do good among other people, but that also as singularly as he surpasses others in dignity, to such a degree he surpass them in deeds and in demeanor. Moreover, he ought to be given the breast of the animal in addition to the shoulder—that is, that he accustom himself to offering God his own breast, which is his intellect—by no means just that in his breast he ponder what is right, but also that by his good example he incline to the same those who observe his behavior. Let him desire nothing of this world above that, nor fear any threat of this present life, but let him meditate upon the indwelling fear of God and despise every blandishment of this world, and also its intimidations, for the delightful sweetness of God.

Therefore, through the sublime voice it was declared in the law that both the priest's shoulders should be firmly wrapped in the liturgical vestment—that is, that he be

ond gefrætwod wið ælce frecenesse ge gæstlice ge men-
nisclice ond wið ælce orsorgnesse besuapen mid ðyssum
mægenum, sua sua Paulus cuæð: "Gað ge gewæpnode ægðer
ge on ða suiðran hond ge on ða winstran mid ðæm wæpnum
ryhtwisnesse." Forðæm ðonne he higað to ðæm godcundum
ðingum anum, ðæt he ne ðyrfe an nane healfe anbugan to
nanum fullicum ond synlicum luste, ne eac ne ðyrfe bion to
up ahæfen for nanum wlencum ne for nanre orsorgnesse, ne
hine ne gedrefe nan wuht wiðerweardes, ne hine ne geloc-
cige nan oliccung to hiere willan, ne hine ne geðrysce nan
wiðermodnes to ormodnesse. Gif ðonne mid nanum ðissa
ne bið onwæced his inngeðonc, ðonne bið hit swutul ðæt
he bið suiðe gerisenlice besuapen mid swiðe wlitige oferbrædelse on bæm sculdrum.

4   Ðæt hrægl wæs beboden ðæt scolde bion geworht of pur-
puran ond of tweobleom derodine ond of twispunnenum
twine linenum ond gerenod mid golde ond mid ðæm stane
iacincta, forðæm ðæt wære getacnod on hu mislecum ond on
hu monigfaldum mægenum se sacerd scolde scinan beforan
Gode, mannum to biesene. Æresð alra glengea ond ymesð
scolde scinan gold on his hrægle—ðæt is ðætte on his mode
scine ealra ðinga fyrmesð ongit wisdomes. Toeacan ðæm
golde ealra glenga fyrmesð on his hrægle wæs beboden ðæt
scolde bion se giem iacinctus, se is lyfte onlicusð on hiwe. Se
ðonne tacnað ðæt eall ðætte ðæs sacerdes ondgit ðurhfaran
mæge, sie ymb ða hefonlican lufan, næs ymbe idelne gilp, ðy
læs him losige ðæt heofenlice ondgit, forðæm ðe he sie ge-
hæfted mid ðæm luste his selfes heringe.

5   Eac ðæm golde ond ðæm line wæs ongemang purpura,
ðæt is cynelic hrægl, forðæm hit tacnað kynelicne anwald.
Be ðæm geðence se sacerd, ðonne he oðre men healice lærð,

always made secure and equipped against every peril, whether spiritual or human, and clothed with these powers against every source of complacency, as Paul said: "Go armed both on the right hand and on the left with the weapons of justice." For this reason, then, he pursues divine matters only, so that he need not deviate in any direction to any foul and sinful desire, nor likewise need be too exalted for any pomp or for any prosperity, nor any adversity oppress him, nor any allurement entice him to desire it, nor disappointment drive him to despair. If, then, his resolve is unweakened by any of these things, it will be plain that he is very aptly fitted out with quite a beautiful coverture on both shoulders.

It was ordained that that garment be made with purple 4 and twice-dyed scarlet and of twice-spun linen thread and adorned with gold and with the stone jacinth, so that it would be symbolized in how various and how manifold virtues the priest should shine before God as an example to humans. First and most important of all ornaments, gold ought to gleam on his vestment—that is, first of all things the comprehension of wisdom ought to gleam in his consciousness. In addition to gold, first of all ornaments on his garment it was commanded that there be the gem jacinth, which is most like the sky in hue. It thus signifies that all that the priest's understanding can penetrate should concern heavenly love, not idle vainglory, so that he not lose that heaven-sent understanding for being captivated by the desire for his own adulation.

In addition to gold and linen there was included purple, 5 which is a royal raiment, as it betokens royal authority. In view of that, let the priest recollect, when he high-mindedly

ðæt he eac on him selfum healice ofðrysce ða lustas his
unðeawa, forðæm ðe he kynelic hrægl hæfð, ðæt he eac sie
kyning ofer his agne unðeawas, ond ða cynelice ofersuiðe.
Ond geðence he simle sie sua æðele sua unæðele suæðer he
sie ða æðelu ðære æfterran acennesse—ðæt is on ðæm fulluhte—ond simle atiewe on his ðeawum ða ðing ðe he ðær
Gode gehet, ond ða ðeawas ðe him mon ðær bebead. Be
ðæm æðelum ðæs gæstes Petrus cuæð "Ge sint acoren kynn
Gode ond cynelices preosthades." Bi ðæm anwalde, ðe we
sculon ure unðeawas mid ofercuman, we magon beon getrymede mid Iohannes cuide ðæs godspelleres, ðe he cuæð,
"Ða ðe hine onfengon, he salde him anwald ðæt hie meahton beon Godes bearn." Ða medomnesse ðære strengio se
salmscop ongeat, ða he cuæð, "Dryhten, suiðe suiðe sint
geweorðode mid me ðine friend, ond suiðe is gestrangod
hiera ealdordom, forðæm ðe ðæt mod ðinra haligra bið
aðened suiðe healice ond suiðe stranglice to ðe, ðonne ðonne
oðrum monnum ðyncð ðæt hie mæstne demm ond mæste
scande ðrowigen, ond hie forsewenuste bioð for worulde."

6   On ðæs sacerdes hrægle wæs toeacan golde ond iacincðe
ond purpuran, dyrodine twegera bleo. Ðæt tacnað ðætte eal
ða god ond ða mægenu ðe heo doð beon gewlitegode mid
ðære lufan Godes ond monna beforan ðæm eagum ðæs
ecean deman, ðætte se spearca ðara godra weorca ðe her
tuinclað beforan mannum, bierne healice liege on ðære inncundan lufan beforan ðæm dieglan deman. Sio lufu ðonne
hio lufað ætsomne ægðer ge God ge his niehstan, hio scinð
suiðe smicere on twæm bleom sua sua twegea bleo godwebb.
Se ðonne, se ðe sua higað ealne weg to andweardnesse his
scippendes, ond agiemeleasað ða giemene his nihstena, oððe

instructs other people, high-mindedly also to repress in himself the impulses of his vices, because he has on a royal garment, for the purpose of his being king over his own vices and royally subduing them. And whether he is of high or low birth, let him always keep in mind the nobility of the second birth—that is, of baptism—and always display in his conduct the qualities that he there promised to God, and the behavior that was required of him. About the nobility of the spirit Peter said, "You are a people chosen for God and of a royal priesthood." About the efficacy with which we ought to surmount our vices, we can be strengthened by the words of the evangelist John when he said, "To those who accepted him he gave the capability of being God's children." The sufficiency of that strength the psalmist acknowledged when he said, "Lord, your friends are highly, highly esteemed by me, and their rule is greatly empowered, because the spirit of your saints is extended very loftily and very firmly to you whenever it seems to other people that they suffer the greatest injury and the greatest disgrace, and they are most despised before the world."

In the priest's garment there is, in addition to gold and jacinth and purple, scarlet color of two dyes. That signifies that all the good and the virtues that they act upon are made more exquisite by the love of God and of humans before the eyes of the eternal judge, that the spark of those good works which here twinkles before men may burn with a loftier flame in indwelling love before the unseen judge. This love, then, which is for both God and his neighbor, shines very appealingly in two tints, just like a textile of two dyes. Whoever thus flies all the way to the presence of his creator and neglects the care of his neighbors, or, conversely, perpetu-

6

eft sua singallice folgað ðære giemenne his niehstena, ðæt he agiemeleasað ða godcundan lufe, ðonne hæfð he anforlæten ðæt twegea bleo godwebb ðæt he habban sceolde on ðæm halgan hrægle, gif he auðer ðissa forlæt. Ac ðonne ðæt mod bið aðened on ða lufan ægðer ge Godes ge his niehstena, ne bið hit ðonne nohtes hwon buton forhæfdnesse anre, ðæt he his lichoman suence ond hlænige.

7   Forðon is beboden toeacan ðæm twiblion godwebbe ðæt scyle beon twiðræwen twin on ðæm mæssegierelan. Of ðære eorðan cymeð ðæt fleax, ðæt bið hwites hiwes. Hwæt mæg ðonne elles beon getacnod ðurh ðæt fleax butan lichoman clænnes, sio sceal scinan of clænre heortan? Forðæm bið gefæsðnod ðæt geðræwene twin to ðæm wlite ðæs mæssehrægles, forðam sio clænnes bið ðonne to ful beorhtum wlite becumen, ðonne ðæt flæsc bið gesuenced ðurh fær-hæfdnesse, ond ðonne betweox oðrum mægenum bið ðionde sio earnung ðæs gesuenctan flæsces, sua sua on ðæm mæssehrægle sciend ongemang oðrum bleon ðæt tweoðræwene twin.

Chapter 15

xv. Hu se lareow sceal bion gesceadwis on his
swigean ond nytwyrðe on his wordum.

Sie se lariow gemetfæsð ond gescadwis ond nyttwyrðe on his wordum, ðætte he ne suigige ðæs ðe nyttwyrðe sie to

ally attends to the care of his neighbors, so that he neglects love of the divine, will have surrendered that textile of two dyes that he ought to have in the sacred vestment, if he neglects either of these. But when consciousness extends to the love of both God and his neighbors, there will be want of nothing but self-denial alone to punish and famish the flesh.

Therefore it is commanded that in addition to the double-dyed textile there ought to be twice-spun linen thread in the liturgical vestment. From the earth comes flax, which is of a white hue. What else can then be signified by the flax but purity of body, which ought to glow from a pure heart? The spun thread is fastened to the beauty of the liturgical vestment for the reason that the purity will then have attained to a very resplendent loveliness when the flesh is afflicted by self-denial, and then among other virtues the merit of the mortified flesh will continue to flourish, just as the twice-spun thread shines among other hues on that liturgical vestment.

Chapter 15

15. How the teacher ought to be prudent in his silence and profitable in his speech.

Let the teacher be moderate and discreet and effectual in his speech, so that he not be silent about what is beneficial

sprecanne, ne ðæt ne sprece ðæt he suigigean scyle, forðæm sua sua unwærlicu ond giemeleaslicu spræc menn dweleð, sua eac sio ungemetgode suige ðæs lareowes on gedwolan gebringð ða ðe he læran meahte gif he sprecende beon wolde. Oft eac ða unwaran lareowas for ege ne durron cleopian, ondrædað him sumra monna unðonc, ne durron forðon ryhtfreolice læran ond unforwandodlice sprecan. Be ðæm sio Soðfæsðness cuæð, "Ne healde ge mid suelcum eornoste ða heorde suelce hirdas scoldon, ac hyrena ðeawe ge fleoð, ond hydað eow mid ðære suigean, sua se hyrra ðonne he ðone wulf gesiehð." Ðæt ilce oðwat Dryhten ðurh ðone witgan, ða he cuæð, "Dumbe hundas ne magon beorcan." Ond eft he cidde, ða he cuæð, "Ne come ge no togenes minum folce ðæt ge meahton standan on minum gefeohte for Israhela folce, ne ge ðone weall ne trymedon ymbe hira hus on ðæm dæge ðe him niedðearf wæs." Ðæt is ðonne ðæt he fare togeanes Israhela folce him mid to feohtanne ðæt he wiðstande mid his spræce ðam unryhtwillendum ðe ðyses middangeardes waldað mid freore ond unforwandodlicre stefne, for gescildnesse his heorde. Ðæt is ðonne ðæt he him mid feohte on ðæm dæge ðe him niedðearf sie, ðæt he wiðstonde ealle mægene ðæm ðe on woh wiellen for ðære ryhtwisnesse lufan. Be ðæm wæs eft gecueden to ðæm scyldegan folce, "Eowre witgan eow witgodan dysig ond leasunga, ond noldon eow gecyðan eowre unryhtwisnesse, ðæt hie eow gebrohten on hreowsunge."

2   Ða godan lareowas beoð oft genemnede on halgum gewritum wietgan, forðæm hie gereccað ðis andwearde lif fleonde, ond ðæt towearde gesueotoligeað. Ða ðonne ðe sio godcundde stefn ðreade, ond cuæð ðæt hie scolden leasunga witgian, ðæt sindon ða ða ðe him ondrædað ðæt hie menn

to be said, nor that he say things which he ought to leave unsaid, for just as incautious and unconsidered speech leads people astray, so also the immoderate silence of the teacher leads into error those whom he could teach, if he would continue to speak. Often, as well, out of timidity, unthinking teachers dare not speak up, but they fear the displeasure of certain persons, and dare not therefore teach with due liberty and speak without hesitation. About that Truth said, "You do not tend the flock with such care as shepherds should, but after the manner of workers on wages you flee and hide yourselves in silence, like the hireling when he sees the wolf." The Lord reproved the same through the prophet when he said, "Mute dogs cannot bark." And again he chided when he said, "You did not come to meet my people so that you could stand in the presence of the nation of Israel in my battle, nor did you reinforce the wall around their house on the day they had need." To go to meet the people of Israel to fight for them, then, is to oppose the unjust who dominate this world by speaking with a free and uninhibited voice for the protection of his flock. To fight for them in their day of need is, then, for love of righteousness to withstand with all one's might those intent on wrong. About this it was likewise said to the guilty people, "Your prophets prophesied folly and lies, and they would not make plain to you your unrighteousness, so that they might bring you to repentance."

Good teachers are in sacred texts often called prophets, 2 because they account this present life transient and they disclose that to come. Those, then, whom the divine voice reproved, and said that they were doomed to prophesy only falsehoods, are those who are afraid to rebuke people for

for hira scyldum ðreagen, ac mid iedelre olicunge orsorgnesse gehataeð ðæm scyldegan, ond mid nanum ðingum nyllað geopenian ðæm syngiendum hiera unryht, ac suigiað
ðara ðreaunga. Ðæt word ðære ðreaunge is cæg, forðæm hit
oft anlycð ond geopenað ða scylde ðe se him self ær nyste se
hie ðurhteah. Be ðæm cuæð Paulus ðæt se lareow sceolde
beon miehtig to tyhtanne on halwende lare, ond eac to
ðreanne ða ðe him wiðstondan wiellen. Eft wæs gecueden
ðurh Zacharias, "Sio æ sceal beon soht on ðæs sacerdes
muðe, ond his weleras gehalðað ðæt andgit, forðæm he bið
Godes boda to ðam folce." Forðam myndgode Dryhten ðurh
Essaiam ðone witgan ond cuæð, "Cleopa ond ne blin; hefe
up ðine stefne sua ðes bime." Forðæm se se ðe ðone sacerd-
had onfehð, he onfehð friccan scire ond foreryneles ða her
iernað beforan kyningum, ond bodigeað hira færelt ond
hiera willan hlydende. Sua sculun ða sacerdas nu faran
hlydende ond bodiende beforan ðæm egeslican deman ðe
him suiðe andrysnlic æfter gæð. Gif ðonne se sacerd bið un-
gerad ðæs lareowdomes, hwæt forstent ðonne his gehlyd?
Hwæt mæg he bodigean ma ðonne se dumba fryccea?

3   Ac for ðeosum wæs geworden ðæt se Halega Gæsð on
tungena onlicnesse gesette ofer ða apostolas, forðæm butan
tweon ðone ðe he gefylð, he gedeð ðæt he bið suiðe hræðe
ymbe hine sprecende. Forðæm wæs beboden Moyse ðæt se
sacerd scolde bion mid bellum behangen—ðæt is ðæt he
hæbbe ða stefne ðære lare, ðy læs he abelge mid ðære suigean ðone dom ðæs sceaweres. Hit is awriten ðæt he scolde
inngongende ond utgongende beforan Gode to ðam halignessum beon gehiered his sueg, ðy læs he swulte. Hit is gecueden ðæt se sacerd scolde sweltan, gif se sueg nære of him
gehiered ægðer ge inngongendum ge utgongendum, forðon

their offenses, and with vain desire to please they promise a carefree existence to the guilty, and in no degree will they expose to the sinful their wrongs, and they speak not a word of reproach. That word of reproach is a key, because often it unlocks and opens the offense of which the perpetrator was not himself cognizant. About that Paul said that the teacher should be forceful at persuading with salutary doctrine, and also at rebuking those who are willing to oppose him. Again it was said through Zachariah, "The law shall be obtained from the priest's mouth, and his lips be the seat of understanding, because he is God's herald to the people." For that reason the Lord admonished through the prophet Isaiah and said, "Cry out and do not cease; raise your voice like a trumpet." For whoever assumes the priesthood assumes the role of clarion crier and of harbinger, those who run before kings and announce their coming and their will with an outcry. So shall priests now go clamoring and announcing before the dread judge who comes after them very menacingly. If, then, the priest is unskilled at teaching, what will his outcry avail? What more can he proclaim than the mute crier?

But for this purpose the Holy Spirit was set over the 3 apostles in the form of tongues, because without a doubt, whomsoever he fills he quite suddenly causes to speak of him. Therefore, Moses was told that bells should be hung on the priest—that is, that he have the voice of instruction, so that by his silence he not provoke the judgment of the Beholder. It is written that as he goes in and out of the sanctuary before God, the sound of him must be heard, or he will die. It is said that the priest must die if the sound of him were not heard both entering and leaving, because he will

he geniet ðone dieglan deman to irre, gif he inngæð butan
ðam swege ðære lare. Hit wæs awriten ðæt ðæs sacerdes
hrægl wære behongen mid bellum. Hwæt elles getacnað ðæs
sacerdes hrægl butan ryht weorc? Dauið se witga ðæt cyðde,
ða he cuæð, "Sien ðine sacerdas gegierede mid ryhtwisnesse."
On ðæs sacerdes hrægle wæron bellan hangiende. Ðæt is
ðæt ða weorc ðæs sacerdes ond eac se sueg his tungan
clypien ymb lifes weg. Ac ðonne se lareow hine gegearwað to
ðære spræce, behalde he hine geornlice ðæt he wærlice
sprece; forðon gif he unendebyrdlice onet mid ðære spræce,
ond wilnað ðæt he ðy wisra ðynce, ðonne is wen ðæt he
gewundige ða heortan ðara gehirendra mid ðære wunde—
ðæt is ðæt he hie gedweleð ond unwislice geiecð ða idelnesse
ðe he of aceorfan sceolde. Be ðæm sio Soðfæsðnes cuæð,
"Habbað ge sealt on ieow, ond sibbe habbað betweoh iow."
Ðurh ðæt sealt is getacnod ða word wisdomes. Se ðonne se
ðe fundige wislice to sprecanne, ondræde he him suiðlice,
ðy læs his spræc gescynde ða anmodnesse ðara ðe ðærto
hlystað. Be ðæm cuæð Paulus, "Ne wilnien ge mare to
witenne ðonne iow ðearf sie, ac witað ðæt ðæt iow gemetlic
sie ond iower ondefenu sien to witenne." Be ðæm wæs gecueden mid ðære godcundan stefne ðæt on ðæs sacerdes
hrægle scoldon hangigan bellan ond ongemang ðæm bellum
reade apla. Hwæt elles is getacnod ðurh ða readan apla buton sio anmodnes ryhtes geleafan? Sua se æppel bið betogen
mid anfealdre rinde, ond ðeah monig corn on innan him
hæfð, sua sio halige cirice unrim folces befehð mid anfealde
geleafan, ond ða habbað suaðeah suiðe misleca geearnunga
ðe ðærinne wunigeað. Forðæm geðence se lariow ðæt he
unwærlice forð ne ræse on ða spræce.

4   Ymbe ðæt ðe we ær spræcon sio Soðfæsðnes ðurh hie

compel the unseen judge to anger if he enters without the sound of teaching. It was written that the priest's garment was to be hung with bells. What else does the priest's garment signify but just works? The prophet David revealed that when he said, "Let your priests be clothed in righteousness." On the priest's vestment were hanging bells. That is, the works of the priest and also the sound of his tongue proclaim the way of life. But when the teacher makes ready to speak, let him be scrupulously careful to speak circumspectly, because if he improperly speaks impetuously and aspires to seem the wiser, it is to be expected that he will wound the hearts of his auditors with that injury—that is, that he will mislead them and stupidly enhance the useless ideas that he ought to excise. About that Truth said, "Have salt within you, and have amity with one another." By salt is signified words of wisdom. Whoever endeavors to speak wisely, let him take every precaution that his words not trouble the unanimity of those listening. About this Paul said, "Do not desire to know more than you need to know, but know what is appropriate to you and in the proportion fitting for you to know." About this it was said by the divine voice that bells should hang on the priest's vestment, and among the bells red apples. What else is signified by the red apples but the unanimity of orthodox faith? As the apple is covered with a single peel and yet contains many seeds, so holy Church encompasses countless nations with a single faith, and those who reside within it nonetheless have quite various merits. Therefore, let the teacher look to it that he not rush forth incautiously when speaking.

We mentioned earlier that Truth himself addressed the 4

selfe cleopade to ðæm apostolum, ond cuæð, "Habbað ge
sealt on iow ond sibbe betweoh iow." Sio anlicnes wæs gecueden ðæt sceolde bion on ðæs sacerdes hrægle ond ða
readan appla ongemang ðam bellum—ðæt is ðætte ðurh eall
ðæt ðæt we ær spræcon sie underfangen ond wærlice gehealden sio anmodnes ðæs godcundan geleafan. Se lareow
sceal mid geornfullice ingehygde foreðencean na ðæt an
ðætte he ðurh hine nan woh ne bodige, ac eac ðæt he nane
ðinga ðæt ryht to suiðe ond to ungemetlice ond to unaberendlice ne bodige, forðæm oft ðæt mægen ðære lare wierð
forloren, ðonne mon mid ungedafenlicre ond unwærlicre
oferspræce ða heortan ond ðæt andgiet gedweleð ðara ðe
ðærto hlystað, ond eac se lariow bið gescinded mid ðære
oferspræce, ðonne he ne conn geðencean hu he nyttwyrðli-
cost læran mæge ða ðe ðærto hlystan willað. Be ðæm wæs
suiðe wel gecueden ðurh Moyses ðætte se wer se ðe ðrowude
oferflownesse his sædes, ond ðæt unnytlice agute, ðæt he
ðonne wære unclæne. Sua eac ða word ðære lare beoð sæd,
ond hi gefeallað on ða heortan ðe hiera hlyst, sua nytt sua
unnyt, suæðer hie beoð. Ðurh ða earan ða word bioð on-
fangen, ond on ðæm mode hie beoð acennedu ðurh ðæt
ondgiet. Forðæm heton woroldwise menn wordsawere ðone
æðelan lareow Paulus. Se ðonne se ðe ðolað flowednesse his
sædes, he bið unclæne gecueden. Sua eac se ðe oferspræce
bið, he bið nohte ðon læs mid ðære besmiten. Gif he ðonne
endebyrdlice his spræce forðbringð, ðonne mæg he cennan
mid ðam ðæt tuder ryhtes geðohtes on ðara tohlystendra
heortan. Gif ðonne unwærlice sio lar toflewð ðurh oferspræce, ðonne bið ðæt sæd unnnyt agoten, næs to nanre
kenninge ðæs cynrenes, ac to unclænnesse ond to ungeris-
num. Be ðam Paulus cuæð, ða he manode his cneoht ðæt he

apostles and said, "Have salt within you and amity with one another." The image was described as having to be on the priest's vestment, and red apples among the bells—that is, that through all that we described earlier, unanimity of religious faith should be adopted and sedulously maintained. With scrupulous regard the teacher is obliged to ensure beforehand not only that he not preach any error, but also that he by no means preach orthodoxy too strongly and excessively and too oppressively, because often the force of instruction is defeated when the heart and the understanding of those listening are confounded by unsuitable and incautious verboseness, and also the teacher is discredited by garrulity when he fails to consider how he can most effectively teach those who are willing to listen. Concerning this, it was quite well said through Moses that the man who experienced a flux of his seed and spilled it to no productive end was unclean. So also words of instruction are seed, and they fall on the heart of one who listens, regardless of whether or not they are profitable. Through the ears words are received, and in the mind they are conceived through the intellect. For this reason, worldly-wise people called the teacher Paul "word sower." Then whoever experiences emission of his seed is called unclean. So, likewise, whoever speaks to excess is not a whit the less defiled by it. If, however, he produces speech in appropriate fashion he can engender with it the progeny of right thinking in the hearts of auditors. If, then, instruction flows out without circumspection through prolixity, the seed is poured out to no purpose, not for any generation of progeny, but for impurity and indecency. About this Paul said, when he exhorted his disciple to per-

scolde standan on ðære lare; he cuæð, "Ic ðe bebeode beforan Gode ond ðæm hælendum Criste, se ðe demende is
cucum ond deadum, ond ic ðe beode ðurh his tocyme ond
ðurh his rice, ðæt ðu stande on ðissum wordum, ond hie lære
ægðer ge gedæftlice ge eac ungedæftlice." Ðeah he cuæde
"ungedæftelice," he cuæð ðeah ær gedæftelice, forðæm sio
ofersmeaung mirð ða unwisan ðe hit gecnawan ne magon,
ond gedeð ða spræce unnytte ðæm tohlystendum ðonne sio
ungedæftnes hit ne cann eft gedæftan.

Chapter 16

XVI. Hu se lareow sceal bion eallum monnum
efnðrowiende ond foreðencende on hiora earfoðum.

Ac sie se lareow eallum monnum se niehsta ond eallum
monnum efnðrowiende on hira gesuincum, ond sie he for
ealle up aðened mid ðære godcundan foresceawunge his
inngeðances, ðætte ðurh ða mildheortnesse his arfæsðnesse
ðæt he tio on hine selfne oðerra monna scylda, ond eac ðurh
ða heanesse ðære sceawunga his inngeðonces he hine selfne
oferstige mid ðære gewilnunge ðara ungesewenlicra ðinga,
ond ðætte he sua healicra ðinga wilnigende ne forsio his
niehstan untrume ond scyldige, ne eft for hiera untrymnesse
ne forlæte ðæt he ne wilnige ðæs hean.

2   For ðysum wæs geworden ðætte Paulus, ðeah ðe he wære
gelæded on neorxna wong, ðær he arimde ða diogolnesse

sist in teaching, "I bid you before God and the savior Christ, who is judge of the living and the dead, to carry on with these words, and teach them both seasonably and unseasonably." Though he said "unseasonably," he nonetheless said "seasonably" first, because excessive scholarliness harms the unlearned, who cannot comprehend it, and makes speaking to an audience useless when unseasonableness cannot by turns render it seasonable.

Chapter 16

16. How the teacher ought to be compassionate to all people and considerate of their troubles.

But let the teacher be everyone's neighbor, and to all people one who commiserates in their hardships, and let him be elevated above all by the divine meditation of his inner being, so that, through the tenderness of his piety, he may take on himself other people's offenses, and also, through the profundity of his examination of his inner being, he may rise above himself with the desire for things invisible, and that, aspiring to such exalted things, he not despise his weak and sinning neighbors, nor on account of their frailty leave off his desire for the lofty.

For this reason it happened that Paul, though he was led 2 into paradise, where he enumerated the mysteries of the

ðæs ðriddan hefones, ond suaðeah for ðære sceawungge ðara ungesewenlicra ðinga, ðeah ðe he up aðened wære on his modes scearpnesse, ne forhogde he ðæt he hit eft gecierde to ðam flæsclican burcotum, ond gestihtode hu men scoldon ðærinne hit macian, ða he cuæð, "Hæbbe ælc monn his wif, ond ælc wif hiere ciorl; ond doo ðæt wif ðæm were ðæt hio him mid ryhte doon sceal, ond he hire sua some, ðy læs hie on unryht hæmen." Ond hwene æfter he cuið, "Ne untreow-sige ge no eow betweoxn, buton huru ðæt ge eow gehæbben sume hwile, ær ðæm ðe ge eowru gebedu ond eowra of-frunga doon wiellen, ond eft sona cirrað to eowrum ryhthæ-mede." Loca nu hu se halega wer, se ðe sua fæsðlice geimpod wæs to ðæm hefenlicum diogolnessum, ond suaðeah for mildheortnesse wæs ðonon gecierred to smeaganne hu flæsclicum monnum gedafonode on hira burcotum ond on hiera beddum to donne; ond sua suiðe sua he wæs up ahæfen to ðæm ungesewenlicum, he ðeah gehwyrfde his heortan eage, ond for mildheortnesse gebigde his mod to untrumra monna diogolnessum. Hefonas he ðurhfor mid his modes sceawunga, ond suaðeah ðone ymbhogan ne forlet ðæs flæsclican beddgemanan; forðæm he wæs gefeged mid ðære lufan Godes ond monna ægðer ge to ðam hiehstum ðingum ge to ðæm nyðemestum. He wæs on him selfum mid ðæs Halgan Gæstes mægene suiðe healice up abrogden, ond ðeah eorðlicum monnum emnlice for arfæsðnesse ond for niedðearfe wæs geuntrumod. Forðæm he cuæð, "Hwa bið geuntrumod ðæt ic ne sie eac geuntrumod? Oððe hwa bið gesciended ðæt ic eac ðæs ne scamige?" Eft he cuæð be ðæm ilcan, "Ðonne ic wæs mid Iudeum ic wæs suelc hie." Ne cuæð he ðæt forðy ðe he wolde his treowa ond his geleafan forlætan suæ suæ hie, ac he wolde atiewan his arfæsðnesse,

third heaven, and yet for the revelation of those things unseen, though the acuity of his mind was sharpened, did not
disdain to train it upon the bedrooms of fleshly beings and
direct how people should conduct themselves there, when
he said, "Let each man have his wife, and each woman her
husband, and let the wife do with the man what she rightly
ought to do, and he with her likewise, lest they turn to adultery." And a little after that he says, "Do not deprive each
other, except perhaps to have for yourselves a little while
before you intend to say your prayers or make your offerings, and immediately return to your conjugal relations."
Now, look how the saintly man, who was so fixedly attached
to the sublime privities, nonetheless for tenderheartedness
was turned from that to considering how it behooved people to conduct themselves in their bedrooms and in their
beds; and as much as his gaze was directed upward to the
unseen, he turned his heart's eye, and out of compassion he
bent his thoughts to the intimate matters of frail humans.
He traversed heaven with contemplation of mind, and yet
he did not neglect reflection upon carnal cohabitation, because he was conjoined by the love of God and men both to
the highest matters and to the lowest. He was in his own
person drawn up so very high by the might of the Holy
Spirit, and yet equally for duteousness and for the need of
earthly beings he showed sympathy. For this reason he said,
"Who is made weak that I am not also weakened? Or who is
corrupted that I do not also feel ashamed of it?" In turn he
said about the same, "When I was among the Jews, I was
such as they." He did not say that because he intended to
give up his faith and devotion as they did, but he wanted to

ða he licette hine selfne ðæt he wære ungeleaffull; ac on ðæm he geleornode hu he scolde oðrum monnum miltsian ðe he geðohte hu he wolde ðæt mon him miltsode gif he suelc wære. Ond eft he cuæð, "Ðeah we nu ofer ure mæð ðencen ond smeagean, ðæt we dooð for Gode; ðonne we hit eft gemetlæcað, ðonne doð we ðæt for eow." He ongeat ðæt he oferstag hine selfne on ðære sceawunge ðære godcundnesse, ond eft hine selfne ofdune astiggende he cuðe gemetgian his hieremonnum.

3   Be ðæm eac Iacobus se heahfæder, ða he smirede ðone stan ðe æt his heafdum læg to tacne ðæt he eft wolde his irfe ðær geteoðian, for ðære gesihðe ðe he on ðæm swefne geseah, ða he æt ðæm stane slæpte. He geseah ane hlædre standan æt him on eorðan. Oðer ende wæs uppe on hefenum, ond æt ðæm uferran ende Dryhten hlinode, ond englas stigon up ond ofdune on ða hlædre. Forðæm ða godan lareowas up sceawiende no ðæt an wilniað secean ond sceawian ðæt halige heafod ðære halgan gesomnunge, ðæt is Dryhten, ac wilnað for mildheortnesse ðæt hie ofdune astigen to his limum.

4   Forðæm Moyses oft eode inn ond ut on ðæt templ, forðæm he wæs ðærinne getogen to ðære godcundan sceawunga, ond ðærut he wæs abisgod ymb ðæs folces ðearfe. Ðærinne he sceawode on his mode ða diogolnesse ðære godcundnesse, ond ðonon ut brohte ðæm folce, ond cyðde hwæt hie wyrcean ond healdan scoldon. Ond symle ymb ðæt ðe hine ðonne tueode, ðonne orn he eft inn to ðæm temple, ond frægn ðæs Dryhten beforan ðære earce ðe se haligdom on wæs ðæs temples. He astealde on ðæm bisene ðæm reccerum ðe nu siendon. Hie sculon, ðonne hie ymb hwæt tueoð ðæs ðe hie ðærute don sculon, cierran eft to hira

show his piety when he presented himself as if he were not a believer; yet he learned how he ought to have compassion for other people by considering how he would like there to be compassion for him if he were such. And again he said, "Though we now meditate and study beyond our due measure, we do it for God; when we again bring it into moderation, we do it for you." He understood that he transcended himself in observing the divine, and he knew how to moderate himself for his disciples by descending.

Regarding the same there is also the patriarch Jacob, 3 when he anointed the stone that lay at his head as a sign that he would subsequently tithe his property there, for the vision that he saw in the dream when he slept by that stone. He saw a ladder by him on the earth. The other end was up in the heavens, and at the upper end the Lord reclined, and angels climbed up and down the ladder. Thus, good teachers with their eyes trained upward desire not only to find out and observe the sacred head of holy Church, which is the Lord, but for compassion they desire to climb down to its limbs.

Moses often went in and out of the temple because he 4 was drawn into it for religious contemplation, and outside he was occupied with the needs of the people. Inside he observed in his mind the mysteries of divinity and from there brought them out to the people, and explained what they were supposed to accomplish and fulfill. And whenever there was something about which he was in doubt, he would run back into the temple and ask the Lord before the ark of the temple in which was the covenant. In that way he set an example to leaders who live now. They ought, when they are in doubt about something they are to do on the outside, to

agnum inngeðonce, ond ðær God ascian, suæ suæ Moyses
dyde beforan ðære earce on ðæm temple. Gif hie ðonne giet
ðær tueonað, gongen ðonne to ðæm halgan gewritum, frine
ðara hwæt hie don oððe læran scylen. Forðæm sio
Soðfæsðnes self—ðæt is Krisð—ða he on eorðan wæs, he
hine gebæd on muntum ond on dioglum stowum, ond on
burgum he worhte his wundru. Mid ðæm he strewede ðone
weg ðære onhyrenesse ðæm godum lariowum, ðæt hie ne
scolden forhyggean ðone geferscipe ðara synfulra ond ðara
ungetydra, ðeh ðe hi selfe wilnien ðæs heahstan. Forðæm
ðonne sio lufu for mildheortnesse nieðer astigeð, ond hio
hie geðied to his niehstena ðearfe, ðonne hio suiðe wunderlice up astigeð; ond sua micle sua hio estelicor ofdune
astigeð, sua hio ieðelicor up astigeð.

5   Suelce hie sculon hie selfe atiowan, ða ðe oðrum fore
beoð, ðætte ða ðe him underðiedde sien him dyrren hira
dieglan ðing for scome geandettan; forðæm ðonne ða yða
ðara costunga ða synfullan ðrowiað, ðæt hi mægen iernan
ond fleon to ðæs lareowes mode him to ondettunge, suæ
suæ cild to his moder greadan, ond ða scylda ðe hie wenað
ðæt hie mid besmitene sien, mid his fultume ond geðeahte
hie mægen aðwean clænran ðonne hie ær ðære costunge
wæren, mid ðæm tearum ðara gebeda aðwægen. Forðæm
eac wæs ðæt ðe beforan ðæm temple stod æren ceac on
uppan twelf ærenum oxum, ðætte ða menn ðe into ðæm
temple gan woldon meahten hira honda ðwean on ðæm
mere. Se ceac wæs sua micel ðæt he oferhelede ða oxan ealle,
buton ða heafudu totodon ut. Hwæt getacniað ðonne ða
twelf oxan buton ða twelf apostolas, ond siððan ealle ða
endebyrdnessa ðara biscopa ðe ðæræfter fylgeað? Bi ðon

turn back to their own conscience and ask God there, just as Moses did before the ark in the temple. If they then still remain in doubt there, let them go to holy scripture and inquire what they ought to do or instruct. For that reason, when Truth itself—that is, Christ—was on earth, he prayed on the mountainside and in remote places, and he worked his miracles in cities. He thereby laid down the course of emulation to be followed by good teachers, that they should not despise the companionship of the sinful and the ignorant, though they themselves should aspire to the highest. For this reason, when love condescends out of compassion, and it applies itself to the needs of one's neighbors, it ascends quite miraculously, and the more gladly it descends, the more easily it ascends.

Likewise, those who are stationed above others ought to 5 make themselves accessible, so that those who are subject to them will dare confess to them their secret affairs out of shame; so that, when the sinful suffer waves of temptation, they will be able to run and take refuge in the teacher's heart to make confession to him, like a child to its mother's bosom, and with his assistance and counsel be able to wash away the offenses by which they consider themselves sullied, growing purer than they were before the temptation, washed in the tears of their prayers. For this reason also there stood before the temple a basin of bronze surmounting twelve brazen oxen, so that people who intended to enter the temple could wash their hands in the reservoir. The basin was so large that it covered the whole of each of the oxen, except that the heads protruded. What, then, did the twelve oxen signify but the twelve apostles, and subsequently all the lines of bishops who succeed them? About

wæs gecueden on ðære æ, "Ne forbinden ge na ðæm ðyrsten-
dum oxum ðone muð." Ðone cwide Paulus geryhte eft to
biscepum ðara openlican weorc we gesioð, ac we nyton
hwelc hira inngeðonc bið beforan ðæm ðearlwisan deman
on ðæm dieglan edleanum. Ða ðeah ðonne hi niðerastigað to
aðweanne hiera niehstena scylda, ðonne hie him ondettað,
hie beoð onlicost suelce hi bæren ðone ceak beforan ðære
ciricean dura, sua sua ða oxan dydon beforan ðæm temple;
ðætte sua hwelc sua inweard higige to gangenne on ða duru
ðæs ecean lifes, he ðonne ondette ælce costunge ðe him on
becume ðam mode his scriftes beforan ðæm temple; ond
suæ suæ ðara monna honda ond fet wæren aðwægene on
ðære ealdan æ on ðæm ceake beforan ðæm temple, sua
ðonne nu we aðwean ures modes honda ond ure weorc mid
ðære ondetnesse. Oft eac gebyreð ðonne se scrift ongit ðæs
costunga ðe he him ondetteð ðæt he eac self bið mid ðæm
ilcum gecostod. Hwæt, ðæt wæter on ðæm ceake wæs gedrefed, ðonne ðær micel folc hiera fet ond honda on ðwogon.
Sua bið ðæs sacerdes mod ðonne ðær bið micel folc on
aðwægen hira scylda ðurh his lare. Ðonne he underfehð ðæt
fenn ðara ðweandra, him ðyncð suelce he forleose ða smyltnesse his clænnesse. Ac nis ðæt na to andrædanne ðæm
hirde, forðæm ðe Dryhten hit eall swiðe smealice geðencð,
ond him forgiefð ðæt he sua micle ieðelicor bið gefriðod
from his agnum costungum sua he mildheortlicor bið gesuenced mid oðerra monna costungum.

this it was said in scripture, "Do not bind up the mouth of thirsty oxen." Paul directed that remark in turn to bishops whose public acts we see, but we do not know what their state of mind will be before the severe judge at the unrevealed expiation. Yet when they condescend to wash away the offenses of their neighbors who confess to them, they are very much as if they supported the basin before the church door, as the oxen did before the temple, so that whoever aspires to enter the door of eternal life ought to admit to his confessor before the temple each temptation that befell him; and just as people's hands and feet were washed under the old law in the basin before the temple, so let us now wash our mind's hands and our deeds by confession. It likewise frequently occurs that, when the confessor understands the temptation that is confided to him, he likewise himself is tempted in the same way. Now, the water in the basin was clouded when a great crowd washed their hands and feet in it. Similar is the priest's mind when many people are cleansed of their offenses in it by his instruction. When he takes on himself the mire of those being washed, it seems to him as if he will lose the tranquility of his purity. But for the shepherd that is nothing to fear, because the Lord considers all of it very minutely and allows him to be so much the more readily disburdened of responsibility for his own temptations, the more compassionately he is afflicted by other people's temptations.

Chapter 17

XVII. Hu se reccere sceal bion ðæm weldondum
monnum for eaðmodnesse gefera,
ond wið ðara yfelena unðeawas stræc
for ryhtwislicum andan.

Se ealdormonn sceal lætan hine selfne gelicne his hieremonnum: he sceal bion hira gefera for eaðmodnesse ðara
ðeah ðe wel don; he sceal bion wið ðara agyltendra unðeawas
up ahæfen for ðæm andan his ryhtwisnesse, ond ðætte he on
nænegum ðingum hine beteran ne do ðæm godum; ond ðeah
ðonne he ongiete ða scylda ðara ðweortiemena, ðonne
geðence he ðone ealdordom his onwealdes; ond eft ongean
ða godan ond ða wellibbendan forsio he his ealdordom suæ
suiðe ðæt he on allum ðingum ða ðe him underðiedde sien
læte him gelice, ond ne wene he nanes ðinges hine selfne
beteran; ond eft wið ða wiðerweardan ne ondræde he ðæt he
begonge his ryhtwisnesse, suæ suæ ic geman ðæt ic io sæde
on ðære bec ðe *Morales Iob* hatte. Ic cuæð ðæt æghwelc
monn wære gelice oðrum acenned, ac sio ungelicnes hira
geearnunga hie tiehð sume behindan sume, ond hira scylda
hi ðær gehabbað. Hwæt, ðonne ða ungelicnesse ðe of hira
unðeawum forð cymeð se godcunda dom geðencð, ðætte
ealle men gelice beon ne magon, ac wile ðæt simle se oðer
beo aræred from ðæm oðrum. Forðæm ealle ða ðe fore
oðrum bieon sculon, ne sculon hi na sua suiðe ne sua oft
geðencean hiera ealderdomes sua hie sculon geðencean hu
gelice hie beoð oðrum monnum on hira gecynde; ond ne

Chapter 17

17. How one in authority ought to be the companion of beneficent people through humility, and vehement in righteous anger against the vices of the bad.

One in authority ought to regard himself as like his charges: he ought to be the companion through humility of those who nonetheless do good; he ought to be towering in the indignation of his righteousness at the vices of wrongdoers, and in no respect hold himself superior to the good; and yet when he perceives the offenses of the perverse, let him consider the authority of his position; and in turn, as regards the good and the upstanding, let him deprecate his authority to the extent that he make himself out to be in all respects like those subject to him, and not suppose himself in any respect better; and again, with the obstinate let him not be too timid to express his righteousness, as I recall that I once said in the book that is called *Moralia in Job*. I said that every person is born equal to every other, but the difference in their merits moves some behind others, and their offenses keep them there. Now, the divine judgment takes into consideration the inequality that arises from their vices, that not all people can be alike, but wills it that one is always raised above the other. Therefore, all who are to be ahead of others ought not to be mindful of their superiority as much or as often as they are mindful of how similar they are in their nature to other people, and not take pleasure in

gefeon hie na ðæt hie ofer oðre menn bion moten sua suiðe sua ðæs ðæt hie oðrum monnum mægen nyttoste beon.

2   Hwæt, hit is gesæd ðæt ure ealdan fæderas wæron ceapes hierdas. Ond eac Dryhten cuæð to Noe ond to his bearnum, "Weahsað ge ond monigfaldiað ond gefyllað eorðan, ond iower ege ond broga sie ofer ealle eorðan nitenu." Ne cuæð he no "ofer oðre men" ac "ofer nietenu"; ða he wæs forboden ofer menn, ða he wæs aliefed ofer nietenu. Se monn is on gecynde betera ðonne dysig nietenu, ac he ne bið na betera ðonne oðre menn. Forðæm hit næs na gecueden ðæt hie ne scoldon oðre menn ondrædan, ac nietenu. Forðæm hit is un-gecyndelicu ofermodgung ðæt se monn wilnige ðæt hine his gelica ondræde, ond suaðeah hit is niedðearf ðæt mon his hlaford ondræde, ond se cneoht his *magister*. Forðæm ðonne ða lareowas ongitað ðæt ða ðe him underðiedde beoð him to hwon God andrædað, ðonne is ðearf ðæt hie gedon ðæt hi huru him menniscne ege ondræden, ðæt hie ne durren syngian ða ðe him ne ondrædað ðone godcundan dom. Ne ofermodgiað ða scirmenn na forðy, ðeah hi for ðyslicum wielnien ðæt hie andrysne sien, forðon hi ne secað na hira selfra gielp on ðam, ac hiora hieremonna ryhtwisnesse hie wilniað, ond ðæm hi wilniað ðæt hie andrysne sien ðæm ðe on woh libbað; ond ofer ða hi sculon ricsian næs na sua ofer menn ac sua sua ofer nietenu, forðon ðe hie be sumum dæle wildorlice beoð. Hie sculon forðy ofdrædde licgean astreahte oðrum monnum underðiodde sua sua nietenu.

3   For ðiosum ðonne oft gebyreð ðæt se reccere on his mode wirð up ahæfen, ond wierð aðunden on ofermetto, ðonne he sua suiðe oðre oferhlifað ðætte ealle licggeað under his willan, ond eall ðæt he bebeodeð bið suiðe hraðe gefylled to

being allowed to hold a place above other people as much as in their having the ability to be of greatest assistance to others.

Now, it is said that our ancestors were herdsmen. And likewise the Lord said to Noah and to his children, "Grow and multiply and fill the earth, and let there be awe and dread of you upon all the beasts of the earth." He did not say "upon other people" but "upon beasts"; while Noah was forbidden it over other people, he was permitted it over beasts. A human is by nature superior to irrational beasts, but he is in no way superior to other humans. Therefore, it was by no means said that other people should fear them, but beasts. And so it is unnatural arrogance that a human should want his equal to fear him, and yet it is necessary that one should fear his lord, and a servant his master. Therefore, when teachers perceive that those in their care fear God too little, they at all events need to induce them to fear human authority, so that they not sin, fearing no divine retribution. Officials do not grow proud on that account, though they wish to be fearsome in the presence of such persons, because they are by no means in pursuit of their own exaltation in doing that, but they desire their subordinates' righteousness, and therefore they wish to be intimidating to those who live in deviousness, and over them they ought to have rule not as if over humans but as if over beasts, for they are to a certain degree bestial. They ought therefore to lie prostrate in fear, subject to other people like beasts.

For these reasons, then, it often happens that the leader grows arrogant in his mind and becomes bloated with pride when he towers over others so much that all are subject to his will, and all that he decrees is performed to his satisfac-

his nytte. Ond gif hwæt welgedones bið, ðonne cnodað him
ðæt ealle ða ðe him underðiedde bioð mid herenesse; ond gif
he hwæt yfeles deð, ne wiðcuið ðam nan mann, ac herigað
oft sua suiðe sua hie hit lean scoldon; ond mid ðy wyrð ðæt
mod besuicen ond genæt mid ðæra olicunga ðe him underðiedde beoð, ðæt he bið up ofer hine selfne ahæfen on his
mode. Ond ðonne he bið utane ymbhringed mid ungemetlicre heringe, he bið innan aidlad ðære ryhtwisnesse, ond
forgiet hine selfne ðonne he tolætt, ond fægnað ongeagn
ðara oðerra word, ond geliefð ðæt he suelc sie suelce he gehierð ðæt his olicceras secgað ðæt he sie, næs suelc suelc
his selfes gescadwisnes sceolde ongietan ðæt he wære. Ac
forsiehð ða ðe him underðiodde beoð, ond ne mæg ongietan
ða ðe him beoð on gecynde ond on ðeawum gelice, ac wenð
ðæt he hæbbe hie oferðungne on his lifes gearnunga sua he
hi hæfð oferstigene mid ðam hliete his anwaldes, ond wenð,
he sua micle ma wite ðonne oðre menn sua he gesihð ðæt he
mare mæg doon ðonne oðre menn. Ond ðonne hine selfne
sua healice up ahefeð on sumum ðingum, ond suaðeah bið
getieged to oðrum monnum mid onlicre gecynde, ðeah
he forsio ðæt he him on locige. Ac sua he wierð self to ðæs
onlicnesse ðe awriten is ðæt he gesio ælce ofermetto, se is
kyning ofer eall ða bearn oferhygde. Se wilnode synderlices
ealdordomes, ond forseah ða geferræddene oðerra engla
ond hira lif, ða he cuæð: "Ic wille wyrcean min setl on
norðdæle, ond wielle bion gelic ðæm hiehstan"; ond ða wunderlice dome gewearð ðæt he geearnode mid his agne
inngeðonce ðone pytt ðe he on aworpen wearð, ða he hine
his agnes ðonces up ahof on sua healicne anwald. Butan
tweon ðonne se monn oferhyð ðæt he beo gelic oðrum monnum, ðonne bið he gelic ðæm wiðerweardan ond ðæm
aworpnan diofule.

tion without delay. And if something admirable is done, all those subject to him ascribe it to him with praise; and if he does something bad, no one criticizes it, but often they praise it as much as they ought to blame it; and thereby his mind is deceived and twisted by the flattery of those subject to him, so that he is elevated above himself in his mind. And when he is surrounded without by limitless praise, he will be voided within of righteousness and will forget himself when he permits it, and takes pleasure in the words of others, and believes he is exactly what he hears those fawning on him say he is, not what his own discernment ought to perceive he is. Yet he scorns those who are subject to him and cannot recognize those who by nature and character are his equals, but he supposes that he has surpassed them in his life's merits as he has transcended them by the chance of his authority, and, he believes, he knows as much more than other people as he sees that he can accomplish more than other people. And then he preens himself so highly in certain respects, and yet he is connected to other people by a like nature, though he disdains to notice them. But in this way he himself comes to be the very image of that one about whom it is written that he who is king over all the children of pride perceives every presumption. He desired sole dominion and despised the companionship of other angels and their place in life when he said, "I will build my seat in the north and will be like the highest"; and then by a marvelous verdict it happened that he attained by his own design the abyss into which he was cast, when he of his own will raised himself to such lofty command. Without a doubt, when someone disdains to be compared to other people, he is like the perverse and outcast devil.

4   Sua sua Sawl Israhela kyning ðurh eaðmodnesse he geearnode ðæt rice, ond for ðæs rices heanesse him weoxon
ofermetto. For eaðmodnesse he wæs ahæfen ofer oðre
menn, ond for ofermettum he wæs aworpen. Dryhten ðæt
gecyðde ða ða he cuæð: "Ða ðu ðe selfum ðuhtest unwenlic,
ða ic ðe gesette eallum Israhelum to heafde." Æresð him
ðuhte selfum ðæt ðæt he wære suiðe unmedeme, ac siððan
he understungen ond awreðed wæs mid ðys hwilendlican
onwalde, he ðuhte him selfum suiðe unlytel ond suiðe
medeme. Forðæm he hine æthof from oðerra monna geferrædenne, ond hine dyde oðrum monnum sua ungelicne.
Forðy he ongeat ðæt he ma mehte ðonne ænig oðer, ða
wende he ðæt he eac mara wære. Ðæt wæs wunderlicu
gemetgung ðætte ða ða he him selfum wæs lytel geðuht, ða
wæs he Gode micel geðuht, ond ða ða he wæs him selfum
micel geðuht, ða wæs he Gode lytel geðuht. Sua oft ðonne
ðæt mod aðint on ofermettum for ðære menige ðæs folces
ðe him underðied bið, hit bið gewemmed mid ðæs anwaldes
heanesse. Ðone anwald mæg wel reccan se ðe ægðer ge hine
habban cann ge wiðwinnan. Wel hine recð se ðe conn wel
stræc bion ond ahæfen wið ða unryhtwisan ond wið ða
scyldgan ond wel emn wið oðre menn, ond he hine na bettran ne deð. Ac ðæt mennisce mod bið oft up ahafen, ðeah
hit mid nane anwalde ne sie underled; ac hu micle ma wenstu
ðæt hit wolde, gif ða wlenca ond se anwald ðær wære to gemenged? Ond ðeah suiðe ryhte stihtað ðone anwald se ðe
geornlice conn ongietan ðæt he of him gadrige ðæt him
stælwierðe sie, ond wið ðæt winne ðæt him dereð, ond ongite hine selfne, ond ongiete ðæt he bið self oðrum monnum
gelic, ond ðeah ahebbe hine ofer ða scyldgan mid andan ond
mid wræce.

Just so, King Saul of the Israelites attained rule by humil- 4
ity, and for the exaltation of that rule there swelled in him
arrogance. For humility he was raised above other people,
and for presumption he was cast out. The Lord revealed
that when he said, "When you were inconsiderable in your
own eyes, I set you at the head of all Israel." At first it
seemed even to him that he was entirely unsuitable, but
once he was sustained and upheld by this ephemeral power,
he seemed to himself so very consequential and worthy. For
that reason, he elevated himself above the society of others
and made himself out to be so unlike other people. Because
he perceived that he could do more than anyone else, he also
supposed that he was greater. It was a remarkable irony that
when he was in his own eyes puny, to God he seemed great,
and when he was in his own eyes great, to God he seemed
puny. Thus, frequently when the mind grows bloated on
self-regard over the sheer number of people subject to it, it
will be spoiled by being exalted to authority. He can well
keep a rein on authority who knows how both to wield it
and to combat it. He will keep it well under his control who
knows to be quite severe and superior to the unrighteous
and the culpable, and quite the equal of other people, and he
does not make himself out to be better. But the human mind
is often full of pretensions, even when it has no foundation
of authority; yet how much more so do you think it would
be if pomp and authority were afforded it? And yet he very
justly wields authority who genuinely knows how to see to it
that he will glean from it what is serviceable to him, and resist what is harmful to him, and that he know himself and
recognize that he is himself like other people, and yet that
he make himself superior to the sinful with vehemence and
severity.

5   We magon eac fullecor ongietan ond tosceadan ða
spræce, gif we sceawiað ða biesene ðæs forman hierdes, ðæt
wæs *sanctus* Petrus. Ðurh Godes giefe he onfeng ðone
ealdordom ðære halgan ciericean, ond ðeah he wiðsoc ðæt
hine mon to ungemetlice weorðode. Ða ða Cornelius for
eaðmodnesse wel dyde ðæt he hine astrehte beforan him, he
ðeah hine selfne ongeat him gelicne, ond cuæð, "Aris, ne do
sua; hu, ne iom ic monn sua ilce sua ðu?" Ac ða ða he ongeat
ða scylde on Annanian ond on Saffiram, suiðe hrædlice he
oðiewde hu micelne onwald he hæfde ofer oðre menn, ða he
hira lif ðurh ða smeanga ðæs Halgan Gæstes ongeat, ond
hine ða mid his worde geslog, ond mid ðy anwalde gecyðde
ðæt he wæs ieldesð ofer ða halgan cirican ond strengesð wið
scylda. Ðæt rice ond ðone anwald he na ne angeat wið Cornelius, ða ða he hine sua suiðlice weorðian wolde; he wolde
him ætfæstan his eaðmetto, ond mid ðy he geearnode ðæt
he ðuhte ðæt he wære his gelica. He cuæð to him ðæt he
wære his gelica: ðær he gecyðde his eaðmodnesse; ond eft on
Annaniam ond on Saffiram gecyðde his nið ond his onwald
mid ðære wræce. Ond eft *sanctus* Paulus, ne ongeat he na
hine selfne beteran oðrum godum monnum, ða ða he cuæð,
"Ne sint we nane waldendas eowres geleafan, ac sint fultemend eowres gefean, forðam ðe ge stondað on geleafan";
suelce he openlice cuæde, "We sint emnlice on ðam ðe we
ongietað ðæt ge stondað." Eft he spræc suelce he nysse ðæt
he a furðor wære ðonne oðre broðor, ða he cuæð, "We sint
gewordene suelce lytlingas betueox eow." Ond eft he cuæð,
"We sint eowre ðeowas for Cristes lufan." Ac ðonne he
gemette ða scylde ðe he stieran scolde, hrædlice he gecyðde
ðæt he wæs *magister* ond ealdormonn. Ðæt he cyðde ða he

We will also be more fully capable of comprehending and 5
appraising these remarks if we observe the example of the
first shepherd, who was Saint Peter. By the grace of God he
received authority over holy Church, and yet he forbade
that he be revered excessively. When Cornelius, out of humility, did well in prostrating himself before him, he, to the
contrary, acknowledged himself his equal and said, "Rise,
and do not do so. Am I not a man the same as you?" But
when he perceived the trespass of Ananias and Sapphira, he
quite readily showed how much authority he had over other
people when he perceived their way of life through the contemplation of the Holy Spirit and assailed him with his
words, and by that power made plain that he was most se-
nior over holy Church and most forceful against transgressions. He did not acknowledge that power and that authority to Cornelius when he wanted so extremely to honor him;
he wanted to impress on him his humility, and therefore he
endeavored to be considered his equal. He said to him that
he was his peer: in that he manifested his humility; and, conversely, with Ananias and Sapphira he manifested his indignation and his power with his retribution. And again, Saint
Paul did not regard himself as superior to other good people
when he said, "We are not dominators over your faith but
facilitators of your gladness, because you abide in faith"; as if
his plain meaning were, "We are equals in what we recognize
you to abide in." Again, he spoke as if he did not know that
he was ever ahead of other brothers when he said, "We have
become like little ones in your midst." And again he said,
"We are your servants for Christ's love." But when he encountered a fault that he ought to correct, he readily made it
known that he was master and overlord. He made that plain

cuæð on his Epistolan to Galatum, "Hwæðer wille ge ðæt ic cume to eow, ðe mid gierde ðe mid monnðwære gæste?"— suelce he cuæde, "hwæðer ic cume ðe mid ege ðe mid lufe?"

6   Ðonne bið ðæt rice wel gereht, ðonne se ðe ðærfore bið suiðor wilnað ðæt he ricsige ofer monna unðeawas ðonne ofer oðre gode menn. Ac ðonne ða ealdermenn ðreageað ða scyldgan, ðonne is him micel ðearf ðæt hie geornlice geðencen ðætte ðurh ða lare ond ðurh ðone ege ðe hie niede don sculon mid hiera anwalde gestiran ðara scylda; ond ðeahhwæðre, ðy læs he his eaðmodnesse forleose, geðence he ðæt he bið self suiðe gelic ðam ilcan monnum ðe he ðær ðreatað ond henð; ond eac we magon suigende geðencean on urum inngehygde, ðeah we hit ne sprecen, ðæt hie beoð beteran ðonne we, ond ðæs wierðe ðæt we hie furðor don, ðeah we to ðam gesette sien ðæt we hie ðreagean scylen, ond ðurh us scylen bion hiora scylda gestiered mid cræfte ond mid lare. Ac eft ðonne we selfe gesyngiað, ne ðreað us nan monn, ne furðum ane worde ne tælð. Forðam we beoð mid Gode sua micle suiðor gebundne sua we for monnum or-sorglicor ungewitnode syngiað buton ælcre wrace. Ac ðonne we ure hieremenn lærað ond ðreageað, sua micle ma we hie gefreogað æfter ðam godcundan dome, sua we her hiera synna wrecað suiðor. Ond suaðeah on ðære heortan is a sio eaðmodnes to healdanne ond eac on weorcum to læranne; ond betuh ðæm twæm is eallenga to geðencenne ðæt we to ungemetlice ða eaðmodnesse ne healden, ðy læs se anweald aslacie ðæs recendomes, ond ðæt we ure hieremenn sua gearige sua we hie eft geegesian mæge. Ðone ealdordom ond ðæt riceter ðe se reccere for monigra monna ðearfe

when he said in his Epistle to the Galatians, "Would you prefer that I come to you with a rod or with a gentle spirit?"—as if he had said, "that I come with intimidation or with love?"

A realm, then, is well governed when the one in command 6 desires more to exercise control over people's shortcomings than over other good people. But when leaders reprove transgressions, it is a firm necessity that they take diligent care, with the instruction and the coercion of the authority which they must apply, to correct those offenses; and yet, lest they cast off their humility, let them consider that they are themselves very like the same people they are then upbraiding and humbling; and also we can think silently to ourselves, without saying it aloud, that they are superior to us, and worthy of our placing them ahead, though we are expected to reprove them, and their offenses should be corrected through our skill and doctrine. Yet, by contrast, when we ourselves sin, no one reproves us or lays blame with even a single word. Therefore, we are so much the more responsible to God, the freer of anxiety we are as we sin with impunity, disburdened of consequences. But when we instruct and rebuke our charges, by so much more will we have exculpated them in accordance with the divine judgment, the more we chastise their sins here. And humility is nonetheless always to be kept in the heart, and also to be taught by deeds; and between the two there is altogether to be considered that we not practice humility excessively, to prevent the authority of leadership from slackening, and that we pardon our dependents to such a degree that we can again command their reverence. The governance and the dominion that the commander assumes for the sake of many

underfehð he hine sceal eowian utan, ond he sceal healdan his eaðmodnesse innan. Eahtige he hine selfne on his inngeðonce suelcne suelcne he ondrætt ðæt he sie. Ond ðeah hit on sumum ðingum getacnad sie ðæt he hwelc gerisenlic wundor wyrcean mæge, gedo he ðeah ðæt his hieremenn ongieten ðæt he sie eaðmod on his inngeðonce, ðæt hi mægen ðæm onhyrigean, ond on his ealdorlicnesse hie ongieten ðæt hie him mægen ondrædan. Ða ðe ofer oðre bioð, giemen hie geornlice ðætte sua micle sua hira onwald bið mara gesewen ofer oðre menn, ðæt hie sua micle ma sien innan geðryccede mid eaðmodnesse, ðy læs ðæt geðoht hine ofersuiðe ond on lustfulnesse his mod geteo hwelces unðeawes, ðæt he hit ne mæge ðonne to his willan gewealdan, forðæm ðe he him ær to unðeawum his agenne willan underðeodde, ond him geðafade ðæt hit mid anwalde him moste oferricsian, ðætte ðæt ofsetene mod mid ðære lustfulnesse his anwaldes ne sie getogen to upahafenesse.

7   Bi ðam wæs suiðe ryhte gecueden ðurh sumne wisne monn; he cuæð to ðæm oðrum, "To ealdormenn ðu eart gesett, ne beo ðu ðeah to up ahafen, ac bio suelce an ðinra hieremonna." Ond eft be ðam ilcan cuæð *sanctus* Petrus, "Ne sint we nane waldendas ðisses folces, ac we sint to bisene gesette urre heorde." Be ðæm ilcan eft sio Soðfæsðness— ðæt is Crist—ðurh hine selfne cuæð, ða he us speon to ðæm hiehstan geearnungum, he cuæð, "Wite ge ðætte ðioda kyningas bioð ðæs folces waldendas, ond ða ðe ðone anwald begað, hi beoð hlafordas gehatene; ne sie hit ðonne na sua betweoxn eow, ac sua hwelc sua wille betweoxn eow fyrmest beon, se sceal beon eower ðegn, ond sua hwelc sua wille betweoxn eow mæst beon, sie se eower ðeow. Sua sua Monnes Sunu," cuæð Crist be him selfum, "ne com he na to ðam on

people he ought to exhibit outwardly, and he ought to keep his humility within. In his private thoughts let him regard himself as being such as he dreads to be. And though it should be made a sign that in some matters he can work certain estimable wonders, let him nonetheless have his auditors know that he is humble in his conscience, so that they can emulate that, and in his lordliness they may perceive that they can feel timidity toward him. Let those who are placed over others take especial care that the greater their authority over other people is perceived to be, to such a greater degree they are inwardly checked by humility, to keep one's imagination from getting the better of him and drawing his mind toward the desire for some vice, so that he cannot then bend it to his will, because he has already made his own will attendant to his vices, and he consented to allowing it to govern him authoritatively, lest the mind, assailed by his appetite for power, be led to self-aggrandizement.

About this it was quite properly said through a certain 7 wise man, who remarked to another, "You are given a place as captain, yet do not be too conceited, but be like one of your subordinates." And on the same subject Saint Peter in turn said, "We are not rulers of this people, but we are set as an example to our flock." About the same, Truth—that is, Christ—in his own person said, when he exhorted us to the highest state of merit, "You should know that kings of nations are rulers of the people, and those who take on authority are called lords; let it not, then, be so among you, but whoever wishes to be first among you ought to be your aide, and whoever wishes to be greatest among you, let him be your servant. Just so the Son of Man," as Christ said of

eorðan ðæt him mon ðenade, ac ðæt he wolde ðenian." For ðeosun illcan is eac gesæd on ðæm godspelle hwelc wite scolde ðrowian se upahafena ðegn æfter ðam anfangnan rice. He cuæð ðonne, "Se yfela ðeow cuið on his mode: Hit bið long hwonne se hlaford cume; ic mæg slean ond ierman mine heafodgemæccan. Itt him ðonne ond drincð mid ðam druncenwillum monnum, ond læt his hlafordes gebod to giemelieste. Ðonne cymð his hlaford on ðæm dæge ðe he ne wenð, ond on ða tiid ðæt he hine ær nat; hæfð hine ðonne siððan for ænne licettere." Ond suiðe ryhte deð for ðære licettunge ðe he licette ðæt he wolde habban ða ðenunga ðeawas ond ðeodscipe to læranne; ond ða he ðæt hæfde, ða wolde he hit habban him to agnum anwalde, ond dyde him ðæt riceter to sida ond to gewunan.

8   Ond suaðeah oft agyltað ða ealdormenn efnsuiðe on ðam ðe he bið to eaðmod ðam yflan mannan, ond læt hine him to gelicne, ond licett wið hie ma to geferrædenne ðonne to ealdordome. Suiðe ryhte se bið geteald to ðæm liceterum se ðe on lareowes onlicnesse ða ðenenga ðæs ealdordomes gecierð to hlaforddome, ond gemacað ðæt his ege ond his onwald wierð to gewunan ond to landsida on his scire. Ond ðeah hwilum giet suiðor hie syngiað on ðam ðe hie healdað ma geferrædenne ond efnlicnesse ðonne ealdordom wið ða yfelan ond ða unryhtwisan. Sua Heli se sacerd dyde. He wæs mid leasre mildheortnesse ofersuiðed, ðæt he nolde witnian his agne suna ða hie agylton, ac beforan ðam ðearlwisan deman he ofslog ægðer ge ða suna ge hine selfne mid ðam ðe he geðafade ða scylde unwitnode. Hit wæs onlicost suelce sio godcunde stemn to him cuæde, "Ðu weorðasð ðine suna ma ðonne me." Ond eft ðurh ðone witgan wæs gecid ðæm hierdum, ða he cuæð, "Ðæt sceap ðæt ðær sceoncforad wæs,

himself, "did not come to earth to be served, but to serve." For this same reason it is said in the gospel what torment the conceited deputy should endure after accepting power. He said, then, "The bad servant says in his mind, 'It will be long until my lord comes; I can beat and abuse my fellows.' Then he will eat and drink with sots, and let his lord's instructions go unheeded. Then his lord will come on a day when he is unexpected, and at a time he will not know beforehand; thereupon he will hold him for a hypocrite." And he will do so quite rightly for the hypocrisy that he pretended that he wished to have the office to teach virtues and community, and when he had it, he wished to have it for the sake of his own power, and made that authority his custom and habitude.

And yet commanders are often equally blameworthy for being too deferential to a bad person and treating him as an equal, and assuming an attitude toward him more of camaraderie than of lordship. Quite properly he is regarded as a hypocrite who under color of a teacher turns the obligations of leadership to overlordship and makes of his overbearingness and his power the law and the custom of the country in his jurisdiction. And yet sometimes they transgress even more who assume conviviality and equality more than authority with the bad and the impious. The priest Eli did so. He was overcome by misguided tenderheartedness, so that he would not correct his own sons when they offended, but before the severe judge he killed both his sons and himself by indulging their offenses without punishment. It was very much as if the divine voice said to him, "You honor your sons more than me." And again through the prophet the shepherds were chided when he said, "The sheep that was

8

131

ne spilcte ge ðæt, ond ðæt ðær forloren wæs, ne sohte ge
ðæt, ne ham ne brohtan." Se bringð ham ðone forlorenan se
ðe mid geornfulnesse ðære hierdelican giemenne ðone ðe
afielð on synne eft gehwyrfð ond arærð ðæt he stent on
ryhtwisnesse. Hwæt, se foreda sconca bið gewriðen mid
ðæm bende, sua beoð ða synna mid ðam lareowdome gebundne. Sua sua sio wund wile toberan, gif hio ne bið gewriðen mid wræðe, sua willað ða synna weaxænde toflowan,
gif hie ne beoð gebundne hwilum mid stræclice lareowdome.

9   Ond suaðeah oft sio wund bið ðæs ðe wierse ond ðy mare,
gif hio bið unwærlice gewriðen, ond him bið ðæt sar ðe ge-
fredre, gif sio wund bið to ungemetlice fæste gewriðen. Sua
is eac ðearf ðæt se lareow, se bið saule læce, ðara synna
wunde stirende gemetlice gewriðe on his hieremonnum,
ond ðeah sua geornlice begaa ða ryhtwisnesse ðæs lareowdomes wið ða gyltendan ðæt he ne forlæte his mildheortnesse. Ond eac him is to giemenne ðæt he ætiewe his hieremonnum ðæt he sie hiera fæder ond reccere on lare, ond
hiera modur on mildheortnesse, ðæt he huru ne sie to stræc
on ðære lare, ne to slæc on ðære mildheortnesse. Sua sua we
io cuædon on ðeawa bocum be Iobe ðæt ægðer wære unnyt
ge mildheortnes ge steor, gif hie anlipe wæron, buton hi
butu ætsomne sien. Forðæm scel bion on ðæm reccere ðæt
he sie ryhtlice ond mildheortlice rædende his hieremonnum
ond mildheortlice witniende. For ðioson ilcan wæs ðætte sio
Soðfæstnes self cuæð—ðæt is Crist—ða he lærde ðurh ða
tielunga ðæs Samaritaniscan ymb ðone gewundedan, ðe
mon lædde helfcuicne to ðæm giesðhuse, ond bæd ðæt mon
scolde ægðer ge win ge ele giotan on his wunde. Witodlice

broken legged you did not bind up, and you did not search for that which went missing, nor bring it home." He brings home the lost who with the diligence of pastoral care turns back and raises up one who falls into sin, so that he abides in righteousness. Now, the broken leg is wrapped in a bandage, just as sins are bound up by the practice of teaching. Just as the wound will open if it is not wrapped in a bandage, sins will sprawl and proliferate if they are not at times bound up with strict doctrine.

And yet often the wound will be the worse for it and the more severe if it is bound up negligently, and one's pain will be the more acute if the wound is bound too tightly. So also it is necessary that the teacher, who is the soul's physician, bind moderately with his correction the wound of sin in those subject to him, and yet diligently practice the righteousness of the post of instructor regarding malefactors in such a way that he does not surrender his compassion. And also he is to take care to convince his charges that he is their father and guide in instruction, and their mother in tenderheartedness, so that he especially is not too severe in instruction, nor too illiberal of compassion. Just so we once said in the books of morals concerning Job that compassion and reproof would both be ineffectual if they were applied exclusively, unless the two were joined. For that reason, it should be such with the guide that he be a just and humane counselor to his adherents, and a tenderhearted scourge. It was about this very matter that Truth itself—that is, Christ —spoke, when he gave instruction by example of the solicitude of the Samaritan for the wounded man who was led half dead to the inn, and it was requested that both wine and oil be poured on his wound. Without a doubt, wine stings

9

ðæt win slit ða wunde, ond se ele hie gesmeð ond gehælð. Ðis is ðearf ðæt se se ðe wunde lacnigean wille giote win on, ðæt sio reðnes ðæs wines ða forrotedan wunde suge ond clænsige, ond eft ele, ðæt se hie lieðe ond gehæle. Sua eac ðam lareowe is to mengenne ða lieðnesse wið ða reðnesse, ond of ðam gemonnge wyrce gemetgunge, ðæt he mid un- gemetlicre grimsunge his hieremonna wunda to suiðe ne slite ne ne ice, ne eft for ungemetlicre mildheortnesse he hie ne læte unwriðena.

10   Suiðe wel ymb ðæt tacnað sio earc on ðære Ealdan Æ. On ðære wæron ða stænenan bredu ðe sio æ wæs on awriten mid Tien Bebodum, ond eac sio gierd mid ðæm bredum, ond eac se sweta mete ðe hie heton *monna,* se him cuom of hefonum. Sua eac, gif ðara haligra gewrita ondgit bið on ðam breostum ðæs godan recceres, ðonne sceal ðær bion gierd— ðæt is ðæt he ðreage his hiremenn. Ond eac sceal bion on ðæm breostum ðæs monnan suetnes—ðæt is ðæt he him sie lieðe. Be ðiosum illcan cuæð Dauið to Gode, "Ðin gierd ond ðin stæf me afrefredon." Mid gierde mon bið beswungen, ond mid stæfe he bið awreðed. Gif ðær ðonne sie gierd mid to ðreageanne, sie ðær eac stæf mid to wreðianne. Sie ðær eac lufu, næs ðeah to hnesce; sie ðær eac reðnes, næs ðeah to stið; sie ðær eac onda, næs ðeah to ungemetlice grim; sie ðær eac arfæsðnes, næs ðeah wandigendre ðonne hit gedafenlic sie; ðætte ðonne sio ryhtwisnes ond sio mildheortnes hi gegadrige on ðæm anwalde ðæs recceres, ond ðæt mod his hieremonna oliccende egesige ond ðreatigende olicce.

the wound and oil relieves and heals it. It is a requirement that whoever will treat the wound pour wine on it, so that the acidity of the wine will draw from and cleanse the infected wound, and in turn pour on oil, to soothe and heal it. So also it is for the teacher to mingle palliation and harshness, and from that mixture forge moderation, in order not to irritate or enlarge his charges' wounds too much with immoderate severity, nor on the other hand leave them unbandaged out of immoderate loving-kindness.

The ark of the Old Covenant stands as an excellent sign of that. In it were the stone tablets on which were inscribed the Ten Commandments, and also the rod with the tablets, as well as the sweet delicacy that they called *manna,* which came to them from the heavens. Thus, likewise, if there is understanding of holy scripture in the breast of the good guide, then there ought to be a rod there—that is, that he discipline his charges. And likewise there ought to be sweetness in such a person's breast—that is, that he be mild to them. About this same, David said to God, "Your rod and your staff comforted me." With a rod one is beaten, and with a staff he is sustained. If, then, there is a rod to discipline with, let there be also a staff to sustain with. Let there also be love, but not too tender; let there be severity, too, but not too harsh; let there also be acrimony, but not too immoderately stern; let there be piety, as well, but not too timid when it is appropriate, so that righteousness and compassion be joined under the control of the guide, and intimidate while soothing the mind of his charges, and soothe while intimidating.

Chapter 18

XVIII. Hu se lareow ne sceal ða inneran giemenne gewanian for ðære uterran abisgunge, ne eft ða uterran ne forlæte he for ðære inneran.

Ne forlæte se reccere ða inneran giemenne ðæs godcundan ðiowdomes for ðære abisgunge ðara uterra weorca, ne eac ne gewanige he na ðone ymbhogan ðære innera scire for ðære abisgunge ðære uterran, ðy læs he sie gehæft mid ðam uterran, oððe eft mid ðam inneran anum abisegad, ðæt he ne mæge ðurhteon his niehstum ðæt he him utan don scolde. Monige ðeah nyllað na geðencean ðæt hi beoð oðrum broðrum ofergesett, ond him fore bion scoldon on godcundum ðingum; ac mid ealre heortan geornfulnesse begongað ða woroldcundan giemenne, ond fægniað ðæs ðæt hie ða habbað to begongenne; ond ðonne, ðonne hie hie ne habbað, dæges ond niehtes hie fundiað to bigietenne, ond beoð suiðe gedrefede on hira mode forðam ðe him ðonne wona bið ðæs ðe hie habban woldon. Ac ðonne him eft gelimpð ðæt hi æmtige beoð ðære scire, ðonne bioð hie suiður on hira mode gesuenced for ðæm æmtan; forðæm ðæt wære his willa ðæt he moste ymb swincan, ond ðyncð him gesuinc ðæt he bið butan woroldgesuincum. Ond sua hit gebyreð, ðonne he fægnað ðæt he sie abisgod mid woroldðingum, ðæt he ne conn oðre læran ða godcundan wisan ðe he læran scolde. Forðon aðreat ða hieremenn ryhtes lifes, ðonne hie

Chapter 18

18. How the teacher ought not to diminish inner responsibilities for outer duties, nor, conversely, neglect the outer for the inner.

Let the leader not neglect inward attentiveness to serving the divine on account of the demands of outward occupations, nor likewise diminish scrutiny of inner governance on account of the demands of the outer, so that he not become captive to the outer, or, conversely, become preoccupied solely by the inner, with the result that he cannot accomplish for his neighbors what he ought to do outwardly for them. Yet many refuse to consider that they are set over other brothers and ought to supervise them in religious matters, but with all their heart's devotion they go about worldly affairs and are delighted to have those things to undertake; and then, when they do not have them, day and night they do their utmost to obtain them and are deeply distressed in their mind because they are without what they would have. But when in turn it happens to one that he is liberated from those duties, he is the more strongly anxious in his mind on account of that leisure, because it would be his preference to be permitted to devote his efforts it, and it seems to him laborious to be free of worldly labors. And so it turns out, when he delights in being occupied with worldly affairs, that he does not know how to teach the religious matters that he ought to teach. Therefore, his charges grow indifferent to the just life when they desire to live spiritually,

wilniað gæstlice libban, be ðæm yfelum bisenum ðe se deð
ðe him fore beon sceolde. Ðonne ætspornað hie, ond weorðað mid ðæm ascrencte. Sua eac ðær ðæt heafod bið unhal
eall ða limu bioð idelu, ðeah hie hal sien, sua eac bið se here
eal idel, ðonne he on oðer folc winnan sceal, gif se heretoga
dwolað; sua eac ðonne se biscep begæð ða ðeninga ðe eorðlice deman sceoldon, ðonne ne tyht nan mon his hieremonna mod ne ne bilt to gæstlicum weorcum, ne nan mon
hiera scylda ne ðreað, ac se hierde bið idel ðe scolde ðære
heorde gieman. Forðy ne magon ða hieremenn begietan ðæt
leoht ðære soðfæstnesse, forðæm ðonne sio giornfulnes
eorðlicra ðinga abisgað ðæt ondgit, ond ablent ðæs modes
eagan mid ðære costunga ðæm folce, sua sua dust deð ðæs
lichoman eagan on sumra mid ðodne.

2   Forðæm suiðe ryhtlice se aliesend monna cynnes, ða he
us stierde urra womba oferfylle, he cuæð, "Behealdað eow
ðæt ge ne gehefegien eowre heortan mid oferæte ond ofer-
drynce ond mid monigfaldre gieminge ðisse worolde"; ond
eac he geicte ðærto ege, ða he cuæð, "ðy læs eow hrædlice on
becume se færlica Domes Dæg." Ðæs dæges tocyme hwelc
he beo he cyðde, ða he cuæð, "He cymð sua sua grin ofer
ealle ða ðe eardiað ofer eorðan." Ond eft he cuæð, "Ne mæg
nan mon twam hlafordum hieran." Ond eac cuæð Paulus, ða
ða he wolde arwierðra monna mod from ðisses middangeardes geferrædenne ateon, suiðe suiðe he him wiðbræd,
ða he cuæð, "Ne scyle nan Godes ðeow hine selfne to ungemetlice bindan on woruldscipum, ðy læs he mislicige ðæm
ðe he ær hine selfne gesealde." Ða ða he lærde ðæt ðære
ciricean ðegnas scoldon stilnesse ðære ðenunga habban, ða
lærde he hi eac hu hie hie geæmettian scoldon oðerra
weorca; he cuæð, "Gif ge ymb woroldcunde domas beon

due to the bad example he sets who ought to be in charge of them. Then they spurn it and are tripped up by that. Just as the limbs are all idle where the head is diseased, though they are all sound, so also the army is all useless when they ought to fight with another body of men if the general blunders; so also when the bishop engages in the services that are proper to worldly judges, no one exhorts the mind of his charges, nor encourages them to spiritual works, nor does anyone rebuke their trespasses, but the shepherd is idle who ought to tend the flock. His subordinates therefore cannot attain the light of truth, because then attention to worldly matters occupies the intellect and blinds the mind's eye of the people with temptation, as dust does the corporeal eye with the winds of summer.

Therefore, quite rightly the savior of humankind, when he forbade us to stuff our bellies, said, "Take care that you not overburden your heart with gluttony and intoxication and with various cares of this world"; and he added menace to that when he said, "lest the fearsome Day of Judgment fall upon you suddenly." Of what sort that day's arrival will be he revealed when he said, "It will come like a snare over all those who inhabit the earth." And again he said, "No one can obey two masters." And also Paul, when he wished to draw the minds of worthy people away from comfortable relations with this earthly existence, rebuked them in the extreme when he said, "No servant of God ought to commit himself too absolutely to mundane affairs, lest he displease the one to whom he has given himself." When he taught that officials of the Church should maintain serenity in their ministration, he taught them also how they ought to free themselves from other tasks; he said, "If you must go about

scylen, ðonne nime ge ða ðe on ðæm hirede unweorðuste
sien, ond settað ða to domerum, ðæt hie stierien ond
stihtien ymb ða eorðlican ðing, ða ðe ne beoð sua suiðe
geweorðode mid ðæm gæstlicum giefum"; suelce he openlice cuæde, "Gedoð ðæt hie sien on ðæm oðrum nytte, gif
hie on ðæm oðrum ne cunnen." Be ðæm eac Moyses sæde,
se ðe wæs Gode sua weorð ðæt he oft wið hine selfne spræc.
Æt sume cierre Githro his sueor, ðeah he hæðen ond
elðiodig wære, hine tælde ond sæde ðæt he on dyslicum gesuincum wære mid ðæs folces eorðlican ðeowote, ac lærde
hine ðæt he gesette oðre for hine to demenne betweox ðæm
folce ymbe hira geflita, ðæt he wære ðæs ðe freorra to ongietanne ða dieglan ond ða gæstlican ðing, ðæt he meahte
ðæt folc ðy wislicor ond ðy rædlicor læran; forðæm ða hlafordas ond ða recceras scoldon ðencean ymb ðæt helicuste,
ond ða underðioddan scoldon don ðæt unweorðlicre.

3   Ða recceras sceolon bion beforan ðæm folce sua sua
monnes eage beforan his lichoman, his weg ond his stæpas
to sceawianne. Ðonne is ðearf ðæt ðæt dust ðisse eorðlican
giemenne ne aðisðrige ðæt eage ðæs recceres, forðæm ealle
ða ðe ofer oðre bioð, bioð heafda ðara ðe ðærunder bioð,
ond ðæt heafod sceal wisian ðæm fotum, ðæt hie stæppen
on ryhtne weg: ufone sceal ðæt heafod giman ðæt ða fet
ne asliden on ðæm færelte, forðæm, gif ða fet weorðað
ascrencte, eal se lichoma wierð gebiged, ond ðæt heafod ge-
cymð on ðære eorðan. Hu gerades mæg ðonne se biscep brucan ðære hirdelican are, gif he self drohtað on ðam eorðlicum
tielongum ðe he oðrum monnum lean sceolde? For ðæm
ryhtan edleane Dryhten ðreade ðurh ðone witgan, ða he
cuæð, "Suelc ðæt folc bið, suelc bið se sacerd." Ðonne bið se

judgment in worldly matters, choose those who are of least regard in the community, and set them up as judges, so that those who are not so very blessed with spiritual gifts should rule and adjudicate about earthly matters"; as if his plain meaning were, "Let them be useful in some matters if they do not know how to be in others." About this also Moses spoke, who was deemed so worthy by God that he himself often spoke with him. On a certain occasion his father-in-law Jethro, though he was a pagan and a foreigner, upbraided him and said that in the worldly service of the people he took part in misguided drudgery, and he advised him to set another in his place to adjudicate among the people in their disputes, so that he would be the freer to understand mystic and spiritual matters, to be able to instruct the people more wisely and expediently, because lords and leaders ought to ponder the loftiest things, and those subject to them should see to the less consequential.

Leaders should be in front of the people as a person's eye 3 is in front of his body, to make out his path and his steps. Then it must be that the dust of this earthly ministry not cloud the eye of the leader, because all who are superior to others are the heads of those inferior, and the head ought to guide the feet, so that they walk the right way: from above, the head ought to ensure that the feet not stumble along the way, because if the feet are tripped up, the entire body gives way, and the head meets the ground. In what way, then, can the bishop be effective in the pastoral office if he engages himself in the worldly occupations that he ought to censure in others? For that very thing the Lord threatened just deserts through the prophet when he said, "Such as the people are, such is the priest." The priest is such as the people are

sacerd suelc suelc ðæt folc bið, ðonne he ðæt ilce deð ðæt hie doð, ond his on ða ilcan wisan tielað ðe hie doð. Ðæt ongeat Heremias se witga, ða ða he suiðe sarlice weop, ond spræc suelce ðæt templ wære eal toworpen. He cuæð, "Eala, hwy is ðis gold adeorcad? Ond ðæt æðeleste hiew, hwy wearð hit onhworfen? Toworpne sint ða stanas ðæs temples, ond licggeað æt ælcre stræte ende." Huæt tacnað ðonne ðæt gold ðe is sua diorwyrðe ofer eall ondweorc, buton ða heanesse ðæs haligdomes? Oððe hwæt getacnað ðæt æðele hiew buton ða arwyrðnes ðære æfesðnesse, ðe eallum monnum is to lufigenne? Hwæt getacniað eac ða stanas ðæs halgan huses buton ðone had ðære halgan endebyrdnesse? Hwæt getacnað eac sio rume stræt butan ðone widan weg ðisses andwerdan lifes? Be ðam ruman wege sio Soðfæsðnes, ðæt is Crist, ðurh hine selfne he cuæð, "Ðæt is suiðe rum weg ond widgille ðe læt to færwyrde." Ac ðonne bið ðæt gold asueartod, ðonne sio halignes monnes lifes bið mid eorðlicum weorcum gewemmed. Ond ðonne bið ðæt æðeleste hiw onhworfen, ðonne se æht ðara godra weorca, ðe he ær beeode, bið gewanod, forðæm ðe menn ær wendon ðæt he æfæsðlice drohtode. Ac ðonne hwelc æfter halgum hade hine selfne fæstlice geimpað on eorðlicum weorcum, ðonne bið hit suelce ðæt fægere hiw ðæs goldes sie onhworfen, ond hit sie ablacod ond forsewen for monna eagum. Ond ða giemmas ðara halignessa licggeað toworpne æfter stræta endum. Ðonne licggeað ða giemmas toworpne æfter strætum, ðonne ða menn ðe hie selfe to ðære ciricean wlite æmtegian sceoldon on ðæm dieglum ðenungum ðæs temples, ðonne hie ute wilniað ðara rumena wega ðisse worulde. Soðlice ða gimmas ðara halignessa to ðæm wæron gemacod ðæt hi scoldon scinan on ðæs hiehstan sacerdes hrægle betwux

when he does the same things they do, and he cultivates the same attainments they do. Jeremiah the prophet perceived that when he wept very bitterly and spoke as if the temple were all cast down. He said, "Oh, why is this gold tarnished? And why has this noblest luster faded? The stones of the temple are scattered and lie at every street's end." Then what does gold signify, which is so costly beyond all substances, but the loftiness of sanctity? Or what does the noble luster signify but the praiseworthiness of piety, which is to be cherished by all people? What, likewise, do the stones of the hallowed building represent but the office of holy orders? What, as well, does the broad street symbolize but the wide way of this present life? About that broad way Truth, which is Christ, said in his own person, "It is a broad and capacious way that leads to perdition." But when the gold is tarnished, the sanctity of a person's life is blemished with mundane deeds. And when the noblest luster is faded, the store of good works which he formerly undertook is depleted, because people formerly supposed that he acted piously. But when someone, after attaining the holy office, applies himself single-mindedly to mundane works, it is as if the lovely luster of gold is faded, and it is blackened and despised in people's eyes. And the gems of the sanctuary lie strewn at streets' ends. The gems lie strewn along the streets when those people who ought to devote their time to the adornment of the Church in the mystical rites of the temple desire the broad ways of this world outside. Certainly, the gems of the sanctuary were fashioned for the purpose of gleaming on the vestment of the chief priest among the

ðam halegestan halignessum. Ac ðonne ða sacerdas to
æfæsðnessum ond weorðunga ures aliesendes ne bædað ða
ðe him underðiedde bioð mid hira lifes geearnungum, ðonne
ne beoð hi na ðære halegestan halignesse gimmas on ðæm
gerenum ðæs biscepes gierelan, ac licggeað toworpne æfter
strætum, ðonne ða hadas ðære halgan endebyrdnesse beoð
forgiefene ðæm widgillan wegum hiera agenra lusta, ond
beoð getigede to eorðlicum tielengum. Eac is to witanne
ðæt he ne cuæð na ðæt ða giemmas wæren forsceadne æfter
ðæm strætum, ac æt ðara stræta endum; forðæm ðeah hie
woroldcundlice drohtigen, hie wiliniað ðæt hie ðyncen ða
betstan, ond ðeah hie gan on ðone ruman weg hiera agnes
willan ond lustfulnesse, hie wilniað ðæt hie mon hæbbe for
ða betstan ond ða halgestan.

4   Ond suaðeah hwilum sint to geðafianne for niedðearfe
ðas eorðlican tielunga, ond næfre ðeah to suiðe ne lufige, ðy
læs hie gehefegien ðæs monnes mod ðe hi to suiðe lufað, ðæt
he for ðære byrðenne gehefegad ond ofersuiðed, ne sie be-
senced of ðæm ymestun to ðæm nioðemestum. Ond suaðeah
monige underfoð heorde, ond ðeah wilniað ðæt hie beon
freo ond æmtige synderlice him selfum to gæstlicum weorcum, ond noldon beon abisgode nane wuht on eorðlicum
ðingum. Ða, ðonne hie eallinga agiemeleasiað ðone ymbhogan woruldcundra ðinga, ðonne ne gefultumað he nawuht to
his hieremonna niedðearfe. Forðæm wyrð oft forsewen ðara
monna lar, ðonne hie tælað ond hatigað hiera hieramonna
unðeawas, ond ne dooð him nan oðer god ðisse weorolde;
forðæm ðæt word ðære lare ne mæg ðurhfaran ðæs wædlan
heortan, gif he næfð ða are ðe he onfon mæge. Ac ðonne
grewð ðæt sæd suiðe wel ðara worda, ðonne sio mildheortnes ðæs lareowes geðwænð ond geleceð ða breost ðæs

holiest sacral objects. But when the priests do not by their life's merits press those placed in their charge to piety and worship of our savior, they are not gems of the holy of holies among the ornaments of the bishop's stole, but they lie strewn along the street when the offices of holy orders are forfeited to the capacious ways of their own desires and are fettered by earthly occupations. It is also to be noted that he by no means said that the gems were scattered along the street, but at the streets' farthest reaches, because although they conduct themselves in secular fashion, they desire to seem the best, and though they go the wide way of their own inclinations and appetite, they desire to be held for the noblest and the holiest.

Nevertheless, at times these earthly occupations are to 4 be tolerated out of necessity, and yet, no one should ever love them excessively, to avoid burdening the mind of one who cares for them too much, so that he, weighed down and overpowered by that burden, is sunk from the highest to the lowest. And yet many assume the care of a flock and nonetheless wish to be free and disengage themselves specially for spiritual works, and would not care at all to be occupied by earthly matters. These, when they entirely fail to pay attention to worldly affairs, in no measure help out with their adherents' needs. Hence, the instruction of these people is often scorned when they criticize and despise the faults of their charges, and do them no other good in this world, because the words of instruction cannot penetrate the heart of someone in need if he has not the graciousness that the other can accept. But the seed of those words grows quite well when the compassion of the teacher moistens and

gehierendes. Forðæm is niedðearf ðæm reccere ðæt he mæge ond cunne oðerra monna inngeðonc giendgeotan ond gewæterian, ond hie eac on hiera niedðearfum utane besio. Sua sculon ða hierdas weallan ymb ða geornfulnesse ðære inneran ðearfe his hieremonna, ðæt he ne forlæte ða giemenne hira uterran ðearfe.

5   Niede sceal bion gebrocen ðæt mod ðara hieremonna, gif se lareow ond se hierde agiemeleasað ðæt he hiera utan ne helpe. Be ðæm se forma hierde *sanctus* Petrus geornfullice monode, ond cuæð, "Ic, eower emnðeowa ond Cristes ðrowunge gewita, ic eow healsige ðæt ge feden Godes heorde ðe under eow is." Suiðe hræðe æfter ðon he gecyðde hwæðer he mænde, ðe ðæs modes foster ðe ðæs lichoman, ða he cuæð, "Ungeniedde, mid eowrum agenum willan, ge sculon ðencean for eowre heorde Godes ðonces, nals na for fraceðlecum gestreonum." Mid ðæm wordum fullice he us warode ond lærde ðætte ðonne hie gefylden ond gebeten ða wædle hiera hieremonna, hie ne wurdon selfe ofslægene mid ðam sueorde ðære gitsunge, ðætte ðonne hira niehstan ðurh hie beoð gereorde ond gearode ðæt hie selfe ne fæsten ðæs hlafes ryhtwisnesse. Ðas ilcan geornfulnesse ðara hierda *sanctus* Paulus aweahte, ða he cuæð, "Se ðe ne gimð ðara ðe his beoð, ond huru Godes ðeowa, he wiðsæcð Godes geleafan, ond he bið treowleas."

6   Ond suaðeah betuoxn ðissum simle is to ondrædenne ond geornlice to behealdenne, ðonne hie ða uterran ðing don sculon, ðæt hie ne sien ðæm innecundan ingeðonce afierrede; forðæm oft ða heortan ðara reccera, sua sua we ær cuædon, ðonne hie mid ðissum hwilendlicum ðingum hie selfe abisegiað, ond ðæm unwærlice ðiowiað, hi ðonne lætað acolian ða innecundan lufan, ond ne ondrædað him na ðæt

sprinkles the breast of the auditor. Therefore, the guide needs to be able and to know how to water and irrigate other people's consciences, and also to see to their external needs. A shepherd ought to brim over with diligent care for the inward wants of his charges in such manner that he not neglect to tend to their outward wants.

The spirit of his charges will of necessity be broken if the 5 teacher and the shepherd neglects to help them materially. About this the first shepherd, Saint Peter, gave earnest warning and said, "I, your fellow servant and witness to Christ's passion, exhort you to feed God's flock, which is in your charge." Quite soon after that he made plain which he meant, feeding the spirit or the body, when he said, "Uncompelled, by your own inclination, you ought to tend to your flock under God's will, by no means for filthy lucre." With these words he alerted us in no partial measure and instructed us that, when they satisfied and remedied the want of their charges, they themselves not be slain with the sword of avarice, so that when their neighbors are succored by them and shown compassion, they not starve themselves of the bread of righteousness. That same watchfulness of shepherds Saint Paul evoked when he said, "Whoever does not tend to those who are his, and especially God's servants, abjures belief in God, and he is without faith."

And yet in the midst of all this, it is continually to be 6 worried over and scrupulously ensured, when they must be about external affairs, that they not grow distant from inward contemplation; because, as we have said already, when the hearts of leaders occupy themselves with these temporal affairs and serve them unreservedly, they cause internal love to grow cool, and they are not concerned about forgetting

hie forgieten ðæt hie underfengon ðone recedom monna saula. Ac hit is ðearf ðætte sio giemen, ðe hie hira hiremonnum utan don scylen, sie wel gemetgod. Be ðæm suiðe wel wæs gecueden to Ezechiele ðæm witgan ðætte ða sacerdas ne scoldon no hiera heafdu scieran mid scierseaxum, ne eft hi ne scoldon hira loccas lætan weaxan, ac hie scoldon hie efsigean mid scearum. Suiðe ryhte ða sacerdas sint gehatene sacerdas, ðæt is on Englisc "clænseras," forðæm hie sculon latteowdom gearwian ðæm geleaffullum ond him sculon fore beon. Ðæt feax ðonne on hira heafde getacnað ða uterran geðohtas, ðæt grewð ond scinð ofer ðæm brægene, ond his mon ðeah ne gefred. Ða giemen ðises andweardan lifes ðæt getacnað: sua giemeleaslice oft sceacað ure geðohtas from us, ðæt we his furðum ne gefredað, ðon ma ðe mon his feax mæg gefredan butan ðam felle, forðæm we oft ymb ungedafenlice wisan smeageað. Ond suaðeah ealle ða ðe for oðrum beon sculon, sculon habban giemenne ðissa uterrena ðinga, ond ðeah ne sien hi to fæste to gebundene. Suiðe ryhte wæs ðæm sacerde forboden ðæt he his heafod sceare, ond eac ðæt he his feax lete weaxan—ðæt is ðæt he ealle ða geðohtas of his mode ne aceorfe ðe he scyle his hieremonnum to nytte habban, ne eft he ne læte forweahsan to suiðe to unnytte ond to unryhte. Be ðæm wæs suiðe wel gecueden ðæt se efsigenda efsode his heafod—ðæt is ðæt he sua geornfullice sie ymb ða giemenne ðissa hwilendlicra ðinga sua sua hit niedðearf sie—ond ðeah sua sua he mæge hie iðelice butan sare of aceorfan ðæt hie to ungemetlice ne forweaxen; ðy læs, ðonne ðæt lif ðæs lichoman bið gescilðed, ðæt innegeðonc sie gebunden ðære heortan for ðære ungemetgunge ðæs ymbehogan ðara uterra ðinga. Sua sindon ða loccas to sparienne ðæm sacerde ðæt hi ða hyde behelien, ond ðeah ðæt he hie forceorfe ær, ær hie on ða eagan feallen.

that they have assumed the superintendence of people's souls. Yet it is a requirement that the care which they are obliged to devote to the external circumstances of their charges remain well within measure. About this it was very well said to the prophet Ezekiel, that priests ought not to shave their heads with razors, nor, conversely, let their locks grow, but they should trim them with shears. Quite rightly are priests called *sacerdas,* which is in English "purifiers," because they ought to furnish leadership to the faithful and take charge of them. The hair on their head then signifies thoughts about the external, since it grows and gleams over the brain, and yet no one feels it do so. It signifies the concerns of this present life: often so unheeded do our thoughts glide from us that we do not even notice it, any more than we notice our hair on the skin, because we often pay attention to negligible things. And yet those who are placed above others ought to pay attention to these external matters, and yet not be too fixedly intent on them. Quite rightly was it forbidden the priest to shave his head, and also to let his hair grow—that is that he was not to cut away all the thoughts of his mind which he ought to have for the benefit of his inferiors, nor, contrariwise, let them grow excessively to the point of futility and impropriety. About this it was quite justly said that the barber was to trim the head—that is, that he be as assiduous about tending to these temporal affairs as is necessary—and yet cut the hair away as liberally as he can without injury, so that it will not grow excessively luxuriant, to prevent, once the well-being of the body is secure, the intellect from being fettered to the heart on account of immoderate attention to external matters. The locks of the priest are thus to be spared to cover the skin, but he should cut them off before they fall into the eyes.

Chapter 19

XVIIII. Ðætte se reccere his godan weorc for gielpe anum ne do, ac ma for Godes lufan.

Betueox ðissum is micel ðearf ðæt se reccere geornlice wacige ond ðence ðæt hine ne cnysse sio wilnung ðæt he scyle monnum licigean; forðam, ðonne he geornlice ongiett ða inneran ond ða gæstlican ðing on his ingeðonce, ond suiðe wel giemeð ðara uterra ðinga, ðæt he ðonne ma ne wilnige ðæt he self licige his hieremonnum ðonne Gode; ðy læs ðonne he mid godum weorcum bið underwreðed, ond from woruldmonnum ongiten suelce he sie ælðiedig on ðiosum middangearde, ðæt he ðonne for ðære wilnunga his agnes gielpes ond heringe ne weorðe ælðiodig from Gode. Se bið eallinga Godes gewinna se se ðe wilnað ðæt he hæbbe ða weorðunga for his godan weorcum ðe God habban sceolde æt ðæm folce. Hwæt, we genoh georne witon ðæt se esne ðe ærendað his woroldhlaforde wifes, ðæt he bið diernes gelires scyldig wið God, ond wið his hlaford eallenga forworht, gif he wilnað ðæt hio hine lufige, ond he hire licige bet ðonne se ðe hine ond ðæt feoh ðider sende. Ac ðonne ðæt selflice gegriepð ðæt mod ðæs recceres, ond he wilnað ungemetlice licigean, ðonne beræst he oft on ungemetlice cueminge, ond bið hwilum to ungemetlice smeðe, hwilum to ungemetlice reðe. Ðonne bið ðæt mod awacod ðæs recceres, ðonne he gesihð ðæt his hieremen agyltað, ond he nyle hie arasian, ðy læs hira lufu aslacige, ond he him ðe wirs licige. Ac ðone gedwolan his hieremonna ðe he stieran sceolde he

Chapter 19

19. That the leader not perform his good works solely for ostentation, but more for love of God.

At the same time, the need is great for the leader to be dutifully vigilant and see to it that the desire to please people does not conquer him; so that, once he intricately understands internal and spiritual matters with his intellect, and tends very well to external matters, he not then himself aim more to please his charges than to please God; lest, once he is supported by good works and is regarded by persons of the world as a stranger on this earth, he then through the allure of his own self-exaltation and adulation become a stranger to God. He is utterly God's adversary who desires to have the honor for his good works that God ought to have from the people. Now, we know well enough that the servant who procures a wife for his earthly master is guilty to God of adultery and altogether treacherous to his master if that servant desires that she love him and that he himself be more pleasing to her than the one who dispatched him there with the money. But when self-regard grips the mind of the leader, and he desires ever so much to be liked, he often rushes headlong into complaisance and is at times excessively smooth, at times excessively rough. The mind of the leader is made pliant when he sees that his inferiors trespass and he refuses to upbraid them, lest their love diminish and he please them less. But often he too greatly indulges the

oft to suiðe geðafað, ðonne he ne dear hie ðreagean for ðære olicunge. Be ðæm wæs suiðe wel gecueden ðurh ðone witgan, "Wa ðæm ðe willað under ælcne elnbogan lecggean pyle ond bolster under ælcne hneccan menn mid to gefonne." Se legeð pyle under ælces monnes elnbogan, se ðe mid liðum oliccungum wile læcnian ða men ðe sigað on ðisses middangeardes lufan, oð ðæt hie afeallað of hiera ryhtwisnessum. Ðonne bið se elnboga underled mid pyle ond se hnecca mid bolstre, ðonne ðæm synfullan menn bið oftogen ðæt hine mon stiðlice arasige. Ðonne hine mon ne cnysð mid nanre reðnesse ne nanre wiðercueðnisse, ðonne geðafað him mon on ðære hnescean olecunge ðæt he hine suiðe softe resð on his agnum gedwolan.

2   Ac ða recceras ðe hira agnes gilpes giernað, ðæm hie geðafigað ðyllic ðe hie ondrædað ðæt him derian mæge æt ðæm gielpe, ond him oftion mæge ðisses eorðlican weorðscipes. Ac ða ðe hi wenað ðæt him nan wuht laðes ne wiðerweardes don ne mæge, ða hie suiðe stiðlice arasigeað, ond mid ealle ofðrysceað; ond hie næfre bilwitlice willað monigean, ac hie ofergietað ðære hirdelican lufan, ond egesiað hie ond ðreatigeað mid onwalde sua sua hlafordas. Ðas ðonne wæron ðurh ðone witgan suiðe ryhtlice geðreade mid ðære godcundan stefne, ða he cuæð, "Ge budon suiðe riclice ond suiðe agendlice." Ðæt is be ðæm ðe ma lufigeað hie selfe ond hiera agenne weorðscipe ðonne hiera Hlafurdes. Hie ðonne ahebbað hie ofer hiera hieremenn, ond ðenceað a hwæt hie don mægen, ond ne ðenceað no hwæt hie don scoldon, ond ne ondrædað ðone dom ðe ðæræfter fylgð; ac suiðe scamleaslice gielpað ðisses hwilendlican onwaldes, ond licað him ðæt hie ðæt unaliefede doð aliefedlice, ond hiera hieremonna him nan ne wiðcuið. Se ðonne ðe wilnað

error of his adherents, whom he ought to correct, when he dare not give them warning on account of flattery. About this it was quite well expressed through the prophet, "Woe unto them who wish to lay a pillow under each elbow and a bolster under each neck, with which to ensnare people." He lays a pillow under each person's elbow who, with pleasant flatteries, wishes to be physician to those people who sink into the love of this world, until they fall from their uprightness. The elbow is propped up by a pillow and the neck by a bolster when a sinful person is denied a stern reprimand. When he is not checked with any severity or at all gainsaid, in soothing softness he is permitted to rest very comfortably in his own folly.

But those leaders who are fond of their own vainglory indulge such things in those who they fear can do harm to their reputation and can deprive them of this earthly reverence. Yet those who they believe can offer them no hostility or opposition they upbraid quite sternly and crush altogether, and they never care to guide them mildly, but they disregard pastoral love and cow them and threaten them with domination, like lords. These, then, were very rightly censured through the prophet by the divine voice when he said, "You commanded very imperiously and very autocratically." That concerns those who love themselves and their own reverence more than their Lord's. They thus elevate themselves above their disciples and always consider what they can do, and they do not consider what they ought to do, and do not fear the judgment that follows from that, but quite without shame they vaunt this ephemeral authority, and it pleases them to perform the unlicensed licentiously, and none of their inferiors contradicts them. Then he who

woh to donne, ond wilnað ðeah ðæt ðæs oðre menn sugigen, he ðonne bið him selfum gewuta ðæt he wilnað ma ðæt hine mon lufige ðonne ryhtwisnesse.

3 Forðæm nan man nis ðe eallunga sua libban mæge ðæt he hwilum ne agylte. Se ðonne wilnað suiður ðæt mon lufge soðfæsðnesse ðonne hine selfne, se ðe wilnað ðæt mon nanre ryhtwisnesse fore him ne wandige. For ðiosum ðingum *sanctus* Petrus anfeng suiðe lustlice *sancte* Paules tælinge. Ond eft Dauið se kyning anfeng suiðe eaðmodlice his agnes ðegnes cease, ðæt wæs Nathan se witga. Forðæm eac ða godan recceras, ðonne hie ne recceað hwæðer mon hie selfe synderlice ond ungemetlice lufige, hie wenað, ðeah hira hieremenn hie mid ryhte heregen for hiera agnum gewyrhtum, ðæt hie ðæt don for lufan ond for eaðmodnesse, nals for his geearnungum. Ðonne is suiðe micel ðearf ðæt we mid micle cræfte betueox ðissum gemetgien ða gemetgunge ðæs reccedomes, ðætte ðonne ðæt mod ðara underðiedra hwæthwugu ryhtlices ongitan mæg, ðæt hit ðonne sua bald sie for his freodome ðæt hit ne gewende on selflice ond on ofermetto, ðonne his hlaford him to ungemetlicne anwald forgiefð his spræcce, ðæt he ðonne forðæm ne forgiete ne ne forlæte his eaðmodnesse.

4 Ond ðeah wel gedafonað ðætte ða godan recceras wilnigen ðæt hie monnum licigen, forðæm ðætte ðurh ða licunga hi mægen gedon ðætte hiera Dryhten licige ðæm folce, ond hie mægen geteon ðurh ða eahtunge ðe hie mon eahtige hira niehstan to ðære soðfæsðnesse lufan — nalles forðæm anum ðe hie wilnigen ðæt hi mon synderlice lufige, ac swelce sio hira lufu si sum weg ðurh ðone hie mægen lædan ða heortan ðe hie gehiran willað to ðære lufan ures scippendes. Ac hit is ðeah suiðe earfeðdæde ðæt mon lustlice ðone lareow

desires to act corruptly, and yet desires that other people leave it unremarked, is his own witness that he desires more to be loved than to be righteous.

For there is no one who can live so perfectly that he does 3 not at times fail. He thus desires righteousness to be loved more than himself who desires that no one vacillate about any point of justice concerning him. For these reasons Saint Peter very willingly accepted Saint Paul's reproof. And again, King David accepted quite meekly the reprimand of his own attendant, who was the prophet Nathan. Therefore also good leaders, while they do not care whether they themselves are personally and immoderately loved, suppose that, though their inferiors properly praise them for their own accomplishments, they do it for love and humility, not at all for their deserts. Thus, it is quite necessary that in the course of all this we regulate the limits of authority with consummate skill, so that when the mind of subordinates is able to recognize some point of justice, it may be so confident in its liberty that it will not turn to self love and pride when the man's lord permits him too unconstrained license to speak, so that he will not therefore forget or cast aside his humility.

And yet it is quite proper for good leaders to wish to 4 please, for by appreciation for them they can make their Lord pleasing to the people, and they can, through the esteem afforded them, draw their neighbors to the love of truth—by no means solely because they desire to be loved in their own person, but as if the love of them might be a certain way by which to lead the hearts that are willing to attend to them to the love of our Creator. And yet it is a most toilsome chore to listen willingly to a teacher who is not

gehieran wille ðe mon ne lufað. Forðon se ðe for oðre beon sceal, he sceal tilian ðæt he licige, forðæm ðæt he mæge beon gehiered. Ond ðeah ða his lufe ne sece he no for him selfum, ðy læs he sie ongieten ðæt he sie wiðerwinna on ðære diegelnesse his geðohtes, ðæs ðe he bið gesewen ðeow on his ðenunge. Ðæt suiðe wel *sanctus* Paulus geopenude, ða he us cyðde ða degolnesse his geornfulnesse, ond cuæð, "Sua sua ic wilnige on eallum ðingum ðæt ic monnum cueme ond licige." Ond suaðeah eft sona he cuæð, "Gif ic monnum cueme ond licige, ðonne ne beo ic no Godes ðeow." Hwæt, ðonne, Paulus ægðer ge licode ge ne licode, forðæm ðe on ðæm ðe he wilnode licigean, nals no he, ðeah ðe he cuæde, ac ðurh hine he wilnode ðæt sio soðfæstnes monnum licode.

Chapter 20

xx. Ðætte se reccere sceal geornlice wietan ðætte oft ða unðeawas leogað ond licettað ðæt hi sien gode ðeawas.

Eac sceal se reccere witan ðæt ða unðeawas beoð oft geliccette to godum ðeawum ond to mægenum ðurh leasunga. Monig mon deð micel fæsten, ond hæfð ðone hlisan ðæt he hit do for forhæfdnesse, ond deð hit ðeah for hneawnesse ond for feohgitsunge. Monig bið agieta his goda ond wilnað mid ðy geearnigan ðone hlisan ðæt he sie rumgiful, ond

loved. Therefore, whoever is to superintend others ought to endeavor to please, so that he can be listened to. And yet then let him not pursue affection for his own sake, so that he not be perceived to be in the privacy of his thoughts an adversary to the one whose servant he appears to be in his official duties. Saint Paul clarified that very well when he revealed his secret preoccupation and said, "Just so I desire in all matters to oblige and please people." And yet, to the contrary, immediately after that he said, "If I oblige and please people, then I am no servant of God." So, then, Paul both pleased and did not please, because in those things in which he wished to please, it was by no means that he pleased, though he said so, but he desired that through him devotion to truth should please people.

Chapter 20

20. That the leader ought to know well that vices often deceive and go in the guise of virtues.

The leader is also to be aware that vices are often disguised as good practices and as virtues through deceit. Many a person does much fasting and has the good repute of doing it for abstinence' sake, and yet does it out of close-fistedness and miserliness. Many a one is prodigal of his goods and desires through that to earn the reputation of being charitable,

wenað menn ðæt he hit do for kystum, ond bið ðeah for gielpe ma ðonne for lufan. Ond oft eac ungemetlico forgifnes bið gelicet, ðæt mon weneð ðæt hit sie mildheortnes. Ond oft eac ungemetlicu irsung bið gelicet, ðæt menn wenað ðæt hit sie ryhtwislic anda. Oft mon bið suiðe rempende, ond ræsð suiðe dollice on ælc weorc ond hrædlice, ond ðeah wenað men ðæt hit sie for arodscipe ond for hwætscipe. Oft mon bið suiðe wandigende æt ælcum weorce ond suiðe lætræde, ond wenað menn ðæt hit sie for suarmodnesse ond for unarodscipe, ond bið ðeah for wisdome ond for wærscipe. Forðæm is micel niedðearf ðæt se reccere ða ðeawas ond ða unðeawas cunne wel toscadan, ðy læs se hneawa ond se gitsigenda fægnige ðæs ðætte menn wenen ðæt he sie gehealdsum on ðæm ðe he healdan scyle oððe dælan; oððe eft se gielpna ond se agita for his goda mierringe gielpe, ond wene ðæt he sie kystig ond mildheort; oððe eft se ðafetere, se ðe wile forgiefan ðæt he wrecan sceolde, to ecum witum geteo his hieremenn; oððe eft se ðe ungemetlice wricð ða scylda, ðæt he self suiður on ðæm ne gesyngige; oððe eft ðæt he ryhtlice ond stiðlice wrecan sceolde, ðæt he ðæt ne forielde, ðy læs se ryhtwislica anda acolige, ðæt he hit eft sua eaðe wrecan ne mæge—ðætte forðy to ungemetlice ne sie geliðod ðæm scyldgan, ðy læs him ðæs godan weorces lean losige ðe he mid ðære steore geearnian sceolde.

and people believe he does it for his excellent character, and yet it is more for self-aggrandizement than for charity. And also boundless forgiveness is feigned, so that it is mistaken for kindheartedness. And, likewise, often intemperate rage is affected, so that it will be mistaken for righteous anger. And often someone is headlong and rushes quite blindly and suddenly into every undertaking, and yet people believe that it is out of decisiveness and vigor. Often someone is quite hesitant about every act, and very irresolute, and people believe that it is out of simplemindedness and indecisiveness, and yet it is out of astuteness and caution. Thus, it is a decided necessity that the leader know how to distinguish well virtues and vices, so that the pinchpenny and the money chaser should not exult in being accounted provident as to what he ought to keep or to give away; or again that the self-admirer and the spendthrift not crow about the depletion of his property, and think that his character is noble and humane; or in turn that one who gives license, who is willing to forgive what he ought to punish, not lead his inferiors to eternal torment; or, contrariwise, that one who punishes wrongs without restraint not himself sin more gravely thereby; or, again, that he not delay about what he ought justly and sternly to punish, lest his righteous anger cool, with the result that he cannot afterward punish it so readily—that things not thus be made too easy for the offender, lest he lose the reward for virtuous conduct which he ought to earn through the penalty.

Chapter 21

XXI. Hu gesceadwis se reccere sceal bion on his
ðreaunga ond on his oleccunga,
ond eac on his hatheortnesse ond
on his monðwærnesse.

Eac is to wietanne ðætte hwilum bið god wærlice to
miðanne his hieremonna scylda ond to licettanne suelce he
hit nyte; hwilum eft to secganne; hwilum, ðeah hit mon
cuðlice wite, hit is to forberanne; hwilum eft smealice ond
geornlice to seccanne; hwilum liðelice to ðreatianne; hwilum
suiðlice ond stræclice to ðrafianne. Monige sint, swa swa we
ær cuædon, ðe mon sceal wærlice liccettan, ond ðeahhwæðre eft cyðan, forðæm þæt hie ongieten ðæt hie mon
tæle, ond ðæt eaðmodlice geðafigen, ond ðonne ða scylda ðe
hie diogollice on him selfum forberað hie geornlice on hiera
agnum ingeðonce sceawigen, ond on him selfum demen ond
wrecen, ond hie forscamige ðæt hie eft sua don; ðonne bið
he self geladod wið hine selfne mid his agenre scame ond
mid his geðylde ond eac mid his recceres. Be ðære ildinge
suiðe wel Dryhten ðreade Iudeas, ða he ðurh ðone witgan
cuæð, "Ge sindon leogende: næron ge no min gemunende,
ne ge no ne geðohton on eowerre heortan ðæt ic suugode,
suelce ic hit ne gesawe." He ilde, ond ðafode ða scylda,
ond ðeah he him gecyðde; ðeah ðe he wið ða scyldgiendan
swugode, he hit him ðeah suigende gesæde.

Chapter 21

21. How discerning the leader ought to be in his condemnation and in his commendation, and also in his indignation and in his clemency.

There is also to be recognized that at times it is good for one carefully to conceal his charges' offenses and to let on as if he knew nothing about it; at times, by turn, to speak; at times, though it is known for a fact, it is to be suffered; at times, in turn, to be investigated studiously and diligently; at times to reprove mildly; at times to censure strongly and severely. There are many, as we said before, about whom one ought carefully to make pretense, and yet, nonetheless, let that be understood, so that they may perceive that they are thought reprehensible, and endure that meekly, and then studiously examine in their own conscience the offenses that they privately tolerate in themselves, and pass judgment on themselves and assign punishment, and feel shame about acting thus again; then he will be exonerated toward himself by his own sense of shame and by his own patience and that of his guide. About such forbearance the Lord reproached the Jews quite aptly when he said through the prophet, "You are liars: you did not keep me in mind, nor did you think at all in your hearts that I was silent, as if I did not see it." He bided his time and tolerated the offense, and yet made that plain to them; though he said nothing to the offenders, yet he told them without speaking.

2   Ac monige scylda openlice witene beoð to forberanne,
ðonne ðæs ðinges tima ne bið ðæt hit mon sidelice gebetan
mæge. Swa se læce, ðonne he on untiman lacnað wunde, hio
wyrmseð ond rotað. Forðæm buton he ðone timan aredige
ðæs læcedomes, ðonne bið hit swutol ðæt se lacnigenda forliesð ðone cræft his læcedomes. Ac ðonne se lareow ieldende
secð ðone timan ðe he his hieremenn sidelice on ðreatigean
mæge, ðonne bið hit swutol ðæt he bierð on his geðylde ða
byrðenne hira scylda. Be ðæm is swiðe wel gecueden ðurh
ðone salmsceop: he cwæð, "Ða synfullan bytledon uppe on
minum hrygge." He sarette ðætte ða synfullan sceoldon byt-
lan on uppan his hrycge, swelce he openlice cuæde, "Ðonne
ic man geryhtan ne mæg ond hine gelæran, ðonne bið me
suelce ic hine bære uppe on minum hrycge."

3   Ac manegu diglu ðing sindon nearolice to smeageanne,
ðætte se reccere mæge ongietan be sumum tacnum on his
hieremonna mode eal ðæt ðær gehyddes lutige, ond on ðæm
anbide ðe he hira fandige, ðæt he mæge hwilum ongietan
micel of lytlum. Be ðæm wæs suiðe ryhte to Ezechiele ðæm
witgan gecueden, "Ðu monnes sunu, ðurhðyrela ðone wag."
"Ða ic ða ðone wah ðurhðyreludne æfde," cuæð se witga, "ða
iewde he me ane duru beinnan ðæm wealle, ond cuæð to me:
Gong inn, geseoh ða scande ond ða wierrestan ðing ðe ðas
menn her doð. Ic ða eode inn, ond geseah ðær ða anlicnessa
eallra creopendra wuhta ond ealra anscunigendlicra nietena,
ond ealle ða heargas Israhela folces wæron atiefrede on ðæm
wage." Hwæt elles meahte beon getacnod ðurh Ezechiel buton ða scirmenn, ond ðurh ðone wah seo heardheortnes ðara
hieremonna? Hwæt is ðonne sio ðyrelung ðæs wages buton scearplicu ond smealicu fandung ðæs modes, ðæt mon
mid ðære ðurhðyrelige ðone weall, ond onluce ða heardan

Still, many transgressions that are openly known are to 2
be suffered when it is not at a time when the matter can be
suitably amended. Just so, when the physician tends a wound
at the wrong time, it will fester and putrefy. Thus, unless he
determines the proper time for treatment, it is plain that
the healer will hinder the effectiveness of his healing. But
when the forbearing teacher looks for the time when he can
suitably chide his charges, it will be plain that in his forbearance he bears the burden of their offenses. About this it is
quite well expressed through the psalmist: he said, "The sinful have built upon my back." He was aggrieved that the sinful should build on top of his back, as if his plain meaning
were, "When I cannot correct someone and instruct him, to
me it is as if I bore him on my back."

But many obscure matters are to be examined minutely, 3
so that the guide can, by certain signs, make out in his
charges' minds all of what lurks hidden there, and attend to
probing them, so that at times he can deduce much from
little. About this it was quite justly said to the prophet Ezekiel, "Son of man, penetrate the wall." "When I had penetrated the wall," said the prophet, "he showed me a certain
door within the wall and said to me, 'Go in, see the depravity and the abominations that people engage in here.' Then
I went in and saw there images of all crawling creatures and
all detestable beasts, and all the idols of the people of Israel
were depicted on the wall." What other could be signified
by Ezekiel than those in governance, and by the wall the cal-
lousness of their subordinates? What is then the penetra-
tion of the wall but piercing and intent probing of the mind,
so that the wall can thus be penetrated and the hard heart

heortan, ond gehnescige? He cuæð, "Ða ic hæfde ðone weall ðurhðyrelod, ða geseah ic duru"; suelce he cuæde, "Ða ic ðære heortan heardnesse mid geornfullicre fandunge ond ascunge ond ðreaunge toslat, ða geseah ic suelce ic gesawe sume duru onlocene, ðurh ða ic geseah on ðæm ðe ic læran scolde ealle ða innemestan geðohtas." Be ðæm wæs suiðe wel gecueden: "Gong inn, ond geseoh ða heardsælða ond ða sconde ðe ðas her doð." Ðæt is ðonne suelce he in gaa ond geseo ða scande, ðonne he ongiet be sumum ðingum oððe ðeawum utanne ætiewdum eall ðæt hie innan ðenceað, ond sua ðurhfærð his ondgit ðæt mod his hieremonna ðætte him bið eall cuð ðæt hie unaliefedes ðenceað. Forðæm wæs eac gecueden, "Ic ða eode inn, ond geseah ða anlicnessa ealra creopendra wuhta ond eac onscuniendlicra nietena." Ða creopendan wuhta getacnigeað ða eorðlican geðohtas. Ða nietenu ðonne beoð hwæthwuguningas from eorðan ahæfen, ond suaðeah onlutað to ðære eorðan forðæm hie sculon bi ðære libban. Ða creopendan ond ða snicendan licgeað mid ealle lichoman on eorðan. Ða nietenu ðonne, ðeah hie maran sien, hie beoð suiður ahæfen from eorðan, ond suaðeah for ðære gewilnunge hiera giefernesse hie simle locigeað to ðære eorðan. Ða creopendan wuhta beinnan ðam wage getacniað ða ingeðoncas ðe wealcað in ðæs monnes mode, ðe æfre willað licgean on ðæm eorðlicum gewilnungum. Ða nietenu ðonne ðe he geseah binnan ðæm wage getacnigeað ðonne mon hwæt ryhtlices ond gerisen- lices geðencð, ðonne ne ligeð he eallinga on ðære eorðan sua ða creopendan wuhta, ac bið hwæthwugu up ahæfen sua ðæt neat from eorðan; ac for ðære gewilnunga woroldgielpes ond gietsunga he onlytt ungerisenlice to ðissum eorðlicum, sua ðæt neat for gifernesse onlyt to ðære eorðan.

opened and made pliant? He said, "When I had penetrated
the wall I saw a door"; as if he were to say, "When I had broken open the hardness of the heart by thorough examination and questioning and reprimand, I saw as if I were looking at a certain door opened through which I made out all
the inmost thoughts of those I was charged to instruct."
About this it was quite well expressed: "Go in and see the
wickedness and the depravity that those here perform." It
is, then, as if he were to enter and see the depravity when he
recognizes, on the basis of certain things or actions outwardly displayed, all that they think inwardly, and his discernment pervades the mind of his charges, so that all of
what is prohibited in their thoughts is plain to him. Therefore it was also said, "Then I went in and saw the likenesses
of all crawling creatures and also detestable beasts." The
crawling creatures signify mundane thoughts. The beasts
then are to some extent raised from the earth, but they incline to the ground because they have to live by it. The
crawling and the slithering lie with their entire body on the
earth. The beasts, then, even if they are larger, are raised
higher from the earth, and yet due to the prompting of their
appetite they are always looking at the ground. The crawling
creatures within the wall signify the inward thoughts that
revolve in someone's mind, and they want always to wallow
in earthly desires. Then the beasts that he saw inside the
wall signify that when someone thinks of something just
and decent, he does not lie altogether on the earth, like
crawling creatures, but is a bit raised from the earth, like an
ox; yet on account of the prompting of worldly vanity and
willfulness he bends without dignity to these earthly things,
the way the ox for its appetite is turned to the earth.

4   Eac wæs gesewen on ðæm wage atifred ealle ða heargas
Israhela folces, ond eac sio gietsung ðe *sanctus* Paulus cuæð
ðæt wære hearga ond idelnesse gefera. Suiðe ryhtlice hit
wæs awriten æfter ðæm nitenum ðæt ða heargas wæron
atiefrede, forðam ðeah ðe ful monige mid gerisenlicum
weorcum arisen from eorðan, mid ungerisenlicum gewilnungum ðissa woroldðinga hie hie selfe alecgeað on eorðan.
Forðy wæs suiðe wel gecueden ðæt hit wære atiefred,
forðæm ðonne mon smeað on his mode ymb hwelc eorðlic
ðing, ðonne deð he suelce he hit amete ond atiefre on his
heortan, ond sua tweolice ond unfæsðlice he atiefreð ðæs
ðinges onlicnesse on his mode ðe he ðonne ymb smeað. Eac
is to wietanne ðæt æresð bið se wah ðurhðyrelod, ond siððan
mon wyrcð duru to. Gif sio ðonne ontyned bið, ðonne mæg
mon geseon gif ðær hwelc dieglu scond inne bið, sua se witga
dyde. Feorrane ðu meaht geseon, gif se wah bið ðyrel, ac ðu
ne meaht geseon hwæt ðærinne bið gehyddes, buton ðu ða
duru ontyne. Sua ðu meaht ælcne unðeaw on ðæm menn
æresð be sumum tacnum ongietan, hwæs ðu wenan scealt,
ær he hit mid wordum oððe mid weorcum cyðe. Sieððan he
hit ðonne mid ðara awðrum cyð, ðonne bið sio duru ðære
unryhtwisnesse ontyned ðæt ðu meaht geseon eall ðæt yfel
openlice ðæt ðærinne lutað.

5   Monige hira ðonne sindon suiðe liðelice to ðreageanne,
ðonne he of yfelum willan ne gesyngað, ac of unwisdome
ond ungewisses oððe ungewealdes oððe of flæsclicum gecynde oððe of wacmodnesse ond of unbieldo oððe of untrymnesse modes oððe lichoman. Forðæm is suiðe micel
niedðearf ðæt mon mid micelre gemetgunge suelcra scylda
ðreaunga geliðige ond gemetgie, forðæm ðe we ealle, ðe
hwile ðe we libbað on ðissum deadlican flæsce, ðære

Also seen depicted on the wall were all the idols of the   4
people of Israel, and also the avarice that Saint Paul said is
the companion of idols and vanity. Quite rightly it was written that after the beasts, idols were depicted, for although
many with fitting deeds rise up from the earth, with improper desires for worldly things they lay themselves to the
ground. Thus, it was quite well put that they were depicted,
because when someone contemplates some worldly matter
in his mind, he does it as if he were painting and depicting it
in his heart, and thus vaguely and indefinitely he depicts in
his mind the image of the thing that he is then contemplating. It is also to be recognized that first the wall is penetrated, and afterward a door is added. If it is opened, one
can see it if there is any hidden depravity inside, as the
prophet did. From a distance you can see it if the wall has
been penetrated, but you cannot see anything hidden within
it unless you open the door. Just so, you can first perceive every vice in the person by certain signs, what you ought to
expect before he reveals it by words or deeds. Then after he
exposes it by either of the two, the door of that unrighteousness will be opened, so that you can see plainly all the evil
that lurks within.

Many a one is to be chastised leniently when he does not   5
sin out of bad intentions but out of naïveté, and unawares or
without volition, or out of the nature of the flesh, or out of
pliancy of character and timidity, or out of indisposition of
mind or body. Therefore, there is urgent need to assuage and
temper with considerable moderation the correction of
such offenses, because all of us, for as long as we inhabit

tidernesse ond ðære hnescnesse ures flæsces we beoð underðiedde. Bi him selfum ælc mon sceal geðencean hu he oðrum
deman wille, ðy læs he sie ongieten ðæt he sie onstyred
ond onæled mid ðæm andan his hieremonna unðeawa, ond
hæbbe hine selfne forgietenne. Be ðæm suiðe wel Paulus us
manode, ða he cuæð, "Gif hwa sie abisegod mid hwelcum
scyldum, ge ðonne ðe gæsðlice sindon gelærað ða suelcan
mid monnðwærnesse gæste; gesceawiað eow selfe, ðy læs
eow becume costung"—suelce he openlice cuæde, "Ðonne
eow misliciað ða mettrumnessa ða ge on oðrum monnum
geseoð, ðonne geðence ge hwæt ge sien ond hwelce ge sien;
forðæm ðæt ge eower mod gemetgien on ðæm niðe, ðonne
ge eow selfum ondrædað ðæt ðæt ge on oðrum monnum
tælað."

6   Ond ðeah sindon monige suiðe suiðe to ðreageanne,
ðonne hie selfe nyllað ongietan hiera scylda, ðæt hi ðonne
gehieren ðreagende of ðæs lariowes muðe hu micle byrðenne hie habbað on hiera scyldum; ðonne hie willað him
selfum ðæt yfel ðæt hie ðurhtugon to suiðe gelihtan, ðæt hie
ðonne ondræden for ðæs lareowes ðreaunga ðæt hie hit him
gehefegigen. Ðæt ðonne bið ðæs recceres ryht ðæt he ðurh
ða stemne his lariowdomes ætiewe ðæt wuldor ðæs uplican
eðles, ond hu moniga digla costunga ðæs ealdan feondes
lutigeað on ðys andweardan life he eac geopenige, ond ðæt
he his hieremonna yfelu to hnesclice forberan ne sceal, ac
mid miclum andan ond reðnesse him stiere, ðy læs he sie
scyldig ealra hira scylda, ðonne him hiera na ne ofðyncð. Be
ðæm wæs suiðe wel gecueden to Ezechiele: "Nim sume tigelan, ond lege beforan ðe, ond writ on hiere ða burg Hierusalem." Ond sona æfter ðæm he cuæð, "Besittað hie utan,

this mortal flesh, are subject to the frailty and vulnerability of our flesh. Each person should gauge how he will judge others by reference to himself, so that he not be perceived as stirred and inflamed with bitterness over his subordinates' vices, and have forgotten himself. Paul admonished us about this quite aptly when he said, "If someone is engaged in any sins, then you who are spiritual instruct such a one with mildness of spirit; keep watch on yourselves, so that temptation not come your way"—as if his plain meaning were, "When the frailties that you see in other people irritate you, consider what you are and of what sort, so that you may temper your mind in its vehemence by having a care as regards yourselves about what you reprehend in other people."

And yet there are exceedingly many who are to be 6 charged when they themselves refuse to recognize their offenses, so that they then may hear from the teacher's mouth what a great burden in offenses they bear, to the end that, when they wish to absolve themselves too thoroughly of the wrong that they have committed, they may fear burdening themselves on account of the teacher's reproof. And so it is the leader's duty through the voice of instruction to make plain the glory of the supernal homeland, and to reveal how many unperceived temptations of the ancient fiend lurk in this present life, and not to indulge his charges' offenses too meekly but to correct them with great indignation and harshness, lest he assume culpability for all their offenses for not being aggrieved at them. About this it was quite well expressed to Ezekiel: "Take a certain tile and lay it before you, and depict on it the city of Jerusalem." And immediately afterward he said, "Lay siege to it, and build another

ond wyrceað oðer fæsten wið hie, ond berað hiere hlæd to, ond send ðærto gefylcio, ond ðerscað ðone weall mid rammum." Ond eft he him tæhte to fultome ðæt he him gename ane iserne hearstepannan, ond sette betweoh hine ond ða burg for iserne weall. Hwæt tacnað ðonne Ezechhiel se witga buton ða lareowas, to ðæm is gecueden, "Genim ðe ane tigelan, ond lege beforan ðe, ond writ on hiere ða burg Hierusalem?" Ða halgan lareowas ðonne him nimað tigelan, ðonne hie ðara eorðlicra monna heortan underfoð to læranne. Ðonne hie lecgeað ða tieglan beforan hie, ðe him beboden wæs ðæt hi scolden ða ceastre Hierusalem on awritan, ðonne hie behealdað ealle ða inngeðoncas hiora modes, ond suiðe geornlice giemað ðæt hie ða eorðlican heortan gelæren, ond him ætiewen hwelc sie ðære uplican sibbe gesiehðe, ond hu on idelnesse man ongiett Godes ðæt hefonlice wundor, gif he ne ongiett hu monega costunga ðæs lytegan feondes him on feallað. Suiðe wel he hit geicte mid ðysum, ða he cuæð: "Ymbsittað ða burg suiðe gebyrdelice, ond getrymiað eow wið hie." Ða halgan lareowas ymbsittað ða tieglan, ðe sio burg Hierusalem on atiefred bið, ðonne hi ðam menniscan mode, ðe ðeah ðæt uplice lif secð, ætiewað hu manega him on ðys andweardum life frecenlice wiðerwearde unðeawas him wiðfeohtað, ond hu æghwelc syn bið sætigende ðæs ðiondan monnes. Ond suæ suæ se here sceolde bion getrymed onbutan Hierusalem, suæ sculon beon getrymed ða word ðæs sacerdes ymbutan ðæt mod his hieremonna.

7   Ond ne sceal he no ðæt an bodigan his hieremonnum hu ða synna him wiðwinnað, ac he him sceal eac cyðan mid hwelcum cræftum he him wiðstondan mæg. Swiðe ryhtlice wæs se eaca ðærto gedon, ða mon to ðæm witgan cuæð,

fortress against it, and bring a ramp to it, and send a host to it, and batter the wall with rams." And again, he instructed him for his own good to take an iron skillet and set it between himself and the city for an iron wall. Then what does the prophet Ezekiel signify but teachers, to whom it is said, "Get yourself some tile, and lay it before you, and inscribe on it the city of Jerusalem"? Holy teachers get themselves tiles when they undertake to instruct the hearts of people in this world. They lay before them the tile on which they were instructed to inscribe the city of Jerusalem when they examine all the inmost thoughts of their mind and take very diligent care to instruct those earthbound hearts, and demonstrate to them the nature of the vision of sublime peace, and how a person recognizes the heavenly wonder of God in vain if he does not recognize how many temptations of the cunning fiend will fall to his lot. He supplemented this quite well with these words that he said: "Besiege the city very spiritedly, and array yourselves against it." Holy teachers besiege the tile on which the city of Jerusalem is depicted when they make plain to the human mind that strives, regardless, toward an elevated existence, how many perilous, perverse vices will assail it in this present life, and how every sin lies in ambush for a person who is managing well. And just as the army was to be arrayed outside of Jerusalem, so ought the word of the priest to be arrayed around the mind of his charges.

And he ought not to preach to his charges only about 7 how sins assail them, but he ought also to explain with what virtues they can repel them. Quite rightly was it added when

"Wyrceað fæsten ymb ða burg." Wiotodlice fæsten wyrcð se halga lariow ymb ða burg ðæs modes ðe he gelærð ðone cræft hu hit mæg costingum wiðstondan, ond him eac gesægð hu ðæm monnum ðe him mægen ond cræft wiexð, hu him eac hwilum eakiað æfter ðæm mægenum ða costunga. Be ðæm wæs suiðe ryhte gecueden, "Berað hire to hlæd, ond ymbsittað hie, ond gað to mid rammum." Ðonne bireð ælc lareow hlæd to ðæs monnes mode, ðonne he him gecyðð hu sio byrðen wiexð ond hefegað. Eac he aræð ceastre wið Hierusalem, ðonne he ðæm ryhtlicum inngeðonce his hieremonna foresægð ða dieglan sætenga ðæs lytegan feondes, ðe he him wenan mæg. Ond eac he bierð rammas ymbutan ðæt mod his hieremonna, ðonne he him gecyð mid hu scearplicum costungum we sint æghwonon utan behrincgde, ond se weall ures mægenes ðurhðyrelad mid ðan scearpan ramman ðara costunga.

8   Ond suaðeah nu, ðeah se lareow ðis eall smealice ond openlice gecyðe, ne forstent hit him noht, ne him nohte ðon ma ne beoð forlætna his agna synna, buton he sie onæled mid ryhtwislicum andan wið his hieremonna scylda. Be ðæm is git suiðe ryhtlice gecueden to ðæm witgan, "Genim ðe ane iserne hierstepannan, ond sete betweoxn ðe ond Hierusalem for iserne weall." Ðurh ða pannan is getacnod se wielm ðæs modes, ond ðurh ðæt isern ðæt mægen ðara ðreatunga. Hwæt is ðienga ðe bieterre sie on ðæs lareowes mode, oððe hit suiður gehierste ond gegremige ðonne se anda ðe for ryhtwisnesse bið up ahæfen? Mid ðisse pannan hierstinge wæs Paulus onbærned, ða he cuæð, "Hwa bið medtrum, ðæt ic ne sie eac for his ðingum seoc? Oððe hwa bið gescended, ðæt me for ðæm ne scamige?" Ond sua hwelc sua mid ðam Godes andan bið onæled, ne bið he for giemeleste gehiened,

it was said to the prophet, "Build a siege wall around the city." For a certainty, the holy teacher builds a siege wall around the city of the mind by teaching the skill of how it can withstand temptations, and telling how in people growing in ability and experience, sometimes in proportion to those abilities, temptations also increase. About this it was quite justly said, "Bring a ramp to it, and besiege it, and attack with battering rams." Every teacher brings a ramp to a person's mind when he explains to him how the burden increases and grows ponderous. Also, he prepares a camp opposite Jerusalem when he forewarns the righteous mind of his charges about the occult stratagems of the sly fiend that they can expect. He positions battering rams around the mind of his charges, as well, when he makes plain with what keen temptations we are surrounded outwardly on all sides, and the wall of our virtue is penetrated by the sharp battering ram of those temptations.

And yet, now, though the teacher may explain all this 8 plainly and in detail, it is of no use to him, nor are his own sins expiated any the more, if he is not inflamed with righteous indignation against his charges' offenses. About this it was said further to the prophet, "Get yourself a certain iron skillet and set it between yourself and Jerusalem for an iron wall." By the pan is signified the fervor of the mind, and by the iron the virtue of reproof. What is there that is bitterer to a teacher's mind or sears and outrages it more than the indignation which is summoned up for righteousness' sake? With the searing of this pan Paul was set ablaze when he said, "Who is infirm that I am not likewise sick for his sake? Or who is disgraced that I do not feel ashamed for that?" And whoever is ablaze with God's indignation will not be

173

ac he bið stranglice wið ða getrymed on ecnesse. Bi ðæm wæs suiðe ryhte gecueden to ðæm witgan, "Sete iserne weall betuh ðe ond ða burh." Ða isernan hierstepannan he tæhte for iserne weall to settanne betuh ðæm witgan ond ðære byrig, forðam nu ða recceras ætiewað sua strangne andan ðy hie wiellað ðæt hie hiene eft hæbben on ðæm ecan life betux him ond hiera hieremonnum to isernum wealle, ðæt is to gewitnesse ðæt hit him ne licode, ðeah he hit gebetan ne meahte.

9   Forðæm ðonne ðæs recceres mod wyrð to reðe on ðære ðreaunga, ðonne abiersð ðær hwilum hwæthwugu ut ðæs ðe he sugian sceolde. Ond oft eac gelimpeð, ðonne he to suiðe ond to ðearllice ðreapian wile his hieremenn, ðæt his word beoð gehwyrfedo to unnyttre oferspræce. Ðonne sio ðreaung bið ungemetgad, ðonne bið ðæt mod ðæs agyltendan mid ormodnesse geðrysced. Forðæm is micel ðearf, ðonne se reða reccere ongiett ðæt he his hieremonna mod suiður gedrefed hæfð ðonne he scolde, ðæt he sona forðæm hreowsige, ðæt he ðurh ða hreowsunga gemete forgiefnesse beforan ðære Soðfæsðnesse ðæs ðe he ðurh ða geornfulnesse his andan gesyngade. Ðæt ilce Dryhten God us bisnade ðurh Moysen, ða he cuæð, "Gif hwa gonge bilwitlice mid his friend to wuda treow to ceorfanne, ond sio æcs ðonne awient of ðæm hielfe, ond sua ungewealðes ofslieð his geferan, he ðonne sceal fleon to anre ðara ðreora burga ðe to friðstowe gesette sint ond libbe, ðy læs hwelc ðara niehstena ðæs ofslægenan for ðæm sare his ehte, ond hine ðonne gefoo ond ofslea." To wuda we gað mid urum freondum sua oft sua we sceawiað ura hieremonna unðeawas; ond bilwitlice we heawað ðone wudu, ðonne we ðara gyltendra scylda mid arfæsð ðes ingeðonces lare anweg aceorfað. Ac sio æcs wint

condemned for negligence but will be powerfully fortified against it for all time. About this it was very aptly said to the prophet, "Set an iron wall between you and the city." He instructed that the skillet be placed for an iron wall between the prophet and the city because leaders, wishing to have it again in the eternal life as an iron wall between themselves and their charges, now show such forceful anger as evidence that it displeased them, though they could not remedy it.

For when the leader's mind grows too fierce in chastise- 9 ment, occasionally there bursts out something that he ought not to mention. And likewise it also often occurs, when he will censure his charges too strongly and severely, that his words will be turned to unproductive oratory. When the criticism is intemperate, the mind of the offender is battered by despair. Therefore, it is imperative that when the harsh guide perceives that he has afflicted the mind of his charges more strongly than he ought, he immediately repent of it, so that by that repentance he find forgiveness in the presence of Truth for having sinned through the ardor of his indignation. The Lord God gave an example of the same through Moses when he said, "If anyone were to go innocently into the forest with his friend to cut wood, and the ax head then separates from the haft, and thus he accidentally kills his companion, he ought to retreat to one of the three cities that are appointed sanctuaries and remain there, lest some one of those nearest allied to the slain pursue him for the injury, and take and kill him." We repair to the woods with our friends as often as we examine our charges' vices; and we innocently hew wood when we cut away the offenders' transgressions under the guidance of pious intent. The

of ðam hielfe, ond eac us of ðære honda, ðonne ðonne sio lar wint on reðnesse suiður ðonne mon niede scyle. Sio æcs wient of ðæm hielfe, ðonne of ðære ðreatunga gað to stiðlico word, ond mid ðam his freond gewundað, oððe ofsliehð, ðonne he hine on unrotnesse oððe on ormodnesse gebringð mid his edwite, ðeah he hit for lufum do, ðæt he geopenige his unðeawas. Suaðeah ðæt geðreatade mod bið suiðe raðe gehwierfed to fiounga, gif him mon to ungemetlice mid ðære ðreapunga oferfylgð suiður ðonne mon ðyrfe. Ac se se ðe unwærlice ðone wuda hiewð, ond sua his freond ofsliehð, him bið nidðearf ðæt he fleo to ðara ðreora burga anre, ðæt on sumere ðara weorðe genered, ðæt he mote libban; ðæt is ðæt he gehweorfe to hreowsunga, ond sua fleo to ðara ðreora burga sumere, ðæt is tohopa ond lufu ond geleafa. Se to anre ðara burga gefliehð, ðonne mæg he bion orsorg ðæs monnsliehtes; ðeah hine ðær meten ða niehstan ðæs ofslæ-genan, ne sleað hi hiene na; forðæm ðonne se ðearla ond se ryhtwisa dema cymð, se ðe hine on urne geferscipe ðurh flæsces gecynd gemengde, ne wriecð he mid nanum ðingum ða scylde on him, forðæm under his forgiefnesse hine ge-frieðode sio lufu ond se geleafa ond se tohopa.

ax head is separated from the haft when too-severe words inform the reproof, and when he wounds or kills his friend he brings him to disquietude or despair with his reproach, even though it is for love that he exposes his faults. Yet the reprimanded mind is quite suddenly led into hatred if it is assailed too immoderately with more reproof than is necessary. But for the one who hews wood negligently and thus kills his friend, it is necessary to retreat to one of those three cities, so that in one of them he will be safe, and as a consequence he will be permitted to live: that is, that he turn to repentance and thus retreat to one of those three cities, which are hope, charity, and faith. The one who escapes to one of those cities can be free of care about homicide: even if those nearest the slain should encounter him there, they will by no means kill him, because when the stern and righteous judge arrives, the one who joined our company through incarnation, he will in no degree exact punishment on him for the offense, because charity and faith and hope furnished him sanctuary under his forgiveness.

Chapter 22

XXII. Hu swiðe se reccere sceal beon
on his smeaunga abisgod ymb ða halgan æ.

Ac eall ðiss aredað se reccere suiðe ryhte, ðonne he for Godes lufum ond for Godes ege deð ðæt ðæt he deð, ond ælce dæge geornfullice smeað ða bebodu halegra gewrita, ðætte on him sie upp aræred se cræft ðære giemenne ymbe ða foresceawunga ðæs hefonlican lifes, ðone singallice ðisse eorðlican drohtunge gewuna wile toweorpan, buton hine sio myndgung ðara haligra gewrita onbryrde. Forðæm se eorðlica geferscipe hine tiehð on ða lufe his ealdan ungewunan, he sceal simle higian ðæt he weorðe onbryrd ond geedniwad to ðæm hefonlican eðle. Ac his mod bið suiðe ieðegende ond suiðe abisgad mid eorðlicra monna wordum, forðam hit is openlice cuð ðætte sio uterre abisgung ðissa woroldðinga ðæs monnes mod gedrefð, ond hine scofett hidres ðædres, oð ðæt he afielð of his agnum willan. Ac him bið ðearf ðæt he hine genime simle be ðære leornunge haligra gewrita, ond be ðam arise. For ðiosum ðingum manade Paulus Timotheum his cniht, ond cuæð: "Ðonne ic cume, ðonne beo ðu abisgad ymbe rædinge." Ond eft Dauit be ðam ilcan spræc, ða he cuæð, "Loca, Dryhten, hu suiðe ic lufige ðine æ; ealne dæg ðæt bið min smeaung."

2   Eft bi ðys ilcan Dryhten bebead Moyse hu he scolde beran ða earce, ða he cuæð, "Wyrc feower hringas ælgyldene, ond ahoh hie suiðe fæste on ða feower hyrnan ðære earce;

Chapter 22

22. How very intent the leader ought to be on his study of divine law.

But the leader carries out all this quite correctly when he does what he does for the love of God and the fear of God, and when every day he studies diligently the injunctions of sacred writings, so that the virtue of attending to the contemplation of heavenly life may be raised up in him, whom habituation to this earthly condition continually aims to cast down unless devotion to sacred writings inspires him. Because the earthly community calls him to the love of his former ill habits, he ought always to endeavor to have renewed inspiration toward the heavenly home. But his mind fluctuates considerably and is deeply occupied with the words of people in this world, for it is patently apparent that the external occupation of these worldly affairs afflicts a person's mind and drives him this way and that, until he falls away of his own accord. But there is a constant need for him to recollect himself by the study of sacred writings and to rise thereby. For these reasons Paul advised his disciple Timothy and said, "When I come, be occupied with reading." And again David was speaking of the same when he said, "See, Lord, how greatly I love your law; all day it is my meditation."

Again regarding this very thing the Lord instructed 2 Moses as to how he ought to transport the ark when he said, "Fashion four rings all of gold and fix them hanging very

ond hat wyrcean twegen stengas of ðæm treowe, ðe is haten *sethim,* ðæt ne wyrð næfre forrotad; ond befoh utan mid golde: ond sting ut ðurh ða hringas bi ðære earce sidan, ðæt hie man mæge beran on ðam, ond læt hi stician ðæron; ne tio hie mon næfre of." Hwæt mæg ðonne elles seo earc tacnian buton ða halgan ciricean, on ðære sculon hangian ða feower hringas on ðam feower hyrnum, ðæt sint ða feower hyrnan ðises middangeardes, binnan ðæm is tobrædd Godes folc, ðæt is utan begyrdd mid ðam feower godspellum? Ða saglas ðonne, ðe mon ða earce big beran sceal, sticiað eallne weg inn on ðam hringum ða earce mid to beranne; ða beoð geworht of ðæm treowe *sethim,* ðæt næfre ne rotað. Sua sindon to seceanne stronge ond unaðrotene lareowas ond ðurhwuniende on ðære lare haligra boca, ða simle sculon bion bodiende ymbe ða anmodnesse ðære halgan gesom-nunga, sua sua ða anbestungnan saglas ða earce berað. Ðæt is ðonne ðæt mon ða earce bere on ðæm saglum, ðætte ða godan lareowas ða halgan gesomnunge lærende ða niwan ond ða ungeleaffullan mod mid hira lare gelæde to ryhtum geleafan. Ða saglas is beboden ðæt scoldon beon mid golde befongne. Ðæt is, ðonne ða lareowas mid wordum oðre menn lærat, ðæt hi eac selfe on hira agnum weorcum biorhte scinen. Be ðam saglum is suiðe gesceadlice gecueden ðæt hie sculon simle stician on ðam hringum, ond næfre ne moton him beon of atogene, forðæm is micel niedðearf ðætte ða ðe beoð gesette to ðære ðenunga ðæs lareowdomes, ðæt hi næfre ne gewiten from ðære geornfulnesse ðære rædinge ond leornunge haligra gewrita. Forðæm is eac gecueden ðætte simle ða ofergyldan saglas sceolden stician on ðæm gyldnum hringum, ðy læs hine ænig wuht gælde ungearowes, ðonne mon ða earce beran scolde. Ðæt is ðonne ðonne ðara

securely on the four corners of the ark, and have two staves made from the tree that is called *shittim,* which never rots, and overlay them with gold, and insert them into the rings on the ark's side, so that it can be carried on them; let them never be pulled out." What else can the ark figure but holy Church, on which the four rings ought to hang from its four corners, which are the four quarters of this earth within which God's people are distributed, who are encompassed by the four gospels? The poles, then, by which the ark ought to be transported, are inserted all the way through the rings for the ark to be carried with; they are made from the tree *shittim,* which will never rot. Just so are to be desired strong and indefatigable teachers, and tenacious in the teaching of holy books, who ought continually to be preaching about the unanimity of the holy congregation, just as the inserted poles support the ark. That the ark is carried on the poles, then, means that good teachers, instructing the holy congregation, by their doctrine lead the new and the unconverted to orthodox belief. It is instructed that the poles be overlaid with gold. That is, when instructors teach other people with their discourse, let them also themselves gleam brightly in their own conduct. About the poles it is quite discerningly said that they should always be thrust into the rings, and they should never be allowed to be drawn out, because it is quite necessary that those who are placed in the service of teaching never desist from the vocation of reading and studying sacred writings. For this reason, it is also said that the gilded poles should remain in the rings, so that nothing unprovided for should cause delay when the ark was to be moved. That is, when a teacher's charges come looking

lareowa hieremenn hwæthwugu gæsðlices to him secað, ond hi frinað, ðonne is suiðe micel scand gif he ðonne færð secende hwæt he sellan scyle, ðonne he iowan scolde ðæt him mon to ascað. Ac ðonne sticiað ða saglas suiðe singallice on ðæm hringum, ðonne ða lareowas simle on hira heortum smeagað ða halgan gewritu. Ond ðonne hi hebbað suiðe arodlice ða earce up, ðonne hi suiðe hrædlice bioð gearwe to læranne ðætte ðonne ðearf bið. Bi ðæm suiðe wel se forma hierde ðære halgan ciricean—ðæt is *sanctus* Petrus—manode oðre hierdas, ða he cuæð, "Bioð simle gearwe to læranne ond to forgiefanne ælcum ðara ðe iow ryhtlice bidde ymbe ðone tohopan ðe ge habbað on eow"; suelce he openlice cuæde, "Ne bregden ge no ða stengas of ðæm hringum, ðy læs sio earc si ungearo to beranne."

for something spiritual from him and inquire of him, it is a considerable disgrace if he goes looking for what he is to give, instead of explaining what is requested of him. But the poles remain inserted perpetually in the rings when teachers unceasingly review the sacred writings in their hearts. And they lift the ark without delay when they are immediately ready to teach whatever is necessary. About this, the first shepherd of holy Church—that is, Saint Peter—advised other shepherds when he said, "Be ever ready to teach and to grant the request of each of those who justly ask you about the hope that you have in yourselves"; as if his plain meaning were, "Do not remove the poles from the rings, lest the ark not be ready to be moved."

BOOK THREE

Chapter 23

xxiii. Hu micel scyle bion ðæt toscead,
ond hu mislice mon scyle menn læran,
mid ðæm cræfte ðæs lareowdomes.

Nu ðonne oð ðiss we rehton hwelc se hierde bion sceal;
nu we him willað cyðan hu he læran sceal, sua sua hit lange
ær us ðære eadegan gemynde wer Gregorius lærde, se wæs
oðrum noman genemned Nanzanzenus. He cuæð, "Ne gedafenað hit no ðæt we ealle menn on ane wisan læren,
forðam hie ne sint ealle anes modes ond anra ðeawa."
Forðæm oft sio ilce lar ðe oðrum hielpeð, hio dereð ðæm
oðrum; sua sua manegra cynna wyrta ond grasu beoð gerad,
sumu neat batigað fore, sumu cuelað; sua sua mid liðre
wisðlunga mon hors gestilleð, sua eac mid ðære illcan wist-
lunga mon mæg hund astyrigean; sua beoð eac monige læcedomas ðe sume adle gelytliað, ond sume gestrongiað; sua eac
hlaf ðe strongra monna mægen gemiclað, he gelytlað cilda.
For ðære ungelicnesse ðara hieremonna sculun beon ungelic
ða word ðæs lareowes, ðæt he hiene selfne geðeode to eallum his hieremonnum, to æghwelcum be his andefne, ond
ðeahwæðre sua suiðe sua he of ðære æwe ond of ðære ryhtan
lare ne cerre. Hwæt cueðe we ðonne hwelce sin ða inngeðoncas monna buton suelce sumere hearpan strengas aðenede,

BOOK THREE

Chapter 23

23. How there ought to be great diversity in, and how differently people should be taught with, the art of instruction.

Heretofore we have discussed what sort the shepherd ought to be; now we intend to explain to him how he ought to teach, just as, long since, the man Gregory of blessed memory instructed us, whose second name was Nanzianzen. He said, "It is not fitting that we teach all people in one manner, since they are not all of the same mind and the same morals." Therefore, often one and the same lesson, which will help one, will harm the other, just as plants and cereals of many sorts are of the nature that some cattle will batten on them, others die; as a horse can be calmed with gentle whistling, and also with identical whistling dogs can be roused; as also there are many remedies which temper some ailments and aggravate others; as also bread that enhances the vitality of strong people curtails that of children. Because of the diversity of his dependents, the words of the teacher ought to be diverse, that he may commit himself to all his charges, to each according to his suitability, and yet as entirely as he can without straying from the law and from correct doctrine. Of what sort, then, shall we say people's consciences are but like the taut strings of some lyre, which

ða se hearpere suiðe ungelice tiehð ond styreð, ond mid ðy gedeð ðæt hi nawuht ungelice ðæm sone ne singað ðe he wilnað? Ealle he gret mid anre honda, ðy ðe he wile ðæt hi anne song singen, ðeah he hie ungelice styrige. Sua sceal æghwelc lareow to anre lufan ond to anum geleafan mid anre lare ond mid mislicum manungum his hieremonna mod styrigean.

2   On oðre wisan mon sceal manian weras, on oðre wif; ond on oðre wisan ealde, on oðre gionge; ond on oðre wisan earme, on oðre eadige; ond on oðre wisan ða bliðan, on oðre ða unrotan; ond on oðre wisan ða underðieddan, on oðre ða ofer oðre gesettan; ond on oðre wisan ða ðeowas, on oðre ða hlafurdas; ond on oðre wisan ða woroldwisan, on oðre ða dysegan; ond on oðre wisan ða scamleasan, on oðre ða scamfæstan; ond on oðre wisan ða ofermodan, on oðre ða wacmodan; ond on oðre wisan ða ungeðyldegan, on oðre wisan ða geðyldegan; ond on oðre wisan ða welwillendan, on oðre ða æfstegan; ond on oðre wisan ða bilwitan, on oðre ða felaspræcan; ond on oðre wisan ða halan, on oðre ða unhalan; ond on oðre wisan ða ðe for ege forberað ðæt hi yfel ne doð, on oðre wisan ða ðe sua aheardigað ðæt hi hit for nanum ege ne forlætað; ond on oðre wisan ða suiðe suigean, on oðre ða felaidelspræcæn; ond on oðre wisan ða slawan, on oðre ða ðe beoð to hrade; ond on oðre wisan ða manðuæran, on oðre ða grambæran; ond on oðre wisan ða eaðmodan, on oðre ða upahæfenan; ond on oðre wisan ða anwillan, on oðre ða ungestæððegan ond unfæsðrædan; ond on oðre wisan ða ofergifran, on oðre ða fæstendan; ond on oðre wisan ða ðe mildheortlice hira agen sellað, on oðre ða ðe æfter oðerra monna ierfe flitað, ond hie reafigeað; ond on oðre wisan ða

the musician plucks and moves in various fashion and thereby sees to it that they produce a tone not at all dissonant to the music that he desires? He touches all with a single hand because he wants them to produce a single tune, though he stirs them differently. So ought every teacher to stir the minds of his charges to a single love and a single faith with a single doctrine and with diverse injunctions.

In one fashion are men to be guided, in another women; 2 and in one fashion the old, in another the young; and in one fashion the needy, in another the well-to-do; and in one fashion the cheerful, in another the fretful; and in one fashion subordinates, in another officials; and in one fashion servants, in another masters; and in one fashion the clever, in another the simpleminded; and in one fashion the shameless, in another the modest; and in one fashion the proud, in another the diffident; and in one fashion the impatient, in another the patient; and in one fashion the benevolent, in another the envious; and in one fashion the pure, in another the voluble; and in one fashion the fit, in another the infirm; and in one fashion those who out of fear forbear to do wrong, in another those who are so hardened that they will not desist for any intimidation; and in one fashion the very quiet, in another idle chatterers; and in one fashion the disinclined, in another those who are too strenuous; and in one fashion the mild, in another the irascible; and in one fashion the humble, in another the haughty; and in one fashion the obstinate, in another the irresolute and yielding; and in one fashion the self-indulgent, in another the abstemious; and in one fashion those who give away their possessions out of compassion, in another those who quarrel over other people's property and steal from them; and in one fashion those

ðe nohwæðer ne oðerra monna ne reafiað, ne hiera agen
rumedlice ne dælað; ond on oðre wisan ða ðe hira agen
rumedlice sellað, ond ne forlætað ðeah ðæt hie oðerra
monna ne reafien; ond on oðre wisan ða ungemodan, on
oðre ða gemodan; ond on oðre wisan ða wrohtgeornan ðe
cease wyrceað, ond on oðre ða gesibsuman.

3   Ond on oðre wisan sint to manianne ða ðe ða word ðære
halgan æ ryhte ne ongietað, on oðre ða ðe hi ryhtlice ongietað, ond ðeah for eaðmodnesse wandiað ðæt hi hit ne
sprecað; ond on oðre wisan ða ðe fullfremede ne beoð
nohwæðer ne on ieldo ne on wisdome, ond ðeah for hrædwilnesse to foð, ond on oðre wisan ða ðe medomlice ond
wel magon læran, ond him ðeah ondrædað for eaðmodnesse,
ðæt hie hit forðy forlætað; ond on oðre wisan ða ðe ðisse
hwilendlican are wilniað, ond him nan gesuinc ne ðyncð ðæt
hi hie hæbben, on oðre ða ðe him ðyncð micel earfoðu ond
micel gesuinc to habbanne, ond hiera suaðeah wilniað; ond
on oðre wisan ða ðe beoð mid synscipe gebundene, on oðre
ða ðe beoð frio ðara benda; ond on oðre wisan ða ðe ða ðurhtogenan synna wepað, on oðre ða ðe ða geðohtan wepað;
ond on oðre wisan ða ðe ða ærgedonan wepað, ond ðeah ne
forlætað, on oðre ða ðe hi forlætað, ond suaðeah ne wepað;
ond on oðre wisan ða ðe ða unaliefedan ðing doð, ond hie
eac herigað, ond on oðre wisan ða ðe hie tælað, ond hi
suaðeah ne forlætað; ond on oðre wisan ða ðe mid sumere
unryhtwilnunga beoð færinga hrædlice ofersuiðede, on oðre
ða ðe on ðære synne ealnuweg licgað, mid geðeahte to gebundene; ond on oðre wisan ða ðe ða lytlan scylda oftrædlice
wyrceað, on oðre wisan ða ðe ða lytlan forgað, ond ðeah

who neither swindle other people of theirs nor liberally distribute their own, in another those who liberally give their own and yet will not desist from robbing other people; and in one fashion the tractable, in another the intractable; and in one fashion the fractious, who sow discord, and in another the peace-loving.

And in one fashion are to be guided those who do not 3 rightly understand holy scripture, in another those who understand it properly and yet for humility hesitate to profess it; and in one fashion those who are mature neither in age nor in understanding, and yet out of rashness have taken it up, in another fashion those who can teach competently and well, and yet out of humility they are afraid, so that on that account they avoid it; and in one fashion those who desire temporal honors, and to whom it seems no struggle to attain them, in another those to whom they seem a significant inconvenience and a strenuous effort to obtain, yet they still desire them; and in one fashion those who are constrained by the bonds of marriage, in another those who are free of those bonds; in one fashion those who weep for sins committed, in another those who weep for the contemplation of it; and in one fashion those who weep for sins priorly committed and yet do not desist, in another those who desist and yet do not weep; and in one fashion those who do impermissible things and also speak well of them, and in another fashion those who deplore them and yet will not quit them; and in one fashion those who are with perilous suddenness overmastered by some illicit desire, in another those who wallow entirely in sin, committed to it consensually; and in one fashion those who frequently commit minor trespasses, in another fashion those who avoid the minor

hwilum ða maran wyrceað; ond on oðre wisan ða ðe nan god nyllað onginnan, on oðre ða ðe hit onginnan willað, ond næfre ne geendigað; ond on oðre wisan ða ðe dearninga yfel doð, ond god eawunga, ond on oðre wisan ða ðe hira god helað ðe hie doð, ond ne reccað ðeah menn wenen ðæt hie yfel don, ond eac mid sumum ðingum gedoð ðæt menn wenað ðæt hi yfel don.

4   Hu nytt rehton we nu ond rimdon ða cæga, buton we eac feawum wordum ætiewen hwæt hie healden, ond sua we swiotolusð mægen æfter gereccan?

Chapter 24

XXIIII. Ðætte on oðre wisan sint to monianne weras, on oðre wif.

On oðre wisan sint to manianne weras, on oðre wif. Ða weras mon sceal hefiglecor ond stiðlecor læran, ond ða wif leohtlecor; forðæm ðæt ða weras higigen to maran byrðenne, ond ða wif mid oleccunga weorðen on gebrohte.

ones and yet occasionally commit major ones; and in one fashion those who do not wish to undertake anything good, in another fashion those who wish to undertake it and never carry it through; and in one fashion those who do evil secretly and good openly, and in another fashion those who conceal the good that they do and do not care whether people think they do ill, and also in some respects cause people to think that they do ill.

To what purpose will we now have mentioned and enumerated the keys unless we additionally indicate in a few words what they keep stored, and explain hereafter as plainly as we can?   4

Chapter 24

24. That men are to be guided in one fashion, women in another.

Men are to be counseled in one fashion, women in another. Men ought to be instructed more firmly and sternly, and women more mildly, to the end that men should apply themselves to a greater burden, and women be persuaded by what is soothing.

Chapter 25

xxv. Ðætte on oðre wisan sint to monianne ða
iungan, on oðre ða ealdan.

On oðre wisan sint to læranne ða iungan, on oðre ða
ealdan; forðæm oftor mid reðre manunga beoð ða iungan
nytwyrðe gedone, ond ða ealdan mid liðelicre bene, sua hit
awriten is on ðære æwe: "Ne ðreata ðu no ðone ealdan, ac
healsa hine sua sua ðinne fæder."

Chapter 26

xxvi. Ðætte on oðre wisan sint to manianne ða
welegan, on oðre ða wædlan.

On oðre wisan sint to manianne ða wædlan, on oðre ða
welegan. Ða wædlan sint to frefranne ond to retanne, ðy læs
hi sien to ormode for hira earfeðum. Ða oðre sint to
breganne, ðy læs hi sien for hiera wlencum to up ahæfene.
To ðæm wædlan wæs gecueden ðurh Dryhten to ðæm witgan, "Ne ondræd ðu ðe, forðæm ðu ne weorðesð gescended."
Ond suiðe hræðe eac æfter ðæm he him olecte, ða he cuæð,
"Ðu earma, ðu ðe eart mid ðy storme ond mid ðære yste
onwend ond oferworpen, ðe ic geceas on ðam ofne ðe ðu on

Chapter 25

25. That the young are to be guided in one fashion, the old in another.

The young are to be instructed in one fashion, the old in another; for the young are more often rendered tractable with harsh admonishment, and the old with gentle entreaty, as it is written in the law: "Do not upbraid an old man, but address him as you would your father."

Chapter 26

26. That the rich are to be guided in one fashion, the poor in another.

In one fashion are the poor to be exhorted, in another the wealthy. The poor are to be solaced and to be gladdened, so that they not be too despondent over their difficulties. The others are to be intimidated, lest out of a sense of grandeur they be too superior. To the poor man it was said through the Lord to the prophet, "Do not be afraid, for you will not be humiliated." And very soon after that he soothed him when he said, "You unfortunates, who are turned aside and laid low by the storm and by the tempest, I have chosen you

THE OLD ENGLISH PASTORAL CARE

wære asoden, ðæt wæs on ðinum iermðum." Ac *sanctus*
Paulus ðreade ða welegan, ða he cuæð to his gingrum,
"Secgað ðæm welegum gind ðisne middangeard ðæt hi to
ofermodlice ne ðencen, ne to wel ne truwigen ðissum unge-
wissum welum." Be ðæm we magon suiðe swutule oncnawan
ðæt se eaðmodnesse lareow, ða ða he ymb ða welegan spræc,
na ne cuæð "Biddað," ac "Secgað, ond bebeodað." Ond eac
we magon oncnawan ðæt, ðæt ða earman ond ða untruman
sient to retanne, ond ða ofermodan ond ða upahafenan ne
sient no to weorðianne, ac ða mon sceal swa micle ma hatan
ðonne biddan sua man ongiet ðæt hie for ðissum woruld-
wlencum bioð suiður up ahafene ond on ofermettum aðundene. Be ðæm Crist cuæð on his godspelle, "Waa ieow welegum, ðe eower lufu eall ond eower tohopa is on eowrum
woruldwelum, ond ne giemað ðæs ecan gefean, ac gefeoð
ealle mode ðisses andweardan lifes genyhte."

2   Ac ðæs is ðearf ðæt mon ðone frefre ðe on ðæm ofne
asoden bið his iermða, ond se is to ðreatiganne ond to
breganne, se ðe bið up ahafen mid ðy gefean ond mid ðy
gielpe ðisse worulde; ðætte ða sorgfullan ongieten ðæt him
becumað ða welan ðe him gehatene sint, ðeah hi hi ðonne git
ne geseon; ond eac ða welegan ongieten ðætte ða welan ðe
hie on lociað ond habbað, ðæt hie ða habban ne magon. Ac
ðæm lareowe is micel ðearf ðæt he ongiete hwa earm sie,
hwa eadig, ond hwone he læran scyle sua earmne, ond hwane
sua eadigne; forðæm oft se welega ond se wædla habbað sua
gehweorfed hira ðeawum ðæt se welega bið eaðmod ond
sorgfull, ond se wædla bið up ahæfen ond selflice. Forðæm
sceal se lareow suiðe hrædlice wendan his tungan ongean
ðæt ðe he ongiet ðæt ðæs monnes inngeðonc bið, forðæm
ðæt se earma upahafena sie mid his wordum geðreatod ond

in the furnace in which you were refined, which was in your sufferings." But Saint Paul rebuked the rich when he said to his disciples, "Tell the wealthy throughout this earth not to be too haughty in their thoughts, nor to trust too well in these precarious riches." From this we can very plainly recognize that the teacher of humility, when he spoke of the rich, did not say, "Ask," but "Tell, and mandate." And also we can recognize that the poor and the ailing are to be gladdened, and the proud and the haughty are not at all to be revered, but they should be so much the more commanded than entreated, the more they are perceived to be haughty about these worldly riches and bloated with pride. About these Christ said in his gospel, "Woe you wealthy, whose affection and confidence is all in your worldly riches, and care not for eternal delight, but celebrate wholeheartedly the abundance of this present life."

But there is need for one refined in the furnace of his sufferings to be comforted, and for one who is elated with the delight and the pomp of this world to be berated and browbeaten, so that those full of care may understand that the riches they have been promised will fall to them, though they do not yet see them, and also the wealthy may recognize that they will not be able to keep the riches they gaze upon and possess. But it is quite necessary for the teacher to recognize who is poor, who rich, and which one he ought to instruct as a pauper, and which as a grandee, since often the wealthy one and the pauper have so altered their bearing that the wealthy one is humble and full of care, and the pauper is haughty and conceited. Therefore, the teacher ought very promptly to attune his tongue to what he perceives a person's attitude to be, so that the haughty indigent may be

2

gescended, ðonne he ongiet ðæt hine ne magon his iermða
geðreatigan ond geeaðmedan.

3   Ac sua micle liðelecor he sceal olecan ðæm welegan eaðmodan sua he ongiet ðæt he eaðmodra bið, ðonne hine ne
magon ða welan forwlencean, ðe ælcne ofermodne oðheb-
bað. Ond oft eac mon sceal ðone welegan ofermodan to him
loccian mid liðelicre olicunga, forðæm ðæt he hine to ryhte
geweeme; forðæm oft hearda wunda beoð mid liðum beðen-
gum gehnescode ond gehælede, ond eac ða wodðraga ðæs
ungewitfullan monnes se læce gestilð ond gehælð mid ðæm
ðæt he him olecð æfter his agnum willan. Ne sculon we eac
forgietan hu hit wæs be Saule ðæm kyninge: ðonne him se
wiðerwearda gæsð on becom, ðonne gefeng Dauid his hearpan, ond gestillde his wodðraga mid ðæm glige. Hwæt mæg
ðonne elles tacnian Saules ungewitfullnes buton ða upahafenesse ðara welegena? Oððe hwæt is elles getacnod ðurh
Dauid buton eaðmodlic lif haligra monna? Forðæm ðonne se
unclæna gæsð becom on Saul, Dauid ðonne mid his sange
gemetgode ða wodðrage Saules. Sua ðonne, ðonne ðæt mod
ðara ricena for upahæfenesse bið to ierre gehwierfed, ðonne
is cynn ðætte we for hira modes hælo olicende hi on smyltnesse gebringen mid ure spræce, sua sua Dauid dyde Saul
mid ðære hearpan.

4   Hwilum eac ðonne mon ðæm ricum cidan sceal, æresð
mon sceal sprecan asciende, suelce he be oðrum menn
sprece ond ascie, ond gehiere hu be ðæm deman wille.
Ðonne mon ðonne ongiete ðæt he ryhte gedemed hæbbe,
ond he wene ðæt he ryht be oðrum gedemed hæbbe, ðonne
secge him mon suiðe gedæftelice for his agnum scyldum,
ðy læs ðæt aðundne mod for ðissum hwilendlicum anwalde
hit gebelge wið ðone ðe him cit, ac ðæt he mid his agnum

berated and put to shame by his words when he recognizes that his sufferings have not served to abase and humble him.

But so much the more mildly he ought to soothe the 3 humble wealthy one, the humbler he perceives him to be, when the riches that exalt every proud person have not served to make him imperious. And often one also ought to win over the proud wealthy one with mild persuasion, to turn him to what is right, because hard sores are often relieved and healed with gentle laving, and also the physician often stills and cures the ravings of a person out of his wits by soothing him according to that person's own wishes. Neither ought we to forget how it was with King Saul: whenever the perverse spirit came over him, David would take up his harp and would still his ravings with music. What else can Saul's madness signify but the self-conceit of the rich? Or what else is meant by David but the humble life of holy people? For when the impure spirit came over Saul, with his song David tempered Saul's paroxysms. So, then, when the mind of the rich out of self-conceit is moved to anger, it is natural that for their mind's health we soothe and bring them to composure with our converse, as David did Saul with the harp.

At times also when the powerful are to be chided, first 4 one ought to speak enquiringly, as if he were referring to and wondering about someone else, and hear what judgment he will pass on that one. When one then perceives that he has given a just assessment, and he believes that he has judged the other fairly, one may very conveniently identify them as his own sins, lest it enrage the mind bloated with this temporal authority against the one who chides him, and so that

wisdome ond mid his agnum wordum ðone suiran gebiege
his agenra ofermetta, ðætte he nane lade ne mæge findan, ac
sie sua mid his agnum wordum gebunden. Forðæm com Nathan to cidanne ðæm cyninge Dauide, ond licette, suelce he
ymb sumes ðearfan ond sumes earmes monnes ryht spræce,
ond sohte ðæs cyninges dom, ond wolde ðæt he æresð hine
be oðrum menn gedemde, ond siððan gehierde his agne
scylde, forðæm ðæt he eft ne meahte ðæm ilcan dome
wiðcueðan. Ond eac se haliga monn ongeat ægðer ge ðæs cyninges scylde ge eac his hatheortnesse ond gedyrstignesse;
wolde hine ða æresð gebindan mid his agenre ondetnesse,
ond forhæl him ðæt he hine eft ðreatian wolde. Sua se læce
hyd his isern wið ðone monn ðe he sniðan wile; wenð, gif he
hit him iewe, ðæt he him nylle geðafigean ðæt he hine sniðe.
Ac grapað suiðe fægre ymbutan ðæt ðæt he sniðan wile, ond
snið swiðe hrædlice. Sua se witga dyde ðone cyning mid his
wordum; ic wene ðæt he hine snide slaulecor, gif he him ær
sæde ðæt he hine sniðan wolde. Ðy hit wæs betre ðæt he
grapude mid ðæm bispelle, ær ðon ðe he cidde, sua se læce
grapað, ond stracað, ond hyt his seax ond hwæt, ær ðon ðe
he stingan wille. Se læce, ðonne he cymð ðone untruman to
sniðanne, æresð he sceawað ðæt cumbl, ond siððan hine
tweonað ymb ðæs untruman geðyld, hwæðer he geðafian
mæge ðæt hine mon sniðe. Hyt ðonne his læceseax under
his claðum oð ðæt he hine wundað; wile ðæt he hit gefrede,
ær he hit geseo; forðæm he wenð, gif he hit ær geseo, ðæt he
hit wille forsacan.

with his own understanding and his own words he bend the neck of his own pride, with the result that he can find no excuse, but is constrained by his own words. For that reason, Nathan came to King David to chide him and let on as if he were talking about a certain poor and a certain wretched person's case, and requested the king's verdict, and wished that he first judge himself on the basis of another person, and afterward hear of his own offense, so that he would not subsequently be able to revoke that same judgment. And that saintly man also recognized both the king's guilt and his irascibility and his rashness; he wanted first to bind him by his own confession, and he concealed from him that he would subsequently reprimand him. So the physician hides his blade from the person on whom he intends to make an incision; he thinks, if he lets him see it, he will not agree to being cut. But he feels very pleasantly around what he intends to cut, and cuts very suddenly. The prophet did so to the king with his words; I think he would have cut him less promptly if he had informed him beforehand that he intended to cut him. Therefore it was better that he felt around with the example before he criticized, just as the physician explores and strokes, and hides his knife and sharpens it before he intends to cut. The physician, when he comes to the point of operating on the patient, first examines the swelling, and then he debates the tractability of the patient, whether he will submit to being cut. Then he hides his medicinal steel under his clothing until he makes the wound, wants him to feel it before he sees it, since he imagines if he sees it beforehand, he will refuse.

Chapter 27

XXVII. Ðætte on oðre wisan sint to manianne ða
gladan, on oðre ða unrotan.

On oðre wisan sint to manianne ða bliðan, on oðre ða
unrotan. Ðæm oferbliðum is to cyðanne ða unrotnessa ðe
ðæræfter cumað, ond ðam unbliðum sint to cyðanne ða gefean ðe him gehatene sindon. Geliorngen ða bliðan on ðære
ðreaunga ðæt hie him ondræden, ond gehieren ða unbliðan
ða lean ðæs gefean ðe hie tohopiað. To ðæm bliðan is gecueden, "Wa eow ðe nu hliehað, forðam ge sculon eft
wepan." Gehieren eac ða unrotan ðone cuide ðe him is to
gecueden ðurh ðone illcan lareow, ðæt is Crist; he cuæð,
"Eft ic eow geseo, ond ðonne blissiað eowre heortan, ond
eowerne gefean eow nan mon æt ne genimð." Monige beoð
ðeah bliðe ond eac unbliðe ðara ðe for nanum woruldðingum
nahwæðer doð, buton for ðæs blodes styringe ond for lichoman medtrymnesse. Suaðeah is ðæm to cyðanne, ðæt hi
hie warenigen ægðer ge wið ða ungemetlican blisse ge wið ða
ungemetlican unrotnesse; forðæm hira ægðer astyreð sumne
unðeaw, ðeah hie ungewealdes cumen of ðæs lichoman
medtrymnesse. Ðæm oferbliðan oft folgað firenlusð, ond
ðæm unrotan ierre. Forðæm is micel niedðearf ðæt mon
hiene wið ðæt irre an ond wið ða ungemetlican sælða ne
warenige, ac eac wið ðæt ðe forcuðre bið, ðe ðæræfter cymð,
ðæt is fierenlusð ond unryhtlicu iersung, ðæt is ðæt mon
iersige on oðerne for his gode. Ðonne is micel ðearf, ðonne

Chapter 27

27. That the cheerful are to be guided in one fashion, the fretful in another.

In one fashion are the cheerful to be advised, in another the dejected. To the overly contented are to be described the asperities that are to come in the hereafter, and to the downcast are to be described the delights that are promised them. Let the complacent learn from that reproof to be afraid, and let the despondent hear about the reward of happiness that they can anticipate. To the lighthearted it is said, "Woe to you who laugh now, for you will in turn weep." Let the dispirited also hear the declaration that is expressed through the same teacher, which is Christ: he said, "I shall see you again, and then your hearts will exult, and no one will deprive you of your joy." Yet many are happy and also unhappy who are not so on account of any worldly circumstances, but for the stirring of the blood and for bodily indisposition. They are nonetheless to be advised to keep watch against both excessive happiness and excessive discontent, for either of them will provoke some immorality or another, even if they proceed unbidden from the body's frailty. Concupiscence often dogs the complacent, and rage the discontented. Therefore, it is a decided necessity to guard not only against rage and against immoderate happiness, but also against what is more deplorable, which follows from these, and that is lewdness and wrongful hatred, which is animus against another for his goods. Then it is an

him mon ðissa tuega hwæðer ondrætt suiður ðonne oðer,
ond wið ðæt wienð, ðæt he sua suiðe wið ðæt winne sua he
on ðæt oðer ne befealle, ðe he him ær læs ondred.

Chapter 28

xxvIII. Ðætte on oðre wisan sint to monianne ða
ealdormen, on oðre wisan ða hieremenn.

On oðre wisan sint ðonne to manianne ða underðioddan,
on oðre ða ofergesettan. Ða underðieddan mon sceal sua
læran ðæt hie elles ne sien genæt ne geirmed, ond ða ofersett-
an mon sceal sua manian ðæt se hiera folgoð hine ne
oðhebbe; ond ða underðioddan ðæt hie wiers ne don ðonne
him man bebeode, ond ða ofergesettan ðæt hi him to
unaberendlice ne beoden; ond ða underðieddan ðæt hi him
eaðmodlice underlicgen, ond ða ofergesettan ðæt hie gemetlice him ofer sien. Ðæt hi magon eac be ðisse bisene
ongietan ðæt him is to gecueden: "Bearn, beo ge underðiodde eowrum ieldrum magum on Dryhtne." Ðæm ofergesettan is to gecueden, "Ne gremigen ge eowru bearn." Geleornigen eac ða bearn ðæt hi sua hieren hira ieldrum sua sua
hie selfe wieten on hira inngeðonce beforan ðæs dieglan deman eagum ðæt hi hit for Gode don, ond æt Gode ða lean
habban willen. Geleornigen eac ða fæderas ond ða hlafurdas
ðæt hie wel libbende gode bisene astellen ðæm ðe him underðiedde sien.

important requirement, when one worries about one of these two more than the other, and struggles with it, not to combat it so strongly that he succumbs to the other, which he had feared less.

Chapter 28

28. That persons of rank are to be guided in one fashion, subordinates in another.

In one fashion are underlings to be counseled, in another those set above them. Subjects ought to be taught in such a way that they are not additionally downtrodden and disheartened, and superiors ought to be warned in such a way that their higher dignity not give them airs; and subjects that they not accomplish less than is demanded of them, and overlords that they not demand of them too intolerably; and subjects that they submit to them humbly, and rulers that they govern them with decency. They can also recognize this by this example which is said to them: "Children, be subject to your elder kinsmen in the Lord." To those who superintend it is said, "Do not aggrieve your children." Let the children also learn to obey their elders in such a way that they themselves know in their inmost thoughts before the eyes of the unseen judge that they do it in God's cause and wish to have reward from God. Let fathers and masters also learn by living well to set a good example to those who are subject to them.

2   Eac sculun wietan ða ofer oðre gesettan ðæt ðæt hie unaliefedes ðurhteoð, ond oðre men bi ðam bieseniað, sua manegra wieta hie beoð wyrðe beforan ðæm oðrum sua sua he monna on won gebrohte, buton he eft self gesuice, ond sua monige gecierre sua he mæsð mæge. Forðæm him is suiðe micel ðearf ðæt he sua micle wærlicor hine healde wið scylda swa he gere witan mæg ðæt he no ana ne forwierð, ðonne he oðrum yfele bisene steleð. Eac sint to manianne ða underðioddan ond ða anlepan menn ðe æmtige beoð ðæs ðæt hie for oðre menn suincen, ðæt hie huru hie selfe ge-healden sua micle ma sua hie æmetegran beoð ðonne oðre menn, ðy læs hie eft wyrðen ðearlwislecor gedemde ðonne oðre menn. Ða ofer oðre gesettan sint to manianne ðæt hie for hira monna gedwolan ne weorðen gedemde, ðonne hie wenað ðæt hie hira selfra gewyrhtum sien clæne. Se æmetiga ond se anlipa is to manianne ðæt he sua micle sorgfulra sie ymb hine selfne, ond sua micle suiður suince sua hine læs oðerra monna giemen bisegað. Ða ofergesettan sint to monianne ðæt hie sua oðerra monna giemenne gefyllen, ðæt hie hie selfe ne forlæten, ond eft ymb hie selfe sua geornfulle ne sien ðæt hie to slawlice ðara ne giemen ðe him befæste sien.

3   Ac ðam ðe ðonne æmetig bið his agenne willan to wyrceane, to ðæm is gecueden, "Ðu slawa, ga ðe to æmett-hylle, ond giem hu hie doð, ond leorna ðær wisdom." Ða ðonne ðe ofer oðre bion sculon sint suiðe egeslice gemanode mid ðy worde ðe mon cuæð: "Sunu min, gif ðu hwæt gehætst for ðinne freond, ðonne hafas ðu ðin wed geseald, ond ðu

Likewise, those who govern others ought to know re- 2
garding whatever interdicted thing they carry out and
thereby give example to someone else, that they are deserving of as many torments before others as they have introduced people to wickedness, unless they themselves desist
and recover as many as they possibly can. Therefore, it is required of one to guard himself against transgressions with
so much the greater care in proportion as he can plainly understand that it is not he alone who will perish when he sets
others a bad example. Likewise, inferiors and single men
who are free of having to work for other people are to be
cautioned that they in particular keep a rein on themselves
by so much the more in proportion as they are at greater
liberty than other people, so that in consequence they not
be judged more severely than others. Leaders are to be
warned to avoid being judged for their followers' mistakes
when they consider themselves pure in their own conduct.
Whoever is master of his own time and a bachelor is to be
exhorted to be all the more careful about himself, and to
work so much the harder as other people's concerns occupy
him less. Those in authority are to be encouraged not to fulfill their duties to other people in such a way as to neglect
themselves, and in turn not to be so solicitous of themselves
as to attend too indifferently to those entrusted to their
care.

But to one who is at liberty to follow his own inclination 3
it is said, "You idler, go to an anthill and make note of what
they do, and learn wisdom there." Those who are to lead
others are very fearsomely warned with this observation
that was made: "My son, if you have pledged something for
your friend, you have given your guarantee, and you are

bist ðonne gebunden mid ðæm wordum ðines agnes muðes, ond gehæft mid ðinre agenre spræce." Hwelc magon beon maran gehat ðonne mon gehate for his freond ðæt he underfoo his saule on his pleoh? Ðæt is suelce he hæbbe befæsð his hond oðrum menn, ðonne he gebint hine selfne to him mid his wordum ðæt he sceal niede ða giemenne ond ða geornfulnesse ymb ðone habban ðe he ær ne ðorfte, forðæm he hine hæfð ðonne gehæftne mid his agnum wordum, suelce he sie mid grine gefangen, ðæt he hine sceal nide tela læran. Ðy him is micel ðearf, ðonne he tela lærð, ðæt he eac tela doo, ond his lif on nan oðer ne wende, on oðer he lærð, forðæm he eft sceal beforan ðæm ðearlwisan deman mid gereccelicre rake gereccan ðæt he ðæt ilce self dyde ðe he oðre menn lærde.

4   Ond eft suiðe hraðe æfter ðæm se ilca Salomon cuæð, "Do, min sunu, sua ic ðe lære: alies ðe selfne; forðæm ðu eart on borg began ðinum friend. Ac iern nu ond onette, awece hine. Ne geðafa ðu ðinum eagum ðæt hie slapige, ne ne hnappigen ðine bræwas." Sua hwa ðonne sua his lif to biesene bið oðrum monnum geset, ne sceal he no ðæt an don ðæt he ana wacie, ac he sceal eac his friend wreccan. Ne ðynce him no genog ðæt he ana wel libbe, buton eac ða ðe he fore beon sceal from ðære slæwðe his synna atio. Ðæt is swiðe wel ðær gecueden, "Ne slapige no ðin eage, ne ne hnappigen ðine bræwas." Ðæt is ðonne ðæt mon his eage læte slapian ðæt mon for his unwisdome ond for his suongornesse ne mæge ongietan ða unðeawas ðara ðe him underðiedde beoð. Ac ðonne hnæppiað ure bræwas, ðonne we hwæthwugu steorweorðes ongietað on ða ðe us underðiedde beoð, ond we gebærað for ure receliesðe swelce we hit nyten;

bound by the words from your own mouth and captive to your own pronouncement." What sort of vow could be greater than to pledge on one's friend's behalf to take responsibility for his soul at his own risk? It is as if he has committed his hand to another person when he binds himself to him with his pledge, so that he must of necessity have care and solicitude for one to whom he was not formerly obliged, because he has made himself captive with his own words, as if he were caught in a snare, so that he must necessarily instruct him well. Thus, it is a firm requirement, when he teaches well, that he also comport himself well and not lead his life in a fashion different from what he teaches, because he will be obliged subsequently in a detailed account to affirm before the severe judge that he himself acted as he instructed other people.

And again very soon after that, this same Solomon said, 4 "Do, my son, as I instruct you: free yourself, for you have incurred an obligation to your friend. But run now and make no delay, awaken him. Do not permit your eyes to sleep, nor your eyelids to droop." Then whoever has his life set as an example to other people is obliged not only to remain awake himself, but also to rouse his friends. Let it by no means seem to him sufficient only that he conduct his life well, but also that he draw away from the indolence of their sins those he is to supervise. In that place it is quite aptly said, "By no means let your eyes slumber, nor your eyelids droop." That one should let his eyes slumber is, then, that for his irresponsibility and his sloth he cannot recognize the vices of those who are subject to him. But when our eyelids droop we perceive something reprehensible in those who are subject to us, and we behave out of indifference as if we were

ðonne hnappige we. Ac ðonne we slapað fæste, ðonne we
nohwæðer ne hit witan nyllað ne hit betan nyllað, ne furðum
ne reccað hwæðer we hit ongieten, ðeah we hit gecnawan
cunnen. Ne slæpð se no fæsðe, ac hnappað, se ðe gecnawan
mæg hwæt tælwierðe bið, ond suaðeah for his modes swongornesse oððe recelieste forwandað ðæt he bete ond ðreage
his hieremenn be ðæs gyltes andefne. Æresð mon hnappað;
gif he ðonne ðære hnappunge ne swicð, ðonne hnappað he
oð he wierð on fæstum slæpe. Sua eac oft gebyreð ðæm ðe
for oðre menn beon sceal, ðonne he hwelc yfel ongiett, ond
ðæt nyle aweg aceorfan, ðæt ðonne æt niehstan hit wyrð to
gewunan ðæt he hit ne mæg gebetan, ne furðum ongietan
ðæt hit ænig yfel sie.

5   Ac ða sint to manianne ðe fore oðre beon sculan, ðæt hie
geornlice ða ymb sion ðe hie ofer beon sculon, ðæt hie ðære
geornfulnesse geearnigen ðæt hie sien ðæm hefonlicum neatum gelice: ða wæron geiewde, sua hit awriten is ðæt hie
wæron ymb eal utan mid eagum besett, ond eac innan ea-
gena full. Sua hit is cynn ðætte ða sien ðe fore oðre beon
sculon, ðæt hie ægðer hæbben eagan innan ge utan, ðæt hi
mægen ðæm inncundan deman on hira agnum inngeðonce
lician, ond eac utane mid godum bisenum hiera agnes lifes
hiera hieremonnum bisenigen, ond ðætte tælwyrðes on him
sie, ðæt hie ðæt tælen, ond hie forðæm ðreagen.

6   Ða underðioddan sint to manianne ðæt hie ðara unðeawas ðe him ofergesette bioð to suiðe ond to ðrisðlice ne
eahtigen, ðeah hie ryhte spræce hæbben hiera yfel on him to
tælanne; ðy læs hie for ðære ryhtlæcinge weorðen up
ahæfene, ond on ofermetto gewiten. Ac hie sient suiðe
georne to maniganne ðæt hi for hira unðeawum hie ne forsion, ne no ðy suiður wið hi ne ðrisðlæcen. Ac gif hie hwæt

unaware of it; then we nod. But when we fall fast asleep we wish neither to acknowledge it nor to rectify it, nor even care whether we perceive it, though we are capable of recognizing it. He by no means sleeps but nods who can recognize what is blameworthy, and yet for indolence of mind or disregard hesitates to correct and reproach his charges in proportion to their culpability. First one nods; if he does not leave off nodding, he dozes until he is deep in slumber. So also it often happens to someone who ought to govern others, when he perceives a certain wrong and does not care to prune it away, that it thereupon becomes such a habit that he cannot rectify it, or even recognize that it is a fault at all.

But those who ought to oversee others are to be warned 5 to observe carefully those in their charge, so that by such diligence they may merit being likened to those heavenly beasts which were described, as it is written, as covered all over with eyes, and also full of eyes on the inside. Thus, it is natural that those who have the care of others should have eyes both within and without, so that they can please the inward judge in their own conscience, and also set a pattern outwardly for their charges with the good example of their own life, and reprove what is reprehensible in them, and correct them that way.

Those in an inferior condition are to be warned not to 6 discuss too much or too brazenly the faults of their superiors, even though they have just cause to find fault with their transgressions, so that for that faultfinding they not grow impudent and stray into pride. But they are very earnestly to be admonished not to despise them for their faults, nor any the more to take liberties with them. But if they perceive

sua healicra yfela on him ongieten ðæt hie hit niede sprecan scylen, ðonne don hie ðæt suiðe diegellice betweoxn him, ond ðeah for Godes ege under ðæm geoke his hlaforddomes ðurhwunigen ond hine for Godes ege weorðigen, sua mon hlaford sceal.

7   Ac gif we nu onginnað reccan ongemong ðissum ymbe Dauides dæda sume, ðonne magon we ðis spel ðe openlicor gereccean. Hit gelamp æt sumum cierre ðæt he wæs gehyd on anum eorðscræfe mid his monnum. Ða Saul hine wolde secean uppe on ðæm munte, ða for he forð bi ðæm scræfe ðæt he on innan wæs, ond he his ðær no ne wende. Ða gewearð hine ðæt he gecierde inn to ðæm scræfe, ond wolde him ðær gan to feltune. Ða wæs ðærinne se ilca Dauid mid his monnum, ðe longe ær his ehtnesse earfoðlice ðolade. Ða cleopedon his ðegnas him to, ond hine bædon, ond geornlice lærdon ðæt he hine ofsloge. Ac he him sona ondwyrde, ond him suiðe stiernlice stierde, ond cuæð ðæt hit no gedæfenlic nære ðæt hie slogon Gode gehalgodne kyning, ond aras ðeah up, ond bestæl hine to him, ond forcearf his mentles ænne læppan to tacne ðæt he his gewald ahte. Hwæt tacnað us ðonne Saul buton yfle hlafurdas? Oððe hwæt Dauid buton gode ðeowas? Swa sua Saul elles ne meahte his wambe geclænsigan buton he to feltune eode, sua eac ne magon ða yflan hlafurdas, ðonne hie underfoð ða yflan geðohtas æt hiera heortan, ða ær alætan ær hie ut aberstað on fullicum weorcum. Sua sua Dauid forbær ðæt he Saul ne dorste ofslean for Godes ege ond for ðæm ealdum treowum, sua doð ða æltæwan mod ðara godra esna. Hie forberað æghwelce unryhte tælinge: sua sua Dauit forbær ðæt he ne slog mid his sueorde Saul, sua hie forberað ðæt hie mid ðæm sueorde hiera tungna tælinge ne sleað hira

something so deeply corrupt that they must of necessity discuss it, let them do it very privately among themselves, and
yet for fear of God persist under the yoke of his governance
and for fear of God show him respect, as one ought to show
his master.

But if we now set out in this context to recount certain of 7
David's affairs, we can explain this lesson more plainly. It
happened on one occasion that he was hidden with his men
in a certain cavern. When Saul went looking for him up in
the mountains, he passed the cavern that he was in, and he
did not guess that he was there. Then it pleased him to turn
into the cavern, and he wished to relieve himself there. This
same David, who long since had endured his persecution by
an effort, was inside with his men. Then his officers addressed him and entreated him, and fervently urged him to
kill him. But he answered them at once and restrained them
very sternly and said that it would be in no way fitting to kill
a king consecrated by God, but he arose and stole up to him
and cut off a corner of his mantle as a sign that he had had
him in his power. What does Saul signify for us but bad masters? And what David but good servants? Just as Saul could
not void his bowels but by visiting the privy, so also when
bad masters admit bad intentions to their heart, they cannot be rid of them before they burst out in foul deeds. Just
as David would not countenance daring to kill Saul for fear
of God and for their association of old, so do the upright
minds of good servants. They avoid any improper criticism:
just as David refrained from attacking Saul with his sword,
so they refrain from attacking their master's conduct with
the sword of their tongues' criticism, though they know to

hlafurdes ðeawas, ðeah hie wieten ðæt hie elles æltæwe ne sin. Ac gif he ðonne eallunge forberan ne mæg for hira agnum unðeawum ond for hiera ungestæððignesse ðæt hie hit ne sciren, ðonne sprecen hie ymbe his ða læstan unðeawas ond ðæt ðeah suiðe diogollice. Sua sua Dauid cearf swiðe digellice suiðe lytelne læppan of Saules mentle his ealdhlafordes, sua doð ða ðe hira hlafordas diegellice tælað, ond ðeah sua sua hit him no ne derige, ne ne egle. Ac gif hwæm gebyrige ðæt he for his agnum unðeawum on ða tælinge his hlafordes befoo, ðonne sceal he hine selfne suiðe suiðlice forðæm tælan ond ðara læstena worda hreowsian. Forðæm hit is awriten ðætte Dauid, ða he ðone læppan forcorfenne hæfde, ðæt he sloge on his heortan, ond suiðe suiðlice hreowsade ðæt he him æfre sua ungeriesenlice geðenigan sceolde, ðeah his ðegnas hine ær lærdon ðæt he hine mid his sweorde sloge. Swa scyle gehwelc mon forberan ðæt he mid ðæm sweorde his tungan his hlaford ne slea—ðæt is, ðeah he hine mid ryhte tælan mæge, ðæt he hit ne doo. Gif him ðonne gewealdes gebyrige oððe ungewealdes ðæt on ðæs hwæt befoo ðe wið his willan sie, ðeah hit on ðæm ealra læstan ðingum sie, ðeah him is ðearf ðæt he his heortan ond his mod mid hreosunga suiðe pinige, ond his agena scylda ongiete, ond him selfum deme suelc wite suelce he wene ðæt his hlaford him deman wolde, gif he hit wiste; forðæm ðonne we agyltað wið ða hlafordas, ðonne agylte we wið þone God ðe hlafordscipe gescop. Be ðæm ilcan cuæð Moyses, ða he gehierde ðæt ðæt folc mænde to him ond Arone ymb hiera earfeðo, ða cuæð he, "Hwæt is eower murcung wið unc? Hwæt sint wit? Wið God ge doð ðæt ge dooð."

the contrary that it is not upright. But if, for their own bad conduct and lack of resolve, they cannot refrain altogether from bringing it to light, let them speak about the least of his faults, and yet that very privately. Just as David quite stealthily cut a very small corner of his old patron's mantle, so likewise do those who censure their masters privately, and yet in such a way as not to harm or aggrieve them. But if it happens to someone that he for his own bad conduct should go about charging his master, he ought to censure himself very strongly for that and repent his every least word. For it is written that David, once he had cut off the corner, battered his heart and bitterly repented ever having served him so unbecomingly, even though his officers had urged him to strike him with his sword. So ought every person to forbear from striking his master with the sword of his tongue—that is, that though he could justly censure him, he refrain from doing it. If it then happens to him, whether or not of his own volition, that he should touch upon something of it that is not to his liking, though it concerns the most trifling matters of all, it is required of him that he severely scourge his heart and his mind with repentance, and acknowledge his own transgressions, and assign himself such penance as he believes his master would assign if he knew, for when we offend against lords, we offend against that God who ordained lordship. About this very thing Moses, when he heard that the people complained to him and Aaron about their trials, said, "What is your complaint against us? What are we? It is against God that you do what you are doing."

Chapter 29

XXVIIII. Ðætte on oðre wisan sint to manianne ða
hlafordas, on oðre wisan ða ðegnas
ond eac ða ðeowas.

On oðre wisan sint to manianne ða ðeowas, on oðre ða
hlafordas. Ða ðeowas sint to manianne ðæt hie simle on him
hæbben ða eaðmodnesse wið hira hlafordas. Ða hlafordas
sint to manianne ðæt hie næfre ne forgieten hu gelic hira
gecynd is, ond hu gelice hi sint gesceapene ðæm ðiowum.
Ða ðiowas sint to monianne ðætte hie hiera hlafordas ne
forsion. Hiera hlafordas hi forsioð, gif hie his willan ond his
bebodu forhyggeað. Ðam hlafordum is eac to cyðanne ðætte
hie wið Gode ofermodgiað for his agenre giefe, gif hie ne
ongietað ðæt ða beoð hira gelican ond hira efngemæccan on
hira gecynde, ða ðe him underðiedde beoð ðurh Godes
gesceafte. Ðæm ðeowan is to cyðonne ðæt he wiete ðæt
he nis freoh wið his hlaford. Ðæm hlaforde is to cyðanne
ðæt he ongiete ðæt he is efnðeow his ðeowe. Ðæm ðeowan
is beboden, ond ðus to cueden: "Beoð ge underðeodde
eowrum woroldhlafordum." Ond eft hit is gecueden, "Ælc
ðara ðe sie under ðæm gioke hlafordscipes, he sceal his
hlaford æghwelcre are ond weorðscipes wierðne onmunan."
Ond eft hit is gecueden, "Ge hlafordas, doð ge eowrum
monnum ðæt ilce be hira andefne ond gemetgiað ðone
ðrean; geðencað ðæt ægðer ge hira hlaford ge eower is on
hefenum."

Chapter 29

29. That lords are to be guided in one fashion, deputies and likewise servants in another.

In one fashion are to be cautioned servants, in another masters. Servants are to be charged always to have within them humility with respect to their lords. Lords are to be admonished never to forget how like their nature is, and how similar to their servants they are made. Servants are to be warned not to despise their master. They despise their master if they reject his desires and his commands. To masters it is also to be made plain that they are arrogant toward God for his own gift if they fail to acknowledge that in their nature they are the equals and the fellow companions of those who are subject to them by God's decree. To the servant it is to be made plain that he should know that he is not independent of his master. It is to be explained to a master that he is to acknowledge that he is his servant's fellow servant. The servant is commanded and spoken to thus: "Be subject to your earthly masters." And again it is said, "Each of those who are under the yoke of overlordship shall deem his master worthy of every honor and obeisance." And again it is said, "You masters, do the same by your people according to their desert, and temper your coercion; remember that both their master and yours is in heaven."

Chapter 30

xxx. Ðætte on oðre wisan sint to manianne ða dolan, on oðre ða wisan.

On oðre wisan sint to manianne ða ðe ðisse worulde lotwrenceas cunnon ond ða lufigeað, on oðre ða medwisan. Ða lytegan sint to manianne ðæt hi oferhycggen ðæt hie ðær wieton; ða samwisan sint to manianne ðæt hie wielnien to wietanne ðæt ðæt hie nyton. Ðæm lytegan is æresð to beleanne hiera selflice, ðæt hie ne wenen ðæt hie sien wiese. On ðæm medwisan is to trymmanne swa hwæt sua hie ongietan mægen ðæs godcundan wisdomes, forðon, ðonne hie nane wuht ne ofermodgiað, ðonne beoð ða heortan suiðe gearwe wisdomes to anfonne. Ac ymb ða lytegan we sculon suiðe suiðe suincan ðæt hie ðone wisdom forlæten ðe him selfum ðyncð ðætte wisdom sie, ond fon to ðæm Godes wisdome ðe him dysig ðyncð. Ne ðarf mon na ðone medwisan læran ðæt he ða lotwrencas forlæte, forðon ðe he hie næfð. Forðæm him is micle ieðre to gestieganne on ðone ryhtan wisdom ðonne ðæm lytegan sie to anbuganne, forðæm ðe he bið ær up ahæfen on selflice for his lotwrencium. Be ðysum illcan cuæð *sanctus* Paulus, "Suelc eower suelce him selfum ðynce ðætte wisusð sie on ðæm lotwrencum, weorðe ðæs æresð dysig, ðæt he mæge ðonan weorðan wis." Be ðam medwisan is gecueden, "Ne sculon ge beon to wise æfter ðæs lichoman luste." Ond eft cuæð Paulus, "Ða ðe woruldmonnum ðynceað dysige, ða geciesð Dryhten, forðæm ðæt he ða lytegan, ðe mid ðissum woroldwrencium bioð up ahæfene,

Chapter 30

30. That the simpleminded are to be guided in one fashion, the clever in another.

In one fashion are to be advised those who are acquainted with the devious ways of this world and value them, in another the simple. The shrewd are to be urged to despise what they know of that; the half-witted are to be persuaded to desire to know what they do not know. The cunning are first to be thwarted of their self-love, so that they do not think themselves wise. In those who are slow of wits is to be encouraged whatever they can understand of divine wisdom, because when they know nothing of hauteur, hearts are quite prepared to accept wisdom. But in regard to the shrewd, we ought to labor very hard to induce them to abandon the cunning that seems to them wisdom and to accept the wisdom of God that seems to them foolish. It is unnecessary to teach the simple to give up devious ways, since they do not have them. Therefore, it is much easier for them to ascend to genuine wisdom than for the knowing person to submit, because he is already swollen with self-regard over his wiles. About such a one Saint Paul said, "Whichever of you seems to himself most learned in devious ways, let him first grow foolish, that he can thereafter grow wise." About the simple it is said, "You ought not to be too learned in the appetites of the body." And again Paul said, "God chooses those who seem foolish to worldly people to put to shame the cunning, who are conceited with this world's

gescende." Ond ðeah oft gebyreð ðæt ða bioð mid liðlicre race gehwyrfde, ond eft ða medwisan oft mid bisenum gehwyrfde. Ðæm lytegan ðonne is betere ðæt hie mid ryhtre race weorðen oferreahte ond mid ðære race gebundene ond ofersuiðde; ðæm medwisan bið genog god ðæt he gecnawe oðerra monna weorc untælwierðe.

2   Be ðæm se æðela lareow *sanctus* Paulus, se sceolde læran ægðer ge wise ge unwise, ða he ongeat ða Ebreas sume wisran, sume medwisran, ða manode he, ond cuæð to ðæm gelæredum ðara aldena boca mid liðelicum wordum: "Ðætte nu foraldod is, ðæt is forneah losad." Ond eft he cuæð to ðæm medwisan ða he ongeat ðæt hie mon mid sumum bisnum manian sceolde, "Ða halgan menn geðafedon on ðisse worlde monig bismer ond monige swyngean ond monige bendas ond carcernu; hie wæron stænde, ond snidene mid snide; hie wæron costade, ond mid sweordum hi wæron ofslægene." Ond eft cuæð Paulus, "Gemunað eowerra foregengena ðara ðe eow bodedon Godes word, ond behealdað hiera lif ond hira forðsiið, ond gongað on ðone geleafan." Forðon he ðus cuæð, ðæt he ða lotwrenceas oferwunne ond oferreahte; ond eac ða medwiisan to maran angienne mid ðære liðelican bisnunga gespone.

wiles." And yet it often happens that they are converted with gentle explanation, and in turn the simple often are converted with examples. For the cunning it is thus better that they be convinced with judicious reasoning and by that reasoning captivated and subdued; for the dull it is good enough to know other people's conduct to be unimpeachable.

About this the noble teacher Saint Paul, who was obliged to instruct both the wise and the unwise, upon recognizing some Hebrews as wiser and some as simpler, guided them with gentle words and spoke to those learned in the old books: "What is now antiquated is nearly vanished." And in turn he said to the simple when he recognized that they ought to be guided by certain examples, "In this world, saintly people suffered many a degradation and many blows and many manacles and prisons; they were stoned and cut with a saw; they were tried, and with swords they were put to death." And again, Paul said, "Remember your predecessors who preached God's word, and consider their life and their death, and walk in faith." He spoke this way to overcome and confute those devious ways, and also to persuade the simple to greater efforts with a gentle example.

Chapter 31

XXXI. Ðætte on oðre wisan sint to manianne ða
scamfæstan, ond on oðre ða scamleasan.

On oðre wisan sint to læranne ða scamleasan, on oðre ða
scamfæstan. Ðæm scamleasan ne wyrð no gestiered butan
micelre tælinge ond miclum ðrean; ða scamfæstan beoð oft
mid gemetlicre lare gebetrode. Ða scamleasa nyton ðæt hie
untela doð, buton hit mon him secge, ond ðeah hit mon him
secge, hie his ne geliefað, buton hie monige menn forðy
tælen. Se scamfæsta hæfð genoh on ðæm to his bettrunge
ðæt his lareow hine suiðe lythwon gemyndgige his unðeawa.
Ðone scamleasan mon mæg ðy bet gebetan ðe hine mon
suiður ðreað ond sciend, ac be ðæm scamfæstan hit is nyttre
ðæt ðæt him mon on tælan wille, ðæt hit mon healfunga
sprece, swelce hit mon hwon gehrine. Be ðæm Dryhten
suiðe openlice tælde ða scamleasan Iudeas, ond cuæð, "Eower nebb sint sua scamleas sua ðara wifa ðe beoð forelegissa."
Ond eft he olehte ðam scamfæstan, ða he cuæð, "Ðære
scame ond ðære scande ðe ðu on iuguðe worhtes ic gedoo
ðæt ðu forgietsð, ond ðæs bismeres ðines wuduwan hades ðu
ne gemansð, forðæm ðæt is ðin waldend ðe ðe geworhte."
Ond eft ða scamleasan Galathas suiðe openlice *sanctus*
Paulus tælde, ða he cuæð, "Eala ge ungewitfullan Galatæ,
hwa gehefegode eow?" Ond eft he cuæð, "Sua dysige ge sint
ðætte ðæt ðæt ge gæsðlice underfengon, ge willað geendigan
flæsclice." Ða scylda ðara scamleasena he tælde, suelce he

Chapter 31

31. That the modest are to be guided in one fashion, the shameless in another.

In one fashion are to be taught the modest, in another the shameless. The impudent person cannot be governed without great reproof and great threats; the bashful are often improved with temperate instruction. The shameless do not know that they are conducting themselves badly unless they are told, and even when they are told, they do not believe it unless many people chide them for it. For the betterment of the modest person it is sufficient for his instructor to give him only a very glancing reminder of his faults. The impudent person can be the better corrected the harder he is pressed and shamed, but with the bashful it is more effective to mention what is blameworthy in him by indirection, as if touching upon a trifle. In this regard the Lord directly rebuked the shameless Jews and said, "Your faces are as impudent as those of women who are harlots." And in turn he soothed the modest when he said, "The shame and the disgrace which you incurred in your youth I shall cause you to forget, and you will not recall the abasement of your widowhood, because it is your ruler who created you." And again Saint Paul reproved the shameless Galatians directly when he said, "Oh, you unthinking Galatians, who has encumbered you?" And in turn he said, "You are so foolish that what you undertook spiritually you intend to finish in the flesh." The offenses of the immodest he censured as if he

efnsuiðe him bære, ond cuæð, "Ic eom suiðe gefeonde on
Dryhten ðætte ge æfre woldon ænig wuht eow selfum wietan, ær ic hit eow wite. Hit is god ðæt ge hit nu witon.
Næron naht æmetige, ðeah ge wel ne dyden." Forðæm he
spræc ðas word ðe he wolde ðara scamleasna scylda tælende
geopenian, ond ðara scamfæstena giemelieste he wolde mid
liðelicum wordum gedieglan.

Chapter 32

XXXII. Ðætte on oðre wisan sint to monianne ða
ofermodan ond ða upahæfenan on hira mode,
on oðre wisan ða earmheortan ond ða wacmodan.

On oðre wisan sint to manianne ða modgan ond ða fortruwodan, on oðre ða unmodgan ond ða unðristan. Ða
fortruwodan, ðonne hie him selfum to suiðe truwiað, hie
forsioð oðre menn, ond eac forcueðað. Ða lytelmodan
ðonne ond ða unðristan, ðonne hie ongietað hiera unbældo
ond hiera unmiehte, hie weorðað oft ormode. Ða modgan
ðonne ond ða fortruwudan, eall hiera agen ðæt hie synderlice ðenceað oððe doð hie wenað ðæt ðæt sie ðæt betste; ac
ða unmodigan ond ða ungedyrstigan wenað ðæt ðæt suiðe
forsewenlic sie ðætte hie doð, ond forðon weorðað oft
ormode.

bore equal culpability when he said, "I rejoice greatly in the Lord that you would ever blame yourselves for anything before I blamed you for it. It is good that you are aware of it now. You were by no means unoccupied, though you did not do well." He said these words for the reason that he wished to lay bare the offenses of the impudent, laying blame, and he wanted to cloak the negligence of the modest with mild words.

Chapter 32

32. That the proud and the haughty in their judgment are to be guided in one fashion, the poor at heart and the diffident in another.

The bold and the brash are to be instructed in one fashion, the timid and the unassertive in another. The brash, when they place too much confidence in themselves, despise other people and also revile them. When those of little pluck and assertiveness recognize their timidity and their impotence, often they turn to despair. As for the bold and the audacious, they regard everything that they as individuals think and do as the best; but the spiritless and the unassertive regard as quite negligible what they do, and therefore often they grow despondent.

2   Ac ðæm lareowe is swiðe smealice to underseceanne be
ðæm weorcum ðara ofertruwedena, ðæt hie him gecyðen
ðætte on ðam ðingum ðe hie him selfum sua suiðe licigað,
ðæt hie Gode misliciað. Swa we magon betst ða gedyrstigan
gelæran ðætte, ðonne hie wenen ðæt hie hæbben betst gedon, ðæt we him ðonne secgen ðæt hie hæbben wierst
gedon—ðætte, ðonne hie wenen ðæt hie ðone gilp ond ðæt
lof begieten hæbben ðæt hie ær wilnodon, ðæt hie ðonne
hæbben mid ðy scame geholode. Hwilum eac, ðonne ða
fortruwudan ond ða anwillan wenað ðæt hie nane scylde
ðurhtogen næbben, ðonne magon we hi sua raðosð to ryhte
gecierran ðæt we him sume opene scylde, ðe ær ðurhtogen
wære, healfunga oðwieten, ðæt hie forðæm scamige, forðæm
of ðære scylde ðe he hine ðonne bereccan ne mæge, he ongiete ða he ðonne deð, ðeah him ðonne ðynce ðæt he nan
yfel ne doo. Ða fortruwodnesse ond ða anwilnesse an
Corinctheum Paulus ongeat suiðe wiðerwearde wið hine,
ond betweoh him selfum suiðe aðundene ond up ahæfene;
sua ðætte sume cuædon ðæt hie wæron Apollan, sume cuædon ðæt hi wæron Saules, sume Petres, sum cuæð ðæt he
wære Cristes. Ac Paulus ða sona ða unclænan scylde beforan
him allum sæde, ðe an hiera ealra gewitnesse gedon wæs,
ond ða giet ungebet; he cuæð, "We gehierdon betueoxn eow
unryhthæmed, ge sua unryht sua we furðum betwuxn hæð-
num monnum ne hierdon, ðæt is ðæt ge sume hæfdon eowre
steopmodur, ond ge ðæs næfdon nane sorge, ond noldon
from eow adon ða ðe ðæt dydon, ac wæron sua up ahæfene
sua ge ær wæron"; suelce he openlice cuæde, "Hwæt wille
ge for eowerre fortruwodnesse ond for eowerre anwilnesse
cueðan, hwæs oððe hwæs ge sien? Forðæm ðe on eowerre
towesnesse ge habbað gecyðed ðæt ge ures nanes ne siendon."

But it is for the teacher to examine in minute detail the 2
doings of the forward, to make it plain to them that in those
respects in which they are so very pleased with themselves
they displease God. Thus, we can best teach the presumptuous by telling them, when they believe they have done best,
that they have done worst—that when they suppose they
have achieved the glory and the adulation that they had desired, they have thereby garnered disgrace. At times also,
when the brash and the willful person believes that he has
committed no offense, we can return him to right thinking
most expeditiously by half holding him to account for some
naked transgression that was committed before, so that he
feels shame over it, to the end that, on the basis of the offense of which he cannot acquit himself, he may recognize
the one that he is committing on that occasion, though at
the time it seems to him that he is doing no wrong. Paul recognized the brashness and the obstinacy of the Corinthians
as set in opposition to him, and that they were quite conceited and high-flown in their own circle, so that some said
that they were of Apollo, some said that they were of Saul,
some of Peter, and one said that he was of Christ. But in the
presence of all Paul identified the impure offense which was
committed in the witness of every one of them and was
as yet unexpiated; he said, "We have heard of fornication
among you, and as wrongful as we have not heard of even
among heathen people, which is that some of you had your
stepmother, and you had no scruples about it, and you would
not send away from you those who did that but were as self-
satisfied as you had been before"; as if his plain meaning
were, "What do you mean to say by your brashness and by
your willfulness, that you are of this one or that one? For by
your laxity you have shown that you are of none of us."

3   Ac ða lytelmodan ond ða unðriestan we magon ðy ieð on
ðæm wege gebringan godra weorca, gif we healfunga ond
ðeah be sumum dæle heora godan weorc secgeað, forðæm,
ðonne we hira yfel tælað, ðæt we eac hira god herigen,
forðæm ðæt we hira modes mearuwnesse gestiðigen mid
ðæm ðæt hie gehiren ðæt we hi herigen, ond ðætte eft sien
hira scylða geðreade mid ðam ðæt we hie tælen. Oft we magon beon sua nyttran æt him, gif we hie myndgiað hira godna
weorca, ond ða secgeað, ond gif we hwæt ongietað on him
ungesceadwislices gedoon, ne sculon we no hi ðreagean
suelce hie hit gedoon hæbben, ðeah hit gedon sie, ac we sculon him forbeodan ðæt hie huru sua ne don, suelce hit ðonne
giet gedon ne sie, forðæm ðæt sio hering ðe we ær heredon
us gefultume ðæt we hie wiðermode ne gedon mid ðære
tælinge, ac ðæt sio hering getrymme ond gemetgige ðæs
wacmodan ond ðæs unðristan monnes mod wið ða tælinge.
Be ðam se ilca Paulus cuæð, ða he ongeat ðæt folc ðe Saloni-
censa hatte, ðæt hie on his lare fæste wæron, ond ðeah he
ongeat ðæt hi gedrefde wæron mid wacmodnesse, forðæm
ðe hie wendon ðæt hit near worulde endunge wære ðonne
hit wære; ða ongon he æresð herigean on him ðæt ðæt he
fæsðrædes wiste, ond sona æfter ðon suiðe liðelice hierdde
ða ðe he unfæsðrade wisse, ond ðus cuæð, "We sculon simle
secgan Gode ðoncas for eow, broður, sua sua hit wel wierðe
is, forðæm ðe eower geleafa hæfð oferðungen suiðe monigra
oðerra monna, ond eower lufu is betweoxn eow suiðe ge-
nyhtsumu, sua ðæt we apostolas sint suiðe gefeonde ealle for
eowrum geleafan ond for eowrum geðylde." Ac sona æfter
ðære liðelican spræce he cuæð, "Ic eow healsige, broður,
for ðæm tocyme Dryhtnes hælendan Kristes ond for ure
gesomnunge ðæt ge no to hrædlice ne sien astyrede from

Yet we can more easily bring the fainthearted and the un- 3
assertive on the way of good works if we remark only in part,
though to some extent, their good works, so that when we
censure their bad deeds we also commend their good, for
the purpose of stiffening the pliancy of their mind by their
hearing that we commend them, and that in turn their offenses are rebuked when we censure them. Thus, we can often be more helpful to them if we recollect their good deeds
and mention them; and if we recognize in them something
indiscreet done, we ought not to upbraid them as if they
have done it, even though it is done, but we ought to forbid
that they ever do so, as if it is still undone, so that the praise
we formerly offered them may help us avoid making them
defiant by that censure, but that the praise may strengthen
and temper the mind of the irresolute and the unassertive in
the face of criticism. About this the same Paul spoke when
he recognized that the people called Thessalonians were
firmly devoted to his doctrine, and yet he perceived that
they were afflicted by faintness of heart because they believed that the end of the world was nearer than it actually
was; then he started by commending in them what resolute-
ness he knew there to be in them, and immediately after
that he very gently lent firmness to those he knew to be irresolute, and thus he said, "We ought continually to say
thanks to God for you, brothers, as is fitting, because your
faith has excelled over many other people, and the love
among you is very profuse, so that we apostles are all delighted at your belief and your endurance." Yet immediately
after these gentle remarks he said, "I beseech you, brothers,
for the coming of the Lord savior Christ and for our congregation, that you not be too suddenly made frantic, nor that

gewitte, ne eow to suiðe ne ondrædað for nanes monnes
wordum ne for nanes witgan gæste, ne ðeah eow hwelc
ærendgewrit cume, suelce hit from us send sie, ond ðæron
cyðe ðæt se Domes Dæg neah sie." Sua gedyde se soðfæsta
lareow ðæt hie æresð gehierdon ða heringe ðe him licode,
forðæm ðæt hie æfter ðæm ðe lusðlicor gehierden ða lare,
ðætte ðæt lof hie to ðæm getrymede ðæt sio manung hie eft
ne ðrycte. Ða he ongeat ðæt hie wæron onstryede mid ðæm
wenan ðæt hi ðæs endes sua neah wendon, ða spræc he
suelce he hit ða giet nyste ðæt hie hit him ða io ondredon, ac
forbead him ðæt hit ne scolde sua weorðan, ond wolde ðæt
hie wenden ðæt hie ðæs ðe untælwyrðran wæren ðe hie wendon ðæt he nyste hira leohtmodnesse ond hira unfæsðrad-
nesse.

Chapter 33

XXXIII. Ðætte on oðre wisan sint to monianne ða
ungeðyldgan, ond on oðre ða geðyldgan.

On oðre wisan sint to manianne ða ungeðyldgan, on oðre
wisan ða geðyldegan. Ðæm ungeðyldedum is to secganne
ðæt hie ne agimeleasigen ðæt hi hira mod gebridligen, ðæt
hi ne hlipen unwillende on ðæt scorene clif unðeawa. Sua hit
oft gebyreð ðæt sio hatheortness ond sio hrædwilnes ðæt
mod gebringð on ðæm weorce ðe hine ær nan willa to ne
spon, ond deð ðeah sua astyred, suelce he hit ungewisses

you fear excessively on account of anyone's words or the spirit of any prophet, even if there should come to you some letter as if it were sent by us proclaiming that the Day of Judgment is near." Thus, the pious teacher first had them hear the commendation that would please them, so that afterward they would listen with a greater will to his doctrine, so that the praise would brace them to such an extent that the admonishment would not subsequently crush them. When he understood that they were agitated by the belief that the end was so nigh, he spoke as if he did not yet know that they were already in fear of it, but forbade that it should happen thus, and he wished that they should believe that they were the less blameworthy for it if they supposed that he did not know of their frivolity and their lack of resolve.

Chapter 33

33. That the patient are to be guided in one fashion, and the impatient in another.

In one fashion are the impatient to be cautioned, in another fashion the patient. The impatient are to be told to be vigilant about keeping their thoughts in check, so that they do not leap over the sheer precipice of vices. It often happens thus that hotheadedness and impulsiveness bring the mind to an act to which no predilection had formerly inclined the person, and nonetheless so incite him that it is as

oððe ungewealdes doo, ðæt him eft gehreoweð, siððan he hit wat. Forðæm him is to secgganne ðæt hie weorðað oft ascrencte on ðæm scyfe ðære styringe hira modes, ðæt hi hira selfra ne agon ðy mare geweald ðe oðerra monna, ond suiðe seldon magon ongietan hira ægen yfel, ær ðon hi hit ðurhtogen habbað. Ac gif he ðonne ðære styringe ne wiðstent, ðonne gescient he ða godan weorc ðe he oft ær on stillum mode ðurhteah, ond sua ungleaulice for ðæm scyfe ðære styringe suiðe hrædlice towierpð ða godan weorc ðe he longe ær foreðonclice timbrede, ond ða geðyld, ðe is modur ond hierde ealra mægena, for ðæm unwrence ðære unge-ðylde forlet, ond eac ðæt mægen ðære soðan lufan he forlet. Hit is awriten on Paules bocum ðæt sio Godes lufu sie geðyld, ond se ðe geðyldig ne sie, ðæt he næbbe ða Godes lufe on him. Forðæm for ðæm unðeawe ðære ungeðylde wirð ut adrifen sio fostermodur ælcre leornunga ond ælces cræftes, ond æghwelces lareowes lar wihxð ðurh his geðylde, æghwelc monn bið onfunden sua micle læs gelæred ðonne oðer sua he bið ungeðyldegra. Ne mæg he no ryhtlice ge-ðyld læran, buton he self geðyldelice oðerra monna tionan geðolige.

2   Hwilum eac gebyreð for ðæm unðeawe ðære ungeðylde ðæt ðæt mod wierð gesticced mid ðære scylde gielpes, ond he ne mæg geðyldgian ðæt he for ðisse worulde sie forsewen, ac gif he hwæt diogollice for Gode to goode gedyde, ðonne ne mæg he geðyldgian ðæt he ðæt forhele, ac wierð ðonon gielpen, ond ongienneð ðonne ðæt cyðan ðonne he ne mæg geðolian ðæt hine menn forsion, ac geopenað hit mid gielpe. Be ðam is awriten ðæt "betera beo se geðyldega wer ðonne se gielpna," forðæm ðe him bið leofre scande to ðolianne

if he does it unwittingly and unwilled, so that he later regrets it, once he realizes it. Therefore, such people are to be told that they are often confounded by the impulse of their mind's urging, that they have no greater control over themselves than other people, and very seldom can they recognize their own misdeed before they have committed it. But if such a one does not resist the impulse, he debases the good works that he often performed at an earlier time with a collected mind, and thus for the impulse of that urging he unwisely casts down the good works that for long he providently built up in the past, and abandons patience, which is mother and shepherd of all virtues, for the swindle of impatience, and also forsakes the virtue of genuine love. It is written in the biblical books of Paul that the love of God is patience, and whoever is impatient does not have the love of God in him. Therefore, the foster mother of all learning and every accomplishment is thrown over for the vice of impatience, and every instructor's teaching grows with his patience, and every person will be found so much the less learned than another to the extent that he is less patient. He cannot properly teach patience unless he patiently bears the abuse of other people.

At times it also happens on account of the vice of impatience that one's mind becomes transfixed by the offense of vanity, and he cannot bear to be scorned before this world, but if he has done something to the good covertly in the sight of God, he cannot bear to conceal it but becomes boastful about it, and begins then to make it public when he cannot tolerate being despised, but trumpets it conspicuously. About this it is written that "the patient man is better than the arrogant," because he would prefer suffering dis-

2

ðonne ðæt god to cyðanne ðæt he deogollice deð, ðy læs he
for ðæm unðeawe ðæs gielpes hit forleose. Ac ðæm gielpnan
bið leofre ðæt he secge on hine selfne gif he hwæt godes wat;
ge ðeah he nyte hwæt he soðes secge, him is ðeah leofre ðæt
he leoge ðonne him mon ænigra ungerisna to wene. Ac he
forlæt ðonne ond towierpð eal ða godan weorc ðe he ær
worhte, ðonne he forlæt ða geðylde.

3   Forðæm wæs suiðe ryhtlice beboden Ezechiele ðæm witgan ðæt he scolde ðone Godes alter habban uppan aholodne
ðæt he meahte on healdan ða offrunga ond ða lac ðe mon
brohte to ðæm weobude; forðæm, gif se weobud ufan hol
nære, ond ðær wind to come, ðonne tostencte he ða lac.
Hwæt elles getacnað ðæt weobud buton ryhtwisra monna
saula? Forðæm ðe nu eal ðæt se ryhtwisa to gode deð, eal hit
bið broht to lacum beforan Godes eagum, sua io wæs eall sio
offrung uppe on ðæt wiebed broht. Hwæt tacnað ðonne ðæt
holh on ðæm weobude buton godra monna geðyld? Forðam,
ðonne mon his mod geeaðmodgað ðæt he wiðerweardnesse
ond scande forbere, ðonne geeacnað he sum holh on his
mode sua sua ðæt weobud hæfð on him uppan. Holh wæs
beboden ðæt sceolde beon on ðæm weobude uppan, forðæm
ðæt wind ne meahte ða lac tostencean, ðe mon on ðæt
weobud legde. Ðæt tacnað ðæt ðæt geðyld sceal gehealdan
ðara gecorenra monna mod, ðætte hit ne astyrige se wind
ðære ungeðylde, ðy læs hit forleose ða godan weorc ðe he ær
geworht hæfde. Wel hit wæs gecueden ðæt ðæt holh sceolde
beon on ðæm weobude anre elne brad ond anre elne long,
forðæm butan tweon se ðe ða geðylde ne forlæt, he gehilt micle anmodnesse. Be ðæm cuæð *sanctus* Paulus, "Bere
eower ælc oðres byrðenne betweoxn eow; ðonne gefylle ge
Godes æ."

grace to advertising the good that he does clandestinely, to avoid debasing it by the vice of vanity. Yet the boastful one would prefer to attribute it to himself if he knows of something good; and even if he does not know that what he says is true, he prefers lying to letting anyone suppose something unseemly about him. But then he repudiates and ruins all the good deeds he has performed previously when he loses patience.

Therefore, the prophet Ezekiel was quite rightly instructed that he was to have the altar of God hollowed out above, so that it could contain the offerings and the gifts which were brought to the altar, because if the altar had no cavity on top and the wind were to come, it would scatter the gifts. What other does the altar signify than the souls of righteous people? For now everything of good that the righteous one does is brought as gifts before the eyes of God, as the entire offering was once brought up onto the altar. What does the cavity in the altar signify but the patience of good people? For when someone humbles his mind to bear contrariety and mockery, he enlarges a certain cavity in his mind such as the altar has on the surface. It was instructed that there ought to be a receptacle in the top of the altar so that the wind could not scatter the gifts that were laid on the altar. That signifies that patience should anchor the minds of the chosen people, so that the wind of impatience not be able to move them, to avoid vitiating the good works that they had already performed. It was well said that the cavity in the altar should be an ell broad and an ell in length, for certainly, whoever does not lose patience retains ample resolve. About this Saint Paul said, "Let each of you bear the other's burden between you; then you will fulfill God's law."

4   Ðæt is ðonne Godes æ ðæt mon hæbbe lufe ond geðyld, ðæt ðonne fullfremmað ða ane þe hie ne forlætað, ðonne hie mon gremeð. Gehieren ða ungeðyldegan ðysne cwyde þe awriten is: "Betra bið se geðyldega wer ðonne se stronga ond se kena, ond strongra bið se ond ðristra þe his agen mod ofercymð ond gewilt ðonne se þe fæste burg abrycð." Læssan sige hæfð se se ða burhware ofercymð, forðon him bioð fremde ða þe he ðær hinð ond ðreatað. Forðæm bið se sige micle mara ðe man mid geðylde gewinð, forðæm sio gesceadwisnes ðonne hæfð ofercumen ðæt mod ond gewielð, swelce he self hæbbe hiene selfne gewildne, ond sio geðyld hæbbe ðæt mod geðreatod ond gecafstrod. Gehieren ða ungeðyldegan hwæt sio Soðfæstnes cwæð to his gecorenum: he cwæð, "On eowrum geðylde ge gehealdað eowra saula." Swæ we sint wunderlice gesceapene ðæt ure mod ond ure gewitt hæfð ðone anwald ures lichoman, ond sio gesceadwisnes hæfð anwald ðæs modes. Forðæm, gif sio gesceadwisnes næfð nanne anwald ðære saule ond ðæs modes, ðonne næfð sio saul ond ðæt gewit nanne anwald ðæs lichoman. Ac sio geðyld is gesett to hierde urre gesceafte. Ðæt us ætiewde Dryhten, þa he us lærde ðæt we sceoldon urra selfra waldan mid ðære geðylde. We magon eac ongietan hu micel sio scyld bið ðære ungeðylde, ðurh þa we forlætað ðone anwald ure selfra, ðone we sceoldon ðurh ða geðylde gehealdan. Gehieren ða ungeðyldegan ðone cwide þe eft be him gecweden is on Salomones bocum: "Se dysega ungeðyldega all his ingeðonc he geypt, ac se wisa hit ieldcað, ond bitt timan." Sio ungeðyld geniet ðone monnan ðæt he geopenað all his ingeðonc, ond ealne ðone gast ut adrifð. Forðæm hiene swæ hrædlice sio gedrefednes ut adrifð ðy hiene ðærinne ne belycð nan ege ðære lare wisdomes. Ac se wisa hilt his spræce

It is God's law, then, to have charity and patience, so that   4
those alone fulfill it who do not lose them when they are
provoked. Let the impatient hear this comment that is written: "Better is the patient person than the strong and the
brave, and he is stronger and more daring who overcomes
his own mind than one who subdues a fortified town." One
who subdues the townsmen has a lesser triumph because
those he humbles and subjugates are strangers to him.
Therefore, the victory that is won with patience is much
greater, because prudence has then conquered the mind and
governs it, as if he himself has gained control of himself, and
patience has subjugated and bridled the intellect. Let the
impatient hear what Truth said to his elect: he said, "In your
patience you will possess your souls." We are marvelously
formed in such a way that our mind and our consciousness
have command of our body, and reason has command of the
mind. Therefore, if reason has no control of the soul and the
mind, the soul and consciousness have no control of the
body. But patience is designated custodian of our nature.
The Lord showed us that when he instructed us to master
ourselves with patience. We can also recognize how great
the offense of impatience is, through which we lose the control of ourselves that we ought to have through patience.
Let the impatient hear the remark that is made about them
in the books of Solomon: "The foolish, impatient one reveals all his inmost thoughts, whereas the wise one delays
and bides his time." Impatience compels the person to
throw wide open all his consciousness and drive into the
open his entire soul. Turmoil drives it out so quickly because
no reverence for the lessons of wisdom confines it within.
But the wise one holds his tongue and awaits his opportu-

ond bitt timan, ond ne wilnað na to hrædlice ðære wræce, ðeah he gegremed sie, ac wyscð ðæt hit him gehreowe, ðæt he hit mæge siððan forgifan. Ond ðeah wite he ðætte ealle scylda þe wið God beoð ungebetta beoð unforgifne on Domes Dæge ond ryhtlice gewrecene.

5 Ac eft sint to manigenne ða geðyldegan ðætte ðæt hie mid hiera wordum ond mid hiera dædum forgiefað ðæt hie ðæt eac on hiera ingeðonce forgifen, ðy læs he mid ðy niðe yfles ingeðonces toweorpe ða mægenu ðæs godan weorces þe he Gode utan anwealglice forgeaf; forðæm, ðonne hit nan man wietan ne mæg hwæðer hit eallinga forgiefen sie, ðætte hit ðonne se ne wrece þe hit wat þe swiður þe he licet mild-heortnesse ond forgifnesse ðær ðær nan ne bið. Ac ðæm geðyldegan ond ðæm forgiefendan is to secganne ðæt he georne wilnige ðæt he ðone mon eft lufian mæge þe him ær abealg, ðonne he hit ðeah forgifan sceal, forðæm, gif sio lufu ne gæð æfter ðære forgifnesse, ðonne wierð ðær feoung, ond se goda cræft ðe he ðær licette ðære forgifnesse wierð behwirfed on wiersan scylde. Be ðæm cwæð *sanctus* Paulus, "Lufu bið geðyldig." Ond sona æfter ðæm he cwæð: "Hio bið mildu." Swiðe sweotule he ætiewde mid ðæm wordum ðætte ðæm monnum ðe we for geðylde hwæt forberan sculon, ðæt we hie sculon eac milde mode lufian. Be ðæm se æðela lareow cwæð, ða he spon his hieremen to ðære geðylde; he cwæð, "Ælc ðweora ond ælc ierre ond unweorðscipe ond geclibs ond tæl sie anumen fram eow." Ða he spræc, swelce he þa uterran yflu hæfde eall geset, ond wende hiene þa to ðæm inneran, ond ðus cwæð, "And ælc yfel forlæte ge on eowrum ingeðonce." Forðæm hit bið unnyt ðæt mon un-weorðunga ond tæl ond geclibs utane forlæte, gif se yfela willa ðone onwald hæfð ðæs ingeðonces, se is modur ælces

236

nity, and never desires too-sudden retaliation, though he may be provoked, and wishes that the other will repent of it, so that he can afterward forgive it. And yet let him know that all transgressions that are unrepented to God will be unforgiven on Judgment Day and justly repaid.

But in turn, the patient are to be advised that whatever they forgive in word and deed, they forgive also in their conscience, to avoid ruining with the malice of bad intentions the efficacy of the good work that they in appearance dedicated entirely to God; so that, though no person can know whether it is completely forgiven, the One who does know may not exact greater retribution for it, the more there is feigning of compassion and forgiveness where there is none. But the patient and the forgiving are to be told to desire earnestly to be able to love once again the person who wronged them, since they are obliged to forgive, because if love does not follow forgiveness, hatred will arise, and the good effect of the forgiveness that they pretend will be turned to a worse offense. About this Saint Paul said, "Love is patient." And directly after that he said, "It is benign." By those words he showed very plainly, regarding those people whom for patience we are obliged to bear with, that we ought also to love them with benign intent. About this the noble teacher spoke when he enticed his disciples to patience; he said, "Let all bitterness and all rage and contempt and protest and condemnation be banished from you." Then he spoke as if he had set in order all external wrongs, and turned then to the internal, and said, "And leave off all wickedness in your mind." For it is pointless to leave off contempt and condemnation and protest externally if ill will, which is the mother

yfeles. Forðæm hit bið unnyt ðæt mon hwelces yfles bogas
snæde, buton mon wille ða wyrtruman forceorfan ðæs
staðoles. Be ðæm sio Soðfæstnes ðurh hie selfe cwæð,
"Lufiað eowre fiend, ond doð ðæm wel þe eow ær hatedon,
ond gebiddað for þa þe eower ehtað ond eow lað doð." Ðæt
is swiðe micel cræft beforan mannum ðæt mon ðæm men
auht forberan mæge þe him wiðerweard sie, ond ðæt is micle
mare beforan Gode ðæt hiene mon siððan mæge lufian.
Forðæm ða lac beoð Gode ealra andfengeost þe beforan his
eagum se lieg ðære lufe forbærnð on ðæm altere godra
weorca, swæ swæ iu mid ðæm heofoncundan fire on ðære
ealdan æ wæron ða lac forbærndu uppe on ðæm altere. Be
ðæm eft Dryhten cwæð to sumum monnum þe hæfdon ða
geðyld, ond næfdon ða lufe; he cwæð, "Hwæt, ðu meaht gesion lytelne cið on ðines broður eagan, ond ne meaht gefredan micelne beam on ðinum agnan." Sio gedrefednes ðære
ungeðylde on ðæm mode, ðæt is se smala cið, ac se yfela willa
on ðære heortan, ðæt is se greata beam. Ðone ungeðyldegan
ðonne suiðe lytel scur ðære costunga mæg onhreran, sua sua
lytel wind mæg ðone cið awecgan, ac ðone yfelan fæsðrædan
willan fulneah nan wind ne mæg awecgan. Be ðæm cuæð
Dryhten, "Ðu licettere, aweorp æresð of ðinum agnum eagan ðone greatan beam, ond cunna siððan hwæðer ðu mæge
adon ðone cið of ðines broður eagan." Suelce he cuæde to
ðæm unryhtwisan mode, ðe innan bið gnornigende, ond
utan licet geðyld: "Adoo æresð from ðe ða byrðenne ðæs
yfelan willan, ond tæl siððan oðerne for his ungeðylde ond
for his leohtmodnesse; forðæm ðonne ðu ne wilnasð ðæt ðu
oferswiðe ond forlæte ða licettunge on ðe selfum, ðonne
meaht ðu ðy wyrs geðyldgian oðres monnes yfel."

of all immorality, has possession of the mind. It is useless to trim away the boughs of evil unless one is willing to cut the root away from its bed. About this Truth said in his own person, "Love your enemies, and act well toward those who have in the past injured you, and pray for those who persecute you and do you wrong." It is a very great merit in the sight of men to be able to be forbearing about something toward a person who is hostile, and it is a much greater one in the sight of God to be able subsequently to love him. For to God those offerings are most acceptable of all which the flame of love immolates before his eyes on the altar of good works, just as formerly under the old law gifts were consumed with heavenly fire upon the altar. About this, the Lord again said to certain people who had patience but not love, "Now, you can see a little mote in your brother's eye and cannot perceive a great beam in your own." The affliction of impatience in the mind, that is the slender mote, but ill will in the heart, that is the great beam. A very light gust of temptation can disturb the impatient, just as a light breeze can move the mote, but there is hardly any wind that can move the evil, obstinate will. About this the Lord said, "You hypocrite, cast first the great beam from your own eye, and try afterward whether you can remove the mote from your brother's eye." It is as if he were saying to the unrighteous mind, which murmurs within, and without feigns patience: "Put first from you the burden of ill will, and afterward censure another for his impatience and his inconstancy; for when you do not desire to conquer and banish the hypocrisy in yourself, you will be worse able to suffer another person's wrongs."

6   Ond oft ðeah gebyreð ðæm geðyldgan, ðeah him mon
hwæt wiðerweardes doo, oððe he hwelce scande gehiere bi
him selfum, ðæt he ðonne nawuht æt ðam cierre ne bið
onstyred, ac gebærð sua geðyldelice suelce he hit hæbbe mid
ealre heortan forlæten. Ac ðonne he hit eft ofman æfter lytlum fæce, ðonne ofðyncð him ðæs ilcan ðe he ær forbær, ond
bið eft onæled mid ðy fyre ðæs sares. Secð ðonne ond smeað
hu he hit gewrecan mæge, ond ða monnðwærnesse ðe he ær
ðurhtogen hæfde eft ðeahtigende on yfel gewend. Ac ðæm
mæg beon suiðe hraðe geholpen from his lareowe, gif he
him sægð hwonon ðæt cymð, ond hu se lytega dioful styreð
gewinn ond gefeoht betweoxn him twam: oðerne he lærð
ðæt he onginne sume scande bi ðæm oðrum oððe sprecan
oððe don, oðerne he lærð ðæt he ða scande forgielde. Ac hit
gebyreð oftosð ðæt se bið ofersuiðed, se ðe ðurh diofles lare
æresð bið onæled mid ðy unryhtan niðe, ðeah he sua ne
wene, ðonne he hit æresð ongind; ond se hæfð oftosð ðone
weorðscipe, se ðe ær geðyldelic ða scande forbær. Ac ðonne
se diobul hæfð ðone ærran gewunnenne, ond he bið under
his geoc gegan, ðonne went he mid ealle cræfte ongen ðæs
oðres geðyld, ðe him ðonne giet wiðwind, ond bið suiðe
sorig, forðæm he on ðæm forman gefeohte hiene ne meahte
ofsceotan mid ðæm bismere, ðe he ðurh ðone oðerne him to
sende. Lætt ðonne an ðæt gefeoht sua openlice sume hwile,
ond ongiend hine diogollice læran, ond slitan his inngeðonc,
ond bit ðære tide, hwonne he ðæs wierðe sie ðæt he hine
besuican mote. Forðæm he hine ne meahte mid openlicum
gefeohte ofersuiðan, sætað ðonne diogollice, ond secð hu
he hine mæge gefon. Se geðyldiga ðonne eft, ðonne ðæt ge-
stilled bið, ðonne went he eft ongean mid his mode, ond

And yet often it happens to one who is patient that, al- 6
though something adverse is done to him, or he hears something disgraceful about himself, he is at the time not at all
discomposed, but he bears it as patiently as if with all his
heart he has let it go. But when he thinks of it again after a
brief while, he resents the very thing that he earlier tolerated, and is at length inflamed with the searing of the injury.
He pursues it then and studies how he can avenge it, and the
dispassion that he had maintained earlier he converts, upon
reflection, to malice. Yet he can be helped by his teacher
very expeditiously if he tells him from what it proceeds, and
how the cunning devil rouses trouble and strife between the
two of them: one he induces to venture to speak or to commit a certain outrage against the other; the other he
prompts to avenge the outrage. But most frequently it happens that the one who by the devil's instruction is first inflamed with unjust enmity will be bested, though he may
not think it will be so when he initiates it, and most often
the one who had suffered the outrage patiently will gain respect. But when the devil has mastered the former, and he
has gone under his yoke, then he will turn all his wiles
against the patience of the latter, who still resists him, and
will be full of anguish that in the earlier struggle he could
not transfix him with the disgrace that he cast at him
through the other. He thus ostensibly abandons the contest
for a time and begins to instruct him furtively, and probes
his mind, and awaits the time when he may be capable of being led astray. Because he cannot triumph over him in an
open fight, in concealment he will lie in wait and look for
a way to get hold of him. The patient one then in turn,
once tranquility is restored, turns back again in his mind

geman ðone demm oððe ðæt bismer, ðæt him ær gedon
wæs, ond ðonne suiðe hrædlice ond suiðe ungemetlice
eahtað eall ðæt him ær gedon wæs, ond hit ðonne suiðe unaberendlic talað, ond mid sua micelre murcunga his agen
mod gedrefð, ðætte oft ðone geðyldegestan scamað ðæs
siges ðe he ofer ðone dioful hæfde mid his geðylde, ond he
ðonne sua gebunden fram ðam diofle sargað ðæs, ond him
ofðyncð ðæt he hit sua emne ond sua geðyldelice forbær ðæt
he ðæt bismer ne forgeald, ond ðencð ðæs timan hwonne he
hit wyrs geleanian mæge.

7   Ac hwam beoð ðonne ðas ðyllecan geliccran ðonne ðæm
folce ðe on clænum felda weorðlicne sige gefeohtað, ond eft
innan hira burgum fæste belocene ðurh hiera giemelieste hie
lætað gebindan, oððe suelce hie ær lægen on longre medtrymnesse, ond hie ðeah gewierpten, ond eft cume an lytel
febbres, ond hie ofslea? Ða geðyldegan sint to manianne
ðætte hie hira heortan getrymigen æfter ðæs miclan sige,
ond ða burg hira modes wið stælherigas behealden, ond mid
wighusum gefæsðnige, suelce he him ðære adle edcier suiður
ondræde ðonne ðone fruman, ðy læs se lytega fiond æfter
fierste suiður fægnige ðæt he hine mid his lotwrencium
besuice, ðeah he hine ær openum gefeohte ofercome, ond
him ðone stiðan suiran forbræce.

and remembers the injury or the insult that had been done to him, and then quite suddenly and quite intemperately he will take account of all that had been done to him, and will then regard it as entirely insupportable, and will flog his own mind with such intense resentment that often the most patient person will feel humiliation over the victory he gained over the devil with his patience, and then, thus taken captive by the devil, he will feel wounded by it, and will feel annoyance that he so flatly and so patiently refrained from repaying the insult, and will reflect upon the time when he can accomplish a worse retribution.

But then whom are such more like than the nation which 7 gains an honorable victory in the open field and then, in turn, securely ensconced in their fortresses, through their heedlessness allow themselves to be taken captive, or as if they had formerly lain in a prolonged ailment, and yet they recovered, and in turn there should come a little bit of fever, and it kills them? The patient are to be warned to steel their heart after so great a victory, and to defend the fortress of their mind against stealthy warfare, and render themselves secure with battlements, as if they dreaded the return of the ailment more than the onset, lest the crafty foe in time celebrate all the more having deceived them with his wiles, though they had before repelled him in open combat, and had broken his stubborn neck.

Chapter 34

XXXIIII. Ðætte on oðre wisan sint to manianne ða welwillendan, ond on oðre ða æfestgan.

On oðre wisan sint to manianne ða welwillendan, on oðre ða æfstegan. Ða welwillendan sint to manianne ðæt hie sua fægenigen oðra monna godra weorca ðæt hie eac selfe ðæs ilcan lyste, ond sua gielpen hiera niehstena dæda ðæt hie him eac onhyrigen. Nimen him bisene on hira godan weorcum, ond icen hie simle mid hira agenum, ðy læs hie sien to oðerra monna gefeohte holde haweras, ond don him selfe nawuht, ond ðonne eft æfter ðam gefeohte sie butan æghwelcum edleane on ðys andweardan life. Se ðe nu on ðæm gefeohte ðisses andweardan lifes nile suincan, ne his selfes plion, he ongiet eft hine selfne ofercymenne ond gesciendne, ðonne he gesiehð ond gehierð ða weorðigan ðe ær wel ongunnon, ða ða he idel wæs. Suiðe suiðe we gesyngiað, gif we oðerra monna welgedona dæda ne lufigað ond ne herigað, ac we nabbað ðeah nane mede ðære heringe, gif we be sumum dæle nellað onginnan ðæt we onhyrigen ðæm ðeawum ðe us on oðrum monnum liciað be dæle ðe we mægen.

2   Forðæm is to secganne ðæm welwillendan monnum ðæt hie habbað sua micle mede oðerra monna godra weorca, gif hie him nan wuht ne onhyrigeað, sua we habbað ðæs hleahtres, ðonne we hliehað gligmonna unnyttes cræftes. We herigað hira cræftas, ond ðeah nyllað hi habban, forðæm we hiera nabbað nan lof. We wundriað hu wel hie liciað for

Chapter 34

34. That the benevolent are to be guided in one fashion, and the envious in another.

In one fashion are the benevolent to be counseled, in another the envious. The kindly disposed are to be encouraged to take such delight in other people's good works that they themselves wish for the same, and to glory so in their neighbors' deeds that they also emulate them. Let them follow their example in their good works and continually add to them with their own, so that they not be loyal spectators to other people's fight, and themselves do nothing, and then in turn after the fight be without reward in this present life. Whoever does not care to labor now in this present life or expose himself to danger will in turn see himself surpassed and disgraced when he sees and hears the deserving ones who did well from the start, while he was idle. We sin very gravely if we do not cherish and acclaim other people's well-done deeds, but we still will not have any reward for that acclaim if we do not to a certain extent care to undertake imitating the practices that please us in other people, to the degree that we are able.

Therefore, benevolent people are to be told that they will have as much reward for other people's good works, if they do not imitate them at all, as we have for laughter when we laugh at the pointless skill of entertainers. We commend their abilities, and yet we do not wish to have them, since we have no regard for them. We are amazed at how well they

hira cræfte, ond ðeah ne wilnigað no ðæt we sua licigen. Ðæm welwillendum is to secganne, ðonne hie gesioð hiera geferena god weorc, ðæt hie eac ðencen to him selfum, ond ne fortruwigen hie for oðerra monna weorcum, ðy læs hie herigen hiera godan weorc, ond onscunigen ðæt hie selfe sua don. Ðæs ðy wyrse wite hie sculon habban on ende ðe him licað ðæt mon wel doo, ond nyllað ðæm onhyrigean be sumum dæle.

3   Ac ða æfstegan sint to manianne ðæt hie ongieten hu blinde hi beoð, ðonne hie beoð unrote for oðerra monna godan weorcum, ond for hira ryhtum gefean beoð unbliðe, forðæm hie beoð suiðe ungesælige, ðonne hie yfeliað, forðæm ðe oðre menn godigað, ond ðonne hie geseoð ðara oðerra gesælða eaciende, ðonne ðyncð him ðæt hie wiellen acuelan for ðære medtrymnesse ðæs oðres gesælignesse, sua he bið genierwed on his mode. Hwa mæg beon ungesæligra ðonne se æfstiga? Ðonne ðu gesiehsð ðæt he bið utan gedrefed, hu micle ma wenstu ðæt he sie innan for ðæs oðres gode? Ðæt god ðæt se oðer ðonne deð, ðæt meahte beon eac his god, ðeah he hit ðonne git don ne meahte, gif he hit wolde lufigean on ðæm oðrum. Ealle ða ðe wunigeað on anum geleafan ond on anum willan, hie beoð sua sua manegu limu on anum menn, ond ælc hæfð ðeah sundernytte, ond ðeah ða limu mislice todælde sin, ælc hira bið on oðres nytte swa some swa on his selfes. Ðonon hit gewyrð ðæt se fot gesiehð ðurh ðæt eage, ond ðæt eage stæpð on ðæm fotum, ða earan gehierað for ðone muð, ond ðæs muðes tunge sceal faran on ðara earena ðearfe, ond sio womb sceal fulteman ðæm hondum, ond sio hond sceal wyrcean for ða wambe. On ðæs lichoman gesceafte we underfengon ealle ða ðenunga ðe we nu ðiowiað ond wyrceað. Forðæm hit is micel

please by their performances, and yet we have no desire to please that way. The benevolent are to be told, when they regard the good works of their fellows, also to examine themselves, and not to presume on the basis of other people's deeds, commending their good works and avoiding doing the same themselves. In the end they will have to undergo the worse punishment the more it pleases them that someone does well, and they do not care to emulate him to some extent.

Yet the envious are to be advised to recognize how blind 3 they are when they are upset about other people's good works and unhappy about their just contentment, because they are very wretched when they suffer over other people's improvement, and when they see the good fortune of others increasing, they feel they want to die for the affliction of someone else's happiness, they are so narrow-minded. Who can be more wretched than the envious person? When you see that he is visibly wracked, how much more so do you suppose he is inside over another's goodness? The good that the other does, then, could also be his good if he were willing to respect it in the other, though as yet he could not do it. All who dwell in one faith and in one will are like so many organs in a single person, and yet each has its own utility, and though the members are variously distributed, each of them is for the others' benefit as much as for its own. Thus it happens that the foot sees through the eye, and the eye walks on the feet, the ears hear for the mouth, and the mouth's tongue must move at the need of the ears, and the belly must assist the hands, and the hand must work for the belly. In the formation of the body we received all the functions that we now serve and perform. Therefore, it is a great

sceand, gif we nyllað licittan ðæt we sien ðæt we sindon,
forðæm butan tweon ðæt bið ure ðæt ðæt we lufigeað on
oðrum monnum, ðeah we hit selfe don ne mægen, ond ðæt
oðre menn on us lufigeað, ðæt bið hira. Geðencen be ðysum
ða æfstigan hu micel mægen bið on ðære lufe, ðæt hio gedeð
ðæt oðerra monna gesuinc ond hira weorc bið ure butan
ælcum gesuince ures lichoman.

4   Ac ðæm æfstegum is to secganne, gif hie hie nyllað healdan wið ðæm æfste, ðæt hie weorðað besencte on ða ealdan
unryhtwisnesse ðæs lytegan fiondes, ðe bi him awriten is
ðætte "for his æfeste deað become ofer ealle eorðan."
Forðæm ðe he hefonrice mid his agenre scylde forworhte,
ða ofðuhte him ðætte menn wæron to ðæm gesceapene, ond
icte ða his agne scylde mid ðæm æfste, ðæt he tiolode menn
forlæran ðæt hie wurden eac forlorene sua he wæs. Eac sint
to læranne ða æfstigan ðætte hie ongieten under hu micelre
frecenesse hie liecgað, ond hu hie iceað hira forwyrd, ðonne
hie of hira heortan nyllað aweorpan ðone æfst, ac hine
healdað, oð ðæt hie afeallað on opene scylde, swæ swæ Cain
dyde. Ne gefiolle he no on swæ opene scylde ðæt he his
broður ofsloge, gif he ær ne geæfstgode ðætte his broður
lac wæron ðancweorðlicor onfongne ðonne his. Be ðam is
awriten ðæt Dryhten besawe to Abele ond to his lacum ond
nolde to Caine ne to his lacum. Ða wearð Cain suiðe
hrædlice irre, ond hnipode ofdune, ond se anda ða ðe he
hæfde to his breðer, forðæm ðe his lac wæron onfangne ond
his næron, se anda wearð to sæde ðæs broðurslæges, forðæm
him eglde ðæt he wæs betra ðonne he, ond ðohte, sua he eft
gedyde, ðæt he hine ofsloge, wurde siððan to ðæm ðe hit
meahte.

shame if we are unwilling to act as if we are what we are, because, without a doubt, what we value in other people is our own, even if we cannot do it ourselves, and what other people cherish in us is theirs. Let the envious deduce from this what great virtue there is in love, that it causes other people's labor and their works to be ours without any bodily labor on our part.

But the envious are to be told, if they are unwilling to   4
guard themselves against envy, that they will be cast down into the ancient iniquity of the cunning fiend, about whom it is written that "for his envy, death encompassed the entire earth." Because he forfeited the kingdom of heaven by his own fault, it rankled him that humans were created for it, and he then aggravated his own offense by that envy, in that he made it his aim to mislead humans, so that they would be as ruined as he was. The envious are also to be instructed to recognize under what great peril they lie, and how they aggravate their ruin when they are unwilling to cast envy out of their heart, but they cling to it until they fall into patent wrongdoing, as Cain did. He would not have sunk to such undisguised villainy as to kill his brother if he had not resented that his brother's offerings were received with greater appreciation than his. About this it is written that the Lord looked upon Abel and his gifts and refused to look upon Cain or his gifts. Then Cain grew very suddenly enraged, and his countenance darkened, and then the anger that he harbored toward his brother, because his gifts were accepted and his own were not, became the seed of his fratricide, because it grieved him that he was better than he, and he determined, as he later did, that he would kill him, come of it what might.

5   Forðæm is to secganne ðæm æfstegum ðætte, ðonne
ðonne hie bioð innan fretene mid ðære adle, ðæt hie forleosað sua hwæt oðres godes sua on him ongieten bið. Be
ðæm is awriten ðætte ðis flæsclice lif sie æfesð, ond he sie
ðære flæsclican heortan hælo, ond ðeah ða ban for him
forrotigen. Hwæt getacnað ðonne ðæt flæsc buton unfæsð
weorc ond hnesce, ond hwæt ða ban buton stronglice geworht weorc? Oft ðeah gebyreð ðætte sume, ða ðe welwil-
lende beoð on monegum weorcum, unfæste beoð ongietene,
ond sume beoð beforan monna eagum gesewen suelce he
fæsðlicu ond stranglecu weorc wyrce, ond ðeah, ðeah he swa
do beforan monnum, for ðam andan oðerra monna godena
weorca, he bið aswunden on innan him selfum. Forðy is wel
gecueden ðætte ðæt flæsclice lif sie ðære heortan hælo,
forðæm se ðe gehielt his unsceaðfulnesse ond his godan willan, ðeah he hwæt tiederlices oððe yfelra weorca utan doo,
he mæg ðæt æt sumum cierre betan. Ac ðæt is suiðe ryhte
gecueden be ðæm banum ðæt hie forrotigen for ðæm æfste,
forðæm for ðæs æfstes scylde forweorðað ða godan weorc,
ðeah ðe hie beforan monna eagum ðyncen trumlice gedon.
Ðæt is ðæt ða ban forrotigen for ðæm æfste ðæt he forleose
sum suiðe god weorc for ðæm æfste.

For that reason the envious are to be told that when they 5
are inwardly consumed by that disease, they lose whatever
other good is recognizable in them. About this it is written
that this carnal life is envy, and it is the carnal heart's salvation, though the bones decay on that account. What, then,
does the flesh signify but unreliable and feeble works, and
what the bones but solidly wrought accomplishments? Yet it
often occurs that some who are benevolent in many works
can be seen to be unreliable, and some appear before people's eyes as if they accomplish solid and robust work, and
yet, though they do so in the sight of many, for resentment
toward other people's good works they are enfeebled within
themselves. For that reason, it is well said that carnal life is
the heart's salvation, because one who preserves his innocence and his good will, though he should publicly commit
some feeble or malign act or other, can at some turn amend
it. But it is quite justly said about the bones that they decay
on account of envy, because for the flaw of envy, good works
perish, even if in people's eyes they seem solidly done. That
is—the bones' decaying for envy—that he invalidates a certain very good work on account of envy.

Chapter 35

xxxv. Ðætte on oðre wisan sint to manienne ða
bilwitan, on oðre ða ðweoran ond ða lytegan.

On oðre wisan sint to manianne ða biliwitan, on oðre ða
lytegan. Ða bilewitan sint to herigenne, forðæm ðe hie simle
suincað on ðæm ðæt hi tieligeað ðæt hie ne sculen leasunga
secgan. Hie mon sceal eac læran ðæt hi hwilum suigien ðæs
soðes, forðæm, sua sua sio leasung simle deret ðæm secggen-
dum, sua dereð eac hwilum sumum monnum ðæt soð to ge-
hierenne. Forðæm ure Dryhten gemetgode mid suigean his
spræce beforan his ðegnum, ða he cuæð, "Fela ic hæbbe eow
to secganne, ac ge hit ne magon nu giet aberan." Ðy sint to
manianne ða bilwitan anfealdan ðætte, sua sua hie ða leasunga nyttwyrðlice fleoð, ðæt hie eac ðæt soð nytwyrðlice
secgen, ond geicen ða god hira anfealdnesse mid wærscipe,
ond sua tilige ðære orsorgnesse mid ðære anfealdnesse
ðætte he ðone ymbeðonc ðæs wærscipes ne forlæte. Be ðam
cwæð se æðela lareow *sanctus* Paulus, "Ic wille ðæt ge sien
wise to gode ond bilwite to yfele." Ond eft be ðæm cwæð
Dryhten ðurh hine selfne to his gecorenum, "Beo ge swa
ware sua sua nædran ond sua bilwite sua culfran." Forðæm
on ðara acorenra monna heortan sceal ðære nædran lytignes
ond hire nið ðære culfran biliwitnesse gescirpan, ond eft
ðære culfran biliwitnesse sceal gemetgian ðære nædran
wærscipe ond hire nið, ðy læs hine se wærscipe ond se anda
gelæde on ealles to micle hatheortnesse, oððe eft sio bi-
lewitnes ond sio anfealdnes hine to ungeornfulne gedoo to
ongietanne, ðy læs he weorðe besolcen.

Chapter 35

35. That the innocent are to be guided in one
fashion, the crooked and the devious in another.

In one fashion are the innocent to be treated, in another
the devious. The innocent are to be commended for always
laboring to make it their practice not to tell untruths. They
should also be taught sometimes to leave the truth unspo-
ken, because just as a lie always harms the teller, so at times
the truth is harmful for certain people to hear. For that reason, the Lord tempered his speech with reserve before his
disciples when he said, "I have much to say to you, but you
are not yet able to bear it." Therefore, simple innocents are
to be advised that, just as they appropriately avoid lies, they
should also speak the truth appropriately and heighten the
virtue of their simplicity with discretion, and promote confidence with simplicity in such a way as not to neglect the
precaution of tactfulness. About this the noble teacher
Saint Paul said, "I want you to be knowledgeable about good
and innocent about evil." And again, about this the Lord
said to his disciples in his own person, "Be as shrewd as ser-
pents and as innocent as doves." For in the hearts of the
elect, the serpent's cunning and its virulence ought to lend
an edge to the innocence of the dove, and in turn the dove's
innocence ought to blunt the serpent's shrewdness and its
injuriousness, so as not to let that shrewdness and bitterness
lead them into all-too-great fervor, or, conversely, not to let
innocence and simplicity render them too indifferent to understanding, so that they grow torpid.

2   Ongean ðæt mon sceal monian ða lytegan, ond him
secgan ðæt hie ongieten hu hefig ðæt twiefalde gesuinc við
ðæt hie him selfe ðurh hira agena scylda hira agnes gewealdes him on geteoð. Ðæt is ðonne ðæt hie eallneg ræswað
ond ondrædað ðæt hi mon tælan wille, ond beoð eallneg mid
ðæm ymbeðoncan abisgode ond ofdrædde. Oðer is ðara ge-
suinca ðæt hi simle seceað endelease ladunga, hu hie ðonne
bereccan mægen. Ac nis nan scild trumra wið ðæt tuiefalde
gesuinc ðonne mon sie untwiefeald, forðæm ðe nawuht nis
ieðre to gesecganne, ne eac to geliefanne ðonne soð. Ac
ðonne hwa on ða leasunga befehð, ðonne ne mæg he of, ac
sceal ðonne niede ðencean hu he hie gelicettan mæge, ond
gewergað ðonne his heortan suiðe hearde mid ðy gesuince.
Be ðæm gesuince spræc se salmscop, ða he cuæð, "Ðæt gesuinc hira agenra welena hie geðrycð." Forðæm se ilca feond
se ðe nu ðæt mod ðurh ða bisuiculan olicunga forlæreð, he
hit eft mid suiðe grimmum edleane geðryscð. Be ðæm wæs
gecueden ðurh Ieremias ðone witgan, "Hie lærdon hira tungan, ond wenedon to leasunge, ond swuncon on unryhtum
weorce"; suelce he openlice cuæde, "Ða ðe meahton Godes
friend beon butan gesuince, hie suuncon ymb ðæt hu hie
meahton gesyngian." Wietodlice, ðonne hwa nyle bielwitlice
libban butan gesuince, he wile geearnian mid his gesuince
his agene deað. Ac monige menn, ðonne him beoð unðeawas on anfundene, ðonne anscunigað hie ðæt mon wite
hwelce hie sien, ond wilniað ðæt hie hie gehyden ond beheli-
gen under ðæm ryfte ðære leasunga, ge furðum ðara scylda
ðe openlice beoð gesewena, hie wilniað ðæt hie scylen hie
beladian sua georne ðætte oft se ðe wilnað hiera unðeawas
arasian, bið openlice besuicen ond ablend mid ðæm miste
ðære leasunga, sua ðæt him fulneah ðyncð ðætte his nawuht
sua ne sie sua sua he ær witodlice be him wende.

To the contrary, the devious ought to be advised and told 2
to recognize how ponderous will be the twofold labor that
they willingly impose on themselves through their own
faults. That is, then, that they always suspect and live in fear
of being blamed, and are always occupied and unnerved by
that expectation. The other of those labors is that they continually seek endless excuses by which to exculpate themselves. But there is no surer safeguard against that twofold
labor than to be sincere, since nothing is easier to speak or
to believe than the truth. Yet once someone takes to telling
lies, he cannot leave off, but then he must by necessity ponder how he can make them plausible, and then he wearies
his heart very tediously with that drudgery. The psalmist
spoke of that toil when he said, "The labor of their own lips
weighs upon them." For the same adversary that now mis-
leads the mind by cunning allurements will in turn afflict it
with very bitter reprisal. About this it was said through the
prophet Jeremiah, "They have trained their tongues and accustomed them to lying, and have toiled at unjust work"; as
if his plain meaning were, "Those who could have been
God's friends without effort labored at being capable of sinning." Plainly, when someone is unwilling to live innocently
without labor, by his labor he wishes to earn his own death.
But many people, when faults are discovered in them, avoid
letting it be known of what sort they are, and desire to obscure and disguise themselves under a veil of deceit; and
even those offenses that are plainly apparent they desire so
earnestly to exculpate themselves of, that often one who is
willing to condemn their vices will be plainly deceived and
blinded by the fog of lies, so that it nearly seems to him that
nothing is as he had believed of him for certain.

3   Be ðæm ryhtlice bi Iudeum wæs gecueden ðurh ðone witgan ymb ðæt synfulle mod ðe hit simle wile ladian; he cuæð
ðæt ðær se iil hæfde his holh. Se iil getacnað ða twiefealdnesse ðæs unclænan modes ðe hit symle lytiglice ladað, sua
sua se iil, ær ðæm he gefangen weorðe, mon mæg gesion
ægðer ge his fet ge his heafod ge eac eall ðæt bodig, ac sona
sua hiene mon gefehð, sua gewint he to anum cliewene, ond
tihð his fet sua he inmest mæg, ond gehyt his heafod, sua
ðætte betwuh hondum ðu nast hwær him awðer cymð, oððe
fet oððe heafod, ond ær, ær ðu his o onhriene, ðu meahtes
geseon ægðer ge fet ge heafod. Swa doð ða lytegan ond ða
unclænan mod: ðonne him bið sum unðeaw on onfunden,
ðonne bið ðæs iles heafud gesewen; ðonne mon mæg ongietan of hwam hit æresð com, ond for hwæm. Ond ðonne
beoð ða fet gesewene, ðonne mon ongiet mid hwelcum
stæpum ðæt nawht wæs ðurhtogen; ac ðeah ðæt unclæne
mod suiðe hrædlice fehð on ða ladunga, ond mid ðære be-
heleð his fet ond ða stæpas his unnyttan weorces. Ðonne he
tiehð his heafod in to him, ðonne he mid wunderlicre ladunga ætiewð ðæt he furðum næfre ðæt yfel ne ongunne.
Sua he hit hæfð mid his lotwrencium bewunden on innan
him selfum, suelce se lareow hæbbe an cliwen on his honda
suiðe nearwe ond suiðe smealice gefealden, ond nyte hwær
se ende sie, sua feor ond sua fæste hit bið gefealden on innan
ðæs synnfullan monnes ingeðonce, ond mid his lote bewunden, ðætte se lareow ðæs yfeles ðe he stieran scolde, ðeah ðe
he hit ær wisðe, ðæt he hit ðonne nat, ond eall ðæt he ær
tælwyrðlices geseah mid ðam forhwirfdan gewunan ðære
unryhtan ladunge he bið amierred ðæt he hit eal endemes
forlæt, ond his nan wuht nat. Wietodlice se il hæfð his holh

Concerning this, in regard to the Jews, pronouncement 3 was justly made through the prophet about the sinful mind's constant desire to exculpate itself, when he said that the hedgehog had its den there. The hedgehog signifies the duplicity of the impure mind that always excuses itself cunningly, just as, before it is captured, both the feet and the head of the hedgehog can be seen, as well as the entire body, but as soon as it is caught it curls itself into a ball and draws its feet in as far as it can, and it hides its head, so that you do not know where between your hands either belongs, feet or head, and before you ever touched it, you could see both feet and head. Thus does the cunning and the impure mind: when a certain vice is discovered in it, the hedgehog's head is visible; then it can be recognized from what it arose and for what reason. And the feet are visible when it can be recognized with what steps the wrongdoing was committed; but then the impure mind quite suddenly seizes on obfuscation and thereupon conceals its feet and the steps of its regrettable deed. It draws its head into itself when, with extraordinary excuses, he makes a show of never even having engaged in that misconduct. With his wiles he has so raveled it up within himself that it is as if the advisor has a ball in his hands, very tightly and very compactly wound up, and does not know where the end is, so thoroughly and so firmly is it wound up within the sinful person's consciousness, and so wrapped in his guile that the advisor, though he knew before of the malignity that he ought to correct, cannot then make it out, and everything of a blameworthy nature that he perceived earlier he finally dismisses, so misled is he by the altered circumstances of the false excuses, and he understands nothing about it. Certainly, the hedgehog has its den in the

on ðæs unnyttan monnes heortan, forðæm ðæt yfelwillende
mod gefielt hit self twiefald on innan him selfum, ond sio
twyfealdnes ðæs yflan willan hiene selfne twyfealdne gefielt
on innan him selfum, ond gehyt hine on ðæm ðiestran mid
ðære ladunge, sua se iil hine selfne gehyt on him selfum.

4   Gehieren ða unclænan ond ða lytegan hu hit awriten is on
Salomonnes bocum ðætte se libbe getreowlice se ðe bilwitlice libbe. Ðæt is se truwa micelre orsorgnesse, biliwitnes
ond anfealdnes his weorca. Gehiraô hwæt of ðæs wisan Salomonnes muðe wæs gecueden: he cuæð ðæt ðæs Halgan
Gæstes lar wille fleon leasunga. Gehiraô eac ðætte ðæræfter
awriten is ðætte he hæbbe his geðeaht ond his sundorspræce
mid ðæm bilwitum ond mid ðæm anfealdum. Ðonne spricð
God to ðæm menn, ðonne he onlieht ðæt mennisce mod
mid his agenre andweardnesse, ond him his dieglan ðing
geopenað. Ðonne is eac gecueden ðætte God sprece to
ðæm bilwitum, ðonne he mid ðæm uplicum ond mid ðæm
dieglum ðingum hira mod onlieht mid ðæm sciman his giefe
ond his fandunga ond eac his tiehtinge—ðæt beoð ðonne
ealles suiðusð ða mod ða ðe nan sceadu ne geðiestrað ðære
twiefaldnesse. Ac ðæt is ðeah syndrig yfel twiefaldra monna
ðætte, ðonne ðonne hie oðre menn mid hira lote bismriað,
ðonne gielpað hie ond fægeniað ðæs, suelce hi sien micle
wærran ond wisran ðonne hie, forðæm ðe hie ne geðenceað
ða ðearlan edlean, ac fægniað irmingas hiera agnes dysiges
ond hearmes. Gehiren eac ða ilcan mid hwelcum ymbeðonce
godcundes onwaldes hie ðreade Soffonias se witga, ða he
cuæð, "Giet cymð se micla ond se mæra ond se egeslica
Godes dæg; se dæg bið irres dæg ond ðiestra dæg ond mistes
ond gebreces ond biemena dæg ond gedynes ofer ealla truma
ceastra ond ofer ealle hea hwammas." Hwæt getacniað

heart of a person of no account, since the malevolent mind wraps itself doubly within itself, and the duplicity of evil intent folds itself double within itself and hides itself in the gloom with excuses, just as the hedgehog hides itself within itself.

Let the impure and the devious hear how it is written in the books of Solomon that whoever lives honestly lives innocently. Innocence and simplicity of conduct are an assurance of great security. Listen to what was said by the mouth of the wise Solomon: he said that the doctrine of the Holy Spirit will flee deceptions. Listen also to what is written afterward, that he has his counsel and his private converse with the innocent and with the simple. God speaks to a person when he illuminates the human mind with his own presence and reveals to it his mysterious ways. Then it is also said that God speaks to the innocent when, by means of supernal and ineffable ways, he illuminates their minds with the brilliance of his grace and his trials, and also his persuasion—that is, most of all, then, those minds that no shadow of duplicity makes dim. But it is an especial wrong of duplicitous people that whenever they make fools of other people with their dishonesty, they crow and revel in it, as if they were much cannier and wiser than they, since they do not consider the grievous reprisal, but the wretches revel in their own folly and ruin. Let those same hear with what reproach of divine reflection the prophet Zephaniah excoriated them when he said, "Yet to come is the great and the momentous and the terrible day of God; that day will be a day of anger and a day of gloom, and a day of fog and of tumult and of trumpets and of outcry over all fortified cities and over all lofty corners." What, then, do the fortified

ðonne ða truman ceastra butan hwurfulu mod, getrymedu ond ymbtrymedu mid lytelicre ladunge, ðæt him ne magon to cuman ða speru ðære soðfæsðnesse—ðæt sindon haligra gewrita manunga? Wið ða speru ðære soðfæstnesse hie hie scildað, ðonne hi mon tælan wile ond arasian for hira unðeawum. Hwæt getacniað ðonne ða hean hwammas buton unclænu ond twiefeald mod? Forðæm ælc wag bið gebieged twiefeald on ðæm heale. Sua bið ðæs monnes heorte: ðonne he ða bilewitnesse ond ða anfealdnesse flihð, he gefielt his mod mid wore ond mid unnytre twiefealdnesse, ond eac ðætte wierse bið, he hine ahefð on his geðohte on gielp ond on ofermetto for ðæm wærscipe his agenre scylde, ond deð his agenne unðeaw him to weorðscipe. Ðonne cymð se Dryhtnes Domes Dæg ond wrace dæg ofer ða truman ceastra ond ofer ða hean hwammas, ðonne ðæt ierre ðæs ytemestan domes ða menniscan heortan towyrpð, ða ðe nu sindon betynede ond getrymede mid lytelicum ladungum wið ða soðfæsðnesse, ond arafað ðæt cliwen ðære twifaldan heortan. Ðonne feallað ða truman ceastra, ðonne ða mod ðe Dryhtne ungeferu sint weorðað gesciende. Ðonne feallað ða hean hwammas, ðonne ða heortan ðe hie ahebbað for ðære tuiefealdnesse ðæs unryhtan wærscipes ðurh ryhtlicne cuide ond dom weorðað ofdune aworpne.

BOOK THREE

cities signify but fickle minds, buttressed and battlemented
with devious excuses, so that the javelins of truth—that is,
the admonitions of holy writings—cannot reach them?
They shield themselves from the javelins of truth when one
intends to scold and reprove them for their vices. What,
then, do the lofty corners signify but impure and duplicitous
minds? For every wall is bent double at the corner. So is that
person's heart: when he shuns innocence and simplicity, he
enfolds his mind with wrongful and unavailing insincerity,
and also, what is worse, he exalts himself in his own opinion
in self-aggrandizement and pride for the canniness of his
own trespass, and turns his own vice to a mark of esteem for
him. There will arrive the Lord's Day of Judgment and day
of retribution over the fortified cities and over the lofty corners when the fury of the endmost judgment will overthrow
human hearts, which are now walled up and armed with devious excuses against truth, and will unravel the skein of the
duplicitous heart. The fortified cities will fall when those
minds that are closed to the Lord will be abased. The lofty
corners will tumble when those hearts that pride themselves
for insincerity and unrighteous cunning will be cast down
through just pronouncement and doom.

Chapter 36

XXXVI. Ðætte on oþre wisan sint to manienne ða
halan, on oðre ða unhalan.

On oðre wisan sint to manianne ða truman, on oðre ða
untruman. Ða truman sint to manianne ðæt hie gewilnigen
mid ðæs licuman trumnesse ðæt him ne losige sio hælo ðæs
modes, ðy læs him ðy wirs sie, gif hie ða trumnesse ðære
Godes giefe him to unnyte gehweorfað, ond ðy læs hie
siððan geearnigen sua micle hefigre wite sua hie nu egeleas-
licor ond unnytlicor brucað ðære mildheortlican Godes
giefe. Forðon sint to manianne ða halan ðæt hie ne forhycgen ðæt hie her on worulde on ðære hwilendlican hælo him
geearnigen ða ecan hælo. Ymb ða hwilendlican tida *sanctus*
Paulus spræc, ða he cuæð, "Nu is hiersumnesse tima ond nu
sint hælnesse dagas." Eac sint to manianne ða halan ðæt hie
Gode wilnigen to licianne ðe hwile ðe hie mægen, ðy læs hie
eft ne mægen, ðonne hie willen. Forðon wæs gesprecen ðurh
ðone wisan Salomonn bi ðæm wisdome ðæt se wisdom wille
sona fleon ðone ðe hine fliehð, ðonne he hine ful oft ær to
him cleopað, ond he forsæcð ðæt he him to cume. Ac eft,
ðonne he ðone wisdom habban wolde, ond his wilnað, ðonne
cuið se wisdom to him, "Ic eow cleopode ær to me, ac ge me
noldon æt cuman; ic ræhte mine hond to eow, nolde iower
nan to locian; ac ge forsawon eall min geðeaht, ond leton
eow to giemeleste, ðonne ic eow cidde. Hwæt sceal ic ðonne
buton hliehchan ðæs, ðonne ge to lose weorðað, ond habban

Chapter 36

36. That the fit are to be guided in one fashion, the infirm in another.

In one fashion are the healthy to be instructed, in another the unhealthy. The healthy are to be advised to desire in bodily health for soundness of mind not to desert them, to prevent worse from happening to them if they render the soundness of God's gift useless to themselves, and so that they not subsequently earn so much heavier punishment in proportion as they now the more casually and the more un-productively enjoy the gift of our benevolent God. There-fore, the hale are to be warned not to disdain to earn eternal well-being here in their temporal well-being in the world. About these fleeting hours Saint Paul spoke when he said, "Now is the time of obedience, and now are the days of sal-vation." The hale are also to be exhorted to desire to please God while they are able, since in turn they may be unable when they so desire. For that reason, it was said about wis-dom through the wise Solomon that wisdom will at once desert whoever deserts it, when it has already called out to him again and again, and he refuses to come to it. But, to the contrary, when he would like to have wisdom, and desires it, wisdom will say to him, "I called you to me formerly, but you were unwilling to come; I extended my hand to you, and none of you was willing to look at it, but you scorned all my counsel and abandoned yourselves to indifference when I chided you. What ought I to do then but to laugh at it when

me ðæt to gamene, ðonne eow ðæt yfel on becymð ðæt ge eow ær ondredon?" Ond eac cuið se wisdom eft, "Ðonne hie to me clipiað, ðonne nylle ic hie gehieran. On uhtan hie arisað, ond me seceað, ac hi me ne findað." Ac ðonne se mon his lichoman hælo forsihð, ðonne ðonne he wel trum bið to wyrceanne ðæt he ðonne wile, ðonne ðonne him eft sio hæl losað, ðonne gefred he æresð hwelc heo to habbanne wæs ða hwile ðe he hi hæfde, ond wilnað hire to late ond on untiman, ðonne he ær nolde hie gehealdan, ða ða he hi hæfde.

2   Forðæm eft suiðe ryhtlice Salomonn cuæð, "Ne læt ðu to ælðiodigum ðinne weorðscipe, ne on ðæs wælhreowan hond ðin gear, ðy læs fremde menn weorðen gefylled of ðinum gesuince, ond ðin mægen sie on oðres monnes gewealdum, ond ðu ðonne sargige forðæm on lasð, ðonne ðin lichoma beo to lore gedon, ond ðin flæsc gebrosnod." Hwa is ðonne from us fremde butan ða awiergdan gæstas, ða ðe from ðæs hefencundan Fæder eðle adrifene sindon? Oððe hwæt is ure weorðscipe on ðissum eorðlicum lichoman buton ðæt we sint gesceapene æfter ðære biesene ures scippendes? Ond hwæt is elles se wælhreowa buton ða aworpnan englas, ðe hie selfe mid hiera ofermettum on deaðes wite gebrohton? Ond on ðone ilcan deað hie wilniað eal moncynn to forspananne ond to forlædanne. Hwæt tacnað ðonne ðæt word elles ðæt mon ne selle his weorðscipe fremdum menn buton ðætte se ðe to Godes bisene gesceapen is, ðonne he ða tid his lifes on gewil ðara awiergdena gæsta gehwierfð? Ond his gear geseleð wælhreowum, se se ðe in yfelra ond wiðerweardra onwald forlæt ða hwile his lifes.

you go to ruin, and to have it as my sport when the ill that you had dreaded happens to you?" And again wisdom will say, "When they call out to me, I will be unwilling to hear them. They will rise in the early hours and look for me, but they will not find me." But when someone disregards his body's health while he is able-bodied enough to do what he then pleases, when at length his health forsakes him, then for the first time he will understand what it was to have it while he had it, and he will desire it too late and in untimely fashion, whereas earlier he did not care to maintain it while he had it.

For this reason again Solomon very justly said, "Do not 2 surrender your worthiness to strangers, nor let your years be captive to one without mercy, lest outsiders be maintained by your labor, and your strength be in the power of someone else, and you then groan for it at the last, when your body is brought to ruin and your flesh decayed." Who, then, are strangers to us but the condemned spirits that were driven out of the homeland of the sublime Father? Or what is our worthiness in this earthly body but that we are formed in the image of our creator? And what else is the one without mercy but the outcast angels, who led themselves into death's torment by their overweening pride? And it is their purpose to seduce and betray all humankind to that same death. Then what else does that phrase refer to, that one ought not to surrender his worthiness to strangers, but to one who is created in God's image when he puts the hours of his living at the disposal of accursed spirits? And he surrenders his years to the merciless who cedes the term of his life to the power of the evil and the injurious.

3   Ond eac cuæð Salomonn ðæt fremde ne scolden beon gefyllede ures mægenes, ond ure gesuinc ne scolde beon on
oðres monnes anwalde. Sua hwa ðonne sua on ðisse worulde
hæfð fulle hæle his lichoman, ond nyle wisdomes ond
cræftes on his mode tiligan, ac suinceð on ðæn ðæt he leornige unðeawas ond fremme, ne fylð se no his agen hus godra
cræfta, ac fremdra hus he fylð, ðæt sint unclæne gæstas.
Wiotodlice ða ðe hira lif on firenluste ond on ofermodnesse
geendigað, ne gefyllað hie godra rim, ac awiergedra gæsta.
Ðonne is æfter ðæm gecueden ðæt he sargige æt niehstan,
ðonne his lichoma ond his flæsc sie gebrosnod, forðæm oft
sio hælo ðæs lichoman on unðeawas wierð gecierred, ac
ðonne he ðære hælo benumen wierð mid monigfaldum sare
ðæs modes ond ðæs flæsces, se lichoma ðonne wierð gedrefed, forðæm sio saul, ðonne hio hire unðonces gebædd
wierð ðæt yfel to forlætanne ðæt hio ær longe on woh hire
agnes ðonces gedyde, secð ðonne ða forlorenan hælo, ond
wilnað ðære, suelce he ðonne wel ond nytwyrðlice libban
wolde, gif he forð moste. Murcnað ðonne forðy ðæt he Gode
nolde ðiowigan ða hwile ðe he meahte, forðon he ðonne
ðone demm his giemelieste mid nanum gesuince gebetan ne
mæg, buton him ðurh his hreowsung ond ðurh Godes miltse
geholpen weorðe. Forðæm cuæð se sealmscop, "Ðonne God
hie slog, ðonne sohton hie hine."

4   Ongean ðæt sint to manianne ða mettruman ðæt hie
ongieten ond gefreden ðæt hie sua micle ma beoð Godes
bearn, ond he hie sua micle ma lufað sua he hie suiður manað
ond suingð, forðæm, gif he ðæm gehiersuman mannum
næfde geteohchad his eðel to sellanne, hwie wolde he hie
mid ænegum ungetæsum læran? Forðæm cuæð Dryhten to
Iohanne ðam godspellere ðurh his engel; he cuæð, "Ic ðreage

And also Solomon said that outsiders should not be main- 3
tained by our strength, and our labor should not be under
the control of another. Then whoever in this world has full
health of body and is unwilling to cultivate wisdom and virtue in his mind, and labors at acquiring and indulging vices,
does not fill his own house with good practices but fills the
houses of strangers, which are impure spirits. Certainly,
those who end their life in self-gratification and in pride do
not fill the ranks of the good but of accursed spirits. Then
after that it is said that he will groan at last, when his body
and his flesh are decayed, because often the body's health is
directed to bad habits, but when he is deprived of health,
with multiple pains of mind and flesh, the body will be afflicted because the soul, when it is compelled against its will
to desist from what for long it had done amiss by its own
volition, will search for that lost health, and desire it, as if
the person were then willing to live well and productively, if
he should be allowed to endure. He will therefore rue it that
he was unwilling to serve God while he could, since then he
cannot remedy the damage of his negligence by any sort of
labor, unless he can help himself through his contrition and
through God's mercy. For that reason the psalmist said,
"When God struck them, then they turned to him."

In contrast to that, the frail are to be advised to under- 4
stand and recognize that they are so much more God's children, and he loves them so much more, the more he chastises and disciplines them, for if he had not determined to
give his homeland to the obedient, why would he instruct
them with any hardships? Therefore, the Lord spoke to
John the Evangelist through his angel, saying, "I rebuke and

ond suinge ða ðe ic lufige." Forðæm eac cuæð Salomonn, "Sunu min, ne agiemeleasa ðu Godes suingan, ne ðu ne beo werig for his ðreaunge, forðæm ðe God lufað ðone ðe he ðreað, ond suingeð ælc bearn ðe he underfon wile." Be ðam ilcan se salmscop cuæð, "Suiðe monigfalde sint ryhtwisra monna earfoðu." Be ðæm eac se eadega Iob cwæð on his earfeðum, ond geomriende cliopode to Dryhtne, ond cuæð, "Gif ic ryhtwis wæs, ne ahof ic me no forðy, ond ðeah ic eom gefylled mid broce ond mid iermðum." Eac is to cyðanne ðæm mettrumum, gif hie willen geliefan ðætte Godes rice hiera sie, ðæt hie ðonne her on worulde ðoligen earfeðu ðæm timum ðe hie ðyrfen, sua sua mon sceal on elðiode. Be ðys ilcan is gecueden on Kyninga bocum, sua sua hit ge-worden wæs, ond eac us to bisene: hit is gecueden ðætte ða stanas on ðæm mæran temple Salomonnes wæron sua wel gefegede ond sua emne gesnidene ond gesmeðde, ær hie mon to ðæm stede brohte ðe hie on standan scoldon, ðætte hie mon eft siððan on ðære halgan stowe sua tosomne ge-sette ðæt ðær nan monn ne gehierde ne æxe hlem ne bietles sueg. Ðæt ðonne tacnað us ðætte we scylen beon on ðisse ælðeodignesse utane beheawene mid suingellan, to ðæm ðæt we eft sien geteald ond gefeged to ðæm gefogstanum on ðære Godes ceastre butan ðæm hiewete ælcre suingean, ðætte sua hwæt sua nu on us unnytes sie, ðætte ðæt aceorfe sio suingelle from us, sua ðætte siððan an sibb Godes lufe butan ælcum ungerade us suiðe fæste gebinde ond gefege tosomne.

5   Ðonne sint eac to manianne ða unhalan ðæt hie geðencen mid hu monigfaldum ungetæsum ond mid hu heardum bro-cum us swingað ond ðreagað ure worldcunde fædras ond hlafordas, forðæm ðe hie wilniað ðæt we him geðwære sien,

discipline those I love." For that reason also Solomon said, "My son, do not make light of God's discipline, and do not weary of his reproach, for God loves whom he reprimands and punishes every child whom he intends to receive." About the same the psalmist said, "Manifold are the tribulations of righteous people." About this also the blessed Job spoke in his trials, and making lamentations cried out to God, and said, "If I was righteous, I did not exult in that, and yet I am filled with tribulation and miseries." It is also to be made plain to the ailing, if they are willing to believe that the kingdom of God will be theirs, that they then shall suffer trials here in the world for the necessary length of time, just as one is obliged in exile. About this same it is narrated in the books of Kings just as it happened, and also as a parable for us: it is said that the stones in the famous temple of Solomon were so well fitted together and so evenly cut and smoothed before they were brought to the place where they were to stand that they were subsequently laid together in that holy place in such manner that neither the stroke of an ax nor the ringing of a hammer was heard there. That, then, signifies to us that in this state of exile we ought to be beaten with scourges, so that we may be accounted fit as keystones in God's citadel without the stroke of any scourge, that the scourge sever from us whatever is now useless in us, so that hereafter a single amity in love of God without any discord may bind and fit us very firmly together.

Invalids are also to be exhorted to consider with how 5 many hardships and with what rough checks our worldly fathers and masters punish and correct us because they want us to be compliant with them, and also to be worthy of their

ond eac hira irfes wierðe sien, ond hie us ðe bliðran beon
mægen. Ac hwelc wite sceal us ðonne to hefig ðyncan ðære
godcundan ðreaunga wið ðæm ðe we mægen geearnian ðone
hefonlican eðel ðe næfre to lore ne weorðeð, ond forðæm
ðæt we mægen forbugan ðæt wite ðæt næfre ne wierð geendod? Forðæm cuæð *sanctus* Paulus, "Ure flæsclican fædras
lærdon us, ond we hie ondredon; hie ðreadon us, ond we
weorðodon hie. Hu micle suiðor sculon we ðonne beon ge-
hiersume ðæm ðe ure gæsta Fæder bið wið ðæm ðæt we moten libban on ecnesse. Ure flæsclican fædras us lærdon to
ðæm ðe hira willa wæs, ac ðæt wæs to suiðe scortre hwile,
forðæm ðe ðios woruld is suiðe lænu, ac se gæsðlica Fæder,
he us lærð nytwyrðlicu ðing to underfonne, ðæt is ðæt we
geearnigen ðæt ece lif."

6   Eac sint to manianne ða mettruman ðæt hie geðencen hu
micel hælo ðæt bið ðære heortan ðæt se lichoma sie
medtrum, forðæm sio medtrymnes ðæt mod gehwierfð
gehwelces monnes hine selfne to ongietanne, ond ðæt
gode mod ðe sio hælo ful oft aweg adriefð ðæt gemynd ðære
medtrymnesse geedniewað, ðætte ðæt mod ðe ofer his mæð
bið up ahæfen gemyne of ðæm suingum ðe ðæt flæsc ðolað
to hwæm eal monncynn gesceapen is. Ðæt wære suiðe ryhte
getacnod ðurh Balaham on ðære lettinge his færeltes, gif he
mid his hiersumnesse Godes stemne ond his gebodum fullice folgian wolde, ond on his willan fore. Baloham ðonne ful
georne feran wolde ðær hine mon bæd, ac his estfulnesse
witteah se esol ðe he on uppan sæt. Ðæt wæs forðæm ðe se
assa geseah ðone engel ongean hine standan, ond him ðæs
færeltes forwiernan, ðone ðe ðæt mennisce mod geseon ne
meahte. Sua eac, ðonne ðæt flæsc bið gelett mid sumum

legacy, and so that they can be more content with us. But then what penalty of divine chastisement ought to seem too severe to us in exchange for our being able to earn the heavenly homeland that will never be lost, and in order for us to avoid that punishment that will never be ended? For this reason Saint Paul said, "Our fathers in the flesh instructed us, and we feared them; they corrected us, and we esteemed them. How much more, then, ought we to be obedient to the one who is Father of our spirits, so that we be allowed to live in eternity? Our fathers in the flesh directed us to accord with their will, but that was for an extremely short while, because this world is exceedingly transient, but the spiritual Father teaches us to take in hand worthwhile pursuits, which is that we merit eternal life."

The indisposed are also to be exhorted to consider how 6 very salutary it is for the heart that the body is ailing, because ill health prompts every person's mind to understand itself, and the good intentions that a sound constitution often drives away are renewed by the recollection of unhealth, so that the mind that is disproportionately vain may be reminded by the chastisement that the flesh suffers to what end all humankind is created. That would have been very correctly typologized by Balaam in the prevention of his journey, if in his obedience he had been willing to follow entirely the voice of God and his behests, and had traveled according to his will. Then Balaam quite conscientiously intended to travel where he was directed, but the ass on which he was seated prevented his compliance. That was because the ass saw the angel standing in front of it and thwarting its passage, which the human mind was unable to see. So also, when the flesh is constrained by a certain hardship, it

broce, hit getacnað ðæm mode for ðære suingan hwæt Godes willa bið, ðone illcan willan ðe ðæt mod hwilum ongietan ne mæg ðe ofer ðæm flæsce sitt, ond his wealdan sceolde, forðæm ðæt flæsc oft lætt ða geornfulnesse ond ðone willan ðæs ðiondan modes her on worulde. Sua mon oft lett fundigendne monnan, ond his færelt gælð, sua gælð se lichoma ðæt mod, oð ðæt he gebrocad wierð mid sumre mettrymnesse, ond ðonne ðurh ða mettrymnesse getacnað se lichoma ðæm mode ðone ungesewenan engel ðe him togenes stent, ond him wiernð his unnyttan færelta ðurh ðæs lichoman mettrymnesse. Be ðæm cwæð *sanctus* Petrus suiðe ryhtlice, "Ðæt dumbe ond ðæt gehæfte neat ðreade ðone witgan for his yfelan willan, ða hit cleopode sua sua monn, ond mid ðy gestierde ðæm witgan his unryhtre ond dyslicre wilnunga." Ðonne ðreað ðæt dumbe neat ðone unwisan monn, ðonne ðæt gebrocode flæsc gelærð ðæt upahæfene mod to ryhttre ond to nyttwyrðre eaðmodnesse. Forðæm ne meahte Balaham geearnian ða Godes giefe ðe he biddende wæs, ða he Israhela folc wirgean wolde ond for hine selfne gebiddan; forðæm he wearð untygða ðe he hwierfde his stemne nales his mod—ðæt wæs ðæt he spræc oðer, oðer ðæt he sprecan wolde.

7   Eac sint ða seocan to monianne ðæt hie ongieten hu micel Godes giefu him bið ðæs flæsces gesuinc, forðæm ðe hit ægðer ge ða gedonan synna aweg aðwiehð, ge hine eac ðara gelett ðe he don wolde, gif he meahte, forðæm ðonne he bið gesargod on ðæs lichoman wundum, ðonne gewyrceað ða wunda on ðæm gebrocodan mode hreowsunge wunda. Bi ðæm is eac awriten on Salomonnes Cuidbocum ðæt sio wund wolde halian, æfter ðæm ðe heo wyrmsde. Ðonne aflewð ðæt sar of ðære wunde mid ðy wormse, ðonne ðæt sar

signifies to the mind by that chastisement what the will of God is, the same will that at times cannot be made out by the mind, which presides over the flesh and ought to govern it, since the flesh often hinders the dedication and the will of the mind faring well in this world. As a person making an effort is often hindered and his progress retarded, so the body hampers the mind, until he is afflicted with a certain ailment, and with that ailment the body renders apparent to the mind the invisible angel that stands in front of it and prevents its ill-advised passage by the infirmity of the body. About this Saint Peter very aptly said, "The mute and captive beast scolded the prophet for his bad intention when it spoke up like a human and thereby diverted the prophet from his wrongful and foolish design." When the mute beast rebukes the unwise person, the afflicted flesh directs the presumptuous mind to just and advantageous humility. It was for that reason that Balaam could not earn the grace of God that he continually prayed for when it was his intention to curse the people of Israel and pray for himself; he was unsuccessful because he applied his voice, not his mind—that is, that he spoke one thing, wishing to speak another.

The sick are also to be exhorted to understand how great 7 a gift of God to them is the distress of the flesh, for the reasons both that it washes away sins committed and also that it forestalls those that one would be willing to commit if he could, because when he is distressed by the body's wounds, the wounds produce in the afflicted mind wounds of contrition. About this it is also said in the book of Proverbs of Solomon that the wound would heal after it suppurated. The pain flows out of the wound with the matter when the

ðære suingellan ðissa woruldbroca aðwiehð ægðer ge ða geðohtan synna ge ða gedonan of ðære saule. Eac cuæð Salomon ðætte ðæt illce beo bi ðæm wundum ðe beoð on innan ðære wambe. Ðære "wambe" nama getacnað ðæt mod, forðæm sua sua sio wamb gemielt ðone mete, sua gemielt ðæt mod mid ðære gescadwisnesse his geðeahtes his sorga. Of Salomonnes Cuidum we namon ðætte ðære "wambe" nama scolde tacnian ðæt mod, ða ða he cuæð, "Ðæs monnes lif bið Godes leohtfæt; ðæt Godes leohtfæt gindsecð ond gindlieht ealle ða diogolnesse ðære wambe"; suelce he cuæde, "Æresð he hiene onlieht mid his leohtfæte, ðonne he hiene gelieffæsð, ond eft he hine onlieht, ðonne he hiene onælð mid ðæm tapure ðæs godcundan lieges"—ðæt bið ðonne, ðonne he deð ðæt he ongiet his agne unnytte ðeawas ond geðohtas ðe wen is ðæt he ær hæfde, ðeah he hit geðencean ne meahte. Ðæt worms ðonne ðara wunda ðæt is ðæt broc ðæs lichoman, ond ðæt sar innan ðære wambe, ðæt tacnað ða sorge ðæs modes. Sio sorg ðonne aswæpð aweg ðæt yfel of ðæm mode. Ðonne we beoð butan ðæm mode on ðæm lichoman gesuencte, ðonne beo we suigende gemanode mid ðære mettrymnesse ura synna to gemunanne, forðæm ðe ðonne bið broht beforan ures modes eagan eall ðæt we ær yfeles gedydon, forðæm sua se lichoma suiður utan ðrowað, sua ðæt mod suiður innan hreowsað ðæs unnyttes ðe he ær dyde. Forðæm gelimpð ðætte ðurh ða openlican wunda ond ðurh ðæt gesewene sar ðæs lichoman bið suiðe wel aðwægen sio diegle wund ðæs modes, forðæm sio diegle wund ðære hreowsunga hælð ða scylðe ðæs won weorces.

8   Eac sint to manianne ða mettruman to ðæm ðæt hie gehealden ða strenge ðære geðylde. Him is to secgeanne ðæt hie unablinnendlice geðencen hu monig yfel ure Dryhten

pain of the scourge of these worldly afflictions washes out of the soul sins both contemplated and committed. In addition, Solomon said that the same pertains to wounds that are inside the belly. The word "belly" signifies the mind, because just as the belly digests food, the mind dissolves its woes with the discernment of its contemplation. It is from the Proverbs of Solomon that we have gathered that the word "belly" ought to signify the mind, when he said, "A person's life is God's lamp; the lamp of God penetrates and illuminates all the mysteries of the insides"; as if his plain meaning were, "First he illuminates him with his lamp when he endues him with life, and again he illuminates him when he ignites him with the taper of the divine flame"—that is, then, when he brings him to recognize the unfit morals and intentions that it is to be expected he formerly harbored, though he could not call them to mind. Then the suppuration of the wounds is affliction of the body, and the pain inside the belly signifies anguish of mind. Then this anguish sweeps evil away out of the mind. When we are, the mind aside, afflicted in body, we are tacitly exhorted by that malady to keep in mind our sins, because then there is brought before our mind's eye all of the ills that we have committed, for the more the body suffers outwardly, the more the mind inwardly repents the vanities that it formerly committed. For that reason it happens that, through the visible wounds and through the evident pain of the body, the unseen wound of the mind is cleansed, because the unseen wound of contrition heals the offense of the wrongful deed.

The ailing are also to be exhorted to maintain the virtue 8 of patience. They are to be told to consider ceaselessly how many ills our Lord and savior suffered among the very

ond ure alisend geðolode mid ðam ilcan mannum ðe he self
gesceop, ond hu fela edwites ond unnyttra worda he forbær,
ond hu manige hleorslægeas he underfeng æt ðæm ðe hine
bismredon. Se ilca se ðe ælce dæg saula gereafað of ðæs ealdan feondes honda, se ilca se ðe us ðwiehð mid ðy halwyn-
dan wætre, se na ne forbeag mid his nebbe ðara triowleasena
monna spatl, ðonne hie him on ðæt nebb spætton. Se ilca
se us gefreoð mid his forespræce from ecum witum, se ilca
suigende geðafode swingellan. Se ðe us sealde ece are betwuxn his engla geferscipe, he geðafode ðæt hine mon mid
fyste slog. Se ðe us gehæleð from ðæm stice urra synna, he
geðafode ðæt him mon sette ðyrnenne beag on ðæt heafud.
Se ðe us oferdrencð mid ðæs ecan lifes liðe, he gefandode
geallan biternesse, ða hine ðyrstte. Se ðe for us gebæd to his
Fæder, ðeah he him emnmiehtig sie on his godhade, ða ða
him mon on bismer to gebæd, ða swugode he. Se se ðe deadum monnum lif gearuwað, ond he self lif is, he becom to
deaðe. For hwy ðonne sceal ænigum menn ðyncan to reðe
oððe to unieðe ðæt he Godes suingellan geðafige for his
yfelum dædum, nu God self sua fela yfeles geðafode, sua sua
we ær cuædon, for monncynne? Hwa sceal ðonne, ðara
ðe hal ond good andgiet hæbbe, Gode unðoncfull beon,
forðæm, ðeah he hine for his synnum suinge, nu se ne for
butan suingellan of ðys middangearde se ðe butan ælcre
synne wæs ond giet is?

people he himself created, and how much scorn and how many insolent words he bore, and how many blows to the cheek he received from those who mocked him. The same one who every day wrests souls from the hands of the ancient adversary, the same one who refreshes us with restorative water, never turned his face from the spittle of the faithless when they spat in his face. The same one who liberates us from eternal torment by his intercession endured the scourge in silence. The same who granted us eternal favor in the company of his angels suffered himself to be beaten with a fist. The one who heals us from the stab wound of our sins abided having a crown of thorns set on his head. The one who intoxicates us with the liquor of eternal life tasted the bitterness of gall when he thirsted. The one who prayed to his Father for us, though he is equipotent in his godhead, maintained silence when they prayed to him in mockery. The one who readies life for the dead, and is himself life, encountered death. Then why ought it seem to anyone too harsh or too difficult to endure God's scourge for his ill deeds, since God himself suffered so many ills, as we have said, for humankind? Then who of those having sound and virtuous understanding ought to be ungrateful to God, for, though God chastises him for his sins, even he who was and ever is without any sin has not now departed this earth without a beating?

Chapter 37

XXXVII. Ðætte on oðre wisan sint to manienne ða ðe him ondrædað Godes swingellan oððe monna, ond forðy forlætað ðæt hie yfel ne doð; on oðre wisan ða ðe beoð swa aheardode on unryhtwisnesse ðæt hi mon ne mæg mid nanre ðreaunge geðreatian.

On oðre wisan sint to monianne ða ðe him suingellan ondrædað, ond forðæm unsceaðfullice libbað; ond on oðre wisan sint to manianne ða ðe on hiera unryhtwisnessum sua aheardode beoð ðæt hie mon mid nanre swingellan gebetan ne mæg. Ðæm is to cyðanne ðe him swingellan ondrædað ðæt hie ðissa eorðlicena goda to suiðe ne gietsien, ðeah hie geseon ðæt ða yfelan hie hæbben ongemong him, forðæm hie sint ægðrum gemæne ge yfelum monnum ge godum; ond ne fleon eac ðis andwearde yfel, suelce hie hit adriogan ne mægen, forðon ðe hit oft gode menn her on worlde dreogað. Eac hie sint to monianne, gif hie geornlice wilnigen ðæt him yfel ðing losie, ðonne beo him suiðe egefull ðæt ece wite— nalles ðeah sua egeful ðæt hie ealneg ðurhwunigen on ðæm ege, ac mid ðam fostre ðære Godes lufan hie sculon up arisan ond weaxan a ma ond ma to lufigeanne ða godcundan weorc. Forðæm Iohannis se godspellere cwæð on his ærendgewrite; he cwæð, "Sio fulfremede Godes lufu adrifeð aweg ðone ege." Ond eft cwæð *sanctus* Paulus, "Ne underfengon ge no ðone Gast æt ðæm fulluhte to ðeowigeanne for ege, ac ge hine underfengon to ðæm ðæt ge Gode geagenudu bearn beon scielen, forðy we cliepiað to Gode, ond cweðað, 'Fæder,

Chapter 37

37. That those are to be guided in one fashion who fear the lash of God or of men, and thus they refrain from doing evil; in another fashion those who are so inured to unrighteousness that they cannot be intimidated by any reproof.

In one fashion are to be instructed those who fear the scourge and therefore live inoffensively; in another fashion are to be instructed those who are so inured to their unrighteousness that no scourge can amend them. Those who fear punishment are to be informed not to long excessively for earthly goods, though they see that the bad have them among them, since they are common to both bad people and good; and also let them not evade present ills, as if they cannot endure them, since good people here in the world often suffer them. They are also to be warned that, if they desire in earnest to liberate themselves from evil things, they should be very much in dread of eternal torment—not, though, so much in dread that they remain ever in terror, but with the nurture of God's love they ought to rise up and grow ever more and more to love godly works. Therefore, John the Evangelist spoke in his letter and said, "The perfect love of God banishes fear." And in turn Saint Paul said, "You did not receive the Spirit at baptism to serve out of fear, but you received it so that you might be adopted children to God, wherefore we call to God and say, 'Father, Father.'"

Fæder.'" Forðæm cwið eft eac se ilca lariow, "Ðær se Dryhtnes gast is, ðær is freodoom." Gif ðonne hwelc mon forbireð his synna for ðæm ege anum ðæs wites, ðonne nafað ðæs ondrædendan monnes mod nanne gastes freodom, forðæm, gif he hit for ðæs wites ege ne forlete, butan tweon he fulfremede ða synne. Ðonne nat ðæt mod ðæt him bið freodom forgiefen, ðonne hit bið gebunden mid ðæs ðeowutes ege. Ðeah monn nu good onginne for sumes wites ege, hit mon sceal ðeah geendigean for sumes godes lufum. Se ðe for ðæm anum god deð ðæt he sumre ðreaunge yfel him ondrætt, se wilnað ðætte nan ðing ne sie ðe he him on-drædan ðyrfe, ðæt he ðy orsorglicor dyrre don unnyttlicu ðing ond unalifedu. Ðonne bið suiðe sweotol ðætte him ðonne losað beforan Gode his ryhtwisnes, ðonne he ðurh his agene geornfulnesse gesyngað unniedenga, ðonne bið suiðe sueotul ðæt he ðæt good na ne dyde ðær he hit for ðæm ege dorste forlætan.

2   Ongean ðæt ðonne sint to monianne ða menn ðe suingel-lan ne magon forwiernan ne na gelettan hiera unryhtwis-nesse. Hie beoð to ðreageanne ond to swinganne mid swa micle maran wite sua hie ungefredelicor beoð aheardode on hiera unðeawum. Oft eac ða swelcan monn sceal forsion mid eallum forsewennessum, ond unweorðian mid ælcre unweorðnesse, forðæm ðætte sio forsewennes him ege ond ondrysnu on gebringe, ond eft æfter ðæm ðæt hiene sio godcunde manung on wege gebringe, ond hine to hyhte ge-hwierfe. Ðonne sint eac ðæm ilcan monnum suiðe ðearllice to recceanne ða godcundan cwidas, ðæt hie bi ðam on-cnawæn, ðonne hie geðencen ðone ecean dom, to hwæm hiera agen wise wirð. Eac hie sculon gehieran ðæt on him

Therefore the same teacher again also says, "Where the spirit of the Lord is, there is liberty." If, then, anyone refrains from sin solely for fear of chastisement, the mind of one who thus fears has no spiritual free will, because if he did not shun it for fear of punishment, without a doubt he would commit the sin. Thus, the mind is not aware that freedom is granted it when it is checked by servile fear. Even if one were now at the beginning to do good for fear of some retribution, one ought nonetheless to complete it for love of some good. Whoever does good only because he fears the bad consequence of a certain retribution desires that there be nothing he need fear, so that he may venture with less apprehension to do detrimental and impermissible things. Then it is quite plain that he is deprived of his innocence before God, for seeing as he will sin of his own free will if unrestrained, it is quite obvious that he would never have done that good if, despite the fear, he might have dared neglect it.

Otherwise are to be warned those people who cannot be 2 restrained or hindered from their immorality by the scourge. They are to be upbraided and chastised with such greater severity in proportion as they are more callously inured to their vices. Additionally, they ought often to be despised with all scorn and demeaned with all contempt, to the end that scorn induce in them fear and deference, and in turn after that religious admonishment set them on their way and direct them toward hope. Then these same people are to have religious precepts recited to them quite forcefully, that they may thereby understand, when they contemplate everlasting damnation, what their own case will come to. They ought in addition to hear that there is fulfilled in them

bið gefylled Salomonnes cwide ðe he cwæð; he cwæð, "Ðeah ðu portige ðone dysegan on pilan, swa mon corn deð mid piilstæfe, ne meaht ðu his dysi him from adrifan." Ðæt ilce sarette se witga, ða ða he cwæð, "Ðu hie tobræce, ond ðeah hie noldon underfon ðine lare." Eft bi ðæm ilcan cwæð Dryhten, "Ic ofslog ðis folc, ond to forlore gedyde, ond hie hie ðeah noldon onwendan from hiera woom wegum"—ðæt is, from hiera yfelum weorcum. Bi ðæm ilcan eft cwæð se witga, "Ðis folc nis no gewend to ðæm ðe hie swingð." Ymb ðæt ilce sargode se witga, sua sua god lareow deð, ðonne he his gingran suingð, gif hit him nauht ne forstent. Be ðæm cwæð se witga, "We lacnodon Babylon, ond hio ðeah ne wearð gehæled." Ðonne bið Babylon gelacnad, nales ðeah fullice gehæled, ðonne ðæs monnes mod for his unryhtum willan ond for his won weorcum gehierð sceamlice ðreaunga, ond sceandlice suingellan underfehð, ond ðeahhwæðre ofer-hygð ðæt he gecierre to bettran.

3   Ðæt ilce eac Dryhten oðwat Israhela folce, ða hie wæron gehergeode ond of hiera earde alædde, ond swaðeah noldon gesuican hiera yfelena weorca, ne hie noldon awendan of hiera won wegum; ða cwæð Dryhten, "Ðiss Israhela folc is geworden nu me to sindrum ond to are ond to tine ond to iserne ond to leade inne on minum ofne"; suelce he openlice cwæde, "Ic hie wolde geclænsian mid ðæm gesode ðæs broces, ond wolde ðæt hie wurden to golde ond to seolufre, ac hie wurdon gehwierfde inne on ðam ofne to are ond to tine ond to isene ond to leade, forðæm ðe hie noldon on ðæm gesuincium hie selfe gecirran to nyttum ðingum, ac ðurhwunedon on hiera unðeawum." Witodlice ðæt ar, ðonne hit mon slihð, hit bið hludre ðonne ænig oðer ondweorc. Sua bið ðæm ðe suiðe gnornað on ðære godcundan suingellan;

the proverb that Solomon spoke when he said, "Though you grind a fool in a mortar, as grain is ground with a pestle, you cannot rid him of his folly." The prophet complained about the same when he said, "You crushed them, and yet they were unwilling to accept your guidance." Again about this very matter the Lord said, "I slaughtered this nation and brought them to destruction, and yet they would not turn from their crooked ways"—that is, from their evil doings. About the same the prophet said, "This nation has not reverted to the one who scourges them." The prophet lamented over this very thing, as a good teacher does when he beats his pupil, if it does not at all improve him. About this the prophet said, "We were physician to Babylon, and yet it was not healed." Babylon is tended but not fully healed when, for its illicit desire and for its perverse deeds, a person's mind hears shameful rebuke and undergoes demeaning punishment, and yet holds it in contempt to be reformed.

For the same cause the Lord upbraided the people of Israel when they were plundered and led out of their land, and yet were unwilling to desist from their bad conduct, and they would not turn from their crooked ways; then the Lord said, "This nation of Israel has become dross to me, and copper and tin and iron and lead in my furnace"; as if his plain meaning were, "I intended to refine them with the smelting of tribulation and wanted to turn them to gold and silver, but inside the furnace they turned to copper and to tin and to iron and to lead, because in that labor they were unwilling to turn themselves to worthwhile pursuits, but they persisted in their vices." Certainly bronze, when it is struck, is louder than any other substance. So it is for one who complains much at divine chastisement: in the midst of

3

he bið on middum ðæm ofne gecirred to are. Ðæt tin ðonne, ðonne hit mon mid sumum cræfte gemengð, ond to tine gewyrcð, ðonne bið hit swiðe leaslice on siolufres hiewe. Sua hwa ðonne sua licet on ðære swingellan, he bið ðæm tine gelic inne on ðæm ofne. Se bið ðonne ðæm isene gelic inne on ðæm ofne, se ðe for ðære suingellan nyle his ðweorscipe forlætan, ac ofan his nihstan his lifes. Ðæt lead ðonne is hefigre ðonne ænig oðer andweorc. Forðy bið inne on ðæm ofne geworden to leade se se ðe sua bið geðrysced mid ðære hefignesse his synna ðæt he furðum on ðæm broce nyle alætan his geornfulnesse ond ðas eorðlican wilnunga. Bi ðæm ilcan is eft awriten, "Ðær wæs suiðe suiðlic gesuinc, ond ðær wæs micel swat agoten, ond ðeah ne meahte monn him of animan ðone miclan rust, ne furðum mid fyre ne meahte hiene mon aweg adon." He us stiereð mid fyres broce, forðæm ðe he wolde from us adon ðone rust urra unðeawa, ac we ðeah for ðæm broce ðæs fyres nyllað alætan from us ðæt rust ðara unnyttra weorca, ðonne we on ðære suingellan nyllað gebetan ure unðeawas. Be ðæm cwæð eft se witga, "Idel wæs se blawere, forðon hiera awiergdan weorc ne wurdon from him asyndred."

4   Eac is to witanne ðætte oft ðæm bið gestiered mid manðwærlicre manunga, ðæm ðe monn mid heardre suingellan gecirran ne mæg, ond ða ðe ne magon ðrouunga gestieran yfelra weorca, eft hie hie forlætað for liðelicre olicunga, sua sua ða seocan, ða ðe mon oft ne mæg gelacnian mid ðæm drencium strangra wyrta gemanges, ða ful oft beoð mid wlacum watre gelacnode, ond on ðære ilcan hælo gebrohte ðe hie ær hæfdon. Sua beoð eac ful oft ða wunda mid ele gehælda, ða ðe mon mid gesnide gebetan ne meahte. Ond eac se hearda stan, se ðe aðamans hatte, ðone mon mid

the furnace he is turned to copper. Tin, then, when it is alloyed by a certain method and worked to pewter, is very deceptively of the appearance of silver. Then whoever plays the hypocrite under castigation is like tin in the furnace. He is like iron inside the furnace who refuses under punishment to discontinue his perversity but grudges his neighbor his life. Lead is heavier than any other substance. Therefore, inside the furnace he is reduced to lead who is so encumbered by the weight of his sins that even under blows he refuses to let go of his compulsion and these earthly desires. About such it is again written, "There was very strenuous labor, and there was much sweat shed, and yet the heavy rust could not be removed from him, nor even with fire could it be purged." He corrects us with fire's tribulation because he would purge from us the rust of our vices, but still, notwithstanding the tribulation of fire, we are unwilling to put away from us the rust of vain doings when under castigation we are unwilling to mend our wrongful ways. About that the prophet again said, "The bellows worked in vain because their damnable deeds were not sundered from them."

It is also to be recognized that those are often made trac- 4 table with gentle prodding who cannot be turned around with hard castigation, and those whom suffering cannot dissuade from ill doings likewise will abandon them for pleasant persuasion, just as the sick who cannot be treated with a drink made of a mixture of strong herbs quite often are treated with tepid water and are brought to the same state of health that they formerly held. So, too, wounds which cannot be improved with surgery are quite often healed with ointment. And, likewise, the hard stone called ada-

nane isene ceorfan ne mæg, gif his mon onhrinð mid buccan blode, he hnescað ongean ðæt liðe blod to ðæm suiðe ðæt hine se cræftega wyrcean mæg to ðæm ðe he wile.

Chapter 38

XXXVIII. Ðætte on oðre wisan sint to manienne ða ðe to swiðe swige beoð, on oðre wisan ða ðe willað to fela idles ond unnyttes gespræcan.

On oðre wisan sint to monianne ða suiðe suigean, on oðre wisan ða ðe beoð aidlode on oferspræce. Ða suiðe suigean mon sceal læran ðætte hie, ðonne ðonne hie sumne unðeaw unwærlice fleoð, ðæt hie ne sien to wyrsan gecirde, ond ðæron befealdne, sua him oft gebyreð, ðonne hie hiora tungan ungemetlice gemidliað ðæt hie beoð micle hefiglicor gedrefde on hiera heortan ðonne ða oferspræcean; forðæm for ðære suigean hiora geðohtas beoð aweallene on hiora mode, forðæm hie hie selfe nidað to healdonne ungemetlice swigean, ond forðæm beoð suiðe forðrycte. Forðæm gebyreð oft ðæt hie beoð sua micle ungestæððelicor toflowene on hiera mode sua hie wenað ðæt hie stilran ond orsorgran beon mægen for hiera suigean. Ac forðæm ðe mon ne mæg utane on him ongietan for hiera suigean hwæt mon tæle, hie

mant, which cannot be cut with any iron, if touched with
billy goat's blood will soften in contact with that mild blood
to such an extent that the craftsman can make of it what
he will.

Chapter 38

38. That those are to be guided in one fashion who are extremely quiet, in another fashion those who talk too much prattle and rubbish.

In one fashion are to be counseled those who are extremely quiet, in another fashion those who waste time with
chatter. The very silent ought to be instructed when they
avoid a certain vice without due circumspection not to turn
to something worse and be implicated in it, since it often
happens to them when they curb their tongue immoderately that they are much more profoundly made anxious in
their heart than the talkative; for their thoughts seethe in
their mind on account of their inexpressiveness, seeing as
they compel themselves to keep inordinately quiet and are
on that account badly distressed. For that reason, it frequently happens that they are so much the more volatile and
distracted in their mind in proportion as they suppose they
can be calmer and more composed for their silence. But because there cannot plainly be recognized in them something
to criticize, on account of their muteness, often they are

beoð innane oft ahafene on ofermettum, swa ðæt hie ða felasprecan forseoð, ond hie for nauht doð, ond ne ongietað na hu suiðe hie onlucað hiera mod mid ðæm unðeawe ofermetta, ðeah hie ðæs lichoman muð belucen; ðeah sio tunge eaðmodlice licge, ðæt mod bið suiðe up ahafen, ond sua micle freolicor he tælð on his ingeðonce ealle oðre menn sua he læs ongitt his agene uncysta.

2   Eac sint to manianne ða suiðe suigean, ðæt hie geornlice tiligen to wietanne ðæt him nis na ðæs anes ðearf to ðenceanne hwelce hie hie selfe utane eowien mannum, ac him is micle mare ðearf ðæt hie geðencen hwelce hi hie innan geeowigen Gode, ond ðæt hi swiðor him ondræden for hiera geðohtum ðone diglan deman, ðe hie ealle wat, ðonne hie him ondræden wið hiera wordum ond dædum hiera geferena tælinge. Hit is awriten on Salomonnes Cwidum, "Sunu min, ongiet minne wisdom ond minne wærscipe, ond behald ðin eagean ond ðin earan to ðæm ðætte ðu mæge ðin geðoht gehealdan." Forðæm nan wuht nis on us unstilre ond ungestæððigre ðonne ðæt mod, forðæm hit gewitt sua oft fram us sua us unnytte geðohtas to cumað, ond æfter ælcum ðara toflewð. Be ðæm cwæð se psalmsceop, "Min mod ond min wisdom me forlet." Ond eft he gehwearf to him selfum, ond wearð on his agenum gewitte, ond cwæð, "Ðin ðeow hæfð nu funden his wisdom, ðæt is ðæt he hine gebidde to ðe." Forðæm, ðonne monn his mod gehæft, ðæt ðæt hit ær gewunode to fleonne hit gemet.

3   Oft eac ða suiðe suigean, ðonne hie monige unnytte geðohtas innan habbað, ðonne weorðað hie him to ðy maran sare innan, gif hie hi ut ne sprecað, ond hwilum gebyreð, gif he hit gedæftelice asægð, ðæt he mid ðy his sorge gebet. Hwæt, we wieton ðæt sio diegle wund bið sarre ðonne sio

inwardly inflated with pride, so that they scorn the talkative and count them worthless, and do not perceive how entirely they lay open their mind to the vice of pride, though they shut the actual mouth; though the tongue rests humbly, the mind is quite full of conceit, and so much the more liberally one criticizes all other people in his thoughts the less he recognizes his own venality.

The excessively quiet are also to be advised to cultivate an awareness that it is by no means necessary solely to consider how they present themselves publicly to men and women, but there is much greater need to consider how they present themselves inwardly to God, and, in respect of their thoughts, to be in greater fear of the unseen judge, who knows them all, than to be in fear of the censure of their fellows for their words and deeds. It is written in the Proverbs of Solomon, "My son, attend to my wisdom and my foresight, and direct your eyes and your ears to the ability to guard your thoughts." For nothing in us is more restless and more inconstant than the mind, since it gets away from us as often as pointless thoughts come to us, and is distracted by each of them. About this the psalmist said, "My wits and my good sense have left me." And afterward he returned to himself and recovered his own wits and said, "Your servant has now met with his good sense, which is that he pray to you." Therefore, when one restrains his mind, it encounters what it had been accustomed to avoiding.

Likewise, frequently when the quiet have many adverse thoughts in them, they experience more pain within if they do not express them, and sometimes it occurs that if they articulate them to a reasonable extent, they assuage their sorrow that way. Now, we know that the internal is more

opene, forðam ðæt worsm ðæt ðærinne gehweled bið, gif hit bið ut forlæten, ðonne bið sio wund geopenod to hælo ðæs sares. Eac sculon weotan ða ðe ma swugiað ðonne hie ðyrfen, ðætte hie hiera sorge ne geiecen mid ðy ðæt hie hiora tungan gehealden. Eac hie sint to manianne, gif hie hiera nihstan lufien swa sua hie selfe, ðæt hie him ne helen for hwy hi hie tælen on hiera geðohte, forðæm sio spræc cymð hiora ægðrum to hælo, forðam ðe hie ægðer ge ðæt gehwelede on ðæm oðrum geopenað ond ut forlæt, ðæt he wierð ðonon gehæled, ge ðone oðerne gelærð, ond his unðeawa gestierð. Se ðe ðonne hwæt yfeles ongiet on his nihstan, ond hit forswugað, he deð sua sua se læce ðe gesceawað his freondes wunde, ond nyle hie ðonne gelacnigan. Hu, ne bið he ðonne swelce he sie his slaga, ðonne he hine mæg gehælan, ond nyle? Forðæm is sio tunge gemetlice to midliganne, nales ungemetlice to gebindanne. Be ðæm is awriten, "Se wisa suigað, oð he ongiet ðæt him bið nyttre to sprecanne." Nis hit nan wundur, ðeah he swugie, ond bide his timan, ac ðonne he nytwyrðne timan ongiet to sprecenne, he forsihð ða swigean, ond spricð eall ðæt he nytwyrðes ongiet to sprecanne. Ond eft hit is awriten on Salomonnes bocum, ðæm ðe *Ecclesiastis* hatton, ðætte hwilum sie spræce tiid, hwilum swigean. Forðæm is gesceadwislice to ðenceanne hwelcum tidum him gecopust sie to sprecanne, ðætte, ðonne ðonne he sprecan wille, he his tungan gehealde ðæt hio ne racige on unnytte spræca, ne eft ne aseolce ðær he nytte sprecan mæg. Be ðæm suiðe wel cwæð se psalmsceop: "Gesete Dryhten hirde minum muðe ond ða duru gestæððignesse." Ne bæd

painful than the open wound, because if the matter that is inflamed within is extracted, the wound will be opened, to the alleviation of the pain. Those who keep their own counsel more than necessary ought likewise to know that they are not to aggravate their sorrow by holding their tongue. They are also to be advised that if they love their neighbors as themselves, they not conceal from them why they criticize them in their thoughts, because such talk serves the well-being of both of them, seeing as it both exposes the inflammation in the other and extracts it, so that he derives healing from that, and teaches the other and corrects his failings. One who perceives something immoral in his neighbor and keeps mum about it is acting like the physician who examines his friend's wound and refuses to heal it. Well, is it not then as if he were his murderer, when he can heal him and will not? Therefore, the tongue is to be bridled seasonably, by no means to be restrained excessively. About this it is written, "The sage holds his tongue until he perceives that it will be more profitable for him to speak." It is no wonder that he keeps still and awaits his moment, but when he recognizes the proper time for speaking, he puts aside his silence and speaks all that he considers it relevant to speak. And again, it is written in the books of Solomon that are called Ecclesiastes that sometimes there is occasion to speak, sometimes to be mute. Therefore, it is to be thought out with prudence at what times it is most fitting for one to speak, so that, when he intends to speak, he manage his tongue in such fashion that it not ramble into idle talk, nor, conversely, shirk when he can speak to the point. About this the psalmist spoke quite well: "May the Lord set a watchman to my mouth and a door of steadfastness." He by no

he no ðæt he hine mid ealle fortynde mid gehale wage, ac he bæd dura to, ðæt he meahte hwilum ontynan, hwilum betynan. Ðy we sculon geleornian ðæt we suiðe wærlice gecope tiid aredigen, ond ðonne sio stemn gesceadwislice ðone muð ontyne, ond eac ða tid gesceadwislice aredigen ðe sio suige hine betynan scyle.

4   Ongean ðæt sint to læranne ða oferspræcean ðæt hie wacorlice ongieten fram hu micelre ryhtwisnesse hie beoð gewietene, ðonne hie on monigfealdum wordum slidrigað. Ac ðæt mennisce mod hæfð wætres ðeaw. Ðæt wæter, ðonne hit bið gepynd, hit miclað ond uppað ond fundað wið ðæs ðe hit ær from com, ðonne hit flowan ne mot ðider hit wolde. Ac gif sio pynding wierð onpennad, oððe sio wering wirð tobrocen, ðonne toflewð hit eall, ond ne wierð to nanre nytte, buton to fenne. Sua deð ðæs monnes mod, ðonne hit gesceadwislice ne can his swigean gehealdan, ac hit abricð ut on idle oferspræce, ond wierð swa monigfealdlice on ðæm todæled, suelce hit eall lytlum riðum torinne, ond ut of him selfum aflowe, ðæt hit eft ne mæge in to his agnum ondgiete ond to his ingeðonce gecirran. Ðæt ðonne bið forðæm ðe hit bið todæled on to monigfealda spræca, suelce he self hine selfne ute betyne from ðære smeaunga his agnes ingeðonces, ond sua nacodne hine selfne eowige to wundigeanne his feondum, forðæm ðe he ne bið belocen mid nanum gehieldum nanes fæstenes. Swa hit awriten is on Salomonnes Cwidum ðætte se mon se ðe ne mæg his tungan gehealdan sie gelicost openre byrig, ðære ðe mid nane wealle ne bið ymbworht. Forðæm sio burg ðæs modes, ðe mid nanre suigean ne bið bityned, sceal suiðe oft gefredan hiere feonda speru, forðæm hio ætieweð hie selfe suiðe opene hiere feondum, ðonne hio hie selfe toweorpeð ut of hiere selfre mid

means asked him to shut him up with a solid wall, but he asked for a door to be added that he could sometimes open, sometimes close. From this we ought to learn very cautiously to select the proper time, and when the voice may open the mouth with discretion, and also to select with prudence the time when silence ought to close it.

To the contrary, the overly talkative are to be trained vigilantly to recognize how far they have strayed from moral demeanor when they career into profuse words. But the human mind has the quality of water. Water, when it is dammed up, swells and rises and struggles toward where it first came from when it cannot flow where it would. But if the reservoir is unpent, or the weir is breached, it all flows away and turns to nothing of use, merely fen. So does a person's mind when it does not know how to maintain silence judiciously, but it breaks out into idle chatter in which it is diffused as variously as if it all were flowing in little rivulets and running away with itself, unable to return to its own sense and to its train of thought. That is, then, because it is scattered in excessively manifold verbiage, as if it were itself barring itself from examining its own train of thought, and thus exposing itself naked to be wounded by its enemies, because it is not secured by the protection of any defenses. Thus, it is written in the Proverbs of Solomon that the person who cannot hold his tongue is most like an open city unenclosed by any wall. For the city of the mind that is not secured by any reserve shall very often feel the missiles of its enemies, since it exposes itself quite bare to its foes when it thrusts itself out

unnyttum wordum, ond hio bið micle ðe ieðre to ofer-feohtanne ðe hio self fieht wið hie selfe mid oferspræce to fultome ðæm wiðfeohtende, forðæm hio bið oft oferfohten butan ælcum gesuince.

5   Oft ðonne ðæt hefige mod glit niðor ond niðor stæp-mælum on unnyttum wordum, oð hit mid ealle afielð, ond to nauhte wirð; forðæm hit ær hit nolde behealdan wið unnyt word, hit sceal ðonne niedinga afeallan for ðæm slide. Æt ærestum lyst ðone monn unnyt sprecan be oðrum monnum, ond ðonne æfter firste hine lyst tælan ond slitan ðara lif bu-tan scylde ðe he ðonne ymb spricð, oð ðæt hit on last of his tungan ut abirst to openum bismere ðæm oðrum. Swa he sæwð ðone sticel ðæs andan, oð ðæt ðærof aweoxð towesnes, ond of ðære towesnesse bið ðæt fyr onæled ðære feounga, ond sio feoung adwæscð ða sibbe. Be ðæm wæs suiðe wel ge-cweden ðurh ðone wisan Salomon, ðætte se se ðæt wæter ut forlete wære fruma ðære towesnesse. Se forlæt ut ðæt wæter, se ðe his tungan stemne on unnyttum wordum lætt toflowan. Ac se wisa Salomon sæde ðætte suiðe deop pol wære gewered on ðæs wisan monnes mode, ond suiðe lytel unnyttes utfleowe. Ac se se ðe ðone wer bricð, ond ðæt wæter ut forlæt, se bið fruma ðæs geflites. Ðæt is ðonne se ðe his tungan ne gemidlað, se towierpð anmodnesse. Eft cwæð Salomon, "Se gemetgað irre, se ðe ðone disigan hætt geswugian."

6   Forðæm se næfre ne mæg ryhtwisnesse ond gesceadwis-nesse healdan, se ðe ofersprecol bið. Ðæt tacnode se salm-sceop, ða he cwæð, "Se oferspræcea wer ne wierð he næfre geryht ne gelæred on ðisse worlde." Eft cwæð Salomon bi ðæm ilcan, "Ne bið næfre sio oferspræc butan synne." Bi ðæm cwæð eac Essaias se witga; he cwæð ðætte sio suyge

of itself with fatuous words, and it is much easier to subdue, inasmuch as it battles itself with prolixity, to the aid of the adversary, for which reason it is often defeated without any effort.

Then, frequently, the torpid mind slips further and fur- 5 ther down by degrees in idle words, until it fails altogether and comes to naught; because it was unwilling to guard itself against idle talk, it then must of necessity fall by that misstep. At first it gives the person pleasure to gossip about other people, and then after a time it gives him pleasure to lambaste and lacerate without cause the lives of those he speaks of, until in the end from his tongue there bursts out patent calumny of others. Thus, he sows the thorn of resentment, until discord grows from it, and by that discord is kindled the fire of hatred, and that hatred extinguishes amity. About this it was quite well expressed through the wise Solomon, that whoever released water was the cause of faction. He releases water who lets the sound of his tongue run away in idle words. But the wise Solomon said that a very deep reservoir was collected in the wise person's mind, and very little frivolity runs out of it. But whoever breaks the weir and lets the water loose is the cause of conflict. That is, then, whoever does not bridle his tongue shatters amity. Again Solomon said, "Whoever bids a fool be silent allays wrath."

Therefore, whoever is verbose can never lay claim to up- 6 rightness and probity. The psalmist indicated that when he said, "The prolix man will never be guided or instructed in this world." Again, Solomon said about the same, "Chattering is never without sin." About this also the prophet Isaiah spoke, saying that silence was the bulwark and fellow

wære ðære ryhtwisnesse fultum ond midwyrhta. Ðæt ðonne tacnað ðætte ðæs modes ryhtwisnes bið toflowen, ðe nele forhabban ða ungemetgodan spræce. Be ðæm cwæð Iacobus se apostol, "Gif hwa teochhað ðæt he æfæst sie, ond nyle gemidlian his tungan, ðæt mod lihð him selfum, forðæm his æfæstnes bið suiðe idlu." Ond eft he cwæð, "Sie æghwelc mon suiðe hræd ond suiðe geornful to gehieranne, ond suiðe læt to sprecenne." Eft bi ðam ilcan he gecyðde hwæt ðære tungan mægen is; he cwæð ðæt hio wære unstille, yfel ond deaðberendes atres full. Ond eft us manode sio Soðfæstnes ðurh hie selfe, ðæt is Crist; he cuæð, "Ælces unnyttes wordes ðara ðe men sprecað hie sculon ryht awyrcean on Domes Dæge." Ðæt bið ðonne openlice unnyt word, ðætte gesced-wise menn ne magon ongietan ðæt hit belimpe to ryhtwis-licre ond to nytwyrðlicre ðearfe auðer oððe eft uferran do-gore oððe ðonne. Gif we ðonne sculon ryht agildan unnyttra worda, hwelc wite wene we ðæt se felaspræcea scyle habban ðe simle on oferspræce syngað?

Chapter 39

XXXVIIII. Ðætte on oðre wisan sint to
manianne ða ðe bioð to late,
on oðre ða ðe bioð to hrade.

On oðre wisan sint to manianne ða ðe beoð to late, on oðre ða ðe beoð to hrade. Ða slawan sint to manianne ðæt

laborer of righteousness. That, then, signifies that the righteousness of the mind that is unwilling to refrain from intemperate speech is dissipated. About this James the apostle said, "If someone persuades himself that he is devout and is unwilling to bridle his tongue, the mind deceives itself, for his devotion is quite worthless." And again he said, "Let every person be very ready and very keen to hear, and very slow to speak." Again, about this very thing he explained what the power of the tongue is: he said that it was restless, evil, and full of mortal venom. And again, Truth exhorted us in its own person, which is Christ, and said, "For every worthless word that people speak, they will render an account on Judgment Day." That is evidently a worthless word when discriminating people cannot recognize that it serves any moral and productive purpose, either in days to come or at that time. If, then, we will be obliged to render an account of worthless words, what punishment do we imagine the prolix ought to have, who continually sin with their jabber?

Chapter 39

39. That those who are too disinclined are to be guided in one fashion, those who are too strenuous in another.

In one fashion are to be cautioned those who are too slow, in another those who are too precipitous. The disinclined

hie ne forielden ðone timan for hiera slæwðe ðe hie tiola on
don mægen. Ða hradan ðonne sint to manianne ðæt hie to
unwærlice ne onetten, ðy læs hie forhradien ðone betestan
timan, ond hiera mede forðæm forleosen. Ðam slawum
ðonne is to cyðanne ðætte oft, ðonne we nellað hwæthwugu
nytwyrðes don, ðonne ðonne we magon, ðætte hwilum eft
cymð sio tid ymb lytel fæc ðætte we ðonne willað, ond
ne magon. Forðæm, ðonne we forslawiað ðone gecopestan
timan, ðætte we ðonne ne beoð onælde mid ðære lustbærnesse ures modes, ðonne bistilð sio slæwð on us, ond ricsað
ðonne ofer us, oð ðæt hio us awyrtwalað from ælcre lustbærnesse godra weorca. Be ðæm wæs suiðe wel gecweden ðurh
Salomon ðone snottran: "Sio slæwð giett slæp on ðone monnan." Se slawa ongit hwæt him ryht bið to donne, swelce he
ealneg wacige, ond swaðeah he aslawað, forðæm ðe he
nawuht ne wyrcð, ac sio slæwð him giet on ðone slæp, cwæð
Salomonn, forðæm, ðeah he ryhtlice ðence, lytlum ond lytlum he forlist ðæt gode andgiet, ðonne he forlætt ða geornfulnesse ðæs goðan weorces. Be ðæm ilcan is eft suiðe ryhte
gecweden, "Ðæt ungeornfulle mod ond ðæt toslopene hyn-
greð"; forðæm hie næfre ne beoð gereorde mid godum weorcum, ne hie nellað hie gehæftan ond gepyndan hiora mod,
swelce mon deopne pool gewerige, ac he læt his mod toflowan on ðæt ofdele giemelieste ond ungesceadwisnesse
æfter eallum his willum, ond ne gehæft hit na mid ðam gesuincium godra weorca, ac hit wirð gewundod mid ðæm
hungre ðæs nyðemestan ond ðæs fulestan geðohtes; ðonne
hit flihð ðæt hit sie gebunden mid ege ond mid lare, ðonne
tostret hit on yfelre ond on unnytte wilnunga, ond hæfð ðæs
suiðe micelne hunger. Be ðæm eft wrat Salomon, ond cwæð:
"Ælc idel mon liofað æfter his agnum dome." Be ðæm ilcan

are to be warned not to delay, on account of their sloth, the occasion when they can do good. The intense, then, are to be warned not to race too recklessly, so that they not act in advance of the best time and forfeit their reward through that. To the sluggish it is to be explained that frequently when we are unwilling to do something useful while we can, sometimes in turn the day will come soon enough when we are willing and cannot. Therefore, when we delay at the most fitting time, so that we are not animated by the inclination of our mind, indolence steals upon us and then holds sway over us, until it extirpates from us any inclination to good works. About this it was very well expressed through the wise Solomon, "Sloth induces sleep in a person." The sluggard recognizes what it is right for him to do, as if he is always awake and yet is lethargic because he works at nothing, but sloth induces sleep in him, said Solomon, because, however virtuous his intentions, little by little he will lose that good sense of his when he sets aside dedication to good work. About this same it is quite justly said, "The uncaring and dissolute mind goes hungry"; for they are never nourished with good works, nor are they willing to restrain and confine their mind, as if damming up a deep pool, but such a one lets his mind stream away into the abyss of heedlessness and indifference in accordance with his every desire, and he will never confine it with the labor of good works, but it will be savaged by the hunger of the basest and foulest thoughts; when it shuns being constrained by fear and doctrine, it will be distracted by corrupt and meretricious desires, for which it will hunger ravenously. About this again Solomon wrote and said, "Every idle person lives according to his own

eft sio Soðfæstnes, ðæt is Crist, he cwæð on his godspelle, "Ðonne an unclæne gast bið adrifen of ðæm men, ðonne bið ðæt hus clæne. Ac gif he eft cymð, ond ðæt hus idel gemett, he hit gefylleð mid suiðe monigum."

2   Oft se slawa, ðonne he agælð ond forielt ðæt weorc ðe him niedðearf wære to wyrceanne, ðonne ðynceað him sumu weorc suiðe hefug, sumu suiðe unwærlico, ond ðonne he wenð ðæt he funden hæbbe hwæt he ryhtlice ondræde, ðonne wile he gereccean ðæt he noht unryhtlice hit ne forslæwde, ðonne him ðyncð ðæt he ryhte lade funden hæbbe. Be ðæm wæs suiðe ryhte gecweden ðurh Salomon ðone snottran, "For ciele nele se slawa erian on wintra, ac he wile biddan on sumera, ond him mon nele ðonne sellan." Ðæt is ðonne ðæt se slawa nylle erian for ciele, ðæt hwa sie gebunden mid hefignesse ðære slæwðe, ðæt hine ne lyste sum nytwyrðe weorc wyrcean. Forðæm is gecweden ðæt se slawa for ðæm ege ðæs cieles nylle erigean, forðæm we oft for ðæm ege lytles yfeles forlætað micel god. Hit is suiðe wel be ðæm gecweden ðæt he eft bedecige on sumera, ond him mon ðonne noht ne selle. Sua bið ðæm ðe nu on godum weorcum ne swæt, ond suiðe ne suinceð: eft ðonne sio sunne, ðæt is Crist, on Domes Dæge on mæstum wielme ætiewð, ðonne bið he idel, gif he on ðæm sumra bidt in-gonges in hefonrice. Be ðæm men wæs eft suiðe wel ge-cweden ðurh Salomon ðone snottran; he cwæð, "Se ðe him ealneg wind ondræt, he sæwð to seldon; ond se ðe him ælc wolcn ondrædt, ne ripð se næfre." Hwæt getacnað ðonne se wind buton ða costunga ðæs awirgdan gæstes, ond hwæt ðæt wolc ðe bið astyred from ðæm winde buton ða wiðerweard-nesse unryhtwisra monna? Se wind drifeð ðæt wolcn. Sua deð se unclæna gæst mid his winde; he onstyreð unryhtwise

dictates." About the same, Truth, which is Christ, said in his gospel, "When a certain impure spirit is driven out of a person, the house is clean. But if it returns and the house is found empty, he will fill it with very many."

Often when the sluggard neglects and delays the work 2 that it is necessary for him to perform, certain efforts seem to him quite cumbersome, some others quite imprudent, and because he thinks he has discovered what he may justly abhor, he will reason that he did not procrastinate unjustly when it seems to him that he has found a reliable excuse. About him it is quite properly remarked through the wise Solomon, "The sluggard is unwilling to plow in winter for the cold, but he will beg in summer, and he will be given nothing." That the sluggard is unwilling to plow for the cold is, then, that whoever is burdened with the torpor of sloth does not care to perform some productive work. It is said that the sluggard for fear of the cold is unwilling to plow because we often for fear of a little bad neglect a great good. It is quite well said about this that he afterward will beg in summer, and he will be given nothing. So it will be for one who does not now sweat and labor hard at doing good works: in turn when the sun, which is Christ, appears on Judgment Day in the greatest heat, it will be in vain if in summer he begs entry into the kingdom of heaven. About such a person it was again very well told through the wise Solomon when he said, "One who is always afraid of the wind will sow too seldom, and he who fears every cloud will never reap." Then what does the wind signify but the urgings of the accursed spirit, and what the cloud that is stirred by the wind but the antagonism of immoral people? The wind drives the cloud. So does the unclean spirit with his wind: he moves unrigh-

men. We cwædon ær ðæt se sceolde lytel sawan, se ðe him
ðone wind ondrede; ond eft lytel ripan, se ðe him ða wolc
ondrede. Ðæt is ðonne ðætte sua hwelc sua him ondræt
oððe deofles costunga oððe yfelra monna ehtnesse, ond
forðy forlæt ðæt he hwæthwugu godes ne do, ðonne nauðer
ne he her ða corn godra weorca ne sæwð, ne he eft nænne
sceaf ne ripð ðæs ecean edleanes.

3   Ongean ðæt is to cyðanne ðæm ðe beoð to hrade, ðonne
hie forhradigað ðone timan godes weorces, ðæt hie forpærað
ðæm edleane, ond oft befeallað on micel yfel, ðonne hie
nabbað ða gesceadwisnesse ðæt hie cunnen ðæs ðinges timan aredian, ne furðum ne giemað hwæt hie don, oððe
hwonne hie hwæt don, ac hwilum hit gebyreð ðæt hie hit eft
ongietað, æfter ðæm ðe hit gedon bið, ðæt hie ær sua don ne
sceoldon. To swelcum monnum Salomon wæs sprecende, ða
he his cnieht lærde; he cwæð, "Sunu min, ne doo ðu nan
wuht butan geðeahte; ðonne ne hriwð hit ðe, ðonne hit gedon bið; ac læt simle gan ðin eagean beforan ðinum fotum."
Ðonne stæppað ða eagan beforan ðæm fotum, ðonne ðæt
ryhte ond ðæt gesceadwislice geðeaht gæð beforan weorcum. Ac se ðe agimeleasað ðæt he ðence, ær ðæm ðe he do,
se stæpð forð mid ðam fotum, ond wincað mid ðæm eagum.
He gæð on ðone weg, ac he nat on hwæt he gæð, ac he wirð
suiðe raðe on fielle. Sua wirð se ðe beforan ðæm stæpum his
weorca ne locað mid ðæm eagum gesceadwisra geðeahtes.

teous people. We said just now that one who feared the wind would sow little, and, conversely, reap little who feared the clouds. That is, then, that whichever person fears either the devil's urgings or the persecution of unjust people, and therefore neglects to do something good, will neither sow the grain of good works here nor in turn reap any sheaf of eternal reward.

To the contrary, it is to be explained to those who are too 3 strenuous that when they are precipitous as to the time of a good deed they spoil its benefits, and they often fall into a great wrong when they do not have the discernment to know how to appoint a time for the matter, nor even care what they are doing or when they do something, but sometimes it happens that they eventually perceive, after it is done, that they should not have done it so soon. To such people Solomon was speaking when he instructed his servant, saying, "My son, do nothing without deliberation; then you will not rue it once it is done; but always let your eyes go before your feet." The eyes step before the feet when proper and discerning reflection precedes action. But whoever neglects to think before he acts steps forth with the feet and shuts the eyes. He walks on the way, but he does not pay attention to what he is walking on, and he will very soon take a tumble. Such is one who does not look ahead of the steps of his actions with the eyes of those prudent at deliberation.

Chapter 40

XL. Ðætte on oðre wisan sint to manienne ða
monðwæran, on oðre ða grambæran.

On oðre wisan sint to manianne ða monðwæran, on
oðre ða grambæran. Forðæm oft gebyreð ðæm monðwæran,
ðonne he wierð riece ofer oðre menn, ðæt he for his
monðwærnesse aslawað, ond wierð to unbeald, forðæm sio
unbieldo ond sio monðwærnes bioð swiðe anlice. Forðæm
oft, ðonne mon læt toslupan ðone ege ond ða lare suiður
ðonne hit ðearf sie for wacmodnesse, ðonne wierð gehne-
scad ðonone sio ðreaung ðæs anwaldes. Ongean ðæt sint to
manianne ða weamodan ond ða grambæran, forðæm, ðonne
hie underfoð ðone folgað, ðonne tyht hie ond gremeð ðæt
ierre ðæt hie wealwiað on ða wedenheortnesse, ond ðurh
ðæt wierð toslieten sio stilnes hiera hieremonna modes, ond
bið gedrefed sio smyltnes hiera lifes. Forðæm, ðonne ðæt
ierre æfð anwald ðæs monnes, ðonne gehriesð he on sume
scylde, sua ðæt he self nat huæt he on ðæt irre deð. Ða irran
nyton hwæt hie on him selfum habbað, ond eac ðætte wierse
is, ðætte hie ful oft wenað ðætte hiera ierre sie ryhtwislic
anda ond manung sumre ryhtwisnesse. Forðæm, ðonne hie
wenað ðæt hiera unðeawas sien sum god cræft, ðonne
gadriað hie hie ond ieceað butan ælcum ege. Oft eac ða
monðwæran weorðað sua besolcne ond sua wlace ond sua
slawe for hira monðwærnesse ðæt hie ne anhagað nane
wuht nyttwyrðes don. Oft eac ða grambæra leogað him selfum, ðonne hie wenað ðæt hie ryhtne andan hæbben. Oft

Chapter 40

40. That the mild are to be guided in one fashion, the irascible in another.

In one fashion are the mild to be guided, in another the wrathful. For it often happens to the mild sort that, when he attains power over other people, he will grow remiss and become too timid, since timidity and gentleness are very much akin. For that reason, frequently when discipline and instruction out of want of will are permitted to grow laxer than is required, the correction wielded by authority will grow forbearing. Contrariwise are to be cautioned the fierce and the passionate, because when they assume authority, anger incites and provokes them so that they wallow in blind rage, and the composure of their charges' minds is thereby ruptured, and the tranquility of their life is thrown into turmoil. As a consequence, when anger takes possession of a person, he falls into a certain error, so that he himself does not know what he does in anger. The enraged do not know what they harbor in themselves, and also, what is worse, they often think that their anger is righteous ardor and a claim to a certain uprightness. As a result, when they regard their vices as a certain desirable quality, they accumulate them and add to them without scruple. Often, as well, the mild grow so dull and so tepid and so torpid for their lenience that they find it inconvenient to accomplish anything productive. Often, as well, the irascible deceive themselves when they suppose that they have just indignation.

eac sio godnes ðære monnðwærnesse bið diegellice gemenged wið sleacnesse. Oft eac ða grambæran wenað ðæt
hiera unðeaw sie sumes ryhtwislices andan wielm. Ac we
sculon manian ða manðwæran ðæt hie hæbben ða monnðwærnesse, ond fleon ðæt ðær suiðe neah liegeð ðære monnðwærnesse, ðæt is sleacnes. Ða grambæran we sculon
monian ðæt hie ongieten hwæt hie on him selfum habbað.
Ða monnðwæran we sculon monian ðæt hie ongieten hwæt
hi nabbað. Ne forlæten ða ierran ðone andan, ac geðencen
ðæt he sie gesceadwislic ond gemetlic. Leorniað hine ða
manðwæran ond lufigað, oð ðæt hie hiene hæbben. Lytligen
ða grambæran hiera gedrefednesse. Ða monðwæran sint to
monianne ðæt hie geornlice tiligen ðæt hie hæbben ryhtwislicne andan. Ða grambæran sint to monianne, ðe wenað
ðæt hie ryhtwislicne andan hæbben, ðæt hie ðone gemen-
gen wið monnðwærnesse. Forðæm us ætiede se Halga Gæsð
ægðer ge on culfran onlicnesse ge on fyres, forðæm ðe ælcne
ðara ðe he gefylð, he hiene onælð ægðer ge mid ðære culfran
bilewitnesse ond mannðwærnesse ge mid ðæs fyres reðnesse. Ne bið se no gefylled ðæs Halgan Gæsðæs se ðe on
ðære smyltnesse his monðwærnesse forlæt ðone wielm ryhtwislices andan, oððe eft on ðæm wielme ðæs andan forlæt
ðone cræft ðære monnðwærnesse.

2   Ic wene ðæt we mægen ðis openlicor gecyðan gif we *sanctus* Paulus lare sume ongemong secgað, forðæm he hæfde
twegen gingran suiðe gelices willan ond on eallum ðingum
suiðe onlice, ond he hie ðeah lærde suiðe ungelice. Oðer hira
wæs haten Timotheus, oðer Titus. He cuæð to ðæm Timo-
theo, "Lære hie, ond healsa, ond tæl hira unðeawas, ond
ðeah geðyldelice." To ðæm Tite he cuæð, "Lær ðæt folc, ond
ðreata, ond tæl, ond hat, ðæt hie wieten ðæt ge sume anwald

Often, too, the virtue of lenience is covertly mingled with indolence. Frequently, as well, the passionate believe that their vice is the heat of a certain righteous fervor. Yet we ought to exhort the mild to maintain their gentleness and shun what lies very near gentleness, which is laxness. We ought to encourage the wrathful to recognize what they harbor in themselves. We ought to exhort the mild to understand what they are without in themselves. Let the angry not relinquish their ardor, but look to it that it is discerning and seasonable. Let the mild learn and value it, until they possess it. Let the passionate mitigate their vehemence. The mild are to be exhorted to endeavor concertedly to possess righteous fervor. The excitable who suppose they have righteous fervor are to be exhorted to mingle it with clemency. The Holy Spirit appeared to us in the form both of a dove and of fire for this reason, that in everyone he enters he inspires both the mildness and the gentleness of the dove and the intensity of fire. He is not filled with the Holy Spirit who in the placidity of his mildness disregards the ardor of righteous fervency, or, conversely, who in the ardor of fervency disregards the virtue of mildness.

I believe that we can explain this more plainly if in passing we say something of Saint Paul's teaching, since he had two followers of very like disposition and in all respects very similar, and yet he counseled them quite differently. One of them was named Timothy, the other Titus. He said to Timothy, "Instruct and admonish them, and censure their vices, and yet patiently." To Titus he said, "Instruct the people, and chide and reprove and command, so that they will know

2

habbað ofer hie." Hwæt mænde *sanctus* Paulus, ða he his lare sua cræftelice toscead, ond ðone oðerne lærde ðæt he him anwald ontuge, oðerne he lærde geðyld, buton ðæt he ongeat Titum hwene monðwærran ond geðyldigran ðonne he sceolde, ond Timotheus he ongeat hatheortran ðonne he sceolde? Titum he wolde onælan mid ryhtwislicum andan; Timotheum he wolde gemetgian. Oðrum he wolde geiecean ðæt him wana wæs, oðrum he wolde oftion ðæs ðe he to fela æfde. Oðerne he draf suiðe geornfullice mid sticele, oðrum he wiðteah mid bridle. Wietodlice se mæra landbegenga— ðæt wæs *sanctus* Paulus—he underfeng ða halgan gesomnunga to plantianne ond to ymbhweorfanne, sua se ceorl deð his ortgeard. Sumu treowu he watrode, to ðæm ðæt hie ðy suiður sceolden weaxan. Sume he cearf ðonne him ðuhte ðæt hie to suiðe weoxsen, ðy læs hie to ðæm forweoxen ðæt hie forseareden, ond ðy unwæsðmbærran wæren. Sumu twigu he lehte mid wætere, ðonne hie to hwon weoxson, ðæt hie ðy suiður weaxan sceolden.

3   Ac ða irsunga sindun suiðe ungelica: oðer bið suelce hit sie irres anlicnes—ðæt is ðæt mon wielle æt oðrum his yfel aðreatigan, ond hine on ryhtum gebringan; oðer bið ðæt ierre ðæt mon sie gedrefed on his mode butan ælcre ryhtwisnesse. Oðer ðara irsunga bið to ungemetlice ond to ungedafenlice atyht on ðæt ðe hio mid ryhte irsian sceall, oðer on ðæt ðe hio ne sceal bið ealneg to suiðe onbærned. Eac is to wietanne ðætte hwæthwugu bið betweoh ðæm irsiendan ond ðæm ungeðyldgan, ðæt is ðæt ða ungeðyldgan ne magon aberan nan wuht ðæs laðes ðe him mon on legð oððe mid wordum oððe mid dædum, ða iersigendan ðonne him to getioð ðæt ðætte hie eaðe butan bion meahton: ðeah

that you hold a certain power over them." What did Saint Paul intend when he differentiated his instructions so markedly, and he directed one to take control, whereas he taught the other patience, except that he regarded Titus as somewhat milder and more patient than he should be, and he regarded Timothy as rasher than he should be? He aimed to inflame Titus with righteous fervor; Timothy he wanted to restrain. In one he wanted to bolster what was in short supply in him, in the other he wanted to diminish what he had in too great abundance. One he drove very determinedly with a goad, the other he curbed with a bridle. Certainly, the great gardener—that was Saint Paul—undertook to plant and cultivate holy Church, as the farmer does his orchard. Some trees he irrigated, so that they would grow more. Some he pruned when it seemed to him that they had grown too much, lest they become so overgrown that they wither and be less fruitful. Some seedlings he hydrated with water when they had grown to such an extent that they could be expected to grow all the more.

But passionate qualities are quite dissimilar: one is as if it 3 were a counterfeit of ire—that is, that one wishes to face down another's wrongdoing and lead him to what is right; the other is the anger whereby one is irritated in his mind without any moral cause. One of these passions is too incommensurately and inappropriately piqued at what it rightly should be angry about; the other is always too strongly incensed at what it ought not to be. It is also to be understood that something distinguishes the irascible and the impatient, which is that the impatient cannot bear any injury laid on them either in word or deed, whereas the wrathful embroil themselves in what they could readily do

hie nan mann mid laðe ne grete, hie wiellað griellan oðre
menn to ðæm ðæt hie niede sculon, ond seceað ða ðe hie
fleoð, ond styrigað geflitu ond geciid, ond fægniað ðæt hie
moten suincan on ungeðwærnesse. Ða suelcan we magon
ealra betest geryhtan mid ðy ðæt we hie forbugen, ðonne
ðonne hie beoð anstyred mid hiera ierre, forðæm, ðonne hie
sua gedrefede bioð, hie nyton hwæt hie ðonne gehierað,
ðeah him mon stiere, ac eft, ðonne hie hie selfe ongietað,
hie onfooð ðære lare sua micle lusðlicor sua him mon ær
geðyldelicor forbær hiera irre, ond sua micle ma scamiað
hiera unðeawes sua hiene mon ær geðyldelicor forbær. Ac
ðæt mod, ða hwile ðe hit bið oferdruncen ðæs ierres, eal ðæt
him mon ryhtes sægð, hit ðyncð him woh. Forðæm eac ðæt
wif ðe Abigall hatte suiðe herigendlice forsuigode ðæt dysig
hiere fordruncnan hlafordes, se wæs haten Nabal, ond
eft, ða him ðæt lið gescired wæs, full herigendlice hio hit
him gecyðde, ond he forðæm sua micle bet his agen dysig
oncnew sua he undruncenra wæs.

4   Sua eac, ðonne ðæt gelimpð ðæt ða iersigendan menn
oðrum monnum oferfylgeað to ðon suiðe ðæt hit him mon
forberan ne mæg, ne sceal mon no mid openlice edwite him
wiðslean, ac bi sumum dæle arwierðelice wandigende suiðe
wærlice stieran. Ðæt we magon openlicor gecyðan, gif
we Æfneres dæda sume her ongemong secgað, hu Assael
hine unwærlice mid anwealde ðreatode, ond him oferfylgde.
Hit is awriten ðæt Æfnere cwæde to Assaele: "Gecier, la,
ond gesuic; ne folga me, ðæt ic ðe ne dyrre ofstingan." He
forhogde ðæt he hit gehierde, ond nolde hine forlætan.
Ða ðydde Æfner hine mid hindewerde sceafte on ðæt

without: even if no one offers them injury, they will provoke other people so much as to compel them by necessity, and they will pursue those who avoid them and stir up contention and quarreling, and they will delight in being able to manufacture discord. Such ones we can best of all correct by avoiding them when they are roused by rage, because when they are thus disturbed, they do not understand what they are hearing when they are checked, but afterward, when they get a grip on themselves, they accept instruction so much the more willingly the more patiently one countenanced their anger, and so much the more are they ashamed of their fault the more patiently they were indulged. But as long as the mind is besotted with anger, everything right that is said to one will seem to him wrong. For that reason, the woman named Abigail very laudably held her tongue about the foolishness of her drunken husband, who was named Nabal, and afterward, when the power of drink had abated in him, very laudably she made it known to him, and he therefore so much the better acknowledged his own folly the soberer he was.

So, also, when it happens that people in a rage attack 4
other people so hard that it cannot be borne, they ought not to be countered with patent abuse but to a certain extent to be handled very attentively with respectful sensitivity. We can explain this more plainly if, in the course of this, we say a certain something about Abner's conduct, how Asahel recklessly threatened him with force and pursued him. It is written that Abner said to Asahel, "Turn, I say, and desist, and do not pursue me, lest I take it upon me to run you through." He disdained to comply and would not leave him. Then Abner ran him through with the blunt end of his spear in the

smælðearme ðæt he wæs dead. Hwæs onlicnesse hæfde
Assael ða buton ðara ðe hiera hatheortnes hie suiðe hrædlice
on færspild gelæd? Ða ðonne hie beræsað on suelce weamodnesse, hie sindon sua micle wærlicor to ferbuganne sua mon
ongiet ðæt hie on maran ungewitte beoð. Ðæs Æfneres
noma ðe ðone oðerne fleah is on ure geðiode "fæder leohtfæt." Ðæt getacnað ðætte ðara lareowa tungan ðe ðæt uplice
leoht bodiað, ðonne hie ongietað hwelcne monnan ge-
suencedne mid irre ond mid hatheortnesse onbærnedne,
ond ðonne forwandigað ðæt hie mid ðæm kycglum hiera
worda ongean hiera ierre worpigen, sua sua Æfner wandade
ðæt he nolde ðane slean ðe hine draf. Sua, ðonne ðonne ða
hatheortan hie mid nane foreðonce nyllað gestillan, ac sua
wedende folgiað hwam sua sua Assael dyde Æfnere, ond
næfre nyllað gesuican, ðonne is micel ðearf ðætte se, se ða
hatheortnesse ofercuman wielle, ðætte he hiene ongean ne
hathierte, ac eowige him ealle stilnesse ongean ðæt, ond
ðeah swiðe wærlice hine pynge mid sumum wordum, ðæt he
on ðæm ongietan mæge be sumum dæle his unðeaw. Forðæm
Æfner, ða ða he ongean ðone cirde ðe hine draf, ne ofstong
he hiene no mid ðy speres orde, ac mid hindewerdum ðam
sceafte. Ðæt is ðonne suelce mon mid forewearde orde
stinge, ðæt mon openlice ond unforwandodlice on oðerne
ræse mid tælinge ond mid ðrafunga. Ðæt is ðonne ðæt mon
mid hindewearde sceafte ðone ðydde ðe him oferfylge, ðæt
mon ðone weamodan liðelice mid sumum ðingum gehrine,
suelce he hine wandigende ofersuiðe. Sua sua Assael suiðe
hrædlice gefeol, sua ðæt ahrerede mod, ðonne hit ongiet
ðæt him mon birgð mid ðære gesceadlican andsuare, hit bið
getæsed on ðæt ingeðonc, ond mid ðære liðelican manunga
to ðam aredod ðæt hit sceal suiðe hrædlice afeallan of ðære

lower abdomen, so that he died. Of whom was Asahel the type but of those whose rage leads them very suddenly to ruin? When they fly into such a passion they are so much the more warily to be avoided the greater the frenzy they are recognized to be in. The name of this Abner who fled from the other is in our language "father's lamp." That signifies that when the tongues of teachers proclaiming the sublime light recognize anyone driven to anger and inflamed with rage, they scruple to launch the darts of their words against their ire, just as Abner hesitated, in that he did not want to strike at the one who was pursuing him. Thus, when the furious are unwilling to compose themselves with any prudence, but thus raging follow someone the way Asahel did Abner and intend never to desist, it is a firm requirement for one who intends to subdue that fury not to grow passionate himself, but to show him all self-composure in return, and yet very cautiously prick him with certain words, so that by that he can recognize his fault to some degree. For that reason, Abner, when he turned toward the one who was pursuing him, by no means stabbed him with the point of the spear, but with the blunt end of the shaft. To charge at another with accusations and with reproof is, then, like thrusting with the pointed tip plainly and unhesitatingly. It is running a pursuer through with the blunt end of the shaft to stroke the infuriated gently with certain words, as if to subdue him by indirection. Just as Asahel fell quite suddenly, so when the disturbed mind perceives that it is being safeguarded by that discerning response, it will be soothed into awareness, and with the gentle prodding made ready to fall

weamodnesse ðe hit ær on ahæfen wæs. Se ðe ðonne sua for-
bygð ðone wielm ond ðone onræs his hatheortnesse, forðæm
ðe hine mon slea mid liðelicre andsuare, ðonne bið his unðeaw ofslægen butan ælcre niedðrafunga, sua sua Assael wæs
dead butan orde.

Chapter 41

XLI. Ðætte on oðre wisan sint to monianne ða eaðmodan, on oðre wisan ða upahæfenan on hira mode.

On oðre wisan sint to manianne ða eaðmodan, on oðre ða
upahæfenan. Ðæm eaðmodum is to cyðanne hu micel sio
heanes is ond hu soðlic ðe hie to hopiað, ond eac habbað.
Ðæm upahæfenum is to cyðanne hwelc nawuht ðes wo-
ruldgielp is ðe hie clyppað ond lufiað, ond his nawuht habbað, ðeah hie wenen ðæt hie hiene hæbben. Gehieren ða
eaðmodan hu ece ðæt is ðæt hie wilniað, ond hu gewitende
ond hu unagen ðæt is ðæt hie onscuniað. Gehieren eac ða
upahæfenan hu gewitende ða ðing sint ðe hie gietsiað, ond
hu eciu ða sint ðe hie forhycgað, ond forleosan willað.
Gehieren ða eaðmodan ðære Soðfæsðnesse stemne, ðæt is
Crist ure lareow; he cuæð, "Ælc ðara ðe bið geeaðmed, he
bið up ahæfen." Gehieren eac ða upahæfenan on hiera mode
hwæt he eft cuæð; he cuæð, "Ælc ðara ðe hine selfne up

quite suddenly from the height of passion to which it had been raised. When one thus turns aside the fit and the eruption of his fury because he is struck by a mild response, his fault is laid low without any need for chastisement, just as Asahel died without a blade.

Chapter 41

41. That the humble are to be guided in one fashion, those exalted in their own conceit in another.

In one fashion are the humble to be advised, in another the proud. To the self-effacing it is to be explained how great and how genuine is the loftiness to which they aspire, and which they also possess. To the haughty it is to be explained what an insignificant thing is this worldly glory that they embrace and cherish, and they possess not a bit of it, though they think they have it. Let the submissive hear how everlasting what they desire is, and how fleeting and impossible to retain is what they avoid. Let the presumptuous also hear how evanescent are the things that they covet, and how everlasting are those that they scorn and want to rid themselves of. Let the meek hear the voice of Truth, which is our teacher Christ, who said, "Each of those who are humbled will be exalted." Let those exalted in their own conceit hear what he said in turn: he said, "Each of those who exalt them-

ahefeð, he wierð gehined." Gehieren ða eaðmodan hwæt Salomon cuæð: "Sio eaðmodnes iernð beforan ðæm gielpe, ond heo cymð ær ær ða wyrðmynðu." Gehieren eac ða upahæfenan on hira mode hu he eft cuæð; he cuæð, "Ær ðæs monnes hryre bið ðæt mod up ahæfen." Gehieren ða eaðmodan hwæt God cuæð ðurh Essaiam ðone witgan; he cuæð, "To hwæm locige ic buton to ðæm eaðmodum ond to ðæm stillum ond to ðæm ðe him ondrædað min word?" Gehieren ða upahæfenan hwæt Salomon cuæð; he cuæð, "Hwæt ofermodgað ðios eorðe ond ðis dusð?" Gehieren ða eaðmodan hwæt on psalmum gecueden is, ðætte Dryhten locige to ðæm eaðmodan. Gehieren ða upahæfenan: "Dryhten ongiet suiðe feorran ða heahmodnesse." Gehieren ða eaðmodan hwæt Crist cuæð: "Ne com ic to ðon on eorðan ðæt me mon ðenode, ac to ðon ðæt ic wolde ðegnian." Gehieren ða upahæfenan hwæt Salomon cuæð; he cuæð ðæt ælces yfles fruma wære ofermetta. Gehieren ða eaðmodan ðætte Crisð ure aliesend hiene selfne geeaðmedde emne oð ðone deað. Gehieren ða upahæfenan hwæt awriten is be hira heafde ond be hiera lareowe, ðæt is dioful: hit is awriten ðæt he sie kyning ofer eal ða oferhydigan bearn, forðæm his ofermedu is fruma ures forlores, ond se orðonc ðe we mid aliesde siendon is Godes eaðmodnes. Se ure fiond ðonne he wæs gesceapen ongemang eallum oðrum gesceaftum, ac he wilnode ðæt he wære ongieten up ahæfen ofer ealle oðre gesceafte. Ac se ure aliesend, ðe mara is ond mærra eallum gesceaftum, he hine gemedomode to bionne betwiux ðæm læsðum ond ðæm gingestum monnum.

2   Ðæm eaðmodum is to cyðanne ðætte, ðonne ðonne hie hie selfe suiðusð eaðmedað, ðætte hie ðonne astigað to Godes anlicnesse. Secgað eac ðæm upahæfenum ðætte,

selves will be humbled." Let the deferential hear what Solomon said: "Humility runs before glory, and it comes before honor." Let those made superior in their own self-regard hear how he spoke again, saying, "Before a person's fall, the mind will be exalted." Let the humble hear what God said through the prophet Isaiah when he said, "On whom do I look but the humble and the peaceable and those who fear my word?" Let the insolent hear what Solomon said when he said, "On what prides itself this earth and this dust?" Let the self-effacing hear what is said in Psalms, that the Lord looks on the lowly. Let the overweening hear: "The Lord recognizes haughtiness from afar." Let the lowly hear what Christ said: "I did not come to earth to be served, but because it was my will to serve." Let the self-satisfied hear what Solomon said: he said that pride was the root of all evil. Let the unassuming hear that Christ our savior humbled himself even unto death. Let the grandiose hear what is written of their head and of their teacher, which is the devil: it is written that he is king over all the children of pride, since his pride is the cause of our fall, and the device by which we are redeemed is God's humility. Our adversary, then, was created along with all other made things, but he desired to be accounted raised above all other creatures. But our savior, who is greater and more glorious than all his creations, humbled himself to be among the lowest and the least.

It is to be explained to the meek that when they abase 2 themselves most, they aspire to a likeness to God. Say also to the conceited that, when they make themselves superior,

ðonne ðonne hie hie selfe up ahebbað, ðæt hie ðonne afeallað on ða biesene ðæs aworpnan engles. Ac hwæt is ðonne
forcuðre ðonne sio upahæfenes? Forðæm, ðonne heo bið
atyht ofer hire andefnu, ðonne bið heo afeorrod suiðe feor
from ðære soðan heanesse. Hwæt mæg ðonne hierre bion
ðonne sio soðe eaðmodnes? Sio, ðonne hio nieðemesð ge-
bygeð, ðonne bið hio gelicosð hiere Dryhtne, se wunað ofer
eallum ðæm hiehstum gesceaftum.

3   Ðonne is ðeah betwux ðissum twam sum ðing ðe mon
wærlice sceal geðencean, ðæt is ðæt sume menn onderfoð
eaðmodnesse hiw, sume ofermodnesse, sua sua hie nyton.
Sume, ða ða wenað ðæt hie eaðmode sien, hie doð for ege
ðone weorðscipe mannum ðe hie Gode don scoldon. Oft eac
ða upahæfenan, ðeah hie hwilum unforwandodlice sprecen,
ðonne hie hwelces unðeawes stiran sculon, ðonne gesugiað
hie for ege, ond tiohchiað ðæt ðæt scyle bion for eaðmet-
tum, ond ðonne hie sprecað, ðonne wenað hie ðæt hie sprecen for unforwandodlicre ond orsorglicre ryhtwisnesse. Ac
hit bið oftor for ðære ungeðylde hiera upahæfenesse. Ða
eaðmodan ðonne bioð oft geðrycte mid ðære synne ðæs
eges, ðonne hie ne durron unðeawas tælan, ond licettað
ðeah ðæt hie ðæt don ðurh eaðmodnesse. Ac ða upahæfenan, ðonne hie licettað ðæt him ne sie nawuhtes cearu ofer
ða ryhtwisnesse, weorðað ðonne unmidlode sua ond aðundene geniedde mid hiera upahæfenesse ðæt hie ða tælað ond
ðreatigað ðe hie ðreatian ne sceoldon, oððe ða ðe hie ðreati-
gan sceoldon suiður ðreatiað ðonne hie sceolden. Forðæm
sint to manianne ða upahæfenan ðæt hie ne sien bealdran
ond orsorgran ðonne hie scylen, ond ða eaðmodan sint to
manianne ðæt hie ne sien suiður underðiedde ðonne hie
mid ryhte scylen, ðy læs ða modgan ða forespræce ðære

they fall after the example of the outcast angel. But what is then more deplorable than arrogance? For when it is indulged beyond due measure it has strayed very far from true superiority. Then what can be loftier than true lowliness? When it bows lowest it is most like its Lord, who occupies a place above all the most superior creatures.

But then there is a certain something between these two which ought to be examined meticulously, which is that some people assume the guise of humility, some of arrogance, without knowing it. Some, when they believe that they are being humble, out of fear render to people the reverence they instead owe to God. Often, likewise, though they sometimes speak without hesitation, when the haughty ought to correct some fault, they fall silent out of trepidation and convince themselves that this must be out of humility, and when they speak they believe that they speak out of forthright and unabashed righteousness. But more commonly it is out of the irrepressibility of their arrogance. The lowly, then, are often constrained by the sin of timidity when they dare not censure vices, and yet they affect to act so out of humility. Yet when the haughty act as if they care for nothing but uprightness, they grow so unrestrained and conceited, compelled by their arrogance, that they upbraid and excoriate people they ought not to criticize, or they rebuke those worthy of reproof more than they ought. Therefore, the presumptuous are to be warned not to be more brazen and self-confident than they ought, and the self-effacing are to be warned not to be more subservient than they ought, to prevent the bold from transforming the

ryhtwisnesse gehwierfen to ofermodnesse, oððe eft ða eaðmodan ðonne hie ma wilniað oðrum monnum underðiedde
beon ðonne hie ðyrfen, weorðen geniedde hiera unðeawas
to herianne ond to weorðianne.

4   Eac is to geðencanne ðætte mon mæg oft ðy bet ða ofermodan ðreatian, gif hie mon ongemang ðære ðreatunga fet
mid sumere heringe. Him mon sceal cyðan ðara goda sum ðe
hie on him habbað oððe ðara sum ðe hie habban meahton,
gif hie næfden. Sua we magon betesð of aceorfan ðæt us on
him mislicað, ðæt we æresð gedon ðæt hie gehieren æt us
hwæthwugu ðæs ðe him licige, ond mid ðy hiera mod getion
to us, ðæt hit sie ðe lusðbærre to gehieranne sua hwæt sua
we him auðer oððe lean oððe læran wiellen. Forðæm hie
beoð to myndgianne ðara goda ðe hie ær dydon, ðæt hie sien
ðe lusðbærran to gehieranne ðæt him mon ðonne beodan
wielle. Swa swa wildu hors, ðonne we hie æresð gefangnu
habbað, we hie ðacciað ond straciað mid bradre handa ond
lemiað, to ðon ðæt we eft on fierste hie moten mid gierdum
fullice gelæran ond ða temian. Sua eac se læce, ðonne he
bietre wyrta deð to hwelcum drence, he hie gesuet mid hu-
nige, ðy læs he ða bieternesse ðære wyrte ðe hine gehælan
sceal æt fruman gefrede, ac ðonne se swæc ðære bieternesse
bið bediegled mid ðære swetnesse, ðonne bið se deaðbæra
wæta on ðæm menn ofslægen mid ðæm biteran drence. Sua
mon sceal on ðæm upahæfenum monnum ðone fruman ond
ðone ingong ðære ðreatunga ond ðære tælinge gemetgian,
ond wið heringe gemengan, ðætte hie for ðære licunga ðære
heringe ond ðære olicunga ðe hie lufigeað eac gaðafigen ða
tælinge ond ða ðreaunga ðe hie onscuniað.

defense of moral standards into arrogance, or, conversely, the humble, when they are willing to be dominated by other people more than they need be, from feeling compelled to applaud and esteem their faults.

Also to be considered is that the proud can often be re- 4 proved more effectively if, in the course of a reprimand, they are sustained with a degree of praise. They ought to have pointed out to them certain of the good qualities they have in them, or certain of those they could have, in the event that they do not have them. Thus, we can best prune away what in them we find unsatisfactory by first letting them hear from us something of what will please them, and thereby dispose their mind to us, so that it may be better inclined to listen to whatever we intend for them of either reproof or instruction. They are accordingly to be reminded of the good that they have done formerly, so that they may be better disposed to listen to what one then wants to impose upon them. Just so, when we have first captured wild horses we pat and stroke them with open palms and subdue them, so that in time we will be able fully to train and tame them with staves. So, also, when the physician adds bitter herbs to some potion, he sweetens it with honey, so that the patient will not at once notice the bitterness of the herb that is intended to heal him; but when the savor of bitterness is concealed by the sweetness, the deadly humor in the person will be counteracted by the bitter drink. Thus, as to conceited people, the design and the commencement of censure and reproof ought to be seasoned and mingled with praise, so that for the satisfaction of the praise and flattery that they enjoy they may also countenance the reproof and blame that they evade.

5   Oft we magon eac ða upahæfenan ðy bet gelæran to urum
willan, gif we him cyðað hu micle ðearfe we hiera habbað,
suelce we maran ðearfe hæbban ðæt hie geðeon ðonne hie
selfe, ond we hie ðonne biddað ðæt hie for urum ðingum
hira unðeawa gesuicen; ðy ieðelicor bið sio upahæfenes to
gode gehwierfed, gif hie ongietað ðæt hiera eac oðre men
ðurfon. Be ðæm se ilca Moyses ðe God self lærde, ond hine
lædde ðurh ðæt westen mid ðy fyrenan sweore on nieht, ond
on dæg mid ðy sweore ðæs wolcnes, he wolde Obab his
sweor ob ðæs hæðendomes siðum alædan, ond hine wolde
underðiodan ælmihtigum Gode; he cuæð, "We willað nu
faran to ðære stowe ðe God us gehaten hæfð, ac far mid us,
ðæt we ðe mægen wel don, forðæm ðe God hæfð suiðe wel
gehaten Israhela folce." Ða andsuarode he him, ond cuæð:
"Ic nelle mid ðe faran, ac ic wille faran to minre cyððe, ond
to ðæm londe ðe ic on geboren wæs." Ða andswarade him
Moyses: "La, ne forlæt us, ac beo ure laðeow; ðu cans eal ðis
westen, ond wasð hwær we wician magon." Ne spræc he
hit no forðy ðe his mod auht genierwed wære mid ðære
uncyððe ðæs siðfætes, forðæm hit wæs geweorðad mid
ðæm andgiete godcundes wisdomes, ond wæs him self
witga, forðam hine God hiewcuðlicor on eallum ðingum ond
ðeawum innan lærde ðonne oðre menn mid his gelomlicre
tospræce, ond utane he hine lærde mid ðæm sweore ðæs
wolcnes. La, ah ðeahhwæðre se foreðancula wer, forðæm ðe
he spræc to ðæm upahæfenan, he bæd his fultumes, swelce
him niedðerf wære; ond bæd ðeah for ðæs oðres ðearfe,
forðæm he tiohchode him ma to fultemanne; he sohte hine
him to latðeowe on ðæm wege, forðæm he teohchode hine
to lædanne on lifes weg. Ac he dyde sua sua ofermod gefera

Often we can also better mold the contemptuous to our 5
will if we let them know what great need we have of them, as
if we have greater need than they themselves that they do
well, and we beg them for our sake to renounce their vices;
arrogance is more readily reformed if they recognize that
other people also have need of them. About this same matter Moses, whom God himself instructed and led through
the wilderness with the pillar of fire by night, and by day
with the pillar of cloud, when he intended to wean his
brother-in-law Hobab from the practices of heathendom,
and he intended to render him subject to almighty God,
said, "We will depart now for the place that God has promised us; but go with us, that we may do well for you, because
God has promised good to the people of Israel." Then he
answered him and said, "I do not care to travel with you, but
I want to repair to my kith and kin, and to the land where I
was born." Then Moses replied to him, "Oh, do not leave us,
but be our guide; you know all this desert, and you know
where we can encamp." He by no means said this because
his mind was at all made anxious by the unfamiliarity of the
way, since it was graced with the understanding of divine
wisdom, and he was himself a prophet, for inwardly God
guided him about all matters and morals more familiarly
than other people with his frequent conversation, and outwardly he guided him with the pillar of cloud. Oh, but nonetheless the prudent man, because he was speaking to the
self-satisfied, requested his help, as if he were in need of it,
and yet asked for the other's sake, since he was determined
to help him more; he asked for him to be his leader on the
way because it was his determination to lead him on the way
of life. But he acted just as a proud fellow does: he should

deð: he sceolde beon ðære spræce sua micle gefægenra sua him mare ðearf wæs, ond ðæs ðe gefægenra ðe he him sua eaðmodlice ond sua arlice to spræc, he sceolde bion him micle ðy eaðmodra ond his larum ðe suiður underðied.

Chapter 42

XLII. Ðætte on oðre wisan sint to manianne ða
anwillan, on oðre ða ungestæððegan
ond unfæsðræda.

On oðre wisan sint to manianne ða anfealdan stræcan, on oðre ða unbealdan. Ðæm anfealdan stræcum is to cyðanne ðæt hie bet ne truwien him selfum ðonne hie ðyrfen, ðonne hi forðy nyllað geðafan beon oðerra monna geðeahtes. Ðæm unbealdum is to cyðanne hu giemelease hie bioð ðonne hie hie selfe to suiðe forsioð, forðæm hie mon æt ælcum cierre mæg for hira leohtmodnesse of hiera agnum geðeahte awendan. Ac ðæm anstræcum is to cyðanne, ðær hie ne wenden ðæt hie selfe beteran ond wisran wæren ðonne oðre menn, ðæt hie ne læten hiera geðeaht ond hiera wenan sua feor beforan ealra oðerra monna wenan. Ac ðæm unbealdum is to kyðanne, gif hie be ænegum dæle wolden geðencean hwæt hie selfe wæren, ðonne ne leten hie no hie eallinga on ælce healfe gebigean, ne furðum no awecggan, ðeah ðe hie mon

have been so much the more pleased with what he said, the greater Moses' need, and being the more pleased for his speaking to him so humbly and so reverently, he ought to have been much the more deferential to him and the more decidedly subject to his guidance.

Chapter 42

42. That the obstinate are to be guided in one fashion, the irresolute and the yielding in another.

In one fashion are the singularly headstrong to be admonished, in another the diffident. It is to be explained to the decidedly unyielding that they should not trust in themselves better than they have need, when on that account they are unwilling to be receptive to other people's opinions. To the pliant it is to be explained how negligent they are when they deprecate themselves too greatly, in that on all occasions they can be dissuaded from their own plans on account of their fickleness. But to the refractory it is to be explained that if they did not think themselves better and wiser than other people, they would not set their opinions and beliefs so far above all other people's. But to the weak willed it is to be explained, if they would to any degree consider what they themselves were, they would never let themselves bend altogether in every direction, nor even ever be

manigfealdlice ond mislice styrede, sua sua wac hreod ond
idel, ðe ælc hwiða windes mæg awecggan. Ac to ðæm anstræcum is gecueden ðurh *sanctus* Paulus, "Ne sculon ge
no ðyncan eow selfum to wise." Ond eft he cuæð to ðæm
unbealdum, "Ne læte ge eow ælcre lare wind awecggan." To
ðæm anstræcum is gecueden ðurh Salomon, "Hie etað ðone
wæsðm hiera ægnes weges." Ðæt is ðonne ðonne hie beoð
gefyllede mid hiera ægnum geðeahte. Eft cuæð Salomon be
ðæm unbealdum, "Dysigra monna mod bið suiðe unemn
ond suiðe ungelic." Ond ðæs wisan monnes mod bið suiðe
emn, ond simle him selfum gelic. He bið simle ryhtes
geðeahtes geðafa, forðæm he bið suiðe arod ond suiðe ge-
reðre on ryhtum weorcum. Ac ðara dysegra monna mod bið
suiðe unemn, forðæm hit gedeð hit self him selfum suiðe ungelic for ðære gelomlican wendinge, forðæm hit næfre eft ne
bið ðæt hit ær wæs.

2   Eac is to wietanne ðætte sume unðeawas cumað of oðrum
unðeawum sua ilce sua hie comon ær of oðrum. Forðy us
is to wietanne ðæt we magon hie sua iðesð mid ðreaunga
gebetan, gif we ðone biteran wille æt ðæm æsprynge for-
wyrceað ond adrygað, forðæm ðære anwilnesse æwilm is
ofermetta, ond of ðære leohtmodnesse cymð sio twiefeald-
nes ond sio unbieldo. Ða anstræcan ðonne sint to monianne
ðæt hie ongieten ða upahæfenesse hiora modes, ond geornlice tiligen ðæt hie hie selfe oferwinnen, ðy læs ðonne hie
oferhyggað ðæt hie sien oferreahte utane mid oðerra manna
ryhtum spellum ond larum, hie ðonne sien innan gehæfte
mid ofermettum. Eac hie sint to manianne ðæt hie geðencen ðætte Crist, ðe simle anes willan wæs ond God Fæder, us
salde bisne urne willan to brecanne, ða he cuæð, "Ne sece ic
no minne willan, ac mines Fæder, ðe me hider sende." Ond

shaken, though they are repeatedly buffeted in different ways, like a pliant and hollow reed which every breath of wind can shake. But to the self-willed it is said through Saint Paul, "You ought not to think yourselves too wise." And in turn he said to the pliant, "Do not let the wind of every doctrine shake you." To the unyielding it is said through Solomon, "They shall eat the fruit of their own way." That is, then, when they are filled with their own opinions. In turn Solomon said about the diffident, "The minds of foolish people are quite uneven and quite diffuse." And the mind of the wise person is quite regular and quite consistent with itself. He is always receptive to proper advice, because he is very active and engaged in just undertakings. But foolish people's minds are quite uneven, because they make themselves very inconsistent with themselves with their continual changes, since they never remain as they were before.

It is also to be recognized that some vices proceed from other vices, just as those earlier ones proceeded from others. Therefore, it is for us to recognize that we can amend them with correction as readily as possible if we stanch and dry up the bitter spring at its source, since the font of self-will is pride, and from caprice arise self-doubt and diffidence. The stubborn, then, are to be cautioned to recognize the presumption of their mind and to work sedulously to master themselves, so that, when they disdain to be convinced outwardly by other people's just arguments and counsel, they not inwardly be made captive to pride. They are also to be urged to consider that Christ, who was ever of one will with God the Father, set us an example for mastering our inclinations when he said, "I am not pursuing my will, but that of my Father, who sent me here." And also he

eac he gehett ðæt he sua don wolde, ðonne he eft come on
ðæm ytemestan dæge, forðæm ðe he wolde ðæt we nu ðe
bett underfengen ðone cræft ðære lare. Ðæt he cyðde, ða he
cuæð, "Ne mæg ic nane wuht don mines agnes ðonces, ac sua
ic deme sua ic minne Fæder gehiere." Ac hwy sceal ænigum
menn ðonne ðyncean to orgellic ðæt he onbuge to oðres
monnes willan, ðonne Godes agen sunu, ðonne he cymð mid
his mægenðrymme to demanne, ond his wuldor to ætie-
wanne, he cyðde ðæt he no ðonne of him selfum ne demde,
ac of ðæm ðe hine sent?

3   Ongean ðæt sint to manianne ða unbealdan ond ða unfæsðrædan ðæt hie hera mod mid stillnesse ond gestæððignesse gestrongien. Sona aseariað ða twigu ðære hwurfulnesse, gif æresð se wyrtruma bið forcorfen æt ðære
heortan—ðæt is sio leohtmodnes. Ðy mon sceal fæsðne
weal wyrcean, ðy mon ær gehawige ðæt se grund fæsð sie,
ðær mon ðone grundweall onlecgge. Ðy sceal eac bion ofersuiðed sio unfæsðrædnes ond sio unbieldo ðara geðohta, ðy
mon hine bewarige wið ða leohtmodnesse. Ðære leohtmodnesse ond ðære leasmodnesse *sanctus* Paulus hine ladode, ða
he cuæð, "Wene ge nu ðæt ic ænigre leohtmodnesse bruce,
oððe ðætte ic ðence æfter woruldluste, oððe wene ge ðæt
ægðer sie mid me ge gise ge nese?" Suelce he openlice cuæde
ðæt hine ne meahte nan scur ðære hwurfulnesse astyrigean,
forðæm he ðære leohtmodnesse unðeawes nan wuht næfde.

promised that he would do so when he came again on the final day, because he wanted us now better to accept the force of this lesson. He made that known when he said, "I cannot do anything of my own volition, but I judge as I hear my Father." But why should it appear to anyone too demeaning to accede to another's will, seeing as God's own son declared that, when he will come in majesty to sit in judgment and to reveal his glory, he would not then judge in his own capacity but in that of the one who will send him?

By contrast, the irresolute and the fickle are to be advised 3 to fortify their mind with composure and steadfastness. The branches of inconstancy quickly wither if first the rootstock is cut away at the pith—that is, frivolity. When a sturdy wall is to be constructed, first it is to be determined that the ground is firm on which the foundation is to be laid. When vacillation and pliancy are likewise to be mastered, caprice is to be checked. Saint Paul cleared himself of suspicion of levity and inconstancy when he said, "Do you now think that I indulge any whim, or that I think in accordance with worldly fashion, or do you suppose that it is with me both 'yes' and 'no'?" It is as if his plain meaning were that no blast of fickleness could move him, because he had nothing of the fault of frivolousness.

Chapter 43

XLIII. Ðætte on oðre wisan sint to manianne
ða ðe hie selfe forgiefað gifernesse,
on oðre wisan ða ðe doð forhæfdnesse.

On oðre wisan sint to manigenne ða gifran, on oðre ða ðe
forhæfdnesse doð, forðæm ðæm ofergifrum wile fylgean
ofersprecolnes ond leohtlicu weorc ond leaslicu ond
wrænnes, ond ðæm swiðe fæstendan oft folgað ungeðyld,
ond hwilum eac ofermetta. Gif ðam gifran ungemetlicu
spræc ne eglde, ðonne ne burne se weliga ðe suiður on ðære
tungan ðe on oðrum limum, se ðe on ðæm godspelle gesæd
is ðætte ælce dæge symblede, ðæt wæs se se ðe cwæð, "Fæder
Habraham, miltsa me, ond onsend Ladzarus, ðætte he
gewæte his ytemestan finger on wættre, ond mid ðæm
gecele mine tungan, forðæm ic eom cwielmed on ðys liege."
Mid ðy worde wæs getacnod ðætte ða ðe ælce dæg symbliað,
on ðære tungan suiður syngiað ðonne on oðrum limum,
forðæm ðe he wæs eall biernende, ond ðeah ða tunga suiðust
mænde, ond him ðære kelnesse bæd.

2   Ond eft ðæm gifrum suiðe hrædlice him willað fylgan
leohtlicu weorc ond unnyt. Ðæt trymeð sio halige æ, ðær
hio cuæð, "Ðæt folc sæt, æt, ond dranc, ond siððan aryson,
ond eodon him plegean." Sua oft se oferæt wierð gehwierfed
to fierenluste, forðæm ðonne sio womb bið full ond aðened,
ðonne bið aweaht se anga ðære wrænnesse. Forðæm wæs gecueden to ðæm lytegan feonde, ðe ðæs ærestan monnes mod

Chapter 43

43. That those who give themselves over to appetite are to be guided in one fashion, those who practice restraint in another fashion.

In one fashion are the voracious to be instructed, in another those who practice self-denial, because garrulousness and trivial and dishonest enterprises and licentiousness will keep the company of the overly wolfish, and impatience often attends the very abstemious, and sometimes also pride. If immoderate speech did not afflict the gluttonous, the wealthy man would not have been inflamed more in the tongue than in other organs, the one about whom it is said in the gospel that he feasted daily, which is the one who said, "Father Abraham, have pity on me, and send Lazarus, that he may wet the tip of his finger in water and with it cool my tongue, for I am anguished in this flame." By these words it is signified that those who feast every day sin more in the tongue than in other members, since he was all aflame, and yet he complained most about his tongue and begged for cooling relief for it.

And in turn, trivial and unproductive endeavors will very 2 soon keep the company of the gluttonous. Holy scripture confirms this, where it says, "The people sat, ate, and drank, and afterward arose and went to amuse themselves." Thus, excessive consumption is often transformed into lechery, because when the belly is full and distended, the goad of licentiousness is stirred. For that reason, it was said by the

ontynde on ðæs æples gewilnunge, ond hit ða gewearp mid synne grine, to ðæm wæs gecueden mid ðære godcundan stemne, "On ðinre wambe ond on ðinum breostum ðu scealt snican"; suelce he openlice cuæde, "On giefernesse ond on unnytum geðohtum ðu ricsasð ofer ða menniscan heortan"; forðæm ðæm ðe on giefernesse ongietene beoð wile folgian fierenlust. Ðæt cyðde se witga, ða he ðæt openlice sæde ðætte sua gewearð, ond ðæt gebiecnede ðæt ða giet diegle wæs; he cuæð, "Koka ealdormon towearp ða burg æt Hierusalem." Ðara koka ealdormon bið sio womb, forðæm eall hiera gesuinc ond hiera ðenung belimpeð to hiere, hu heo weorðe mid swotlecustum mettum gefylled. Ða weallas ðonne Hierusalem getacniað ða mægenu ðære saule. Ða mægenu beoð aræredu mid wilnunge to ðære uplican sibbe. Ac ðara koka ealdormon towierpð ða weallas Hierusalem. Ðæt is, ðonne ðonne sio wamb bið aðened mid fylle for giefernesse, ðonne towierpð hio ðurh fierenlustas ða mægenu ðære saule.

3   Ongean ðæt ðonne is to cyðanne ðæm fæstendum, gif ðæs modes forhæfdnes ful oft mid ungeðylðe ne ascoke ða sibbe of ðæm sceate ðære smyltnesse, ðonne ne cuæde *sanctus* Petrus to his cnihtum sua sua he cuæð; he cwæð, "Nu ge habbað geleafan, wyrceað nu god weorc, ond habbað ðonne wisdom, ond on ðam wisdome habbað forhæfdnesse, ond eac lærað, ond huru on ðære forhæfdnesse geðylde." Ne cuæde he no sua, gif he ne ongeate ðæt him wæs ðæs wana, ac forðy ðe he ongeat ðæt sio ungeðyld oft dereð ðæm mannum ðe micle forhæfdnesse habbað, ða lærde he ðæt hie huru sceoldon ða habban toeacan ðære forhæfdnesse. Gif eac sio scyld ðara ofermetta ne gewundode ðy oftor ðæt mod ðæs fæstendan, ðonne ne cuæde no *sanctus* Paulus, "Se

divine voice to the false fiend who first opened for the human mind the way to desiring the apple and then made it stumble with the snare of sin, "On your belly and on your breast you shall crawl"; as if its plain meaning were, "In appetite and idle thoughts you will rule over the human heart"; because lust will attend one who is gripped by ravenousness. The prophet showed this when he plainly foretold what turned out so and revealed what was yet obscure; he said, "The commander of cooks laid low the city at Jerusalem." The commander of cooks is the belly, for all their labor and their service is on its behalf, how it may be filled with the most savory morsels. Then the walls of Jerusalem signify the virtues of the soul. The virtues are built up with the desire for celestial peace. But the commander of cooks casts down the walls of Jerusalem. That is, when the belly is distended with its fill by greediness, by its licentiousness it overthrows the virtues of the soul.

By contrast, then, it is to be explained to the fasting, if 3 abstemiousness of mind did not very often out of impatience displace peace from the shelter of tranquility, then Saint Peter would not have spoken to his disciples as he did speak, saying, "Now that you have belief, perform good works and possess wisdom, and in that wisdom possess abstinence, and also teach it, and especially in abstinence patience." He would not have spoken so if he had not perceived that they were wanting in it, but since he understood that impatience often troubles someone who has great self-restraint, he instructed that they especially should possess that as well as self-restraint. In addition, if the fault of pride did not more often impair the mind of the abstinent, Saint Paul would not have said, "Whoever chooses to fast ought

ðe fæstan wille, ne tæle he no ðone ðe ete." Ond eft he cwæð to Kolosensum, ða he ongeat ðæt hie gulpun hiera fæstennes, "Oft ðonne mon ma fæst ðonne he ðyrfe, ðonne eoweð he utan eaðmodnesse, ond for ðære ilcan eaðmodnesse he ofermodgað innan micle ðy hefelicor." Gif ðæt mod ful oft ne aðunde on ofermettum for ðære forhæfdnesse, ðonne ne talode se ofermoda Phariseus to sua micle mægene ða forhæfdnesse sua he dyde, ða he cwæð, "Ic fæste tuwa on wican."

4   Ongean ðæt sint to manianne ða ofergifran, ðeah hie ne mægen ðone unðeaw forlætan ðære gifernesse ond ðære oferwiste, ðæt he huru hine selfne ne ðurhstinge mid ðy sweorde unryhthæmedes, ac ongiete hu micel leohtmodnes ond leasferðnes ond oferspræc cymeð of ðære oferwiste, ðy læs he hit mid ðæm oðrum yfele geiece, ond eac ðonne he his wambe sua hnesclice oleceð, ðæt he forðæm ne weorðe wælhreowlice gefangen mid ðæm grinum uncysta. Ac we sculun geðencean, sua oft sua we ure hand doð to urum muðe for giefernesse ofergemet, ðæt we geedniwiað ond gemyndgiað ðære scylde ðe ure ieldesta mæg us on forworhte, ond we beoð sua micle fier gewitene fram urum æfterran mæge ðe us eft geðingode, sua we oftor aslidað on ðæm unðeawe.

5   Ongean ðæt sint to manianne ða fæstendan ðæt hie huru geornlice giemen, ðær ðær hie fleoð ðone unðeaw ðære gifernesse, ðætte of ðæm gode ne weorðe wyrse yfel akenned: ðætte, ðonne ðonne ðæt flæsc hlænað, ðæt mod ne beræse on ungeðyld, ond ðonne sie unnyt ðætte ðæt flæsc sie oferswiðed, gif ðæt mod bið mid ðæm ierre oferswiðed. Oft eac, ðonne ðæt mod ðæs fæstendan bið mid ðy irre ofseten, ðonne cymð sio blis seldhwanne, suelce hio sie cuma

not to condemn one who eats." And again he said to the Colossians, when he perceived that they boasted of their fasting, "Frequently when someone abstains more than is needful, he outwardly displays humility, and for that same humility he grows so much the more profoundly proud within." If the mind did not quite often swell in pride over abstinence, the proud Pharisee would not have accounted abstemiousness so great a virtue as he did when he said, "I fast twice weekly."

By contrast, the gluttonous are to be warned that even if   4 they cannot forgo the sin of appetite and overeating, they at least should not run themselves through with the sword of fornication, but understand what great caprice and spiritual laxity and volubility come from stuffing themselves, so that they not compound it with that other evil, and also that when they pamper their belly so tenderly they not by that means be cruelly caught in the trap of indecencies. But we ought to have it in mind, as often as we put our hand to our mouth for excess of appetite, to renew and call again to memory the offense by which our most ancient kinsman ruined us, and that we are so much the further removed from our nearer Kinsman who interceded for us, the more frequently we stray into that vice.

In opposition to that, the fasting are to be warned to take   5 especially concerted care, wherever they fly from the vice of appetite, that a worse offense not be born out of that good: that, when the flesh grows lean, the mind not bolt to impatience, and it turn out to be in vain that the flesh is overcome if the mind is overcome by anger. Often, likewise, when the mind of one who fasts is assailed by anger, happiness visits seldom, as if it were a guest or a stranger, because

oððe elðeodig, forðæm ðæt mod bið mid ðy ierre gewemmed, ond forðæm forliesð ðæt god ðære forhæfdnesse,
forðæm ðe he hine no ne beheold wið ða gæstlican scylde.
Be ðæm wæs suiðe ryhte gecueden ðurh ðone witgan, "On
eowrum fæstendagum bið ongieten eower willa." Ond sona
ðæræfter he cuæð, "To gemotum ond to gecidum ond to
iersunga ond to fystgebeate ge fæstað." Willa belimpð to
blisse simle ond ðæt fystgebeat to irre. On iedelnesse ðonne
bið se lichoma mid fæstenne gesuenced, ðonne ðæt mod bið
forlæten ond onstyred ond todæled ungedafenlice ond unendebyrdlice on unðeawas. Ond ðeah hie sint to manianne
ðæt hie no hiera fæsten ne gewanigen, ne eft ne wenen ðæt
hit anlipe full healic mægen sie beforan ðæm dieglan deman,
ðy læs hie wenen ðæt hit anlipe micellre geearnunge mægen
sie, ond ðonne weorðen on hiera mode forðy to up ahæfene.
Be ðæm wæs gecueden ðurh Essaias ðone witgan, "Ne geceas ic no ðis fæsten, ac ðyllic fæsten ic geceas: brec ðæm
hyngriendum ðinne hlaf, ond ðone widfarendan ond ðone
wædlan læd on ðin hus."

6   Be ðæm we magon geðencean, hu lytelu sio forhæfdnes
bið gesewen, gif hio ne bið mid oðrum goodum weorcum
geiced. Be ðæm cuæð Iohel se witga, "Gehalgiað eower
fæsten." Ðæt is ðonne ðæt mon his fæsten gehalgige, ðæt
he hit geice mid oðrum godum weorcum; ðonne mæg he
eowian ðær Gode suiðe gelicweorðe forhæfdnesse. Forðæm
is to cyðanne ðæm fæstendum ðæt hie wieten ðæt hie ðonne
Gode suiðe licwyrðe forhæfdnesse briengað, ðonne hie
ðearfendum monnum sellað hiera ondliefene ðone dæl ðe hi
him selfum oftioð. Ac us is suiðe geornlice to gehieranne
hwæt Dryhten ðreatigende cuæð to Iudeum ðurh Sacharias
ðone witgan; he cuæð, "Eall ðæt ðæt ge fæstun ond weopun

the mind is corrupted by wrath and therefore loses the
benefit of self-denial, since one did not safeguard himself
against that spiritual wrong. About this it was quite accurately said through the prophet, "On your days of fasting
your will is realized." And immediately after that he said,
"You fast for conflict and for wrangling and for passion and
for fistfights." Will appertains always to happiness and fistfights to ire. In vain, then, is the body mortified by fasting
when the mind is set loose and agitated and diffused by vices
in unseemly and chaotic fashion. And yet they are to be exhorted not to abate their fast, nor, by contrast, to believe
that it is a quite singularly exalted virtue in the sight of the
unseen judge, lest they believe that it is a virtue of un-
matched high merit and therefore grow too self-satisfied in
their mind. About this it was said through the prophet Isaiah, "I never chose this fast, but such fasting as this I chose:
break your bread with those who hunger, and open your
house to the homeless and the destitute."

In respect to this, we can consider what little regard is ac-   6
corded self-restraint if it is not augmented with other good
works. About this the prophet Joel said, "Consecrate your
fast." To consecrate one's fast is to augment it with other
good works; then by that one can show God a quite acceptable fastidiousness. For this reason, the fasting are to be advised to know that they are bringing a very appreciable self-
denial to God when they give to needy people the portion of
their sustenance that they themselves forgo. But we need to
attend conscientiously to what the Lord said in rebuke of
the Jews through the prophet Zachariah: he said, "All that
you have fasted and wept in the fifth and in the seventh

on ðæm fiftan ond on ðam siofoðan monðe nu hundsiofan-
tig wintra, ne fæste ge ðæs nawuht me, ond ðonne ge æton,
ðonne æte ge eow selfum, ond ðonne ge druncon, ðonne
druncon ge eow selfum." Ne fæsð se no Gode ac him selfum,
se ðe ðæt nyle ðearfum sellan ðæt he ðonne on mæle læfð, ac
wile hit healdan eft to oðrum mæle, ðæt he eft mæge his
wambe mid gefyllan.

7   Ac sua he sceal etan ðætte hine sio gewilnung ðære gifernesse of his modes fæsðrædnesse ne gebrienge, ne eft sio
ðræsðing ðæs lichoman ðæt mod ne ascrence mid upahæfenesse. Gehieren ða oferetolan ða word ðe Krist of his agnum
muðe cuæð; he cuæð, "Behealdað eow ðæt eowre heortan ne
sin gehefegode mid oferæte ond druncennesse ond on to
monigfaldum ymbehogan ðisse worulde, ðy læs eow on ðæm
weorcum gemete se reða ond se egeslica dæg, se cymð ofer
ealle eorðwaran ungeðinged, sua sua grin." Gehieren eac ða
fæstendan hwæt he eft cuæð; he cuæð, "Ne geunclænsað
ðæt no ðone mon ðæt on his muð gæð, ac ðæt ðæt of his
muðe gæð, ðæt hine geunclænsað." Gehieren ða oferetolan
hwæt *sanctus* Paulus cuæð: "Fulga nu se mete ðære wambe
willan, ond sio wamb ðæs metes, ðonne towyrpð God
ægðer." Ond eft he cuæð, "Ne gewunigen ge to oferetolnisse
ond to oferdruncennisse." Ond eft he cuæð, "Se ofermete ne
befæsð us næbre Gode." Gehieren eft ða fæstendan hwæt
he to him cuæð; he cuæð ðæt ðæm clænum wære eal clæne,
ond ðæm unclænum nære nan wuht clæne. Gehiren eft ða
oferetolan hwæt he to him cuæð; he cuæð ðætte hira wamb
wære hiera god, ond hie dydon hiera bysmer him to
wyrðscipe. Gehieren eac ða fæstendan hwæt he to him
cuæð; he cuæð ðæt ðæm forhæbbendum hwilum gebyrede
ðæt hie gewieten of hiera geleafan, ond forbeodað monnum

months now these seventy years, you were not fasting for me at all, and when you ate, you ate for yourselves, and when you drank, you drank for yourselves." He fasts not for God but for himself who is unwilling to give to the poor what he leaves of a meal, but wishes to keep it in turn for another meal, so that he can fill his belly with it again.

But he ought to eat in such a way that the cravings of the appetite not lead him away from his firmness of intent, nor, by contrast, the denial of the flesh make the mind miscarry with self-regard. Let gluttons hear the words that Christ spoke from his own mouth, saying, "Take care that your hearts not be burdened with repletion and drinking and in too many concerns of this world, lest the fierce and terrible day encounter you in the midst of that, the day that will arrive unanticipated for all the inhabitants of earth, like a trap." Let the fasting hear what he in turn said, saying, "What goes into a person's mouth does not defile him, but what comes out of his mouth defiles him." Let the voracious hear what Saint Paul said: "Now, if food fulfills the will of the belly, and the belly that of food, God will destroy them both." And again he said, "Do not accustom yourselves to excessive eating and inebriation." And again he said, "Extravagant consumption will never commend us to God." Let the abstinent hear what he said to them: he said that to the pure all things were pure, and to the impure nothing was pure. Let gourmands in turn hear what he said to them: he said that their belly was their god, and they made of their disgrace a mark of honor. Let those who fast also hear what he said to them: he said that sometimes it would happen to the abstemious that they would depart from their faith, and forbid people to wed, and deny them the foods that God

ðæt hie hiwien, ond ða mettas ðe God self gesceop to etanne geleaffullum monnum, ðæm ðe ongietað soðfæsðnisse, ond Gode ðonciað mid goodum weorcum his giefa. Gehieren ða oferetolan hwæt *sanctus* Paulus cwæð; he cuæð ðæt hit wære good ðæt mon foreode flæsc ond win for bisene his broðrum. Gehiren ða fæstendan hwæt he eft cuæð; he cuæð ðæt ge moston drincan gewealden wines for eowres magan mettrymnesse. Forðæm he ðæt cuæð ðæt he wolde ðæt ða oferetolan geleornoden ðæt hie to ungemetlice ne wilnoden flæscmetta, ond eft ða fæstendan ne forsawen ða etendan, forðæm ðe hie ðære Godes giefe brucað ða ðe oðre forberað.

Chapter 44

XLIIII. Ðætte on oðre wisan sint to manianne ða ðe
hiora agnu ðing mildheortlice sellað,
ond on oðre wisan ða ðe ðonne giet wilniað
oðerra monna gereafigan.

On oðre wisan sint to manianne ða ðe hira god mild-heortlice sellað, on oðre wisan ða ðe ðonne giet flietað æfter oðera monna, ond hie reafiað. To manienne sint ða ðe hiera mildheortlice sellað ðætte hie ne aðinden on hiora mode to ðæm ðæt hi hi hæbben ofer ða ðe hie hiora sellað, ne hie selfe ðy beteran ne taligen ðe ða oðre, ðeah ða oðre be him libben. Ac ða eorðlican hlafordas sint to ðæm gesette ðæt

himself created for devout people to eat, those who acknowledge righteousness and with good works give thanks
to God for his gifts. Let those who eat excessively hear what
Saint Paul said: he said that it would be good to forgo meat
and wine as an example to one's brothers. Let the abstinent
hear what he in turn said: he said that you are allowed to
drink a modicum of wine for your stomach's health. He said
that because he wanted the gluttonous to learn not to crave
meat too excessively, and, conversely, those who fast not to
despise those who eat for availing themselves of that gift of
God that others forgo.

Chapter 44

44. That those who compassionately give away their own things are to be guided in one fashion, and those who still desire to steal from other people in another fashion.

In one fashion are to be counseled those who generously
give away their goods, in another fashion those who still
contend for other people's, and rob them. Those who generously give their own are to be exhorted not to pride themselves in their mind to such an extent that they hold themselves superior to those to whom they give theirs, nor count
themselves better than the others, even though the others
live by their generosity. But earthly lords are appointed for

hie ða endebyrdnesse ond ða ðegnunga hiora hieredum gebrytnige, ond hie gerecce, ond ðæt folc is to ðæm gesett ðæt hie scylen be hira rædum libban. Ðæm hlafordum is beboden ðæt hie him doon ðæt hira ðearf sie, ond ðæm ðegnum is beboden ðæt hie him ðæt to genyhte don ðæt hie him sellen. Ond ðeah oft agyltað ða hlafordas, ond ða menn wuniað on Godes hyldo ða ðe ryhtwise beoð, ond ða habbað his unhyldo ðe hit him bryttian sceoldon, ond ða beoð butan ierre ðe be hiera giefum libban sculon. Eac sint to manienne ða ðe ðonne mildheortlice sellað ðæt hie ðonne habbað, ðæt hie ðonne angieten ðæt hie sint gesette ðæm hefencundan Gode to ðeningmannum, to dælanne ðas lænan god. Forðæm hie hie sculon sua micle estelicor dælan sua hie ongietað ðæt him lænre ond unagenre bið ðæt hie ðær dælað, forðæm hie magon ongietan ðæt hie beoð to hiera ðenunga gesette Godes giefe to dælanne. Hwy sculon hie ðonne beon forðæm up ahæfene ond aðundene on hira mode? Him wære ðonne micel ðearf ðæt hie leten Godes ege hie geeaðmedan.

2   Ond eac him is micel ðearf ðæt hie geornlice geðencen ðæt hie to unweorðlice ne dælen ðæt him befæsð bið, ðy læs hie awuht sellen ðæm ðe hie nan wuht ne sceoldon, oððe nan wuht ðæm ðe hie hwæthwugu sceoldon, oððe eft fela ðam ðe hie lytel sceoldon, oððe lytel ðæm ðe hie micel sceoldon, ðy læs hie unnytlice forweorpen ðæt ðæt hie sellen for hira hrædhydignesse, oððe him eft hefiglice ofðynce ðæs ðe hie sealdon, ond hi scylen selfe beon biddende, ond forðy weorðen geunrotsode, oððe hie eft her wilnigen ðara leana ðæs ðe hie on ælmessan sellað, ðy læs sio gidsung ðæs lænan

the purpose of determining the ranks and the duties of their dependents and supervising them, and the people are placed so as to be obliged to live by their dictates. Lords are mandated to do for them what their need demands, and subjects are mandated to content themselves with what they give them. And yet often lords are in the wrong, and the people, who are righteous, persist in God's favor, and those have his displeasure who are to distribute it to them, and those are without his anger who are obliged to live by the lords' liberality. Then those who generously give what they have are also to be admonished to recognize that they are appointed stewards of the celestial God to distribute these ephemeral goods. Therefore, they ought to distribute them the more munificently, the better they understand that what they disburse there is lent them and is not for their keeping, since they can see that they are given as their commission to deal out God's gifts. Then why should they be haughty and conceited in their attitude on that account? It would then be no small requirement for them to let the fear of God lend them humility.

And likewise there is great need for them to arrange carefully not to distribute too inequitably what is entrusted to them, so that they do not give anything to those who ought to be given nothing, or nothing to those who ought to be given something; or, alternatively, give much to those who ought to receive little, or little to those who deserve much, so that for their impetuousness they not squander uselessly what they give, or in time profoundly regret having given, and they be obliged themselves to be beggars and on that account grow dispirited; or, again, desire to have reward here for the alms they give, so that the craving for ephem-

2

lofes adwæsce ðæt leoht ðære giofolnesse, oððe eft sio giofolness sie gemenged wið unrotnesse, oððe he eft for ðæm giefum, ðe him ðonne ðynceð ðæt he suiðe wel atogen hæbbe, his mod suiður fægnige ond blissige ðonne hit gemetlic oððe gedafenlic sie. Ac ðonne hie hit eall ryhtlice gedæled hæbben, ðonne ne teon hie nan wuht ðæs lofes ond ðæs geðonces to him, ðy læs hie hit eal forleosen, ðonne hie hit gedæled hæbben, ne him selfum ne tellen to mægene hiora freodom.

3   Ac gehieren hwæt awriten is on ðæm ærendgewrite *sancte* Petres: "Gif hwa ðenige, ðenige he suelce he hit of Godes mægene ðenige, næs of his selfes, ðy læs he to ungemetlice fægenige for his godum weorcum." Ac gehieren hwæt awriten is on Kristes bocum; hit is awriten, "Ðonne ge eall hæbben gedoon ðæt eow beboden is, ðonne cueðe ge ðæt ge sien unnytte ðeowas, forðæm ge ðæt an worhton ðæt ge niede scoldon." Ond eft, ðy læs ða rummodnessa sio unrotnes gewemme, gehieraðd ðone cuide ðe *sanctus* Paulus cuæð to Corinctheum: he cuæð ðætte ðone gladan giefan God lufode. Ond eft, ðy læs hie for ðæm gedale ðæs feos wilnigen ðisses lænan lifes, gehieren hie ðone cwide ðe on Cristes bocum awriten is, ðæt is ðæt sio winestre hand ne scyle witan hwæt sio suiðre do. Ðæt is, ðonne ðonne he his ælmessan dælð, ðæt ðær ne sie wið gemenged nan gielp ðisses andweardan lifes, ne he ne scrife ðæs hlisan buton hu he ryhtosð wyrce. Ne he ne gieme hwelce hylde he mid ðære ælmessan gewriexle, ac gehiren hwæt awriten is on Cristes bocum; he cuæð, "Ðonne ðu hæbbe gegearwod underngiefl oððe æfengiefl, ne laða ðu no ðærto ðine friend, ne ðine broðor, ne ðine cuðan, ne ðine welegan neahgeburas, ðy læs

eral praise will douse the light of generosity; or, again, generosity be mingled with malaise; or, again, on account of the gifts that it seems to them they have disposed of very well, their mind should feel greater delight and satisfaction than is fit or proper. But when they have judiciously distributed it all, let them not lay claim to any praise and thanks for themselves, in order not to vitiate it completely when they have distributed it, nor let them account their liberality a virtue themselves.

But let them hear what is written in the Epistle of Saint 3 Peter: "If anyone serves, let him minister as if he were serving by the power of God, not of himself, lest he take immoderate satisfaction in his good works." But let them hear what is written in the books of Christ, where it is written, "When you have done everything that is required of you, say that you are worthless slaves, since you accomplished only what you ought by necessity." And again, to prevent anxiety from tainting largesse, hear the dictum that Saint Paul spoke to the Corinthians: he said that God loved the cheerful giver. And again, to prevent their desiring this fleeting acclaim for the distribution of wealth, let them hear the charge inscribed in the books of Christ, which is that the left hand ought not to know what the right does. That is, when they distribute their alms, let there be no grasping after glory in this present life mingled with it, nor ought they to care for repute, but for how they may do what is fittest. Nor ought they to have regard for whatever favor they may earn by alms, but let them hear what is written in the books of Christ: he said, "When you have prepared a morning meal or an evening meal, do not invite your friends to it, nor your brothers, nor your intimates, nor your wealthy neighbors,

hie ðe don ðæt selfe. Ac ðonne ðu feorme gierwe on ælmessan, laða ðærto wædlan ond wanhale ond healte ond blinde; ðonne bis ðu eadig, forðæm hie nyton mid hwam hie hit ðe forgielden."

4   Ond ðætte mon ðonne ðurhteon mæge, ðæt he ðæt ne forilde, ac gehieren hwæt awriten is on Salomonnes bocum: hit is awrieten ðæt mon ne scyle cweðan to his friend, "Ga, ond cum to morgenne, ðonne selle ic ðe hwæthwugu," gif he hit him ðonne sellan mæge. Ond eft, ðy læs mon unnytlice mierre ðæt ðæt he hæbbe, gehieren menn ðisne cwide: "Heald ðine ælmessan, ðy læs ðu hie forweorpe." Ond eft ða ðe to lytel sellað ðæm ðe micles ðorfton, sculon gehieran *sancte* Paules cuide; he cuæð, "Se ðe lytel sæwð, he lytel ripð." Ond ðeah ne selle mon to fela ðæm ðe lytles ðyrfe, ðy læs hwa him self weorðe to wædlan, ond him ðonne gehreowe sio ælmesse. Be ðam cwæð *sanctus* Paulus, "Ne beo ge oðrum monnum sua gifole ðæt hit weorðe eow selfum to gesuince, ac ofer ðæt ðe ge selfe genog hæbben, sellað ðæt ðearfum, ond mid ðy hiera wædle gebetað, ðætte sua ielce sua hie beoð her gefyllede mid ure genyhtsumnesse, we beon eac mid hiera genyhtsumnesse." Ðæt is ðonne hiera genihtsumnes Godes milts, ða geearnað se se on his gæste bið wædla. Ac ðonne ðæs sellendan mod ne cann ða wædelnesse geðolian, ðonne him micles oftogen bið ðæs ðe he habban wolde; ðonne oncann he hiene selfne for ðære hrædhydignesse ðe he ær to fela sealde. Forðy mon scel ær geðencean, ær he hwæt selle, ðæt he hit eft forberan mæge butan hreowe, ðy læs he forleose ða lean ðæs ðe he ær sealde, ond ðæt mod eac weorðe wirs forloren ðurh ða gnornunga. Gehieren eac ða ðe nan wuht ne sellað ðæm ðe hie lytles

lest they do the same for you. But when you prepare a repast, out of charity invite the poor to it and the sick and the lame and the blind; then you will be blessed, since they will not know how they can repay you for it."

And what can be accomplished, then, ought not to be put off, but listen to what is written in the books of Solomon: it is written that a person ought not to say to his friend, "Go away and come back tomorrow; then I will give you something," if he can give it to him then. And again, to prevent someone's scattering futilely what he has, let people hear this saying: "Keep your alms, lest you squander them." And, in turn, those who give too little to those who have had need of much ought to hear Saint Paul's pronouncement when he said, "Who sows little, reaps little." And yet too much ought not to be given to one who has need of little, to avoid someone's making a pauper of himself and then regretting the almsgiving. About this Saint Paul said, "Do not be so munificent to other people that it creates hardship for yourselves, but what you have beyond what is sufficient for yourselves, give to the needy, and with it mitigate their poverty, so that just as they are here filled with our abundance, let us be, too, with their abundance." Their abundance, then, is God's mercy, which a person will earn who is poor in spirit. But when the mind of the giver does not know how to countenance poverty, once he is deprived of a great part of what he wished to have, he will be indignant with himself for the rashness of having given too much. Therefore, one must determine before giving something away that he can forgo it without regret, so that he not lose the reward for what he had given, and the intent be even worse vitiated by complaining. Let them also hear, those who give nothing to

hwæthwugu scoldon, hwæt to him gecweden is on ðæm
godspelle; hit is gecweden, "Sele ælcum ðara ðe ðe bidde."
Eft gehieren ða ða ðe hwæthwugu sellað ðæm ðe hie nane
wuht ne scoldon, hwæt to him gecueden is on Salomonnes
bocum: hit is gecueden: "Sele ðin good, ond na ðeah ðam
synnfullum. Doo wel ðæm eaðmodum, ond ðam arleasum
nan wuht." Ond eft hit is gecweden on Tobius bocum, "Sete
ðin win, ond lege ðinne hlaf ofer ryhtwisra monna byrgenne,
ond ne et his nan wuht, ne ne drinc mid ðæm synfullum." Se
ðonne itt ond drincð mid ðæm synfullum, ond him selð his
hlaf ond his win, se ðæm unryhtwisan fultumað, ond hine
arað, forðæm ðe he unryhtwis bið. Sua eac monige welige
menn on ðys middangearde lætað cuelan hungre Cristes
ðearfan, ond fedað yfle gliigmenn mid oferwiste, ond beoð
ðæm to ungemetlice kystige. Ða ðonne ðe hira hlaf sellað
ðæm synfullum ðe ðearfende beoð—nalles no forðæm ðe
hie synnfulle beoð, ac forðæm ðe hie menn beoð ond
ðearfende beoð—ne selð se no synfullum his hlaf, ac ryht-
wisum, gif he on him ne lufað his yfel, ac his gecynd, ðæt is
ðæt he bið man swa same sua he.

5 Eac sint to manianne ða ðe nu hiera mildheortlice sellað,
ðæt hie geornlice giemen ðæt hie eft ða synne ne gefremmen ðe hie nu mid hira ælmessan aliesað, ðy læs hie eft scilen
don ðæt selfe. Ne fortruwige he hiene æt ðære cipinge, ne
wene he no ðæt Godes ryhtwisnes sie to ceape, swelce he
hie mæge mid his peningum gebygcgean, ond don siððan
suelc yfel suelce hie willen butan ælcre oðerre wrace, ða
hwile ðe hie peningas hæbben mid to gieldanne. Mare is ðæt
mod ðonne se mete, ond se lichoma ðonne ðæt hrægl. Ac
ðonne hwa ægðer ge mete ge hrægl ðearfendum rumodlice

those to whom they ought to give a little of something, what is said to them in the gospel: it is said, "Give to everyone who asks you." In turn let them hear, those who give something to people who ought to be given nothing, what is said to them in the books of Solomon: it is said, "Give away your goods, and yet not to the sinful. Do well by the humble, and do nothing for the wicked." And again it is said in the books of Tobias, "Set out your wine and lay out your bread on the tombs of righteous people, and neither eat nor drink any of it with the sinful." Then one who eats and drinks with the sinful, and gives them his bread and his wine, comes to the aid of the immoral because he is immoral. So, also, many wealthy people in this world let Christ's needy die of hunger, and they feed unsavory entertainers to excess and are extravagantly generous to them. Those, then, who give their bread to the sinful who are needy—not at all because they are sinful, but because they are people, and needy—are not giving their bread to the sinful but to the righteous, if they love in them not their immorality but their nature, which is that they are people as well as they.

Those who compassionately give away their goods are 5 also to be urged to take diligent care that they not again commit the sin they now expiate with their alms, or they will be obliged to do the same again. Let them not presume to bargain, nor to think that God's righteousness is a commodity such as they can buy with their wealth, and afterward do such misdeeds as they please without any other punishment, as long as they have the wherewithal to pay for it. The spirit is more than sustenance, and the body more than clothing. But when someone generously gives both food and clothing to the needy, and defiles his spirit and his

selð, ond his mod ond his lichoman mid unryhtwisnesse besmit, ðonne selð he Gode ða læsðan ryhtwisnesse, ond oftiehð him ðære mæstan, ðonne he syngað on his mode ond on his mægene, ond selð ðeah his ælmessan: selð Gode his æhta, ond hine selfne diobule.

6   Ongean ðæt sint to manigenne ða ðe ðonne giet wilniað oðre menn to reafigeanne, ðæt hie geornlice gehieren ðone cuide ðe gesæd is on ðæm godspelle, ðæt Dryhten cueðan wille, ðonne he cymð to ðæm dome; he cuið, "Me hyngrede, ond ge me nawuht ne sealdun etan. Me ðyrste, ond ge me ne sealdon drincan. Ic wæs cuma, ond ge me noldon onfon. Ic wæs nacod, ond ge me noldon bewreon. Ic wæs untrum ond on cearcerne, ond ge min noldun fandian." Ðæm monnum is gehaten ðæt he wille cueðan, "Gewitað from me, awiergde, on ece fyr, ðæt wæs gegearwod diofle ond his englum." Ne scirð he no hwæðer hie reafoden, oððe hwelc oðer yfel fremeden, ond swaðeah cwið ðæt hie scylen bion gehæfte on ecum fyre. Be ðæm we magon geðencean hu micles wites ða beoð weorðe ðe oðre menn reafiað, nu ða sua micel wite habbað ðe hiora agen ungesceadwislice healdað. Nu ða sua micel wite habbað ðe hira agen nyllað sellan, geðenceað ðonne hwelces wites ge wenen ðæm ðe oðre men reafiað. Hwæt wene ge hwæt sio ðurhtogene unryhtwisnes geearnige, nu sio unðurtogene arfæsðnes swa micel wite geearnað?

7   Gehieren ða reaferas, ða ðe higiað wið ðæs ðæt hie willað oðre menn bereafian, hwæt be him gecweden is: hit is gecweden, "Wa ðæm ðe ealnig gaderað an hine selfne ðæt hefige fenn, ond gemonigfaldað ðætte his ne bið." Ðæt is

body with improbity, he is giving to God the least measure of righteousness and withholding from him the greatest when he sins in his mind and in his bodily powers, and yet distributes his alms: he gives his possessions to God and himself to the devil.

In contrary fashion are to be warned those who are then still willing to rob other people, for them to listen attentively to the words that the gospel says the Lord will speak when he comes to judgment, saying, "I hungered, and you gave me nothing to eat. I thirsted, and you did not provide me with drink. I was a stranger, and you would not take me in. I was naked, and you would not clothe me. I was sick and in prison, and you did not visit me." To these people it is promised that he will say, "Depart from me, you accursed, into everlasting fire, which was prepared for the devil and his angels." He does not distinguish whether they robbed or what other wrongdoing they committed, and yet he says that they are to be confined to fire without end. We can imagine how deserving of eternal suffering are those who defraud other people, considering that those will have such grave suffering who, without exception, keep their own possessions. Considering that those who are unwilling to give away their own will have such severe punishment, think, then, what torment you may expect for those who cheat other people. What do you suppose unrighteousness committed will merit, seeing as rectitude neglected will earn so stark a retribution?

Let swindlers, those who are intent on their desire to cheat other people, hear what is said of them: it is said, "Woe unto one who continually collects on himself heavy mud and multiplies what is not his." That someone amasses

6

7

ðonne ðæt monn gadrige ðæt ðicke fenn on hine, ond hine mid ðy gehefegige, ðæt se gitsere him on geheapige ða byrðenne eorðlicra æhta mid unryhte, ond his worðig ond his land mid unryhte ryme. Ac hi scoldon gehiran ðone cwide ðe bi him gecweden is in Essaies bocum; hit is gecweden, "Wa eow ðe gadriað hus to huse, ond spannað ðone æcer to ðæm oðrum oð ðæs landes mearce, swelce ge ane willen gebugean ealle ðas eorðan"; swelce he openlice cwæde: "Hu feor wolde ge nu ryman eower land? Wolde ge nu ðæt ge næfden nanne gemacan on ðys gemænan middangearde? Ðu cuist nu ðæt ðu wille geswican ðonne, ær ðe ðu genoh hæbbe. Hwonne bið ðæt, ðæt ðe swa ðynce, oððe hwonne bið ðæt, ðæt ðu nyte hwæðer ðu maran wilnige? A ðu findst wið hwone ðu meaht flitan." Ac gehiere ge feohgietseras hwæt be eow gecweden is on Salomonnes bocum: hit is gecweden, "Ne wyrð se gitsere næfre full feos, ond se ðe woruldwelan lufað ungesceadwislice, ne cymð him of ðæm nan wæsðm." Ac him meahte cuman, gif he hi to swiðe ne lufode, ond he hi wel wolde dælan. Ac forðæm ðe he hi her lufað ond hielt, he hi eac her forlæt butan ælcum wæsðme ond ælcum edleane. Ac ða ðe wilniað ðæt hi her beon gefylde mid eallum welum ond mid ðæm willan beoð onælede, hie sculon gehieran ðone cwide ðe be him gecweden is on Salomonnes bocum; hit is gecweden, "Se ðe æfter ðæm higað ðæt he eadig sie on ðisse worulde, ne bið he unsceaðful," ac ða hwile ðe he giernð ðæt he his weolan iece, he agiemeleasað ond forgiet ðæt he forbuge his synna. Swa swa fleogende fugel, ðonne he gifre bið, he gesihð ðæt æs on eorðan, ond ðonne for ðæm luste ðæs metes he forgiet ðæt grin ðæt he mid awierged wirð; swa bið ðæm gitsere. He ge-

thick mud on himself and burdens himself with it, then, is that the acquisitive person freights himself wrongfully with the weight of earthly possessions and unjustly fattens his estate and his lands. But they ought to hear the pronouncement that is made of them in the books of Isaiah, where it is said, "Woe unto you who add house to house and annex one field to the other as far as the land's end, as if you intend to occupy all the earth alone"; as if his plain meaning were, "How far would you enlarge your lands? Would you now like to have no peer in this community of earth? You say now that you intend to leave off before you have enough. When will it be that it appears so to you, or when will it be that you do not know whether you desire more? You will always find someone with whom to compete." But you money chasers should hear what is said about you in the books of Solomon: it is said, "The rapacious will never be sated with money, and one who loves terrestrial riches indiscriminately will reap no fruit from them." But he could benefit if he did not love them excessively, and if he were willing to distribute them appropriately. But because he loves and withholds them here, he will also leave them here without any benefit or any recompense. But those who desire to be glutted here with all riches and are inflamed with that desire ought to hear the assessment that is made of them in the books of Solomon: it is said, "Whoever aims to be prosperous in this world will never be innocent," but as long as he sets his heart on magnifying his wealth, he neglects and forgets to desist from his sins. Just as a bird in flight, when it is greedy and sees carrion on the ground, out of desire for the food will ignore the snare by which it will be throttled, so will it be for the rapa-

sihð ðone welan ðe he wilnað, ond he ne geliefð ðæs grines ðe he mid gebrogden wyrð, ær ðon he hit gefrede.

8   Ac ða ðe wilniað ðisses middangeardes gestreona, ond nyllað wietan ðone demm ðe him æfter cuman sceal, hie sculon gehieran ðone cwide ðe bi him gecweden is on Salomonnes bocum; hit is gecweden, "Ðæt ierfe ðæt ge ærest æfter hiegiað, æt siðesðan hit bið bedæled ælcre bledsunge." On ðys andweardan life we onginnað æresð libban to ðæm ðæt we æt ytemestan onfon sumne dæl bledsunge. Se ðonne ðe wilnað ðæt he wolde on ðæm angienne his lifes woroldspedig weorðan mid unryhte, se hine wile selfne bedælan ðære bledsunge ond ðæs weolan on ðæm ytemestan dæge. Ac ðonne hie wilniað ðurh ða nawhtgitsunga ðæt hie hira woruldspeda ieicenn, ðonne weorðað hie bedælede ðæs ecean eðles ures Fæder. Ac ða ðe wilniað feola to begietanne, ond eac ða ðe magon begietan eall ðæt hie wilniað, gehieren hwæt Krist self cuæð: he cwæð, "Hwæt forstent ænigum menn ðæt, ðeah he mangige ðæt he ealne ðisne middangeard age, gif he his saule forspildt?" Swelce sio Soðfæsðnes openlice cwæde, "Hwelc fremu bið menn ðæt he gestriene eal ðæt him ymbutan sie, gif he forliesð ðæt him on innan bið, swelce he eall gegadrige ðætte his ne sie, ond forspilde hine selfne?" Ac mon mæg ðy hraðor ðara reafera gitsunga gestillan, gif se lareow him gerecð hu fleonde ðis andwearde lif is, ond hie gemyndgað ðara weligera ðe lange striendon, ond lytle hwile brucon; hu hrædlice se færlica deað hie on lytelre hwile bereafode ðæs ðe hi on langre hwile mid unryhte strindon. Ðeah hie hit hrædlice ætsomne ne gestriendon,

cious. He sees the riches that he desires, and he fails to credit the snare with which he will be entangled before he feels its effect.

But those who desire this world's riches, and who refuse 8 to acknowledge the harm that will visit them afterward, ought to hear the point that is made about them in the books of Solomon, where it is said, "The legacy that you pursue at the start will in the end be bereft of every blessing." In this present life, at the start, we set out to live so that, in the end, we may receive some degree of blessing. Then whoever desires unjustly to become materially endowed at the outset of his life will deprive himself of blessing and wealth on the final day. But when through corrupt avarice they desire to amplify their material abundance, they grow estranged from the everlasting abode of our Father. But let those who desire to acquire much, as well as those who are able to acquire all they desire, hear what Christ himself said: he said, "What does it avail anyone though he bargain for the possession of this entire earth if he bring his soul to ruin?" It is as if Truth were plainly to say, "What benefit is there to a person if he should acquire everything outside him if he loses what is within him, as if he were to amass everything that is not his and to impoverish himself?" But the acquisitiveness of swindlers can be subdued more expeditiously if the teacher impresses upon them how fleeting this present life is and reminds them of those wealthy people who took long to amass riches and enjoyed them but a brief interval of time, and how suddenly unforeseen death deprived them in a short while of what they had by injustice amassed over a long while. Though they did not amass it in its entirety all at once, they lost it in

hie hit ðeah swiðe hrædlice ætsomne forluron, ond his nawht mid him ne læddon, buton ða synne ðara yfelena weorca hie brohton to Godes dome. Ac hit mæg eaðe gesælan, gif we him swelc secgað, ðæt hie eac mid us ða oðre tælen, ond hie ðonne eft hira selfra gescamige, ðonne hie gemunað ðæt hie ðæt ilce doð ðæt hie on ðæm oðrum tældon.

Chapter 45

XLV. Ðætte on oðre wisan sint to monianne ða ðe nohwæðer ne oðerra monna ne wilniað, ne hiora agen nyllað sellan; on oðre wisan ða ðe willað sellan ðæt hi gestrinað ond ðeah nyllað geswican ðæt hi oðre men ne reafigen.

On oðre wisan sint to manianne ða ðe nauðer ne oðerra monna ne wilniað, ne hira agen nyllað sellan; on oðre ða ðe hira agen willað sellan, ond ðeah ne magon forlætan ðæt hie oðre menn ne reafigen. Ac ða ðonne ðe hira agen nyllað sellan, ne eac oðerra monna ne gitsiað, hie sint to manianne ðæt hie geornlice geðencen ðæt ðios eorðe, ðe him ðæt gestreon of com, eallum mannum is to gemanan geseald, ond forðæm eallum mannum bringð gemænne foster. Hwæt, se ðonne unryhtlice talað, se ðe talað ðæt he sie unscyldig, gif he ða good, ðe us God to gemanan sealde, him

its entirety all at once, and they took nothing of it with them, but they brought the sins of their base deeds to God's judgment. But it can readily come to pass, if we say such things to them, that they also, along with us, will deplore others, and then be ashamed of themselves when they remember that they are doing the very thing that they deplored in those others.

Chapter 45

45. That those who neither desire other people's
property nor care to give away their own
are to be guided in one fashion;
in another fashion those who are willing to
give what they acquire and yet will not
desist from robbing other people.

In one fashion are to be admonished those who desire to give away neither other people's goods nor their own, in another those who are willing to give away their own and yet cannot desist from robbing other people. But then those who are unwilling to bestow their own goods and also do not covet other people's are to be advised to consider well that this earth, from which their wealth derives, is given to all people in common and therefore furnishes all people with common sustenance. Now, then, he judges amiss who accounts himself upright if he appropriates all to himself the

synderlice ægnað. Ac ðonne hie nyllað sellan ðæt ðæt hie underfengon, ðonne mæstað hie hie selfe on hira niehstena
cwale, forðæm hie nealice swa fela ðearfena ofsleað swa hie
iðelice mid hiera ælmessan gehelpan meahton, gif hie
woldon. Forðæm, ðonne ðonne we ðæm ðearfum hiera
niedðearfe sellað, hiera ægen we him sellað, nalles ure;
ond ryhtlicor we magon cweðan ðæt we him gielden scylde
ðonne we him mildheortnesse don.

2   Forðæm sio Soðfæstnes, ðæt is Crist, ða ða he lærde ðæt
mon ælmessan wærlice sellan sceolde, ða cwæð he, "Giemað
ðæt ge eowre ryhtwisnesse ne don beforan monnum." To
ðæm cwide belimpð eac ðæs psalmscopes sang ðe he sang,
ða he cwæð, "Se todælð his god, ond selð ðearfum, his
ryhtwisnes wunað on ecnesse." Nolde he no ða rummodnesse hatan mildheortness, ac ryhtwisnes, forðæm ðætte us
from ðæm gemænan gode geseald bið, hit is cynn ðæt we
ðæs eac gemænelice brucen. Be ðæm cwæð Salomon, "Se ðe
ryhtwis bið, he bið a sellende, ond no ne blinð." Eac hie sint
to maniene ðæt hie geornlice geðencen ðætte se fiicbeam,
ðe on ðæm godspelle gesæd is ðætte nanne wæsðm ne bære,
stod unnyt; forðæm him wearð ierre se goda wyrhta forðæm
he ofergreow ðæt land butan wæsðme. Ðonne ofergrewð se
fiicbeam ðæt lond, ðonne se gitsere hyt ond heleð to unnytte
ðæt ðæt manegum menn to nytte weorðan meahte. Swa se
fiicbeam ofersceadað ðæt lond ðæt hit under him ne mæg
gegrowan, forðæm hit sio sunne ne mot gescinan, ne he self
nanne wæsðm ðærofer ne bireð, ac ðæt land bið eal unnyt
swa he hit oferbræt, swa bið ðæm unnytwyrðan ond ðæm
unwisan menn, ðonne he mid ðære scande his slæwðe

goods that God gave us in common. But when they are un-willing to give what they have received, they fatten them-selves on the slaughter of their neighbors, because they kill nearly as many of the needy as they readily could have helped with their alms, had they cared to. Therefore, when we supply the needs of the poor, we are giving them their own, not ours at all, and we can say with greater justice that we are repaying them a debt than that we are showing them generosity.

For that reason, when Truth, which is Christ, instructed that alms should be distributed with circumspection, he said, "Look that you not practice your righteousness in the sight of men." To that precept pertains also the song that the psalmist sang, saying, "Whoever distributes his belong-ings and gives to the poor, his righteousness will endure in perpetuity." He was unwilling to call generosity mercy, but righteousness, because it is natural that what is given to us from the common good we also employ in common. About that Solomon said, "One who is righteous is ever giving, and never ceases." They are also to be exhorted to consider care-fully that the fig tree which is said in the gospel to have borne no fruit stood useless; the good laborer grew impa-tient with it because it took up land unproductively. The fig tree takes up land when the avaricious person hides and consigns to uselessness what could be of benefit to many people. Just as the fig tree casts its shadow on the ground so that there can be no growth underneath it, since the sun is not permitted to light it up, nor does the tree itself produce any fruit above it, but all the ground is useless, it overspreads it so, in like fashion it is with the unenterprising and the un-wise person when he with the disgrace of his sloth sprawls

2

oferbræt ða scire ðe he ðonne hæfð, ond ðonne nauðer ne ðone folgað self nytne gedon nyle, ne ðone tolætan ðe hine ðurh ða sunnan goodes weorces giendscinan wille, ond nytwyrðne ond wæsðmbærne gedon wille.

3 Ac manigra manna gewuna is ðæt hie hie mid ðissum wordum ladiað, ond cueðað: "We brucað ures ægnes, ne gitsige we nanes oðres monnes. Gif we nauht ðæs ne dooð ðe us mon mid goode leanian ðyrfe, ne do we eac nan woh ðe us mon fore tælan ðurfe." Ac forðæm hie cueðað ðas word, ðe hie belucað hiera modes earan ongean ða godcundan lare. Hwæt, se weliga ðe on ðæm godspelle getæld is, ond him bi gecweden is ðæt he ælce dæge symblede, ond mid micelre wiste wære gefeormod, ond ælce dæge geglenged mid pur-puran ond mid hwitum hrægle, nis hit no gesæd ðæt he forðy getæled wære ðy he oðre menn reafode, ac forðy ðe he his ægenes ungemetlice breac, ond oðrum monnum nawuht ne sealde; ond ðeah æfter ðisse worulde he underfeng helle wite, nalles no forðy ðe he awuht unaliefedes dyde, ac forðæm ðe he ðæs aliefdan nan wuht nolde forlætan, ac his swiðe ungemetlice breac, ond hine selfne eallinga gesealde ðiossum woruldwelum.

4 Eac sint to manianne ða fæsðhafulan ðæt hie ongieten ðæt ðæt sindon ða forman læððo ðe hie Gode gedoon mæ-gen, ðæt hie ðæm nawuht ne don ðe him eall sealde ðæt hie habbað. Be ðæm cwæð se psalmscop, "He ne sealde Gode nanne metsceat for his saule ne nænne geðingsceat wið his miltse." Ðæt is ðonne se medsceat wið his saule ðæt he him gielde god weorc for ðære giefe ðe he him ær sealde. Be ðæm ilcan cwæð Iohannes se godspellere, "Ælc treow mon sceal ceorfan, ðe goode wæsðmas ne birð, ond weorpan on fyr,

over the office that he then holds, and then is willing neither himself to exercise authority productively nor to delegate it to one who is willing to light it up with the sun of good works and intends to make it productive and fruitful.

But it is the habit of many people to excuse themselves 3 with these words and to say, "We rely on our own and do not covet anyone else's. If we do nothing that need be repaid us with good, neither do we do anything wrongful for which we need be reproved." But they speak these words because they shut their mind's ear to religious instruction. Now, concerning the rich man of whom the gospel tells, and about whom it is said that he feasted every day and was entertained with great lavishness, and each day adorned with garments of purple and white, it is not said that he was censured because he robbed other people but because he enjoyed his own without reserve and gave nothing to other people; and though after this world he received the punishment of hell, it was by no means because he had done anything unlawful but because he would not part with anything lawful, but enjoyed it very extravagantly and dedicated himself entirely to worldly opulence.

The close-fisted are also to be enjoined to recognize that 4 it is the foremost injury they can offer God to do nothing for him who gave them everything they have. About that the psalmist said, "He gave God no propitiation for his soul, nor any ransom to gain his mercy." The propitiation for his soul, then, is that he render him good works for the gift that he had bestowed on him. About this very thing John the Evangelist said, "Every tree shall be hewn that bears no good

ond forbærnan. Nu is ðonne sio æxs aset on ðane wyrttruman ðæs treowes." Ac ondræden him ðone dynt swa neah,
ða ðe nauht to gode ne doð, ond ðeah wenað ðæt hie sien
unscyldige, forðæm ðe hie nan lað ne doð. Ac him is ðearf
ðæt hie forlæten ða orsorgnesse ond ðæt dysig hiera slæwðe,
ðy læs hie wyrðen awyrtwalode of ðys andwerdan life. Swa
swa ðæt treow ðe ða wyrtruman beoð færcorfene forsearað,
swa hie magon ondrædan ðæt him weorðen ða wyrttruman
færcorfene on ðys andweardan life, gif hie for hiera giemel-
iste nyllað beran ða bleda godra weorca.

5   Ongean ðæt sint to manianne ða ðe willað sellan ðæt ðæt
hie habbað, ond ðeah nyllað forlætan ðæt hie oðre menn ne
reafigen. Hie sint to manigenne ðæt hie geðencen, ongemang ðæm ðe hie wilniað ðæt hie gifule ðyncen, ðæt hie for
ðæm godan hlisan ðy forcuðran ne weorðen, ðy læs him gebyrige, swa swa we ær bufan cwædon, ðonne hie hiera ægen
ungesceadwislice ond ungemetlice dælen, ðæt hie ðonne for
wædle weorðen on murcunga ond on ungeðylde, ðæt hie eft
ongiennen gietsian ond reafian for hiera wædle. Hwelc mæg
him mare unsælð becuman ðonne him becymð ðurh ða
ælmessan, gif he hie to ungemetlice dælð, ond ðurh ðæt
wyrð eft gietsere? Hu, ne bið he ðonne swelce he sæwe good,
ond him weaxe of ðæm ælc yfel? Ac hie sint ærest to manianne ðæt hie cunnen hiora ægen gesceadwislice gehealdan,
ond siððan ðæt hie oðerra monna ne giernen, forðæm ðe na
se ðorn ðære gitsunga ne wyrð forsearod on ðæm helme, gif
se wyrttruma ne bið færcorfen oððe forbærned æt ðæm
stemne. Swa wyrð eac gestiered ðæm gitsere ðæs reaflaces,
gif he ær ðæm gedale cann gemetgian hwæt hine anhagige to
sellanne, hwæt he healdan scyle, ðæt he eft ðæt good ðære

fruit, and cast into the fire and burned. Now the ax is set to the root of the tree." But let those fear so imminent a blow who do nothing to the good and yet believe themselves guiltless because they do no harm. Yet there is need for them to shed the security and the folly of their inactivity, against their being uprooted from this present life. Just as the tree withers of which the roots have been severed, so they can well fear that their roots will be severed in the present life if for their heedlessness they are unwilling to bear the fruit of good works.

Contrariwise are to be cautioned those who are willing to give what they have and yet are unwilling to leave off defrauding other people. They are to be advised to look to it that, while desiring to seem generous, they not for the sake of that good repute grow even more villainous, to prevent its happening to them, as we said above, when they distribute their possessions indiscriminately and immoderately, that they then for poverty fall into depression and discontent, so that they again begin to covet and rob on account of their poverty. What greater misfortune can affect someone than one resulting from almsgiving if he distributes too intemperately and through that becomes again acquisitive? Why, is it not then as if he were to sow good and from it there were to grow for him every ill? But they are first to be advised to know how to keep their own discriminately, and afterward that they not long for other people's, because the thorn of covetousness will not wither on the crown of the tree if the root is not severed or burned at the trunk. Thus, someone desirous of plunder can be controlled if, before distributing it, he knows how to limit what it is proper for him to give and what he ought to keep, so that he need not

mildheortnesse ne ðyrfe gesciendan mid gidsunge ond mid
reaflace. Siððan hie ðonne ðæt geleornod hæbben, ðonne
sint hie siððan to læranne hu hie scilen mildheortlice dælan
ðæt ðæt hie ofer ðæt habbað ðe hie hiora gitsunge mid gestillan sculon; forðæm, gif hie sua ne doð, ðonne sculon hie
eft niedenga gadrian oðer ierfe on ðæs wriexle ðe hie ær for
mildheortnesse ond for rummodnesse sealdon, swelce hie
setten ða synne wið ðære ælmessan. Oðer is ðæt hwa for
hreowsunge his synna ælmessan selle, oðer is ðæt he forðy
syngige ond reafige ðy he tiohchie ðæt he eft scyle mid ðy
reaflace ælmessan gewyrcean. Ac ðæt nis nan ælmesse,
forðæm hio nanne swetne wæsðm forð ne bringð, ac sona on
ðæm wyrtruman abiteriað ða bleda.

6   Forðæm Dryhten ðurh Essaias ðone witgan forcwæð
swelce ælmessan, ond ðus spræc: "Ic eom Dryhten; ic lufige
ryhte domas, ond ic hatige ða lac ðe beoð on woh gereafodu." Ond eft he cwæð, "Arleasra offrung bið awierged,
forðæm hie beoð brohte of unryhtum gestreonum ond of
mandædum." Ond oft bið genumen on ðearfendum monnum ðæt ðæt hie ðonne wenað ðæt hie Gode sellen. Ac
Dryhten gecyðde ðurh Salomon ðone snottran hu micel his
irsung æfter ðære dæde bið, ða he cwæð, "Se ðe me bringð
lac of earmes monnes æhtum on woh gereafodu, ðonne bið
ðæt swelce hwa wille blotan ðæm fæder to ðance ond to
lacum his ægen bearn, ond hit ðonne cwelle beforan his
eagum." Hwæt bið ðonne unaberendlicre to gesionne ðonne
ðæs bearnes cwalu beforan ðæs fæder eagum? Be ðæm we
magon ongietan mid hu micle irre Dryhten geðyldegað ða
ælmessan ðe him man of reaflace bringð, nu he hie tealde
gelice ðæs bearnes cwale beforan ðæs fæder eagum. Ac ða

again spoil the virtue of compassion with avarice and rob-
bery. Then, after they have learned that, they are to be
taught how they ought to distribute compassionately what
they have beyond what they require for satisfying their
greed; because if they do not do so, they will be obliged by
necessity to amass again a fortune in exchange for the one
that they previously gave away out of compassion and generosity, as if they were offsetting the sin by the act of giving.
It is one thing for someone to give alms out of contrition for
his sins, another for him to sin and extort because he has resolved that he shall perform almsgiving with the plunder.
But that is no almsgiving, because it produces no sweet
fruit, but all at once the fruits will turn bitter on the rootstock.

For that reason the Lord rejected such almsgiving 6
through the prophet Isaiah, and thus spoke: "I am the Lord;
I love just pronouncements, and I despise gifts that are
plundered in iniquity." And again he said, "The offerings of
the impious are an abomination, because they derive from
tainted riches and from heinous deeds." And often there is
taken from needy people what some believe they are giving
to God. But the Lord declared through the wise Solomon
how great will be his wrath over the deed, when he said, "If
someone offers me gifts plundered in iniquity from a poor
person's belongings, it is as if someone were to sacrifice a father's own child to him in gratitude and tribute, and were to
kill it before his eyes." What, then, is more unbearable to
watch than the slaughter of a child before its father's eyes?
From this we can infer with how much animosity the Lord
will regard offerings brought to him out of rapine, now that
he has characterized them as like the killing of a child be-

reaferas geðenceað swiðe oft hu micel hie sellað, ond suiðe seldon hie willað gemunan hu micel hie nimað, swelce hie ða metsceattas rimen ðe hie Gode sellen, ond ða scylda willen forgietan ðe hie wið hiene geworhton. Ac hie sceoldon ge-hieran ðone cwide ðe awriten is in Ageas bocum ðæs witgan: he cwæð, "Se ðe medsceattas gaderað, he legeð hie on ðyrelne pohchan." An ðyrelne pohchan se legð ðæt he to metsceatte sellan ðencð, se ðe wat hwær he hiene leget, ond nat hwær he hiene forliesð. Swa bið ðæm ðe witan willað hwæt hie sellað, ond nyllað wietan mid hwelcum woo hie hit gestriendon oððe forworhton. Forðæm hie doð swelce hie hit on ðyrelne pohchan fæten, forðæm hie gemunan ðone tohopan ðe hie to ðæm gestreonum habbað, ond forgietað hira demm ðe him of ðæm gestreonum cymð, oððe coom.

Chapter 46

XLVI. Ðætte on oðre wisan sint to manianne ða geðwæran, on oðre ða ungeðwæran.

On oðre wisan sint to manigenne ða gesibsuman, on oðre ða ungesibsuman. Ða ungesibsuman sint to manigenne ðæt hie gewisslice wieten ðæt hie na on to ðæs manegum

fore its father's eyes. But thieves contemplate quite frequently how much they give, and quite seldom are they inclined to recall how much they take, as if they were counting up the wages they are devoting to God and are intent on ignoring the offenses they have committed against him. But they ought to hear the pronouncement written in the books of the prophet Haggai: he said, "One who collects wages puts them into a purse riddled with holes." Whoever knows where he is putting it and does not know where he is losing it puts what he intends to give as payment into a purse riddled with holes. Thus it is with those who are willing to acknowledge what they are giving and unwilling to acknowledge with what deviousness they acquired or squandered it. Therefore, they are doing as if they thrust it into a purse full of holes, because they keep in mind the expectations that they have for those riches, and they ignore the harm that will be visited upon them by those valuables, or has been visited upon them.

Chapter 46

46. That the tractable are to be guided in one fashion, the intractable in another.

In one fashion are the peaceable to be instructed, in another the belligerent. The quarrelsome are to be counseled to know for a certainty that they are not in possession of so

goodum cræftum ne beoð, ðæt hie æfre mægen gæsðlice beon, gif hie ðurh ungemodnesse agiemeleasiað ðæt hie anmode beon nyllað on ryhte ond on gode. Hit is awriten on *sancte* Paules bocum ðætte ðæs gæstes wæsðm sie lufu ond gefea ond ryhtwislicu sibb. Se ðe ðonne ne giemð hwæðer he ða sibbe healde, ðonne forsæcð he ðone wæsðm his gæstes. Eft cwæð *sanctus* Paulus: "Ðonne betweoxn eow bið yfel anda ond geflitu, hu ne beoð ge ðonne flæsclice?" Ond eft he cuæð, "Seceað sibbe ond god to eallum mannum; butan ðære ne mæg nan man God gesion." Ond eft he manode, ond cuæð: "Geornlice gebinde ge eow tosomne mid anmodnesse ond mid sibbe, ðæt ge sien gelices modes swa ge sint gelices lichoman, sua sua ge ealle sint gelaðode to anum tohopan." To ðæm gebanne ðæs tohopan nan monn mæg cuman, butan he ðider ierne mid anmodnesse wið his niehstan.

2   Ond ðeah wel manige onfoð synderlicre giefe, ond ðonne ofermodgiende forlætað ða giefe ðe mare is, ðæt is sio anmodnes. Sua sua manige doð, gemidliað hiera giefernesse, ond atemiað hira lichoman ðæt hie magon bet fæstan ðonne oðre, ond ðonne for ðæm goodan cræfte forleosað ðone ðe betera bið ðonne sio forhæfdnes, ðæt is anmodnes. Ac se ðe wille ascadan ða forhæfdnesse from ðære anmodnesse, geðence se ðone cwide ðe se psalmscop cuæð; he cwæð: "Lofiað God mid tympanan ond on *choro.*" Se tympano bið geworht of drygum felle, ond ðæt fell hlyt, ðonne hit mon sliehð, ond on ðæm *chore* beoð manige menn gegadrode anes hwæt to singanne anum wordum ond anre stefne. Se ðonne se ðe his lichoman swencð, ond ða anmodnesse wið his niehstan forlæt, se hereð Dryhten mid timpanan, ond nyle mid *choro.*

many good qualities as ever to be able to be spiritual if through contentiousness they grow heedless, so that they refuse to live harmoniously in what is right and good. It is written in the books of Saint Paul that the fruit of the spirit is love and delight and the peace of the pious. Then anyone who does not care whether he maintains peace renounces the fruit of his spirit. Again Saint Paul said, "When there is wrongful spite and contention between you, are you not then devoted to the flesh?" And again he said, "Have as your aim peace and good for all people; without that, no one can see God." And again he admonished and said, "Bind yourselves intently to one another with concord and with peace, so that you may be of like mind, as you are of like body, just as you are all called to a single hope." To the summons of that hope, no one can come unless he flies there in concurrence with his neighbor.

And yet quite a few receive a singular gift, and then out of 2 arrogance surrender that gift which is greater, which is like-mindedness. Many do just so, curbing their appetite, and mastering their body so that they can fast with a better will than others, and then for that good quality they lose the one that is better than abstemiousness, which is amity. But whoever thinks it right to separate self-denial from like-mindedness, let him consider the words that the psalmist spoke, saying, "Praise God with timbrel and in chorus." The timbrel is made of dry hide, and the hide sounds when it is beaten, and in the chorus many people are assembled to sing something or other with a single text and a single voice. Then whoever punishes his body and neglects amity with his neighbor praises God with timbrel, and will not in chorus.

3   Oft eac, ðonne hwone mara wisdom up arærð ðonne oðre
menn, ðonne wile he hiene ascadan from oðerra monna geferrædenne, ond sua micle sua he ma wat, ond wisra bið
ðonne oðre menn, sua he ma dysegað, ond suiður wienð wið
ðone cræft ðære anmodnesse. Ac hie sceoldon gehieran
ðone cuide ðe sio Soðfæsðnes self cwæð; he cwæð, "Habbað
sealt on eow, ond habbað sibbe betweoxn eow." Ðæt sealt he
nemde for wisdom, forðæm he wolde ðæt we hæfden ægðer
ge sibbe ge wisdom, forðæm hit ne beoð nane cysta ne nan
cræft ðæt mon hæbbe wisdom, ond nylle wilnian sibbe.
Forðæm sua sua he bet wat, swa he wyrs agylt, ond maran
demm gedrihð him selfum mid ðæm lote. He mæg hine ðy
læs beladian ðæt he næbbe wite geearnod ðy he meahte
mid his wisdome wærlice ða synne forbugan, gif he wolde.
Ac him wæs swiðe ryhte to gecueden ðurh Iacobus ðone
apostol; he cwæð, "Gif ge hæbben yfelne andan on eow ond
teonan ond geflitu on eowrum mode, ne gilpe ge no, ne ne
fægniað ðæs, ond ne flitað mid eowrum leasungum wið ðæm
soðe. Forðæm se wisdom nis ufan cumen of hefenum, ac he
is eorðlic ond wildiorlic ond eac diofullic." Ac se se ðe of
Gode cymð, he bið godes willan ond gesibsum. Ðæt is ðonne
ðæt he sie clænes willan ond goodes, ðæt he clænlice ond
ryhtwislice ongiete ðæt ðæt he ongiete. Ðæt is ðonne ðæt
he gesibsum sie, ðæt he hiene nan wuht ne ahebbe ofer his
gelican, ne from hiera geferrædenne ne aðiede.

4   Ðæm ungesibsuman is to cyðanne ðæt hie wieten ðætte
swa lange sua hie beoð from ðære lufe aðied hiera niehstena,
ond him ungemode beoð, ðætte hie nan wuht godes ne
magon ða hwile Gode bringan to ðances. Be ðæm is awriten
on Cristes bocum: "Gif ðu wille ðin lac bringan to ðæm

Frequently, as well, when greater insight places someone 3
above other people, he will want to remove himself from
other people's company, and the more he knows, and the
wiser he is than other people, the more foolish he, and the
more he counters the virtue of concord. But they ought to
hear the pronouncement that Truth himself spoke, saying,
"Have salt within you, and have amity with one another."
Salt he invoked in token of wisdom, because he wanted us to
have both amity and wisdom, seeing as it is no merit and no
virtue to have wisdom and refuse to promote concord.
Therefore, the better he understands, the worse he is culpable, and he incurs greater injury to himself by that device.
All the less can he clear himself of having merited punishment as he could for all his wisdom have avoided the sin
conscientiously, had he cared to. But it was spoken quite
pertinently of him through James the apostle when he said,
"If you have reprehensible enmity among you, and animus
and quarrelsomeness in your mind, do not boast of it or
revel in it, and do not set your lies in contention with the
truth. For such wisdom does not proceed from heaven, but
it is earthbound and bestial, and also demonic." But what
comes from God is benevolent and peaceable. To be of pure
and good will, then, is to understand with purity and piety
what one understands. To be peaceable, then, is in no way to
place oneself above one's fellows, nor to stand aloof from
their society.

The contentious are to be told to know that, as long as 4
they are alienated from the love of their neighbors and are
at odds with them, for that time they can offer nothing of
good that will please God. About such it is written in the
books of Christ: "If you intend to bring your gift to the altar,

371

wiofude, ond ðu ðonne ryhte ofðence hwæthwugu ðæs ðe
ðin niehsta ðe wiðerweardes gedon hæbbe, forlæt ðonne an
ðin lac beforan ðæm weofude, ond fer ærest æfter him; læt
inc geseman ær ðu ðin lac bringe; brieng siððan ðin lac."
Ðæt is ðæt hwa fare mid his mode æfter his niehstan, ond
him unne ðæt he to ryhte gecierre. Of ðissum bebode we
magon geðencean hu unaberendlic gylt sio towesnes bið,
ðonne ða lac forðæm beoð forsacene. Nu man ælc yfel mæg
mid goode adilegian, is ðæt ðonne formicel scyld ðæt gedeð
ðætte nan good ne bið andfenge, buton mon ær ðæt yfel
forlæte.

5   Ac ða ungesibsuman sint to maniene, gif hie nyllen hiera
lichoman earan ontynan to gehieranne ða godcundan lare,
ðæt hie ontynen hiera modes eagan, ond giemen ðissa
eorðlicna gesceafta, hu ða fuglas, ðe him gelice beoð, ond
anes cynnes beoð, hu gesibsumlice hie farað, ond hu seldon
hie willað forlætan hiera geferrædenne, ond eac ða dumban
nietenu, hu hie hie gadriað heapmælum, ond hie ætsomne
fedað. Nu we magon gecnawan on ðara ungesceadwisra
nietena gesibsumnesse hu micel yfel sio gesceadwislice gecynd ðurh ða ungesibsumnesse gefremeð, ðonne he on
gesceadwislicum ingeðonce forliesð ðæt ða dumban nietenu
gehealden habbað on hiera gecynde.

6   Ongean ðæt sint to manienne ða gesibbsuman, ðonne hie
lufigað ða sibbe ðe hie her habbað suiður ðonne hit ðearf sie,
ond ne wilniað na ðæt hie to ðære ecean sibbe becumen. Ac
sio stillnes ðe hie ðær wilniað oft swiðe hefelice dereð hira
ingeðonce, forðæm swa him ðios stillnes ond ðios ieðnes ma
licað, sua him læs licað ðæt ðæt hie to gelaðode sindon, ond
sua hienne swiður lysð ðisses andweardan lifes, swa he læs
secð ymb ðæt ece. Be ðysum ilcan cwæð Crist ðurh hiene

and you then plainly recall something irksome to you that your neighbor has done, leave your gift before the altar, and first go in search of him; let the two of you be reconciled before you make your offering; then present your gift." That is that someone should go with all his heart in search of his neighbor and give him the opportunity to put matters right. From this injunction we can infer what an intolerable offense discord is, when gifts are rejected on account of it. Since every wrong can be blotted out by good deeds, it must be a very great wrong that causes no good deed to be acceptable unless the wrong is first righted.

But the quarrelsome are to be urged, if they refuse to unstop their body's ears to hear religious doctrine, to open their mind's eyes and observe the creatures of this world, how birds which are alike and of one species travel so amicably, and how seldom they will give up their companionship, and likewise the mute beasts, how they gather in herds and feed together. Now, we can recognize from the cooperation of irrational animals how great a wrong the rational nature commits through contentiousness, when one in his rational mental capacity surrenders what mute beasts keep steady in their nature.

Otherwise are to be exhorted the peaceable when they cherish the peace that they have here more than is needful and never desire to obtain everlasting peace. But the serenity that they thus desire often quite severely mars their turn of mind, because the more this tranquility and this ease satisfy them, the less they are devoted to those things to which they are called, and the more they delight in this present life, the less they are directed to the eternal. About this same, Christ spoke in his own person when he distinguished

selfne, ða ða he ðas eorðlican sibbe toscead ond ða hefonlican, ond his apostolas spon of ðissum andweardan to ðæm
ecan; he cuæð, "Mine sibbe ic eow selle, ond mine sibbe ic
læte to eow"; swelce he cwæde, "Ic eow onlæne ðas gewitendan, ond ic eow geselle ða ðurhwuniendan." Gif ðonne ðæs
monnes mod ond his lufu bið behleapen eallunga on ða
lænan sibbe, ðonne ne mæg he næbre becuman to ðære ðe
him geseald is. Ac swa is ðios andwearde sib to habbanne
ðæt we hie sculon lufian, ond ðeah oferhyggean, ðy læs ðæt
mod ðæs ðe hie lufað on synne befealle, gif he hie to ungemetlice lufað.

7   Eac sint to manianne ða gesibsuman ðæt hie to ungemetlice ðære sibbe ne wilnigen, ðy læs hie for ðære wilnunga
ðisse eorðlican sibbe forlæten untælde oðerra monna yfele
unðeawas, ond hiene ðonne selfne swa aðiede from ðære
sibbe his scippendes mid ðære geðafunga ðæs unryhtes—ðy
læs, ðonne he him ondrædt ða towesnesse utane, he sie innan asliten from ðæm geðoftscipe ðæs incundan deman.
Hwæt is elles ðios gewitendlice sibb, buton swelce hit sie
sum swæð ðære eccean sibbe? Hwæt mæg bion dyslicre
ðonne hwa lufige hwelcre wuhte spor on ðæm duste, ond ne
lufige ðæt ðætte ðæt spor worhte? Be ðæm cwæð Dauid, ða
he hine eallunga geðiedde to ðæm geðoftscipe ðære incundan sibbe; he cyðde ðæt he nolde habban nane gemodsum-
nesse wið ða yfelan, ða he cuæð, "Hu ne hatige ic ða ealle,
Dryhten, ða ðe ðe hatigað? Ond for ðinum feondum ic
aswand on minum mode, ond mid ful ryhte hete ic hie
hatode, forðæm hie wæron eac mine find." Swa mon ðonne
sceal fullfremedlice Godes fiend hatigean, ðætte mon lufige
ðæt ðæt hie beoð, ond hatige ðæt ðæt hie doð. He sceal
weorðan his life to nytte mid ðy ðæt he næte his unðeawas.

earthly peace and heavenly while directing his apostles from the present to the eternal, saying, "My peace I give to you, and my peace I leave to you"; as if his plain meaning were, "I lend you what is temporary, and I shall give you what is permanent." If, then, a person's mind and his devotion are fixed entirely on this impermanent peace, he can never attain to the one he is to be given. But this present peace is to be possessed in such a way that we love it and yet hold it in contempt, to prevent the mind of one who loves it from falling into sin if he loves it too unseasonably.

The congenial are also to be exhorted not to desire peace 7 excessively, so that for the desire of peace in this world they not leave uncensured other people's bad conduct and then alienate themselves from the peace of their creator by tolerating iniquity—lest, by living in dread of outward discord, they inwardly cut themselves off from communion with the indwelling judge. What else is this temporal peace but as if it were a trace of everlasting peace? What can be more absurd than for someone to cherish the track of something in the dust and not cherish what left the track? About this David spoke when he dedicated himself entirely to accord with inner peace; he indicated that he would have no intimacy with those who are evil when he said, "Do I not hate all those, Lord, who hate you? And in my mind I shrank from all your enemies, and with wholly just despite I hated them, because they were also my enemies." To hate God's enemies perfectly, one ought to love what they are and hate what they do. One ought to convert such a one's life to good use by censuring his vices.

8   Ac hu wene we hu micel scyld ðæt sie ðæt monn aðreote
ðære nætinge yfelra monna, ond nime sume sibbe wið ða
wierrestan, nu se witga ðæt brohte Gode to lacum ond to of-
frunga ðæt he ðara yfelena feondscipe ongean hine selfne
aweahte for Gode? Forðæm wæs ðætte Leuis kynn gefengon
hiera sweord, ond eodon ut ðurh ðone here, sleande ða
scyldgan; ond forðæm hit is awriten ðæt hiera honda wæren
gehalgode Gode, forðæm ðe hie ne sparodan ða synfullan, ac
slogon. Be ðæm wæs eac ðætte Fines forseah his neahgebura
freondscipe, ða he ofslog his agenne geferan, ða he hine for-
læg wið ða Madianiten, ond ða forlegisse he mid ofslog, ond
swa mid his ierre he gestilde Godes ierre. Ond eft cwæð
Crist ðurh hine selfne, "Ne wene ge no ðæt ic to ðæm come
on eorðan ðæt ic sibbe sende on eorðan, ac sweord."
Forðæm, ðonne we us unwærlice geðiedað to yfelra monna
freondscipe, ðonne gebinde we us to hiera scyldum. Be ðys
ilcan wæs ðætte Gesaphað, se ðe ær on eallum dædum
his lifes wæs to herigenne, fullneah mid ealle forwearð for
Achabes freondscipe. He wæs geleahtrad from Gode: ðurh
ðone witgan him wæs to gecweden, "Ðu fultemodes ðæm
arleasum, ond ðu gemengdest ðinne freondscipe wið ðone
ðe hatode God, ond mid ðæm ðu geearnode Godes irre, ðær
ða godan weorc ær næren on ðe mette; ðæt wæs ðæt ðu
adydes ða bearwas of Iudea londe." Be ðæm we magon gehieran ðætte sua micle sua we us swiður geðiedað ond ge-
modsumiað to ðæra yfelena freondscipe, ðætte we swa micle
fier beoð ðæm hiehstan ryhte aðiedde.

9   Eac sint to monigenne ða gesibsuman ðæt hie him ne ondræden ðæt hie ðas lænan sibbe ongean hie selfe gedrefen

Yet how great a fault shall we suppose it is to be indiffer- 8
ent to reprimanding malignant people and to making a degree of peace with the worst, considering that the prophet
presented it as a gift and an offering to God that he incited
the enmity of the vicious against himself on God's behalf? It
was for that reason that the Levites grasped their swords
and went out through the host, striking the culpable, and it
is for this reason that it is written that their hands were consecrated to God, that they did not spare the sinful but
struck them. For this it was also that Phineas spurned his
neighbors' friendship when he killed his own companion
who had sinned with the Midianite woman, and the harlot
he killed alongside him, and thus with his anger he stilled
God's anger. And again Christ said in his own person, "Do
not believe that I came into the world to bring peace on
earth, but a sword." For when we inadvisably join in friendship with wrongdoers, we bind ourselves to their offenses.
For this same reason it was that Jehoshaphat, who had previously been praiseworthy in all the deeds of his life, very
nearly perished entirely for Ahab's friendship. He was reproved by God: through the prophet he was told, "You lent
aid to the dishonorable, and you exchanged friendship with
one who hated God, and thereby you would have earned
God's anger if good had not formerly been evident in you;
that was that you removed the groves from the land of the
Jews." By this we can make out that by so much the more
that we attach ourselves to and consent to the friendship of
wrongdoers, so much the further are we alienated from the
highest righteousness.

The peace-loving are also to be warned not to fear dis- 9
turbing this impermanent peace with themselves by their

mid ðære ðreaunga, ðonne hit to cymð ðæt hie hit sprecan sculon. Ond eft hie sint to manianne ðæt hie ðeah ða sibbe anwealge on innan him gehealden, ða ðe hie utane mid ðære ðrafunga gedrefað. Ægðer ðara Dauid sægde ðæt he swiðe wærlice beheolde, ða he cwæð, "Ic lufode ða ðe sibbe hatodon, ond ðonne ic him cidde, ðonne oncuðon hie me butan scylde." Hie oncuðon hiene for ðære cease, ond he wæs ðeah hiora freond. Ne aðreat hine no ðæt he ða dysegan ne tælde, ond ðeah ðe hie hine tældon, he hie lufode. Be ðys ilcan cwæð eft Paulus, "Ic wolde, gif hit swa beon meahte, ðæt ge wið ælcne monn hæfden sibbe eowres gewealdes." Forðæm he cwæð, "gif hit swa beon meahte," ond eac he cwæð, "iowres gewealdes," forðæm he wisse ðæt hit bið swiðe unieðe ægðer to donne: ge wið ðone to cidanne ðe yfel deð, ge eac sibbe wið to habbenne. Ac us is swiðe micel ðearf, ðeah ðeos hwilendlice sibb for ure cease gedrefed weorðe on ðæra yfelena monna mode, ðæt hie ðeah on ussum eallunga gehealden sie. Forðæm he cwæð bi ðære sibbe, "iowres gewealdes," forðæm sio sib mid ryhte beon sceal ægðer ge on ðæs cidendan monnes mode ge on ðæs geðafiendan. Gif hio ðonne of oðres gewite, on ðæs oðres hio ðurhwunige. Be ðæm se ilca Paulus on oðre stowe monode his gingran, ond ðus cwæð: "Swa hwa swa urum wordum ond gewritum hieran nylle, do hit mon us to witanne, ond nabbe ge nanne gemanan wið hine, forðæm ðætte hine gesceamige." Ond eft æfter ðæm he cwæð, "Ne scule ge wið hine gebæran swa swa wið feond, ac ge him sculon cidan swa swa breðer"; swelce he openlice cwæde, "Forlætað ða uterran sibbe, ond habbað ða innerran fæste, ðætte eower unsibb geeaðmede ðæs synnigan mod, swaðeah ðæt sio sib of eowre heortan ne gewite, ðæah hiere mon ne recce."

reproach when it comes to it that they are obliged to speak. And in turn they are to be advised nonetheless to maintain peace undisturbed within them when outwardly they cause agitation by their censure. David said that he very carefully maintained both of these when he said, "I loved those who hated peace, and when I chided them, they were indignant with me without cause." They were indignant with him for the chiding, and yet he was their friend. He never shrank from rebuking the foolish, and though they criticized him, he loved them. About this same, Paul in turn said, "I would wish it, if it could be so, that as far as you are concerned, you would be at peace with every person." He said, "if it could be so," and also he said, "as far as you are concerned," because he knew that it is extremely difficult to do both: both to reprove one who does wrong and also to maintain peace with him. Yet, though this temporal peace may be disrupted in the mind of evildoers on account of our criticism, we have great need that it be perfectly maintained in our own. About this peace he said, "as far as you are concerned," because with justice there ought to be peace in the mind both of the rebuker and of the rebuked. If it should be missing from that of one, it must persist in the other's. About that, this same Paul advised his disciples in another place: "Whoever is unwilling to comply with our words and missives, let us be informed, and have nothing to do with him, so that he will be ashamed." And again after that he said, "You ought not to behave toward him as toward an enemy, but you should remonstrate with him like brothers"; as if his plain meaning were, "Cast aside superficial peace and maintain inner peace unwaveringly, so that your antagonism may humble the mind of the sinful, provided that peace not depart from your heart, even though it go unheeded."

Chapter 47

XLVII. Ðætte on oðre wisan sint to monianne ða wrohtgeornan, on oðre ða gesibsuman.

On oðre wisan sint to monigenne ða ðe wrohte sawað, on oðre ða gesibsuman. Ða wrohtgeornan sint to manigenne ðæt hie geðencen hwæs folgeras hie sindon. Be ðæm aworpnan engle is awriten on ðæm godspelle ðæt he sewe ðæt weod on ða godan æceras. Forðy wæs bi him gecweden, "Sum mon ðis dyde ðe ure feond wæs." Be ðæs ilcan feondes limum is ðus gecweden ðurh Salomon: "Aworpen man bið a unnyt, ond gæð mid wo muðe, ond bicneð mid ðæm eagum, ond trit mid ðæm fet, ond spricð mid ðæm fingre, ond on wore heortan bið yfel donde, ond on ælce tid saweð wrohte." Her we magon gehieran, ða he be ðæm wrohtgeornan secgean wolde, ðæt he hine nemde se aworpna. Forðon, gif he ær on ðæs ofermodan engles wisan innan his geðance of Godes gesiehðe ne afeolle, ðonne ne become he no utane to ðæm sæde ðære wrohte. Be ðæm is ryhtlice awriten ðæt he bicne mid ðæm eagum, ond sprece mid ðæm fingrum, ond trit mid ðæm fet; forðæm ðe innor bið se hierde, ðæt is se willa, se hielt ða leomu utan. Forðæm, ðonne mon ða fæstrædnesse his modes innan forlist, ðonne bið he hwilum swiðe ungestæððiglice astyred utane on his limum, ond gekyðð on ðære styringe ðara telgena utane ðæt ðær ne bið nan fæstnung on ðæm wyrtruman innan.

Chapter 47

47. That the fractious are to be guided in one fashion, the peaceable in another.

In one fashion are to be counseled those who sow discord, in another the peaceable. The fractious are to be urged to consider whose disciples they are. About the outcast angel it is written in the gospel that he sowed weeds in good fields. Therefore it was said of him, "Some person did this who was our enemy." About that same enemy's members it is said through Solomon as follows: "An apostate is always worthless and goes about with a wicked mouth, and gestures with his eyes, and treads with the foot, and speaks with the finger, and is an evildoer in his crooked heart, and at all times spreads contention." Here we can hear that, when he cared to say something about the contentious person, he called him an apostate. For if in the manner of the proud angel he had not internally in his thoughts fallen from the sight of God, he would not externally have become the seed of contention. About him it is accurately written that he gestures with the eyes, and speaks with the fingers, and treads with the foot, because deeper inside is the shepherd, which is the will, which controls the external members. Therefore, when someone loses steadiness of mind within, he will at times be quite erratically agitated outwardly in his members, and will show by the agitation of the branches that there is no stability in the rootstock within.

2 Ac gehiren ða wrohtsaweras hwæt awriten is on ðæm godspelle: hit is awriten, "Eadige beoð ða gesibsuman, forðon hie beoð Godes bearn genemde." Be ðæm worde we magon geðencean, nu ða sint Godes bearn genemned ðe sibbe wyrcað, ðætte ða sindon butan tweon diofles bearn, ðe hie toweorpan willað, forðæm ðe ælc ðara ðe hine mid unryhte ascadan wille from ðære geðwærnesse, he wile forlætan ðære lufan grennisse, ond forsearian on ðære un-geðwærnesse. Forðæm, ðeah he hwelcne wæstm forðbrenge godes weorces, gif he ne bið of godum willan ond of untwie-faldre lufan ongunnen, ne bið he nawuht. Geðencen be ðissum ða wrohtsaweras hu monigfaldlice hie gesyngiað, ðonne hie ðæt an yfel ðurhtioð, ond mid ðæm anum yfele aterað of ðære menniscan heortan ealle ða godan cræftas. Mid ðam anum yfele hie gefremmað unrim oðerra yfela, forðam ða ðe ða wrohte sawað, hie adwæscað ða sibbe, ðe modor is ealra godra cræfta. Forðon ðe nan cræft nis Gode deorwyrðra ðonne sio lufu, ne eft ðæm deofle nan cræft leoftælra ðonne hie mon slite. Swa hwa ðonne swa ða wrohte bið sawende, ond mid ðy ða sibbe ofslihð on his geferan, he bið hiewcuðlice ðeow ðæm Godes feonde, ðe simle wiðbritt ðæm untruman mode ðære sibbe ðe he self forlet, ond hine mid ðæm forworhte, oð he ofdune afeoll, ond nu giet wilnað ðæt he us ðone weg fordikige, ðæt we ne mægen astigan on ðone weg ond on ða are ðe he of afeoll.

3 Ongean ðæt sint to manienne ða ðe ða sibbe sawað, ðæt hie swa micel weorc to recceleaslice ond to unwærlice ne don, ond huru ðær ðær hie nyton hwæðer sio sibb betre be-twux gefæstnod bið, ðe ne bið, forðæm swa swiðe swa hit dereð ðætte ænig wana sie ðære sibbe betwux ðæm goodum, swa swiðe hit eac dereð ðæt hio ne sie gewanod betwux ðæm

But let sowers of discord hear what is written in the gos- 2
pel: it is written, "Blessed are the peacemakers, for they will
be called children of God." From these words we can deduce, seeing as those who promote peace are called God's
children, that those who want to subvert it are, without a
doubt, the devil's children, because everyone who wishes
without cause to hold himself aloof from concord will forfeit the greenness of love and will wither in discord. Therefore, though he may produce a certain fruit of good work, if
it does not originate in goodwill and indubitable charity, it
will amount to nothing. From this, let incendiaries deduce
how multiply they sin when they perform that one misdeed,
and with that one misdeed rip from the human heart all
good qualities. With that one wrong they cause untold other
wrongs, because those who foment schisms extinguish
peace, which is the mother of all good qualities. For no quality is dearer to God than amity, and, conversely, no practice
more agreeable to the devil than to shatter amity. Whoever
is a sower of discord, then, and thereby annihilates the peace
of his fellows, is a servant and intimate of God's adversary,
who continually deprives the unprepared mind of the peace
that he himself forfeited, and thereby ruined himself, so
that he fell down and now still longs to block the way for us,
so that we cannot ascend the path and reach the dignity
from which he fell.

To the contrary, those who sow peace are to be exhorted 3
not to perform so great a work too heedlessly and too incautiously, and particularly where they do not know whether or
not it is better to broker peace, because as very harmful as it
is that there be any deficiency of amity between the good, to
the same degree it causes harm to the bad not to diminish it

yfelum. Forðæm, gif ða ðweoran ond ða unryhtwisan hiera yfel mid sibbe gefæstnigað, ond tosomne gemengað, ðonne bið geiced hiera mægen, ond hiora yfelum weorcum gefultumod, forðon swa micle swa hie gemodsumeran bioð betwux him, swa hie beoð bealdran ða godan to swenceanne. Be ðæm wæs ðætte sio godcunde stemn cwæð to ðæm eadgan Iobe ymb ða bodan ðæs idlan fætes, ðæt is se awirgda Antexrist; hio cwæð, "His flæsces lima clifað ælc on oðrum." Ond eft hio dyde sciella to bisene his heorðcneohtum, ond ðus cwæð: "Ælces fisces sciell bið to oðerre gefeged, ðæt ðær ne mæg nan æðm ut betwuxn." Swa eac ða his folgeras: swa hie unwiðerweardran ond gemodran beoð, swa hie swiður hlecað tosomne, ond eac fæstor tosomne beoð gefegde to godra monna hienðe. Swa eac se se ðe ða unryhtwisan tosomne sibbað, he seleð ðære unryhtwisnesse fultom ond mægen, forðæm hie magon ða godan swa micle swiður geswencean swa hie hiora anmodlicor ehtað. Be ðæm cwæð se æðela lareow *sanctus* Paulus, ða he geseah ðæt folc Phariseo ond Saducia anmodlice his ehtan; he tiolode hie betwux him to toscadanne, ond ðus cwæð: "Hwæt do ge, broðor, doð esnlice. Hu, ne eom ic eower gefera, ond eom Fariseisc swa same swa ge? Ond forðæm min monn eht ðe ic bodige ymb ðone tohopan deadra monna ærestes." Forðæm he cwæð ða word, forðæm ða Saducie antsacodon ðære æriste æfter deaðe, ond ða Farisseos geliefdon ðære æriste, swa swa ða halgan gewritu bodiað. Swa he tosced ðara ehtera anmodnesse ðe hine ær woldon fordon, ond Paulus com gesund ðonon.

4 Eac sint to manianne ða ðe on ðam beoð abisgode ðæt hie

between them. For if the perverse and the unrighteous consolidate their criminality with peace and join forces, their
effectiveness will be heightened and their bad deeds furthered, because the more in agreement they are among
themselves, the more brazen they will be about afflicting
the good. It was about this that the divine voice spoke to the
blessed Job concerning the messengers of the empty vessel,
which is the accursed Antichrist, saying, "The members of
his flesh cleave one to another." And again it drew the analogy of scales to his henchmen and spoke thus: "Every fish's
scale is joined to another, so that no air can escape between
them." So also with his followers: the more uncontentious
and the more complaisant they are, the more cohesive they
will be, and also the more firmly united in the degradation
of good people. So, likewise, whoever reconciles the impious to one another lends aid and capability to impiety, since
they can trouble the good so much the more severely in proportion as they persecute them with greater unanimity.
About this the noble teacher Saint Paul spoke when he saw
that the sects of the Pharisees and the Sadducees persecuted him in concert; he attempted to drive a wedge between them, and spoke thus: "What you do, brothers, do
manfully. Now, am I not your fellow, and am a Pharisee the
same as you? And I stand trial because I preach about the
hope of the resurrection of the dead." He spoke those words
because the Sadducees denied the resurrection after death,
and the Pharisees believed in the resurrection, as holy scripture proclaims. He shattered the unanimity of those persecutors who had intended to destroy him, and Paul emerged
from that unscathed.

Those who are engaged in cultivating peace are also to be   4

sibbe tiligað, ðæt hie ærest tilgen to kyðanne ðæm unge-
sceadwisum modum hu sio lufu beon scyle ðære inweard-
lican sibbe, ðy læs him æfter firste sio uterre sib derige;
forðon, ðonne ðonne hie geðencað ða ryhtan lufe, ðæt hie
eac geðencen ðæt hie ne weorðen beswicene mid ðære uterran lufe, ond ðonne hie ongitað ða godcundan sibbe, ðætte
sio eorðlice sib hi ne geteo to wirsan. Ond eft ðonne sume
yfele menn swa gerade beoð ðæt hie ne magon godum monnum derian, ðeah hie willen, ðonne is betere ðeah ðæt mon
eorðlice sibbe betwux ðæm fæstnige, oð ðæt hie mægen
ongietan ða uplican sibbe; ðætte hie ðurh ða menniscan
sibbe mægen astigan to ðære godcundan sibbe—ðeah hio
him ðonne giet feorr sie, forðæm ðæt yfel hiera unryhtwisnesse hie hæfð ðonne giet ahierde—ðætte hie ðonne
gemonnðwærige sio lufu ond sio geferræden hiora niehstena,
ond hie to beteran gebrenge.

Chapter 48

XLVIII. Ðætte on oðre wisan sint to manianne ða ðe
ða halgan æ ryhtlice ongietan ne cunnon, on oðre
wisan ða ðe hie ryhtlice ongietað ond ðeah for
eaðmodnesse swugiað ðæt hi hi ne bodigeað.

On oðre wisan sint to manigenne ða ðe ða halgan æ
ryhtlice ongietan ne cunnon, on oðre ða ðe hie ryhtlice ongietan cunnon, ond ðeah for eaðmodnesse swigiað ðæt hie

urged first to make an effort to explain to undiscerning minds how the love of inward peace ought to be, to prevent, after a time, outward peace from causing them harm, so that when they contemplate genuine love they also beware coming to be deceived by outward love, and when they understand divine peace, earthly peace not attract them to the inferior sort. And again, when certain malevolent people are so circumstanced that they cannot harm good people, though they would like to, it is better nonetheless that worldly peace be established between them until they can understand sublime peace, so that through human peace they can aspire to divine peace—though it is then still far off from them, because the malignance of their impiety has as yet hardened them—so that the love and the companionship of their neighbors may then refine them and bring them to a better condition.

Chapter 48

48. That those who cannot rightly understand divine law are to be guided in one fashion, in another fashion those who understand it properly and yet for humility remain silent, not professing it.

In one fashion are to be advised those who cannot rightly understand divine law, in another those who understand it properly and yet for humility remain silent, not professing

hie ne bodiað. Ða sint to maniene ðe ða æ ryhtlice ne ongietað, ðætte hie geðencen ðætte hie ðone halwendan drync
ðæs æðelan wines ne gehwyrfen him selfum to attre, ond
ðæt isen ðæt hie menn mid lacnian sculdon, ðæt hie mid
ðæm hie selfe to feore ne gewundigen, ðy læs hie mid ðy tole
ðæt hale lic gewierden ðe hie sceoldon mid ðæt unhale aweg
aceorfan. Eac hie sint to manigenne ðæt hie geðencen ðæt
ða halgan gewritu sint us to leohtfatum gesald, ðæt we mægen geseon hwæt we don scylen on ðisse niht, ðæt is ðis andwearde lif, swa swa ðæt leohtfæt lieht on nieht urum eagum,
ðætte ða gewritu on dæg liehten urum mode. Ac ðonne hwa
ne cann ða ryhtlice ongietan, ðonne bið him ðæt leoht aðies-
trod. Ne gehwyrfde hine næfre ðæt unryhtwise ingeðonc to
ðæm won andgiete, gif he ær nære on ofermettum aðunden.
Ac ðonne hie wenað ðæt hie wisran sien selfe ðonne oðre,
ðonne forhyggeað hie ðæt hie folgien oðrum monnum æfter
bettran andgiete, ond wilniað ðæt hie gegitsien ond gelicet-
ten æt ðæm ungetydum folce wisdomes naman. Higiað
ðonne ealle mægene ðæt hie ðæt gedwellen ðæt oðre menn
ryhtlice ond gesceadwislice ongieten habbað, ond hira agen
unryht willað mid ðy getrymman.

2   Be ðæm wæs swiðe wel gecweden ðurh Amos ðone witgan; he cwæð, "Hie snidon ða Galatiscan wif ðe bearneacene
wæron, ond woldon mid ðy geryman hira landgemæru."
Ðæt folc wæs gehaten Galað on Ebrisc, ðæt is on Englisc
gewitnesse heap, forðæm eal sio gesomnung ðære halgan
ciricean ðurh ondetnesse hielt ða gewitnesse ðære soðfæsðnesse. Ðy is swiðe ryhte getacnod ðurh Galates naman sio
halige gesomnung, forðæm ðe ealle ða geleaffullan bodiað be
Gode ðæt soð is. Ðonne getacniað ða geeacniendan wif ða
saule ðe ða gebodu angietað, ond hie mid godcundlicre lufan

it. Those who understand the law properly are to be warned to look that they not turn the salutary drink of the noble wine to poison against themselves, and that they not wound themselves fatally with a blade with which they ought to heal people, so that, with that implement with which they ought to cut away what is unsound, they not harm the healthy body. They are also to be charged to consider that holy texts are given to us as lamps, so that we can see what we ought to do in this night, which is this present life, the way a lamp provides light for our eyes, so that scripture may illuminate our mind by day. But when someone cannot understand it correctly, the light is dimmed for him. Yet perverse intent would never have led him to deficient understanding if he had not previously been inflated with pride. But when they believe that they themselves are wiser than others, they scorn to follow other people in search of better understanding, but by greed and hypocrisy they desire to attain the name of wisdom from the ignorant masses. With all their might, then, they endeavor to obscure what other people rightly and perceptively have understood, and they wish in that way to lend support to their own error.

About this it was quite aptly spoken through the prophet 2 Amos, who said, "They ripped open the pregnant women of Gilead and wanted thereby to extend their borders." That nation was called Gilead in Hebrew, which is in English "Heap of Witness," because through confession the entire congregation of holy Church holds witness to truth. Thus, quite rightly is the holy congregation signified by the name of Gilead, because all the faithful profess what is true about God. Then the women with child stand for souls that understand his biddings and accept them with divine love: if the

underfoð: gif ðæt underfangne andgit to ryhtre tide bið
forðbroht, ðonne bið hit mid ðy ðurhtogenan weorce gedon,
swelce hit sie geboren. Ðæt is ðonne ðæt mon his mearce
bræde, ðæt mon his hlisan ond his naman mærsige. Ac
ðonne mon snið ða bearneacnan wif on Galað hira mearce
mid to rymanne, ðonne ða gedwolmenn mid wore lare
ofsleað ðæt mod geleaffullra monna, ðonne ðonne hit
furðum ryht andgiet underfangen hæfð, ond him hwæthwugu sio soðfæsðnes on geeacnod bið, ær ðæm ðe hit full-
boren sie, ond willað mid ðy gedon ðæt hie mon hlige
wisdomes, mid ðy ðe hie ofsniðen mid ðy seaxe hefiglices
gedwolan ða unborenan bearn, ðe ðonne furðum beoð mid
wordum geeacnode on geleaffullra mode. Ac hie wilniað
mid ðy ðæt hie mon herige, ond cweðe ðæt hie sin wise
lareowas. Ac gif we wilnigen ðæt hie ðæs wos geswicen,
ðonne sculon we hie ealra ðinga ærest ond geornost læran
ðæt hie ne wilnigen leasgielpes, forðæm, gif se wyrttruma
ðære upahafenisse ærest wyrð forcorfen, ðonne bið hit sona
swutol ðæt ða twigu forseariað ðære unryhtan lare.

3   Eac hie sint to manigenne ðætte hie ðurh hiera gedwolan
ond ðurh hiera ungeðwærnesse ða Godes æ, ðe us forbiet
diofulum to offrianne, ðæt hie ða ilcan æ ne gehwierfen to
diofulgielde. Be ðæm Dryhten siofigende cwæð ðurh Ossei
ðone witgan; he cwæð, "Ic him sealde hwæte ond win ond
oele ond gold ond siolfor; ic him sealde genog, ond ðæt hie
worhton to diofulgieldum Bale hiera gode." Ac ðonne we underfoð ðone hwæte æt Gode, ðonne we ongietað inweardlice
ða æ, ond onwreoð ða dieglan cwidas, swelce we nimen ðone
clænan hwæte, ond weorpen ðæt ceaf onweg. Ond ðonne us
selð God his win, ðonne he us oferdrencð mid ðære lare
dioplices andgites. Ond ðonne he us selð his ele, ðonne he us

understanding received is produced at the appropriate time, it will be accomplished by performance of labor, as if it were born. To extend one's borders, then, is to magnify one's renown and one's name. But the pregnant women of Gilead are ripped open to extend their borders when heretics with corrupt doctrine eviscerate the mind of devout people just when their mind has comprehended the rudiments of proper understanding, and truth has gestated a little in them, before it is fully delivered, and they wish wisdom to be ascribed to them for their cutting out with the knife of weighty error the unborn children which are at that time just conceived in the mind of the devout. But they desire to be lauded for that and accounted wise teachers. Yet if we want them to desist from this outrage, we ought, first of all and most concertedly, to teach them not to crave vainglory, because if the root of this presumption is first severed, then it will soon be evident that the offshoots of illegitimate doctrine will wither.

They are also to be warned that, through their error and 3 through their fractiousness, they not pervert to idolatry God's law, which forbids us to offer to demons. About this the Lord spoke in complaint to the prophet Hosea, saying, "I gave them wheat and wine and oil and gold and silver; I gave them abundance, and they fashioned it to idols for their god Baal." But we receive wheat from God when we comprehend the law penetratingly and explicate the obscure passages as if we were preserving the pure wheat and discarding the chaff. And God imparts to us his wine when he intoxicates us with the enlightenment of profound understanding. And he gives us his oil when he reveals his

his bebodu openlicor gecyð, ond mid ðæm ure lif liðelice
ond getæslice fereð. Ond ðonne he us seleð micel siolfor,
ðonne he us selð micle getyngnesse ond wlitige spræce ymb
soðfæsðnesse to cyðanne. Ðonne he us gewelegað mid
golde, ðonne he ure heortan onlieht ond gebierht mid ðæm
sciman healices angietes. Ðis is eall ryhtwisra monna offrung Gode, ac hit briengað eal ða gedwolmen Bale, mid
ðæm ðe hie hiora hieremonna mod gedwellað, ond eall hiera
andgit forhwirfað mid hiera wore lare. Ðonne hie doð ðone
hwæte ond ðæt win ond ðone ele ond ðæt siolfor to diofulgieldum, ðonne hie ða gesibsumnesse ond gesceadwisnesse
to gedwolan ond to ungeðwærnesse gehwyrfað. Forðæm hie
sint to manigenne ðæt hie geornlice geðencen, ðonne hie
mid forhwirfede mode ðære sibbe bebod gehwierfað to ungeðwærnesse, ðæt hie ðonne hie selfe ofsleað from lifes
wordum mid ryhtum Godes dome.

4   Ongean ðæt sint to manigenne ða ðe ða word ðære halgan
æ ryhtlice ongietan cunnon, ond hie swaðeah eaðmodlice
nyllað læran. Hie sint to manigenne ðæt hie hie selfe ongieten on ðæm halgum gewritum, ær ðæm ðe hie oðre læren,
ðy læs hie eahtigen oðerra monna dæda, ond forgieten hie
selfe; ond ðonne hie eal ða halgan gewritu ryhtlice ongiten
hæbben, ðæt hie ne forgiten hwæt bi ðæm upahæfenum gecweden is. Hit is gecweden, "Dysig bið se læce ond untyd ðe
wilnað ðæt he oðerne mon gelacnige, ond nat ðæt he self bið
gewundad." Forðæm sint to monigenne ða ðe eaðmodlice
nyllað læran Godes word, ðætte ðonne ðonne hie ða untruman lacnian willað, ðætte hie ær gesceawigen ðæt ater hiera
agenra mettrymnessa on him selfum, ðy læs hie selfe acwe-
lan, ðær ðær hie ða oðre lacniað. Ac hie man sceal manian
ðæt hie geðencen ðætte hie selfe ne geunðwærigen ðæm

commandments more plainly, and that way orders our life smoothly and mildly. And he bestows on us much silver when he gives us great eloquence and oratory to proclaim truth. He enriches us with gold when he enlightens and illuminates our heart with the brilliance of exalted understanding. All of this is the offering of upright people to God, but heretics offer all of it to Baal, in that they lead astray the understanding of their charges and pervert their judgment entirely with their corrupt doctrine. They devote the wheat and the wine and the oil and the silver to devil worship when they transform amity and probity to error and discord. Therefore, they are to be charged to consider attentively, when with perverted intent they convert the commandments of peace to faction, that they annihilate themselves by means of the words of life, by the just sentence of God.

In opposition to that are to be counseled those who 4 rightly know how to interpret the words of holy scripture and nonetheless refuse to teach them humbly. They are to be exhorted to recognize themselves in holy texts before they teach others, to prevent their deliberating about other people's deeds and ignoring themselves; and when they have accurately comprehended all the holy texts, not to forget what is said about the haughty. It is said, "Foolish and inept is the physician who desires to heal other people and does not recognize that he is himself wounded." Therefore, those who refuse to teach God's word humbly are to be told that when they intend to heal the ailing, they ought first to observe in themselves the poison of their own infection, so that in healing others they not themselves die. But they ought to be exhorted to look that they not themselves

wordum ðe hie læra mid ðy ðæt hie oðer don, oðer hie
læra. Ac gehieren hwæt awriten is on ðæm ærendgewrite
sancte Petres; hit is awriten, "Swa hwa swa sprece, sprece
he Godes worde, swelce ða word no his ne sien, ac Godes."
Gif hit ðonne Godes word bioð, næs his, forhwy sceal hwa
ðonne bion ahæfen on ðæm, swelce hit his agenu word sien?
Ac hie scoldon gehieran ðone cuide ðe *sanctus* Paulus cwæð
to Corintheum; he cwæð, "Sua sua of Gode beforan Gode
we sprecað on Criste." Se ðonne spricð of Gode beforan
Gode, se ðe ongiet ðæt he ða word ðære lare from Gode onfeng, ond ðurh ða wilnað Gode to liciganne, nalles mannum.
Hie sculon gehieran ðone cuide ðe awriten is on Salomonnes
bocum: hit is awriten ðætte God anscunige ælcne ofermodne man. Se ðonne ðe mid Godes wordum his agenne
gielp secð, he wile reafian ðone ðe hie him sealde his anwaldes; ond ne ondræt him no, ðeah ðe he do God behindan
hine, ðeah ðe him God geafe ðæt ðæt ðær mon hereð.

5 Eac hie sculon gehieran hwæt to ðæm lareowum gecweden is ðurh Salomon: hit is gecweden, "Drinc ðæt wæter
of ðinum agenum mere, ond ðætte of ðinum agnum pytte
aflowe, ond læt ðine willas iernan wide, ond todæl hie, læd
hie gind ðin lond, ond gegier ðæt hie iernen bi herestrætum,
ond hafa hie ðeah ðe anum, ðy læs elðiodige hie dælen
wið ðe." Ðonne drincð se lareow ðæt wæter of his agnum
mere, ðonne he gehwirfð æresð to his agnum ingeðonce to
hladanne ðæt wæter—ðæt is to wyrceanne ðæt ðæt he lærð.
Ðonne he drincð of ðæm wielme his agnes pyttes, ðonne he
bið self geðwæned ond wel gedrenced mid his agnum wordum. Swiðe wel wæs ðios spræc mid ðy geieced ðe Salomon
cwæð, "Læt forð ðine willas, ond todæl ðin wætru æfter

contradict the words that they preach by doing one thing and teaching another. But let them hear what is written in the Epistle of Saint Peter, where it is written, "Whoever speaks, let him speak God's word as if the words were not his, but God's." Then if they are God's words, not his, why ought anyone to be conceited about them, as if they were his own words? But they ought to hear the point that Saint Paul made to the Corinthians when he said, "As from God, before God we speak in Christ." Then he speaks from God before God who understands that he received the words of instruction from God, and through them desires to please God, not humans. They ought to hear the pronouncement that is written in the books of Solomon: it is written that God abominates every proud person. Then whoever pursues his own glory with God's words aims to defraud the one who gave him his authority, and has no scruples about placing himself before God, though God gave him what is held in esteem there.

They ought likewise to hear what is said to teachers 5 through Solomon: it is said, "Drink the water from your own cistern, and which flows from your own well, and let your springs run wide, and divide them, and channel them throughout your land, and arrange for them to run along the highroads, and yet keep them to yourself alone, lest strangers divide them with you." The teacher drinks the water from his own cistern when he turns first to his own understanding to draw water—that is, to practice what he teaches. Then he drinks from the freshet of his own well when he is himself refreshed and well irrigated with his own words. This passage was quite well enlarged upon by Solomon's saying, "Let your springs flow forth, and disperse your waters

herestrætum." Ðæt is ðætte se lareow ærest sceal self drincan of ðæm wille his agenre lare, ond siððan geotan mid his
lare ðæt ilce wæter on his hieremonna mod. Ðæt is ðonne
ðæt mon his wætru ut læte, ðæt se lareow mid ðy cræfte his
lareowdomes utane on oðre menn giote, oð ðæt hie innan
gelærede weorðen. Ðæt is ðonne ðæt mon his wætru todæle
æfter cyninga herestrætum, ðæt mon ða godcundan spræce
ðære menigo ðæs folces todæle gemetlice ælcum be his andefne. Ac forðon ðe oft sio wilnung ðæs idlan gielpes gegripð
ðæt mod ðæs lareowes, ðonne he ongiet ðæt ða Godes word
manegum menn liciað ðe ðurh his muð beoð gesprecen,
forðæm wæs gecweden ðæt ðæt we ær sædon ðurh Salomon
ðone snotran; he cwæð, "Ðeah ðu ðin wætru todæle, hafa
hie ðeah ðe self, ond ne sele elðiodigum hira nawuht." He
mænde ða awiergedan gæstas. Bi ðæm spræc Dauid swiðe
cuðlice on psalmum, swa he hit oft acunnad hæfde: he cwæð,
"Elðiodige arison wið me, ond wunnon wið me, ond swiðe
stronge wæron ða ðe min ehton." We cwædon ær ðæt Salomon cwæde ðæt mon sceolde his wætru todælan, ond ðeah
him self eall habban, swelce he openlice cwæde, "Eow is
micel ðearf ðæt ge swa ætfeolen ut ðære lare, swa swa ge
eow innan ne geðieden to ðæm awiergedum gæstum ðurh
upahafenesse eowres modes, ðy læs ge ðurh ða ðenunga ðara
Godes worda to eow forlæten eowre fiend, ðy læs eow ðonon
awuht gemænes weorðe." Ac ðonne we doð ægðer—ge we ða
wætru todælað æfter cyninga herestrætum, ge eac us selfe
habbað—ðonne ðonne we swiðe wide ut togeotað ða lare,
ond suaðeah ðurh ða ne wilniað woruldgielpes.

along the highroads." That is that the teacher ought first himself to drink from the spring of his own doctrine, and afterward with his instruction pour that same water into the mind of his charges. That one releases his waters is, then, that the teacher infuses other people outwardly with the craft of his pedagogy, until they have inwardly grown learned. That waters are dispersed along the kings' high-ways, then, is that religious discourse is distributed to the multitude of the people in just proportion, to each accord-ing to his ability. But desire for vain prestige frequently grips the mind of the teacher when he perceives that many people are pleased by the words of God that are delivered through his mouth, and for that reason was stated what we said be-fore was spoken through the wise Solomon when he said, "Though you should divide your waters, keep them to your-self, and give nothing of them to strangers." He meant con-demned spirits. About these David spoke very intelligibly in Psalms, as he had learned it from frequent experience: he said, "Strangers have risen against me and assailed me, and very strong were those who persecuted me." We said earlier that Solomon said that waters should be dispersed and yet kept all to oneself, as if his plain meaning were, "There is great need for you to apply yourselves outwardly to teaching in such a way that you not associate yourselves with con-demned spirits through arrogance of mind, lest in the minis-tration of God's words you allow your enemies means to you, and there develop by that means anything in common between you." But we do both—we both disperse the waters along the kings' highways and also keep them to ourselves—when we let learning flow out far and wide and yet do not desire from it worldly glory.

Chapter 49

XLVIIII. Ðætte on oðre wisan sint to manianne ða
ðe medomlice cunnon læran, ond ðeah for
miclum ege ond for micelre eaðmodnesse
forwandiað, ond on oðre wisan ða ðe ðonne giet
to ðæm gewintrede ne beoð ne geðiegene,
ond ðeah for hrædhydignesse bioð to gegripene.

On oðre wisan sint to maniane ða ðe medomlice læran
magon, ond ðeah for micelre eaðmodnesse him ondrædað;
on oðre ða ða ðe unmedome bioð to ðære lare oððe for
gioguðe oððe for unwisdome, ond ðeah for hira fortruwodnesse ond for hira hrædwilnesse beoð to gescofene. Ða
ðonne sint to manigenne ðe nyttweorðlice læran meahton,
ond ðeah for ungemetlicere eaðmodnesse hit onscuniað. Hi
sint to manigenne ðæt hie be ðæm læssan ðingum ongieten
hu suiðe hie gesyngiað on ðæm maran. Hwæt, hie witon, gif
hiera niehstan friend weorðað wædlan, ond hie feoh habbað,
ond his ðonne him oftioð, ðæt hie beoð ðonne fultemend to
hiera wædle. Hwy ne magon hie ðonne geðencean, gif hie on
ðæm gesyngiað, hu micle swiður hie gesyngiað, ðonne hie
oftioð ðære lare ðæm synfullum broðrum, swelce hie gehyden lifes læcedom, ond his forwirnen ðæm cwelendum
monnum? Be ðæm cwæð Salomon, "Hu nytt bið se forho-
lena cræft oððe ðæt forhydde gold?" Oððe gif hwelc folc bið
mid hungre geswenced, ond hwa his hwæte gehyt ond
oðhielt, hu ne wilt he ðonne hiera deaðes? Be ðissum magon
ongietan ða lareowas hwelces wites hi wyrðe bioð, ðonne hie

Chapter 49

49. That those who know how to teach tolerably well, and yet for extreme trepidation and for extreme self-doubt are reluctant, are to be guided in one fashion, in another fashion those who are not yet sufficiently mature or experienced, and yet out of rashness they have undertaken it.

In one fashion are to be advised those who can teach tolerably well, and yet out of great humility are afraid; in another those who are incompetent at teaching, either for their youth or for ignorance, and yet out of presumption and out of audacity have thrust themselves into it. Those, then, are to be admonished who can teach effectively, and yet out of excessive abashedness avoid it. They are to be directed to understand by lesser matters how greatly they sin in greater ones. Now, they know, if their nearest friends become paupers, and they have money and yet withhold it from them, they are contributing to their poverty. Why can they not then conceive, if they sin in such a case, how much more they sin if they withhold doctrine from erring brothers, as if they were to hoard vital medicine and deny it to dying people? About this Solomon said, "Of what use is hidden ability or buried gold?" Or if a certain province is plagued by famine, and someone hides and withholds his wheat, does he not then desire their death? From this, teachers can conclude what sort of punishment they will merit when

lætað ða sawla acwellan for hungre hira worda, ond hie
nyllað hie fedan mid ðæm hlafe ðære giefe ðe hie onfengon.
Bi ðæm wæs swiðe wel gecweden ðurh Salomon, "Se ðe
his hwæte hytt, hine wiergð ðæt folc." Ðæt is ðonne ðæt
mon his hwæte ahyde, ðæt se lareow gehyde ða word ðære
halegan lare. Forðæm he for ðære anre scylde ðære swigan
bið awierged ond fordemed from ðæm folce, forðæm he
manigne gelæran meahte, gif he wolde. Hwæt we magon
geðencean, gif hwelc god læce bið ðe wel cann wunda sniðan,
ond ðonne gesihð ðæt his hwam ðearf bið, ond ðonne for his
slæwðe agiemeleasað ond forwirnð ðæt he his helpe, ðonne
wille we cweðan ðæt he sie genog ryhtlice his broðor deaðes
scyldig for his agenre slæwðe. Nu ðonne, nu ða lichomlican
læcas ðus scyldige gerehte sint, nu is to ongietanne æt hu
micelre scylde ða beoð befangne ða ðe ongietað ða wunda on
ðæm modum, ond agiemeleasiað ðæt hi hi lacnigen, ond
mid hiera wordum sniðen. Be ðæm wæs swiðe wel gecweden
ðurh Ieremias ðone witgan; he cwæð, "Awierged bið se mann
se ðe wirnð his sweorde blodes." Ðæt is ðonne ðæt mann
forwierne his sweorde blodes, ðæt hwa forwirne his lare ðæt
he mid ðære ne ofslea ðæs flæsces lustas. Eft cwæð Moyses
be ðæm ilcan, "Min sweord itt flæsc."

2   Gehieren eac ða ðe on innan him gedigliað ond gehydað
ða godcundan lare ðone egeslican Godes cwide ðe to him gecweden is, forðæm ðæt se ege ðone oðerne ege ut adrife; ðæt
is ðonne se cwide hu mon ðæt feoh befæste ðæm ciepemen
ðe he scolde forð sellan to wæstme, ond ða forðy ðe he forwandode ðæt he swa ne dyde, ða ageaf he hit to unðances,
ond his eac hæfde micelne dem. Eac hi sculon gehiran ðætte

they allow souls to be killed out of hunger for their words, and they refuse to feed them with the bread of the gift that they have received. About this it was very well put through Solomon, "One who hoards his wheat will be cursed by the people." To hoard one's wheat, then, is for the teacher to hoard the words of holy doctrine. For the sole offense of his silence he will be cursed and condemned by the people, because he could teach many if he cared to. Now, we can reason, if there is a certain good physician who is very knowledgeable about surgery for wounds, and then he sees that there is someone in need of it, and yet for his indolence is heedless and neglects to help him, we will say with sufficient justice that he is responsible for his brother's death, due to his own inaction. Now, then, given that healers of the body are thus to be held accountable, it can now be recognized in how great culpability those are implicated who understand the wounds in the mind and neglect to heal them and make incisions with their words. About this it was quite well spoken through the prophet Jeremiah, who said, "Cursed is the man who withholds his sword from bloodshed." That someone withholds his sword from bloodshed is that he withholds his teaching, so that with it he does not dispatch fleshly desires. Again, about the same Moses said, "My sword will devour flesh."

Let those who obscure and conceal religious doctrine 2 within themselves hear the terrible pronouncement of God that is spoken to them, so that fear of this may drive out that other fear: that is, then, the story about how money was entrusted to a merchant which he was to lend at interest, and when he neglected to do so, he returned it without thanks and also had great misfortune from it. They ought

sanctus Paulus geliefde ðæt he swa micele unscyldigra wære his niehstena blodes swa he læs wandade ðæt he hira unðeawas ofsloge. Hi magon gehieran be ðæm cuide ðe he cwæð; he cwæð, "Hwæt, ge sint ealle mine gewietan ðæt ic eom clæne ond unscildig nu giet to dæg eowres ælces blodes, forðæm ic næfre ne forwandode ðæt ic eow ne gecyðde eall Godes geðeaht." Eac hi sculon gehieran hu *sanctus* Iohannes wæs gemanod mid ðæs engles stemne, ða ða he cwæð to him, "Se ðe gehire ðæt hine mon clipige, clipie he eac oðerne, ond cweðe, 'Cum.'" Ðæt is, se ðe ongiete ðæt he sie gecieged mid godcundre stemne, ðætte he eac cigende ond lærende oðre ðider tio ond laðige ðider he getogen bið, ðy læs he finde ða duru betynede ongean hine, ðonne he cume, gif he cume idelhende to, ond ða mid him ne brenge, ðe he ðider laðian scolde. Hie scoldon gehieran hu Essaias se witga hreowsigende hine selfne tælde, ða he wæs onæled mid ðy upcundan leohte; he cwæð, "Waa me ðæs ic swigode." Eac hie sculon gehieran ðætte ðurh Salomon is gehaten ðæm monnum ðe lustlice ond unslawlice lærað ðæt ðæt hie ðonne cunnon, ðæt is ðæt him scyle hiera wisdom bion geieced ond gemanigfalðod. Salomon cuæð, "Ðæs monnes sawl ðe wel spricð, hio bið amæst, ond swa hwa swa oðerne drencð, he wirð self oferdruncen." Swa eac se ðe ut wel lærð mid his wordum, he onfehð innan ðæs inngeðonces fætnesse, ðæt is wisdom. Swa eac se ðe ne wirnð ðæs wines his lare ða mod mid to oferdrencanne ðe hine gehieran willað, he bið eac oferdrenced ond wel afed mid ðæm drence mislicra ond monigfaldra giefa. Hwæt, we hirdon ðætte Dauid brohte Gode

likewise to hear that Saint Paul believed that he was so much the less guilty of his neighbors' blood the less he hesitated to flog their vices. They can hear it by this utterance which he spoke, saying, "Now, you are all my witnesses that I am clean and guiltless to this very day of the blood of each of you, because I never neglected to make plain to you God's entire design." They ought also to hear how Saint John was exhorted by the voice of an angel, who said to him, "Let him who hears that he is called also call another and say, 'Come.'" That is that someone who perceives that he is summoned by a divine voice should also by summoning and teaching draw and invite others to where he is drawn, to prevent his finding the doors shut to him when he comes, if he arrives empty-handed and does not bring with him those he ought to invite there. They ought to hear how the prophet Isaiah blamed himself contritely when he was inflamed with the sublime light, saying, "Woe unto me that I have held my peace." They ought likewise to hear what, through Solomon, is promised to those people who with a will and without want of energy teach what they then know how to teach, which is that their wisdom will be increased and multiplied in them. Solomon said, "The soul of a person who speaks blessings will be fattened, and whoever intoxicates another will himself be intoxicated." Thus, likewise, one who teaches well outwardly with his words will inwardly receive stoutness of mind, which is wisdom. Thus, also, one who does not decline to intoxicate with the wine of his instruction the mind of those who are willing to listen to him will also be intoxicated and well sustained with the drink of various and manifold gifts. Now, we have heard that David brought it as

to lacum ðæt ðæt he ða lare ne hæl ðe him God geaf. Ðæt he cyðde, ða he cwæð, "Dryhten, ðu wast ðæt ic ne wyrne minra welera, ond ðine ryhtwisnesse ic ne diegle on minre heortan; ðine hælo ond ðine ryhtwisnesse ic secgge."

3   Gehierað hwæt on *Cantica Canticorum* is awriten, ðæt se brydguma scolde sprecan to ðære bryde: he cwæð, "Hlyst hider, ðu ðe eardasð on freondes orcgearde, ond gedoo ðæt ic mæge gehiran ðine stemne." Ðæt is sio halige gesomnung Godes folces, ðæt eardað on æppeltunum, ðonne hie wel begað hira plantan ond hiera impan, oð hie fulweaxne beoð. Ðæt bið ðonne ðæt mon his stemne gehiere, ðonne ða gecorenan menn giornfulle bioð his worda to gehlystanne. Ond ðonne wilnað se brydguma, ðæt is Crist, ðæt he gehire ða stemne ðære bryde, ðæt is Cristenra monna gesomnung, ðonne he ðurh gesceadwisra ond him gecorenra monna mod him to clipað, ond hie lærð ðurh hiora muð. Eac hie sculon gehieran hwæt Moyses dyde, ða he ongeat ðæt God wæs ðæm folce ierre; he bebead ðæt menn namen hiora sweord Godes andan mid to wrecanne, ond cwæð ðæt ða scolden bion synderlice Godes ðegnas, ða ðe unwandiende ðara scyldegena gyltas ofslogen. He cwæð, "Se ðe Godes ðegn sie, ga hider to me, ond do his sweord to his hype, ond gað from geate to geate ðurh midde ða ceastre, ond ofslea ælc mon his broður ond his freond ond his nihstan." Ðæt is ðonne ðæt mon his sweord doo ofer his hype, ðæt mon ða geornful-nesse his lare læte furður ðonne his flæsces lustas, ond ðæs gieme ðæt he unaliefede lustas ond lara atemige ond oferwinne, ðonne he wilnað ðæt he haligdom lære. Ðæt is ðonne ðæt mon ierne from geate to oðrum, ðæt he ierne ðreatigende from ðara unðeawa ælcum to oðrum, ðe deað mæge ingan on ðæs monnes mod. Ðæt is ðonne ðæt mon

an offering to God that he did not keep hidden the instruction that God had given him. He made that plain when he said, "Lord, you know that I will not restrain my lips, and I will not conceal your uprightness in my heart; I will proclaim your salvation and your righteousness."

Hear what is written in Song of Songs, which the bridegroom is supposed to have spoken to the bride: he said, "Listen here, you who linger in a friend's garden, and let me hear your voice." It is the holy congregation of the people of God which lingers in apple orchards when they well cultivate their shoots and their grafts until they are mature. That is, then, that his voice is heard when the elect are devoted to listening to his words. And the bridegroom, which is Christ, desires to hear the voice of the bride, which is the communion of Christian people, when he calls them to him through the minds of discerning people of his selection, and he teaches them through their mouth. They should likewise hear what Moses did when he understood that God was angry with the people: he directed men to take their swords with which to wreak God's anger, and said that they should be God's singular servants who unhesitatingly cut down the sins of the guilty. He said, "Whoever is God's servant, let him come here to me and place his sword at his hip, and go from gate to gate through the midst of the camp, and let each man kill his brother and his friend and his neighbor." To put one's sword to one's hip, then, is to value the scrupulousness of one's teaching above the desires of the flesh and to look that he subdue and master illicit desires and doctrines when he wishes to teach holiness. To run from one gate to the other, then, is to run rebuking from each to every other vice through which death can gain entry to a person's

ierne ðurh midde ða ceastre, ðætte mon sua emn sie betweox Cristenum folce on ðære ðreaunga hiera scylda ðæt
he nauðer ne nanum men ne olicce, ne he nanes monnes
oleccunga ne recce. Be ðæm wæs swiðe ryhtlice gecweden
ðæt mon scolde ofslean his broður ond his freond ond his
niehstan. Ðonne mon ofslihð his broður ond his friond ond
his niehstan, ðonne he for nanre sibbe ne wandað ðæt he
ða gyltas ne wrece on scyldegum monnum. Nu se is ðonne
gehaten Godes ðegn se ðe mid ðæm andan onæled bið
godcundre lufan unðeawas to ofsleanne. Hu ne wiðsæcð se
ðonne eallunga Godes ðegn to bionne, se ðe wiðsæcð ðæt he
ne ðreage swa he swiðusð mæge woruldmonna unðeawas?

4   Ongean ðæt sint to manianne ða ðe nabbað nawðer ne
ildo ne wisdom to ðon ðæt hie mægen oððe cunnen læran,
ond hi ðeah forhradiað ðæt hie hit ongiennað, ðy læs hie him
selfum fordikigen ðone weg ðære bote, ðe him on fierste
becuman meahte, ðonne hi him to tioð ða byrðenne swa
micelre ðenunge swa hrædlice. Ac ðonne hie him ær tide to
tioð ðæt hi ne magon ne ne cunnon, ðonne is him to ondræ-
danne ðæt him weorðe to lore ðæt hie to ryhtre tide gefol-
gian meahton, ðæt is se wisdom, ðe hie ær tide wilniað ond
eowiað, ac he him wyrð ðonne swiðe ryhtlice to lore. Hwæt,
hie magon geðencean ðæt fugla briddas, gif hie ær wilniað to
fleoganne, ær hira feðra fulweaxene sin, ðætte sio wilnung
hie geniðrað ðe hi ær up ahefð, oð hie forweorðað.

5   Eac hie sint to manigenne ðæt hie geðencen, gif mon
on niwne weall unadrugodne ond unastiðodne micelne hrof
ond hefigne onsett, ðonne ne timbreð he no healle ac hryre.
Eac hi sint to manigenne ðæt hi geðencen ðætte ða wif ðe ða
geeacnodan bearn cennað ðe ðonne git fulborene ne bioð,

mind. To run through the middle of the camp, then, is to be so impartial between Christian folk in the reproof of their offenses that he neither flatter any person nor credit anyone's flattery. About this, it was quite properly said that one's brother and his friend and his neighbor were to be killed. When someone kills his brother and his friend and his neighbor, he does not allow any bond to make him hesitate to castigate the wrongdoing of the guilty. Now, then, he is called God's servant who is inflamed with the indignation of divine love to strike down vices. Does he not refuse entirely to be God's servant who refuses to rebuke to his utmost ability the vices of worldly people?

Contrariwise, those who have neither the maturity nor 4 the wisdom sufficient to be able or to know how to teach, and yet they are headlong about beginning it, are to be exhorted not to block for themselves the way to the remedy which in time could fall to their lot when they take upon themselves the onus of so great an office so precipitately. But when they take upon themselves too soon what they cannot do or do not know how to do, they are to dread their losing what could serve them at the proper time, which is wisdom, which they desire to manifest prematurely, but it will then quite justly be lost to them. Now, they can consider that if the fledglings of birds desire to fly before their wings are full grown, the desire that had lifted them up will bring them down, until they meet their end.

They are also to be advised to consider that if a large and 5 heavy roof is placed on a new wall not yet dried and hardened, then no hall is built, but a ruin. They are also to be urged to consider that pregnant women who give birth to children that are not yet fully developed fill not houses with

ne fyllað hie no mid ðæm hus ac byrgenna. For ðissum ðingum wæs ðætte Crist self, ðe swiðe hrædlice meahte getrymian ðone ðe he wolde, sealde bisene ðæm lareowum to ðæm ðæt ða unlæredan ne scoldon læran: siððan he his cnihtas gelæred hæfde ðone cræft ðæs lareowdomes, he cwæð swaðeah, "Sittað eow nu giet innan ceastre, oð ðæt ge weorðen fullgearowode mid ðæm gæsðlican cræfte." Ðonne we sittað innan ceastre, ðonne we us betynað binnan ðæm locum ures modes, ðy læs we for dolspræce to widgangule weorðen. Ac eft ðonne we fullgearowode weorðað mid ðæm godcundan cræfte, ðonne bio we of ðære ceastre ut afærene—ðæt is of urum agnum ingeðonce—oðre men to læranne. Be ðys ilcan cwæð Salomon to iongum monnum, "Ðu gionga, bio ðe uniðe to clipianne ond to læranne, ge furðum ðina agna spræca, ond ðeah ðe mon tuwa frigne, ge-bid ðu mid ðære andsware, oð ðu wite ðæt ðin spræc hæbbe ægðer ge ord ge ende." For ðissum ilcan ðingum wæs ðætte ure aliesend, ðeah he on hefenum sie scieppend ond engla lareow, nolde he ðeah on eorðan bion monna lareow, ær he wæs ðritiges geara eald, forðæm ðe he wolde ðæm fortruwo-dum monnum andrysno halwendes eges on gebrengean; ðeah ðe he self gegyltan ne meahte, nolde he ðeah ær bodian ða giefe ðæs fulfremedan lifes, ær ðæm ðe he self wære ful-fremedre ielde. Hit is awriten on ðæm godspelle ðætte ure hælend, ða he wæs twelfwintre, wurde beæftan his meder ond his mægum innan ðære ceastre Hierusalem. Ac eft ða his mægas hine sohton, ða fundon hie hiene tomiddes ðara wietena ðe ðær wisoste wæron in Hierusalem, hlys-tende hiora worda, ond frinende hiora lara. Ðonne is us ðæt swiðe wocorlice to geðenceanne ðætte ure hælend, ða ða he twelfwintre wæs, ða wæs he gemet sittende tomiddes ðara

them, but tombs. For these reasons it was that Christ himself, who could without hindrance have confirmed whomever he wished, gave an example to teachers to the effect that the uneducated ought not to teach: after he had taught his disciples the craft of teaching, he nonetheless said, "Stay longer in the town, until you are fully prepared with spiritual ability." We stay within the town when we close ourselves off within the cells of our mind, so that for fatuous talk we not wander excessively. But in turn when we grow fully prepared with divine ability, we will have departed from the town— that is, from our own introspection—to teach other people. About this very matter Solomon said to young people, "Young man, do not let it be unforced that you speak out and teach, even on your own behalf, and though you are asked twice, delay the reply until you know that your response has both a start and a finish." For these very reasons it was that our redeemer, though in heaven he is creator and instructor of angels, refused to be an instructor of humans before he was thirty years of age, since he intended to inculcate in presumptuous people a regard for wholesome fear: though he could not himself err, he nonetheless did not wish to preach the grace of the life of perfection before he was himself of the age of perfection. It is written in the gospel that when our savior was twelve years old, he remained behind within the city of Jerusalem when his mother and his relations departed. But when his family returned to look for him, there in the company of those elders who were wisest in Jerusalem they found him, listening to their words and inquiring about their doctrines. Then it is for us to reflect very attentively that our savior, when he was twelve years of age, was found sitting amid teachers inquiring, not teaching,

lareowa frignende, nalles lærende; forðæm he us wolde ðæt
to bisene don ðætte ða unlæredan ne dorsten læran, nu he
ðonne wolde cniht bion, ond wolde ðæt hiene mon lærde—
se ilca se ðe ða ær lærde ðe hine ða lærdon mid ðæm cræfte
ðæs godcundan anwaldes. Ond eft Paulus cwæð to his
cnihte, "Bebiod ðis ond lære, ond ne forsio nan mon ðine
gioguðe." We sculon wietan ðætte oft bið on halgum ge-
wrietum genemned midfeorh to giuguðhade. Ðæt we magon sweotolor ongietan, gif we Salomones cuida sumne her
ongemong eowiað; he cwæð, "Bliðsa, cniht, on ðinum
gioguðhade." Gif he hit ðonne ne tiohchode eall to anum,
ðonne ne nemde he ðone cniht ægðer ge "cniht" ge "giong
man."

Chapter 50

L. Ðætte on oðre wisan sint to manianne ða ðe
woroldare wilniað, ond hie ðonne orsorglice
habbað, ond on oðre ða ðe woroldare
wilniað, ond ðonne hie gewilnode habbað,
hie ðonne mid micelre earfoðnesse
ond mid micle broce on wuniað.

On oðre wisan sint to manianne ða ðe eall orsorglice be-
gitað ðisse worulde ðæt ðæt hie wilniað; on oðre wisan ða ðe
ðisses andweardan middangeardes wilna ond welena wilniað, ond swaðeah mid sumum wiðerweardum brocum hiora

because he wished to set an example for us that the untaught not presume to teach, seeing as he was then willing to be a disciple and was willing to be taught—the very one who had endowed with the power of religious authority those who then instructed him. And again Paul said to his disciple, "Prescribe and teach this, and let no one impugn your youth." We ought to recognize that in sacred discourse, young adulthood is often referred to as youth. We can understand this with greater clarity if, in this context, we present a certain observation of Solomon, who said, "Delight, my boy, in your youth." If he had not regarded it as all the same, he would not have called the boy both "boy" and "young man."

Chapter 50

50. That those who desire worldly success, and already have it securely, are to be guided in one fashion, and in another fashion those who desire worldly success, and once they have come to desire it, they persist in a state of extreme difficulty and of extreme care.

In one fashion are to be instructed those who obtain effortlessly all that they desire of this world, in another fashion those who desire the gratifications and the riches of this present existence and yet are defeated of them by certain

him bið færwirned. Ða ðonne sint to manienne ðe simle habbað ðisse worulde ðæt ðæt hie wilniað ðæt hie ne agiemeleasien, ðonne hi hit eall hæbben, ðæt hie ne secen ðone ðe him to eallum gefultemað, ðy læs hie lufigen ðas elðiodignesse ofer hiora ægenne eðel, ond hiora mod eal ahon on ðæt ðe him her gelæned bið, ond ðy læs hie gedwelle sio gehydnes ond ða getæsu ðe hie on ðæm wege habbað, ðæt hie forgieten hwider hie scylen, ond ðy læs hie for ðæm fægeran monan ðe hi on niht gesioð forhycgen ðæs dæges bierhto ond ðære sunnan. Eac hi sint to monienne ðætte hie no ne geliefen ðætte ða willan ond ða getæsu ðe him on ðisse worulde becumað, ðætte ðæt sien ða lean ðe him God getiohchod hæfð, ac bið ðissa iermða frofor, ond ða lean bioð on ðæm ecean life ðæs ðe we to gode doð. Forðy we sculon ure mod getrymman wið ðisses middangeardes oliecunga, ðy læs we hie mid ealle mode lufigen, ond us mid ealle hiere underðieden. Ac se se ðe ðas orsorgnesse ðe he her hæfð ne forswið mid ðære gesceadwisnesse his ingeðonces ond mid ðære lufan ðæs beteran lifes, ðonne gehwierfð he ða olecunga ðisse gewitendan worulde him to ecum deaðe. For ðissum ðingum wæs ðætte Ezechiel se witga ðreade Israhela folc, ond cwæð ðæt hie wolden weorðan forlorene ond oferwunnene mid orsorgnesse, swa swa Idumeas wæron, forðæm hi to swiðe bliðsodon on ðisses middangeardes orsorgnesse. Ac Dryhten hie ðreade ðurh ðone witgan, ða he cwæð, "Hie dydon min land him selfum to ierfelonde mid gefean ond mid ealre heortan ond mid ealle mode." Be ðæm wordum we mægon gehieran ðæt hie wæron swiðe suiðlice getælde, næs no forðæm ðe hie fægnodan, ac forðæm ðe hie mid ealre heortan ond mid ealle mode fægnodan. Be ðæm cwæð Salomon, "Giongra monna dolscipe hi ofslihð, ond dysigra

adverse mishaps. Those, then, who always have what they desire of this world are to be warned not to neglect, while they have it all, to search out the one who helps them to it all, so that they not value this exile over their own country and devote their attention entirely to what is lent them here; to avoid letting the ease and the comforts that they have along the way mislead them, so that they forget where they ought to be bound; and lest for the lovely moon that they observe at night they despise the brightness of day and of the sun. They are also to be warned not to believe that the gratifications and the comforts that fall to their lot in this world are the rewards that God has appointed for them, but they are solace for these miseries, and the rewards for what good we do will be in eternal life. For that reason, we ought to fortify our will against the flatteries of this existence, so that we not care for them wholeheartedly and enthrall ourselves to them entirely. But whoever does not vanquish these luxuries that he has here with discernment of conscience and devotion to the better life will convert the blandishments of this ephemeral world to everlasting death. For these reasons it was that the prophet Ezekiel lambasted the people of Israel and said that they would be lost and overcome by luxury, as the Edomites were, because they delighted overmuch in a carefree existence. But the Lord reproved them through the prophet when he said, "They have turned my land to their own inheritance with rejoicing and with all their heart and with all their mind." By these words we can make out that they were very strenuously condemned not because they rejoiced, but because they rejoiced with all their heart and with all their mind. About this Solomon said, "The waywardness of young people will kill

monna orsorgness hi fordeð." Be ðæm ilcan cwæð *sanctus* Paulus, "Sien ða hæbbendan swelce hie nowiht hæbben, ond ða ðe ðisses middangeardes notigað swelce hi his no ne notigen"; ðæt is ðætte we swa lufigen ðisne uterran ond ðisne eorðlican fultum ðætte we forðæm from ðære wilnunga ond from ðære geornfulnesse ðære godcundan lufan ure mod ne awenden, ðy læs us weorðe to wope ond to elðiodignesse ðæs ecean lifes ðæt ðæt us on ðisse elðiodignesse to fultume ond to are gelæned is; ðætte we ne fægnigen, swelce we gesælige sien for ðissum gewitendan ðingum, ðonne ðonne we betweox ðæm ongieten hu earme we bioð ðara ecena ðinga.

2   Be ðissum ilcan cwæð Salomon on *Cantica Canticorum* ðære bec be ðære halgan gesomnunge: he cwæð, "Dryhtnes winestre hand is under minum heafde, ond his swiðre hand me beclipð." Sio winestre hand Godes he cwæð wære under his heafde. Ðæt tacnað orsorgnesse ðisses andweardan lifes. Ða hand ðonne geðrycð sio incunde lufu ðæs uplican lifes. Sio swiðre hand hine ðonne beclipð, ðonne ðonne he hine gehielt on ðæm willan ðæt he mid ealre estfulnesse lufað ðæt ece lif. Eft wæs gecueden ðurh Salomon ðone snottran ðætte on his swiðran handa wære lang lif, ond on his winestran wære wela ond wyrðmynt. Ða he lærde hu we ægðer lufian sceolden, ða he mæt ðone welan ond ðone wyrðmynd to ðære winestran handa. Eft be ðæm ilcan cwæð se psalmsceop, "Gehæle me ðin sio swiðre." Ne cwæð he no "ðin sio winestre hond," ac "ðin sio swiðre." Mid ðæm he gecyðde ðæt he ne mænde ðis andwearde lif, ac ðæs ecean lifes hælo he sohte. Be ðæm ilcan is eft awriten on *Exodo,* ðæt is Moyses boc; hit is awriten, "Ðin swiðre hand, Dryhten, gebræc ðine feond." Ða ðonne ðe Godes fiond bioð, ðeah hi on ðære

them, and the complacency of foolish people will be their ruin." About the same Saint Paul said, "Let those who possess be as if they possessed nothing, and those who have use for this world as if they had no use for it"; that is, that we value this external and this earthly solace in such fashion that, for its sake, we not avert our mind from desire for and diligence about love of the divine, so that what is lent us as a relief and a favor in this exile not become for us grief and exile from eternal life; that we not be contented, as if we were made happy by these impermanent things, while in the midst of them we recognize how poor we are in things that are without end.

About just this Solomon spoke in the book Song of Songs 2 about the holy congregation: he said, "The Lord's left hand is under my head, and his right hand embraces me." The left hand of God, he said, was under his head. That signifies easy circumstances in this present life. The indwelling love of sublime life, then, presses the hand. The right hand embraces him when he maintains in himself the desire to love eternal life with complete devotion. Again it was said through the wise Solomon that in his right hand was long life, and in his left were wealth and honor. He instructed how we are to love each when he compared wealth and honors to the left hand. In turn, about this same the psalmist said, "Let your right hand save me." He by no means said "your left hand" but "your right." He thereby made it plain that he did not mean this present life, but he looked forward to the felicity of life everlasting. About this same it is written in Exodus, which is the book of Moses, "Your right hand, Lord, shattered your enemy." Those, then, who are God's enemies, though they have flourished on the

winstran handa bion geðigene, hi beoð mid ðære swiðran tobrocene—ðæt is ðætte oft ðis andwearde lif up ahefeð ða yfelan, ac se tocyme ðære ecan eadignesse hie geniðrað.

3 Ðy sint to manienne ða ðe on ðisse worulde orsorglice libbað, ðæt hie geornlice ongieten ðætte sio orsorgnes ðisses andweardan lifes hwilum bið to ðæm gelæned ðæt hie sien ðurh ða to beteran life getogene, hwilum to ðæm ðæt hie sien ðy swiður on ecnesse gesciende. Forhwam wæs elles Canonea land Israhela folce gehaten, buton forðæm ðe ðæt ungetyde folc nolde geliefan ðeah him mon feorr land on fierste gehete, gif him sona ne sealde sum on neaweste se him ðæt mare gehett? Ond eac forðæm ðætte hie ðy fæsðlicor ond ðy untweogendlicor gelifden ðara ecena ðinga, swa hwanne swa him ða gehete, ðy læs hi mid ðæm gehatum ond mid ðæm tohopan anum hi spone to ðære giefe, ac eac mid ðære giefe he hi teah on ðone tohopan. Ðæt eac gecyðde se psalmsceop swiðe openlice, ða he cwæð, "He him sealde ricu oðerra kynrena, ond manigra folca gestreones hie wieoldon, to ðon ðæt hi his ryhtwisnesse geheolden, ond his æ sohten." Ac ðonne ðæt mennisce mod Godes glædmodnesse mid godum weorcum ne geandsworað, ðonne bið he swiðe ryhtlice mid ðæm gehined ðe mon wenð ðæt he mid gearod sie. Be ðæm wæs eft gecweden ðurh ðone salmsceop, "Ðu hie geniðrades, ða hi hi selfe up ahofon." Swa, ðonne ðonne unnyttan men ða godcundan gife nyllað leanian mid ryhtum weorcum, ac willað hi selfe her mid ealle fordon mid ðære fortruwunga ðæs toflowendan welan ond orsorgnesse, ond ðonon ðe hi utan bioð ahæfene, ðanon hie bioð innan afeallene. Be ðys ilcan wæs eac gecweden be ðæm welegan ðe gesæd is ðætte on helle ðrowude; hit wæs gecweden, "Ðu onfenge ðin god eal her on worulde." Forðæm anfehð se yfla

left hand, are shattered with the right—which is that this present life often exalts the bad, but the coming of everlasting contentment will lay them low.

Therefore, those who live without care in this world are 3 to be charged to recognize in earnest that easy circumstances in this present life are sometimes lent to draw them to a better life, sometimes to confound them all the more in eternity. Why else was the land of Canaan promised to the people of Israel but that that ignorant nation refused to believe it when they were promised a far country in time, unless he who promised them that greater country had not at once given them one nearby? And also so that they would believe more firmly and freer of doubt in eternal things whenever he promised them to them, so that he would not entice them to that gift with promises and hopes alone, but by means of the gift he drew them to that hope. The psalmist also explained this quite plainly when he said, "He gave them the realms of other nations, and they controlled the wealth of many peoples, that they should maintain his righteousness and pursue his law." But when the human mind does not respond to God's beneficence with good works, it will be justly abased by what is supposed to honor it. About that it was again said through the psalmist, "You cast them down when they exalted themselves." Just so, when idle people refuse to repay divine gifts with appropriate works but wish to ruin themselves here altogether with misplaced confidence in flowing riches and security, and on that account are outwardly arrogant, for that they will be inwardly cast down. Regarding this same, it was likewise said about the rich man who suffered in hell, "You received all your store of good here in the world." The bad person receives anything

auht goodes on ðisse worulde ðæt he eft ðy maran yfles on ðæm toweardan life onfo, gif he her nolde for ðæm goode to Gode gecierran.

4   Angean ðæt sint to manigenne ða ðe ðises middangeardes wilna ond weolena wilniað, ond him swaðeah sum wiðerweardnes his forwiernð, ond hi geswencð on ðisse worulde. Ða sint to manienne ðæt hie geornlice geðencen mid hu micelre giefe ofer him wacað se scippend ond se stihtere ealra gesceafta, ðonne he hi nyle lætan to hiera agnum wilnungum. Swa swa se læce, ðonne he ðæm siocan ne truwað, ond wenð ðæt his gehelpan ne mæge, ðonne aliefð he him eal ðæt ðæt hine lysð to donne ond to ðycganne, ac ðæs ðe he wenð ðæt he gehelpan mæge, ðæm he forwiernð swiðe feola ðæs ðe he wilnað. Hwæt, we eac wiernað urum cildum urra peninga mid to plegianne, ðæm ilcum ðe we eft tiochiað urne eard ond urne eðel ond ure ierfe eall ætsomne to te forlætanne, ond hie tiochiað us to ierfeweardum to habbanne. Ac nimen him nu be ðisse bisene gefean ond tohopan ðære ecan ierfeweardnesse, ða ðe sio wiðerweardnes ðisses andweardan lifes geeaðmet: ac gif hi God næfde on ecnesse getiochod to gehælanne, ðonne ne gebridlode he hi no mid swa swiðlicre ðreaunga his lare.

5   Eac sint to manigenne ða ðe ðissa hwilendlicra ðinga wilniað, ond him ðeah sum broc ond sumu wiðerweardnes hiera forwiernð, ðætte hie geornfullice geðencen ðætte oft ryhtwise menn mid ðys hwilendlican anwealde weorðað up ahæfene, oð hie ðurh ðone anwald weorðað mid synnum gefangne, sua sua mid sume grine, swa swa we ær herbiufan sædon on ðisse ilcan bec bi Dauide ðæm Godes dirlinge ðæt he wære ryhtwisra ða ða he ðegn wæs ðonne he wære siððan he kyning wæs. Ða ða he ðegn wæs, he mette his feond, ond

good in this world only so that he may get more that is bad in the life to come, if he refuses for that good to turn to God.

Otherwise are to be advised those who desire the gratifications and riches of this existence, and yet some disappointment prevents it, and they struggle in this world. They are to be urged to consider carefully with how great a grace the creator and ruler of all creatures is watching over them when he refuses to grant them their own desires. Just so the healer, when he despairs of a sick person and believes that he cannot help him, allows him everything that he wishes to do and to have, but he forbids a great deal of what he desires to someone whom he believes he can help. Look how we likewise do not allow our children to play with our money, the very ones to whom we intend to leave our land and our home and our legacy, and whom we plan to have as our heirs. But let them derive from this example satisfaction and hope of an everlasting legacy, those whom the reverses of this present life chasten: yet if God had not determined to save them for all time, he would by no means have checked them so harshly with the severity of his discipline. 4

Those who desire these temporal things and yet are frustrated of them by some ill fortune and some adversity are likewise to be instructed to consider attentively that pious people often grow arrogant with this temporal power, until through that power they become enmeshed in sin, as if with a kind of net, just as in this very book we said above about God's favorite, David, that he was more righteous when he was an officer than he was after he became king. When he was an officer he encountered his enemy, and yet for fear of 5

ðeah for Godes ege ond for ryhtwisnesse lufum he hine ne
dorste ofslean. Ac eft siððan he kyning wæs, for lare ond for
tiehtinge his agenes firenlustes he ofslog ond besirede his
getreowne ðegn. Hwa mæg ðonne æhta oððe anwaldes oððe
weorðscipes wilnian butan plio, nu se swelc plioh ðæron gefor, se ðe his no ne wilnode? Hwa mæg ðonne for ðyllecum
bion gehealden butan miclum gesuince ond miclum plio, nu
se on ðæm rice on swelce synne befioll, se ðe God self to
ðæm rice geceas? Eac hie sint to manigenne ðæt hie geðencen hu hit awriten is be Salamonne, hu he æfter swa miclum
wisdome afioll, emne oð ðæt he dioflum ongan gieldan. Nis
hit no gesæd ðæt he ænig wuht wiðerweardes on ðys middangearde hæfde, ær ðæm þe he afeol; ac siððan him se wisdom to forlæten wæs eallunga he forget hine selfne ond ða
lare ond ðone ðiodscipe ðe he geliornode, swa ðæt he his
nan geswinc habban nolde ne læsse ne mare.

Chapter 51

LI. Ðætte on oðre wisan sint to manianne ða
ðe beoð gebundne mid synrædenne,
on oðre wisan ða ðe freo
bioð ðara benda.

On oðre wisan sint to manienne ða ðe mid synnrædenne
bioð gebundene, on oðre ða ðe ðara benda bioð frio. Ða sint

God and for love of ethical behavior he dared not kill him. But in turn after he was king, under the dictates and inducement of his own lust he killed and betrayed his trusty officer. Then who can desire goods and power and dignity without peril, seeing as he who never desired them encountered such peril in that way? Who, then, can be safe in regard to such without much struggle and much danger, seeing as he in authority fell into such a sin, whom God himself had appointed to that authority? They are also to be advised to consider how it is written about Solomon: how, after having been possessed of so much wisdom, he fell away, even to the extent that he began to sacrifice to devils. It is not said that he had any sort of hardship in this existence before he stumbled, but after wisdom had been granted him, he wholly forgot himself, and the learning and the discipline that he had acquired, so that he refused to be troubled with it, neither more nor less.

Chapter 51

51. That those who are constrained by the bonds of matrimony are to be guided in one fashion, in another fashion those who are free of those bonds.

In one fashion are to be cautioned those who are held by the bonds of matrimony, in another those who are free of

to manigenne ðe mid ðæm gebundene bioð, ðonne ðonne
hie betwuh him ðenceað hu hiera ægðer oðres willan don
scyle, ðæt hira swa tilige ægðer oðrum to licianne on hiera
gesinscipe, ðæt hi ne mislicien hiera scippende; ond ðæt hie
swa wyrcen ðisses middangeardes weorc ðæt hie ne forlæten
to wilnianne ðara ðe Godes sien, ond swa gefeon ðissa and-
weardena goda ðæt hi him eac geornlice ondræden ða ecan
yflu, ond swa eac ðara yfela ðisse worulde hiofen ðæt hi huru
hiora tohopan anwealgne gefæstnigen to ðæm ecum godum;
ond ðonne hie ongieten hu gewitendlic ðis andwearde bið
ðæt ðæt hie her doð, ond hu ðurhwunienede ðæt bið ðæt hi
wilniað, ðætte ðonne nawðer ne nan yfel ðisses middangeardes hiora mod ne gebrece ne nan god hie ne beswice,
ac se gefea ðara hefonlicena goda hi gehierde wið ðæm bro-
cum—ond eft se wena ðara toweardena yfela on ðæm
toweardan dome hie geegesige on ðære orsorgnesse. Forðæm ðæt mod ðara Cristenra gesamhiwena, ðætte bið ægðer
ge trum ge untrum ond ne mæg fullice forsion ðas hwilendlican ðing, he mæg ðeah hine formengan to ðæm ecum mid
his willan, ðeah he ðonne giet on ðæs flæsces lustfulnesse
licge, mid ðæm ðæt he hine getrymige ond gefylle mid ðæm
uplican tohopan. Ond ðeah he hæbbe hwæt eorðlices ond
mennisclices him on gewunan on ðys wege—se weg is ðis
andwearde lif—ne forlæte he ðeah ðone tohopan ðæt he becume to Gode for his godan willan, ond swaðeah ne fulga he
eallunga ðæs lichoman wilnunga, ðy læs he eallunga afealle
ðonon ðe he fæsðlicost tohopian scolde.

2   Ymb ðæt reahte Paulus swiðe wel mid feaum wordum on
his ærendgewrite to Corinctheum; he cuæð, "Ða ðe wif
hæbben, sien ða swelce hie nan hæbben, ond ða ðe wepen,
sien ða swelce hi no ne wepen, ond ða ðe fægnigen, sien ða

those bonds. Those who are constrained by them are to be directed, when they consider between them how each ought to do the other's will, endeavoring each to please the other in their marriage, not to displease their maker; and to work at the tasks of this existence in such manner as not to cease to long for those that are of God, and to delight in these present benefits in such a way as also to dread everlasting ills, and likewise to deplore the ills of this world in such fashion particularly as to fix their hopes entirely on eternal benefits; and when they understand how ephemeral is what they presently do and how enduring will be what they desire, to let neither any ill of this world break their spirit nor any benefit mislead them, but let their delight in heavenly benefits steel them against reverses—and, conversely, belief in future ills at the judgment to come unsettle them in contentment. For the spirit of Christian married couples, which is both secure and insecure and cannot fully despise these temporal things, can nonetheless take part in the eternal with a will by bracing and filling itself with lofty hope, even though that spirit lies as yet in the appetites of the flesh. And though it may have something of the earthly and the human in its manner on this way—the way is this present life—let it not, however, abandon the hope that it may come to God for its good will, and yet not entirely fulfill the impulses of the body, to avoid its falling entirely from what it ought most firmly to hope in.

About this, Paul gave quite good directions in brief words 2 in his Epistle to the Corinthians, saying, "Let those who have a wife be as if they have none, and those who weep be as if they do not weep, and those who are glad as if they are

swelce hi no ne fægnigen." Se ðonne hæfð wif swelce he nan
næbbe, se ðe hit hæfð for licumlicre frofre, ond ðeah for
ðæm bryce ond for ðære lufe hine ne awent from bettrum
weorcum. Se hæfð eac wif swelce he nan næbbe, se ðe ongiet
ðætte eal ðas andweardan ðing bioð gewitendlicu, ond ðeah
for niedðearfe hæfð giemenne his flæsces, ond hwæðre mid
micelre wilnunga his gæstes giernð ðæs ecan gefean. Ðæt is
ðonne ðæt mon wepe, ond ne wepe, ðæt mon ða iermðo
ðisses middangeardes wepe, ond swaðeah wite ðæt he sceal
bion afrefred, ond blissian on ðæm ecum gefean. Ond eft is
ðæt mon blissige ond ne blissige ðæt mon ahebbe his mod of
ðissum eorðlican to ðæm hefonlican, ond ðeah ne forlæte
ðæt he him ne ondræde ðæt he afealle of ðæm uplican to
ðæm niðerlican. Ymb ðæt swiðe wel ðærryhte æfter rehte
sanctus Paulus, ða he cwæð, "Ðyses middangeardes ansien
ofergæð"; swelce he openlice cwæde, "Ne sculon ge no eallunga to swiðe lufian ðisne middangeard, forðam, ðeah ge
hine lufigen, he eow ne mæg ealneg standan. On idelnisse ge
fæstniað eower mod on him, forðæm ðe he eow flihð, ðeah
ge hine lufigen swelce he wunigende sie."

3   To manigenne sint ða gesomhiwan, ðeah hira hwæðrum
hwæthwugu hwilum mislicige on oðrum, ðæt hie ðæt geðyldelice forberen; ond gebidde hira ægðer for oðer ðæt hie
mægen ðurh ðæt weorðan gehælede, forðæm hit awriten
is, "Berað eowre byrðenna gemænelice betwux iow, ðonne
gefylle ge Godes æ." Sio lufu ðonne is Godes æ: sio æ ond
sio lufu us briengað monig god from Criste, ond ure yfelu
geðyldelice forbierð. Ac ðonne we onhyrigað Criste, ond eac
ða onhyringe gefyllað, ðonne we lustlice sellað oðrum ðæt
ðæt us God selð, ond geðyldelice forberað hiora yfelu. Ða
gesinhiwan mon sceal manian, ond eac gehwelcne mon, ðæt

not glad." Then he has a wife as if he has none, who has her for the solace of the body and yet does not, for that use and that love, turn away from nobler works. He likewise has a wife as if he has none, who understands that all these present things are fleeting and yet he must of necessity care for his flesh, and nonetheless with prodigious desire of the spirit yearns for everlasting joy. Then this it is to weep and not to weep: to lament the wretchedness of this existence and yet to know that one shall be comforted and exult in everlasting delight. And in turn, to be glad and not be glad is to elevate one's mind from the worldly to the sublime, and yet not cease to fear falling from the lofty to the base. About this Saint Paul gave very good instructions directly afterward when he said, "The form of this world will pass away"; as if his plain meaning were, "You are not to love this existence altogether too well, for though you may love it, it cannot persist forever. In vain do you fix your mind on it, because it will recede from you even though you love it as if it were enduring."

The married are to be advised that, although each of 3 them may on occasion dislike something about the other, they should bear it patiently, and let each of them pray for the other so that they might be saved by that means, because it is written, "Bear your burdens together between you; then you will fulfill God's law." Love, then, is God's law: the law and love bring us many favors from Christ, and he bears our ill doings patiently. But we emulate Christ, and likewise perfect our imitation, when with pleasure we give to others what God gives to us and with patience bear their wrongs. Married couples, as well as each individual, are to be

hie no læs ne geðencen hwæt oðre men him forberað ond geðafiað, ðonne hie geðenceað hwæt hi oðrum monnum forberað; forðæm ðe he mæg micle ðy ieð adreogan ða tionan ðe him oðre men doð, gif he wile gemunan ða ðe he oðrum monnum deð.

4   Eac sint to manigenne ða gesinhiwan ðæt hi gemunen ðæt hie for nanum oðrum ðingum ne bioð gesomnode, buton forðæm ðæt hie sculon bearna strienan. Forðæm hi sculon geðencean, gif hie to oftrædlice ond to ungemetlice hie gemengað on ðæm hæmede, ðæt hie ne bioð no on ryhtum gesinscipe, gif hie ðæt on gewunan habbað, ac forðæm ðe hie gewemmað ðone aliefedan gesinscipe mid ðære unliefedan gemengnesse, him is micel niedðearf ðæt hie mid oftrædlicum gebedum ða scylde adiligien. Forðæm wæs ðæt se getyda læce ðæs hefonlican læcedomes, ðæt wæs *sanctus* Paulus, ægðer ge ða halan lærde ge ðam unhalum læcedom eowde, ða he cwæð, "God bið men ðæt he sie butan wife." Ond eft he cwæð, "God bið mannum ðæt ælc hæbbe his agen wif, ond ælc wif hire ceorl, ðy læs hi on un-ryht hæmen." Ægðer he dyde, ge he egesode ða ðe on unryht hæmdon, ge he liefde ðæm ðe hit forberan ne meahton, forðæm ðætte ða ðe gestondan ne meahton, gif hi afeallan scolden, ðæt hi afeollen on ðæt hnesce bedd ðæs gesin-scipes, næs on ða heardan eorðan ðæs unryhthæmdes. Ond eft he cwæð to ðæm untrumum, "Agife se wer his wife hire ryht on hira gesinscipe, ond swa same ðæt wif ðæm were." Ac æfter ðæm ðe he hwelcehwugu gerisenlice leafe dyde ðæm gesinhiwon hira willan to fremmanne, he cwæð, "Ne cweðo ic no ðæt ðæt ic ær cwæð bebeodende, ac lærende ond geðafigende." Ða he spræc gelicost ðæm ðe hit hwelc-hwugu syn wære, ða he cwæð ðæt he hit forgiefan wolde ond

exhorted to devote no less consideration to what other people tolerate and accept in them than they devote to what they tolerate in other people, since one can much the more readily endure the injuries that other people inflict on him if he is willing to remember those that he inflicts on others.

Married couples are also to be advised to recall that they 4 are wedded for no other reason than to engender children. Therefore, they are to reflect that if they engage too frequently and too intemperately in copulation, they are not in a state of true matrimony, supposing they make a habit of it, but because they profane legitimate matrimony with illegitimate relations, it is sorely needed that they expiate the offense with frequent prayer. It was for that reason that the learned physician of heavenly healing, which was Saint Paul, both instructed the fit and administered medicine to the weak when he said, "It is good for a man to be without a woman." And again he said, "It is good for men to have each his own wife, and each woman her husband, lest they commit fornication." He did two things, inasmuch as he both put fear into those who fornicated and gave leave to those who could not forbear, for the purpose that if those who could not stand should fall, they would fall on the soft bed of matrimony, not on the hard ground of fornication. And again he said to the weak, "Let a man give his wife what is her right in their marriage, and likewise the woman her husband." Yet after granting a degree of due leave to married couples to do their will, he said, "I say what I have said not as a commandment but as edification and indulgence." He spoke most nearly as if it were some sort of sin when he said that he was willing to forgive and indulge it. The fault is the

geðafian. Forðæm bið sio scyld ðy hraðor gehæled, forðæm ðe hio ne bið unliefedo, ac ðeah hio aliefedu sie, ne sceal hi mon to ungemetlice began.

5 Ðæt us getacnode Loth swiðe wel on him selfum: ða he fleah ða biernendan ceastre Sodoman, ond com to Segor, ða ne dorste he nawuht hrædlice ut of ðære ceastre faran up on ða muntas. Mid ðæm ðe he fleah ða birnendan Sodoman, he getacnode ðæt we sculon fleon ðone unliefedan bryne ures lichoman. Sio heanes ðonne ðara munta getacnað ða clæn-nesse ðære forhæfdnesse. Ða ðonne bioð swelce hi eardigen upp on ðæm munte ða ðe bioð gesponnene to gesinscipe, ond ðeah ne bioð na gemengde buton ðonne hi wilniað bearn to gestrienanne. Ðonne hie stondað up on ðæm munte, ðonne ðæt flæsc nauht elles ne secð to ðæm oðrum buton tudor. Ðæt is ðæt mon stonde on ðæm munte ðæt ðæt flæsc ne sie flæsclice to ðæm oðrum gefæsðnod. Ac monige bioð ðara ðe hie gehealdað wið unryhthæmed, ond swaðeah his agenra ryhthiwena ne brycð swa swa he mid ryhte sceolde. Loth for ut of Sodoman to Segor, ond ðeah ne com he nauht hraðe on uppan ðæm muntum. Swa, ðonne ðonne mon forlæt ðæt wyrreste lif, ond ne mæg ðeah ðonne git cuman to ðæm betstan, ne ða forhæfdnesse gehealdan ðæs hean gesinscipes, ðonne bið ðæt swa swa Segor stod on midwege betweox ðæm muntum ond ðæm merscum ðe Sodoma on wæs. Sio Segor gehælde Loth fleondne. Swa deð sio Segor ðæs medemestan lifes: ða ðe hire to befleoð hio gehæld. Ac ðonne ða gesinhiwan hi gemengað ðurh unge-metlice unforhæfdnesse, ðær ðær hi ðone fiell fleoð ðære synne, ðonne magon hie ðeah weorðan gehælede suiðe ieðe-lice ðurh forgiefnesse ond ðurh gebedu, swa swa Loth funde ða lytlan ceastre, ond hine ðæron wið ðæt fyr gescilde. Ðæt

more readily remitted because it is not illicit, yet although it is sanctioned, it ought not to be engaged in with excessive license.

Lot indicated that to us quite well in his own person: when he fled the burning city of Sodom and came to Zoar, he by no means dared go at once out of the city and up into the mountains. In fleeing the burning Sodom, he indicated that we ought to flee the proscribed ardor of our body. Then the altitude of the mountains signifies the purity of abstinence. And so it is as if they reside up on the mountain, those who are joined in matrimony and yet are commingled only when it is their desire to beget children. They stand up on the mountain when the flesh solicits nothing else from the other but progeny. That one stands on the mountain is that the flesh is not brought into contact with the other carnally. But there are many who guard themselves against fornication, and yet they do not enjoy their lawful union the way they rightly should. Lot went out of Sodom to Zoar, and yet by no means did he at once ascend the mountains. Similarly, when one gives up the worst way of living and nonetheless cannot yet attain to the best, nor sustain the continence of high matrimony, it is similar to how Zoar stood midway between the mountains and the fens among which Sodom lay. Zoar saved Lot in his flight. So does the Zoar of the most middling life: it saves those who take shelter in it. But when a wedded pair are coupled in intemperate self-indulgence, they accordingly retreat from the precipice of sin, since they can still be saved quite readily through forgiveness and prayers, just as Lot found out that little city and shielded himself from the fire. The life of married couples, even if it

lif ðara gesinhiwena, ðeah hit ful wundorlic ne sie on mægenum weoruldwilnungum to wiðstondanne, hit mæg ðeah
bion orsorglic ælcra wita. Forðæm cwæð Loth to ðæm engle,
"Her is an lytele burg swiðe neah, ðær ic mæg min feorh on
generian. Hio is an lytel, ond ðeah ic mæg ðæron libban." He
cwæð ðæt hio wære swiðe neah, ond ðeah genog fæst on
his hælo. Swa is ðæt lif ðara gesinhiwena. Nis hit naht feor
ascaden from ðisse worulde, ne eac noht fremde ðære ecan
hælo, forðæm for ðære dæde ðe hie doð betwuh him hi beoð
gefriðode mid oftrædlicum gebedum betwuh him, swelce
hie sien on sumere lytelre byrig belocene. Be ðæm wæs
swiðe ryhte gecweden ðurh ðone engel to Lothe: "Ðinre
bene ic wille nu onfon, ond for ðinre bede ic ne toweorpe ða
burg ðe ðu fore spricsð." Swa bið ðæt lif ðara gesinhiwena.
Ne bið hit no fordemed beforan Gode, gif ðær gebedo æfter
fylgeað. Ymb ða illcan gebedo *sanctus* Paulus manode, ond
ðus cwæð: "Ne fornime incer noðer oðer ofer will, butan be
geðafunge ðæm timum ðe he hine wille gebiddan, ac geæm-
tigeað inc to gebedum."

6   Ongean ðæt sint to manigenne ða ðe ne beoð gebundne
mid ðæm gesinscipe, ða sint to manienne ðæt hie swa micle
ryhtlecor ða hefonlican bebodo healden swa hie orsorgran
bioð ðisses middangeardes ymbhogena, forðæm hie nan
gespann ðæs flæsclican gesinscipes ne gebiegeð on ðisse
worulde, ne se aliefeda gesinscipe hi ne gehefegað. Ðonne is
him micel ðearf ðætte sio unliefde byrðen ðissa eorðlicena
sorga hi ne geðrysce, ðætte hie swa micle gearran finde se
ytemesta dæg, ðonne he cume, swa hi her æmtegran bioð;
ond ðonne hi geæmetgade bioð ðæt hie magon bet don
ðonne oðre menn, ond hit swaðeah agiemeleasiað, ðæt hie
ðonne ðurh ðæt ne geearnigen wyrse wite ðonne oðre menn.

is unremarkable as regards the strength to withstand worldly appetites, can nonetheless be secure against all punishments. Hence, Lot said to the angel, "Here is a certain little city quite close by, in which I can preserve my life. It is a small one, and yet I can survive in it." He said that it was quite close by, and yet secure enough for his safety. Such is the life of married couples. It is not far removed from this world, nor yet at all alien to eternal salvation, because for the deed they do between them they are granted sanctuary with frequent prayers between them, as if they were walled up within some small city. About that it was quite aptly expressed to Lot through the angel: "I am willing now to receive your prayer, and at your request I shall not destroy the city for which you intercede." Such is the life of married couples. It is not condemned before God if prayers accompany it. About these same prayers Saint Paul gave advice and spoke thus: "Do not one of you deprive the other against the other's will, unless by consent for the times when that one wishes to pray, but make time, the two of you, for prayers."

Otherwise are to be cautioned those who are not bound 6
in marriage, who are to be advised that they observe the heavenly commandments so much the more strictly as they are freer of the cares of this existence, since no yoke of carnal union bears down on them in this world, nor does lawful matrimony weigh upon them. Then they have great need that the unlawful weight of earthly troubles not burden them, that the ultimate day find them so much the readier as they here are at greater leisure; and when they are unoccupied, so that they can do better than other people, and yet they squander the opportunity, that they not then earn from that worse punishment than other people. But they should

Ac hi scoldon gehiran hwæt Paulus cwæð, ða ða he sume men manode to ðære giefe Godes ðiowdomes. Ne cwæð he ðeah no ðæt ðæt he cwæð forðæm ðe he gesinscipe tælde, ac forðæm ðe he wolde ða sorga aweg adrifan ðisses middangeardes of his hieremonna mode ða ðe bioð aweaxene of ðæm gesinscipe. He cwæð, "Ðis ic cweðe for eowerre ðearfe, ðy læs ic eow mid ænige grine gefoo. Ic eow secgge hwæt eow arwyrðlicost is to beganne, ond hu ge fullecost magon Gode ðiowian ðæt eow læst ðinga ne mierð." Forðæm of ðæm gesinscipe weaxað eorðlice ymbhogan ond sorga, forðæm se æðela ðioda lareow his hieremen to betran life spon, ðy læs hi mid eorðlicre sorge wurden gebundne. Forðæm, ðonne se Godes ðiow on ðæt gemearr ðære woruldsorga befehð, ðeah he ðonne hæbbe beflogen ðone gesinscipe, ðonne næfð he no beflogen ða byrðenne.

7   Eac sint to manienne ða Godes ðiowas ðæt hie ne wenen ðæt hie butan ðæm demme stranges domes hi gemengan mægen wið ða æmtegan wifmen. Ða Paulus ðæt yfel ðære forlegnesse on swa manegum awiergdum leahtrum loh, he gecyðde hwelc sio scyld bið, ða he cwæð, "Nawðer ne ða wohhæmendan, ne ða ðe diofulgieldum ðiowiað, ne ða unfæsðradan, ðe ne magon hira unryhthæmdes geswican, ne ða ðiofas, ne ða gietseras, ne ða druncenwillnan, ne ða wiergendan, ne ða reaferas Godes rice ne gesittað." Ond eft he cwæð, "Ðæm wohhæmerum demeð Dryhten." Forðæm hi sint to manigenne, gif hie ða halwendan forhæfdnesse gehabban ne mægen, ond ða scuras ðære costunga adreogan ne mægen, ðæt hie wilnigen ðære hyðe ðæs gesinscipes. Forðæm hit is awriten ðæt hit sie betere ðæt mon gehiewige ðonne he birne, forðæm butan synne he mæg gehiwian, gif he hit ær ne forhet. Ac se ðe mare god gehet ðonne he ær

hear what Paul said when he exhorted certain people to the grace of serving God. He said what he said not to condemn marriage, but because he wanted to drive away from the mind of his disciples the cares of this existence that are produced by wedlock. He said, "This I say for your need, not to catch you with any snare. I say to you what is most admirable for you to go about, and how you can most perfectly serve God, so that not the least thing will hinder you." Because earthly cares and sorrows stem from marriage, the noble teacher of nations persuaded his charges to a better life, to save them from becoming saddled with earthly trials. For when the servant of God faces the impediment of worldly woes, even though he has then avoided wedlock, he has not avoided its burdens.

God's servants are also to be warned not to suppose that 7 they can mingle with unmarried women without the consequence of harsh judgment. When Paul condemned the evil of fornication among so many abominable crimes, he identified what sort of fault it is when he said, "Neither fornicators nor idolaters nor the weak willed who cannot desist from their fornication, nor thieves, nor the rapacious, nor drunkards, nor those who curse, nor swindlers will inhabit the kingdom of God." And again he said, "The Lord will judge adulterers." Therefore, they are to be advised, if they cannot maintain wholesome continence and cannot bear up under the torrents of temptation, to desire the haven of matrimony. For it is written that it is better for a person to marry than to burn, since he can marry without sin if he has not renounced marriage beforehand. But one who has committed himself to a greater good than he was formerly

dyde, he gedeð mid ðæm ðæt læsse god unaliefed ðæt he ær dyde. Hit is awrieten on ðæm godspelle ðæt nan mon ne scyle don his hond to ðære sylg, ond hawian underbæc. Ne ðon ma se ðe gehat gehæt, ne wene he ðæt he sie a ðy near hefonrice, gif he hine from went ðæm gehatum. Forðæm se ðe hine selfne maran godes behæt, ond ðonne forlæt ða maran god, ond went hine to ðæm læssum, ðonne bið hit swutol ðæt he bið fromlociende oferswiðed.

Chapter 52

LII. Ðætte on oðre wisan sint to manienne ða ðe
gefandod habbað ðara flæsclicra synna,
on oðre wisan ða ðe ðæs
noht ne cunnon.

On oðre wisan sint to manienne ða ðe ongietað ond witon hiera lichoman synna, on oðre ða ða ðe hie nyton. Ða sint to manienne ðe hiera lichoman synna onfunden habbað, ðæt hie huru æfter ðæm scipgebroce him ða sæ ondræden, ond ðæt forlor hira frecennesse, ðonne hie hit oncnawen, ðæt hi hit onscunigen; ðætte ða ða ðe mildheortlice bioð gehealdne æfter hiora ðurhtogenum synnum, ðætte hi eft unwærlice to ne gecierren, ond ðonne swelten. Forðæm is gecweden to ðære syngiendan sawle, ðe næfre hire synna geswican nyle, "Ðu hæfst forlegisse andwlitan, forðæm ðe no ne sceamað." Ðeah hie sint to manienne ðæt hie geornlice giemen, ðeah hi ðæt god hira gecynde gehal nolden

ВУBBBB

committed to, in doing so renders unattainable the lesser good that was his before. It is written in the gospel that no one shall put his hand to the plow and look back. No more should one who has sworn a vow suppose that he will ever be nearer the kingdom of heaven if he breaks that vow. Therefore, it is plain that one who commits himself to a greater good and then renounces that greater good and turns to a lesser will be defeated in looking away.

Chapter 52

52. That those who have had experience of the sins of the flesh are to be guided in one fashion, in another fashion those who have no acquaintance with such.

In one fashion are to be instructed those who are cognizant of and familiar with the sins of their body, in another those who are ignorant of them. Those who have discovered the sins of their body are to be warned after shipwreck at least to live in dread of the sea, and, once they recognize it, to shun the loss threatened by the danger to them, so that those who are mercifully safeguarded after the commission of their sins not heedlessly revert and die. For that reason, it is said to the sinning soul that refuses ever to desist from sinning, "You have the countenance of a harlot, since you are shameless." They are nonetheless to be enjoined to take concerted care, though they refused to preserve whole the

gehealdan, ðæt hi hit huru tobrocen gebeten. Him is ðearf ðæt hie geðencen hu micel menigu ðæra getreowfulra bið, ðe ægðer ge hi selfe clæne gehealdað, ge eac oðre of hira ge-dwolan ahwierfað. Ac hwæt cweðað hi ðonne, ðonne ða oðre stondað on anwalgre hælo, ond hie nyllað æfter yfelre dæde gecierran? Oððe hwæt cweðað hi, ðonne ða oðre briengað ægðer ge hie selfe ge eac oðre mid hiora bisenum to hefon-rice; ond hie, ðonne him God ðone first alefð, ond him hira yfel forbierð, nyllað furðum hie selfe briengan? Ac hie sint to manienne ðæt hie gemunen hwæt hi godes ær forleton ðæs ðe hi don meahton, ðæt hi huru ðonne forbugen ðæt andwearde yfel. Be ðæm cwæð Dryhten to ðæm gewunde-dum modum ðurh Ezechiel ðone witgan, swelce he to Iu-deum spræce, ond he ðara gedonena scylda eft gemyndgade, forðæm ðe he wolde ðæt hi sceamode ðæt hie eft on ðære oðerre worulde wæren unclæne. He cwæð ðæt hi hi forlæ-gen on Egiptum on hira gioguðe, "Hi wæron ðær forlegene, ond ðær wæron gehnescode hiera breost, ond forbrocene ða dela hiora mægdenhades." On Egiptum beoð hira breost gehnescod, ðonne hi ða scandlican lustas ðisses middan-geardes mid hira modes willan underhnigað. Ond eft on Egiptum bioð forbrocene ða wæstmas ðæra dela, ðonne ðæt gecyndelice gewitt ærest sume hwile bið on him selfun anwalg untosliten, oð ðæt hit bið gewemmed mid ðæm ðe hit cnyssað on unryhta wilnunga, ond hit toterað.

2   Forðæm sint to manienne ða ðe hiera synna onfunden habbað, ðætte hie mid wacore mode ongieten æfter hira misdædum mid hu miclum godum willan Dryhten tobræt ðone greadan his mildheortnesse ongen ða ðe to him ge-cierrað, swa swa he ðurh Ieremias ðone witgan cwæð; he

good in their nature, that they at least mend what is broken. They have need to consider how massive is the congregation of the faithful, who both keep themselves pure and divert others from their folly. But what will they say when those others abide in complete security, and they refuse to deviate from their vile doings? Or what will they say when the others conduct both themselves and others by their example to the kingdom of heaven, and they, while God allows them time and suffers their wrongdoing, refuse to conduct even themselves there? But they are to be encouraged to recall what good they formerly neglected which they might have done, so that they then at least escape that present wrong. About this the Lord spoke to wounded spirits through the prophet Ezekiel, as if he were speaking to the Jews, and he called to mind again offenses committed, because he wanted them to be ashamed of being unclean again in that other world. He said that they were prostituted in Egypt in their youth: "They were prostituted there, and their breasts were made tender, and the teats of their virginity were shattered." Their breasts are made tender in Egypt when they submit to the disgraceful appetites of this existence with willful intent. And, in turn, in Egypt the fruits of their paps are shattered when the inbred conscience first for a time remains whole and entire on its own, until it is impaired by dashing against proscribed desires, and it becomes tattered.

Therefore, those who have had experience of these sins 2 are to be advised to acknowledge with receptive mind with what good will the Lord, after their misdeeds, opens the embrace of his compassion to those who return to him, as he declared through the prophet Jeremiah, saying, "If a certain

437

cwæð, "Gif hwelc wif forlæt hiere ceorl, ond nimð hire
oðerne, wenestu recce he hire æfre ma, oððe mæg hio æfre
eft cuman to him swa clænu swa hio ær wæs? Hwæt, ðu
ðonne eart forlegen wið manigne copenere, ond swaðeah ic
cweðe, 'Gecier eft to me,'" cwæð Dryhten. He gereahte
ðone ryhtestan dom be ðæm forlegenan ond ðæm aworpnan
wife, ond swaðeah us gecyðde, gif we æfter ðæm hryre urra
scylda to him gecierdon, ðæt us wære gearo his miltsung,
næs ðæt ryht. Of ðissum wordum we magon oncnawan, nu
he us sparað mid swa micelre mildheortnesse, ðonne we ge-
synngiað, ond ðonne giet nyllað æfter ðære scylde to him
gecierran, ðæt we ðonne eft mid micle dysige syngiað, nu sio
Godes miltsung is swa micul ofer ða dysegan, ðæt hiene na
ne aðriet ðæt he hi to him ne laðige, æfter ðæm ðe hie gesyn-
god habbað. Be ðære miltsunga æfter ðære laðunga is swiðe
wel gesæd ðurh Essaias ðone witgan; hit is gecweden to ðæm
wiðerweardan men, "Ðin eagan weorðað gesionde ðinne be-
biodend, ond ðin earan gehirað under bæc." Eall moncynn
wæs to Gode gewend, ða ða hi ærest gesceapene wæron on
neorxna wonge; ond he ða hie manode andwearde, ond him
forgeaf ðæt hie moston stondan on frioum anwalde, ond
him getæhte hwæt hi on ðæm don sceolden, hwæt ne
scolden. Ða giet stodon men to him gewende. Ac ða hie
wendon hiera bæc to him, ða hi ofermodgiende his gebod
forhogdon. Ond ðeah, ðeah hi hine oferhogden, ne forhogde
he hi no ne ne forlet: ðæt he gecyðde, ða ða he him sealde æ,
ond hi mid ðære ham gelaðode, ond oft sende his englas us
ham to spananne to him, ond on ðissum deadlican flæsce he
hine selfne æteowde. Ða he ðis eal dyde, ða he stod æfter us
gewend, ond clipode æfter us, ðeah we from him gewende
wæren; ond ðeah he oferhogod wære, he us eft laðude to his
hyldo.

woman leaves her husband and takes another, do you suppose he will ever again assume responsibility for her, or will she ever after be able to come to him as pure as she was before? Now, then, you have been debauched with many a lover, and yet I say, 'Return to me,'" said the Lord. He rendered the fittest judgment on the adulterous and spurned wife, and yet he declared, if we should return to him after the lapse of our misdeeds, that his mercy would be ready for us instead of that judgment. From these words we can infer, since he will spare us with such immense tenderness, that when we sin and then still refuse to return to him after the trespass, we sin again with the utmost folly, seeing as God's mercy for the foolish is so prodigious that he never tires of calling them to him after they have sinned. About this mercy that follows his calling them to him, it was well said through the prophet Isaiah: it is said to the recalcitrant person, "Your eyes will be trained on your master, and your ears will listen behind you." All humankind was attentive to God when they were first created in paradise, and at that time he advised them in person and granted them the ability to exercise free will, and he instructed them what they ought to do with it, and what not. Humans were then still attentive to him. But they turned their back on him when in arrogance they despised his commandments. And yet, though they scorned him, he neither scorned nor abandoned them: he showed this when he gave them the law and with that invited them home, and he frequently sent his angels to entice us home to him, and he revealed himself in this mortal flesh. When he did all this, he stood turned toward us and called after us, though we had turned away from him, and though he was scorned, he again offered his good graces.

3   Ac swa swa we nu ðis reahton be eallum monnum, swa hit mæg æghwelc mon be him anum geðencean, forðæm ðe æghwelc mon ðe his bebod ond his forbod ongiet, he bið swelce he beforan him stonde, ær ðæm ðe he gesyngige. Ðonne giet he stent beforan him, ðonne he hine ne forhygeð, ac for his ege forbierð ðæt he ne syngað. Ac ðonne he forlæt his godnesse ond his unsceaðfulnesse, ond gecist unryhtwisnesse, ond ða gefremeð, ðonne went he his hrycg to him. Ac ðeah ðonne giet him fylgð God, ond him æfter cliopað, ðonne he hine monað æfter ðære gedonan scylde, ond hine spænð ðæt he to him gecierre. Ða scylda he nyle gesion, ond ðone fromweardan he ciegeð, ond ðone greadan his arfæstnesse ond his frofre he gebræt ongean ða ðe to him gecierrað. Ðonne we gehirað under bæc ðæs maniendes stemne, ðonne we to him gecierrað—ðonne ðonne he us ciegeð huru æfter urum scyldum, ðonne he us æfter cliopað, ðeah we ær nolden æfter his lare. Hit is cyn ðæt we ure scomigen, ðonne he us æfter cliopað, gif we us nyllað ondrædan his ryhtwisnesse, forðæm we hine mid swa micle maran unryhte ond dysige oferhycgeað swa he læs forhogað ðæt he us ðonne giet to him spane, siððan we hiene oferhycggeað.

4   Ongean ðæt sint to manigenne ða ðe ðonne giet ungefandod habbað flæsclicra scylda, ðætte hie swa micle swiðor ðone spild ðæs hryres him ondræden ðonne ða oðre swa hi ufor stondað ðonne ða oðre. Hi sint to manienne ðæt hi witen swa swa hie on hira stede gestondað swa him mare gescot ond ma flana hiera feonda to cymð. Forðæm he ongit swa micle swiður him on feohtan swa he hine selfne untrumran gefred on his lichoman. Ac gif he ðonne ðæm wiðstent, ðonne ongit he swa micle maran sige on him selfum swa

Yet as we have related this about all people, so every per- 3
son can take thought about himself individually, because for
everyone who understands what is required of him and what
forbidden him, it is as if he were standing in God's presence
before he sins. He still stands before him when he does not
despise him but for fear of him refrains from sinning. But
when he relinquishes his goodness and his innocence and
chooses immorality, and engages in it, he turns his back on
him. But yet, God then still accompanies him and calls after
him when he admonishes him after the offense has been
committed and urges him to turn back to him. He refuses to
see the offense, and he calls out to the resistant, and the embrace of his clemency and his solace he opens wide to those
who turn to him. We listen to the voice of exhortation from
behind when we turn to him after he calls to us even after
our trespasses—when he calls after us even though we had
refused to abide by his instructions. It is natural that we
should feel shame when he calls after us if we refuse to fear
his righteousness, since we scorn him with so much greater
injustice and folly the less he scorns still to draw us to him
after we have shown him contempt.

Otherwise are to be exhorted those who have not as yet 4
had experience of carnal sins, that they by so much more
than others dread the ruin of that fall the higher they stand
above others. They are to be advised to understand that inasmuch as they occupy the position they do, so there will be
directed at them more missiles and darts from their foes.
Therefore, he will perceive assaults on him so much the
more, the weaker he feels of body. But if he then resists
them, he will realize in himself so much the greater triumph

he unieð wiðstod. Ac hie sint to manienne ðæt hie unablinnendlice ðara leana wilnigen, ond lustlice ðæt geswinc ðæra
costunga ðe hi ðrowiað hi forsion ond geðolien, ond buton
tweon hi geliefen ðara leana; forðæm, gif hie geðenceað
ðara gesælða ðe him ungeendode æfter ðæm geswincum becuman sculon, ðonne ðyncað him ðy leohtran ða geswinc ðe
hi ofergan sculon. Hi sculon gehieran hwæt ðurh Essaias
ðone witgan gecweden is; he cwæð, "Ðis cwið Dryhten: Ða
afyrdan, ða ðe behealdað minne ræstedæg, ond geceosað
ðæt ic wille, ond minne freondscipe gehealðað, ic him selle
on minum huse, ond binnan minum wealle, wic ond beteran
noman ðonne oðrum minum sunum oððe dohtrum." Hwæt
elles getacniað ða afyrdan buton ða ða ðe ofðryscað ða
styringe ðæs flæsclican lustes, ond of him selfum aceorfað
unryhtlico weorc? Ðæm monnum is gecyðed hwelce stowe
hi moton habban beforan urum Fæder, swa swa we ær cwædon, ðæt hie sceolden habban ece eardungstowe on ðæs
Fæder huse furðor ðonne his ægnu bearn. Hi sculon gehieran hwæt ðurh *sanctus* Iohannes gecweden is; he cwæð,
"Ðæt sindan ða ða ðe mid wifum ne beoð besmitene, ond
hira mægeðhad habbað gehealdenne. Ða folgiað ðæm
lambe, swa hwær swa hit færð. Ða singað ðone sang ðe nan
mon elles singan ne mæg, buton ðæt hundteontig ond feo-
wertig ond feower ðusendo." Ðæm is sundorlic sang to singanne mid ðæm lambe on ecnesse beforan eallum geleaffullum, ond to blissianne for hira flæsces clænnesse, ðætte ða
oðre gecorenan ðone song gehiran mægen, ðeah ðe hine swa
singan ne mægen, ond for ðæm lufum ðe hi to him habbað,
ond for ðæm weorðscipe ðe hi gesioð ðæt hie habbað hi fægnigen, ond emnswiðe him blissigen, ðeah hie ða geearnunga
næbben ðæt hi ðone weorðscipe habban mægen.

the less easy it was to resist. But they are to be encouraged to desire the rewards without cease and to hold at nothing and to endure gladly the effort occasioned by the temptations they endure and to trust in the rewards free of uncertainty, because if they consider the boundless happiness that must fall to their lot after those labors, the hardships they must undergo will seem to them less onerous. They are to hear what is proclaimed through the prophet Isaiah, who said, "This says the Lord: Eunuchs who observe my day of repose and choose as I wish and hold fast my friendship I will give a place in my house and within my walls and a better name than to my other sons and daughters." What other is signified by eunuchs than those who suppress the stirrings of carnal lust and who cut away from themselves immoral conduct? To these people it is declared what sort of place they will be permitted before our Father, as we said before that they should have everlasting quarters in the Father's house surpassing those of his own children. They ought to hear what is pronounced through Saint John, who said, "These are the ones who are undefiled with women and have maintained their chastity. They follow the Lamb wherever it leads. They will sing the song that no man else can sing but the one hundred forty-four thousand." It will be for them to sing a singular song with the lamb for all time before all the faithful, and to exult in the purity of their flesh, so that the other elect can hear the song, though they cannot sing it so, and for the love they harbor for them and for the distinction that they see them enjoy they will be jubilant, and they will exult to the same degree they do, though they will not have the merited privilege of being able to receive that distinction.

5   Gehieren eac ða ðe ungefandod habbað ðara flæsclicana scylda hwæt sio Soðfæsðnes ðurh hie selfe cwæð bi ðære clænnesse; he cwæð, "Ne underfoð no ealle men ðas lare." Mid ðæm worde he cyðde ðæt hit is se hiehsta cræft, forðæm he cwæð ðæt hine ealle ne gefengen, ond eac sæde ðæt he unieðe wære to gehealdenne, ond eac cyðde hu wærlice hi hine healdan scolden, ðonne hie hine underfangen hæfden.

6   Eac sint to manienne ða ðe ungefandod habbað ðæs lichoman scylda ðæt hie witen ðæt se mægðhad is hirra ðonne se gesinscipe, ond swaðeah hi sint to læranne ðæt hi hi ne ahebben ofer ða oðre; ac læten ðæt lif ðæs mægðhades beforan ðæm oðrum, ond hine selfne biæftan, ond ne forlæte ðeah ðæt lif ðe he wat ðætte betere bið, ond behealde hine selfne ðæt he hine ne ahebbe on idelnesse. Hi sint to manienne ðæt hi ongieten ðætte oft gebyreð ðætte ðæt lif ðara gesinhiwena oferstigð ðæt lif ðæs mægðhades, ðonne hi underfoð ægðer ge forhæfdnesse ge eaðmodnesse furðor ðonne hie gehaten, ond ða oðre ne begað furðum hira ægne endebyrdnesse. Be ðæm wæs swiðe wel gecweden ðurh Essaias ðone witgan to ðære byrig ðe Sidon hatte, sio stod bi ðære sæ: ðæ cwæð se witga, "Ðios sæ cwið ðæt ðu ðin scamige, Sidon"; swelce sio burg ða wære ðurh ðæs sæs stemne to scame geworden. Swa bið ðis eorðlice lif oft yðgiende swa swa sæ, ond ðeah bið oft swiðe acorenlic, ond ðæt oðer swiðe aworpenlic, ðætte fæstre bion scolde ond trumlicre. Oft weorðað monige æfter ðæs lichoman scylde to Gode gecerred, ond hi ðonne swa micle fæsðlicor gestaðoliað on godum weorcum swa hi hi selfe synnigran ongietað. Ond oft ða, ða ðe on clænnesse hiora lichoman gehealdenne

Let those who have no experience of the transgressions 5
of the flesh hear also what Truth said in his own person
about purity, saying, "By no means will all people embrace
this guidance." With this remark he stipulated that it is the
highest virtue, because he said that not everyone might attain to it, and likewise said that it was difficult to maintain,
and also indicated how warily they must keep it when they
had achieved it.

Those who are inexperienced in the trespasses of the 6
body are likewise to be advised to know that virginity is superior to marriage, and yet they are to be taught not to hold
themselves superior to others; but let them acknowledge
the life of chastity as superior to others, and themselves inferior, and yet not renounce the life that they know to be
better, and keep watch on themselves so that they not ag-
grandize themselves out of vanity. They are to be encouraged to understand that it often happens that the life of
married couples surpasses the life of virginity when they undertake both continence and humility beyond their vows,
and the others do not observe even their own order's rule.
About this it was well put through the prophet Isaiah to the
city called Sidon, which stood by the sea: then the prophet
said, "This sea tells you to be ashamed, Sidon," as if the city
had been put to shame by the voice of the sea. So life in the
world often is tumultuous, like the sea, and yet it is often
quite preferable, and the other quite contemptible, which
ought to be more secure and more robust. Oftentimes,
many revert to God after a transgression of the body, and
then they ground themselves the more securely in good
works the more sinful they perceive themselves to be. And,
frequently, as regards those who have maintained the purity

habbað, swa swa hi læsse ongietað on him selfum ðæs ðe him hreowan ðyrfe, swa swa hie swiður wenað ðæt him genog sie on hira lifes clænnesse, ðonne hira mod ne beoð onhæt mid nanre manunge ðære hreowsunga. Ðonon wyrð oft Gode leofre ðæt lif ðætte æfter his synnum onæled bið mid hreowsunga ðonne ðæt clæne ond ðæt unsceaðfulle for slæwðe ond for orsorgnesse. Be ðæm cwæð ðæs deman stemn, ðæt is Crist, be Marian ðære forlegisse, "Hire sint forgifena swiðe manega synna," forðæm ðe hio swiðe hreowsade. Ond eft he cwæð, "Mara gefea wyrð on hefonum for anum hreowsiendum ðonne ofer nigon ond hundnigontig ryhtwisra ðæra ðe him nan ðearf ne bið hreowsunga." Ðæt we magon swutolor ongietan ond hræðor bi urum agnum gewunan, gif we willað ongietan ðone dom ures agnes modes. Hwæt, we witon ðæt we ma lufiað ðone æcer ðe ær wæs mid ðornum aswogen, ond æfter ðæm ðe ða ðornas beoð aheawene, ond se æker bið onered, bringð godne wæsðm—ma we lufiað ðone ðonne ðone ðe stent on clænum lande, ond bið unwæsðmbære oððe ungefynde corn bringð oððe deaf.

7   Eac sint to manienne ða ðe ungefandod habbað ðissa flæsclicena scylda, ðæt hie ne wenen for hira clænnesse ðæt hie sien beforan ðæm hirrum hadum, forðæm ðe hi nyton ðeah hi sin behindan ðæm ðe læssan hades bioð, ond hie wenað ðæt hie beforan bion scylen; forðæm ðe on ðæm dome ðæs ryhtwisan deman onwent sio geearnung ðone had ond ða geðyncðo. Hwa is nu ðæra ðe gesceadwis sie, ond to ðæm gleaw sie ðæt he swelces hwæt tocnawan cunne, ðætte nyte ðætte on gimma gecynde carbunculus bið diorra ðonne iacinctus? Ond swaðeah ðæt bleoh ðæs welhæwnan iacintes

of their body, the less they recognize in themselves for which they need to repent, the more they suppose that the purity of their life will suffice them, when their mind is not made ardent by any exhortation to penitence. Hence, that life often turns out to be dearer to God which, pursuant to sinning, is inflamed with contrition, than the pure and innocent one, on account of laxity and indifference. About this the voice of the judge, which is Christ, said concerning the harlot Mary, "Very many sins are forgiven her," because she repented greatly. And again he said, "There is more rejoicing in heaven over a single penitent than over ninety-nine righteous who have no need of repentance." We will be capable of understanding this more plainly and readily by comparison to our own habits if we are willing to examine the prejudices of our own mind. Now, we know that we value more the field which was formerly choked with thorns, and after the thorns have been cleared and the field cultivated, produces a good crop—we value it more than one that lies on good land and is unfruitful or produces worthless or stunted grain.

Those who are unacquainted with these carnal offenses 7 are likewise to be warned not to suppose that for their purity they are to be preferred to the superior orders, since they do not know it even if they rank behind those who are of an inferior order, and they suppose that they must be preferred, for in the estimation of the righteous judge, merit alters rank and distinction. Who is there among the discerning and who is so sharp-witted as to know how to distinguish something of such a character, that he does not know that in the nature of gems, the carbuncle is more precious than the jacinth? And yet the color of the finely hued

bið betera ðonne ðæs blacan carbuncules, forðæm ðæs ðe
sio endebyrdnes ond ðæt gecynd forwiernð ðæm iacinte, se
wlite his beorhtnesse hit eft geiecð, ond eft, ðeah ðe ðæt gecynd ond sio endebyrdnes ðæs carbuncules hine up ahebbe,
his blioh hine gescent. Swa bið on ðisse menniscan gecynde
manige on beteran hade ond on beteran endebyrdnesse
wyrsan, ond on wyrsan hade ond on wyrsan endebyrdnesse
beteran; swa ðætte oft on læwedum hade ond on læwedum
girelan mid godum weorcum ond mid ryhte life man ofer-
ðihð ðone munuchad, ond ða oðre, ðe ðone hierran had habbað, ðonne hi nyllað ðæm ðeawum ond ðæm geearningum
folgian, ðonne gewaniað hie ðone had ond gewemmað.

Chapter 53

LIII. Ðætte on oðre wisan sint to manianne
ða ðe ða geworhtan synna wepað,
on oðre ða ðe ða geðohtan wepað.

On oðre wisan sint to manienne ða ðe hiera geworhtan
synna wepað, on oðre ða ðe hira geðohtan wepað. Ða sint to
manienne ðe hira geworhtan wepað, ðætte hie ða gedonan
yfelu mid fullfremedre hreowsunga aðwean, ðy læs hi sin
to swiðe gebundne mid ðæm ðurhtogenum scyldum, ond
ðonne to lange forelden ðæt hi hi ne anbinden mid ðære
hreowsunge. Be ðæm is awriten on ðæm nigon ond hundsiofantigoðan sealme, "God us drencte swiðe gemetlice mid

jacinth is nobler than that of the pale carbuncle, because what rank and nature deny the jacinth, the beauty of its brilliance by turns supplies to it, and, conversely, though the carbuncle's rank and nature exalt it, its hue demeans it. Just so, among the human race, many of nobler order and of nobler rank are ignobler, and many of ignobler order and ignobler rank nobler, so that often one in lay condition and lay garb will by good works and virtuous living surpass the monastic orders, and the latter, who belong to that higher order, degrade and blemish their order when they refuse to adhere to its morals and standards.

Chapter 53

53. That those who weep for sins committed
are to be guided in one fashion,
in another who weep for those contemplated.

In one fashion are to be counseled those who weep over their sins that are committed, in another those who weep over those contemplated. Those who weep for their deeds are to be advised to wash away with perfect contrition the wrongs done, to avoid being too firmly bound to the offenses perpetrated, and then delay too long unbinding themselves with penitence. About this it is written in the seventy-ninth psalm, "God very fitly gave us tears to drink,"

tearum," swa ðætte æghwelces mannes mod swa micle oftor
wære geðwæned mid hreowsunge tearum swa swa he gemunde ðæt hit oftor wære adrugod from Gode on his synnum. Hi sint eac to manienne ðæt hi unaðrotenlice ða gedonan synna gelæden beforan hira modes eagan, ond ðonne hi
hi gesewene hæbben, gedon ðæt hie ne ðyrfen bion gesewene æt ðæm nearwan dome. Be ðæm cwæð Dauid on
psalmum, "Ahwyrf, Dryhten, ðin eagan from minum synnum." Ond lytle ær he cwæð, "Mine misdæda bioð simle beforan me"; swelce he cwæde, "Ic ðe bidde ðæt ðu no ne locige on mine synna, forðæm ðe ic self him ealneg on locige."
Be ðæm eac cwæð Dryhten ðurh Essaias ðone witgan,
"Ðinra synna ne weorðe ic gemunende, ac gemun ðu hiora."
Forðæm hie sint to manienne ðæt hi ælce synne geðencen
ðæra ðe hi gemunan mægen, forðæm, ðonne hie for anre
hwelcre hreowsiað, ðonne hreowsiað hie for ealle. Be ðæm is
swiðe wel gecweden ðurh Ieremias ðone witgan; ða ða he
ðæra Iudea misdæda ealle apinsode, he cwæð, "Todælnessa
ðara wætera utleton min eagan." Todældu wæteru we lætað
ut of urum eagum, ðonne we for synderlecum synnum syn-
derleca hreowsunga doð: forðæm ðe hie ne magon ealneg
ealla on ane tid emnsare hreowan, ac hwilum an, hwilum
oðru cymð sarlice to gemynde; ond ðonne he wierð mid
ðære anre onstyred, ðonne wyrð he eallra geclænsod.

2   Eac hie sint to manienne ðæt hi gelefen ond baldlice ge-
truwien ðæt hi ða forgiefnesse habbað for ðære hreowsunga
ðe hi wilniað, ðy læs hi to ungemetlice sien gewægde mid
ðære hreowsunga. Ne gedyde næfre se mildheorta Dryhten,
ne an his mode ne gebrohte swelce hreowsunga, gif he hit
æfter ðæm auht swiðe wrecan wolde. He gecyðde swiðe
mildheortlice ðæt he him deman nolde, ða he gedyde ðæt hi

so that every person's mind would be washed with tears of repentance so much the oftener, the oftener he recalled that it had been dried up by God in the midst of his sins. They are also to be admonished to lead tirelessly before their mind's eye those sins committed, and when they have examined them, ensure that they need not be examined at the straitened judgment. About this David said in the Psalms, "Avert, Lord, your eyes from my sins." And a little before, he said, "My misdeeds are ever before me"; as if he had said, "I pray you not to look on my sins, for I myself look on them continually." About this likewise the Lord said through the prophet Isaiah, "I shall not keep in mind your sins, but you recall them." They are to be exhorted to contemplate every sin that they can recall, because when they repent each one, they repent all. About this it is quite well told through the prophet Jeremiah; when he weighed all the misdeeds of the Jews, he said, "My eyes shed divisions of waters." We shed divided waters from our eyes when we perform individual repentance for individual sins, since they cannot all invariably be repented of at once with equal suffering, but sometimes one, sometimes another comes painfully to mind, and when the mind becomes troubled by that one, it will be cleansed of all.

They are also to be encouraged to believe and confidently 2 trust that, on account of repentance, they have the forgiveness they desire, to prevent their being too immoderately encumbered with penitence. The benevolent Lord would never have caused or introduced to his mind such contrition if he intended after that to punish anything very arduously. He made it plain quite mercifully that he did not intend to

him selfe ær beforan demdan. Be ðæm is awriten on ðæm feower ond hundnigontigoðan psalme; hit is gecweden, "Wuton cuman ær his dome andettende." Ond eft hit wæs gecweden ðurh *sanctus* Paulus, "Ðær we us selfum demden, ðonne ne demde us no God."

3 Ond eft hi sint to manienne ðæt hi swa hopigen to ðære forgiefnesse ðæt hie for ðære orsorgnesse to unwærlice ne aslawien. Forðæm oft ðæt lytige dioful ðæt mod ðæt he mid ðære synne ascrenceð, ðonne he gesihð ðæt hit unrot bið for ðæm hryre his synna, ðonne forspenð he hit mid ðære wolberendan oliccunge. Ðæt wæs mid ðære biesene getacnod ðe Dinan gedon wæs Iacobes dohtor. Hit is awriten ðæt Dina wære ut gangende sceawian ðæs londes wif. Ða hi ða geseah Sihhem, Emmores sunu ðæs Ebreiscan, se wæs aldormon ðæs londes, ond ða gelicode hio him, ond he hi genam niedenga, ond hire mid gehæmde. Ond ða wæs his mod gehæft mid ðæm mædene, ond he ða hi swa unrote oleccende to him geloccode. Ðonne gæð Dine ut sceawian ða elðiodigan wif, ðonne hwelces monnes mod forlæt his ægne tilunga, ond sorgað ymb oðerra monna wisan, ðe him nauht to ne limpð, ond færð swa wandriende from his hade ond of his endebyrdnesse. Sihhem, ðæs landes ealdorman, geniedde ðæt mæden Dinan, ða he hie gemette swa wandrian. Swa deð se dioful ðæt mod ðæt he gemet on unnyttum sorgum: he hit awiert. Sihhemes mod wæs ða gehæft to Dinan. Swa ðæt dioful, ðonne he gesihð ðæt mod on ðæm ilcan unryhtan willan ðe he bið, ond ðonne eft gesihð ðæt hit ðæs hreowsað, ðonne gebringð he beforan ðæs modes eagan idle orsorgnesse ond tohopan, forðæm ðæt he him oftio ðære nyttwyrðan unrotnesse. Be ðæm wæs swiðe ryhtlice gecweden ðætte Sihhem Dinan liðelice olehte, ða ða he hi geunrotsod

judge him when he caused him to judge himself first. About this it is written in the ninety-fourth psalm, where it is said, "Let us anticipate his judgment by confessing." And again, it was said by Saint Paul, "If we were to judge ourselves, God would not judge us at all."

And, in turn, they are to be warned not so to trust in for- 3 giveness that out of insouciance they grow too unguardedly lax. For often, when the crafty devil sees that the mind he has made stumble with sin is made anxious over the misstep of its offenses, he distracts it with noxious persuasion. This was illustrated by the example of what was done to Jacob's daughter Dinah. It is written that Dinah was out walking to see the women of the country. She was seen by Shechem, the son of Hamor the Hebrew, who was governor of that province, and he found her pleasing, and he took her by compulsion and lay with her. And then his mind was capti- vated by the young woman, and in her distress he soothed her, coaxing her to him. Dinah goes out to see the foreign women when each person's mind leaves off its own endeav- ors and troubles itself with other people's affairs which in no way concern it, and goes thus straying from its ambit and from its station. Shechem, the governor of the province, forced the young woman Dinah, whom he encountered wandering thus. So does the devil to the mind that he en- counters in useless occupations: he defiles it. Shechem's mind was then captivated by Dinah. So the devil, when he observes the mind entertaining the same indecent desires that he does, and then in turn sees that it is repentant, leads before the mind's eye empty complacency and trust, to rid it of that wholesome anxiety. Concerning this, it was quite creditably said that Shechem soothed Dinah gently after he

hæfde. Swa deð ðæt dioful ðæm mode: hwilum he gedeð ðæt
him ðyncð ðæt hit nan scyld ne sie ðæt ðæt he deð; hwilum
he gedeð ðæt him ðyncð, ðeah hit scyld sie, ðæt oðre men
hefiglicor syngien; hwilum he fortruwað to swiðe Godes
mildheortnesse; hwilum him ðyncð ðæt he hæbbe fierst ge-
nogne to hreowsianne. Ond ðonne ðæt beswicene mod ymb
ðyllic ðencð, ðonne wyrð hit amierred from ðære incundan
hreowe, to ðon ðæt hit nan god ne gemete, forðæm him nan
yfel ne hriwð. Ac hit wyrð swa micle swiður beswicen mid
ðæm witum swa hit nu swiður gefihð on his yfelum.

4   Ongean ðæt sint to manienne ða ðe ða geðohtan synna
wepað, ðæt hie geornlice giemen on ðære degelnesse hira
modes hwæðer him ðæt geðoht cume of færlicum luste, ðe
of wilnunga ond geðafunga, ðæt hie swa gesyngeden.
Forðæm hit oft gebyreð ðæt ðæt mod wyrð gecostod of ðæs
flæsces lustfulnesse, ond ðeah ðæt mod wiðstent ðæs flæsces
lustfulnesse, swa ðætte se ilca lust ðe hine geunrotsað on
ðære degelnesse his modes hine eft gerotsat, gif he him
wiðstent. Oft eac folgað ðæm mode swa grundleaslicu costung, ond hit swa forswilgð, ðæt hit mid nanre wiðerweardnesse hire ne wiðstent, ac geðafigende folgað ðære costunga.
Ðonne hit bið onstyred mid ðære lustbærnesse, ond hit onhagað to ðæm ðingum, ðonne forlæt hit hrædlice ða weorc
ðæs inneran godan willan, ðonne hit onhagað to ðæm uterran. Ac ðonne ðæt gesihð se ryhta dom ðæs ðearlwisan deman, ðonne ne bið hit no swa swa geðoht syn, ac swa ðurhtogen, forðæm ðe ðæt ðætte hine ne onhagode utane forð to
brenganne mid weorcun, innane he hit geðafode, ond
ðurhteah mid ðy weorce ðæs fulfremedan willan.

had made her distraught. So does the devil to the mind: at times he makes it seem to one that what he is doing is no misdeed; at times he makes it seem to him that though it may be a sin, other people sin more grievously; at times he has excessive confidence in God's compassion; at times it seems to him that he has time enough to repent. And when the deluded mind thinks after such a fashion, it will be prevented from inward penitence, so that it may meet with no good, since it repents no evil. But it will be so much the more betrayed with punishments, the more it takes satisfaction in its wrongdoing.

Otherwise are to be advised those who weep for sins contemplated, that they give careful heed in the privacy of their mind to whether the thought comes to them out of sudden pleasure or whether it was with a will and by consent that they thus sinned. For it frequently happens that the mind will be tempted by the impulsiveness of the flesh, and yet the mind will resist the flesh's avidity, so that the same appetite that disturbed one in the privacy of his mind will in turn lend him composure if he withstands it. Often, too, such fathomless temptation will pursue the mind and consume it so, that it will not confront it with any resistance but will pursue the enticement consensually. When it is aroused by pleasurableness, and opportunity for those things presents itself, it will soon renounce the workings of inner good will when opportunity for outer will presents itself. But when the just appraisal of the severe judge observes it, it will not be regarded as contemplated, but as performed, because what opportunity did not permit him to bring to pass outwardly in performance, he consented to inwardly and performed by the workings of fully formed desire.

5   We habbað geascod from urum ærestan mæge Adame
ðæt us is from him gecynde ðæt we ælc yfel on ðrio wisan
ðurhtion: ðurh gespan, ond ðurh lustfulnesse, ond ðurh
geðafunga. Ðæt gespan bið ðurh dioful; sio lustbærnes bið
ðurh ðone lichoman; sio geðafung bið ðurhtogen ðurh ðone
gæst. Se sætere, ðæt is se dioful, he hine spænð on woh. Se
lichoma hine ðonne him underðied mid ðære lustfulnesse,
oð ðæt se gæst bið oferwunnen mid ðære lustfulnesse, ðæt
he hit geðafað. Swa swa sio nædre on neorxna wonge, ærest
hio lærde Euan on woh, ond Eue hi hire underðiodde mid
lustfulnesse, swa swa lichoma. Ða wæs Adam, swa swa se
gæst, ðurh gespan ðære næddran ond ðurh Euan lustbærnesse oferswiðed, ðæt he geðafode ða synne. On ðæm ge-
spane we magon ongietan ða synne, ond mid ðære lustfullnesse we bioð genedode, ond mid ðære geðafunge we bioð
gebundne. Ac ða sint to manienne, ða ðe ða geðohtan synna
hreowsiað, ðæt hie geornfullice giemen on hwelce ðæra
synna hie befeollen, forðæm ðæt hi mægen ongean ðæt be
ðæm ilcan gemete hreowsian ðe hi on hira inngeðonce ongieten ðæt hie gesyngoden, ðy læs him to hwon hreowen ða
geðohtan synna, oð ðæt hi hi fulfremmen. Ond swaðeah we
hi scylen manian ond bregean ðæt we hi on ormodnesse ne
gebringen, ðy læs hi wyrs don. Forðæm oft se mildheortaa
Dryhten swiðe hrædlice ða geðohtan synna aweg aðwihð,
ðonne he him ne geðafað ðæt hi hi ðurhtion moten. Be ðæm
he mæg witan ðæt hi bioð hrædlice forgiefene, ðonne he
him ne geðafað ðæt hi to ðæm weorce becumen, ðæt he him
ðonne ðearlur deman scyle. Be ðæm is swiðe wel gecweden
ðurh ðone psalmsceop on ðæm an ond ðritigoðan psalme:
he cwæð, "Ic wille secgan ongean me selfne min unryht,
Dryhten, forðæm ðu forgeafe ða arleasnesse minre heortan." Ða he hæfde befæst Gode his synna, ða he getiohchod

We have learned from our first father Adam that, by 5 nature inherited from him, we perform every wrong in three ways: through suggestion, and through pleasure, and through consent. Suggestion is through the devil; pleasure is through the body; consent is realized through the spirit. The lurking assailant, which is the devil, entices one to corruption. The body then makes him subservient to pleasure, until the spirit is mastered by delectation, so that he consents to it. Just as the serpent in paradise first seduced Eve, and Eve succumbed to pleasure, so the body. Then Adam, like the spirit, was vanquished through the suggestion of the serpent and through Eve's inclination, so that he countenanced the sin. In the suggestion we can conceive the sin, and by pleasure we are compelled, and by consent we are caught. But those who repent of sins contemplated are to be admonished to make careful note of which of these sins they have fallen into, so that they can correspondingly do penance in the same measure that they in their conscience perceive themselves to have sinned, so that they not do too little penance for meditated sins, until they have committed them. And yet we should warn and alarm them in such a way as not to lead them into despair, lest they do worse. For that reason, the merciful Lord often washes away at once sins of thought when he does not consent to one's being allowed to carry them out. By that one can understand that they are soon forgiven, seeing as God will not suffer them to be realized, so that he would then be obliged to judge them more severely. About this it is well told through the psalmist in the thirty-first psalm: he said, "Against myself I will tell my injustice, Lord, because you have forgiven the cruelty of my heart." He had entrusted his sins to God when he had

æfde ðæt he him ondettan sceolde. Ða cyðde se witga hu
ieðelic bið to forgiefenne sio geðohte synn, ða he cwæð ðæt
hio him sona forgiefen wære swa he geðoht hæfde ðæt he hi
ondettan wolde. Ðæt ilce ðæt he getiohchod hæfde to bid-
danne he cwæð ðæt him wære ær forgiefen. Forðæm sio
synn ne wearð ðurhtogen mid nanum weorce, forðæm ne
com seo hreowsung to nanre ðrowunge, ac sio geðohte
hreowsung adrygð ða geðohtan synne of ðæm mode.

Chapter 54

LIIII. Ðætte on oðre wisan sint to monianne
ða ðe ða ðurhtogenan synna wepað,
ond swaðeah ne forlætað, on oðre wisan ða
ðe hie no ne hreowsiað, ond hie ðeah forlætað.

On oðre wisan sint to manienne ða ðe ða gedonan synna
wepað, ond hi ðeah ne forlætað; on oðre wisan ða ðe hi forlætað, ond swaðeah no ne hreowsiað. Ða sint to manienne
ðe ða gedonan synna wepað, ond hi swaðeah ne forlætað,
ðæt hi geornlice ongieten ðæt hi on idelnesse tiliað hi selfe
to clænsianne mid ðy wope, ðonne hi eft mid unryhte life
hie besmitað; swelce hi hi mid ðære hreowsunga to ðæm
aðwean ðæt hi hi mægen eft afylan. Be ðæm is awriten ðæt
se hund wille etan ðæt he ær aspaw, ond sio sugu hi wille
sylian on hire sole æfter ðæm ðe hio aðwægen bið. Hwæt, se

resolved to confess them. The prophet revealed how easy it is for a sin of thought to be pardoned when he said that it was forgiven him as soon as he had thought that he wished to confess. He said that the very thing that he had resolved to request had already been granted him. Because the sin never came to be realized in performance, repentance did not lead to suffering, but the contemplated penitence wipes away the contemplated sin from the mind.

Chapter 54

54. That those who weep for sins performed and yet do not desist from them are to be guided in one fashion, in another fashion those who are unrepentant and yet desist.

In one fashion are to be admonished those who weep for sins committed, and yet they do not desist from them, in another fashion those who desist and yet do not repent. Those who weep for sins committed and yet fail to give them up are to be charged to acknowledge that it is futile for them to endeavor to purge themselves with weeping if they again defile themselves with an immoral way of life, as if they were washing themselves in contrition so as to be able to befoul themselves again. About this it is written that the dog will eat what it earlier spewed, and the sow will wallow in mud after it has been washed. Now, the dog will vomit the

hund wile aspiwan ðone mete ðe hine hefegað on his breostum, ond ðæt ilce ðæt he for hefignesse aspaw, ðonne he hit eft frit, ðonne gehefegað hine ðæt ilce ðæt hine ær gelihte. Swa bið ðæm ðe ða gedonan yfelu hreowsiað, ðonne hi ðæt yfel mid ondetnesse him of aweorpað ðætte hira modes innað yfele ond hefiglice mid gefylled wæs, ond ðonne eft foð to ðæm ilcan ond fætað in æfter ðære ondetnesse ðæt ilce yfel ðæt hi ær mid ðære ondetnesse ond hreowsunga ut awurpun. Swa ðet swin, ðeah hit aðwægen sie, gif hit eft filð on ðæt sol, ðonne bið hit fulre ðonne hit ær wæs, ond ne forstent ðæt ðweal nauht, ðeah hit ær aðwægen wære. Swa bið ðæm ðe his gedonan synna wepeð, ond hi swaðeah ne forlæt: hefigran scylde ond hefigran witum he hine underðiet, gif he hit ne forlæt. Forðæm he forhogde ða forgifnesse ðe he mid ðære hreowsunga begiten hæfde, forðæm ðe he wealwode on ðæm gedrofum wætere; ond ðæt ðæt he ær mid ðære hreowsunga geclænsode he beforan Godes eagum eft afylde. Be ðæm is eft awriten on Salomonnes bocum; hit is awriten, "Ne eftga ðu ðin word on ðinum gebede." Ðæt is ðonne ðæt mon eftgige his word on his gebede, ðæt mon æfter his hreowsunga gewyrce ðæt he eft scyle hreowsian. Be ðæm is eac gecweden ðurh Essaias ðone witgan; he cwæð, "Aðweað iow, ðæt ge sin clæne." Hwæt, se ðonne ne recð hwæðer he clæne sie, ðe ne sie, se ðe æfter ðære hreowsunga hine ryhtlice ond clænlice nyle gehealdan. Ealne weg hi hi ðweað, ond ne beoð hie næfre clæne, ðeah hi ealneg wepen; ealneg hi wepað, ond æfter ðæm wope hi gewyrceað ðæt hi moton eft wepan. Be ðæm is gecweden ðurh sumne wisne mon, "Gif hwa on hand nimð hwæt unclænes, ond hine æfter ðæm aðwihð, ond ðonne eft fehð on ðæt ilce ðæt he ær feng, hwæt forstent him ðonne

food that hangs heavy on its breast, and when it again devours the same that it vomited for its heaviness, the same thing burdens it that it was formerly disburdened of. So it is with those who repent of wrongs done when by confession they cast off from them the evil with which the innards of their mind were foully and ponderously stuffed, and then after confession they partake of the same and cram in the very ills that they had cast up through confession and penance. As with the swine, though it is washed, if it falls again into the mire, it will be filthier than it was before, and the bath is to no purpose, even though it had been washed. So it is for one who weeps for his sins committed and yet does not refrain from them: he will subject himself to heavier culpability and heavier punishment if he persists in them. He abused the forgiveness that he had obtained by contrition because he wallowed in muddy water, and what he had made pure before God's eyes by repentance he again begrimed. About this it is again written in the books of Solomon: it is written, "Do not repeat your words in your prayer." To repeat one's words in his prayer is, after penance, to do what will again require penance. About this it is said by the prophet Isaiah, "Wash yourselves so that you are clean." Now, then, he does not care whether or not he is clean who after penance refuses to maintain himself in piety and in purity. They continually wash themselves and are never clean, though they weep without end; they weep without end, and after the tears, they do such that they must weep again. About this it is said by a certain sage, "If someone takes something unclean in hand and after that washes himself, and then again takes hold of the same thing that he previously grasped, what good does the prior cleansing do him?" He is washed

461

ðæt ærre ðweal?" Se bið aðwægen of unclænnesse, se ðe aðwihð mid hreowsunga his unclænnesse. Se ðonne gehrinð eft ðære unclænnesse ðe syngað æfter his hreowsunga.

2 Ac ða sint to manienne ðe ða gedonan scylda hreowsiað, ond hi ðeah ne forlætað, ðæt hi ongieten ðæt hie beoð beforan ðæs dieglan deman eagum gelice ðæm monnum ðe swiðe eaðmodlice onginnað beforon ricum monnum, ond him swiðe olleccað ða hwile ðe hi him beforan beoð, ond eft, ðonne hi him beæftan beoð, ðonne doð hi him to demme ond to fiondscipe ðæt ðæt hi magon. Hwæt is ðæt, ðæt mon hreowsige his synna, buton ðæt mon eowað Gode his eaðmodnesse ond his treowa ond his hiersumnesse? Oððe hwæt is ðæt, ðæt mon æfter his hreowsunga syngige, buton ðæt, ðæt he deð feondscipe ond ofermetto ond unhiersumnesse ðæm ilcan Gode ðe he ær olehte? Swa swa Iacobus sæde se apostol, ða he cwæð, "Swa hwa swa wille bion ðisse weorlde freond to ungemetlice, he bið gehaten Godes feond." Ða ðonne sint to manienne ðe ða gedonan scylda wepað, ond hi swaðeah ne forlætað, ðætte hi ongiten ðætte oft bið swiðe idel ond unnyt ðara yfelena manna hreowsung, ðonne hi æfter ðæm ne tiliað nauðer ne god to donne ne yfel to forlætanne. Swa bið eac swiðe oft synleas yfel geðoht ðæm godum, ðonne hi hit mid weorcum ne ðorhtioð. Swa wundorlice hit todælð ond gemetgað se godcunda wisdom be hira ægðeres geearnungum, swa ðætte ða yflan betwix eallum hira yflum ðe hi fullice gefremmað hi fortruwiað, ond hi on ofermetto ahebbað for ðæm lytlan gode ðe hi geðenceað, ond no ne anginnað to wyrceanne; ond eft, ða godan, ðonne hi beoð onstyrede mid ðæm yflum geðohtum ðe hi næfre nyllað ðurhtion, ðonne beoð hi geeaðmedde, ond forsioð hi selfe for ðæm lytlan yfele, ond ne forleosað

clean of defilement who washes away his impurity with repentance. He then again touches the foul thing who sins after his penance.

But those who repent the trespasses they have committed, and yet do not put them aside, are to be advised that, before the eyes of the unseen judge, they are like those people who behave quite humbly before powerful people and flatter them excessively all the time they are in their presence, and in turn, behind their backs, do them whatever injury and spitefulness they can. What is it to repent one's sins but to show God one's humility and his fidelity and his obedience? Or what is it to sin after repentance but to engage in enmity and arrogance and disobedience to the very God whom one previously supplicated? Just so the apostle James spoke when he said, "Whoever will be too completely a friend of this world will be called God's enemy." Those, then, who weep for sins committed, and yet do not give them up, are to be advised to recognize that the repentance of bad people is often quite vain and futile when they afterward practice neither to do good nor to avoid bad. So, likewise, an evil thought is often without sin for the good when they do not carry it through in performance. Divine wisdom distinguishes and measures out the deserts of either of them so marvelously that the bad in the midst of all the wrongs that they carry to completion grow presumptuous and preen themselves in their self-regard for the little good that they meditate and never undertake to perform; and, in turn, when the good are disturbed by the bad thoughts that they will never be willing to bring to fruition, they are humbled and despise themselves for that minor infraction, and they

nauht ðurh ðæt hira ryhtwisnesse, ac hi hi geiecað mid ðære eaðmodnesse.

3   Hwæt, Balam cwæð, ða he geseah ða wicstowa ðara ryhtwisena Israhela, "Geweorðe min lif swelce ðissa ryhtwisena, ond geweorðe min ende swelce hira." Ac eft, ða sio anbryrdnes hine alet, ða funde he swiðe yfel geðeaht ond searwa ymb hira lif; forðæm hine gehran sio gitsung, he forget ðone freondscipe wið Israhele. Hwæt, *sanctus* Paulus cwæð ðæt he gesawe oðerne gewunan ond oðerne willan on his limum, ond se wære feohtende wið ðæm willan his modes, ond hine gehæftne lædde on synne gewunan; sio, he cwæð, wære on his limum. Forðæm wæs *sanctus* Paulus gecostod mid his modes untrumnesse ðæt he ongeate his synna, ond forðæm wære ðy strangra on godum weorcum. Forhwy bið se synfulla onbryrd mid ðære hreowsunga, ond ne bið no ðy ryhtwisra; oððe forhwy bið se ryhtwisa gecostod mid yfle geðohte, ond ne bið ðeah gewemmed mid ðære scylde; buton forðy ðe ðæm synfullan nauht ne helpað his godan geðohtas, forðæm ðe he næfð gearone willan untweogendne to ðæm weorce, ne eft ðæm ryhtwisan ne deriað his yflan geðohtas, forðæm ðe he næfð gearone willan ðæt woh to fulfremmanne?

4   Ongean ðæt sint to manienne ða ðe hira synna forlætað, ond hi ðeah ne betað ne ne hreowsiað, ðæt hi ne wenen, ðeah hi hira synna forlæten, ðæt hi God him forlæte, gif hi hi mid nanum ðingum ne betað ne ne hreowsiað. Swa se writere, gif he ne dilegað ðæt he ær wrat, ðeah he næfre ma nauht ne write, ðæt bið ðeah undilegod ðæt he ær wrat. Ond swa eac se ðe oðrum bismer cwið, oððe deð: ðeah he geswice, ond hit næfre eft ne do, ðeah hit bið gedon ðæt

464

lose nothing of their uprightness by that, but they add to it by that humility.

Now, Balaam said, when he saw the encampments of the 3 righteous Israelites, "May my life turn out like that of these righteous, and my end turn out like theirs." But in turn, when the inspiration left him, he devised very malign purposes and schemes against their lives; because covetousness took hold of him, he failed to remember his friendship with Israel. Now, Saint Paul said that he saw another regimen and another will in his members, and it was in conflict with the will of his intellect and had led him captive to the regimen of sin, which, he said, was in his members. Saint Paul was tempted in his weakness of mind so that he might recognize his sins and for that reason would be the firmer in adherence to good conduct. Wherefore is the sinner inspired to penitence and yet is none the more ethical; or wherefore is the virtuous person tempted by an evil idea and yet is unsoiled by the offense; but because the good thoughts of the one offer him no help, since he has no ready, determined inclination to act, nor, in turn, do wrongful thoughts of the other injure the virtuous person, since he has no ready inclination to bring that wrong to fulfillment?

Those who cease their sinning and yet neither atone nor 4 repent are, contrariwise, to be advised not to expect that, since they have put aside their sinning, God has put it aside, supposing they neither atone for it nor repent it in any way. Thus, if a scribe does not expunge what he wrote before, even should he never write anything more, what he wrote before will stand unblotted. And so also with one who speaks of or treats another with insults: though he should finish with it and never do it again, what he did is still done

he dyde, ond unðingad, gif he hit ne bet; ac he sceal ða ofermodlican word mid eaðmodlicum wordum gemetgian, gif he wið ðone oðerne geðingian wile. Wenstu, gif hwa oðrum hwæt gieldan sceal, hwæðer he hine mid ðy gehealdan mæge ðæt he him nauht mare on ne nime, ne ðæt ne gielde ðæt he ær nam? Swa us bið æt Gode, ðonne we wið hine gesyngiað: ðeah we næbre eft swa ne don, gif we ðæt gedone mid nanum ðingum ne betað ne ne hreowsiað, ne bio we no ðæs sicore; gif us ðæt ne mislicað ðæt us ær licode, ðonne ne bið hit no us færgiefen, ðeah we nu nauht yfeles ne don on ðisse worulde. Ne sculon we ðeah forðy bion to orsorge, gif we nauht to gode ne doð, forðæm ðe swiðe fela unalifedes we oft geðenceað. Hu mæg se ðonne bion orsorg se ðe him self wat ðæt he gesyngað?

5   Hwelce iðnesse hæfð God æt urum witum, oððe hwelcne weorðscipe hæfð he æt urre ðrowunga, butan ðæt he wile gehælan ða wunde urra scylda mid strangum læcedome, gif he ne mæg mid liðum, ðætte us biterige sio hreowsung, swa swa us ær swetedon ða synna? Ond swa swa we sigon ær on ðæt unaliefede, oð ðæt we afeollon, swa we sculon nu forberan ðæt aliefede, oð ðæt we arisen; ðætte ðæt mod ðætte wæs abisegad mid unryhtre blisse si eft abisegad on halwyndre ond on ryhtlicre hreowsunga, swa ðætte ðæt mod ðætte sio upahæfenes ond ða ofermetto gewundedon eft gehæle sio eaðmodnes ond sio forsewennes his selfes. Be ðæm cwæð Dauid on ðæm feower ond hundsiofantigoðan psalme, "Ic cwæð to ðæm unryhtwisum, 'Ne do ge unryhtwislice,' ond cwæð to ðæm ðe ðær syngedon, 'Ne hebbe ge to up eowre hornas.'" Ðonne ahebbað ða synfullan swiðe up hira hornas, ðonne hi hi næfre nyllað geeaðmedan to ðæm ðæt hie ongieten hira unryhtwisnesse, ond ða hreowsian. Be

and uncompensated if he makes no amends; but he must season overbearing words with words of humility if he intends to be reconciled with the other. Do you imagine that someone who is in debt to someone else can clear himself by taking on no more debt, without repaying what he had borrowed? So it is for us before God when we sin against him: even if we never again behave so, if we neither atone for nor somehow repent of what is done, we will not be free of its peril; if we are not averse to what we formerly enjoyed, it will not be forgiven us, even if we do nothing else reprehensible in this world. Yet we ought not on that account to feel too secure if we do nothing in the way of good, since we often contemplate a great deal of what is disallowed. Then how can he feel secure who himself knows that he sins?

What satisfaction does God derive from punishing us, or 5 what honor accrues to him from our sufferings, but that he intends to heal the wounds of our wrongs with strong medicine if he cannot with mild, so that penance may seem to us bitter, just as sins formerly seemed sweet? And just as we formerly sank into what is prohibited, until we fell, so now we ought to forgo what is permissible, until we rise, so that the mind that was occupied with unethical enjoyment may in turn be occupied with wholesome and virtuous penitence, so that the mind that hauteur and pride wounded may in turn be healed by humility and self-abnegation. About this David said in the seventy-fourth psalm, "I said to the unrighteous, 'Do not act unrighteously,' and said to those who sinned, 'Do not raise your horns too high.'" The sinful raise their horns up high when they refuse ever to demean themselves by recognizing their immorality and

467

ðæm wæs eft gecweden on ðæm fiftegoðan psalme, "Ða ge-
drefedan heortan ond ða geeaðmeddan, ne forsihð hi næfre
Dryhten." Swa hwa ðonne swa his synna hreowsað, ond hi
swaðeah ne forlæt, se gedrefð his heortan, ond ðeah ofer-
hygð ðæt he hi geeaðmede. Se ðonne, se ðe his synna forlæt,
ond hi swaðeah ne hreowsað, se hine eaðmed, ond nyle ðeah
his mod gedrefan. Be ðæm cwæð *sanctus* Paulus on his
ærendgewrite to Corinctheum: he cwæð, "Ge wæron ær on
yflum weorcum, ac ge sint nu geclænsode ond gehalgode";
forðæm ðe æghwelc man bið æfter ðære hreowsunga his
synna clænra ðonne he ær wæs, ær he gesyngade. Be ðæm
cwæð *sanctus* Petrus, ða he geseah manige men ormode for
hira ærron yflun: he cwæð, "Hreowsiað ond weorðað ge-
fulwade eower ælc." Ærest he lærde ðæt hi hreowsodon,
ond siððan ðæt hi wurden gefullwode, swelce he cwæde,
"Hreowsiað ærest on eowrum mode, ond siððan æfter fierste aðweað eow, ond geclænsiað mid eowrum tearum." Hu
mæg se bion orsorg ðære wrace his scylda, se ðe nu agiemeleasað ðæt he hreowsige his synna? Hu mæg he hira bion orsorg, nu se hiehsta hierde ðære halgan ciricean cwæð ðætte
sio hreowsung scolde bion ær ðæm fulwihte? Se fullwuht
ðone mon geclænsað from his synnum, ond ealra ðinga
swiðosð ða synna adwæscð.

repenting. About these it was again said in the fiftieth psalm, "The Lord will never despise troubled and self-effacing hearts." Then whoever repents his sins and yet does not desist from them, troubles his heart and yet does not deign to humble it. Then the one who stops his sinning, and yet does not repent it, effaces himself and yet refuses to trouble his mind. About these Saint Paul spoke in his Epistle to the Corinthians: he said, "You were formerly ill demeaned, but now you are made pure and sanctified"; because everyone is, after repentance for his sins, cleaner than he was before he sinned. About this Saint Peter spoke when he saw many people in despair over their former misdeeds: he said, "Repent and be baptized, every one of you." He first prescribed that they repent and afterward that they be baptized, as if he were to say, "Repent first in your mind, and then after a time wash and cleanse yourselves with your tears." Who can feel secure from retribution for his offenses who neglects now to repent of his sins? How can he feel secure about them now that the chief pastor of holy Church said that contrition ought to precede baptism? Baptism cleanses a person of his sins and of all things most thoroughly remits sins.

Chapter 55

LV. Ðætte on oðre wisan sint to monianne ða
ðe ða unaliefedan ðing ða ðe hi doð
herigað, on oðre ða ðe hi tælað
ond swaðeah doð.

On oðre wisan sint to manienne ða ðe ðæt unliefde herigað, ond eac doð; on oðre ða ðe hit leað, ond swaðeah doð.
Ða sint to manienne, ða ðe ægðer ge hit doð ge hit herigað,
ðæt hi ongieten ðæt hi oft swiðor gensyngiað mid ðæm
wordum ðonne hi don mid ðæm dædum; forðæm, ðonne
hi yfel doð, ðonne doð hi ðæt him anum, ac ðonne hi hit
heriað, ðonne lærað hi hit ælcne ðara ðe hit gehierð herian.
Forðy hi sint to manienne, ðonne hi licettað ðæt hi willen
astyfecian ðæt yfel on him selfum, ðæt hi hit ðonne ne dyrren sæwan on oðrum monnum; ac ðæt him ðynce genog on
ðæm ðæt hi hit selfe dydon.

2   Ond eft hi sint to manienne, ðeah hi him nyllen ðæt ondrædan ðæt hi yfele sien, ðæt hi huru scamige ðæt men
witen hwelce hi sin. Forðæm oft ðæt yfel ðæt forholen bið,
hit bið fleonde, forðæm, ðonne ðæt mod sceamað ðæt hit
mon wite, ðonne mæg hit eaðe gesælan æt sumum cierre
ðæt hine eac scamige ðæt he hit wyrce. Hwæt, ælc unryhtwis mon, swa he scamleaslicor his yfel cyð, swa he freolicor hit ðurhtiehð, ond hit him aliefedlicre ðyncð. Swa hit
him ðonne aliefedlicre ðyncð, swa he ðær diopor on gedyfð.

Chapter 55

55. That those who speak well of the illicit things
they do are to be guided in one fashion,
in another those who deplore them
and yet do them.

In one fashion are to be cautioned those who speak admiringly of the proscribed and also engage in it, in another those who deplore it and yet do it. Those who both do it and applaud it are to be urged to recognize that they sin much more frequently by their words than by their deeds, because when they commit a wrongful act, they bring it upon themselves alone, but when they commend it, they teach it to everyone who hears it approved. For that reason they are to be warned, when they pretend to want to suppress that wrong in themselves, not to venture to plant the seed of it in others, but to let it seem sufficient that they themselves have done it.

And again they are to be advised, although they have no 2 concern about being immoral, to feel shame that people should know what sort they are. Iniquity concealed is often temporary, because when the mind feels shame to have it known, it can easily turn out on this or that occasion that it will feel shame about perpetrating it. Well, then, the more shamelessly any unethical person airs his wrongdoing, the more unconstrainedly he carries it out, and the more acceptable it seems to him. The more acceptable it seems to him, the deeper he plunges into it. About this it is written in

Be ðæm is awriten on Essaies bocum, "Hi lærdon hira synna swa swa Sodome dydon, ond hi hi nan wuht ne hælon." Gif Sodome hira synne hælen, ðonne ne syngodon hi na butan ege, ac hi forleton eallinga ðone bridels ðæs eges, ða hi ne scrifon hwæðer hit wære ðe dæg ðe niht, ðonne ðonne hi syngodon. Be ðæm is eft awriten on Genesis ðætte swiðe wære gemanigfalðod Sodomwara hream ond Gomorwara. Se cliopað, se ðe dearninga syngað; ac se hremð, se ðe openlice ond orsorglice syngað.

3   Ongean ðæt sint to manienne ða ðe hira synna onscuniað, ond hi swaðeah ne forlætað, ðæt hi foreðonclice ongieten hu hi hi willen beladian on ðæm miclan dome, ðonne hi hi nyllað her beladian mid ðæm ðæt hi him selfum demen, ond hiora agna scylda on him selfum wrecen. Hwæt bioð hi elles buton liceteras, ðonne hi tælað ðæt ðæt hi nyllað forlætan? Ac hie sint to manienne ðæt hi ongieten ðæt hit bið se degla Godes dom ðæt hi eft ðy mare wite hæbben ðe hi gere witon ðæt hi on ðweorh doð, ond ðeah nyllað geswican, ne nan wuht ymb ðæt swincan ðæt hi hit mægen forlætan. Swa hi hit ðonne swutolor witon, swa hi swiður forweorðað, forðæm ðe hi onfengon ðæt leoht ðæs ondgietes, ond ðeah noldon forlætan ða ðistro ðæs won weorces, ac ðæt andgiet ðæt him God sende to fultome hi agimeleasedon. Ðæt ilce andgit bið eft on gewitnesse hira yfela æt ðæm dome, ond geiecð hira witu ðætte him ær wæs onsended mid to dielgianne hira synna. Ac forðæm ðe hi her syngiað, ond hit him no ne hreowð, hi gehrinð her sumu wracu ær ðæm ecum

the books of Isaiah, "They professed their sins as did the Sodomites, and they in no way concealed them." If the Sodomites had concealed their sins, they would not have sinned without care, but they relinquished the bridle of care altogether when they paid no regard to whether it was day or night when they sinned. About this it is again written in Genesis that the outcry of the Sodomites and Gomorrans was greatly amplified. Anyone who sins in private gives voice to it, but one makes an outcry who sins publicly and free of compunction.

By contrast, those who despise their sins and yet do not give them up are to be warned to devote forethought to how they intend to exculpate themselves at the great judgment, seeing as they refuse to acquit themselves here by judging themselves and punishing their own sins in themselves. What else are they but hypocrites when they deplore what they refuse to relinquish? But they are to be advised to understand that it is the unrevealed judgment of God that they in turn are to have greater punishment for knowing with certainty that they are engaging in immorality and yet refuse to put a halt to it or to devote any effort to being capable of giving it up. The more plainly they know, the more certainly they will perish, since they received the illumination of understanding and yet refused to leave behind the dimness of perverse conduct, but ignored the good sense that God sent them in aid. That very understanding will in turn stand witness to their crimes at the judgment, and what had been sent them with which to blot out their sins will amplify their torments. But because they sin here and do not repent, a certain kind of retribution will touch them here in advance of those torments without end, so that they

witum ðæt hi ne sien freo ne orsorge on ðæm anbide ðæs
maran wites. Ac swa micle hi onfoð ðær mare wite swa hi her
gearor witon ðæt hi untela doð, ond hit ðeah nyllað forlætan.
Be ðæm cwæð Crist on his godspelle, "Se ðegn, se ðe wat his
hlafordes willan, ond ðonne nyle wyrcean æfter his hlafordes
willan, he bið manigra wita wyrðe." Be ðæm ilcan cwæð eac
se salmscop on ðæm feower ond fiftiogoðan psalme: he
cwæð, "Hi sculon gan libbende on helle." Ða ðe libbende
bioð, hi witon ond ongietað hwæt ymb hi gedon bið; ða
deadan ne magon nan wuht witan. Ða bioð genemde deade,
ond ða stigað on helle, ða ðe nyton hwonne hi untela doð; ac
ða ðe hit witon, ond swaðeah doð, ða gað libbende ond wi-
tende on helle.

Chapter 56

LVI. Ðætte on oðre wisan sint to monianne ða ðe
swiðe hrædlice bioð oferswiðde mid sumre
unryhtgewilnunge, on oðre wisan ða ðe longe ær
ymbðeahtigeað, ond hit ðonne on lasð ðurhtioð.

On oðre wisan sint to manienne ða ðe mid færlice luste
bioð oferswiðde, on oðre ða ðe lange ymbðenceað ond
ðeahtiað, ond swa weorðað beswicene. Ða ðonne sint to
manienne ðe mid færlice luste bioð beswicene, ðæt hi ongieten ðæt hi ælce dæg beoð on ðæm gefeohte ðisses andweardan lifes. Ac ðæt mod ðætte ne mæg gesion ða flane ær

will not be free or without care in anticipation of that greater punishment. But they will receive so much the greater penalty the more certainly they know that they do wrong here and refuse to relinquish it. About this Christ said in his gospel, "The servant who knows his master's will and refuses to act according to his master's will shall be deserving of many punishments." About the same the psalmist spoke in the fifty-fourth psalm: he said, "They shall enter living into hell." Those who are living know and understand what is being done with them, whereas the dead can know nothing. Those are called dead and then make their way to hell who do not know when they are doing wrong, but those who know it and yet do it enter hell alive and aware.

Chapter 56

56. That those who are very suddenly overmastered by some illicit desire are to be guided in one fashion, in another fashion those who consider it for quite a while beforehand and then at length do it.

In one fashion are to be instructed those who are overpowered by a sudden passion, in another those who consider and debate for long, and so yield to seduction. Those who are seduced by a sudden impulse are to be advised to recognize that they are engaged every day in the conflict of this present life. Yet the mind that cannot detect the arrow

hit sie gewundad, hit beðearf ðæt hit hæbbe simle on honda ðone scield Godes eges, ond him symle ondræde ða diglan gescotu ðæs sweocolan feondes, ond hine wærlice healde on ðære byrg his modes wið nihtlicum gefeohtum, forðæm ðe hi willað simle on ðistrum feohtan. Ac ðæt mod ðætte næfð singale sorge hit self to behealdanne, ðonne bið hit on sume healfe open to wundianne; forðæm se lytega feond swa micle ieðelicor ðæt mod gewundað swa he hit ongiet nacodre ðære byrnan wærscipes. Forðy sint ða to manienne ða ðe mid hrædlice luste bioð oferswiðde, ðæt hie to georne ne giemen ðissa eorðlicena ymbhogena, forðæm ðe hi ne magon ongietan mid hu manegum unðeawum hi beoð gewundode, ða hwile ðe hi to ungemetlice smeagað ymb ðas eorðlecan ðing.

2   Be ðæm sæde Salomon ðæt se mon sceolde cweðan, se ðe wæs slæpende gewundad, "Hi me wundedon, ond ic hit ne gefredde; hi me drogon, ond ic hit nyste; ond sona swa ic anwoc, swa wilnode ic eft wines." Swa bið ðæt mod slæpende gewundad swa hit ne gefret, ðonne hit bið to gimeleas his agenra ðearfa. Ac ðæt mod ðætte bið mid unðeawum oferdrenced, hit ne mæg ongietan ða toweardan yfelo, ne furðum ða nat ðe hit deð. Hit mon drægð swa hit ne gefret, ðonne ðonne hit iernð on ða unaliefedan unðeawas, ond hit swaðeah ne onwæcneð to ðon ðæt hit eft on ierne mid hreowsunga, ac hit wilnað ðæt hit to ðon onwæcne ðæt hit mæge eft weorðan oferdruncen; forðæm, ðeah ðæt mod slæpe godra weorca, hit wacað hwæððre on ðæm ymbhogum ðisse worlde, ond wilnað ðæt hit sie oferdruncen his agnes willan. Swa hit gebyreð ðæt ðæt mod slæpð ðæs ðe hit wacian sceolde, ond wacað ðæs ðe hit slapan scolde.

3   Be ðæs modes slæpe wæs ær awriten on ðære ilcan Salomonnes bec; hit wæs awriten ðæt hit wære swelce se stiora

before it is wounded needs always to have in hand the shield of the fear of God and ever to dread the unseen missiles of the devious foe and guard himself warily in the fortress of his mind against skirmishes in the night, since their will is always to fight in the dark. Yet the mind that does not take continual pains to defend itself will be exposed to injury from one quarter or another, since the treacherous enemy injures the mind much more readily the more he finds it bare of the mail shirt of vigilance. Therefore, those who are overcome by sudden urgings are to be advised not to care too sincerely about the concerns of this world, since they cannot conceive with how many vices they will be wounded as long as they devote excessive attention to worldly affairs.

About this Solomon said that one who was injured while sleeping may be supposed to have said, "They injured me, and I did not feel it; they dragged me, and I had no idea; and as soon as I awoke, I wanted wine again." The sleeping mind is wounded in such a way that it does not feel it when it is negligent of its own requirements. But the mind that is made drunk with vices cannot recognize evils to come, nor even know those that it is perpetrating. It is dragged so that it does not feel it when it runs into prohibited practices, and it nonetheless fails to rouse itself to run back in repentance, but it desires to rouse itself so that it can again become drunk, because although the mind is asleep to good works, it is nonetheless vigilant in its attention to this world, and of its own accord desires to be inebriated. Thus it occurs that the mind sleeps through what it should wake for and wakes for what it should sleep through.

About the sleep of the mind it was written earlier in the same book of Solomon that it was as if the helmsman slept

2

3

477

slepe on midre sæ, ond forlure ðæt stiorroður. Ðæm stiorere
bið gelicost se mon ðe ongemong ðisses middangeardes
costungum ond ongemong ðæm yðum unðeawa hine agimeleasað. Se deð swa se stiora ðe ðæt stiorroðor forliesð, se ðe
forlæt ðone ymbhogan ond ða geornfulnesse ðe he mid stioran scolde ðære sawle ond ðæm lichoman. Se bið swiðe onlic
ðæm stioran ðe his stiorroðor forliest on sæ, se ðe forlæt
ðone foreðonc his gesceadwisnesse ongemong ðæm bisegum
ðisses middangeardes. Ac gif se stiora his stiorroðor gehilt,
ðonne cymð he orsorglice to lande, hwilum ðeah ongean
wind ond ongean ða yða, hwilum mid ægðrum. Swa deð ðæt
mod, ðonne hit wacorlice stiereð ðære sawle: sume unðeawas hit ofertrit, sume hit ær gesihð, ond utan becierð; ðæt is
ðæt hit ða gedonan unðeawas swincende gebete, ond ða
ungedonan foreðoncelice becierre, swa se stiora deð: sume
ða yða he becerð mid ðy scipe, sume hit oferstigð.

4   Ymb ðæt is eft gecweden on ðæm Salomones bocum ðe
we hatað *Cantica Canticorum;* be ðæm strengestan cempum
ðæs uplican eðles hit is gecweden, "Hæbbe eower ælc his
sweord be his ðeo for nihtlecum ege." Ðonne mon hæfð his
sweord be his ðio, ðonne mon temeð his unaliefde lustas
mid ðæm wordum ðære halgan lare. Ond sio niht getacnað
ða ðistro ðære blindnesse urre tidernesse. Forðæm ðe nan
mon ne mæg on niht gesion hu neah him hwelc frecenes sie,
him is ðearf ðæt he hæbbe his sweord be his hype. Swa sculon ða halgan weras simle stondan gearuwe to gefohte wið
ðæm lytegan fiende, forðæm hi him ondrædað ða frecenesse
ðe hi ne gesioð. Be ðæm is eft gecweden on ðære Salomones
bec ðe we hatað *Cantica Canticorum:* hit is gecweden, "Ðin
nosu is swelce se torr on Libano." Ðæt is ðæt we oft gestin-
cað mid urum nosum ðæt we mid urum eagum gesion ne

amid the sea and lost the helm. Very like the helmsman is one who relinquishes control of himself in the midst of the temptations of this world and among the waves of vices. As the helmsman loses the helm, so does one who abandons the care and devotion with which he ought to steer soul and body. Quite like the steersman who loses the helm at sea is one who renounces the providence of his discretion among the distractions of this existence. But if the steersman keeps hold of his rudder, he will come securely to land, though at times against wind and waves, at times with them both. So does the mind when it pilots the soul vigilantly: some vices it treads down, some it spies ahead and turns from, which is that he works hard at atoning for those committed and providently steers past those uncommitted, as the helmsman does: some waves he turns the ship from, some he surmounts.

This is again spoken of in the books of Solomon that we 4 call Song of Songs; about the strongest champions of the supernal realm it is said, "Let each of you have his sword by his thigh for alarms in the night." One has his sword by his thigh when he tames his forbidden impulses with the words of holy doctrine. And night signifies the gloom of our frailty's blindness. Because at night no one can see how near to him any threat is, he has need to keep his sword by his hip. So ought holy men to stand ever ready to combat the fraudulent fiend, since they fear the peril they do not see. This is again spoken of in the book of Solomon that we call Song of Songs; it is said, "Your nose is as the tower on Mount Lebanon." That is, often with our nose we detect the scent of what we cannot see. With the nose we distinguish and

magon. Mid ðæm nosum we tosceadað ond tocnawað gode
stencas ond yfele. Hwæt is elles getacnod ðurh ða nosu buton se foreðonc ond sio gesceadwisnes ðara godena manna?
Hwæt elles getacnað se hea torr on Libano buton ðone hean
foreðonc ond ða gesceadwisnesse ðara godena monna, ða
sculon ongietan ða costunga ond ðæt gefeoht, ærðæm ðe hit
cume, ðæt hi mægen ðy fæstor gestondan, ðonne hit cume?
Forðæm ðe ælc here hæfð ðy læssan cræft ðonne he cymð,
gif hine mon ær wat, ær he cume. Forðæm he gesihð ða
gearwe ðe he wende ðæt he sceolde ungearwe findan, him
wære ðonne ieðre ðæt he hira ær gearra wende ðonne he
hira ungearra wende, ond hi ðonne gearuwe mette.

5   Ongean ðæt sint to manienne ða ðe ær ðenceað to syn-
gianne, ond ymbðeahtiað, ær hi hit ðurhtion, ðæt hi ongiten
mid foreðonclicre gesceadwisnesse ðæt hi onælað ðearlran
dom wið him mid ðæm ðæt hi her ymb ðæt yfel ðeahtiað, ær
hi hit don, ond hi beoð mid swa micle strengran cwide ðæs
domes geslægene swa hi beoð fæstor gebundne mid ðæm
bende ðæs yflan geðeahtes. Micle hrædlicor hi wæren aðwægene ðæra scylda mid ðære hreowsunga, gif hi færlecor
syngoden unbeðohte. Ac hi beoð ðæs ðe lator ðe hi oftor
ymbðeahtiað; forðæm, gif ðæt mod eallunga ær ne forsawe
ða ecan edlean, ðonne ne gesirede hit no ðæt hit ðurhtuge
swelce synne. Swa micel toscead is betwuh ðære beðohtan
synne, ðe mon longe ymbsireð, ond ðære ðe mon færlice
ðurhtiehð; swa ðætte se se ðe ða synne gesireð, ægðer ge
gesyngað, ge eac syððan hwilum on ormodnesse gewit.
Forðæm ne tælde Dryhten ða twa scylda gelice. Ðæt he
cyðde, ða he cwæð ðurh Ieremias ðone witgan, "Healdað
eow ðæt ge ne onælen min ierre mid eowrum searwum, ðæt

differently identify good and bad odors. What else is meant by the nose but the providence and probity of good people? What else is signified by the high tower on Mount Lebanon but the high foresight and discernment of good people, who should recognize the temptation and the contest before it arrives, so that they can stand the firmer when it comes? For every army is less effective when it arrives if its arrival is anticipated. Because it sees those prepared whom it expected to find unprepared, it would have been easier for it to have expected the prepared than to have expected the unprepared and then to have encountered them ready.

Contrariwise, those who plan beforehand to sin, and deliberate before acting, are to be warned to recognize with discerning forethought that they will provoke a severer judgment against them for having contemplated that wrong here before committing it, and they will be struck with so much the starker pronouncement of justice in proportion as they are the more firmly constrained by the bond of that wrongful premeditation. They would be much more readily washed clean of those offenses by penitence if they had sinned on impulse, without thinking. But they will be the less readily so, the more frequently they make designs, because if the mind had not altogether disdained the everlasting retribution, it would not have schemed to perform such a sin. So great is the distinction between the considered sin that is long contemplated and one that is perpetrated of a sudden, that one who hatches a plot to sin both commits the crime and also sometimes afterward falls into despair. For that reason, the Lord did not censure the two offenses alike. He demonstrated this when he said through the prophet Jeremiah, "Take care that you not inflame my wrath

ge hit ne mægen eft adwæscan." Be ðæm ilcan he cwæð eft ierrenga ðurh ðone ilcan witgan; he cwæð, "Ic wrice on eow æfter eowrum geðeahte." Ðy ne wricð Dryhten no gelice ða gesiredan synne ond ða færlice ðurhtogenan, forðæm sio gesirede syn bið ungelic eallum oðrum synnum. Ac sio ðe hrædlice ðurhtogen bið, sio bið hwilum for giemeleste, hwilum for untrymnesse modes oððe lichoman. Sio ðonne ðe longe gesired bið, sio cymð symle of yflum ingeðonce. Be ðæm wæs gecweden swiðe ryhte ðurh ðone psalmscop on ðære heringe ðæs eadgan weres, ond on ðæm forman psalme, hit is gecweden ðæt he no ne sæte on ðæm wolberendan setle. Forðæm wæs ðis gecweden ðe hit is swiðe gewunelic ðætte domeras ond rice menn on setelum sitten. Se ðonne sit on woles setle, se ðe yfel wyrcð mid geðeahte. Ond se sit eac on wolberendum setle, se ðe gesceadwislice tocnawan con god ond yfel, ond ðeah geleornað ðæt he deð ðæt yfel. Se sit, swelce he sitte on ðæm stole ðæs forhwierfdan gemotes, se ðe hine up ahefeð on ða ofermetto swelcre unryhtwisnesse ðætte he fullfremme hwelc yfel huru ðurh geðeaht. Forðæm swa micle swa se bið beforan ðe on ðæm stole sitt ðæm oðrum ðe ðær ymb stondað, swæ bið sio syn ðe longe ær geðoht bið, ond ðonne ðurhtogen, ofer ða ðe færlice geðoht bið, ond ðonne ðurhtogen. Forðæm sint to manianne ða ðe lange ymbsieriað ðæt hi ongieten hu micel wite hi sculun habban beforan ðæm oðrum, forðæm ðe hi nu nyllað bion ðara synnfullena geferan, ac willað bion hira ealdormenn.

with your schemes, so that you cannot extinguish it again." About the same he spoke again angrily through the same prophet, saying, "I shall visit retribution upon you in accordance with your stratagems." The Lord does not punish alike the devised sin and the impulsively committed because the devised sin is unlike all other sins. But one impulsively committed is sometimes performed out of carelessness, sometimes out of indisposition of mind or body. One that is long connived at always proceeds from bad intentions. About this it was spoken quite correctly through the psalmist in praise of a blessed man, and in the first psalm it is said he did not sit in the pestilential seat. This was said because it is quite usual for judges and powerful people to sit in seats. He sits in a seat of pestilence, then, who works evil by set purpose. And he likewise sits in a pestilential seat who knows how to distinguish good and evil with discrimination, and yet studiously does evil. He sits as if sitting in the chair of a corrupt court who exalts himself in the pride of such unrighteousness that he brings to fruition every wrong by special design. Therefore, by as much as he who sits in that seat is superior to those who stand about, so is the sin that is meditated long beforehand and then perpetrated higher in rank than those which are suddenly conceived and then performed. For that reason, those who long devise schemes are to be advised to understand how much punishment they shall have in excess of others, because they now refuse to be the equals of the sinful but intend to be their leaders.

Chapter 57

LVII. Ðætte on oðre wisan sint to monienne
ða ðe oftrædlice lytla scylda wyrceað,
on oðre wisan ða ðe hi gehealdað
wið ða lytlan scylda, ond ðeah
hwiltidum afellað on hefegum scyldum.

On oðre wisan sint to manienne ða ðe oftrædlice syngiað,
ond ðeah lytlum scyldum; on oðre wisan ða ðe hie wið ða
læssan scylda bewareniað, ond ðeah hwilum afeallað on
micla scylda. Hi sint to manienne, ðonne hi oft syngiað,
ðeah hi lytlum syngien, ðæt hie ma ðencen hu manega synna
hi fremmað ðonne hi ðencen hu micle hi hie gefremmen;
ond gif hi oferhycgen ðæt hi him ondræden hiora lytlan
synna, ðonne ðonne hi hi gesioð, ondræden hi him huru,
ðonne hi hi rimað. Swiðe lytle beoð ða dropan ðæs smalan
renes, ac hi wyrceað ðeah swiðe micel flod ond swiðe
strongne stream, ðonne hi gegaddrode beoð, forðon ðe hira
bið swiðe fela. Swiðe lytlum sicerað ðæt wæter ond swiðe
degellice on ðæt hlece scip, ond ðeah hit wilnað ðæs ilcan ðe
sio hlude yð deð on ðære hreon sæ, buton hit mon ær ut
aweorpe. Swiðe lytle bioð ða wunda on ðæm hreofan lice,
ond ðeah, gif sio hreofl hit eal ofergæð, hio gedeð ðæt ilce
ðæt sio micle wund gedeð on ðæm breostum. Be ðæm is
awriten on Salomonnes bocum ðætte se, se ðe nylle onscunian his lytlan scylda, ðæt he wille gelisian to maran. Ond gif
he agiemeleasað ðæt he ða lytlan hreowsige, ond hwilum
forcierre, he wile afeallan on ða miclan, ðeah hit late sie.

Chapter 57

57. That those who frequently commit minor trespasses are to be guided in one fashion, in another fashion those who hold out against minor transgressions and yet occasionally fall into weighty offenses.

In one fashion are those who sin frequently to be cautioned, and yet through minor infractions, in another fashion those who secure themselves against lesser offenses and yet at times fall into major transgressions. They are to be advised when they sin often, though they sin in small ways, to devote more thought to how many sins they commit than they devote to how great are the ones they commit, and if they disdain to feel alarm about their minor sins when they take stock of them, let them be alarmed at least when they number them. Very small are the drops of a fine rain, yet they form a great torrent and a very powerful current when they come together, because they are very numerous. Water seeps in very small amounts and quite imperceptibly into a leaky ship, and yet it tends to the same end as a loud wave on a rough sea if it is not bailed out in time. Quite small are the lesions on a scabrous body, and yet if scabs cover it completely, it has the same effect that a great wound in the chest has. About this it is written in the books of Solomon that one who declines to evade his small offenses will drift into greater ones. And if he neglects to repent of the little ones and sometimes avoid them, he will fall into grievous ones, though it be slowly.

2   Ac hi sint to manienne, ðonne hi oft syngiað lytlum, ðæt
hie geornlice ongieten ðæt mon oft wyrs gesyngað on ðæm
lytlum synnum ðonne on ðæm miclum, forðæm hi mon onginð swa micle ær betan swa hie mon ær ongiet; ac ða lytlan
mon ne gelefð to nanre synne, ac nimð hi to gewunan, ond hi
ðonne ðy earfoðlicor gebet. Ðonon cymð oft ðætte ðæt mod
him ærest na ne ondræt ða lytlan scylda, ne, ðonne on last,
ða miclan. Ac hit gewunað to ðæm synnum oð hit becymð to
sumum ealdordome ðara scylda, ond ðonne swa micle læs
onscunað ða miclan swa hit ær orsorglicor gewunode to
ðæm lytlum, ond him ða læs ondred.

3   Ongean ðæt sint to manienne ða ðe hi gehealdað wið ða
lytlan scylda, ond hwilum ðeah gedufað on ðæm miclum; hi
sint to manienne ðæt hi geornlice hi selfe ongieten, forðæm
ðe hiora mod bið swiðe oft up ahæfen, forðæm ðe hi hi habbað swa wærlice gehealden wið ða lytlan scylda. Ac him
is ðearf ðæt hi for ðære orsorgnesse ne ðurhtion hefigran
scylda—ðæt is ðæt hi for hira upahæfennesse ne befeallen
on ðone pytt ofermetta, ðy læs hi forswelge sio swelgend
ðære upahæfenesse; forðæm oft, ðonne hi oferswiðað utane
ða lytlan scylda, hi aðindað innane on idlum gilpe. Ond
ðonne ðæt mod bið innan oferswiðed mid ðæm ofermettum, hi toflowað swiðe hræðe ut, ond ætiewað on openum
yfle. Forðæm sint to manienne ða ðe hi wið ða lytlan scylda
gehealdað, ond ðeah hwilum gedufað on ðæm miclum; hi
sint to manienne ðæt hi hi behealden ðæt hi innan ne afeallen ðonon ðe hi wenað ðæt hi utan stonden, ðy læs sio
upahæfenes for ðære lytlan ryhtwisnesse him weorðe to
wege micelre scylde æfter ðæs ðearlwisan deman dome ond

But when they repeatedly commit venial sins they are to   2
be admonished to understand very well that one often sins
more egregiously with little infractions than with great, because the sooner one recognizes them, the sooner he begins
to atone for them; whereas he regards the little ones as no
sin but makes a habit of them and then atones for them with
so much greater difficulty. From this it often arises that the
mind first fails to worry about little transgressions, and then
subsequently big ones. But it grows accustomed to those
sins, until it arrives at something of an authorization for sinning, and then it refrains from great offenses so much the
less as it formerly habituated itself with less concern to
small ones and is the less in dread of them.

To the contrary, those who refrain from small offenses   3
and yet sometimes plunge into large ones are to be counseled genuinely to understand themselves, because their
mind is often quite conceited about having restrained themselves so cannily from small trespasses. But it is necessary
for them not to perpetrate weightier sins on account of that
security—that is, that they not for their self-congratulation
fall into the pit of pride, lest the maw of insolence swallow
them up, because often when they outwardly vanquish the
little sins, they grow inwardly bloated with specious self-
congratulation. And when the mind within is overmastered
by pride, it very soon seeps out and appears as patent evil.
Therefore, those who resist small transgressions and yet
sometimes plunge into large ones are to be warned to take
care that they not inwardly fall from where they believe they
outwardly stand, to avoid letting self-satisfaction over a little virtuousness become for them the route to major trespass after the verdict and sentence of the severe judge. But

edleane. Ac ðonne hi wenað ðæt hi of hira ægnum mægene hi hæbben gehealden wið ða lytlan scylda, ðonne weorðað hi swiðe ryhtlice forlætene from Gode, oð ðæt hi afeallað on maran scylda; forðæm ðæt hi ongiten feallende ðæt hie ær hiora agnes ðonces ne stodon, ðætte ðæt mod, ðe ær wæs up ahæfen for lytlum gode, si ðonne gebiged to miclum yfele.

4   Ac hi sint to manienne ðæt hie ongieten ðæt hie oft ge-syngiað giet wyrs on ðæm ðæt hi hi wareniað wið ða lytlan scylda ðonne hi don on miclum scyldum; forðæm ðe hi licet-tað hie unscyldge, ðonne hi hi wæreniað wið ða lytlan. Ac hi hi ne ladiað nowiht, ðonne hi wyrcað ða miclan ond ða openan. Ðæt is open yfel beforan Gode ðæt mon ða miclan do, ac ðæt is licettung haligdomes for monnum ðæt mon ða lytlan forga, ond ða miclan do. Be ðæm wæs gecweden on ðæm godspelle to Fariseum ðæt hi wiðbleowen ðære fleo-gan, ond forswulgun ðone olfend, swelce he openlice cwæde, "Ða lytlan yflu ge fleoð, ond ða miclan ge fretað." Ðæt is ðæt ilce ðæt eft wæs getæled ðurh ðone muð ðære Soðfæstnesse, ðæt is Crist: he cwæð, "Ge tiogoðiað eowre mintan ond eowerne dile ond eowerne kymen, ond lætað untiogoðad ðætte diorwyrðre is eowra oðra æhta, ond ða bebodu ðe giet maran sint on ðære æwe ge no ne healdað: ðæt is ryht dom ond mildheortnes ond treowa." Nis us nawht recceleaslice to gehiranne ðætte he nemde ða undiorestan wyrta ðe on wyrttunum weaxe, ond ðeah swiðe welstincenda. Ðurh ðone stenc sint getacnode ða liceteras, ðe willað habban ðone hlisan haligdomes, ond don ðeah lytel godes; ond ðeah hi formicel god ne don, hi wilniað ðæt hi micel ðyncen, ond hi mon widherge.

when they suppose that they have preserved themselves from small infractions by their own ability, they will quite justly be forsaken by God, until they fall into greater immorality, so that in falling they may recognize that they did not previously stand by their own ability, so that the mind that formerly prided itself on a little goodness may be made to submit in the face of immense ills.

Yet they are to be advised to recognize that they often sin 4 still more gravely in keeping aloof from peccadilloes than they do in major transgressions, since they pretend to be innocent when they preserve themselves from minor ones. But they can offer no excuse when they commit great and unconcealed wrongs. It is patent evil before God to perpetrate great ones, but it is pretense of sanctity before men to forgo the small and commit the great. About this it was said to the Pharisees in the gospel that they blew away the fly and swallowed the camel, as if plainly to say, "You shun little wrongs and devour big ones." It is the same that again was rebuked through the mouth of Truth, which is Christ: he said, "You tithe your mint and your dill and your cumin and leave untithed what is costlier than your other possessions, and the commandments that are yet greater in the law you do not keep: that is, true justice and mercy and trustworthiness." We are not to hear without due attention that he named the herbs of least worth that grow in gardens, and yet which are very aromatic. By the fragrance are signified hypocrites who want a reputation for sanctity and yet do little good; and though they do no very grand good, they yearn to be thought grand and to be extolled far and wide.

Chapter 58

LVIII. Ðætte on oðre wisan sint to monianne
ða ðe nan wuht godes ne onginnað,
on oðre wisan ða ðe hit onginnað
ond wel ne geendiað.

On oðre wisan sint to manienne ða ðe nan god ne onginnað; on oðre ða ðe hit onginnað, ond no ne geendiað. Ða
ðonne ðe nan god ne onginnað, ne sint hi no to lærenne
hwæt hi don scylen, ær him si belagen ðæt hi ðonne doð;
forðæm ðe hi nyllað underfon ðæt uncuðe ðæt hi gehirað,
buton hi ær ongieten hu frecenlic ðæt is ðæt hi cunnon;
forðæm nan mon ne bitt oðerne ðæt he hine rære, gif he self
nat ðæt he afeallen bið; ne eac se, se his wunde sar ne gefret,
ne wilnað he nanes læces. Forðy him is ærest to cyðanne hu
idel ðæt is ðæt hi lufiað ond hu unnytt, ond siððan him is to
reccanne hu nyttwyrðe ðæt is ðæt hi forlæten habbað. Ærest
hi sculon ongietan ðæt hi fleon ðæt ðæt hi lufiað; ðonne magon hi sið ieðelice ongietan ðæt ðæt is to lufianne ðæt hi ær
flugon. Micle ðy bet hi underfoð ðæt uncuðe, gif hi on ðæm
cuðan gewislice ongietað hwæt ðæron tælwyrðes bið. Ðonne
hi leorniað mid fulre estfulnesse ða soðan god to secanne,
ðonne hi mid fulle gesceade ongietað ðæt ðæt wæs leas ond
idelnes ðæt hi ær heoldon.

2   Ac gehiren hi ðæt ðas andweardan god bioð from ælcre

Chapter 58

58. That those who undertake nothing good are to be guided in one fashion, in another fashion those who undertake it but do not finish it properly.

In one fashion are to be advised those who undertake no good, in another those who undertake it and do not carry it through. Those, then, who take in hand nothing good are not to be instructed what they ought to do before they are reproved for what they are then doing, because they will be unwilling to take on the unfamiliar that they hear about unless they first understand how reprehensible is what is familiar to them; for no one asks to be helped up if he does not himself know that he has fallen; neither does one who does not notice the pain of his injury desire any physician. Therefore, it is first to be made plain to them how vain is what they love, and how useless, and thereafter they are to be informed how important is what they have given up. First they ought to understand to turn from what they cherish; then they will subsequently be able to understand readily that what they previously turned from is to be valued. They will accept much better the untried if they recognize what is deplorable in the tried. They will learn to pursue the true good with full devotion once they recognize with full discernment that what they adhered to before was falsehood and vanity.

But let them hear that this present good will very soon be 2

491

lustfulnesse swiðe hrædlice gewitende, ond swaðeah sio scyld ðe hi ðurh ða lustfullnesse ðurhtioð ungewitendlice bið ðurhwuniende mid wræce; ond nu ðæt ðæt hie lyst hi sculon nedenga forlætan, ond ðeah ðæt hi nu nedenga forlætað him bið eft to wite gehealden. Oft ðeah weorðað men swiðe halwendlice afærde mid ðæm ilcan ðingum ðe hi ær unnytlice lufedon: ðonne ðæt geslægene mod gesihð swa healicne dem his agnes hryres, ond ongit hine selfne on swelcre frecennesse ond on swelcne spild forlæd, ðonne wiðtremð he, ond onhupað, ond ondræt him þæt ðæt he ær lufode. Leornað ðonne to lufianne ðæt he ær forhogde. Be ðæm wæs gecweden to Ieremie ðæm witgan, ða he wæs onsended to læranne; hit wæs gecweden, "Ic hæbbe ðe nu todæg gesetne ofer rice ond ofer ðioda ðæt ðu hi toluce ond toweorpe ond forspilde ond tostence ond getimbrie ond geplantige." Forðæm, buton he ðæt woh ær towurpe ne meahte, he noht nytwyrðlice ðæt ryht getimbrian; forðæm, buton he of his hieremonna mode ða ðornas ðære idlan lufan ær up atuge, unnyt he plantode on hi ða word ðære halgan lare. Forðæm wæs eac ðætte *sanctus* Petrus ærest towearp ðæt ðæt he eft timbrede. Ðæt wæs ða ða he Iudeas nolde nan wuht læran hwæt hi don scolden, ac him cidde for ðæm ðe hi ær dydon, ond ðus cwæð: "Ðone Nazareniscan hælend—ðæt wæs afandod wer betwux eow on mægenum ond tacnum ond foretacnum, ða worhte Dryhten ðurh hine ongemang eow—ðone ge beswicon ðurh unryhtwisra monna honda, ond ofslogon ond ahengon ðurh eower geðeaht, swa swa hit God æt fruman wisse, ond ðeah geðafode; se ilca God hine eft aweahte to onliesanne ða gehæftan on helle." Forðæm him ætwat Petrus ða dæde ðe he walde, siððan hi

bereft of all enjoyment, and yet the guilt that they incur through that enjoyment will persist inescapably, with consequences, and what they now take pleasure in they must forfeit under compulsion, and yet what they now forfeit under compulsion will be reserved for their punishment. Yet people often quite beneficially come to be alarmed by the very things that they formerly loved: when the stricken mind sees such deep ruin in its own fall, and one perceives that he has been misled into such peril and such desolation, he will step away and retire, and he will fear what he formerly loved. He will learn then to love what he formerly despised. About this it was said to the prophet Jeremiah when he was sent to teach, saying, "I have now today appointed you over kingdoms and over nations, that you shatter them and level and annihilate and scatter and build and plant." For unless he first leveled the wicked he could by no means effectively build the just; for unless he first uprooted from the mind of his disciples the thorns of idle affections, it would have been useless for him to plant in them the words of holy doctrine. It was likewise for this reason that Saint Peter first tore down what he afterward constructed. That was when he refused to instruct the Jews what they ought to do but chided them for what they had been doing, and spoke thus: "The Nazarene savior—that was a man approved among you by powers and wonders and signs which the Lord worked among you through him—him you betrayed into the hands of vicious people, and beat and crucified him through your contrivance, just as God knew from the beginning and yet permitted; none other but God raised him again to release the prisoners of hell." Peter condemned those deeds because he wanted, after they understood their bloodthirst-

ongeaten hiora wælhreownesse, ðæt hi wæren gedrefde ond geeaðmedde, ond ðæs ðe nytweorðlicor gehierden ða halgan lare, ðe hi ær wilnodon ðæt hi gehiran mosten. Ða andwyrdon him ða Iudeas, ond cwædon, "Hwæt magon we his nu don, broður Petrus?" Petrus andswarode, ond cwæð, "Doð ærest hreowsunga, ond weorðað siððan gefullwade." Ða edniwunge ond ða lare hi swiðe hrædlice forsawen, ðær hi ær ne ongeten ðone hryre ond ða toworpennesse hira wælhreownesse ðurh his ðreaunga.

3   Gelicost ðæm ðe *sancte* Paule wæs, ða him ðæt leoht com of hefonum, ond hine gebregde: næs him no ða giet to gecweden hwæt he mid ryhte ðonon forð don scolde, ac him wæs gesæd hwæt he ær to unryhte dyde. Ac ða he swa gebreged on eorðan feoll, ond ascode, ond cwæð, "Hwæt eart ðu, Dryhten?" ða wæs him swiðe hraðe geandwyrd, "Ic eom se Nazarenisca hælend, ðe ðu ehtst." Ond ða cwæð he, "Dryhten, hwæt hætst ðu me gedon?" Ða ondwyrde him Dryhten, "Aris, ond gong to geonre byrig; ðe mon sægð ðær hwæt ðu don scealt." Loca nu, hu Dryhten wæs sprecende of hefonum to his ehtere, ond hine ðreade for his ærgedonan weorcum. Ær ðæm ðe he him sæde hu he hine forð healdan sceolde, ða wæs gehroren sio upahæfenes Paules ond eal ða weorc ðe he ðurh ða worhte. Ond sona æfter ðæm hryre ðære upahæfennesse, he ongan timbran eaðmodnesse. Ða ða he wilnode lare æt Gode, ða gefeoll se egeslica ehtere to ðon ðæt he swa micle stranglicor arise swa he hefiglicor afeoll. Swa sint to teweorpanne ærest ða ðe nan god ær ne dydon ðurh ðreaunge of ðære heardnesse hiora yfelnesse, to ðæm ðæt hi sien eft on firste arærde ond gestonden on ryhtum weorce. Forðæm we ceorfað heah treowu on holte,

494

iness, for them to be anxious and humbled, and on that
account to listen more profitably to the holy doctrine that
they had desired to be permitted to hear. Then the Jews answered him and said, "What can we do about it now, brother
Peter?" Peter replied and said, "First repent, and afterward
be christened." They would very soon have held in contempt
the rebirth and the doctrine had they not first, through his
condemnation, acknowledged the downfall and ruin occasioned by their cruelty.

It was quite like that for Saint Paul when the light from 3
heaven came to him and terrified him: he was by no means
yet told what he was to do thenceforth with justice, but he
was told what he had done without justice. But when he fell
to the ground thus terrified and asked, "Who are you, Lord?"
he was very promptly answered: "I am the Nazarene savior,
whom you are persecuting." And then he said, "Lord, what
are you telling me to do?" Then the Lord answered him,
"Arise and go to that city over there; you will be told there
what to do." See, now, how the Lord was speaking from
heaven to his persecutor and upbraided him for previous actions. Before he told him how he should conduct himself
thenceforth, Paul's self-satisfaction was laid low, along with
all the deeds he had done through it. And immediately after
the razing of his exaltedness he began to build up humility.
When he desired direction from God, the fearsome persecutor fell in order that he might rise much more soundly the
more heavily he had fallen. Just so, those who have done no
good are first to be cast down through rebuke of the hardened state of their immorality, so that they may in time
afterward be raised and made to stand in righteous work.
We fell tall trees in the forest to raise them up again in a

ðæt we hi eft up aræren on ðæm botle, ðær ðær we timbran willen, ðeah we hi forhrædlice to ðæm weorce don ne mægen for grennesse, ær ðæm ðe hi adrugien. Ac swa swa hi swiður adrygde bioð on eorðan swa hi mon mæg orsorglicor up fegean.

4   Ongean ðæt sint to manienne ða ðe næbre nyllað fulfremman ðæt god ðæt hi onginnað, ðæt hi ongieten mid wærlice ymbeðonce ðætte, ðonne ðonne hi forlætað hiora willes ond hiora gewealdes ða god ðe hi getiohchod æfdon to donne, ðæt hi ðonne mid ðy dilgiað ða ðe hi ær ongunnon; forðæm, gif ðæt ne wexð ðæt hie tiohhiað to donne, ðonne wanað ðæt ðæt hi ær dydon. Ac ælces mannes mod on ðys middangearde hæfð scipes ðeaw. Ðæt scip wile hwilum stigan ongean ðone stream, ac hit ne mæg, buton ða rowend hit teon, ac hit sceal fleotan mid ðy streame; ne mæg hit no stille gestondan, buton hit ankor gehæbbe, oððe mon mid roðrum ongean tio; elles hit gelent mid ðy streame. Swa deð sio forlætnes ðæs godan weorces. Hio winð wið ða god ðe mon ær gedon hæfð, buton mon simle swincende ond wyrcende sie god weorc oð ende. Be ðæm wæs gecweden ðurh Salomon ðone snotran; he cwæð, "Se ðe his willum for his slæwðe forlætt his godan weorc, he bið gelicost ðæm men ðe his towirpð." Be ðæm wæs eac gecweden ðurh Iohannis ðone godspellere to ðære ciricean biscepe ðe Sardis hatte; he cwæð, "Bio ðu wacor, ond gebet ða weorc ðe deadlicu sint in ðe: ne mette ic no ðin weorc fullfremed beforan minum Gode." Forðæm he cwæð ðæt he forðy ne funde his weorc fulfremed beforan Gode, ða ðe he ær worhte, forðæm ðe he ða ne worhte, ða ðe he ða wyrcean sceolde. Swa eac, gif we ne gebetað ðæt on us deadbæres is ðurh synna, ðonne acwilð ðæt ðætte on us ær lifde ðurh god weorc.

building where we want to erect one, though we cannot apply them to the construction all at once, on account of their being still green before they have dried. But the more they have dried on the ground, the more confidently they can be joined.

To the contrary, those who are never willing to complete   4 the good that they begin are to be advised to understand with careful reflection that, when they willingly and under no compulsion renounce the good things that they had resolved to do, they thereby nullify what they had begun, because if what they purpose to do does not reach maturity, what they did earlier will decay. But the mind of every person in this world has the character of a ship. A ship will sometimes move against the current, yet it cannot unless oarsmen propel it, but it must float with the current; it cannot remain still unless it has an anchor or is controlled with oars; otherwise, it will proceed with the current. So does the abandonment of the good work. It strives against the good that had been previously accomplished unless one is continually toiling and working at good deeds to the very end. This was spoken of through the wise Solomon, who said, "One who for his indolence willingly gives up his good work is most like the person who destroys it." This was also spoken of through the evangelist John to the bishop of the church that is called Sardis when he said, "Be vigilant, and amend those works that are moribund in you: I have not found your works completed before my God." He said that he had not found his works completed before God, those that he then had performed, because he had not performed the deeds that he ought to have performed. So, also, if we do not remedy what is moribund in us through sin, we will kill what formerly lived in us through good works.

5   Eac hi sint to manienne ðæt hi geornlice geðencen ðætte hit bið wyrse ðæt mon a onginne faran on soðfæstnesse weg, gif mon eft wile ongean cierran, ond ðæt ilce on faran. Forðæm, gif us ne lyst ðæra ærrena yfela ðe we ær worhton, ðonne ne gælð us nan ðing te fullfremmanne ða godan weorc ðe we nu wyrceað. Ac hi scoldon gehiran ðone cwide ðe awriten is on ðæm ærendgewrite *sancte* Petres. Hit is awriten ðæt him wære betere ðæt hi no soðfæstnesse weg ne ongeaten, ðonne hi underbæc gecerden, siððan hi hine ongeaten. Eac hi sculon gehiran ðone cwide ðe be him awriten is on ðæm bocum ðe hatton *Apocalipsin:* hit is awriten ðæt se engel cwæde be ðæm biscepe to *sancte* Iohanne, "Eala, wære he auðer, oððe hat, oððe ceald. Ac forðon ðe he is wlaco, ond nis nauðer ne hat ne ceald, ðeah ic hine supe, ic hine wille eft ut aspiwan of minum muðe." Se ðonne bið wearm, nalles wlaco, ðe god geornlice onginð, ond eac geendað. Ac se bið ceald ðe nan god ne onginð. Ac swa swa ðæt cealde ærest onginð wlacian, ær hit ful wearm weorðe, swa eac ðæt wearme wlacað, ær hit eallunga acealdige. Swa eac se ðe forlæt ðone cele ungetreownesse, ond wyrð wlacra treowa, ond nyle ðonne ðæt wlæce oferwinnan, ond wearmian oð he wealle— butan tweon, se ðe to lange ond to fæste wunað on ðæm wlacum treowum, he geortreowð ðæt he æfre mæge on welme weorðan, oð ðæt he mid ealle acolað; ond ðeah he ær truwige, ðonne he ceald bið, ðæt he mæge wearm weorðan, he geortriewð, ðonne he wlacu bið, gif he to longe on ðæm stent. Swa eac se ðe nu giet on synnum is, næfð he no forlæten ðone truwan ond ðone tohopan his gehwearfnesse; ac se, se ðe æfter his gehwerfnesse to lange wlæc bið, ðonne

They are also to be urged to consider earnestly that it is 5 worse for someone ever to begin to travel the way of truth if afterward he will turn back and cover the same ground. For if we are not inclined to the earlier wrongs that we formerly committed, nothing will hinder us from completing the good works in which we are now engaged. But they should hear the pronouncement that is written in the Epistle of Saint Peter. It is written that it would be better for them never to have acknowledged the way of truth than to have turned back once they had acknowledged it. They should also hear the observation that is written about them in the books that are called Apocalypse: it is written that the angel said about the bishop to Saint John, "Oh, that he would be one or the other, either hot or cold. But because he is indifferent and is neither hot nor cold, if I taste him I will subsequently spit him out of my mouth." Someone, then, is warm, not indifferent, who begins something good diligently and likewise completes it. But he is cold who begins nothing good. Yet just as something cold first begins to grow tepid before it turns fully warm, so also something warm grows tepid before it goes entirely cold. So also one who renounces the chill of disbelief and grows to be of tepid faith and refuses then to transcend that tepidness and be heated till he boils—without a doubt, one who too long and too immutably remains of tepid faith will despair of ever being able to come to a boil, until he cools altogether; and though earlier, when he is cold, he has faith that he can become warm, when he is tepid he will despair of being warm if he remains too long in that condition. So, likewise, one who is still in a state of sin has not abandoned the trust and the hope of his conversion; but for one who, after his conversion, is tepid

lytlað him se tohopa ðe he hæfde, ða he synful wæs. Forðæm
wilnað God to ælcum men ðæt he sie oððe wearm oððe
ceald, ðy læs he for wlæcnesse sie ut aspiwen. Forðæm se
cealda ðencð to wearmianne, ond se wearma welð on godum
cræftum, ðy læs he sie wealg for wlæcnesse, ond forðæm
weorðe ut aspiwen. Forðæm ælc wæter bið ðy unwerodre to
drincanne, æfter ðæm ðe hit wearm bið, gif hit eft acolað,
ðonne hit ær wære, ær hit mon o ongunne wleccan.

Chapter 59

LVIIII. Ðætte on oðre wisan sint to monianne
ða ðe diegellice yfel doð, ond god openlice,
ond on oðre wisan ða ðe willað helan
ðæt hi to gode doð, ond of sumum
ðingum openlice cyðað ðæt hie willað
ðæt men wenen ðæt hi yfle beon.

On oðre wisan sint to manienne ða ðe yfel degellice doð,
ond god openlice; on oðre wisan ða ðe ða god helað ðe hi
doð, ond ne reccað hwæt him mon ymbe ræswe. Ða ðonne
sint to manienne, ða ðe yfel degellice doð, ond god openlice,
ðæt hi geðencen hu hrædlice se eorðlica hlisa ofergæð, ond
hu unanwendendlice se godcunda ðurhwunað. Hi sint to
manienne ðæt hi on ðara ðinga ende hiora modes eagan
afæstnien, ond gesion ðætte ðis mennisce lof swiðe hrædlice
gewit, ond se uplica dema ond se eca ða deglan scylda ealla

for too long, the hope that he had when he was sinful will diminish. Therefore, God wills for every person that he be either warm or cold, lest he spit him out for tepidness. For one who is cold thinks about warming up, and one who is warm boils in good works, to avoid being bland for tepidness and therefore being spewed out. For all water, once it is warm, should it cool again, is less sweet to drink than it was before it ever began to grow tepid.

Chapter 59

59. That those who do evil secretly and good
openly are to be guided in one fashion,
in another fashion those who wish to
conceal what they do for the good and for
certain reasons make it perfectly plain
that they wish people to think them evil.

In one fashion are to be warned those who do evil in private and good in public, in another fashion those who conceal the good that they do and do not care what is thought of them. Those, then, who do evil in private and good in public are to be told to consider how suddenly worldly judgment passes away, and how immutably divine judgment endures. They are to be advised to fix their mind's eye on the end of things and see that this human esteem departs quite suddenly, and the supernal and eternal judge is aware of all

wat, ond simle bið gearo to ðæm edleanum. Ac ða dieglan yfel habbað ecne gewutan on ðæm godcundan deman; ac ða god ðe hi openlice doð beforan monnum beoð fulneah swelce hi sien butan gewitnesse, forðæm hi næbbað ece gewitnesse. Ac hi habbað ece gewitnesse ðara yfela ðe hi diegellice doð, ðonne hi heolað from monnum ðæt hi secggan scoldon, ond secgað ðæt hi heolan scoldon. Be swelcum monnum cwæð Dryhten ðæt hi wæren gelicost deadra manna byrgennum, ða bioð utan oft swiðe wlitige geworhte, ond bioð innan swiðe fule gefylde. Swa bioð ða ðe hira god eowiað beforan monnum, ond hira yfel helað on innan him selfum: hi licettað, ond woldon lician for manna eagum utane buton godum weorcum innane. Ac hi sint to manienne ðæt hi ne forsion ða god ðe hi doð, ac wenen him maran mede to ðonne hi wenað. To swiðe hi hi forsioð, gif hi him maran mede to ne wenað ðonne eorðlices lofes, ond him ðær genog ðyncð. Hi sellað wið to lytlum weorðe ðæt ðæt hi meahton hefonrice mid gebycggan: sellað wið manna lofe. Be ðæm cwæð Dryhten on his godspelle ðæt ðæt wære hira med. Ac forðæm ðe hi ðæt god openlice doð, ond ðæt yfel diegellice, hi tacniað mid ðæm ðæt men scylen onscunian ðæt ðæt hie degellice doð, ond lufian ðæt hi openlice doð: for ðære bisene hi libbað ðeah oðrum monnum, ond cwelað him selfum.

2   Ongean ðæt sint to manienne ða ðe god diegellice doð, ond swaðeah on sumum weorcum geliccetað ðæt hi openlice yfel don, ond ne reccað hwæt men be him sprecen. Hi sint to manienne ðæt hi mid ðære licettunge oðrum monnum yfle bisene ne astellen, ðeah hi self teladon ðæt hi mid ðære

private shortcomings and is ever ready for retribution. Yet private misdeeds have an everlasting witness in the divine judge, but the good things that they do in the open before men are very nearly as if they are unobserved, because they have no eternal witness. Yet they have an eternal witness to the evils that they perpetrate in private when they conceal from people what they ought to declare, and declare what they ought to conceal. About such people the Lord said that they were very like the sepulchers of dead persons, which are often made quite lovely on the outside and are on the inside filled with what is quite putrid. So are those who display their goodness before people and conceal their badness within themselves: they make pretense and would like to please outwardly before people's eyes, lacking good works inwardly. But they are to be warned not to despise the good that they do, but to expect for themselves greater reward for it than they do expect. They dismiss it excessively if they do not expect more reward for it than worldly praise, and that seems to them sufficient. They sell at too paltry a price that with which they could buy the kingdom of heaven, selling it for men's acclaim. About this the Lord said in his gospel that that was their reward. But because they do good in public and evil in private, they give the example thereby that people ought to avoid what they do in private and admire what they do in public: in providing that example they live to others and die to themselves.

Otherwise are to be counseled those who do good in private and yet by some actions give the appearance of doing evil in public, and do not care what is said of them. They are to be warned not to set a bad example for other people by that pretense, even if they themselves did not make it their

licettunga oðre men ne dwellen ne him ne derigen, ðy læs hit
sie ongieten ðæt hie lufigen hi selfe swiður ðonne hiora
niehstan, swelce hi hie selfe drencen mid wine, ond ðæm
oðrum sellen attor. Ac ðonne hi ða yflan bisne openlice doð,
ond ðæt god degellice, ðonne ne helpað hi mid oðrum ðara
nauht hira niehstum, mid oðrum hi him deriað. Forðæm swa
hwa swa hilð his godan weorc, forðæm ðe he wile fleon idel
gielp, ðonne ne læt he nanne oðerne æfter him on ða godan
weorc, ðonne he nyle ða bisne oðrum eowian ðe he mid
ryhte eowian sceal. He deð swelce he plantige treowu,
ond ceorfe of ða wyrtruman. Be ðæm cwæð Crist on his
godspelle, "Doð eower godan weorc beforan mannum, ðæt
hi mægen weorðian eowerne Fæder ðe on hefonum is." Ac
swaðeah is awriten on ðæm ilcan bocum ungelic cwide
ðissum, ðæt is ðæt he cwæð, "Behealdað eow ðæt ge ne don
eowre ryhtwisnesse beforan monnum, ðy læs hi eow herien."
Ac hwæt wile ðæt nu beon weorca ðæt us on oðerre stowe
forbiet ðæt we hit beforan mannum don, on oðerre lærð,
buton ðæt we hit forðæm helen, ðæt us mon ne herige, ond
forðy yppen, ðæt mon God herige, ond oðre men ða ilcan
bisne underfon? Ac ðær ðær us God forbead ðæt we ure
ryhtwisnesse beforan monnum dyden, he us gecyðde forhwy
he hit forbead, ða he cwæð, "ðy læs hi eow herigen." Ond eft
ða he us het ðæt we hit beforan monnum dyden, ða cwæð he
sona ðæræfter, "to ðon ðæt hi weorðigen eowerne Fæder ðe
on hefonum is." On ðæm twæm wordum he us getacnode
for hwelcum ðingum we sceolden ure godan weorc helan,
ond for hwelcum we hi sceolden cyðan, forðæm ðætte ælc
mon, swa hwæt swa he for gode don wolde, ðæt he hit ne do
for ðæm anum ðæt hine man herige, ac ma for Gode. For
ðæm ðingum bið ælc god weorc god, sie swa open swa degle,

aim by that dissembling to mislead and injure other people, lest it be perceived that they love themselves more than their neighbor, as if they were to serve themselves wine to drink and give others poison. But when they set a bad example in the open and do good privately, by the one they in no degree help their neighbors, and by the other they injure them. Therefore, whoever conceals his good works with the intention of avoiding vacuous ostentation does not lead others after him in good works when he declines to show others the example he rightly ought to show. He does as if he were to plant trees and cut them off at the root. About this Christ said in his gospel, "Do your good works before men, so that they can do honor to your Father who is in heaven." And yet in the same books there is written a pronouncement different from this, which is that he said, "Do not practice your uprightness before men, lest they praise you." But what is to be made of works such that in the one place we are forbidden to do them before men, yet in the other it is required, but that we conceal them so that we not be praised, and advertise them so that God may be glorified and so that other people should follow that very example? Yet at the same time that God forbade us to practice our righteousness before men he revealed why he forbade it when he said, "lest they praise you." And in turn, when he enjoined us to practice it before men, after that he immediately said, "so that they do honor to your Father who is in heaven." By those two phrases he indicated for which reasons we ought to conceal our good works and for which we ought to make them known, to the end that each person not do whatever good he would like to do solely to be praised, but more for God. For these reasons every good work is

swæðer hit sie. Ðonne se mon no his ægenne gielp mid ne
secð, ac ðæs uplican Fæder, ðeah he hit openlice do, he hit
gediegleð mid ðy ðæt he hæfð ðæs gewitnesse ðe he ðær
cweman ðencð ðæt he hit for Gode dyde, næs for gielpe.

3   Ac se ðonne se hit degellice deð, ond ðeah wolde ðæt he
wurde arasod, ond siððan forðy hered, ðeah hit ðonne nan
mon nyte, swaðeah hit bið beforan monnum gedon, emne
swelce hit sie on ealra ðara gewitnesse gedon ðe he on his
mode wilnode ðæt hit hereden. Forðæm hit is betere, swa
swa we ær cwædon, ðætte ælc mon adryge of oðerra monna
mode ðone wenan be him ælces yfeles, swa swa he butan
synne fyrmest mæge, forðæm, gif he swa ne deð, ðonne
scencð he ða scylde mid ðære bisene ælcum ðara ðe him
ænges yfles to wenð. Forðæm hit gebyreð oft, ðonne hwa ne
recð hu micles yfeles him mon to wene, ðeah he self nan yfel
ne do, ðæt he ðeah gesyngað ðurh ða ðe be him bisniað. Be
ðæm cwæð *sanctus* Paulus to his giongrum, ða ða he sumun
liefde to ðicgganne ðætte he nolde ðæt hi ealle ðigden, ðy
læs ða untruman be him bisneden, ond ðurh ðæt wurden
astyrede mid ðæra costunga hwelcra ðe hi eft wiðstondan ne
meahton. Forðæm he cwæð, "Lociað nu ðæt ðios eowru leaf
ne weorðe oðrum monnum to biswice." Ond eft he cwæð be
ðæm ilcan "Ðonne forwyrð ðin broður for ðinum ðingum,
for ðone ær Crist geðrowade. Swa ðonne ge gesyngiað wið
eowre broðer, ond ofsleað hira untruman gewit, ðonne gesyngige ge wið God." Ðæt ilce mænde Moyses, ða he cwæð,
"Ne cweðe ge nan lað ðæm deafan." Ond eft he cwæð, "Ne
screnc ðu ðone blindan." Se ðonne cwið yfel ðæm deafan, se
ðone æfweardan tælð, gif he hine unscyldigne wat. Ond se

good, regardless of whether it is public or private. When one pursues not his own glory by it but the supernal Father's, even though he does it publicly, he conceals it in that he has the witness of the one he intends to please that he did it for God, not for glory.

But regarding one who does it in private and yet would 3 like to be found out, and therefore subsequently admired, even if no one happens to know it, it is still done before men, just as if it were done in the witness of all those whom he in his heart desired to praise it. Therefore, it is better, as we said earlier, that each person wipe away from other people's minds the supposition about him of any evil, as best he can without sin, for if he does not do so, by his example he pours the libation of his offense to all those who suppose any evil of him. For it often happens, when someone does not care how much evil is supposed of him, even if he himself performs no evil, that nonetheless he sins by the example he sets. About this Saint Paul spoke to his disciples when he permitted some of them to partake of what he did not want all of them to partake of, to avoid inducing the weak to take example by them and thereby come to be disturbed by such temptations as they would not afterward be able to withstand. Therefore he said, "Take care that this license of yours not come to be a snare for other people." And again he said about the same, "Then your brother will perish on your account, for whom Christ formerly suffered. Thus, when you sin against your brothers and wound their weak intellect, you sin against God." Moses meant the same when he said, "Say nothing ill to the deaf." And in turn he said, "Do not cause the blind to stumble." He, then, speaks ill to the deaf who disparages the absent if he knows him to be blame-

screncð ðone blindan, ðe ðone ungesceadwisan mirð mid ðy
ðe he his god degelice deð, ond ðeah licet swelce he yfel do.

Chapter 60

LX. Ymbe ðæt, hu mon monige scyndan scyle to
ðæm ðætte his godan dæda ne weorðen
to yflum dædum.

Ðis sint nu ða lara ðe ðæs modes hierdas ond ðære sawle
sceolon ealle men læran ðæt hi ealneg hæbben ða sealfe
gearuwe ðe to ðære wunde belimpe ðe hi ðonne gesion.
Forðæm hit bið swiðe geswincful ðæt mon ælcne mon scyle
on sundrum læran, hit is ðeah earfoðre ealle ætsomne to
læranne, forðæm ðe he sceal gemetgian swa cræftelice his
stemne ðætte he æghwelcum men finde ðone læcedom ðe
him to gebyrge, forðæm ðe ða mettrymnessa ne beoð ealra
manna gelica; ond huru ðæt he self do swa swa he oðre lærð,
forðon ðæt he mæge self gan orsorglice betwuxn oðerra
monna unðeawas, swa swa scearp sweord ða wunde tosceat
on tu, ond gæð gehalre ecgge forð; ond ðæt he huru swa
egesige ða ofermodan, ðæt he ða eaðmodan mid ðy to swiðe
ne fære; ond swa lære ða oðre eaðmetta, swa he ðone ege to
swiðe ðæm oðrum ne geiece; ðæt he swa frefre ða eaðmodan, swa ða ofermodan ne weorðen unmidlode; ond swa lære

less. And he causes the blind to stumble who injures the undiscerning by doing good in private and yet acting as if he is doing evil.

Chapter 60

60. Regarding how many are to be encouraged not to let their good deeds turn to bad deeds.

These, now, are the instructions that shepherds of the heart and of the soul ought to convey to all people, so that they always have ready the salve appropriate to the wound that they are examining. For it is very laborious to be obliged to teach each person individually, yet it is more difficult to teach all in concert, because one has to tailor his discourse so artfully that he finds for each person the cure appropriate to him, since not all people's infirmities are alike; and particularly that he himself do as he teaches others, so that he can himself go free of concern in the midst of other people's vices, the way a sharp sword wounds, cleaving the flesh in two, and departs with edge intact; and that he especially intimidate the proud is such a way that he not thereby frighten the humble excessively; and that he teach humility to the one in such a way that he not intensify the timidity of the others; that he encourage the humble in such a way that the proud not grow unbridled; and that he exhort the inactive

ða slawan geornfulnesse godes weorces, swa he ða geornful-
lan to ungemetlice ne geswence; ond swa tilige hira geswinc
to gemetgianne, swa he ða idlan ne gedo orsorge, ðæt hi
forðy ne aslawien; ond ðæt he swa stiere ðæm ungeðylde-
gum irsunga, swa he ðone hnescan ðafettere on recceleste ne
gebrenge; ond ðeah swa tilige hi to onælenne, swa hi ða
hatheortan ne forbærnen; ond swa eac ða uncystigan cysta
lære, swa he ða cystgan on merringe ne gebringe; ond swa eft
ða rummodan fæsthafolnesse læren, swa hi ða uncystegan
on yfelre hneawnesse ne gebrengen; ond swa læren ða wifga-
lan gesinscipe, swa hi ða forhæbbendan ne gebrengen on unryhthæmde; ond swa ða forhæbbendan læren forhæfdnesse,
swa hie ne forsion ðone gesinscipe; ond swa wilnigen to
oleccanne ðæm godum, ond hi to herianne, swa hi huru ne
oleccen ðæm yflum; ond swa herien ðæt mæste god, swa hi
ðæt læste ne forsion; ond eft swa herie ða ðe lytel god doð,
ðæt hi ne wenen ðæt hi genog don.

Chapter 61

LXI. Ymbe ðæt, hu mon ænne mon scyndan scyle
ðonne he yfle costunga monege ðrowað.

Ð æt bið eac swiðe hefig broc ðæm lareowe ðæt he scyle
on gemænre lare, ðær ðær he eall folc ætsomne lærð, ða lare

to diligence about good deeds in such a way as not to goad
the assiduous to excess; and that he endeavor to moderate
their efforts in such a way as not to discourage the indolent,
so that they therefore shirk; and that he so curb the annoyance of the impatient as not to lead the mild, permissive
sort into recklessness, and yet endeavor so to inspire them
as not to inflame the hot hearted; and, likewise, that he
teach liberality to the illiberal in such a way as not to lead
the generous into profligacy; and, in turn, that he so teach
thrift to the generous as not to lead the illiberal into reprehensible miserliness; and that he so instruct the lecherous in
marital union as not to lead the chaste into fornication; and
that he so instruct the chaste in self-denial that they not despise marital union; and that he so devise to compliment the
good and applaud them as certainly not to compliment the
bad; and that he so acclaim the greatest good as not to over-
look the least; and, in turn, that he praise those who do little
good in such degree that they not believe they are doing
enough.

Chapter 61

61. Regarding how a lone individual is to be
encouraged when he suffers many evil temptations.

It is also a grave trial for the teacher in communal instruction, when he teaches all the people together at once, that

findan ðe hi ealle behofigen, forðæm hira unðeawas bioð swiðe ungelice; ond ðeah bið giet earfoðre ælcne on sundrum to læranne, forðæm ðe manege bioð ðe hæbbað ða unðeawas ealle ðe mon eallum monnum forbeodan sceolde. Oft eac gebyreð ðætte sume bioð to ungemetlice bliðe for sumum gesælðum, oððe for ðæs blodes styringe, ond eft swiðe hræðe for sumum ungesælðum to ungemetlice unbliðe. Forðæm is to giemanne ðæm lareowe ðæt he swa swiðe stiere ðære unrotnesse ðæt he to swiðe ne geiece ða ungemetlican blisse; ond eft swa gemidlige ða blisse ðe of ðære orsorgnesse cymð ðæt sio unrotnes to swiðe ne weaxe ðe of ðære færlican gedrefednesse cymð, oððe of yfles blodes flownesse. Forðæm oft ða oferbliðan weorðað gedrefde for ungemetlicre onettunga, ðonne him hwæthwugu wiðstent ðæt hi ne magon swa hrædlice forðbrengan ðæt hi tiohhiað swa hi woldon. Swa eac ða swiðe unrotan bioð oft gedrefde mid ungemetlice ege, ond ðeah hwilum bioð genedde mid sumre fortruwodnesse ðæt hi onginnað ðæt ðæt hi willað. Swa ðonne sceal se *magister* gemetgian ðone færlican ege ðæt ðær ðeah ne weaxe to ungemetlice beldo, ond swaðeah swa ðrycce ða belde on ðæm oferbliðum ðæt ðær ðeah ne weaxe on him sio ofðrycnes ðæs eges, ðe cymð of ðæs yflan blodes flownesse.

2   Hwelc wundor is ðæt, ðeah ðæs modes læcas behealden ðas lare, ðonne ðæs lichoman læcas habbað swelce gesceadwisnesse on hira cræfte? Ac hwilum ðeah ofðrycð ðone lichoman ungemetlicu mettrymnes. Ongean swelce mettrymnesse mon beðorfte stronges læcedomes, ðær se mettruma lichoma hine adreogan meahte. Forðæm is ðæm læce swiðe

he must discover the lesson that they all require, because their vices are quite various; and yet it is even more challenging to teach each individually, since there are many who have all the vices which ought to be forbidden all people. Likewise, it frequently happens that some are too inordinately glad over certain strokes of good fortune, or for the stirring of the blood, and, conversely, very suddenly too immoderately sad over certain misfortunes. Therefore, it is for the teacher to take care that he manage distraught feelings to such a degree that he not excessively promote unbridled happiness; and, by turns, so to mitigate the happiness that springs from freedom from care that the discouragement that results from sudden distress or from bad circulation of the blood not increase too disproportionately. Accordingly, the excessively cheerful often become distressed out of inordinate haste, when something prevents them from being able as quickly as they would like to accomplish what they are trying to accomplish. Likewise, the very unhappy are often afflicted with excessive timidity, and yet sometimes they are compelled by a certain overconfidence to undertake what they will. The master ought, then, so to keep in check sudden timidity, that it not give rise to excessive bravado, and nonetheless so to suppress boldness in the overly happy that there not fall on them the heavy hand of timidity, which comes from bad circulation of the blood.

What wonder is it that physicians of the soul should assume this mode of instruction, when physicians of the body have such subtlety in their craft? And yet sometimes excessive infirmity distresses the body. Against such a disorder there would be need of strong medicine if the ailing body could endure it. For the healer is very assiduously to take

geornlice to giemanne ðæt he swa strangne læcedom selle
ðæm seocan, swa he mæge ða mettrymnesse mid geflieman,
ond eft swa liðne swa se tydra lichoma mæge astandan, ðy
læs he ægðer afierre of ðæm lichoman ge ða mettrymnesse
ge eac ðæt lif. Ac ðonne he deð ðæm siocan swiðe gescead-
wislicne fultum, ðonne he afliemð æt anum cierre ða mettrymnesse, swa ðæt he ðeah ðæm lichoman ne dereð. Ac
forhwy ne mæg ðonne micle ma ðæs modes læce gehælan ða
adle ðæra unðeawa monigra monna mid anre lare, ðonne swa
micle manigfaldran bioð ðæs modes læcedomas ðonne ðæs
lichoman? Ond ðeah ðæs lichoman læcas oft æt anum cierre
ægðer doð, ge ðæm lichoman gebeorgað, ge eac ða mettrymnesse afliemað.

Chapter 62

LXII. Ðætte hwilum ða leohtan scylda
bioð beteran to forlætenne,
ðy læs ða hefigran weorðen ðurhtogene.

Oft eac gebyreð ðætte twegen unðeawas hreosað on
ænne man, oðer læssa, oðer mara. Forðæm sceal ðæs modes
læce ær tilian ðæs ðe he wenð ðæt ðone mon ær mæge ge-
brengan on færwyrde. Hwilum ðeah, ðær ðær mon oðres
tiolað, ðær weaxð se oðer. Forðæm sceal se gesceadwisa læce
lætan ær weaxan ðone læssan, ond tilian ðæs maran, oð ðæt

care that he dispense to the sick as potent medicine as he can to allay the ailment, and, at the same time, no more potent than the feeble body can endure, to avoid driving out of the body both the disease and life. But he lends the sick highly astute care when concurrently he quells the affliction without harming the body. But for what reason cannot the healer of the spirit, then, much the more so treat with a single prescription the illness of the vices of many people, when the medicines for the soul are so much more numerous than those for the body? And yet physicians of the body often do both at one stroke: preserve the body and dislodge the disease.

Chapter 62

62. That sometimes petty offenses
are better to leave unaddressed,
lest graver ones come to be carried through.

In addition, it frequently happens that two kinds of immorality fall upon a single person, one minor, one major. Therefore, the physician of the spirit ought to attend first to the one that he believes will first lead the person to ruin. At times, though, when one is treated, the other will increase. In that event, the prudent healer ought first to let the lesser grow and attend to the greater until the occasion

sio tid cume ðæt he ðæs oðres tilian mote, buton he begra ætgæddre getilian mæge. Ne gaderað he no mid ðy un-ðeawas, ac tilað ðæs gewundedan werpe ðe he bewitan sceal, oð ðæt he hine fullice gehælan mæge. Oft weorðað ða ofer-swiðde mid unryhthæmde ða ðe ne magon forlætan hira gifernesse. Oft eac gebyreð ðæm ðe him ægðer ðissa on-drædað, gif hi hi wið ægðer gehealdað, ðæt hi befeallað on idelgielp, forðæm ðe nan mon ne mæg nauðer ðissa swa for-lætan ðæt ðæt oðer ne weaxe. Hwæðres ðonne ðara yfela is betere ær to tilianne, buton swæðres swæðer frecenlicre is? Forðy is betere ðæt mon læte sume hwile weaxan ðæt idel-gielp, oð ðæt mon fullice mæge getilian ðæs unryhthæmdes. Forðæm cwæþ *sanctus* Paulus to his cnihte, ða he ongeat ðæt he wolde oðer twega, oððe ða giet yfel don, oððe mid his gode him wilnian lofes; ða cwæð he, "Gif ðu wille ðæt ðu ne ðyrfe ðe ondrædan ðinne hlaford, do tela: ðonne hereð he ðe." Ne scyle ðeah nan mon for ðæm anum ðingum don ðæt ðæt he to gode deð, ðæt he ne ðyrfe his hlaford ondrædan, ne eft for ðæm anum ðe he wilnige eorðlices lofes. Forðæm se æðela lareow *sanctus* Paulus, ða he ongeat ðæt he ægðer ne meahte his cniht gelæran ge ðæt ðæt he yfel forlete, ond eac ðæt he forðy nanes lofes ne wilnode, ða liefde he him ðone gielp to sumre hwile, ond forbead ðæt yfel. Ða he him ge-ðafode ðone gielp, ða forbead he him ðæt yfel, for ðæm ðæt he ðy ieð meahte ðæt oðer forlætan ðe he on ðæm oðrum hæfde ðæt hine lyste.

arises when he is free to treat the other, if he cannot attend to both at once. He will not thereby pile up vices, but he will promote the recovery of the injured one on whom it is his duty to attend, until he can cure him altogether. Those who cannot shed their gluttony are often undone by fornication. It frequently happens, as well, to those who are wary of both of these, if they hold out against both, that they succumb to self-regard, since no one can so renounce either of these that the other will not increase. Which of the two is then better to attend to first but whichever poses the greater danger? It is thus better to let self-satisfaction grow for a time, until fornication can be handled decisively. For this reason, Saint Paul spoke to his disciple when he understood that he would do one of two things, either go on doing what is bad or desire esteem for his doing good; he said, then, "If you want not to need fear your Lord, do good: then he will esteem you." Yet no one ought to do the good that he does for the sole purpose of not having to fear his Lord, nor, conversely, for the sole reason that he craves worldly esteem. Thus, the noble teacher Paul, when he perceived that he could not induce his disciple both to avoid what is bad and also not to desire any reverence for it, allowed him the self-congratulation for a time and forbade the sin. When he indulged the self-conceit he forbade him the sin, so that he could the more easily give up the one as in the other he had what pleased him.

Chapter 63

LXIII. Ðætte ða untruman mod mon
ne scyle ellenga to healice læran.

Þæm lareowe is to wietanne ðæt he huru nanum men
mare ne beode ðonne he acuman mæge, ðy læs se rap his
modes weorðe to swiðe aðened, oð he forberste. Forðæm sio
hea lar is betere manegum monnum to helanne, ond feawum
to secgganne. Be ðæm cwæð sio Soðfæstnes ðurh hi selfe,
ðæt is Crist: he cwæð, "Hwa wenstu ðæt sie to ðæm getreow
ond to ðæm wis brytnere ðæt hine God gesette ofer his
hired, to ðæm ðæt he him to tide gemetlice gedæle ðone
hwæte?" Ðurh ða gemetgunge ðæs hwætes is getacnod
gemetlico word, ðy læs hira mon ma geote on ðæt undiope
mod ðonne hit behabban mæge, ðæt hit ðonne oferflowe.
Be ðæm cwæð *sanctus* Paulus, "Ic ne mæg no to eow sprecan
swa swa to gæstlicum, ac swa swa to flæsclicum; forðæm ge
sint giet cilderu on eowrum geleafan, ðy ic sceal sellan eow
giet mioloc drincan, nalles flæsc etan." Forðæm wæs eac
ðætte Moyses behelede ða ofermætan bierhto his ondwlitan
beforan ðæm folce, ða he com from ðære dieglan spræce
Dryhtnes, forðæm ðe he ða giet nolde hi læran ða diegelnesse ðære halgan æ, ne hi ða giet ne meahton hi ongietan.
Forðæm wæs eac beboden ðurh Moyses, gif hwa adulfe pytt,
ond ðonne forgiemeleasode ðæt he hine betynde, ond ðær
ðonne befeolle on oððe oxa oððe esol, ðæt he hine scolde
forgieldan. Swa eac swa hwa swa becymð to ðæm hiehstan

Chapter 63

63. That weak minds ought
not to be taught all too loftily.

It is for the teacher to understand, at all events, not to ask of anyone more than he can sustain, so that the cord of his mind will not grow overly strained, until it snaps. Thus, lofty teaching is best withheld from the majority of people and expressed to the minority. About this Truth spoke in his own person, which is Christ: he said, "Who do you suppose is so trustworthy and perceptive a steward that God will set him at the head of his household, to distribute wheat to them at the proper time?" By the measuring of wheat is expressed measured words, lest more of them be poured into a shallow mind than it can accommodate, so that it then spills over. About this Saint Paul said, "I can by no means speak to you as to the spiritual but as to the carnal: because you are still children in your faith, I shall as yet give you milk to drink, not flesh to eat." It was for this reason as well that Moses hid the exceeding brilliance of his countenance before the people when he came from private converse with the Lord, that he did not yet want to instruct them in the mysteries of holy law, nor could they yet comprehend them. For this reason it was also enjoined through Moses that if anyone dug a pit and then neglected to enclose it, and either an ox or an ass fell into it, he would have to pay compensation for it. So, as well, whoever attains to the highest erudition and then does

wisdome, ond ðonne ne forhilð ða diogolnesse ðæs godcundan wisdomes ðæm dysegum, he bið scyldig geteald, gif he gebrengð auðer oððe clænne oððe unclænne on ormodnesse.

2   Be ðæm cwæð Dryhten to ðæm eadgan Iobe, "Hwa sealde kokke wisdom?" Ðæt getacnað ðætte æghwelc ðæra halgena lareowa ðe nu lærað on ðære ðisternesse ðisses middangeardes habbað onlicnesse ðæm kokkum, ðe on ðistrum niehtum crawað. Ðonne græt se lareow swa swa kok on niht, ðonne he cwið "Nu us is tima ðæt we onwæcnen of slæpe." Ond eft, ðonne he cwið, "Onwæcnað, ge ryhtwisan, ond ne syngiað ma." Ðæs cocces ðeaw is ðæt he micle hludor singð on uhtan ðonne on dægred. Ac ðonne hit nealæcð dæge, ðonne singð he smælor ond smicror. Swa sceal ælc gesceadwis lareow opene lare ond swutole ðæm ðiestrum modum bodian, ond nane wuht ðære dieglan ond ðære diopan lare ðonne giet cyðan. Ac siððan hi gesion ðætte ða ðistran mod ðæra dysegena monna auht nealæcen ðæm leohte ðære soðfæstnesse, ðonne sculon hi him eowian diogolran ond diopran lara of halgum bocum.

not shield the mysteries of divine philosophy from the vacuous will be accounted guilty if he leads either the clean or the unclean into desperate straits.

About this the Lord said to the blessed Job, "Who made the cock wise?" This signifies that all the holy teachers who now teach in the dimness of this world bear a resemblance to cocks that crow in the gloom of night. The teacher, then, cries out like a cock in the night when he says, "Now is the hour for us to awake from sleep." And also when he says, "Awake, you righteous, and sin no more." The cock's habit is to sing much louder in the predawn than at daybreak. And as day approaches, it sings more finely and elegantly. So ought every prudent teacher to preach candid and plain guidance to dim minds, and nothing of arcane and profound instruction reveal then as yet. But after they see that the cloudy minds of dull-witted people are at all approaching the light of truth, they ought to reveal to them the more mysterious and more profound tutelage of holy books. 2

Chapter 64

LXIIII. Be ðæm weorcum ðæs lareowes ond be his wordum.

Hit is nu ðearf ðæt we for lufum eft cierren betwuxn oðrum spræcum to ðæm ðe we ær spræcon: ðæt is ðætte ælc lareow swiðor lære mid his weorcum ðonne mid his wordum. Hwæt, se kok ðe we ær ymb spræcon, ær ðæm ðe he crawan wille, hefð up his fiðru, ond wecð hine selfne, ond hine selfne bet. Swa is ðearf ðæt se lareow ærest awecce hine selfne, ðæt he wacie on ðære geornfulnesse godra weorca, ðy læs he oðre awecce mid his wordum, ond him self aslawige godra weorca. Ac hudenige ærest hine selfne, oð he wacige, ond ahrisige siððan oðre to geornfulnesse godra weorca. Ðaccige hine selfne mid ðæm fiðrum his geðohta; ðæt is ðæt he behealde ðurh ða wæccan his smeaunga ærest hwæt on him selfum unnyttes sie, ond ðreage ærest hine selfne ðearlwislice on his geðohte, ond siððan mid his lare geedniwige oðerra monna lif. Ærest he sceal wrecan on him selfum his agnu yfelu ond ða hreowsian, ond siððan oðerra monna cyðan ond wrecan. Ærest hi sculon eowian on hiora agnum weorcum eall ðæt hi eft læran willað mid hiora wordum, swa ðætte ða weorc clipien ær, ær ða word.

Chapter 64

64. Of the conduct of the teacher and his words.

It is now necessary that, out of charity, in the course of other discourse we return to what we discussed earlier: that is, that every teacher instructs more by his actions than by his words. Now, before the cock that we mentioned previously intends to crow, it lifts its wings and rouses itself and beats itself. It is similarly necessary for the teacher first to rouse himself, that he be vigilant in his diligence as to good works, and not to rouse others with his words while he himself languishes as to his good works. But let him first shake himself awake and afterward stir up others to devotion to good deeds. Let him pummel himself with the wings of his thoughts: that is, that he first observe through the vigilance of his contemplation what is objectionable in himself and first castigate himself severely in his conscience, and thereafter by his guidance make other people's lives new. First he must discipline in himself his own wrongs and repent of them, and afterward expose and discipline other people's. They shall first exhibit in their own behavior all that they in turn intend to teach with their words, so that their behavior proclaims first, before the words.

BOOK FOUR

Chapter 65

LXV. Đonne hwa ðis eall gefylled hæbbe,
hu he ðonne sceal hine selfne geðencan ond
ongietan, ðy læs hine auðer
oððe his lif oððe his lar to up ahebbe.

Oft eac ða lareowas weorðað onstyrede mid diegelre blisse, ðonne hi ongietað ðæt hi gemetlice ond medomlice lærað. Ac him is ðonne micel ðearf ðæt he hine hrædlice selfne gewundige mid ðy ege ðæt he him ondræde, ðy læs he weorðe up ahæfen for his wordum; ðætte ðær ðær he oðerra monna wunda lacnað, he self ne weorðe aðunden on upahæfennesse for ðære giemeleste his hælo; ðæt he hine selfne ne forlæte, ðær he oðerra freonda tilige, ond him self ne afealle, ðær ðær he oðre tiolað to ræranne. Forðæm oft ða cræftas ond ða mægenu weorðað te færwyrde ðæm ðe hi hæfð, ðonne hi for hira giemeleste hie fortruwiað on ðæm cræftum ðe hi hæbbað, ond hi nyllað iecan: ðonne weorðað hi him to færwyrde, forðæm simle ða cræftas winnað wið ðæm unðeawum. Ac ðæt mod oft oleccð him selfum, ond ðonne for ðære oleccunga forlæt ðone ege his selfes ymbeðances. Đonne gerest ðæt mod hit orsorglice on ðære fortruwunga. Đonne cymð se lytega sætere to ðæm slawan mode, ond ateleð him eall ðæt he ær to gode gedyde, ond geræcð him ðonne to geleafsuman ðæt he sie se gesælgosta

BOOK FOUR

Chapter 65

65. When someone has fulfilled all of this, how he then ought to regard and understand himself, lest either his conduct or his teaching exalt him excessively.

Frequently, as well, teachers are moved by a secret delight when they perceive that they teach fitly and effectively. But then it is a pressing requirement that one at once inflict on himself the oppression of fearing that he will grow arrogant over his eloquence; that in the course of healing other people's wounds, he not himself grow inflated with self-conceit through neglect of his own well-being; that he not betray himself while cultivating the friendship of others, and not pull himself down while trying to raise others. Thus, talents and abilities often turn ruinous for those who possess them when, for their recklessness, they feel excessive security in the skills they possess, and they have no regard for augmenting them: then they will become their ruin, since talents are always at war with vices. Yet the mind often flatters itself, and for that flattery abandons the constraint of introspection. Then the mind rests free of concern in its self-confidence. Then the cunning seducer comes to the indolent mind and recounts to him all that he did formerly to the good, and renders him too credulous about being the most

on eallum cræftum ofer ealle oðre men, oð ðæt he wyrð
aðunden ond up ahæfen on his mode. Ond ðonne beforan
ðæs ryhtwisan Deman eagum him wyrð ðæt gemynd ðæra
mægena ond ðæra cræfta to swiðe diopum seaðe, ond he
ðær ðonne swiðe hefiglice on gefielð, forðæm ðe he afelð beforan ðæm Gode ðe eaðmodnesse lareow is, ðonne he hine
up ahefeð beforan him selfum for his cræftum. Be ðæm wæs
gecweden ðurh Ezechiel ðone witgan; he cwæð, "Astig eft
ofdune ðonan ðe ðu wenst ðæt ðu wlitegost sie"; swelce he
openlice cwæde, "For ðæm wlite ðinra cræfta ðu wurde up
ahæfen, ond ðonan ðu wyrst geniððrad."

2   Eft se ilca witga sæde bispell bi Hierusalem, ond tælde
ðæt mod ðe for his cræftum ofermodgede, ða he cwæð,
"Dryhten cwið to ðisse byrg: 'Ðu wære fulfremed on minum
wlite, ond ða fortruwdes ðu ðe forðæm, ond forlæge ðe ðines
ægnes ðonces.'" Ðonne bið ðæt mod up ahæfen for ðære
fortruwunga his cræfta, ðonne hit for hiora geearnunga
gilpð, ond orsorglice fægnað on him selfum. Ac ðurh ða for-
truwednesse hit wyrð getogen to ðon ðæt hit wyrð forlegen
on ofermettum. Ærest se awiergda gæst hit lærð utane ðone
gielp, oð ðæt he ingæð ðurh ða ofermetta, ond hit siðða n
gebregð on manegum unðeawe. Be ðæm worde is to ðenceanne ðe he cwæð to ðæm burgwarum: "Ge eow forlægon
eowres ægnes ðonces." Ðæt is ðætte ðæt mod sona swa hit
God forsihð, swa secð hit his agenne gielp, ond gæderað him
ðonne selfum to lofe eall ðæt god ðæt him forgiefen wæs to
Godes lofe; wilnað mid ðy to gebrædenne his ægen lof, ond
higað wið ðæs ðæt he wolde hu he eallum monnum weorð-
fullicost ond wunderlicost ðuhte. Se bið forlegen on his
agnum willan se ðe hine selfne diofle befæst, ond Dryhten

fortunate in endowments above all other people, until he grows inflated and self-conceited in his mind. And then before the eyes of the righteous judge the thought of those abilities and those virtues will turn for him to a very deep pit, into which he will plummet quite heavily, because he will fall before that God who is the teacher of humility when he exalts himself in his own estimation of his talents. This was spoken of through the prophet Ezekiel, who said, "Climb back down from believing that you are most beautiful"; as if his plain meaning were, "For the fineness of your virtues you grew exalted, and from that place you will be cast down."

Again, the same prophet delivered a parable about Jerusalem and rebuked the heart that had grown proud over its talents when he said, "The Lord said to this city, 'You were perfect in my loveliness, and then you presumed because of that, and you prostituted yourself of your own accord.'" The mind is self-conceited out of presumption over its virtues when it vaunts their merits and indulges in self-satisfaction without check. Yet through that presumption it will be led on to the extent that it is prostituted in pride. First the condemned spirit teaches self-satisfaction outwardly, until he penetrates through that pride and thereupon seduces it with many vices. Those words are to be contemplated that he spoke to the citizens: "You prostituted yourselves of your own accord." That is that as soon as the mind disregards God, it pursues its own glory and arrogates to its own acclaim all the good that was granted it to God's acclaim; it desires in that way to magnify its own preeminence and busies itself with wanting to appear most praiseworthy and most admirable to all people. One prostitutes himself by his own consent who commits himself to the devil and forsakes

forlæt for mennisces lofes wilnunga. Be ðæm cwæð Dauid
on ðæm siofan ond hundsiofantiogoðan psalme; he cwæð,
"Dryhten geðafode ðæt hiora mægen ond hiora cræft wære
gehæft, ond hiora wlite wære on hira feonda honda." Gehæft bið hiora cræft, ond hira wlite on hiora feonda hond
gelæd, ðonne se ealda feond onwald hæfð ðæs beswicenan
modes for ðære upahæfennesse, ðonne hit hit up ahefð for
godum weorcum. Se lytega fiond wile fondian ælces monnes
mid ðære upahæfennesse for godum weorcum, ge furðum
ðara acorenra monna mod he wile costian, ðeah he hit fullice
beswican ne mæge. Forðæm ælc mod swa hit bið up ahæfen
swa bið hit forlæten from Gode, ond sona swa hit bið forlæten from Gode, swa bið hit gedrefed mid diofles ege.

3   Be ðæm cwæð Dauid eft on ðæm nigon ond twen-
tiogoðan psalme; he cwæð, "Ic wende on minum wlencum
ond on minum forwanan, ða ic wæs full ægðer ge welona ge
godra weorca, ðæt ðæs næfre ne wurde nan ende." Ac siððan
he ongeat ðæt he wæs aðunden on upahæfennesse for his
godan weorcum, ða gecyðde he swiðe hræðe æfter ðæm
hwæt he siððan dreag, ða he cwæð: "Dryhten, ðu ahwyrfdes
ðinne ondwlitan from me; ða wearð ic gedrefed"; swelce he
openlice cwæde, "Ic wende ðæt ic wære swiðe strong on
manegum cræftum, ac ic ongeat swiðe hraðe, siððan ðu me
forlete, hu untrum ic wæs." Ond eft he cwæð on ðæm eahta
ond hundælleftiogoðan psalme; he cwæð, "Ic swor swa swa
ic getiohhod hæfde ðæt ic wolde gehealdan ðine domas ond
ðine ryhtwisnesse, Dryhten." Ac he ongeat swiðe hraðe, ða
he gemette ða gedrefednesse, ðæt hit næs on his agnum onwalde ðæt he meahte gehealdan ðæt ðæt he ær gehet ond
swor. Ond ða wende he hine sona to his gebede, ond sohte
him ðær fultum to, ond cwæð, "Ic eom gehened æghwonane

God out of desire for human esteem. David referred to this in the seventy-seventh psalm when he said, "The Lord consented to their virtue and their ability being held captive, and their beauty being given into the hands of their enemies." Their ability is held captive and their beauty given into the hands of their enemies when the ancient foe has control of the deluded mind on account of self-conceit when it exalts itself for its good works. The cunning fiend will make trial of every person with self-regard on account of good works, and he will even tempt the minds of the elect, even if he cannot delude them altogether. Therefore, by as much as every mind is exalted, by so much is it alienated from God, and as soon as it is alienated from God, it is assailed by the devil's intimidation.

About this David spoke again in the twenty-ninth psalm, 3 saying, "I supposed in my splendor and in my abundance, when I was full both of riches and of good works, that there would never be an end of it." But once he understood that he was swollen with arrogance for his good works, he made known very soon after that what he subsequently experienced, when he said, "Lord, you turned your face from me; then I suffered affliction"; as if he were to say plainly, "I believed that I was very powerful in many abilities, but very soon I came to see, once you abandoned me, how feeble I was." And again he said in the one hundred eighteenth psalm, "I swore just as I had determined that I would maintain your judgments and your righteousness, Lord." But he understood very soon, when he encountered adversity, that it was not within his own capacity to maintain what he had formerly vowed and sworn. And then he turned at once to prayer and looked for solace there, and said, "I am abased on all sides and in all things, Lord; but

ond on æghwam, Dryhten; ac gecwuca me æfter ðinum wordum, Dryhten." Swa oft sio godcunde gemetgung, ær ðæm ðe hio ðæm men selle cræftas ond mægen, hio him geeowað his untrymnesse, ond his unmehta hine gemyndgað, ðy læs he hine up ahebbe for his cræftum. Forðæm eac wæs gecweden to Ezechiele ðæm witgan ðæt he wære monnes sunu, ær ðæm ðe him wæren geeowad ða hefonlican ðing, swelce hine God openlice manode, ond him to cwæde: "Ne beo ðu to up ahæfen on ðinum mode for ðæm ðingum ðe ðu gesihst, ac geðenc wærlice hwæt ðu eart; ond ðeah ðu ðæt hehste ðurhfare, ne forgiet ðu ðeah ðæt ðu man eart, ac geðenc ðone bridel ðinre mettrymnesse swiðe geornlice on ðe selfum, ðeah ðu sie up ofer ðine mæð ahæfen."

4   Forðæm is micel ðearf ðæt we ures modes eagan gecerren to ðære sceawunga urre untrymnesse. Ðonne us fullicost oleccað ða cræftas ond ða mægenu, ðonne is us micel ðearf ðæt we eaðmodlice ofdune anluten mid urum mode, ond halwendlice geðencen ða god ðe we forgiemeleasodon, næs ða we dydon, ðætte ure mod ðy fæstre ond ðy strenge beforan Gode sie on ðæm cræftum for ðære eaðmodnesse ðe we hit mid gewundiað, ðonne we gemunað ure giemeleste. Forðæm oft se ælmiehtiga God forlet ðæt mod his gecorenra gesyngian on sumum lytlum ðingum, ðeah hi on manegum sien fullfremede, ðæt hi him ondræden, ond murkien for hira unfullfremednesse, ðeah hi beorhte scinen on sumum wunderlicun cræftum, ðæt hi hi for ðæm miclum ðingum ne mægen to up ahebban, ða hwile ðe hi ne magon gebetan ðæt lytle, ðy læs hi dyrren ofermodgian for ðæm æðelestum weorcum, ða hwile ðe hi ne magon oferswiðan ða ytemestan yfelu.

animate me in accordance with your word, Lord." Just so, often the divine dispensation, before it bestows talents and abilities on a person, confronts him with his feebleness and makes him aware of his shortcomings, so that he not preen himself on his advantages. For that reason also it was said to the prophet Ezekiel, before the workings of the heavens were revealed to him, that he was the son of man, as if God were to give him undisguised warning and say to him, "Do not be too self-impressed in your mind over things that you will see, but consider carefully what you are; and though you explore the sublime, do not forget that you are a man, but keep in mind the constraint of your frailty very responsibly within yourself, despite your being raised above your station."

For that reason, it is of the first importance that we di- 4 rect our mind's eyes to the contemplation of our frailty. When talents and abilities most abundantly flatter us, then it is that we need especially to bow down our mind humbly, and give salutary thought to the good things we have neglected, not those we have performed, so that our psyche may be the firmer and the stronger in those accomplishments in the sight of God for the humility with which we wound it when we recall our lapses. Almighty God often leaves the minds of his elect faulty in some small matter, though they are perfect in many respects, for the purpose that they fear him and lament their imperfection, even though they shine brilliantly in certain admirable traits, so that they cannot, on account of important matters, grow too conceited as long as they cannot remedy the unimportant, to prevent their presuming to pride themselves on the noblest accomplishments while they are unable to triumph over the most peripheral ills.

GREGORY'S EPILOGUE

Loca nu, ðu goda wer Iohannes, hu fægerne ond hu wlitigne monnan ic hæbbe atæfred, swa unwlitig writere swa swa ic eom, ðær ic hæbbe getæht hwelc hierde bion sceal. To ðæm ic wæs gened mid ðinre tælnesse, ðæt ic nu hæbbe manege men gelæd to ðæm stæðe fullfremednesse on ðæm scipe mines modes, ond nu giet hwearfige me self on ðæm yðum minra scylda. Ac ic ðe bidde ðæt ðu me on ðæm scipgebroce ðisses andweardan lifes sum bred geræce ðinra gebeda, ðæt ic mæge on sittan oð ic to londe cume, ond arær me mid ðære honda ðinra geearnunga, forðæm ðe me hæfð gehefegad sio byrðen minra agenra scylda.

GREGORY'S EPILOGUE

Look, now, my good man John, what a fine and lovely person I have depicted, unlovely writer as I am, where I have taught what kind of person a shepherd ought to be. I was compelled to it by your criticism, so that I have now conveyed many people to the shore of perfection in the ship of my mind and yet still wander myself on the rough seas of my faults. But I pray you will extend to me in the shipwreck of this present existence the plank, as it were, of your prayers, that I may sit on it till I come to land, and raise myself with the hand of your merits, since the burden of my own deficiencies has weighed heavy on me.

OLD ENGLISH VERSE EPILOGUE

Ðis is nu se wæterscipe   ðe us wereda God
to frofre gehet   fold-buendum.
He cwæð ðæt he wolde   ðæt on worulde forð
of ðæm innoðum   a libbendu
5 wætru fleowen,   ðe wel on hine
gelifden under lyfte.   Is hit lytel tweo
ðæt ðæs wæterscipes   wel-sprynge is
on hefon-rice,   ðæt is Halig Gæst.
Ðonan hine hlodan   halge and gecorene,
10 siððan hine gierdon   ða ðe Gode herdon
ðurh halgan bec   hider on eorðan
geond manna mod   missenlice.
Sume hine weriað   on gewit-locan,
wisdomes stream,   welerum gehæftað,
15 ðæt he on unnyt   ut ne tofloweð.
Ac se wæl wunað   on weres breostum
ðurh Dryhtnes giefe   diop and stille.
Sume hine lætað   ofer land-scare
riðum torinnan;   nis ðæt rædlic ðing,
20 gif swa hlutor wæter,   hlud and undiop,
tofloweð æfter feldum   oð hit to fenne werð.
Ac hladað iow nu drincan,   nu iow Dryhten geaf
ðæt iow Gregorius   gegiered hafað
to durum iowrum   Dryhtnes welle.
25 Fylle nu his fætels,   se ðe fæstne hider

OLD ENGLISH VERSE EPILOGUE

This is now the fount that the God of hosts promised us, inhabitants of earth, as a solace. He said that it was his will that ever-living waters should flow from the hearts of those who, under the heavens, well trusted in him. There is little doubt that the fount's source is in the kingdom of heaven, which is the Holy Spirit. The holy and the elect drew it from there after those who obeyed God prepared it through holy books here on earth in various ways for human hearts. Some dam it up in the mind's reservoir, wisdom's stream, hold it captive with lips, so that it will not flow away to no use. But the well remains deep and still in a man's breast through the grace of the Lord. Some let it disperse in rivulets over the countryside; that is not a well-considered thing if water so pure is scattered murmuring and shallow among the fields until it forms a fen. But draw it for you to drink, now that the Lord has granted Gregory the grace to have directed to your door the Lord's spring. Let whoever has brought

kylle brohte,   cume eft hræðe.
Gif her ðegna hwelc   ðyrelne kylle
brohte to ðys burnan,   bete hine georne,
ðy læs he forsceade   scirost wætra,
30   oððe him lifes drync   forloren weorðe.

a sound vessel here fill his pitcher and return soon.
If any courtier here has brought a leaking pitcher to this
brook, let him repair it with care, lest he spill the clearest of
waters or lose the liquor of life.   30

Note on the Text

The only more or less complete manuscript of the Old English *Pastoral Care* from Alfred's reign to survive to the present day is Oxford, Bodleian Library, MS Hatton 20 (H), made in the closing years of the ninth century. Another manuscript of about the same date, London, British Library, Cotton MS Tiberius B. xi, lacking more than a dozen chapters at the end, is now destroyed, except for a few charred fragments reproduced in facsimile by Ker, but before its loss a copy was made by Franciscus Junius, now Oxford, Bodleian Library, MS Junius 53 (C); see N. R. Ker, ed., *The Pastoral Care; King Alfred's Translation of St. Gregory's "Regula pastoralis,"* Early English Manuscripts in Facsimile 6 (Copenhagen, 1956). One leaf became detached from this manuscript before Junius copied it, and the folio is now preserved as Kassel, Landesbibliothek, MS Anhang 19 (K). A third parchment, London, British Library, Cotton MS Otho B. ii (C2), made about 1000, was badly damaged in the Cottonian fire of 1731; roughly half of the work is legible in what remains. On three post-Alfredian manuscripts at Cambridge, see the introduction to the facsimile edited by Ker, *King Alfred's Translation,* 11–12. The Hatton manuscript, it should be said, is full of erasures, additions, and alterations of various dates, on which see below.

The basis of the text ultimately is Sweet's edition of the Hatton manuscript, as transcribed by the *Dictionary of Old English;* the departures from Sweet's text in the latter of the two, it is to be hoped, have all been remedied here. To the text have been applied the corrections supplied or prescribed by N. R. Ker in the 1958 reprint of Sweet's edition and those prescribed by Kim (with contributions by Ker), to the extent that reasonable certainty could be derived from the latter; Henry Sweet, ed. and trans., *King Alfred's West-Saxon Version of Gregory's Pastoral Care,* vol. 1, Early English Text Society, o.s., 45 (London, 1958), especially p. xi, and Suksan Kim, "A Collation of the Old English MS Hatton 20 of King Alfred's *Pastoral Care,*" *Neuphilologische Mitteilungen* 74 (1973): 425–42. It should be noted that Sweet's stated aim was to remove all the many scribal changes made to the text except those of the original copyists and to restore original readings. It should be observed, however, that he did not follow this practice faithfully, admitting to the text without brackets many interlinear additions, presumably regarding them as the additions of the original scribes. Aside from the alterations mentioned above, his text generally is retained here; exceptionally, a small number of alterations has been made on the basis of the facsimile edited by Ker, but no systematic attempt has been made to alter the results of Sweet's judgment as to which emendations to the text are attributable to the original scribes. Also, as frequently but not consistently in Sweet's text, variants and missing text are supplied here and there from other manuscripts, almost always from C, which is the only manuscript here collated extensively with H. Abbreviations have been silently expanded, accents in the manuscript omitted, and spacing and punctuation altered to conform to modern standards for the editing of Old English texts, though the spacing and punctuation are not always in agreement with Sweet's.

Although chapter numbers are supplied in H, the work is not there divided into books, despite the consideration that the Old English translation includes a rendering of Gregory's rationale for dividing the work so (see the *Dedicatory Letter of Gregory*). For ease of comparison with Gregory's Latin, the Old English is here divided into books. In Gregory's work, the numbering of chapters begins anew with each book, so that after the first book the chapter numbers in the Old English and the Latin are not congruent. To avoid complicating navigation within the volume, series conventions will not allow the corresponding book and chapter numbers of Gregory's work to be indicated in the translation here. The correspondences are these: Old English chapters 12–22 are equivalent to Latin Book Two, chapters 1–11; Old English chapters 23–64 are equivalent to Latin Book Three, chapters 1–40, with Old English chapters 24–26 corresponding to chapter 2 of the Latin; and Old English chapter 65 is equivalent to Latin Book Four.

Sigla

H = Oxford, Bodleian Library, MS Hatton 20

C = Oxford, Bodleian Library, MS Junius 53

K = Kassel, Landesbibliothek, MS Anhang 19

C2 = London, British Library, Cotton MS Otho B. ii

Notes to the Text

Table of Contents

Book One

7.3	bisene *C*: biwene *H*
	fundiað *C*: fandiað *H*
8.title	wilniað *C*: wilnað *H*
8.1	biscephad *C*: biscephade *H*
8.2	gehered: gehiered *H*; gehened *C*
9.1	god *C*: od *H*
	beon: beom *H*; bion *C*
	aled *C*: keled *H*
10.1	ongienne: ongiene *H*; onginne *C*
10.2	ðurh his *C*: ðurhis *H*
11.3	suelce: suel *H*; swelce *C*
	gesomnung ðurh *C*: gesomnung dur *H*
	costung *C*: costug *H*
11.6	se hæfð *C*: seðe hæfð *H*
	aflihð *C*: aslihð *H*
	ðurhteo *C*: ðurteo *H*
	ðonne he ðurh *C*: ðonne he ður *H*
	ðæt mod *C*: ða mod *H*
11.7	ðe bið: se bið *H*; þe bið *C*
	ne mæg mid: he mæg mid *HC*
	mæg ðurhteon *C*: mæg ðurteon *H*

Book Two

13.1	ðonne is *C*: ðone is *H*
13.2	ðæt he ðara *C*: ðæt hie ðara *H*
	mennisce *C*: menisce *H*
14.1	hrofe godcundra *C*: hrofe godcunra *H*
14.2	oðrum flæsce *C*: odrum flæsce *H*
14.5	cynelice: cynelican *H*; kynelice *C*
14.7	beboden toeacan *C*: toeacan *H*
15.1	gebringð *C*: gebrinð *H*
15.2	iedelre: ieðelre *H*; idelre *C*
15.3	Ðurh *C*: Durh *H*
15.4	wordsawere *C*: wordsceawere *with* c *underpuncted H*
16.1	ond eallum monnum *C*: ond eallum monum *H*

mildheortnesse *C*: mildheornesse *H*
eac ðurh: eac *HC*
sceawunga *C*: scaewunga *H*
ðætte he *C*: ðætte hie *H*

16.2   ðær he: he *H*; þær he *C*
flæsclicum monnum *C*: flæsclicum monum *H*

16.4   wunderlice up astigeð: wunderlice up astigen *HC, the last word*
altered to astigeð *H*

16.5   he eac self *C*: eac self *H*

17.1   ryhtwisnesse: ryhtwisnes *H*; ryhtwysnesse *C*
ealdordom *C*: ealðordom *H*
ðætte ealle *C*: ðæte ealle *H*

17.3   suelc suelc: suelc scuelc *H*; swelc swelc *C*
he gesio *C*: he *H*
forseah *C*: forsieh *H*

17.4   for ofermettum *C*: fær ofermettum *H*

17.6   scyldgan *C*: scylgan *H*
on sumum *C*: on on sumum *H*
ne mæge *C*: mæge *H*

17.7   druncenwillum *C*: drucenwillum *H*
ryhte *C*: ryht *H*

17.8   ðeah hwilum *C*: ðeahwilum *H*
eft ðurh *C*: eft ður *H*
ðæm hierdum *C*: hierdum *H*
forlorenan *C*: folorenan *H*
wræðe *C*: wræde *H*

17.9   mengenne *C*: monianne *H*

18.1   ne habbað: habbað *H*; nabbað *C*
soðfæstnesse *C*: soðfæsnesse *H*

18.2   stierien *C*: strienen *H*
Moyses sæde *C2*: Moyses *HC*

18.3   ðurh hine: ður hine *H*; ðurh hiene *C*
suelce ðæt: suelc ðæt *H*; swelce ðæt *C*
hi na: hira *H*; hie na *C*
woroldcundlice: woroldcunlice *H*; worldcundlice *C*

18.4   onfon: on beon *H*; on bion *C*

18.5	selfe C: self H
	ðurhtugon C: ðurtugon H
18.6	sie ymb C: sie ym H
19.3	forgiefð: forgief H; forgifð C
21.3	heargas C: hearga H
	snicendan C: scnicendan H
21.6	ðurhtugon C: ðurtugon H
21.7	wiðstondan C: wistondan H
	ðurhðyrelad: ðurhðyrelað H; ðurhðyrelod C
21.9	anre ðara ðreora: anra ðara ðreora HC
	anre ðara burga: anra ðara burga HC
22.1	ðone C: ðonne H
	onbryrd C: onbryd H
22.2	anbestungnan C: anbestungne H

Book Three

23.1	hieremonnum C: hieremonum H
23.2	gesettan ond C: gesettan H
	felaspræcan ond: felaspræcan H; felaspræcean ond C
	manðuæran: manðuæra H; manðwæran C
26.4	hatheortnesse C: hatheornesse H
27.1	manianne C: mananne H
	bliðan on oðre C: bliðan onðre H
	ne warenige: warenige H; warnige C
	ondrætt: onðrætt H; ondræt C
28.1	underðieddan: unðerðieddan H; underðioddan C
28.2	gewyrhtum C: gewyrhtu H
	eft ymb C: eft H
	geornfulle ne: geornfulle HC
28.4	suiðe hraðe æfter ðæm: suið hraðe H; swiðe hræðe æfter ðæm C
	swiðe wel C: swiwel H
28.7	wið ðone C: wiðone H
	ond Arone C: Arone H
29.1	Ðæm ðeowan is to cyðonne ðæt he wiete ðæt he nis freoh wið his hlaford C: *omitted* H

30.1	manianne ða C: manne ða H
	samwisan C: sanwisan H
	ðyncð C: ðync H
	to anbuganne: to to anbuganne H; to anbugonne C
31.1	forelegissa C: forelegnissa H
32.1	ðætte C: ðæte H
32.2	wiðerwearde: wiðerweardne HC
32.3	gestiðigen mid C: gestiðigen mið H
33.title	ungeðyldgan: ungeðylgan H; ungeðyldegan C
33.1	is C: his H
	læran C: læra H
33.2	geðyldgian C: geðylgian H
	forsewen C: foresewen H
33.3	broht C: beorht H
33.4	geðyld ðæt: *lacuna in H begins hereafter, text supplied from C*
	eowrum: eorum C
33.5	dryhten: dryhte C
	micelne beam: *H resumes*
	oferswiðe C: oferswið H
33.7	ðurh hiera C: ðurhiera H
34.1	onhyrigen C: ohyrigen H
34.2	hie habbað C: habbað H
34.4	suiðe: suið H; swiðe C
34.5	ðætte ðonne ðonne hie beoð innan fretene mid ðære adle ðæt hie forleosað C: *omitted H*
	unsceaðfulnesse C: unsceadfulnesse H
	ðeah he C: ðeahe H
35.2	ðurh hira: ðurhira H; ðurh hiera C
35.3	ðæt ðær C: ðær ðær H
	ond sio twyfealdnes ðæs yflan willan hiene selfne twyfealdne gefielt on innan him selfum C: *omitted H*
35.4	sprece C: spræce H
	monna ðætte C: monna ðæte H
36.1	hælo forsihð C: hælo H
36.2	awiergdan: awierdan H; awiergedan C
	from ðæs C: from H

547

ne selle *C*: selle *H*

awiergdena: awierdan *H*; awiergedan *C*

36.5 geearnigen *C*: gearnigen *H*

36.6 mennisce *C*: menisce *H*

ongietan ne *C*: ongietan *H*

lichoman *C*: lichoma *H*

36.7 ðonne he bið *C*: he bið *H*

godcundan *C*: gocundan *H*

37.1 Ðæm *C*: ðæt *H*

he cwæð *C*: Ic cwæð *H*

37.3 ðonne hit mon *C*: ðonne *H*

38.1 orsorgran *C*: orsorgtran *H*

38.3 mid ealle *C*: elle *H*

38.4 deð *C*: ðeð *H*

monnes mod *C*: monnes *H*

Ðæt ðonne *C*: Ðætte ne *H*

on to *C*: ond to *H*

feondum *C*: feonðum *H*

38.5 ymb spricð *C*: ymb sricd *H*

towesnesse *C*: towesnesnesse *H*

39.1 ond ðonne *C*: ond donne *H*

se ðe him: se de him *H*; se þe him *C*

Ðæt is *C*: Hwæt is *H*

39.3 gesceadwisnesse *C*: gesceadwisnesnesse *H*

40.1 unbieldo *C*: bieldo *H*

forðæm ðonne hie underfoð ðone folgað ðonne tyht hie ond gremeð *C*: *omitted H*

ierre *C*: hierre *H*

eac ðæt *C*: ðæt *H*

40.4 him mon *C*: mon *H*

ferbuganne: oferbuganne *H*; ferbugonne *C*

ac eowige him ealle stilnesse ongean ðæt, ond ðeah swiðe *C*:
omitted H

suelce mon: suelc mon *H*; swelce mon *C*

41.1 Essaiam *C*: essaim *H*

41.2   heo bið: bið *H*; hio bið *C*
         affeorod: *lacuna in C begins hereafter*
41.3   ðæt hie sprecen: sprecen *H*
         unmidlode: unmidlod *H*
         oððe ða ðe: oððe ðe *H*
         orsorgran: orsorgra *H*
         ma wilniað: wilniað *H*
         hiera: hera *H*
41.4   læran: læra *H*
         straciað: straciad *H*
         handa: hanða *H*
41.5   hine wolde: hie wolðe *H*
         mid ðære: miðære *H*
         hine lærde: hine ne lærde *H*
42.title ungestæððegan: gestæððegan *H*
42.1   suiðe arod: suið arod *H*
         ðara dysegra: ðara *H*
42.2   hie comon: he comon *H*
         us is: is *H*
         ofermettum: ofermetum *H*
42.3   forcorfen: focorfen *H*
         ðæt is sio: ðæt sio *H*
43.1   symbliað: symblað *H*
         on oðrum: onðrum *H*
43.2   ðonne bið: ðonne bid *H*
         nytum geðohtum: *C resumes with these words (wanting* un-)
         ricsasð: ricsað *H*; ricsast *C*
43.3   forhæfdnesse *C*: fohæfdnes *H*
43.4   mid ðæm *C*: miðæm *H*
43.6   druncon ge *C*: drucon ge *H*
44.title wilniað *C*: wilniad *H*
44.2   hæbben *C*: hæbbe *H*
         tellen *C*: telen *H*
44.3   lofes *C*: lifes *H*
44.4   ða ðe nan: ða nan *H*; ða þe nan *C*

ðæm to *C*: to *H*

44.5   unryhtwisnesse *C*: unryhwisnesse *H*

44.7   ðætte his *C*: ðæte his *H*

ðu wille *C*: wille *H*

geswican ðonne *C*: geswican ðon *H*

hwæðer: hwæder *H*; hwiðer *C*

A *C*: ac *H*

ðone cwide *C*: ðon cwide *H*

44.8   he wolde *C*: wolde *H*

gemyndgað *C*: gemydgað *H*

dead hie *C*: dead he *H*

45.1   to gemanan *C*: tege man *H*

45.4   fæsðhafulan: fæsðhafula *H*; fæsthafolan *C*

45.5   unsælð *C*: unslæwð *H*

bringð: bring *H*; brengeð *C*

45.6   bringð: bring *H*; brengð *C*

46.title   wisan *C*: wisa *H*

46.1   ungesibsuman *C*: ungesibsibsuman *H*

ungemodnesse *C*: ungemodnes *H*

forsæcð *C*: forsencð *H*

cuman *C*: cunnan *H*

46.3   arærð *C*: aræð *H*

geearnod: geearnoð *H*; geearnad *C*

aðiede: ðiede *HC*

andweardan lifes *C*: andweardan *H*

46.6   ðurhwuniendan *C*: ðurhwiniendan *H*

ðonne ne *C*: ðonn ne *H*

46.8   ðætte leuis *C*: ðæt eleuis *H*

agenne *C*: ane *H*

47.1   ðære wrohte *C*: ðære *H*

47.3   Fariseisc *C*: Fariscisc *H*

eht *C*: eft *H*

48.1   ðæt isen *C*: isen *H*

48.2   snidon *C*: sindon *H*

48.3   ryhtwisra *C*: ryhwisra *H*

48.4	ryhtlice *C*: ryhlice *H*
	oðerra *C*: oðer *H*
48.5	of his *C*: of is *H*
49.title	wisan *C*: wisa *H*
	miclum *C*: milum *H*
49.1	unmedome *C*: umedome *H*
49.3	ðine stemne: *so ends C*
49.5	midfeorh: mid feorwe *HK*
50.1	gehwierfð: gehwierf *H*
	ðæt is ðætte: ðætte *H*
50.2	ðonne ðonne: ðonne ðone *H*
	gecyðde: gecyde *H*
50.3	israhela: israhe *H*
	cwæð: cwæ *H*
	he mid: mid *H*
	helle: hele *H*
	life onfo: life *H*
50.4	aliefð: alief *H*
	ðegn: ðeng *H*
51.1	become to: become *H*
51.2	afrefred: afrefed *H*
51.3	monig god: monigod *H*
	ne geðencen: ne ne geðencen *H*
51.4	niedðearf: nieðearf *H*
51.5	betwuh: be betwuh *H*
	butan be: butan *H*
51.6	ne mierð: mierð *H*
	ðeah he: ðea he *H*
51.7	on swa: swa *H*
52.2	forlegen: folegen *H*
	eft to: efto *H*
52.4	hi ofergan: ofergan *H*
	hundteontig: hunteontig *H*
52.6	ongietað: ongietad *H*
53.2	hreowsunga: hreowsnga *H*

	demde: dem *H*
53.5	underðiodde: underðiode *H*
54.title	ða ðe ða: ða ðe *H*
54.1	hi forlætað: hi folætað *H*
54.2	ofermetto: ofermeto *H*
54.3	gewemmed: gewemed *H*
54.5	unryhtwisum: uryhtwisum *H*
56.title	unryhtgewilnunge: unryhtgewilnung *H*
56.1	manegum: magum *H*
56.5	cyðde: cyde *H*
57.1	hi hi rimað: hihrimað *H*
	awriten on: awriten o *H*
57.3	forswelge: foswelge *H*
58.2	afandod: afandon *H*
	him ða: hin ða *H*
58.3	sægð ðær: sægð ðara *H*
58.4	to manienne: toma manienne *H*
	godspellere: godspllere *H*
59.1	beforan: beforum *H*
	sellað: selað *H*
59.2	ðeah hi: ðeahi *H*
59.3	hwelcra: hwelcre *H*
	screncð: screnc *H*
61.1	mæge: mæg *H*
61.2	swelce mettrymnesse: swelce metrymnesse *H*
	mettrymnesse ge: metrymnesse ge *H*
	mettrymnesse afliemað: mettrynesse afliemað: *H*

BOOK FOUR

65.1	oðerra: oðer *H*
65.3	openlice: openlic *H*
	gemyndgað: gemydgað *H*
65.4	forlet: folet *H*
	beorhte: beorte *H*

GREGORY'S EPILOGUE

I hæfð: hæf *H*

OLD ENGLISH VERSE EPILOGUE

II halgan: halga *H*

Notes to the Translation

VERSE PROLOGUE

1–16   The speaker is to be understood to be the book itself, in a conceit employed also in the verse prologue to Bishop Wærferth's Old English version of Gregory's *Dialogi,* and perhaps that to the Old English Boethius, two other works of the Alfredian period. Despite the assessment of Sweet, echoed by others, that these verses are "curious doggrel," they are, in reality, formally unexceptionable, without metrical or alliterative defect by classical standards, though a few are of uncommon scansional types; Henry Sweet, ed. and trans., *King Alfred's West-Saxon Version of Gregory's Pastoral Care,* 2 vols., Early English Text Society, o.s., 45, 50 (London, 1871), vol. 2, p. 473.

EPISTOLARY PREFACE

title   *This book is to go to Worcester*: The Hatton manuscript (H) is addressed to Wærferth, bishop of Worcester, who at Alfred's prompting translated another of Gregory's works, the *Dialogi.* Other known copies of the *Pastoral Care* were addressed to Wulfsige, bishop of Sherbourne, and Heahstan, bishop of London; and a note in the margin of C indicates that copies had been sent to Plegmund, archbishop of Canterbury, and Swithulf, bishop of Rochester, in addition to Wærferth. In C the letter heading reads, "Ðis is seo forespræc hu S. Gregorius ðas boc gedihte þe man *Pastoralem* nemnað" (This is the preface how Saint Gregory composed this book, which is called *Pastoralis*).

4 *the law*: Holy scripture.

6 *a certain pointer*: "Pointer" is the term used here to render Old English *æstel*, almost certainly a borrowing of a posited Latin **hastella* (little spear) and glossed *indicatorium* by Ælfric. It thus appears to refer to such a wand as was used to keep track of the text as it was read aloud. The rich Alfred Jewel, on which is inscribed a legend that may be translated "Alfred commanded that I be made," is generally thought to be the handle of one of these wands mentioned by Alfred.

 fifty crowns: The term *mancessa* is here rendered "crowns," a nearly equivalent value, as a *mancus* was a coin worth thirty pence, one eighth of a pound.

DEDICATORY LETTER OF GREGORY

1 *Dearest brother*: The dedicatory letter's Latin salutation, which precedes these words and is left untranslated in the Old English, is addressed to one *Ioanni coepiscopo* (fellow bishop John), who is most commonly identified as John, bishop of Ravenna, a known correspondent of Gregory. For references and an alternative identification, see Bruno Judic, Floribert Rommel, and Charles Morel, eds. and trans., *Grégoire le grand: Règle pastorale*, Source Chrétiennes 381, 382 (Paris, 1992), vol. 1, p. 16n3.

3 *the craft of teaching*: Old English *cræft* renders Latin *artem*, a misreading of Gregory's *arcem* (citadel).

BOOK ONE

1.title *teaching*: Pastoral duties are various, and although they include teaching, the vocabulary that Gregory uses to refer to a bishop makes plain that he means not just a teacher but someone in a position of authority. In the Old English translation such a person is with some frequency referred to simply as a teacher.

1.1 *They aim to be approached . . . at assemblies*: Christ's words here are a paraphrase of Matthew 23:6–7; similar is Mark 12:38–39.

 They ruled . . . them: Hosea 8:4.

 The eternal and unseen judge . . . dignity of his forbearance: The sense of the Latin is that at the same time God grants such people prestige he does not recognize them, for those whom he permissively tolerates he surely does not recognize by a judgment of reproof.

And though they may work many wonders in that office: Gregory meant that it was Christ who had performed wonders, though he did not say so explicitly.

Depart from me . . . you are: Luke 13:27.

These shepherds have no understanding: Isaiah 56:11.

they had my law . . . me: Jeremiah 2:8.

Whoever does not recognize . . . him: 1 Corinthians 14:38.

1.2 *If the blind . . . pit*: Matthew 15:14.

May their eyes . . . bent: Psalms 69:23(68:24).

2.1 *You trampled . . . unsullied*: Ezekiel 34:18.

Bad priests are the people's ruin: Hosea 9:8.

2.2 *the grade of holy orders*: An ordained ministry, such as bishophood or priesthood.

Whoever beguiles . . . sea: Matthew 18:6.

3.1 *Brother, do not let . . . teachers*: James 3:1.

the Jews came . . . compulsion: See John 6:15.

3.2 *King Saul at first . . . dishonored him*: See 1 Samuel 10:21–23; 13:7–15; 15:17–30, 34–35.

David . . . Uriah: See 2 Samuel 11:2–22.

when he had him . . . old: See 1 Samuel 24:3–4.

4.1 *My son, do not . . . efforts*: Sirach 11:10.

Hezekiah . . . the foreign emissaries: See 2 Kings 20:12–20; Isaiah 39:1–7.

4.2 *the Babylonian king*: Nebuchadnezzar. See Daniel 3–4.

5.1 *No one ought . . . bushel*: Matthew 5:15.

Do you love me . . . if you love me: John 21:15.

If Christ died . . . again: 2 Corinthians 5:15.

5.2 *Should someone die . . . unshod*: Deuteronomy 25:5–10.

Go and announce . . . see me: Matthew 28:10.

See to your feet . . . books: Ephesians 6:15.

7.1 *Oh, oh, oh, Lord . . . speaking*: Jeremiah 1:6.

I am ready. Send me: Isaiah 6:8.

two commandments: See Mark 12:30–31.

this life of difficulties: This, rendering the reading in C, is closer in meaning to Gregory's "per activam vitam" (through an active life) than the reading of H, "ðys eorðlican life" (this earthly life).

7.2   *the coals of the altar*: See Isaiah 6:6.

     Moses fulfilled both of these conditions . . . dominion: See Exodus 3–4.

8.1   *Whoever desires . . . noble work*: 1 Timothy 3:1.

     It is incumbent . . . reproach: 1 Timothy 3:2.

9.1   *But the mind's eyes will all at once be turned back to former occupations*: Gregory's point, rather, is that for its own sake the mind's eye *must* revisit former occupations when it aspires to office. The translator's failure to understand this is what prompted the preceding sentence, an addition to what Gregory says, in an attempt to rationalize Gregory's reference to recalling former deeds.

9.2   *an experienced one does not have confidence in himself*: In Gregory's "etiam peritus se nauta confundit" (even an experienced sailor is confounded), *confundit* has been confused with *confidit* (has confidence) in the Old English translation.

9.3   *the napkin that Christ . . . gospel*: See Luke 19:20; compare Matthew 25:18.

     Pharisees: See Matthew 23:13.

10.1   *You summoned me . . . here*: Isaiah 58:9.

10.2   *But let everyone examine himself meticulously*: The Latin corresponding to these and the following words ending the chapter is so placed in some manuscripts of Gregory's text, whereas in others it correctly opens the following chapter.

11.1   *if he had any blemish . . . hydrocele*: See Leviticus 21:17–21. "White spot" renders Old English *fleah*, Latin *albuginem* (albugo or leukoma, a whitening of the cornea, though the word can also refer to a cataract); "impetigo" renders Old English *teter* (tetter, a skin disease), Latin *impetiginem*; hydrocele is swelling of the scrotum.

11.2   *The Lord will direct . . . darkness*: 1 Samuel 2:9.

> *when he has accustomed himself . . . decay*: Gregory's Latin means, more precisely, "when intermittent habit is not raised to a constant state of virtue."
>
> *Reach forth your disused hands . . . sound*: Hebrews 12:12.

11.3   *Your nose is . . . Lebanon*: Song of Songs 7:4.

11.4   *I am bowed . . . abased*: Psalms 38:6(37:7).

> *Their seed fell . . . fruit*: Luke 8:14.

11.5   *are often desiccated*: The Latin has *atteritur* (is rubbed, is worn).

> *Anoint your eyes . . . see*: Revelation 3:18.
>
> *They said that . . . foolish*: Romans 1:22.

11.6   *Never let any temptation . . . human*: 1 Corinthians 10:13.

> *the root of every evil . . . avarice*: See 1 Timothy 6:10.

11.7   *The condition of hydrocele results . . . deformed*: The condition described by Gregory is referred to as *ponderosus* (weighty, massive), with the same intent as *herniosus* in the Vulgate (literally, "ruptured," Leviticus 21:20). As Gregory develops the metaphor, the lecherous man is weighed down by continually thinking about the act never committed, just as the herniated man is ruptured by the weight of the bowels. In identifying the condition as hydrocele, the Old English translator has been obliged to alter the metaphor.

Book Two

12.1   *cord*: The idea of a rope or cord seems to have been suggested to the translator by literal interpretation of the word *constringitur* (is bound).

13.1   *Make yourselves clean . . . vessels*: Isaiah 52:11.

13.2   *inscribed on Aaron's chest*: See Exodus 28:15–29.

> *rationale*: The rationale, or breastplate, of judgment was a square wallet worn by the priest on his chest, five or six inches on a side, set with twelve precious stones representing the twelve tribes of Israel.
>
> *twelve patriarchs*: That is, the sons of Jacob, progenitors of the twelve tribes of Israel.

About that it is written . . . truth: See Exodus 28:30.

14.1   *You who intend . . . mountain*: Isaiah 40:9.

14.2   *holy scripture dictates that the priest . . . flesh*: See Leviticus 7:30–34 and Exodus 29:22, 26–27.

that he do good among other people: The Latin means instead, "that he do good among bad people."

he ought to be given . . . shoulder: See Leviticus 10:14.

14.3   *liturgical vestment*: See Exodus 28:1–14.

Go armed both on the right hand . . . justice: 2 Corinthians 6:7.

14.4   *jacinth*: Although jacinth is now the name given to yellow zircon, in antiquity it referred to a blue stone, probably sapphire. In using the word *hyacinthus,* Gregory appears to be referring to the color blue, as in the Vulgate, rather than to a gemstone of that color.

14.5   *And whether he is of high or low birth . . . required of him*: What Gregory says, rather, is that he must repress vices in himself, seeing as he always observes the nobility of his inmost regeneration.

You are a people . . . priesthood: 1 Peter 2:9.

To those who . . . children: John 1:12.

Lord, your friends . . . before the world: The first two clauses render Psalms 139(138):17.

14.6   *eternal*: The Latin has *interni* (inward), apparently mistaken for *aeterni.*

But when consciousness extends . . . the flesh: That is, when the individual loves both God and his neighbor, the only quality further required of him will be self-denial.

15.1   *You do not tend . . . wolf*: John 10:12.

Mute dogs cannot bark: Isaiah 56:10.

You did not come . . . need: See Ezekiel 13:5.

Your prophets prophesied . . . repentance: Lamentations 2:14.

15.2   *forceful at persuading . . . oppose him*: See Titus 1:9.

The law shall . . . people: Malachi 2:7. The Old English translation follows the uncorrected recension of Gregory's text, in which the quotation is attributed to Zachariah, though it is Malachi who is cited in the revised Latin recension. The corrections

supplied in this latter recension were most likely made by
Gregory himself, chiefly by the substitution of citations of the
Vulgate for those of the Old Latin Bible.

Cry out and . . . trumpet: Isaiah 58:1.

15.3   *in the form of tongues*: See Acts 2:3.

as he goes in and out . . . die: See Exodus 28:35.

Let your priests . . . righteousness: Psalms 132(131):9.

Have salt within you . . . one another: Mark 9:50.

Do not desire to know more . . . you to know: Compare Romans 12:3.

among the bells red apples: See Exodus 28:34. Corresponding to
"apples," Gregory's Latin has *malo Punico* (pomegranate).

15.4   *the man who experienced a flux . . . unclean*: See Leviticus 15:2.

word sower: *Seminiverbius*, Acts 17:18.

I bid you . . . unseasonably: 2 Timothy 4:1–2.

16.1   *through the profundity of his examination*: Old English *ðurh*
(through), corresponding to Latin *per*, is missing from the manuscripts.

16.2   *though he was led into paradise*: See 2 Corinthians 12:2–4.

enumerated: Here Old English *arimde* is a "false friend," mistrans-
lating Latin *rimatur* (probes).

Let each man have . . . adultery: 1 Corinthians 7:2–3.

Do not deprive . . . relations: 1 Corinthians 7:5.

Who is made weak . . . ashamed of it: 2 Corinthians 11:29.

When I was . . . as they: 1 Corinthians 9:20.

Though we now meditate . . . for you: 2 Corinthians 5:13.

16.3   *the patriarch Jacob*: See Genesis 28:12–22.

16.4   *Moses often went in and out . . . people*: Compare Exodus 33:7–11.

he prayed on the mountainside: See Luke 6:12.

16.5   *so that those who are subject to them . . . shame*: The Latin means,
rather, "lest they be ashamed to confess." The Old English appears to be a mistranslation rather than the result of scribal error, and no extant Latin manuscript is in error at this point.

basin of bronze: See 1 Kings 7:25.

Do not bind up . . . oxen: Deuteronomy 25:4; 1 Corinthians 9:9; 1
Timothy 5:18.

17.1   *Moralia in Job*: Gregory's *Morals on the Book of Job*, a commentary on the book of Job in thirty-five books, is his most influential work. It is also sometimes called *Magna moralia (The Great Morals)*. The passages alluded to here will be found in *S. Gregorii Magni Moralia in Job*, ed. Marc Adriaen, Corpus Christianorum, Series Latina 143A–C (Turnhout, 1979–1985), 21.15.22–24 (vol. 143A, p. 1082) and 26.26.44–46 (vol. 143B, pp. 1298–1302).

17.2   *Grow and multiply . . . of the earth*: Genesis 9:1–2.

17.3   *he who is king . . . presumption*: See Job 41:34.
       I will build . . . highest: Isaiah 14:13–14.

17.4   *When you were inconsiderable . . . Israel*: 1 Samuel 15:17.

17.5   *Rise, and do . . . as you*: Acts 10:26.
       Ananias and Sapphira: See Acts 5:1–5.
       We are not dominators . . . faith: 2 Corinthians 1:24.
       We have become . . . midst: 1 Thessalonians 2:7.
       We are your servants . . . love: 2 Corinthians 4:5.
       Would you prefer . . . spirit: 1 Corinthians 4:21.

17.6   *And though it should be made a sign . . . wonders*: Here the Old English misrepresents the Latin, which says that one in authority should let his followers know by certain becoming signs that he is humble.

17.7   *You are given . . . subordinates*: Sirach 32:1.
       We are not rulers . . . flock: 1 Peter 5:3.
       You should know . . . serve: Matthew 20:25–28.
       The bad servant . . . hypocrite: Matthew 24:48–51.

17.8   *The priest Eli did so*: See 1 Samuel 4:17–18.
       You honor your sons more than me: 1 Samuel 2:29.
       The sheep that was broken legged . . . home: Ezekiel 34:4.

17.9   *books of morals concerning Job*: See *Moralia In Job* 20.5.14 (see note on 17.1 above), Corpus Christianorum, Series Latina 143A, p. 1012.
       Samaritan: See Luke 10:33–4.

17.10 *the rod*: Aaron's rod. See Hebrews 9:4; Exodus 7:9–12; Numbers 17:6–7.
       Your rod and your staff comforted me: Psalms 23(22):4.

18.2   *Take care that . . . earth*: Luke 21:34–5.
       No one can obey two masters: Luke 16:13.

No servant of God ... given himself: 2 Timothy 2:4.

If you must ... earthly matters: 1 Corinthians 6:4.

Moses ... Jethro: See Exodus 18:17–23.

18.3　*Such as the people are, such is the priest*: Hosea 4:9.

Oh, why is this ... end: Lamentations 4:1.

It is a broad ... perdition: Matthew 7:13.

to be held for the noblest and the holiest: The translator omits after this a comparison that Gregory draws between the stones of which the temple was constructed and men in sacred orders who devote themselves to worldly matters.

18.5　*I, your fellow servant ... lucre*: 1 Peter 5:1–2.

Whoever does not tend ... faith: 1 Timothy 5:8.

18.6　*priests ought not to shave ... shears*: See Ezekiel 44:20.

sacerdas: This is the plural of Old English *sacerd*, a borrowing of Latin *sacerdos*, which etymologically means "one who makes sacred."

the intellect from being fettered to the heart: The meaning of the Latin is, rather, "lest the intent of the heart be impeded," though there is some uncertainty at this point in the Latin as regards textual authority.

19.1　*Woe unto them ... people*: Ezekiel 13:18.

19.2　*You commanded very imperiously ... autocratically*: Ezekiel 34:4.

19.3　*Saint Peter very willingly accepted Saint Paul's reproof*: See Galatians 2:11.

King David ... Nathan: See 2 Samuel 12:7–13.

19.4　*Just so I desire ... people*: 1 Corinthians 10:33.

If I oblige ... God: Galatians 1:10.

20.1　*or, again, that he not delay ... through the penalty*: It is not plain whether the Old English means that it is the offender or his spiritual advisor who will lose the reward for virtuous conduct. In the corresponding Latin, reference is made only to the danger of acting too soon or too late.

21.1　*You are liars ... not see it*: Isaiah 57:11.

21.2　*The sinful have built upon my back*: Psalms 129(128):3.

21.3　*Son of man ... depicted on the wall*: Ezekiel 8:8–10.

21.4　*the avarice that Saint Paul ... idols*: See Colossians 3:5.

21.5   *If someone is engaged . . . come your way*: Galatians 6:1.

21.6   *Take a certain tile . . . rams*: Ezekiel 4:1–2.

       sublime peace: According to one interpretation, Jerusalem means "city of peace."

21.8   *Who is infirm . . . for that*: 2 Corinthians 11:29. Compare 16.2 above.

21.9   *If anyone were to go . . . kill him*: Deuteronomy 19:5–6.

       three cities, which are hope, charity, and faith: The association of the cities of refuge with these three virtues seems to be original with Gregory. It appears earlier in his *Moralia in Job* 10.7.

22.1   *When I come . . . reading*: 1 Timothy 4:13.

       See, Lord, how greatly . . . meditation: Psalms 119(118):97.

22.2   *Fashion four rings . . . pulled out*: Exodus 25:12–15. Hebrew *shiṭṭim* is the plural of *shiṭṭah* (acacia).

       Be ever ready . . . yourselves: 1 Peter 3:15.

Book Three

23.1   *Heretofore we . . . injunctions*: In the Latin text, the words corresponding to the first paragraph of the Old English are marked as a prologue, the chapter proper beginning with the second paragraph.

       It is not fitting . . . morals: See Gregory Nanzianzen, *Theological Orations* 2.16, 2.28–31 (*Grégoire de Nazianze: Discours,* ed. and trans. Jean Bernardi, Sources Chrétiennes 247 [Paris, 1978], 111, 127–31). This work is similar to the present one and was apparently an inspiration for Pope Gregory.

24–26   Chapters 24, 25, and 26 are treated as a single chapter (chapter 2) of Book 2 in the Latin text.

25.1   *Do not upbraid . . . father*: 1 Timothy 5:1.

26.1   *Do not be afraid . . . humiliated*: Isaiah 54:4.

       You unfortunates . . . tempest: Isaiah 54:11.

       I have chosen you . . . sufferings: Isaiah 48:10.

       Tell the rich . . . riches: 1 Timothy 6:17.

       Woe you wealthy . . . life: Luke 6:24.

26.3   *King Saul . . . David*: See 1 Samuel 16:23.

26.4   *Nathan . . . King David*: See 2 Samuel 12:1–12.

27.1   *Woe to you . . . weep*: Luke 6:25.

         I shall see you . . . joy: John 16:22.

         to guard not only against rage: The editorial insertion of *ne* (not) into the text is demanded not only by the otherwise peculiar *an* (only) but by the Latin, which has *non solum* (not only).

28.1   *Children, be subject . . . Lord*: Ephesians 6:1 and Colossians 3:20.

         Do not aggrieve your children: Colossians 3:21.

28.2   *unless they themselves . . . possibly can*: This is the translator's addition.

28.3   *You idler . . . there*: Proverbs 6:6.

         My son . . . pronouncement: Proverbs 6:1–2.

28.4   *Do, my son . . . droop*: Proverbs 6:3–4.

28.5   *heavenly beasts . . . inside*: See Revelation 4:6.

28.7   *certain of David's affairs*: See 1 Samuel 24:2–4.

         battered his heart: See 1 Samuel 24:5.

         such penance as he believes his master would assign if he knew: The Latin refers, rather, to dreading the judgment of God.

         What is your complaint . . . doing: Exodus 16:8.

29.1   *Be subject to your earthly masters*: Colossians 3:22.

         Each of those . . . obeisance: 1 Timothy 6:1.

         You masters . . . in heaven: Ephesians 6:9.

30.1   *Whichever of you . . . wise*: 1 Corinthians 3:18.

         You ought not to be . . . wiles: 1 Corinthians 1:26–27.

30.2   *who was obliged to instruct . . . the unwise*: See Romans 1:14.

         What is now antiquated is nearly vanished: Hebrews 8:13; compare Jeremiah 31:31–34.

         In this world, saintly people suffered . . . death: Hebrews 11:36–37.

         Remember your predecessors . . . faith: Hebrews 13:7.

31.1   *Your faces are . . . harlots*: Jeremiah 3:3.

         The shame and . . . created you: Isaiah 54:4–5.

         Oh, you unthinking Galatians . . . flesh: Galatians 3:1–3.

         I rejoice greatly . . . well: Philippians 4:10.

32.2   *some said that they were of Apollo*: See 1 Corinthians 1:12 and 3:4.

         We have heard . . . before: 1 Corinthians 5:1–2.

32.3   *We ought continually . . . endurance*: 2 Thessalonians 1:3–4.

I beseech you . . . near: 2 Thessalonians 2:1–2.

33.1   *the love of God is patience*: See 1 Corinthians 13:4.

every instructor's teaching grows with his patience: See Proverbs 19:11.

33.2   *the patient man is better than the arrogant*: Ecclesiastes 7:9.

33.3   *Let each of you bear . . . law*: Galatians 6:2.

33.4   *Better is the patient . . . town*: Proverbs 16:32.

In your patience . . . souls: Luke 21:19.

The foolish, impatient one . . . time: Proverbs 29:11.

33.5   *the One who does know*: The Latin makes it plain that the reference is to God.

Love is patient . . . benign: 1 Corinthians 13:4.

Let all bitterness . . . mind: Ephesians 4:31.

Love your enemies . . . wrong: Matthew 5:44.

Now, you can see . . . own: Matthew 7:3.

You hypocrite . . . eye: Matthew 7:5; Luke 6:41–42.

33.6   *the one who by the devil's instruction . . . gain respect*: The Latin says, rather, that whereas the devil has already conquered the initiator of the conflict, he is conquered by the one who bears the insult patiently.

34.1   *without reward in this present life*: Old English *andweardan* (present) is apparently an error for *toweardan* (future), as implied by Gregory's Latin.

34.4   *for his envy . . . earth*: Wisdom 2:24.

the Lord looked upon Abel . . . or his gifts: See Genesis 4:4–5.

34.5   *this carnal life is envy*: Compare Proverbs 14:30, where the import rather is that a tranquil heart gives life to the body, whereas envy rots the bones. The Old English here departs from Gregory's Latin.

35.1   *I have much to say . . . bear it*: John 16:12.

I want you to be . . . evil: Romans 16:19.

Be as shrewd . . . doves: Matthew 10:16.

35.2   *The labor of their own lips . . . them*: Psalms 140:9(139:10).

They have trained . . . work: Jeremiah 9:5.

35.3   *the hedgehog had its den there*: See Isaiah 34:15, "Ibi habuit foveam ericius." In translations of Isaiah 34:15, the Hebrew word rendered as *ericius* (hedgehog) in the Old Latin Bible and the Vulgate is translated as "great owl" or "arrowsnake," or similar, though the ancient versions take it to refer to the hedgehog or the porcupine.

35.4   *whoever lives honestly lives innocently*: See Proverbs 10:9.
     the doctrine of the Holy Spirit will flee deceptions: See Wisdom 1:5.
     he has his counsel . . . simple: See Proverbs 3:32.
     Yet to come is . . . corners: Zephaniah 1:14–16.

36.1   *Now is the time . . . salvation*: 2 Corinthians 6:2.
     I called you . . . dreaded happens to you: Proverbs 1:24–26.
     When they call . . . find me: Proverbs 1:28.

36.2   *Do not surrender . . . decayed*: Proverbs 5:9–11.

36.3   *When God struck . . . him*: Psalms 78(77):34.

36.4   *I rebuke and discipline those I love*: Revelation 3:19. It is now generally regarded as improbable that the author of the Apocalypse of John was John the Evangelist.
     My son, do not make light . . . receive: Hebrews 12:5–6.
     Manifold are the tribulations . . . people: Psalms 34:19(33:20).
     If I was righteous . . . miseries: Job 10:15.
     the stones in the famous temple . . . heard there: See 1 Kings 6:7.

36.5   *Our fathers in the flesh . . . life*: Hebrews 12:9–10.

36.6   *Balaam*: See Numbers 22:22–23.
     The mute and captive beast . . . design: 2 Peter 2:16.

36.7   *the wound would heal after it suppurated*: See Proverbs 20:30.
     wounds that are inside the belly: See Proverbs 20:27.
     A person's life . . . insides: Proverbs 20:27.

37.1   *The perfect love . . . fear*: 1 John 4:18.
     You did not receive . . . Father: Romans 8:15.
     Where the spirit . . . liberty: 2 Corinthians 3:17.
     Then it is quite plain . . . neglect it: Most of the Old English sentence here does not correspond to anything explicit in the Latin, and the Old English is obscure, as illustrated by Sweet's more literal rendering, "It is very evident that his righteousness before God is lost, when he sins unnecessarily of his own desire, when it is very evident that he did not do good, when from fear he durst neglect it" (*King Alfred's West-Saxon Version*,

vol. 1, pp. 263, 265). Rather, the sense appears to be that the subject's righteous actions are of no worth in God's eyes because he would have preferred to sin and never do good, but his fear compelled him to act responsibly.

37.2   *Though you grind . . . folly*: Proverbs 27:22.
   You crushed them . . . guidance: Jeremiah 5:3.
   I slaughtered this nation . . . ways: Jeremiah 15:7.
   This nation has not reverted . . . them: Isaiah 9:13.
   We were physician . . . healed: Jeremiah 51:9.

37.3   *This nation of Israel . . . furnace*: Ezekiel 22:18.
   There was very strenuous labor . . . purged: Ezekiel 24:12.
   The bellows worked . . . them: Jeremiah 6:29.

38.2   *My son, attend . . . thoughts*: Proverbs 5:1.
   My wits and my good sense have left me: Psalms 40:12(39:13).
   Your servant has now . . . you: 2 Samuel 7:27.
   it encounters what it had been accustomed to avoiding: Gregory's meaning is that the heart is found which had been accustomed to fleeing. The translator has omitted reference to the heart.

38.3   *The sage holds . . . speak*: Sirach 20:7.
   sometimes there is occasion . . . mute: See Ecclesiastes 3:7.
   May the Lord set . . . steadfastness: Psalms 141(140):3.

38.4   *The person who cannot hold . . . wall*: Proverbs 25:28.

38.5   *whoever released water was the cause of faction*: See Proverbs 17:14.
   Whoever bids a fool . . . wrath: Proverbs 26:10.

38.6   *The prolix man . . . world*: Psalms 140:11(139:12).
   Chattering is never without sin: Proverbs 10:19.
   silence was the bulwark . . . righteousness: See Isaiah 32:17.
   If someone persuades . . . worthless: James 1:26.
   Let every person . . . speak: James 1:19.
   he said that it . . . venom: See James 3:8.
   For every worthless word . . . Judgment Day: Matthew 12:36.

39.1   *Sloth induces sleep in a person*: Proverbs 19:15.
   The uncaring and dissolute mind goes hungry: Proverbs 19:15.
   Every idle person . . . dictates: The Old English here rather freely renders Gregory's "In desideriis est omnis otiosus" (Every idle person is desirous), which is quoted widely in the patrology, apparently first in the letters of Jerome, and is ascribed to various

books of scripture, most often to Proverbs 21:25, of which it renders the sense but is not scriptural *per se*.

When a certain impure spirit . . . many: See Matthew 12:43–45.

39.2   *The sluggard is unwilling . . . nothing*: Proverbs 20:4.

One who is always . . . reap: Ecclesiastes 11:4.

39.3   *My son, do nothing . . . done*: Sirach 32:24.

but always let . . . feet: Proverbs 4:25.

40.1   *The enraged do not know what they harbor in themselves*: Gregory says, rather, that the enraged do not know what in their anger they inflict on themselves.

in the form both of a dove and of fire: See Matthew 3:16 and Acts 2:3.

40.2   *Instruct and admonish . . . patiently*: 2 Timothy 4:2.

Instruct the people . . . them: Titus 2:15.

40.3   *the woman named Abigail*: See 1 Samuel 25:2–38.

40.4   *Abner . . . Asahel*: See 2 Samuel 2:22–23.

41.1   *Each of those who are humbled . . . will be humbled*: Luke 18:14.

Humility runs before glory . . . honor: Proverbs 15:33.

Before a person's fall . . . exalted: Proverbs 16:18.

On whom do I look . . . word: Isaiah 16:2.

On what prides . . . dust: Sirach 10:9.

the Lord recognizes . . . afar: Psalms 138(137):6.

I did not come . . . serve: Matthew 20:28.

pride was the root of all evil: See Sirach 10:15.

he is king over all the children of pride: See Job 41:25.

41.5   *We will depart . . . encamp*: Numbers 10:29–31.

But he acted . . . guidance: The point of the corresponding Latin is not that Hobab acted foolishly but to explain Moses's reasons for speaking as he did.

42.1   *You ought not . . . wise*: Romans 12:16.

Do not let . . . you: Ephesians 4:14.

They shall eat . . . way: Proverbs 1:31.

The minds of foolish people . . . diffuse: Proverbs 15:7.

foolish people's minds: Old English *dysegra* (foolish) is supplied on the basis of Latin *stultorum* in Gregory's text.

42.2   *I am not pursuing . . . here*: John 5:30; compare John 6:38.

I cannot do anything . . . Father: John 5:30.

42.3   *Do you now think . . . "yes" and "no"*: 2 Corinthians 1:17.

43.1   *Father Abraham . . . flame*: Luke 16:24.

43.2   *The people sat . . . themselves*: Exodus 32:6.

         On your belly . . . crawl: Genesis 3:14.

         The commander of cooks laid low . . . Jerusalem: See 2 Kings 25:8–10. Here for "commander of cooks" the Vulgate reads *princeps exercitus* (commander of the army), but Gregory follows the *Vetus Latina* (Old Latin Bible) reading *princeps coquorum,* a misinterpretation of the Hebrew *Rab-tabbachim* ("chief of the bodyguard," or, more literally, "chief of the slaughterers"), the title of Nabuzaradán, Nebuchadnezzar's viceroy in Jerusalem after the capture of the city in 587 BCE.

43.3   *Now that you . . . patience*: 2 Peter 1:5–6.

         Whoever chooses to fast . . . eats: Romans 14:3.

         Frequently when someone . . . within: Colossians 2:23.

         I fast twice weekly: Luke 18:12.

43.5   *Often, likewise . . . benefit of self-denial*: The meaning of the Latin is instead that when the abstemious manage to avoid anger, sometimes they are corrupted by a foreign joy and thereby lose the good effect of abstinence.

         On your days . . . fistfights: Isaiah 58:3–4.

         I never chose . . . destitute: Isaiah 58:5–7.

43.6   *Consecrate your fast*: Joel 2:15.

         All that you . . . drank for yourselves: Zachariah 7:5–6.

43.7   *Take care that your hearts . . . trap*: Luke 21:34–35.

         What goes into a person's mouth . . . defiles him: Matthew 15:11.

         Now, if food . . . both: 1 Corinthians 6:13.

         Do not accustom . . . inebriation: Romans 13:13.

         Extravagant consumption will . . . God: 1 Corinthians 8:8.

         to the pure . . . was pure: See Titus 1:15.

         their belly was . . . honor: See Philippians 3:19.

         it would happen . . . gifts: See 1 Timothy 4:1–3.

         it would be good . . . brothers: See Romans 14:21.

         you are allowed . . . health: See 1 Timothy 5:23.

44.1   *Lords are mandated . . . demands*: In the Latin, Gregory draws comparison to a household in which servants are of various ranks, and those with greater authority are likelier to offend their

master than the others. The Old English text misconstrues
this.

44.3   *If anyone serves . . . works*: 1 Peter 4:11.

When you have done . . . necessity: Luke 17:10.

God loved the cheerful giver: See 2 Corinthians 9:7.

this fleeting acclaim: The reading *lofes* (acclaim) of C is superior to
lifes (life) in H, corresponding to the Latin *laudem*.

the left hand . . . does: Matthew 6:3.

When you have prepared . . . for it: Luke 14:12–13.

44.4   *Go away and come back . . . something*: Proverbs 3:28.

Keep your alms: The corresponding Latin, "Sudet eleemosyna in
manu tua" (Let the alms gather sweat in your hand), though of
no biblical authority, is treated as scriptural already in early
sources, including Augustine: see *Didachè: Insegnamento degli
apostoli*, ed. Giuseppe Visonà (Milan, 2000), 114n and 202; and
Sancti Aurelii Augustini Enarrationes in Psalmos, vol. 3, Corpus
Christianorum Series Latina 40 (Turnhout, 1956), 1462 and
1509.

Who sows little, reaps little: 2 Corinthians 9:6.

Do not be . . . their abundance: 2 Corinthians 8:13–14.

Their abundance, then . . . in spirit: This is the translator's addition.

Give to everyone who asks you: Luke 6:30.

Give away your goods . . . wicked: Sirach 12:5–6.

Set out your wine . . . sinful: Tobit 4:18.

44.5   *The spirit is more . . . clothing*: Luke 12:23; Matthew 6:25.

44.6   *I hungered, and you gave . . . angels*: Matthew 25:41–43. Gregory
does not say that the final part of the quotation was promised;
rather, it was said earlier than the rest, in verse 41. That is, the
translator has mistaken *praemittit* (puts before) for *promittit*
(promises).

44.7   *Woe unto one who continually collects . . . his*: See Habakkuk 2:6.

Woe unto you who add house . . . alone: Isaiah 5:8.

You will always . . . compete: Old English *a* (always) in C (compare
ac, "but" in H) corresponds to Gregory's *semper*.

The rapacious will never be sated . . . them: Ecclesiastes 5:9.

Whoever aims to be prosperous . . . innocent: Proverbs 28:20.

44.8   *The legacy that you pursue . . . blessing*: Proverbs 20:21.

        What does it avail . . . ruin: Matthew 16:26.

45.2   *Look that you not practice . . . men*: Matthew 6:1.

        Whoever distributes his belongings . . . perpetuity: Psalms 112(111):9.

        One who is righteous . . . ceases: Proverbs 21:26.

        the fig tree which is said . . . useless: See Luke 13:6–9.

45.3   *the rich man of whom . . . white*: See Luke 16:19.

45.4   *He gave God . . . mercy*: See Psalms 49:7–8(48:8–9).

        Every tree shall be hewn . . . tree: Luke 3:9. The speaker is not John
           the Evangelist but John the Baptist; Gregory refers only to *Io-*
           hannes, without further specification.

45.6   *I am the Lord . . . iniquity*: Isaiah 61:8.

        The offerings of the impious . . . deeds: Proverbs 21:7.

        If someone offers . . . eyes: Sirach 34:24.

        One who collects . . . holes: Haggai 1:6.

46.1   *the fruit of the spirit is love . . . pious*: Galatians 5:22.

        When there is wrongful spite . . . flesh: 1 Corinthians 3:3.

        Have as your aim . . . God: Hebrews 12:14.

        Bind yourselves intently . . . hope: Ephesians 4:3–4.

46.2   *Praise God with timbrel and in chorus*: Psalms 150:4.

46.3   *Have salt within you . . . another*: Mark 9:50.

        If you have reprehensible enmity . . . demonic: James 3:14–15.

46.4   *If you intend to bring . . . present your gift*: Matthew 5:23–24. Mat-
           thew refers instead to one's having offended, rather than hav-
           ing been offended.

46.6   *My peace I give . . . leave to you*: John 14:27.

46.7   *Do I not hate . . . enemies*: Psalms 139(138):21–22.

46.8   *the Levites grasped their swords*: See Exodus 32:27–28.

        Phineas spurned . . . God's anger: See Numbers 25:7–8.

        Do not believe . . . sword: Matthew 10:34.

        You lent aid . . . Jews: 2 Chronicles 19:2–3.

46.9   *I loved those . . . cause*: Psalms 120:6–7(119:7).

        I would wish it . . . person: Romans 12:18.

        Whoever is unwilling . . . brothers: 2 Thessalonians 3:14–15.

47.1   *those who sow discord . . . the peaceable*: The distinction of subject
           between this chapter and the preceding, as drawn by Gregory,

and which is partly obscured in the Old English translation, is between, on the one hand, the belligerent and the peace-loving (46) and, on the other, sowers of discord and peacemakers (47).

Some person did this . . . enemy: Matthew 13:28.

An apostate is always worthless . . . contention: Proverbs 6:12–14.

47.2   *Blessed are the peacemakers . . . God*: Matthew 5:9.

47.3   *The members of his flesh . . . another*: Job 41:14. Gregory equates Leviathan with the Antichrist.

Every fish's scale . . . them: Job 41:7.

Now, am I not . . . dead: Acts 23:6. The sentence "What you do, brothers, do manfully" appears to represent an interpretation of Paul's exclamation "Viri, fratres" (Men, brethren!).

48.title   *and yet for humility remain silent, not professing it*: The chapter heading and first sentence represent a misinterpretation of what Gregory says, since he is concerned not with those who are too humble to preach, even though they understand the Bible, but (as correctly represented later in the Old English translation of the chapter) with those who understand the Bible yet are not humble.

48.2   *They ripped open . . . borders*: Amos 1:13.

Heap of Witness: That is, a cairn. See Genesis 31:48.

48.3   *They are also to be warned . . . demons*: Gregory reasons that by promoting discord, ignorant preachers turn God's law into a sacrifice to Satan, as is made plain farther down in the Old English translation.

I gave them wheat . . . Baal: Hosea 2:8.

48.4   *Foolish and inept is the physician . . . wounded*: Compare Luke 4:23, "Medice, cura te ipsum" (Physician, heal thyself).

Whoever speaks . . . God's: 1 Peter 4:11.

As from God, before God we speak in Christ: 2 Corinthians 4:17.

God abominates every proud person: See Proverbs 16:5.

48.5   *Drink the water . . . you*: Proverbs 5:15–17.

Strangers have risen . . . persecuted me: Psalms 54:3(53:5).

49.1   *Of what use . . . gold*: Sirach 20:32.

One who hoards . . . people: Proverbs 11:26.

Cursed is the man . . . bloodshed: Jeremiah 48:10.

My sword will devour flesh: Deuteronomy 32:42.

49.2   *how money was entrusted . . . from it*: See Matthew 25:14–30.

Now, you are . . . design: Acts 20:26–27.

Let him who hears . . . "Come": Revelation 22:17.

Woe unto me . . . peace: Isaiah 6:5.

The soul of a person . . . intoxicated: Proverbs 11:25.

Lord, you know . . . righteousness: Psalms 40:9–10(39:10–11).

49.3   *Listen here, you who linger . . . voice*: Song of Songs 8:13.

Whoever is God's servant . . . neighbor: Exodus 32:26–27.

49.5   *Stay longer in the town . . . ability*: Luke 24:49.

Young man, do not let . . . finish: Sirach 32:7–8(10–11).

when our Savior was . . . doctrines: See Luke 2:42–46.

Prescribe and teach this . . . youth: 1 Timothy 4:11–12.

young adulthood: Old English *midfeorh* is literally "midlife." The scribe mistook *mid* for the preposition meaning "with," which demands the dative case, and accordingly he altered nominative *feorh* to dative *feorwe*. The former is restored here.

Delight, my boy, in your youth: Ecclesiastes 11:9. Here the Vulgate has "Laetare ergo iuvenis in adulescentia tua." The age designated by *adulescentia* (youth) follows *pueritia* (childhood) and precedes *juventus* (young adulthood); Gregory's point is that Timothy need not be thought an adolescent at the time of Paul's writing to him (which would contradict his injunction that the immature should not preach).

50.1   *They have turned . . . mind*: Ezekiel 36:5.

The waywardness of young people . . . ruin: Proverbs 1:32.

Let those who possess . . . it: 1 Corinthians 7:30–31.

50.2   *The Lord's left hand . . . me*: Song of Songs 2:6.

in his right hand . . . honor: See Proverbs 3:16.

Let your right hand save me: Psalms 108:6(107:7).

Your right hand . . . enemy: Exodus 15:6.

50.3   *He gave them . . . law*: Psalms 105(104):44–45.

You cast them down . . . themselves: Psalms 73(72):18.

You received all your store . . . world: Luke 16:25.

50.5   *When he was . . . kill him*: See 1 Samuel 24.

he began to sacrifice to devils: See 1 Kings 11.

51.2 *Let those who have a wife . . . glad*: 1 Corinthians 7:29–30.
The form of this world will pass away: 1 Corinthians 7:31.

51.3 *Bear your burdens . . . law*: Galatians 6:2.

51.4 *It is good for a man to be without a woman*: 1 Corinthians 7:1.
It is good for men to have . . . fornication: 1 Corinthians 7:2.
Let a man give . . . husband: 1 Corinthians 7:3.
I say what I have said . . . indulgence: 1 Corinthians 7:6.

51.5 *Here is a certain little city . . . in it*: Genesis 19:20.
I am willing now . . . intercede: Genesis 19:21.
Do not one of you . . . prayers: 1 Corinthians 7:5.

51.6 *This I say . . . hinder you*: 1 Corinthians 7:35.

51.7 *Neither fornicators nor idolaters . . . God*: 1 Corinthians 6:9–10.
The Lord will judge adulterers: Hebrews 13:4.
it is better . . . to burn: 1 Corinthians 7:9.
no one shall put . . . back: See Luke 9:62.

52.1 *You have the countenance . . . shameless*: Jeremiah 3:3.
But they are to be encouraged . . . present wrong: The Latin says, rather, that they are to contemplate past offenses and avoid future ones.
About this the Lord spoke . . . other world: The meaning of the Latin is, more precisely, that the Lord rebuked minds corrupted in this world so that they would be ashamed to be defiled in the future.
They were prostituted . . . shattered: Ezekiel 23:3.
the teats of their virginity were shattered: Latin *fractae sunt* is in the Old English translation given its commoner sense, though the intended meaning in the Latin is "were crushed" or "were bruised."

52.2 *If a certain woman . . . "Return to me"*: Jeremiah 3:1.
Your eyes will be trained . . . you: Isaiah 30:20–21.

52.4 *Therefore, he will perceive . . . resist*: The Old English translator has misunderstood the Latin, which pertains to Satan, indicating that he chafes against refusal more violently the more firmly his temptations are resisted.
This says the Lord . . . daughters: Isaiah 56:4–5.
These are the ones . . . thousand: Revelation 14:3–4. On the identity

of the one hundred forty-four thousand, see Revelation 7:2–17 and 14:1–5.

52.5   *By no means . . . guidance*: Matthew 9:11.

52.6   *This sea tells you . . . Sidon*: Isaiah 23:4.
          Very many sins are forgiven her: Luke 7:47.
          There is more rejoicing . . . repentance: Luke 15:7.

52.7   *for their purity . . . superior orders*: The Old English here miscon-
          strues the Latin, which instead concerns the pretense of the
          chaste to greater sanctity than that of inferiors who are more
          devout.
          carbuncle: This is any sort of red gemstone, very commonly gar-
          net. On the jacinth, see the note to 14.4.

53.1   *God very fitly . . . drink*: Psalms 80:5(79:6).
          Avert, Lord . . . sins: Psalms 51:9(50:11).
          My misdeeds are ever before me: Psalms 51:3(50:5).
          I shall not keep . . . them: Isaiah 43:25–26.
          My eyes shed . . . waters: Lamentations 3:48.

53.2   *Let us anticipate . . . confessing*: Psalms 95(94):2.
          If we were . . . all: 1 Corinthians 11:31.

53.3   *Dinah was out walking . . . country*: See Genesis 34:1–3; *Ebreiscan*
          (Hebrew) is a mistranslation of *Hevaei* (Hivite).

53.5   *Against myself I . . . heart*: Psalms 32(31):5.

54.1   *the dog will eat . . . washed*: 2 Peter 2:22; compare Proverbs 26:11.
          Do not repeat . . . prayer: Sirach 7:15.
          Wash yourselves so . . . clean: Isaiah 1:16.
          If someone takes . . . him: Sirach 34:30.

54.2   *Whoever will be . . . enemy*: James 4:4.

54.3   *May my life . . . theirs*: Numbers 23:10.
          he saw another regimen . . . members: See Romans 7:23.

54.4   *if we do nothing in the way of good*: Here "good" is an error for
          "bad," to judge by the Latin, the meaning of which is that even
          if someone committed no sinful act in his lifetime, he would
          not be free of sinful thoughts, and since there is thus no secu-
          rity in this life, how can someone who has actually committed
          wrongful acts feel secure without having repented them?

54.5   *we ought to forgo what is permissible*: Gregory's meaning is that showing restraint even in what is permissible will help one to rise.

I said to the unrighteous . . . high: Psalms 75:4(74:5).

The Lord will never . . . hearts: Psalms 51:17(50:19).

You were formerly . . . sanctified: 1 Corinthians 6:11.

Repent and be baptized . . . you: Acts 2:38.

Baptism cleanses a person . . . remits sins: Gregory's point is that even though baptism washes away the stain of all sins, repentance is still necessary, according to Peter.

55.2   *They professed their sins . . . them*: Isaiah 3:9.

      the outcry of the Sodomites . . . amplified: See Genesis 18:20.

55.3   *The servant who knows . . . punishments*: Luke 12:47.

      They shall enter living into hell: Psalms 55:15(54:16).

56.2   *They injured me . . . again*: Proverbs 23:35.

56.3   *it was as if the helmsman slept . . . helm*: See Proverbs 23:34.

56.4   *Let each of you have . . . night*: Song of Songs 3:8.

      Your nose is . . . Mount Lebanon: Song of Songs 7:4.

56.5   *Take care that you not inflame . . . again*: Jeremiah 4:4.

      I shall visit retribution . . . stratagems: Jeremiah 23:2.

      he did not sit in the pestilential seat: See Psalms 1:1.

57.1   *one who declines to evade . . . ones*: See Sirach 19:1.

57.4   *they blew away . . . camel*: See Matthew 23:24.

      You tithe your mint . . . trustworthiness: Matthew 23:23.

58.2   *what they now forfeit . . . punishment*: The Latin says, rather, that what pains them will be reserved for their punishment.

      I have now today appointed . . . plant: Jeremiah 1:10.

      The Nazarene savior . . . hell: Acts 2:22–24.

      Then the Jews answered . . . christened: Acts 2:37–38.

58.3   *Who are you, Lord . . . what to do*: Acts 9:5–7 and 22:8–10.

58.4   *One who for his indolence . . . destroys it*: Proverbs 18:9.

      Be vigilant, and amend . . . God: Revelation 3:2. On John the Evangelist as the author of Revelation, see the notes on 36.4.

58.5   *it would be better for them . . . acknowledged it*: See 2 Peter 2:21.

      Oh, that he would be . . . mouth: Revelation 3:15–16.

      For all water . . . tepid: This is the Old English translator's addition.

59.1   *they were very like the sepulchers . . . putrid*: See Matthew 23:27.
        that was their reward: See Matthew 6:2.

59.2   *lest it be perceived . . . neighbor*: That is, they love their neighbor
        less than themselves if by their bad example they lead him
        astray.
        Do your good works . . . heaven: Matthew 5:16.
        Do not practice your uprightness . . . you: Matthew 6:1.

59.3   *Take care that this license . . . people*: 1 Corinthians 8:9.
        Then your brother will perish . . . God: 1 Corinthians 8:11–12.
        Say nothing ill . . . stumble: Leviticus 19:14.

60.title *How many are to be encouraged . . . bad deeds*: The Latin instead in-
        dicates that the chapter concerns teaching many at once in
        such a way as to encourage virtues without promoting vices.

60.1   *and particularly that he himself . . . edge intact*: The meaning of the
        Latin is that, rather, while it is suited to the needs of a diverse
        audience, preaching should not itself be diverse, but, like a
        sword, it should cut the swellings of vices on both sides — that
        is, one prescription should serve to correct opposed kinds of
        behavior.

61.title *How a lone individual . . . temptations*: The Latin makes it plain
        that this chapter concerns instructions to an individual who is
        subject to contrary bad impulses.

61.2   *But for what reason . . . for the body*: The sense of the Latin is in-
        stead to question why moral instruction cannot have efficacy
        of two opposing sorts, seeing as a single medicinal prescription
        can have such.

62.1   *If you want not to need fear . . . you*: Romans 13:3.

63.1   *Who do you suppose . . . time*: Luke 12:42. Compare Matthew 24:45.
        I can by no means speak . . . eat: 1 Corinthians 3:1.
        Moses hid . . . countenance: See Exodus 34:29–35.
        if anyone dug a pit . . . for it: See Exodus 21:33–34.
        the clean or the unclean: The meat of oxen is permitted to be eaten
        under Mosaic law, but not that of asses.

63.2   *Who made the cock wise*: Job 38:36.
        Now is the hour . . . sleep: Romans 13:11.
        Awake, you righteous . . . more: 1 Corinthians 15:34.

Book Four

65.1   *Climb back down from believing . . . beautiful*: Ezekiel 32:19.

65.2   *The Lord said to this city, . . . accord*: Ezekiel 16:14–15.
       The Lord consented . . . enemies: Psalms 78(77):61.

65.3   *I supposed in my splendor . . . of it*: Psalms 30:6(29:7).
       Lord, you turned your face . . . affliction: Psalms 30:7(29:8).
       I swore just . . . Lord: Psalms 119(118):106.
       I am abased on all sides . . . Lord: Psalms 119(118):107.
       the son of man: See Ezekiel 2:1, 2:3, 2:6, 2:8, etc. *(filius hominis)*.

Gregory's Epilogue

1   *my good man John*: On the identity of John, see the notes to the
      Dedicatory Letter of Gregory, above.

Old English Verse Epilogue

1–30   As with the *Verse Prologue* (to which see the note), the poetic
      form of the *Verse Epilogue* is faultless by classical standards. The
      inspiration for the image of the spring will be found in 48.5.

Bibliography

The bibliography is highly selective. For full bibliographical coverage of the earlier scholarship, consult Stanley B. Greenfield and Fred C. Robinson, *A Bibliography of Publications on Old English Literature to the End of 1972* (Toronto, 1980). For subsequent publications, see the annual bibliographies in the journals *Anglo-Saxon England* and *Old English Newsletter.*

Editions and Translations

Carlson, Ingvar, ed. *The Pastoral Care: Edited from British Museum MS. Cotton Otho B.ii.* Completed by Lars-G. Hallander, with Mattias Löfvenberg and Alarik Rynell. 2 vols. Stockholm Studies in English 34, 48. Stockholm, 1975–1978.

Judic, Bruno, Floribert Rommel, and Charles Morel, eds. and trans. *Grégoire le grand: Règle pastorale.* 2 vols. Sources Chrétiennes 381, 382. Paris, 1992.

Ker, N. R., ed. *The Pastoral Care; King Alfred's Translation of St. Gregory's "Regula pastoralis": Ms. Hatton 20 in the Bodleian Library at Oxford, Ms. Cotton Tiberius B.XI in the British Museum, Ms. Anhang 19 in the Landesbibliothek at Kassel.* Early English Manuscripts in Facsimile 6. Copenhagen, 1956.

Schreiber, Carolin. *King Alfred's Old English Translation of Pope Gregory the Great's "Regula pastoralis" and Its Cultural Context.* Münchener Universitätsschriften 25. Frankfurt am Main, 2003.

Sweet, Henry, ed. and trans. *King Alfred's West-Saxon Version of Gregory's Pastoral Care.* 2 vols. Early English Text Society, o.s., 45, 50. London, 1871. Reprinted with contributions by N. R. Ker. London, 1958.

Further Reading

Bately, Janet. "Did King Alfred Actually Translate Anything? The Integrity of the Alfredian Canon Revisited." *Medium Ævum* 78 (2009): 189–215.

Bremmer, Rolf H., Jr., Kees Dekker, and David F. Johnson, eds. *Rome and the North: The Early Reception of Gregory the Great in Germanic Europe.* Mediaevalia Groningana, n.s., 4. Paris, 2001.

Clement, Richard W. "King Alfred and the Latin Manuscripts of Gregory's *Regula pastoralis.*" *Journal of the Rocky Mountain Medieval and Renaissance Association* 6 (1985): 1–13.

———. "The Production of the *Pastoral Care:* King Alfred and His Helpers." In *Studies in Earlier Old English Prose,* edited by Paul E. Szarmach, 129–52. Albany, NY, 1986.

Discenza, Nicole G. "Alfred the Great: A Bibliography with Special Reference to Literature." In *Old English Prose: Basic Readings,* edited by Paul E. Szarmach, 463–502. New York, 2000.

Godden, Malcolm. "The Alfredian Project and Its Aftermath: Rethinking the Literary History of the Ninth and Tenth Centuries." *Proceedings of the British Academy* 162 (2009): 93–122.

———. "Did King Alfred Write Anything?" *Medium Ævum* 76 (2007): 1–23.

Jeffery, C. D. "The Latin Texts Underlying the Old English *Gregory's Dialogues* and *Pastoral Care.*" *Notes and Queries,* n.s. 27 (1980): 483–88.

Kim, Suksan. "A Collation of the Old English MS Hatton 20 of King Alfred's *Pastoral Care.*" *Neuphilologische Mitteilungen* 74 (1973): 425–42.

Shippey, T. A. "Wealth and Wisdom in King Alfred's *Preface* to the Old English *Pastoral Care.*" *English Historical Review* 94 (1979): 346–55.

Waite, Gregory. *Old English Prose Translations of King Alfred's Reign. Annotated Bibliographies of Old and Middle English Literature 6.* Woodbridge and Rochester, NY, 2000.

Index

Names cited simply by chapter and paragraph are in the main text of the translation. Otherwise, one of the following abbreviations will be found: VP = *Verse Prologue;* EP = *Epistolary Preface;* TC = *Table of Contents;* DL = *Dedicatory Letter of Gregory;* GE = *Gregory's Epilogue;* VE = *Old English Verse Epilogue.*